ESSENTIALS OF AMERICAN POLITICS

Second Edition

ROBERT J. SPITZER
SUNY CORTLAND

BENJAMIN GINSBERG
JOHNS HOPKINS UNIVERSITY

THEODORE J. LOWI
CORNELL UNIVERSITY

MARGARET WEIR
UNIVERSITY OF CALIFORNIA, BERKELEY

W. W. NORTON & COMPANY

NEW YORK • LONDON

W.W. Norton & Company has been independent since its founding in 1923, when William Warder Norton and Mary D. Herter Norton first published lectures delivered at the People's Institute, the adult education division of New York City's Cooper Union. The Nortons soon expanded their program beyond the Institute, publishing books by celebrated academics from America and abroad. By mid-century, the two major pillars of Norton's publishing program—trade books and college texts—were firmly established. In the 1950s, the Norton family transferred control of the company to its employees, and today—with a staff of four hundred and a comparable number of trade, college, and professional titles published each year—W. W. Norton & Company stands as the largest and oldest publishing house owned wholly by its employees.

Copyright © 2006, 2002 by W. W. Norton & Company, Inc.

All rights reserved
Printed in the United States of America

Composition by TSI Graphics
Manufacturing by Quebecor/Taunton
Editor: Stephen Dunn
Director of Manufacturing, College: Diane O'Connor
Project Editor: Chris Granville
Editorial Assistant: Kelly Rolf
Book Designer: Chris Welch
Copy Editor: Andy Saff

Library of Congress Cataloging-in-Publication Data

Essentials of American Politics / Robert J. Spitzer . . . [et al.].—2nd ed.
     p. cm.
  Includes bibliographical references and index.
  ISBN 0-393-92673-7 (pbk.)
  1. United States—Politics and government—Textbooks. I. Spitzer, Robert J., 1953-

JK276.E77 2005
320.473—dc22

W. W. Norton & Company, Inc., 500 Fifth Avenue, New York, N.Y. 10110
www.wwnorton.com

W. W. Norton & Company Ltd., Castle House, 75/76 Wells Street, London W1T 3QT

1 2 3 4 5 6 7 8 9 0

To
Teresa Spitzer
Sandy, Cindy, and Alex Ginsberg
Angele, Anna, and Jason Lowi
Nicholas Ziegler

CONTENTS

3 FEDERALISM   51

5 PUBLIC OPINION AND THE MEDIA 123

8 CONGRESS 223

10 BUREAUCRACY 285

11 THE FEDERAL COURTS 311

12 DOMESTIC POLICY 341

13 FOREIGN POLICY   369

APPENDIX   A1

PREFACE

This book proudly stands on the shoulders of the previous works of Benjamin Ginsberg, Theodore Lowi, and Margaret Weir. Yet it is a new and different book, organized around several distinct objectives, to provide a clear, concise understanding of American government and politics. First, this book maintains a single conceptual focus: the relationship between the citizen and the government. Every important question raised in the book stems from the key issue of how people relate to their government, and, in turn, how the government reacts, regulates, and responds to the people. Second, the book's analysis includes historical treatment of political institutions and processes. Modern political relations are a product of America's political culture and can be best understood in a historical context. We ignore history at our peril. It is difficult to understand the modern strong presidency, for example, without knowing how much weaker the institution was in the early decades of American history.

Third, this book is structured and organized to help the reader grasp key ideas and facts without sacrificing complexity or talking down to the reader. The objective of learning about key ideas is a goal that is entirely compatible with clarity. To that end, each chapter begins with a single main idea that emphasizes an important lesson or principle. More specific key concepts are also listed at the start of each chapter. The major headings and subheadings in each chapter are written in sentence form not only to organize but to summarize and clarify the key ideas to come. Pop-up captions accompany tables and charts to help the reader extract the important information from visual presentations of data. In addition, the book is peppered with both contemporary and historical examples to engage the reader and illustrate key ideas and arguments.

As the book's title says, the objective is to provide the "essentials," both in concept and fact. The authors hope the reader finds that this goal has been met.

Special thanks are extended to W. W. Norton Vice President Steve Dunn, who organized and shepherded this project with skill and diplomacy, and to Aaron Javsicas, Mikael Awake, Andy Saff, and Deb Dintino. Further thanks are owed to colleagues Sheldon Goldman, Nancy Kassop, Jerry O'Callaghan, and Henry Steck, and to two sharp-eyed former students: Jennifer Lodico from SUNY Cortland and Breton Perry from Cornell.

1

INTRODUCTION: THE CITIZEN AND THE GOVERNMENT

MAIN MESSAGE

Understanding American politics means understanding the relationship between the citizen and the government.

M ost Americans do not think of politics as a high priority. In a way, this is understandable, because most Americans do not see much of a link between the government and their daily lives. In addition, when things are going well—no major wars, no economic depression, no riots in the streets—people see little need to demand action from their government.

Key Concepts

1. Even though the relationship between the citizen and the government is central to American government, the government does not necessarily do what the majority of the people want.

2. Government affects our lives every day.

3. Different types of government are defined by how powerful the government is and how free the people are.

4. Politics in America changed when more people won the right to participate.

5. Liberty, equality, and democracy are core American values, though they often come into conflict.

When the country does face a national crisis, political decisions suddenly become much more important to the average citizen. The September 11, 2001, terrorist attacks show vividly how events can change attitudes about the government. In a nationwide survey of over 276,000 first-year college students conducted in 2003, 34 percent said that "keeping up with political affairs" was either "very important" or "essential" to them. Although 34 percent might seem like a low number, it was up from the record low of 28 percent reported in 2000. Since 9/11, this number has increased each year. The percentage of first-year students who reported discussing politics frequently in 2003 was 22.5 percent— the highest reported since 1994.[1] The continuing war on terrorism, the war in Iraq, heightened security measures at airports and other places where large numbers of people gather, and renewed discussion of reinstituting the military draft are all specific examples of political issues that have become highly visible in the lives of Americans since 9/11.

Yet even in times when politics seems far removed from students' daily lives, it turns out that much of what students think about is political. Figure 1.1 shows an array of first-year college student attitudes from 2003. Although being "very well-off financially" is by far the most important goal, all the others are, in some way, political.

 Important Life Goals of College Freshmen

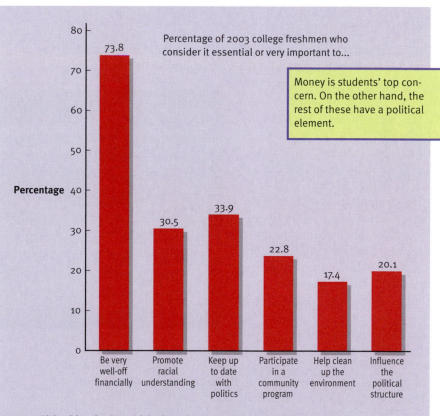

Percentage of 2003 college freshmen who consider it essential or very important to...

Money is students' top concern. On the other hand, the rest of these have a political element.

- Be very well-off financially: 73.8
- Promote racial understanding: 30.5
- Keep up to date with politics: 33.9
- Participate in a community program: 22.8
- Help clean up the environment: 17.4
- Influence the political structure: 20.1

SOURCE: Higher Education Research Institute, UCLA, Annual Freshman Survey, 2003.

Yet the government affects people's lives in good times as well as bad. One important reason for citizens to pay attention to their government in good times is to make sure that the government does not make decisions that might result in unjustified wars, riots, or an economic downturn. The numerous ways in which government affects people daily are nicely summarized in Box 1.1, which shows how many of the typical routine events in the life of an average college student are affected by the hand of government. "Picturing Politics" on pages 6–7 details the web of government influences that affect a graduate making his or her way in the work world.

In this chapter, and in this book, we will argue that the key to understanding American government is to understand the relationship between the citizen and the government. This does *not* mean that every government decision is based on what the majority of people want. In fact, there are many instances when the government makes decisions contrary to what most people want.

Sometimes the government contradicts public opinion because well-placed, influential elites exert a great deal of influence over those who make decisions—a circumstance that riles most Americans. Other times, the government may oppose majority wishes because it is acting to protect the fundamental civil or political rights of a few—a circumstance that most citizens would support, at least in principle. The point is that politics takes on a different character according to the extent to which people are informed and involved. In order to understand this complex relationship, we must begin with an understanding of "citizen," "government," and how the two relate to each other. We will then consider three key values that organize American politics: liberty, equality, and democracy.

Citizenship Is Based on Knowledge of and Participation in Politics

Beginning with the ancient Greeks, citizenship has meant membership in one's community. In fact, the Greeks did not even conceive of the individual as a complete person. The complete person was the public person, the *citizen;* noncitizens and private persons were referred to as *idiotés.* Participation in public affairs was virtually the definition of citizenship. Contrary to the way we think of the term today, citizenship was not defined as voting. Although voting was not excluded, the essence of citizen participation was talking. As one political philosopher put it, "What counts is argument among the citizens. . . . [T]he citizen who makes the most persuasive argument gets [his or her] way but can't use force, or pull rank, or distribute money; [the citizen] must talk about the issues at hand. . . . Citizens must come into the forum with nothing but their arguments."[2] Involvement in the public debate is the central, quintessential right of citizenship. Following the Greek idea, the First

Box 1.1   The Presence of Government in the Daily Life
of a Student at "State University"

Time of Day	Schedule
7:00 AM	Wake up. Standard time set by the national government.
7:10 AM	Shower. Water courtesy of local government, either a public entity or a regulated private company. Brush your teeth with toothpaste, with cavity-fighting claims verified by federal agency. Dry your hair with electric dryer, manufactured according to federal government agency guidelines.
7:30 AM	Have a bowl of cereal with milk for breakfast. "Nutrition Facts" on food labels are a federal requirement, pasteurization of milk required by state law, freshness dating on milk based on state and federal standards, recycling the empty cereal box and milk carton enabled by state or local laws.
8:30 AM	Drive or take public transportation to campus. Air bags and seat belts required by federal and state laws. Roads and bridges paid for by state and local governments, speed and traffic laws set by state and local governments, public transportation subsidized by all levels of government.
8:45 AM	Arrive on campus of large public university. Buildings are 70 percent financed by state taxpayers.
9:00 AM	First class: Chemistry 101. Tuition partially paid by a federal loan (more than half the cost of university instruction is paid for by taxpayers), chemistry lab paid for with grants from the National Science Foundation (a federal agency) and smaller grants from business corporations made possible by federal income tax deductions for charitable contributions.
Noon	Eat lunch. College cafeteria financed by state dormitory authority on land grant from federal Department of Agriculture.
2:00 PM	Second class: American Government 101 (your favorite class!). You may be taking this class because it's required by the state legislature or because it fulfills a university requirement.
4:00 PM	Third class: Computer lab. Free computers, software, and Internet access courtesy of state subsidies plus grants and discounts from IBM and Microsoft, the costs of which are deducted from their corporate income taxes; Internet built in part by federal government. Duplication of software protected by federal copyright laws.
6:00 PM	Eat dinner: hamburger and french fries. Meat inspected by federal agencies for bacteria.
7:00 PM	Work at part-time job at the campus library. Minimum wage set by federal government, books and journals in library paid for by state taxpayers.
10:00 PM	Go to local bar. Purchase and consumption of alcohol regulated by state law and enforced by city police.
11:00 PM	Go home. Street lighting paid for by county and city governments, police patrols by city government.
11:15 PM	Watch TV. Networks regulated by federal government, cable public-access channels required by city law. Weather forecast provided to broadcasters by a federal agency.
Midnight	Put out the garbage before going to bed. Garbage collected by city sanitation department, financed by "user charges."

Amendment to the U.S. Constitution makes freedom of speech the primary right of American citizenship.

Today, voting is considered the building block of **citizenship,** as it is the method by which Americans choose their elected leaders. Yet there are many other ways citizens can influence their government, from serving on a jury, to lobbying, to writing a letter to the editor of a local newspaper, to engaging in a public rally or protest. The point of these activities is to influence the government. It is to the nature of government that we now turn.

> **citizenship** informed and active membership in a political community

Government Is Made Up of the Institutions and Procedures by Which People Are Ruled

Government is the term generally used to describe the formal institutions through which a land and its people are ruled. To govern is to rule. A government may be as simple as a tribal council that meets occasionally to advise the chief, or as complex as the vast establishments, with their forms, rules, and bureaucracies, found in the United States and the countries of Europe. A more complex government is sometimes referred to as "the state." In the history of civilization, governments have not been difficult to establish. There have been thousands of them. The hard part is establishing a government that lasts. Even more difficult is developing a stable government that promotes liberty, equality, and democracy.

> **government** institutions and procedures through which a territory and its people are ruled

DIFFERENT FORMS OF GOVERNMENT ARE DEFINED BY HOW POWERFUL THE GOVERNMENT IS AND HOW FREE THE PEOPLE ARE

Governments vary in their structure, in their size, and in the way they operate. Two questions are of special importance in determining how governments differ: Who governs? And how much government control is permitted?

In some nations, government power is held by a single individual, such as a king or dictator, or by a small group of powerful individuals, such as military leaders or wealthy landowners. Such a system of government normally pays little attention to popular preferences; it tends to hold power by violence or the threat of violence and is referred to as an **authoritarian** system. A system of government in which the degree of control is even greater is a **totalitarian** system, where the government not only exercises great power, but seeks to impose its will by suppressing any and all other groups and individuals in society that might pose a challenge to its power. Nazi Germany under Adolf Hitler and the Soviet Union under Joseph Stalin are classic examples of totalitarian rule.

In contrast, a **democracy** is a political system where popular wishes and preferences regularly and systematically shape who controls the government and what the government does. Under such a system, **constitutional government** is the norm, in that governmental power is both described in, and limited by, a governing constitution. At times, an authoritarian government might

> **authoritarian government** a system of rule in which the government recognizes no formal limits but may nevertheless be restrained by the power of other social institutions
>
> **totalitarian government** a system of rule in which the government recognizes no formal limits on its power and seeks to absorb or eliminate other social institutions that might challenge it
>
> **democracy** a system of rule that permits citizens to play a significant part in the governmental process, usually through the election of key public officials
>
> **constitutional government** a system of rule in which formal and effective limits are placed on the powers of the government

PICTURING

The Role of Government in Your Daily Life

When you shower in the morning, the water comes to you courtesy of your local government, either from a public entity or from a regulated private company.

On your way to campus, you drive over roads and bridges paid for by state and local governments. The speed and traffic laws are also set by state and local governments.

POLITICS

Once on the campus of the large public university you attend, you enter one of its many buildings. Seventy percent of those buildings are financed by state taxpayers.

The sandwich you eat for dinner contains meat inspected by federal agencies, and the TV stations you flip through with your remote are also regulated by the federal government.

bend to popular wishes, and as we have already pointed out, democratic governments do not automatically follow the wishes of the majority. The point, however, is that these contrasting systems of government are based on very different assumptions and practices (see Box 1.2).

Americans have the good fortune to live in a nation in which limits are placed on what governments can do and how they can do it. But such constitutional democracies are relatively rare in today's world; it is estimated that only twenty or so of the world's nearly two hundred governments could be included in this category. And constitutional democracies were unheard of before the modern era. Prior to the eighteenth and nineteenth centuries, governments seldom sought—and rarely received—the support of their ordinary subjects. The available evidence strongly suggests that the ordinary people had little love for the government or for the social order. After all, they had no stake in it. They equated government with the police officer, the bailiff, and the tax collector.[3]

Beginning in the seventeenth century, in a handful of Western nations, two important changes began to take place in the character and conduct of government. First, governments began to acknowledge formal limits on their power. Second, a small number of governments began to provide the ordinary citizen with a formal voice in public affairs—through the vote. Obviously, the desirability of limits on government and the expansion of popular influence were at the heart of the American Revolution in 1776. "No taxation without representation" was hotly debated from the beginning of the Revolution through the adoption of the modern Constitution in 1789. But even before the Revolution, a tradition of limiting government and expanding citizen participation in the political process had developed throughout western Europe. Thus, to understand how the relationship between rulers and the ruled was transformed, we must broaden our focus to take into account events in Europe as well as in America. We will divide the transformation into its two separate parts. The first is the effort to put limits on government. The second is the effort to expand the influence of the people through access to government and politics.

LIMITING GOVERNMENTS ENCOURAGED FREEDOM

The key force behind the imposition of limits on government power was a new social class, the bourgeoisie. *Bourgeoisie* is a French word for freeman of the city, or *bourg*. Being part of the bourgeoisie later became associated with being "middle class" and with being in commerce or industry. In order to gain a share of control of government, joining or even displacing the kings, aristocrats, and gentry who had dominated government for centuries, the bourgeoisie sought to change existing institutions—especially parliaments—into instruments of real political participation. Parliaments had existed for centuries, but were generally controlled by the aristocrats. The bourgeoisie embraced parliaments as means by which they could exert the weight of their superior numbers and growing economic advantage against their aristocratic rivals. At the same time, the bourgeoisie sought to place restraints on the capacity of governments to threaten

Constitutional, Authoritarian, and Totalitarian Governments

Box 1.2

Most Western democracies have constitutions that actually define the limits and scope of governmental power. But the mere existence of a constitution does not, by itself, define a regime as constitutional. Some governments have constitutions that they ignore. At least until recently, this was the case in such eastern European nations as Romania and Bulgaria. In the true constitutional setting, the actual processes of government follow the forms prescribed by the constitution, and groups in society have sufficient freedom and power to oppose efforts by the government to overstep these limits. The governments in the United States and western Europe provide the best examples.

Authoritarian governments must sometimes be responsive to a small number of powerful social groups and institutions such as the army, but such governments recognize no formal obligations to consult their citizens or to respect limits on their actions. Examples of authoritarian governments in the recent past include Spain under the leadership of General Francisco Franco and Portugal under Prime Minister Antonio Salazar.

Totalitarian governments can be distinguished from both democratic and authoritarian governments by the lack of any distinction between the government and other important social institutions. Indeed, totalitarian governments generally seek to destroy all other social institutions—for example, churches, labor unions, and political parties—that may function as rival sources of power. Examples of totalitarian governments include the Third Reich in Germany under Hitler in the 1930s and 1940s and the government of the Soviet Union under Stalin between the 1930s and 1950s.

In recent years, a number of authoritarian regimes in eastern Europe, including the Soviet Union and its satellite states, faced severe economic hardship and popular discontent. After 1989, most of these regimes, including those in Czechoslovakia, Poland, Hungary, East Germany, and the Soviet Union itself, collapsed and were replaced by new, democratically elected governments.

these economic and political interests by placing formal or constitutional limits on governmental power.

Although motivated primarily by the need to protect and defend their own interests, the bourgeoisie advanced many of the principles that became the central underpinnings of individual liberty for all citizens—freedom of speech, freedom of assembly, freedom of conscience, and freedom from arbitrary search and seizure. It is important to note here that the bourgeoisie generally did not favor democracy as we know it. They were advocates of electoral and representative institutions, but they favored property requirements and other restrictions so as to limit participation to the middle classes. Yet once these institutions of politics and the protection of the right to engage in politics were established, it was difficult to limit them to the bourgeoisie.

EXPANSION OF PARTICIPATION IN AMERICA CHANGED THE POLITICAL BALANCE

In America, the expansion of participation to ever-larger segments of society, seen mostly in the expansion of voting rights, occurred because of pressure from those who were not a part of the political process, as well as from those already in power who tried to gain political advantage by "lining up the unwashed," as one American historian put it.[4] In the first thirty years of America's history, for example, property qualifications for voting kept most white males out of the voting booths (obviously, African Americans and women did not win the right to vote until much later). In the 1820s, leaders like Andrew Jackson came to power by helping to put an end to property qualifications. These millions of grateful new voters threw overwhelming support behind Jackson and what came to be known as "Jacksonian democracy."

This pattern of suffrage expansion by groups hoping to derive some political advantage has been typical in American history. After the Civil War, one of the chief reasons that Lincoln's Republican Party moved to enfranchise newly freed slaves was to use the support of the former slaves to maintain Republican control over the defeated southern states. Similarly, in the early twentieth century, upper-middle-class "Progressives" advocated women's suffrage because they believed that women were likely to support the reforms espoused by the Progressive movement.

POLITICS MEANS HAVING A SAY IN WHAT HAPPENS

Expansion of participation means that more and more people have a legal right to take part in politics. Politics is an important term. In its broadest sense, "politics" refers to conflicts over the character, membership, and policies of any organization to which people belong. As Harold Lasswell, a famous political scientist, once put it, politics is the struggle over "who gets what, when, how."[5] Although politics is a phenomenon that can be found in any organization, our concern in this book is more narrow. Here, **politics** will be used to refer only to conflicts and struggles over the leadership, structure, and policies of governments. The goal of politics, as we define it, is to have a share or a say in the composition of the government's leadership, how the government is organized, or what its policies are going to be. Having a share is called **power** or influence.

Politics can take many forms, including everything from voting, to sending letters to government officials, to lobbying legislators on behalf of particular programs, and participating in protest marches and even violent demonstrations. A system of government that gives citizens a regular opportunity to elect the top government officials is usually called a **representative democracy** or **republic.** A system that permits citizens to vote directly on laws and policies is often called a **direct democracy.** At the national level, America is a representative democracy in which citizens select government officials but do not vote on legislation. Some states, however, have provisions for direct legislation through popular referendum. For example, California voters in 1995 decided to bar undocumented immigrants from receiving some state services.

politics conflict over the leadership, structure, and policies of governments

power influence over a government's leadership, organization, or policies

representative democracy/ republic a system of government in which the populace selects representatives, who play a significant role in governmental decision making

direct democracy a system of rule that permits citizens to vote directly on laws and policies

America Is Built on the Ideas of Liberty, Equality, and Democracy

A few fundamental values underlie the American system. These values are reflected in such founding documents as the Declaration of Independence, the Constitution, and the Bill of Rights. The three values on which the American system of government is based are liberty, equality, and democracy.

LIBERTY MEANS FREEDOM

No ideal is more central to American values than liberty. The Declaration of Independence defined three inalienable rights: "life, liberty and the pursuit of happiness." The preamble of the Constitution likewise identified the need to secure "the blessings of liberty" as one of the key reasons for drawing up the Constitution. For Americans, **liberty** means both personal freedom and economic freedom. Both are closely linked to the idea of **limited government.**

> **liberty** freedom from government control
>
> **limited government** a government whose powers are defined and limited by a constitution

The Constitution's first ten amendments, known collectively as the Bill of Rights, above all preserves individual personal liberties and rights. In fact, liberty has come to mean many of the freedoms guaranteed in the Bill of Rights: freedom of speech and writing, the right to assemble freely, and the right to practice religious beliefs without interference from the government. Over the course of American history, the scope of personal liberties has expanded, as laws have become more tolerant and as individuals have successfully used the courts to challenge restrictions on their individual freedoms. Far fewer restrictions exist today on the press, political speech, and individual moral behavior than in the early years of the nation. Even so, conflicts persist over how personal liberties should be extended and when personal liberties violate community norms. For example, one of the most contentious issues in the last thirty years has been that of abortion. Whereas defenders of the right to choose abortion view it as an essential personal freedom for women, opponents view it as murder—something that no society should allow.

In addition to personal freedom, the American concept of liberty means economic freedom. Since the founding, economic freedom has been linked to capitalism, free markets, and the protection of private property. Free competition, unfettered movement of goods, and the right to enjoy the fruits of one's labor are all essential aspects of economic freedom and American capitalism.[6] In the first century of the Republic, support for capitalism often meant support for the doctrine of *laissez faire* (translated literally as "to leave alone"). **Laissez-faire capitalism** allowed very little room for the national government to regulate trade or restrict the use of private property, even in the public interest. Americans still strongly support capitalism and economic liberty, but they now also endorse some restrictions on economic freedoms to protect the public. Federal and state governments now deploy a wide array of regulations in the name of public protection. These include health and safety laws, environmental rules, and workplace regulations. Not surprisingly, fierce disagreements often

> **laissez-faire capitalism** an economic system in which the means of production and distribution are privately owned and operated for profit with minimal or no government interference

erupt over what the proper scope of government regulation should be. What some people regard as protecting the public, others see as an infringement of their own freedom to run their businesses and use their property as they see fit.

EQUALITY MEANS TREATING PEOPLE FAIRLY

equality of opportunity a widely shared American ideal that all people should have the freedom to use whatever talents and wealth they have to reach their fullest potential

The Declaration of Independence declares as its first "self-evident" truth that "all men are created equal." As central as it is to the American political creed, however, equality has been a less defined ideal than liberty because people interpret "equality" in different ways. Most Americans share the ideal of **equality of opportunity**—that is, the notion that each person should be given a fair chance to go as far as his or her talents will allow. Yet it is hard for Americans to reach agreement about what constitutes equality of opportunity. Must past inequalities be remedied in order to ensure equal opportunity in the present? Should inequalities in the legal, political, and economic spheres be given the same weight? In contrast to liberty, which requires limits on the role of government, equality implies an obligation of the government to the people.[7]

political equality the right to participate in politics equally, based on the principle of "one person, one vote"

Americans do make clear distinctions between political equality and social or economic equality. **Political equality** means that members of the American political community have the right to participate in politics on equal terms. Beginning from a very restricted definition of political community, which originally included only propertied white men, the United States has moved much closer to an ideal of political equality that can be summed up as "one person, one vote." Broad support for the ideal of political equality has helped expand the American political community and extend the right to participate to all. Although considerable conflict remains over whether the political system makes it harder for some people to participate and easier for others and about whether the role of money in politics has drowned out the public voice, Americans agree that all citizens should have equal rights to participate and that government should enforce that right.

In part because Americans believe that individuals are free to work as hard as they choose, they have always been less concerned about social or economic inequality. Many Americans regard economic differences as the consequence of individual choices, virtues, or failures. Because of this, Americans tend to be less supportive than most Europeans of government action to ensure equality. Yet when major economic forces, such as the Great Depression of the 1930s, affect many people or when systematic barriers appear to block equality of opportunity, Americans support government action to promote equality. Even then, however, Americans have endorsed only a limited government role designed to help people get back on their feet or to open up opportunity.

DEMOCRACY MEANS THAT WHAT THE PEOPLE WANT MATTERS

The essence of democracy is the participation of the people in choosing their rulers and the people's ability to influence what those rulers do. In a democracy, political power ultimately comes from the people. The idea of placing power in the hands of the people is known as **popular sovereignty.** In the United States, popular sovereignty and political equality make politicians accountable to the people. Ideally, democracy envisions an engaged citizenry prepared to exercise its power over rulers. As we saw earlier, the United States is a representative democracy, meaning that the people do not rule directly but instead exercise power through elected representatives. Forms of participation in a democracy vary greatly, but voting is a key element of the representative democracy that the American Founders established.

American democracy rests on the principle of **majority rule** with **minority rights.** Majority rule means that the wishes of the majority determine what government does. The House of Representatives—a large body elected directly by the people—was designed in particular to ensure majority rule. But the Founders feared that popular majorities could turn government into a "tyranny of the majority" that would violate individual liberties. Concern for individual rights has thus been a part of American democracy from the beginning. The rights enumerated in the Bill of Rights and enforced through the courts provide an important check on the power of the majority.

popular sovereignty a principle of democracy in which political authority rests ultimately in the hands of the people

majority rule/minority rights the democratic principle that a government follows the preferences of the majority of voters but protects the interests of the minority

AMERICAN POLITICAL VALUES CONFLICT

The ideals of liberty, equality, and democracy can be interpreted in many different ways. Moreover, these ideals can easily conflict with one another in practice. When we examine American history, we can see that there have been large gaps between these ideals and the practice of American politics. We can also see that some ideals have been prized more than others at different historical moments. But it is also clear that as Americans have engaged in political conflict about who should participate in politics and how political institutions should be organized, they have called upon these ideals to justify their actions. So, for example, affirmative action programs, or laws designed to prevent discrimination against the handicapped, such as the Americans with Disabilities Act, may promote equality but may also infringe upon the liberty of employers to hire whomever they wish.

Conversely, in the name of equality or liberty, courts often hand down verdicts that undo decisions of democratically elected legislatures and even decisions reached in popular votes. Principles that seem universal in the abstract become more complicated in operation. In the process of resolving conflicts among core beliefs, America's political principles change and evolve. Even core values should be understood as works in progress rather than immutable facts.

Summary

The key to understanding American government is to understand the relationship between the citizen and the government. Americans often do not take their citizenship seriously, especially when times are good. Yet the government shapes people's daily lives far more than they realize.

Governments can take many forms. Throughout most of history, and throughout much of the world today, the most common form of government has been undemocratic. The idea of democratic governance is a relatively new one. America was founded on democratic beliefs, but the nation was less democratic two hundred years ago than it is today.

America's core values of liberty, equality, and democracy did and do shape its political struggles. All are noble goals, but they often conflict.

For Further Reading

Craig, Stephen C., and Stephen Earl Bennett, eds. *After the Boom: The Politics of Generation X.* Lanham, MD: Rowman and Littlefield, 1997.

Dahl, Robert. *How Democratic Is the American Constitution?* New Haven, CT: Yale University Press, 2002.

Delli Carpini, Michael X., and Scott Keeter. *What Americans Know about Politics and Why It Matters.* New Haven, CT: Yale University Press, 1996.

Hochschild, Jennifer L. *Facing Up to the American Dream: Race, Class, and the Soul of the Nation.* Princeton, NJ: Princeton University Press, 1995.

Huntington, Samuel P. *American Politics: The Promise of Disharmony.* Cambridge, MA: Harvard University Press, 1981.

Lasswell, Harold. *Politics: Who Gets What, When, How.* New York: Meridian Books, 1958.

McClosky, Herbert, and John Zaller. *The American Ethos: Public Attitudes toward Capitalism and Democracy.* Cambridge, MA: Harvard University Press, 1984.

Nie, Norman H., Jane Junn, and Kenneth Stehlik-Barry. *Education and Democratic Citizenship in America.* Chicago: University of Chicago Press, 1996.

Nye, Joseph S., Jr., Philip D. Zelikow, and David C. King, eds. *Why People Don't Trust Government.* Cambridge, MA: Harvard University Press, 1997.

Putnam, Robert. *Making Democracy Work: Civic Traditions in Modern Italy.* Princeton, NJ: Princeton University Press, 1993.

de Tocqueville, Alexis. *Democracy in America.* Trans. Phillips Bradley. New York: Knopf, Vintage Books, 1945; orig. published 1835.

Study Outline

Government Is Made Up of the Institutions and Procedures by Which People Are Ruled

1. Governments vary in their structure, in their size, and in the way they operate.
2. Beginning in the seventeenth century, two important changes began to take place in the governance of some Western nations: governments began to acknowledge formal limits on their power, and governments began to give citizens a formal voice in politics through the vote.
3. Political participation can take many forms: the vote, group activities, and even direct action, such as violence or civil disobedience.

America Is Built on the Ideas of Liberty, Equality, and Democracy

1. Three important political values in American politics are liberty, equality, and democracy.
2. At times in American history there have been large gaps between the ideals embodied in Americans' core values and the practice of American government.
3. Many of the important dilemmas of American politics revolve around conflicts over fundamental political values. One such conflict involves the ideals of liberty and democracy. Over time, democracy promotes stronger, more active government, which may threaten liberty.

Practice Quiz

1. The famous political scientist Harold Lasswell defined politics as the struggle over
   a) who gets elected.
   b) who gets what, when, how.
   c) who protests.
   d) who gets to vote.

2. The bourgeoisie championed
   a) democracy.
   b) "taxation without representation."
   c) limitations on government power.
   d) societal revolution.

3. The principle of political equality can be best summed up as
   a) "equality of results."
   b) "equality of opportunity."
   c) "one person, one vote."
   d) "equality between the sexes."

4. Which of the following is an important principle of American democracy?
   a) popular sovereignty
   b) majority rule/minority rights
   c) limited government
   d) All of the above are important principles of American democracy.

5. Which of the following is not related to the American conception of "liberty"?
   a) freedom of speech
   b) free enterprise
   c) freedom of religion
   d) All of the above are related to liberty.

Critical Thinking Questions

1. What type of government does the United States have? Is it the most democratic government possible? Do citizens make the decisions of government or do they merely influence them? Describe the ways in which citizens in America participate in politics.

2. Think of some examples that demonstrate the gaps between the ideals of America's core political values and the practice of American politics. Describe how such gaps were reconciled in the past. Identify one current gap between Americans' values and their political practices. How might this discrepancy be reconciled?

Key Terms

authoritarian government (p. 5)
citizenship (p. 5)
constitutional government (p. 5)
democracy (p. 5)
direct democracy (p. 10)
equality of opportunity (p. 12)
government (p. 5)
laissez-faire capitalism (p. 11)
liberty (p. 11)
limited government (p. 11)
majority rule/minority rights (p. 13)
political equality (p. 12)
politics (p. 10)
popular sovereignty (p. 13)
power (p. 10)
representative democracy (or republic) (p. 10)
totalitarian government (p. 5)

2

THE FOUNDING AND THE CONSTITUTION

MAIN MESSAGE

The Constitution defines the relationship between citizens and the government, and it reflects both high principle and self-interest.

The story of America's founding and the Constitution is generally presented as something both inevitable and glorious: it was inevitable that the American colonies would break away from England to establish their own country successfully; and it was glorious in that it established the best of all possible forms of government under a new Constitution, which was easily adopted and quickly embraced, even by its critics. In reality, though, America's successful breakaway from England was by no means assured, and the Constitution that we revere today as

Key Concepts

1. The Constitution balances individual freedom with governmental power.

2. British laws that hurt American economic interests pushed the colonies toward independence.

3. The country's first founding under the Articles of Confederation failed because it created a national government that was too weak.

4. The new Constitution of 1787 combined selfish interests and high principle.

5. The new Constitution gave vast new powers to the national government, but it also sharply limited those powers.

6. The new Constitution was highly controversial at first, and as a result, a Bill of Rights was added to calm the critics' fears.

7. Later constitutional amendments dramatically changed the relationship between Americans and the government.

one of the most brilliant creations of any nation was in fact highly controversial. Moreover, its ratification and durability were often in doubt. George Washington, the man revered as the father of the country and the person chosen to preside over the Constitutional Convention of 1787, thought the document produced that hot summer in Philadelphia would probably last no more than twenty years, at which time leaders would have to convene again to come up with something new.

That Washington's prediction proved wrong is, indeed, a testament to the enduring strength of the Constitution. But none of the Founders was Moses, and the Constitution was no Ten Commandments, carved by lightning in stone. The Constitution was a product of political bargaining and compromise, formed very much in the same way political decisions are made today. This fact is often overlooked because of what historian Michael Kammen has called the "cult of the Constitution"—a tendency of Americans, going back more than a century, to venerate blindly, sometimes to the point of near worship, the Founders and the document they created.[1] As this chapter will show, the Constitution reflects political self-interest, but high principle, too. It also defines the relationship between American citizens and their government.

The proposed new system of government faced considerable opposition. The objections raised by opponents of the proposed constitution—who called themselves Antifederalists—were profound and important. The Antifederalists thought that the state governments would be able to represent the people much better than the national government could. They also were concerned that the officials of a large and powerful government would inevitably abuse their authority. The Antifederalists understood the basic problem of freedom and power and feared that the powers given to the national government to do good would sooner or later be turned to evil purposes.

The founding era was also the period during which Americans first confronted the great question of who was to be included and who was to be excluded from full citizenship. The answer given by the Founders—all white men were entitled to full citizenship rights—was an extremely democratic position for its time. America was one of the few nations that extended citizenship so broadly. Yet the founding generation did not resolve the question once and for all. Over the ensuing two hundred years, as we shall see, the question of who is and who is not a full citizen of the United States has been debated many times and has never been completely resolved.

In this chapter, we will first assess the political backdrop of the American Revolution, which led to the Declaration of Independence and the establishment of a governmental structure under the Articles of Confederation. We will then consider the conditions that led to the Constitutional Convention of 1787 and the great issues that were debated by the framers. Next, we will examine the Constitution that ultimately emerged as the basis for the national government. The framers sought to create a powerful national government, but guarded against possible misuse of that power through the separation of powers, federalism, and the Bill of Rights. We will then examine the first hurdle that the Constitution faced, the fight for ratification. Two sides, the Federalists and the Antifederalists, vigorously debated the great political issues and principles at stake. The resolution of this debate created the framework for a national government that has lasted more than two hundred years. We will then look at how the Constitution has changed over the past two centuries. The framers designed an amendment process so that the Constitution could change, but the process has succeeded only on rare occasions. Finally, we will ask what liberty, equality, and democracy meant to the framers of the Constitution. Although the framers established a system of government that would eventually allow each of these political values to thrive, they championed liberty as the most important of the three.

Narrow Interests and Political Conflicts Shaped the First Founding

The American Revolution and the American Constitution were outgrowths of a struggle among competing economic and political forces within the colonies. Five sectors of society had interests that were important in colonial politics: (1) the New England merchants; (2) the southern planters; (3) the "royalists"—holders of royal lands, offices, and patents (licenses to engage in a profession or business activity); (4) shopkeepers, artisans, and laborers; and (5) small farmers. Throughout the eighteenth century, these groups were in conflict over issues of taxation, trade, and commerce. For the most part, however, the southern planters, the New England merchants, and the royal office and patent holders—groups that together made up the colonial elite—were able to maintain a political alliance that held in check the more radical forces representing shopkeepers, laborers, and small farmers. After 1750, however, by seriously threatening the interests of New England merchants and southern planters, British tax and trade policies split the colonial elite, permitting radical forces to expand their political influence, and set into motion a chain of events that culminated in the American Revolution.[2]

BRITISH TAXES HURT COLONIAL ECONOMIC INTERESTS

Beginning in the 1750s, the debts and other financial problems faced by the British government forced it to search for new revenue sources. This search rather quickly led to the Crown's North American colonies, which, on the whole, paid remarkably little in taxes to their parent country. The British government reasoned that a sizable fraction of its debt arose from the expenses it had incurred in defense of the colonies during the recent French and Indian wars (1756–63), as well as from the continuing protection that British forces were giving the colonists from Indian attacks and that the British navy was providing for colonial shipping. Thus, during the 1760s, England sought to impose new, though relatively modest, taxes upon the colonists.

Like most governments of the period, the British regime had limited ways in which to collect revenues. The income tax, which in the twentieth century has become the single most important source of governmental revenues, had not yet been developed. For the most part, in the mid-eighteenth century, governments relied on tariffs, duties, and other taxes on commerce, and it was to such taxes, including the Stamp Act, that the British turned during the 1760s.

The Stamp Act and other taxes on commerce, such as the Sugar Act of 1764, which taxed sugar, molasses, and other commodities, most heavily affected the two groups in colonial society whose commercial interests and activities were most extensive—the New England merchants and the southern planters. Under the famous slogan "no taxation without representation," the merchants and planters together sought to organize opposition to these new taxes. In the course of the struggle against British tax measures, the planters and merchants broke with their royalist allies and turned to their former adversaries—the shopkeepers, small farmers, laborers, and artisans—for help. With the assistance of these groups, the merchants and planters organized demonstrations and a boycott of British goods that ultimately forced the Crown to rescind most of its new taxes.

From the perspective of the merchants and planters, the British government's decision to eliminate most of the hated taxes represented a victorious end to their struggle with the parent country. They were anxious to end the unrest they had helped to arouse, and they supported the British government's efforts to restore order. Indeed, most respectable Bostonians supported the actions of the British soldiers involved in the Boston Massacre (1770). In their subsequent trial, the soldiers were defended by John Adams, a pillar of Boston society and a future president of the United States. Adams asserted that the soldiers' actions were entirely justified, provoked by "a motley rabble of saucy boys, Negroes and mulattos, Irish teagues and outlandish Jack tars." All but two of the soldiers were acquitted.[3]

Despite the efforts of the British government and the better-to-do strata of colonial society, political strife persisted. The more radical forces representing shopkeepers, artisans, laborers, and small farmers, who had been mobilized and energized by the struggle over taxes, continued to agitate for political and social change within the colonies. These radicals, led by individuals such as Samuel Adams, a cousin of John Adams, asserted that British power supported an unjust political and social structure within the colonies, and began to advocate an end to British rule.[4]

POLITICAL STRIFE RADICALIZED THE COLONISTS

The political strife within the colonies was the background for the events of 1773–74. In 1773, the British government granted the politically powerful East India Company a monopoly on the export of tea from Britain, eliminating a lucrative form of trade for colonial merchants. To add to the injury, the East India Company sought to sell the tea directly in the colonies instead of working through the colonial merchants. Tea was an extremely important commodity in the 1770s, and these British actions posed a mortal threat to the New England merchants. Together with their southern allies, the merchants once again called upon their radical adversaries for support. The most dramatic result was the Boston Tea Party of 1773, led by Samuel Adams.

This event was of decisive importance in American history. The merchants had hoped to force the British government to rescind the Tea Act, but they did not support any demands beyond this one. They certainly did not seek independence from Britain. Samuel Adams and the other radicals, however, hoped to provoke the British government to take actions that would alienate its colonial supporters and pave the way for a rebellion. This was precisely the purpose of the Boston Tea Party, and it succeeded. By dumping the East India Company's tea into Boston Harbor, Adams and his followers goaded the British into enacting a number of harsh reprisals. Within five months after the incident in Boston, the House of Commons passed a series of acts that closed the port of Boston to commerce, changed the provincial government of Massachusetts, provided for the removal of accused persons to England for trial, and most important, restricted movement to the West—further alienating the southern planters, who depended upon access to new western lands. These acts of retaliation confirmed the worst criticisms of England and helped radicalize Americans. Radicals such as Samuel Adams and Christopher Gadsden of South Carolina had been agitating from more violent measures to deal with England. But it was Britain's political repression that fanned support for independence.

Thus, the Boston Tea Party set into motion a cycle of provocation and retaliation that in 1774 resulted in the convening of the First Continental Congress—an assembly of delegates from all parts of the country—that called for a total boycott of British goods and, under the prodding of the radicals, began to consider the possibility of independence from British rule. The eventual result was the Declaration of Independence.

THE DECLARATION OF INDEPENDENCE EXPLAINED WHY WE WANTED TO BREAK WITH ENGLAND

In 1776, the Second Continental Congress appointed a committee consisting of Thomas Jefferson of Virginia, Benjamin Franklin of Pennsylvania, Roger Sherman of Connecticut, John Adams of Massachusetts, and Robert Livingston of New York to draft a statement of American independence from British rule. The Declaration of Independence, written by Jefferson and adopted by the Second Continental Congress, was an extraordinary philosophical and political document. Philosophically, the Declaration was remarkable for its assertion that certain rights, called "unalienable rights"—including life, liberty, and the pursuit of happiness—could not be abridged by governments. In the world of 1776, a world in which some kings still claimed to rule by divine right, this was a dramatic statement. Politically, the Declaration was remarkable because, despite the differences of interest that divided the colonists along economic, regional, and philosophical lines, the Declaration identified and focused on problems, grievances, aspirations, and principles that might unify the various colonial groups. The Declaration was an attempt to identify and articulate a history and set of principles that might help to forge national unity.[5] It also explained to the rest of the world why American colonists were attempting to break away from England.

THE ARTICLES OF CONFEDERATION CREATED OUR FIRST NATIONAL GOVERNMENT

Having declared their independence, the colonies needed to establish a governmental structure. In November of 1777, the Continental Congress adopted the **Articles of Confederation and Perpetual Union**—the United States's first written constitution. Although it was not ratified by all the states until 1781, it was the country's operative constitution for almost twelve years, until March 1789.

Articles of Confederation America's first written constitution; served as the basis for America's national government until 1789

The Articles of Confederation was a constitution concerned primarily with limiting the powers of the central government. The central government, first of all, was based entirely in a Congress. Since it was not intended to be a powerful government, it was given no executive branch. Execution of its laws was to be left to the individual states. Second, the Congress had little power. Its members were not much more than delegates or messengers from the state legislatures. They were chosen by the state legislatures, their salaries were paid out of the state treasuries, and they were subject to immediate recall by state authorities. In addition, each state, regardless of its size, had only a single vote.

The Congress was given the power to declare war and make peace, to make treaties and alliances, to coin or borrow money, and to regulate trade with the Native Americans. It could also appoint the senior officers of the United States army. But it could not levy taxes or regulate commerce among the states. Moreover, the army officers it appointed had no army to serve in because the nation's armed forces were composed of the state militias. Probably the most unfortunate part of the Articles of Confederation was that the central government could not prevent one state from discriminating against other states in the quest for foreign commerce.

confederation a system of government in which states retain sovereign authority except for the powers expressly delegated to the national government

In brief, the relationship between the Congress and the states under the Articles of Confederation was much like the contemporary relationship between the United Nations and its member states, a relationship in which the states retained virtually all governmental powers. It was properly called a **confederation** because, as provided under Article II, "each state retains its sovereignty, freedom and independence, and every Power, Jurisdiction and right, which is not by this confederation expressly delegated to the United States, in Congress assembled." Not only was there no executive, there also was no judicial authority and no other means of enforcing the Congress's will. If there was to be any enforcement at all, the states would do it for the Congress.[6]

The Failure of the Articles Made the "Second Founding" Necessary

The Declaration of Independence and the Articles of Confederation were not sufficient to hold the new nation together as an independent and effective nation-state. From almost the moment of armistice with the British in 1783, moves were afoot to reform and strengthen the Articles of Confederation.

AMERICA'S WEAKNESS AT HOME MADE IT WEAK ABROAD

There was a special concern for the country's international position. Competition among the states for foreign commerce allowed the European powers to play the states against one another, which created confusion on both sides of the Atlantic. At one point during the winter of 1786–87, John Adams of Massachusetts, a leader in the independence struggle, was sent to negotiate a new treaty with the British, one that would cover disputes left over from the war. The British government responded that, since the United States under the Articles of Confederation was unable to enforce existing treaties, it would negotiate with each of the thirteen states separately.

At the same time, well-to-do Americans—in particular the New England merchants and southern planters—were troubled by the influence that "radical" forces exercised in the Continental Congress and in the governments of several of the states. The colonists' victory in the Revolutionary War had not only meant the end of British rule, but also significantly changed the balance of political power within the new states. As a result of the Revolution, one key segment of the colonial elite—the royal land, office, and patent holders—was stripped of its economic and political privileges. In fact, many of these individuals, along with tens of thousands of other colonists who considered themselves loyal British subjects, left for Canada after the British surrender. And while the pre-Revolutionary elite was weakened, the pre-Revolutionary radicals were now better organized than ever before and were the controlling forces in such states as Pennsylvania and Rhode Island, where they pursued economic and political policies that struck terror into the hearts of the pre-Revolutionary political establishment. In Rhode Island, for example, between 1783 and 1785, a legislature dominated by representatives of small farmers, artisans, and shopkeepers had instituted economic policies, including drastic currency inflation, that frightened business and property owners throughout the country. Of course, the central government under the Articles of Confederation was powerless to intervene.

THE ANNAPOLIS CONVENTION WAS KEY TO CALLING A NATIONAL CONVENTION

The continuation of international weakness and domestic economic turmoil led many Americans to consider whether their newly adopted form of government might not already require revision. In the fall of 1786, many state leaders accepted an invitation from the Virginia legislature for a conference of representatives of all the states. Delegates from five states actually attended. This conference, held in Annapolis, Maryland, was the first step toward the second founding. The one positive thing that came out of the Annapolis Convention was a carefully worded resolution calling on the Congress to send commissioners to Philadelphia at a later time "to devise such further provisions as shall appear to them necessary to render the Constitution of the Federal Government adequate to the exigencies of the Union."[7] This resolution was drafted by Alexander Hamilton, a thirty-four-year-old New York lawyer who had played a significant role in the Revolution as George Washington's secretary and who would play a still more significant role in framing the Constitution and forming the new government in the 1790s. But the resolution did not necessarily imply any desire to do more than improve and reform the Articles of Confederation.

SHAYS'S REBELLION SHOWED HOW WEAK THE GOVERNMENT WAS

It is quite possible that the Constitutional Convention of 1787 in Philadelphia would never have taken place at all except for a single event that occurred during the winter following the Annapolis Convention: Shays's Rebellion.

Daniel Shays, a former army captain, led a mob of farmers in a rebellion against the government of Massachusetts. The purpose of the rebellion was to prevent foreclosures on their debt-ridden land by keeping the county courts of western Massachusetts from sitting until after the next election. The state militia dispersed the mob, but for several days Shays and his followers terrified the state government by attempting to capture the federal arsenal at Springfield, provoking an appeal to the Congress to help restore order. Within a few days, the state government regained control and captured fourteen of the rebels (all were eventually pardoned). In 1787, a newly elected Massachusetts legislature granted some of the farmers' demands.

Although the incident ended peacefully, its effects lingered and spread. George Washington summed it up: "I am mortified beyond expression that in the moment of our acknowledged independence we should by our conduct verify the predictions of our transatlantic foe, and render ourselves ridiculous and contemptible in the eyes of all Europe."[8]

The Congress under the Confederation had been unable to act decisively in a time of crisis. This provided critics of the Articles of Confederation with precisely the evidence they needed to push Hamilton's Annapolis resolution through the Congress. Thus, the states were asked to send representatives to Philadelphia to discuss constitutional revision. Delegates were eventually sent by every state except Rhode Island.

THE CONSTITUTIONAL CONVENTION DIDN'T START OUT TO WRITE A NEW CONSTITUTION

Delegates selected by the state governments convened in Philadelphia in May 1787, with political strife, international embarrassment, national weakness, and local rebellion fixed in their minds. Recognizing that these issues were symptoms of fundamental flaws in the Articles of Confederation, the delegates soon abandoned the plan to revise the Articles and committed themselves to a second founding—a second, and ultimately successful, attempt to create a legitimate and effective national system of government. This effort occupied the convention for the next five months.

A Marriage of Interest and Principle Scholars have for years disagreed about the motives of the Founders in Philadelphia. Among the most controversial views of the framers' motives is the "economic interpretation" put forward by historian Charles Beard and his disciples.[9] According to Beard's account, America's Founders were a collection of securities speculators and property owners whose only aim was personal enrichment. From this perspective, the Constitution's lofty principles were little more than sophisticated masks behind which the most venal interests sought to enrich themselves.

Contrary to Beard's approach is the view that the framers of the Constitution *were* concerned with philosophical and ethical principles. Indeed, the framers did try to devise a system of government consistent with the dominant philosophical and moral principles of the day. But, in fact, these two views belong together; the Founders' interests were reinforced by their principles. The convention that drafted the American Constitution was chiefly organized by the New England merchants and southern planters. Although the delegates representing these groups did not all hope to profit personally from an increase in the value of their securities, as Beard would have it, they did hope to benefit in the broadest political and economic sense by breaking the power of their radical foes and establishing a system of government more compatible with their long-term economic and political interests. Thus, the framers sought to create a new government capable of promoting commerce and protecting property from radical state legislatures. At the same time, they hoped to fashion a government less susceptible than the existing state and national regimes to populist forces hostile to the interests of the commercial and propertied classes.

The Great Compromise The proponents of a new government fired their opening shot on May 29, 1787, when Edmund Randolph of Virginia offered a resolution that proposed corrections and enlargements in the Articles of Confederation. The proposal, which showed the strong influence of fellow Virginian James Madison, was not a simple motion, but a package of fifteen resolutions that, in effect, created a new government. Randolph later admitted it was intended to be an alternative draft constitution, and it did in fact serve as the framework for what ultimately became, after much debate and amendment, the Constitution. (There is no verbatim record of the debates, but Madison was present during virtually all of the deliberations and kept full notes on them.[10])

The portion of Randolph's motion that became most controversial was called the **Virginia Plan.** This plan provided for a system of representation in the national legislature based upon the population of each state or the proportion of each state's revenue contribution to the national government, or both. (Randolph also proposed a second branch of the legislature, but it was to be elected by the members of the first branch.) Since the states varied enormously in size and wealth, the Virginia Plan was heavily biased in favor of the large states.

While the convention was debating the Virginia Plan, additional delegates were arriving in Philadelphia and were beginning to mount opposition to it. Their resolution, introduced by William Paterson of New Jersey and known as the **New Jersey Plan,** did not oppose the Virginia Plan point for point. Instead, it concentrated on specific weaknesses in the Articles of Confederation, in the spirit of revision rather than radical replacement of that document. Supporters of the New

Virginia Plan a framework for the Constitution, introduced by Edmund Randolph, which called for representation in the national legislature based upon the population of each state

New Jersey Plan a framework for the Constitution, introduced by William Paterson, which called for equal state representation in the national legislature regardless of population

Jersey Plan did not seriously question the convention's commitment to replacing the Articles. But their opposition to the Virginia Plan's scheme of representation was sufficient to send its proposals back to committee for reworking into a common document. In particular, delegates from the less-populous states, which included Delaware, New Jersey, Connecticut, and New York, asserted that the more populous states, such as Virginia, Pennsylvania, North Carolina, Massachusetts, and Georgia, would dominate the new government if representation were determined by population. The smaller states argued that each state should be equally represented in the new regime regardless of that state's population.

The issue of representation was one that threatened to wreck the entire constitutional enterprise. Delegates conferred, factions maneuvered, and tempers flared. James Wilson of Pennsylvania told the small-state delegates that if they wanted to disrupt the union they should go ahead. The separation could, he said, "never happen on better grounds." Small-state delegates were equally blunt. Gunning Bedford of Delaware declared that the small states might look elsewhere for friends if they were forced. "The large states," he said, "dare not dissolve the confederation. If they do the small ones will find some foreign ally of more honor and good faith, who will take them by the hand and do them justice." These sentiments were widely shared. The union, as Oliver Ellsworth of Connecticut put it, was "on the verge of dissolution, scarcely held together by the strength of a hair."

Great Compromise the agreement reached at the Constitutional Convention of 1787 that gave each state an equal number of senators regardless of its population, but linked representation in the House of Representatives to population

The outcome of this debate was the Connecticut Compromise, also known as the **Great Compromise.** Under the terms of this compromise, in the first branch of Congress—the House of Representatives—the representatives would be apportioned according to the number of inhabitants in each state. This, of course, was what delegates from the large states had sought. But in the second branch—the Senate—each state would have an equal vote regardless of its size; this provision addressed the concerns of the small states. This compromise was not immediately satisfactory to all the delegates. Indeed, two of the most vocal members of the small-state faction, John Lansing and Robert Yates of New York, were so incensed by the concession that their colleagues had made to the large-state forces that they stormed out of the convention. In the end, however, both sets of forces preferred compromise to the breakup of the Union, and the plan was accepted.

The Question of Slavery: The Three-Fifths Compromise   Important as the Great Compromise was, the notion of a **bicameral** (two-chambered) legislature was no novelty in 1787. Some of the states had had bicameral legislatures for years. A far more fundamental issue had to be confronted before the Great Compromise could take place: the issue of slavery.

bicameral having a legislative assembly composed of two chambers or houses; opposite of unicameral

Many of the conflicts that emerged during the Constitutional Convention were reflections of the fundamental differences between the slave and the non-slave states—differences that pitted the southern planters and New England merchants against one another. This was the first premonition of a conflict that would almost destroy the Republic in later years.

More than 90 percent of the country's slaves resided in five states—Georgia, Maryland, North Carolina, South Carolina, and Virginia—where they accounted for 30 percent of the total population. In some places, slaves outnumbered nonslaves by as much as ten to one. If the Constitution were to embody any principle of national supremacy, some basic decisions would have to be made about the place of slavery in the general scheme. Madison hit on this point on several occasions as different aspects of the Constitution were being discussed. For example, he observed,

> It seemed now to be pretty well understood that the real difference of interests lay, not between the large and small but between the northern and southern states. The institution of slavery and its consequences formed the line of discrimination.[11]

Northerners and Southerners eventually reached agreement through the **Three-fifths Compromise.** The seats in the House of Representatives would be apportioned according to a "population" in which five slaves would count as three free persons. The slaves would not be allowed to vote, of course, but the number of representatives would be apportioned accordingly.

The issue of slavery was the most difficult one faced by the framers and nearly destroyed the Union. Although some delegates believed slavery to be morally wrong, an evil and oppressive institution that made a mockery of the ideals and values espoused in the Constitution, morality was not the issue that caused the framers to support or oppose the Three-fifths Compromise. Whatever they thought of the institution of slavery, most delegates from the northern states opposed counting slaves in the distribution of congressional seats. Wilson of Pennsylvania, for example, argued that if slaves were citizens they should be treated and counted like other citizens. If, on the other hand, they were property, then why should not other forms of property be counted toward the apportionment of representatives? But southern delegates made it clear that if the northerners refused to give in, they would never agree to the new government. William R. Davie of North Carolina heatedly said that it was time "to speak out." He asserted that the people of North Carolina would never enter the Union if slaves were not counted as part of the basis for representation. Without such agreement, he asserted ominously, "the business was at an end." Even southerners such as Edmund Randolph of Virginia, who conceded that slavery was immoral, insisted upon including slaves in the allocation of congressional seats. This conflict between the southern and northern delegates was so divisive that many came to question the possibility of creating and maintaining a union of the two. Pierce Butler of South Carolina declared that the North and South were as different as Russia and Turkey. Eventually, the North and South compromised on the issue of slavery and representation. Indeed, northerners even agreed to permit a continuation of the odious slave trade until 1808 to keep the South in the Union. The price paid to placate southern slaveholders was to provide a political reward—greater representation in the House of Representatives to slaveholders. As such, the Three-fifths Compromise was an early example of what is now called **institutional racism.** In due course, Butler proved to be correct, and a bloody war was fought when the disparate interests of the North and the South could no longer be reconciled.

Three-fifths Compromise the agreement reached at the Constitutional Convention of 1787 that stipulated that for purposes of the apportionment of congressional seats, every slave would be counted as three-fifths of a person

institutional racism rules or laws that protect or perpetuate the oppression of racial groups

The Constitution Created Both Bold Powers and Sharp Limits on Power

The political significance of the Great Compromise and the Three-fifths Compromise was to reinforce the unity of the mercantile and planter forces that sought to create a new government. The Great Compromise reassured those who feared this new governmental framework would reduce the importance of their own local or regional influence. The Three-fifths Compromise temporarily defused the rivalry between the merchants and planters. Their unity secured, members of the alliance supporting the establishment of a new government moved to fashion a constitutional framework consistent with their economic and political interests.

In particular, the framers sought a new government that, first, would be strong enough to promote commerce and protect property from radical state legislatures such as Rhode Island's. This became the constitutional basis for national control over commerce and finance, as well as for the establishment of national judicial supremacy and the effort to construct a strong presidency. Second, the framers sought to prevent what they saw as the threat posed by the "excessive democracy" of the state and national governments under the Articles of Confederation. This led to such constitutional principles as bicameralism (division of the Congress into two chambers), **checks and balances,** staggered terms in office, and indirect election (selection of the president by an **electoral college** rather than by voters directly, and senators by state legislatures). Third, the framers, lacking the power to force the states or the public at large to accept the new form of government, sought to identify principles that would help to secure support. This became the basis of the constitutional provision for direct popular election of representatives and, subsequently, for the addition of the **Bill of Rights** to the Constitution. Finally, the framers wanted to be certain that the government they created did not pose even more of a threat to its citizens' liberties and property rights than did the radical state legislatures they feared and despised. To prevent the new government from abusing its power, the framers incorporated principles such as the **separation of powers** and **federalism** into the Constitution. Let us assess the major provisions of the Constitution's seven articles (listed in Box 2.1) to see how each relates to these objectives.

checks and balances mechanisms through which each branch of government is able to participate in and influence the activities of the other branches. Major examples include the presidential veto power over congressional legislation, the power of the Senate to approve presidential appointments, and judicial review of congressional enactments

electoral college the presidential electors from each state who meet after the popular election to cast ballots for president and vice president

Bill of Rights the first ten amendments to the Constitution, which guarantee certain rights and liberties to the people

separation of powers the division of governmental power among several institutions that must cooperate in decision making

federalism a system of government in which power is divided, by a constitution, between a central government and regional governments

THE LEGISLATIVE BRANCH WAS DESIGNED TO BE THE MOST POWERFUL

The Constitution provided in Article I, Sections 1–7, for a Congress consisting of two chambers—a House of Representatives and a Senate. Members of the House of Representatives were given two-year terms in office and were to be elected directly by the people. Members of the Senate were to be appointed by the state legislatures (this was changed in 1913 by the Seventeenth Amendment, which instituted direct election of senators) for six-year terms. These terms were staggered so that the appointments of one-third of the senators would expire every

The Seven Articles of the Constitution

BOX 2.1

1. The Legislative Branch

House: two-year terms, elected directly by the people.

Senate: six-year terms (staggered so that only one-third of the Senate changes in any given election), appointed by state legislature (changed in 1913 to direct election).

Expressed powers of the national government: collecting taxes, borrowing money, regulating commerce, declaring war, and maintaining an army and a navy; all other power belongs to the states, unless deemed otherwise by the elastic ("necessary and proper") clause.

Exclusive powers of the national government: states are expressly forbidden to issue their own paper money, tax imports and exports, regulate trade outside their own borders, and impair the obligation of contracts; these powers are the exclusive domain of the national government.

2. The Executive Branch

Presidency: four-year terms (limited in 1951 to a maximum of two terms), elected indirectly by the electoral college.

Powers: can recognize other countries, negotiate treaties, grant reprieves and pardons, convene Congress in special sessions, and veto congressional enactment.

3. The Judicial Branch

Supreme Court: lifetime terms, appointed by the president with the approval of the Senate.

Powers: include resolving conflicts between federal and state laws, determining whether power belongs to the national government or the states, and settling controversies between citizens of different states.

4. National Unity and Power

Reciprocity among states: establishes that each state must give "full faith and credit" to official acts of other states, and guarantees citizens of any state the "privileges and immunities" of every other state.

5. Amending the Constitution

Procedure: requires approval by two-thirds of Congress and adoption by three-fourths of the states.

6. National Supremacy

The Constitution and national law are the supreme law of the land and cannot be overruled by state law.

7. Ratification

The Constitution became effective when approved by nine states.

two years. The Constitution assigned somewhat different tasks to the House and Senate. Although the approval of each body was required for the enactment of a law, the Senate alone was given the power to ratify treaties and approve presidential appointments. The House, on the other hand, was given the sole power to originate revenue bills.

The character of the legislative branch was directly related to the framers' major goals. The House of Representatives was designed to be directly responsible to the people in order to encourage popular consent for the new Constitution and to help enhance the power of the new government. At the same time, to guard against "excessive democracy," the Constitution checked the power of the House of Representatives with that of the Senate, whose members were to be appointed by the states for long terms rather than be elected directly by the people. The purpose of this provision, according to Alexander Hamilton, was to avoid "an unqualified complaisance to every sudden breeze of passion, or to every transient impulse which the people may receive."[12] Staggered terms of service in the Senate, moreover, were intended to make that body even more resistant to popular pressure. Since only one-third of the senators would be selected at any given time, the composition of the institution would be protected from changes in popular preferences transmitted by the state legislatures. This would prevent what James Madison called "mutability in the public councils arising from a rapid succession of new members."[13] Thus, the structure of the legislative branch was designed to contribute to governmental power, to promote popular consent for the new government, and at the same time to place limits on the popular political currents that many of the framers saw as a radical threat to the economic and social order.

The issues of power and consent were important throughout the Constitution. Section 8 of Article I specifically listed the powers of Congress, which include the authority to collect taxes, to borrow money, to regulate commerce, to declare war, and to maintain an army and navy. By granting Congress these powers, the framers indicated very clearly that they intended the new government to be far more powerful than its predecessor. At the same time, by defining the new government's most important powers as belonging to Congress, the framers sought to promote popular acceptance of this critical change by reassuring citizens that their views would be fully represented whenever the government exercised its new powers.

As a further guarantee to the people that the new government would pose no threat to them, the Constitution implied that any powers not listed were not granted at all. This is the doctrine of **expressed power.** The Constitution grants only those powers specifically expressed in its text. But the framers intended to create an active and powerful government, and so they included the **elastic clause,** sometimes known as the necessary and proper clause, which signified that the enumerated powers were meant to be a source of strength to the national government, not a limitation on it. The national government could use each power with the utmost vigor, but could seize upon no new powers without a constitutional amendment. In the absence of such an amendment, any power not enumerated was conceived to be "reserved" to the states (or the people).

expressed powers specific powers granted to Congress under Article I, Section 8, of the Constitution

elastic clause Article 1, Section 8, of the Constitution (also known as the necessary and proper clause), which enumerates the powers of Congress and provides Congress with the authority to make all laws "necessary and proper" to carry them out

THE EXECUTIVE BRANCH CREATED A BRAND NEW OFFICE

The Constitution provided for the establishment of the presidency in Article II. As Hamilton commented, the presidential article aimed toward "energy in the Executive." It did so in an effort to overcome the natural tendency toward stalemate that was built into the bicameral legislature as well as into the separation of powers among the three branches. The Constitution afforded the president a measure of independence from the people and from the other branches of government—particularly the Congress.

In line with the framers' goal of increasing power to the national government, the president was granted the power to receive ambassadors from other countries, which has amounted to the power to "recognize" other countries. The president was also given the power to negotiate treaties, although their acceptance required the approval of the Senate. The president was given the unconditional right to grant reprieves and pardons, except in cases of impeachment. And the president was provided with the power to appoint major departmental personnel, to convene Congress in special session, and to veto congressional enactments. (The veto power is formidable, but it is not absolute, since Congress can override it by a two-thirds vote.)

The framers hoped to create a presidency that would help the federal government operate more efficiently. At the same time, however, the framers sought to help the president withstand excessively democratic pressures by creating a system of indirect rather than direct election through a separate electoral college.

THE JUDICIAL BRANCH WAS A CHECK ON TOO MUCH DEMOCRACY

In establishing the judicial branch in Article III, the Constitution reflected the framers' preoccupations with nationalizing governmental power and checking radical democratic impulses while guarding against potential interference with liberty and property from the new national government itself.

Under the provisions of Article III, the framers created a court that was to be literally a supreme court of the United States, and not merely the highest court of the national government. The most important expression of this intention was granting the Supreme Court the power to resolve any conflicts that might emerge between federal and state laws. In particular, the Supreme Court was given the right to determine whether a power was exclusive to the national government, concurrent with the states, or exclusive to the states. In addition, the Supreme Court was assigned jurisdiction over controversies between citizens of different states. The long-term significance of this provision was that as the country developed a national economy, it came to rely increasingly on the federal judiciary, rather than on the state courts, for the resolution of disputes.

Judges were given lifetime appointments in order to protect them from popular politics and from interference by the other branches. This, however, did not mean that the judiciary would remain totally impartial to political considerations or to the other branches, for the president was to appoint the judges, and the Senate to approve the appointments. Congress would also have the power to create inferior (lower) courts, to change the jurisdiction of the federal courts, to add or subtract federal judges, and even to change the size of the Supreme Court.

No direct mention is made in the Constitution of **judicial review**—the power of the courts to render the final decision when there is a conflict of interpretation of the Constitution or of laws between the courts and Congress, the courts and the executive branch, or the courts and the states. The Supreme Court eventually assumed the power of judicial review. Its assumption of this power was based not on the Constitution itself but on the politics of later decades and the membership of the Court.

judicial review the power of the courts to declare actions of the legislative and executive branches invalid or unconstitutional. The Supreme Court asserted this power in *Marbury v. Madison*

NATIONAL UNITY AND POWER SET THE NEW CONSTITUTION APART FROM THE OLD ARTICLES

Various provisions in the Constitution addressed the framers' concern with national unity and power, including Article IV's provisions for comity (reciprocity) among states and among citizens of all states. Each state was prohibited from discriminating against the citizens of other states in favor of its own citizens, with the Supreme Court charged with deciding in each case whether a state had discriminated against goods or people from another state. The Constitution restricted the power of the states in favor of ensuring enough power to the national government to give the country a free-flowing national economy.

The framers' concern with national supremacy was also expressed in Article VI, in the **supremacy clause,** which provided that national laws and treaties "shall be the supreme law of the land." This meant that all laws made under the "authority of the United States" would be superior to all laws adopted by any state or any other subdivision, and the states would be expected to respect all treaties made under that authority. The supremacy clause also bound the officials of all state and local governments as well as the federal government to take an oath of office to support the national Constitution. This meant that every action taken by the United States Congress would have to be applied within each state as though the action were in fact state law.

supremacy clause Article VI of the Constitution, which states that laws passed by the national government and all treaties are the supreme law of the land and superior to all laws adopted by any state or any subdivision

THE CONSTITUTION ESTABLISHED THE PROCESS FOR AMENDMENT

The Constitution established procedures for its own revision in Article V. Its provisions are so difficult that the document has been successfully amended only seventeen times since 1791, when the first ten amendments were adopted. Thousands of other amendments have been proposed in Congress, but fewer than forty of them have even come close to fulfilling the Constitution's requirement of a two-thirds vote in Congress, and only a fraction have gotten anywhere near adoption by three-fourths of the states. Article V also provides that the Constitution can be amended by a constitutional convention. Occasionally, proponents of particular measures, such as a balanced-budget amendment, have called for a constitutional convention to consider their proposals. Whatever the purpose for which it would be called, however, such a convention would presumably have the authority to revise America's entire system of government.

THE CONSTITUTION SET FORTH RULES FOR ITS OWN RATIFICATION

The rules for the ratification of the Constitution were set forth in Article VII. Nine of the thirteen states would have to ratify, or agree upon, the terms in order for the Constitution to pass.

THE CONSTITUTION LIMITS THE NATIONAL GOVERNMENT'S POWER

As we have indicated, although the framers sought to create a powerful national government, they also wanted to guard against possible misuse of that power. To that end, the framers incorporated two key principles into the Constitution: the separation of powers and federalism. A third set of limitations, in the form of the Bill of Rights, was added to the Constitution to help secure its ratification when opponents of the document charged that it paid insufficient attention to citizens' rights.

The Separation of Powers   No principle of politics was more widely shared at the time of the 1787 founding than the principle that power must be used to balance power. The French political theorist Baron de la Brède et de Montesquieu (1689–1755) believed that this balance was an indispensable defense against tyranny, and his writings, especially his major work, *The Spirit of the Laws,* "were taken as political gospel" at the Philadelphia Convention.[14] The principle of the separation of powers is not stated explicitly in the Constitution, but it is clearly built on Articles I, II, and III, which provide for the following:

1. Three separate and distinct branches of government (see Figure 2.1).
2. Different methods of selecting the top personnel, so that each branch is responsible to a different constituency. This is supposed to produce a "mixed regime," in which the personnel of each department will develop very different interests and outlooks on how to govern, and different groups in society will be assured some access to governmental decision making.
3. Checks and balances—a system under which each of the branches is given some power over the others. Familiar examples are the presidential veto power over legislation, the power of the Senate to approve presidential appointments, and judicial review of acts of Congress (see Figure 2.2).

One clever formulation of the separation of powers is that of a system not of separated powers but of "separated institutions sharing power,"[15] thus diminishing the chance that power will be misused.

Figure 2.1   **Separation of Powers**

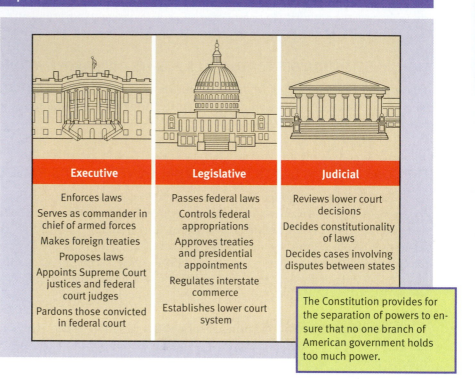

Executive	Legislative	Judicial
Enforces laws	Passes federal laws	Reviews lower court decisions
Serves as commander in chief of armed forces	Controls federal appropriations	Decides constitutionality of laws
Makes foreign treaties	Approves treaties and presidential appointments	Decides cases involving disputes between states
Proposes laws	Regulates interstate commerce	
Appoints Supreme Court justices and federal court judges	Establishes lower court system	
Pardons those convicted in federal court		

The Constitution provides for the separation of powers to ensure that no one branch of American government holds too much power.

Federalism   Compared to the confederation principle of the Articles of Confederation, federalism was a step toward greater centralization of power. The delegates agreed that they needed to place more power at the national level, without completely undermining the power of the state governments. Thus, they devised a system of two sovereigns—the states and the nation—with the hope that competition between the two would be an effective limitation on the power of both.

The Bill of Rights   Late in the Philadelphia Convention, a motion was made to include a list of citizens' rights in the Constitution. After a brief debate in which hardly a word was said in its favor and only one speech was made against it, the motion was almost unanimously turned down. Most delegates sincerely believed that since the federal government was already limited to its expressed powers, further protection of citizens was not needed. The delegates argued that the states should adopt bills of rights because their greater powers needed greater limitations. But almost immediately after the Constitution was ratified, there was a movement to adopt a national bill of rights. This is why the Bill of Rights, adopted in 1791, comprises the first ten amendments to the Constitution rather than being part of the body of it. We will have a good deal more to say about the Bill of Rights in Chapter 4.

Check and Balances   Figure 2.2

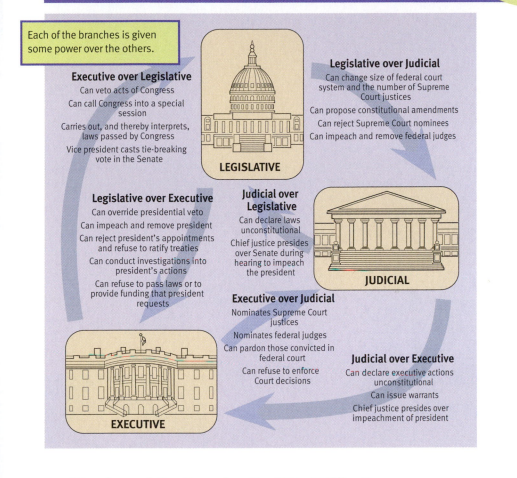

Each of the branches is given some power over the others.

Executive over Legislative
Can veto acts of Congress
Can call Congress into a special session
Carries out, and thereby interprets, laws passed by Congress
Vice president casts tie-breaking vote in the Senate

LEGISLATIVE

Legislative over Judicial
Can change size of federal court system and the number of Supreme Court justices
Can propose constitutional amendments
Can reject Supreme Court nominees
Can impeach and remove federal judges

Legislative over Executive
Can override presidential veto
Can impeach and remove president
Can reject president's appointments and refuse to ratify treaties
Can conduct investigations into president's actions
Can refuse to pass laws or to provide funding that president requests

Judicial over Legislative
Can declare laws unconstitutional
Chief justice presides over Senate during hearing to impeach the president

JUDICIAL

Executive over Judicial
Nominates Supreme Court justices
Nominates federal judges
Can pardon those convicted in federal court
Can refuse to enforce Court decisions

Judicial over Executive
Can declare executive actions unconstitutional
Can issue warrants
Chief justice presides over impeachment of president

EXECUTIVE

Ratification of the Constitution Was Difficult

The first hurdle faced by the new Constitution was ratification by state conventions of delegates elected by the people of each state. This struggle for ratification was carried out in thirteen separate campaigns. Each involved different people, moved at a different pace, and was influenced by local as well as national considerations. Two sides faced off throughout the states, however; the two sides called themselves Federalists and Antifederalists (see Table 2.1). The **Federalists** (who more accurately should have called themselves "Nationalists" but who took their name to appear to follow in the revolutionary tradition) supported the Constitution and preferred a strong national government. The **Antifederalists** opposed the Constitution and preferred a federal system of government that was decentralized; they took their name by default, in reaction to their better-organized opponents. The Federalists were united in their

Federalists those who favored a strong national government and supported the constitution proposed at the American Constitutional Convention of 1787

Antifederalists those who favored strong state governments and a weak national government and who were opponents of the constitution proposed at the American Constitutional Convention of 1787

PICTURING

The Separation of Powers in Action

In the wake of 9/11, Congress authorized the president "to use all necessary and appropriate force against those nations, organizations, or persons he determines planned, authorized, committed, or aided the terrorist attacks" or "harbored such organizations or persons." Bush responded by ordering U.S. armed forces to Afghanistan to subdue al Qaeda and the Taliban regime. During this operation, thousands of alleged enemy combatants were captured by American and allied forces.

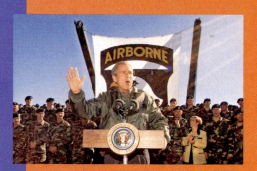

Article I of the U.S. Constitution gives Congress the power to declare war and raise and regulate the armed forces. Even the president, as commander in chief of the military, must obey Congress if Congress chooses to assert its constitutional authority.

A twenty-two-year-old American citizen of Saudi origin named Yaser Hamdi was captured in Afghanistan in 2001 by U.S. forces, designated an "enemy combatant," and detained in a Virginia jail without trial.

Hamdi's lawyer, Frank Dunham, argued that the president was violating Hamdi's constitutional rights as an American citizen by jailing him without access to an attorney or trial. The government countered that during wartime the executive branch had the right to restrict the access of enemy combatants to the court system and that the court had no authority to review such detentions.

POLITICS

The Supreme Court ruled that while Congress had authorized the president's power to detain enemy combatants, the government's detention of Hamdi was in violation of his right to an impartial trial and access to counsel. Hamdi was released to Saudi Arabia in fall 2004.

In its decision, the majority of the Court wrote that "a state of war is not a blank check for the President when it comes to the rights of the Nation's citizens." The Court's decision exemplifies its ability to check the power of the executive and legislature, one of the many ways that separation of powers works in the U.S. government.

Table 2.1   Federalists versus Antifederalists

	FEDERALISTS	ANTIFEDERALISTS
Who were they?	Property owners, creditors, merchants	Small farmers, frontiersmen, debtors, shopkeepers
What did they believe?	Believed that elites were best fit to govern; feared "excessive democracy"	Believed that government should be closer to the people; feared concentration of power in hands of the elites
What system of government did they favor?	Favored strong national government; believed in "filtration" so that only elites would obtain governmental power	Favored retention of power by state governments and protection of individual rights
Who were their leaders?	Alexander Hamilton James Madison George Washington	Patrick Henry George Mason Elbridge Gerry George Clinton

support of the Constitution, while the Antifederalists were divided as to what they believed the alternative to the Constitution should be.

During the struggle over ratification of the Constitution, Americans argued about great political issues and principles. How much power should the national government be given? What safeguards were most likely to prevent the abuse of power? What institutional arrangements could best ensure adequate representation for all Americans? Was tyranny to be feared more from the many or from the few?

FEDERALISTS AND ANTIFEDERALISTS FOUGHT BITTERLY OVER THE WISDOM OF THE NEW DOCUMENT

During the ratification struggle, thousands of essays, speeches, pamphlets, and letters were written in support of and in opposition to the proposed Constitution. The best-known pieces supporting ratification of the Constitution were the eighty-five essays written, under the name of "Publius," by Alexander Hamilton, James Madison, and John Jay between the fall of 1787 and the spring of 1788. These **Federalist Papers,** as they are collectively known today, defended the prin-

Federalist Papers a series of essays written by James Madison, Alexander Hamilton, and John Jay supporting the ratification of the Constitution

ciples of the Constitution and sought to dispel fears of a national authority. The Antifederalists published essays of their own, arguing that the new Constitution betrayed the Revolution and was a step toward monarchy. Among the best of the Antifederalist works were the essays, usually attributed to New York Supreme Court justice Robert Yates, that were written under the name of "Brutus" and published in the *New York Journal* at the same time the Federalist Papers appeared. The Antifederalist view was also ably presented in the pamphlets and letters written by a former delegate to the Continental Congress and future U.S. senator, Richard Henry Lee of Virginia, using the pen name "The Federal Farmer." These essays highlight the major differences of opinion between Federalists and Antifederalists. Federalists appealed to basic principles of government in support of their nationalist vision. Antifederalists cited equally fundamental precepts to support their vision of a looser confederacy of small republics. Three areas of disagreement were representation, majority tyranny, and governmental power.

Representation   The Antifederalists believed that the best and most representative government was that closest to the people, what we would think of as local and state governments. These smaller, more homogeneous governing units would provide "a true picture of the people . . . [possessing] the knowledge of their circumstances and their wants."[16] A strong national government could not represent the interests of the nation as effectively, the Antifederalists argued, because the nation as a whole was simply too large and diverse.

The Federalists, on the other hand, thought that some distance between the people and their representatives might be a good thing, because it would encourage the selection of a few talented and experienced representatives to serve in a national legislature who could balance the wishes of the people with their own considered judgment. In James Madison's view, representatives would not simply mirror society; rather, they must be "[those] who possess [the] most wisdom to discern, and [the] most virtue to pursue, the common good of the society."[17]

Tyranny of the Majority   Both Federalists and Antifederalists feared **tyranny**— unjust rule by the group in power. But each painted a different picture of what kind of tyranny to fear.

tyranny oppressive and unjust government that employs cruel and unjust use of power and authority

The Antifederalists feared that tyranny would arise from the tendency of governments to become more "aristocratic," wherein a few individuals in positions of authority would use their positions to gain more and more power over the people. For this reason, Antifederalists were sharply critical of those features of the Constitution that limited direct popular influence over the government, including the election of senators by state legislatures, election of the president by the electoral college, and selection of federal judges by the president and the Senate. Judges, who are appointed for life, were seen as an especially dire threat: "I wonder if the world ever saw . . . a court of justice invested with such immense powers, and yet placed in a situation so little responsible," protested Antifederalist Brutus.[18]

For the Federalists, tyranny in a republic was less likely to come from aristocrats, and more likely to come from the majority. They feared that a popular majority, "united and actuated by some common impulse of passion, or of interest, adverse to the rights of other citizens," would attempt to "trample on the rules of justice."[19] Those features of the Constitution opposed by the Antifederalists were the very ones that the Federalists defended as the best hope of avoiding tyranny. The sheer size and diversity of the American nation, as represented in the two houses of Congress, would provide a built-in set of balances that would force competing interests to moderate and compromise.

Governmental Power A third difference between Federalists and Antifederalists was over the matter of governmental power. Both sides agreed on the principle of **limited government,** but they differed on how best to limit the government.

limited government a government whose powers are defined and limited by a constitution

Antifederalists wanted the powers of the national government to be carefully specified and limited. Otherwise, it would "swallow up all the power of the state governments." Antifederalists bitterly attacked the supremacy clause and the elastic clause of the Constitution, saying that these provisions gave the national government dangerously unlimited grants of power. They also insisted that a bill or rights be added to the Constitution to place limits on the government's power over citizens.

Federalists favored a national government with broad powers. They insisted that the new government must have the power to defend the nation from foreign threats, guard against domestic strife and insurrection, promote commerce, and expand the nation's economy. Federalists agreed that such power could be abused, but that the best safeguard against such abuse was through the Constitution's internal checks and controls, not by keeping the national government weak. As Madison said, "[T]he power surrendered by the people is first divided between two distinct governments [federal and state], and then the portion allotted to each subdivided among distinct and separate departments. Hence, a double security arises to the rights of the people. The different governments will control each other, at the same time that each will be controlled by itself."[20] The Federalists considered a bill of rights to be unnecessary, although this Antifederalist demand was eventually embraced by Federalists, including Madison.

BOTH FEDERALISTS AND ANTIFEDERALISTS CONTRIBUTED TO THE SUCCESS OF THE NEW SYSTEM

In general, the Federalist vision of America triumphed. The Constitution adopted in 1789 created the framework for a powerful national government that for more than two hundred years has defended the nation's interests, promoted its commerce, and maintained national unity. In one notable instance, the national government fought and won a bloody war to prevent the nation from breaking apart. And despite this powerful government, the system of internal checks and balances has functioned reasonably well, as the Federalists predicted, to prevent the national government from tyrannizing its citizens.

Although they were defeated in 1789, the Antifederalists present us with an important picture of a road not taken and of an America that might have been.

Would the country have been worse off if it had been governed by a confederacy of small republics linked by a national administration with severely limited powers? Were the Antifederalists correct in predicting that a government given great power in the hope that it might do good would, through "insensible progress," inevitably turn to evil purposes? The verdict of history supports both the Federalist blueprint for American government and the Antifederalist concern for individual rights. In modern politics, many Americans continue to identify with the Antifederalist suspicion of government and its powers. Yet the success of the Federalist plan that has prevailed for over two hundred years surely supports the idea that government is less a "necessary evil" than it is, in historian Garry Wills's phrase, "a necessary good."[21]

Constitutional Amendments Dramatically Changed the Relationship between Citizens and the Government

The Constitution has endured for more than two centuries as the framework of government because it has changed. Without change, the Constitution might have become merely a sacred but obsolete relic of a bygone era.

AMENDMENTS: MANY ARE CALLED, FEW ARE CHOSEN

The need for change was recognized by the framers of the Constitution, and the provisions for **amendment** incorporated into Article V were thought to be "an easy, regular and Constitutional way" to make changes, which would occasionally be necessary because members of Congress "may abuse their power and refuse their consent on that very account . . . to admit to amendments to correct the source of the abuse."[22] Madison made a more balanced defense of the amendment procedure in Article V: "It guards equally against that extreme facility, which would render the Constitution too mutable; and that extreme difficulty, which might perpetuate its discovered faults."[23]

amendment a change added to a bill, law, or constitution

Experience since 1789 raises questions even about Madison's more modest claims. The Constitution has proven to be extremely difficult to amend. In the history of efforts to amend the Constitution, the most appropriate characterization is "many are called, few are chosen." Between 1789 and 1996, more than eleven thousand amendments were formally offered in Congress. Of these, Congress officially proposed only twenty-nine, and twenty-seven of these were eventually ratified by the states. But the record is even more severe than that. Since 1791, when the first ten amendments, the Bill of Rights, were added, only seventeen amendments have been adopted. And two of them—Prohibition and its repeal—cancel each other out, so that for all practical purposes, only fifteen amendments have been added to the Constitution since 1791. Despite vast changes in American society and its economy, only twelve amendments have been adopted since the Civil War amendments in 1868.

Four methods of amendment are provided for in Article V:

1. Passage in House and Senate by two-thirds vote; then ratification by majority vote of the legislatures of three-fourths (thirty-eight) of the states.
2. Passage in House and Senate by two-thirds vote; then ratification by conventions called for the purpose in three-fourths of the states.
3. Passage in a national convention called by Congress in response to petitions by two-thirds of the states; ratification by majority vote of the legislatures of three-fourths of the states.
4. Passage in a national convention, as in (3); then ratification by conventions called for the purpose in three-fourths of the states.

(Figure 2.3 illustrates each of these possible methods.) Since no amendment has ever been proposed by national convention, methods 3 and 4 have never been employed. And method 2 has only been employed once (the Twenty-first Amendment, which repealed the Eighteenth, or Prohibition, Amendment). Thus, method 1 has been used for all the others.

Now it should be clear why it has been so difficult to amend the Constitution. The requirement of a two-thirds vote in the House and the Senate means

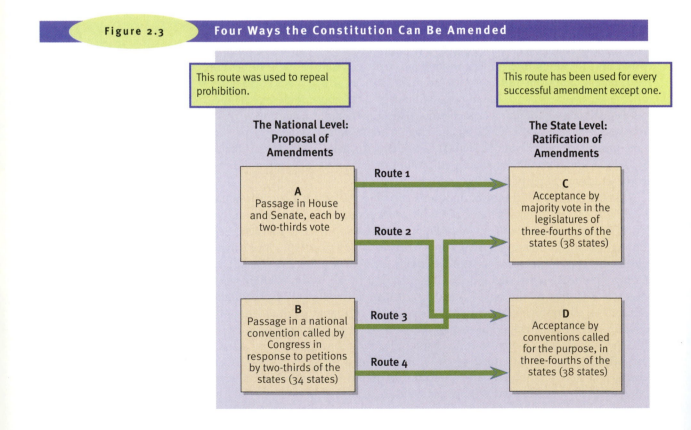

Figure 2.3   **Four Ways the Constitution Can Be Amended**

This route was used to repeal prohibition.

This route has been used for every successful amendment except one.

The National Level: Proposal of Amendments

The State Level: Ratification of Amendments

A
Passage in House and Senate, each by two-thirds vote

B
Passage in a national convention called by Congress in response to petitions by two-thirds of the states (34 states)

Route 1
Route 2
Route 3
Route 4

C
Acceptance by majority vote in the legislatures of three-fourths of the states (38 states)

D
Acceptance by conventions called for the purpose, in three-fourths of the states (38 states)

that any proposal for an amendment in Congress can be killed by only 34 senators or 136 members of the House. What is more, if the necessary two-thirds vote is obtained, the amendment can still be killed by the refusal or inability of only thirteen out of fifty state legislatures to ratify it. Since each state has an equal vote regardless of its population, the thirteen holdout states may represent a very small fraction of the total American population.

THE TWENTY-SEVEN AMENDMENTS ARE ABOUT POWER AND PEOPLE

Based on an examination of the few amendments successfully added to the Constitution, it would appear that only a limited number of changes needed by society can actually be made through the Constitution. Most efforts to amend the Constitution have failed because they were simply attempts to use the Constitution as an alternative to legislation for dealing directly with a public problem. A review of the successful amendments provides two insights: first, it gives us some understanding of the conditions underlying successful amendments; and second, it reveals a great deal about what constitutionalism means. The first ten amendments will be discussed in Chapter 4.

Five of the seventeen amendments adopted since 1791 are directly concerned with the expansion of the electorate and, thus, political equality (see Table 2.2). The Founders were unable to establish a national electorate with uniform voting qualifications. They decided to evade it by providing in the final draft of Article I, Section 2, that eligibility to vote in a national election would be the same as "the Qualification requisite for Elector of the most numerous

Amending the Constitution to Expand the Electorate   Table 2.2

AMENDMENT	PURPOSE	YEAR PROPOSED	YEAR ADOPTED
XV	Extended voting rights to all races	1869	1870
XIX	Extended voting rights to women	1919	1920
XXIII	Extended voting rights to residents of the District of Columbia	1960	1961
XXIV	Extended voting rights to all classes by abolition of poll taxes	1962	1964
XXVI	Extended voting rights to citizens aged 18 and over	1971	1971*

*The Twenty-sixth Amendment holds the record for speed of adoption. It was proposed on March 23, 1971, and adopted on July 5, 1971.

PICTURING

The Federal Marriage Amendment

The Constitution has evolved through the amendment process—a process that continues today. In 2003 some conservatives, in an attempt to override several states' laws permitting gay marriage, began a push to pass the Federal Marriage Amendment, a constitutional amendment that defined marriage as a union legal only between a man and a woman, which would effectively ban gay marriages. In early 2004 conservatives stepped up their efforts in response to the Massachusetts Supreme Judicial Court's decision to grant marriage rights to gay and lesbian couples and San Francisco mayor Gavin Newsom's decision to give marriage licenses to gay and lesbian couples. In both Massachusetts and California, opinion was divided on the issue.

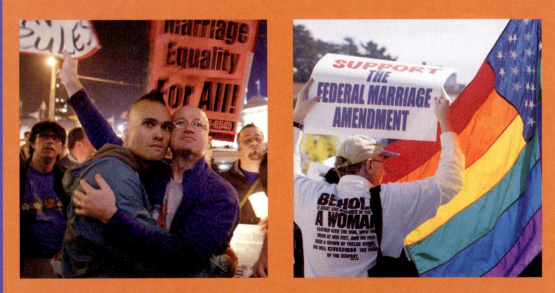

The Massachusetts State House was the scene of protests both for (above left) and against (above right) gay marriage.

POLITICS

Protests for (above left) and against (above right) gay marriage were also held in California.

In July 2004, the amendment was defeated in the U.S. Senate. Opinion polls showed that although a large majority of Americans oppose gay marriage, many also oppose amending the Constitution to outlaw the practice. In line with the polls, senators expressed reluctance to alter the Constitution to include a divisive social issue, especially at the expense of tampering with existing state prerogatives over marriage law. In general, attempts to legislate through the amendment process have proven unsuccessful throughout American political history.

branch of the state Legislature." Article I, Section 4, added that Congress could alter state regulations as to the "Times, Places, and Manner of holding Elections for Senators and Representatives." Nevertheless, this meant that any important *expansion* of the American electorate would almost certainly require a constitutional amendment.

Six more amendments are also electoral in nature, although they are not concerned directly with voting rights and the expansion of the electorate (see Table 2.3). These six amendments are concerned with the elective offices themselves (the Twentieth, Twenty-second, and Twenty-fifth) or with the relationship between elective offices and the electorate (the Twelfth, Fourteenth, and Seventeenth). One could conclude that one effect was the enhancement of democracy.

Another five amendments have sought to expand or to delimit the powers of the national and state governments (see Table 2.4).[24] The Eleventh Amendment protected the states from suits by private individuals and took away from the federal courts any power to take suits by private individuals of one state (or a foreign country) against another state. The other three amendments in Table 2.4 are obviously designed to reduce state power (Thirteenth), to reduce state power and expand national power (Fourteenth), and to expand national power (Sixteenth). The Twenty-seventh put a limit on Congress's ability to raise its own salary.

Table 2.3   **Amending the Constitution to Change the Relationship between Elected Offices and the Electorate**

AMENDMENT	PURPOSE	YEAR PROPOSED	YEAR ADOPTED
XII	Provided separate ballot for vice president in the electoral college	1803	1804
XIV	(Part 1) Provided a national definition of citizenship*	1866	1868
XVII	Provided direct election of senators	1912	1913
XX	Eliminated "lame duck" session of Congress	1932	1933
XXII	Limited presidential term	1947	1951
XXV	Provided presidential succession in case of disability	1965	1967

*In defining *citizenship,* the Fourteenth Amendment actually provided the constitutional basis for expanding the electorate to include all races, women, and residents of the District of Columbia. Only the "eighteen-year-olds' amendment" should have been necessary, since it changed the definition of citizenship. The fact that additional amendments were required following the Fourteenth suggests that voting is not considered an inherent right of U.S. citizenship. Instead, it is viewed as a privilege.

Amending the Constitution to Expand or Limit the Power of Government

Table 2.4

AMENDMENT	PURPOSE	YEAR PROPOSED	YEAR ADOPTED
XI	Limited jurisdiction of federal courts over suits involving the states	1794	1798
XIII	Eliminated slavery and eliminated the right of states to allow property in persons	1865*	1865
XIV	(Part 2) Applied due process of Bill of Rights to the states	1866	1868
XVI	Established national power to tax incomes	1909	1913
XXVII	Limited Congress's power to raise its own salary	1789	1992

*The Thirteenth Amendment was proposed January 31, 1865, and adopted less than a year later, on December 18, 1865.

Summary

Political conflicts between the colonies and Britain, and among competing groups within the colonies, led to the first founding as expressed by the Declaration of Independence. The first constitution, the Articles of Confederation, was adopted one year later (1777). Under this document, the states retained their sovereignty and the central government had few powers and no means of enforcing its will. The national government's weakness led to the Constitution of 1787, the second founding.

Many interests competed to shape our modern governing system. This competition was especially fierce between the Federalists, who supported the new, stronger government, and the Antifederalists, who favored a weaker government in the style of the Articles of Confederation. Both sides realized that the stakes in this struggle were great—a stronger federal government could open the door to tyranny and the limiting of individual liberty. The solution to the problem of how to protect individual liberty while still giving the government the powers it needed included separated powers, internal checks and balances, federalism, and the inclusion of the Bill of Rights. This allowed the government to promote commerce, protect property, limit the powers of the states (which had been far greater under the Articles of Confederation), and win popular consent for the new government. These mechanisms continue to define the relationship between citizens and their government.

This chapter also sought to gain an appreciation of constitutionalism itself. In addition to describing how the Constitution is formally amended, we analyzed the twenty-seven amendments in order to determine what they had in common. We found that, with the exception of the two Prohibition amendments, all amendments were oriented toward some change in the framework or structure of government. The Prohibition Amendment was the only adopted amendment that sought to legislate by constitutional means.

For Further Reading

Beard, Charles. *An Economic Interpretation of the Constitution of the United States.* New York: Macmillan, 1913.

Bellesiles, Michael A. *Arming America.* New York: Knopf, 2000.

Cohler, Anne M. *Montesquieu's Politics and the Spirit of American Constitutionalism.* Lawrence, KS: University Press of Kansas, 1988.

Farrand, Max, ed. *The Records of the Federal Convention of 1787.* 4 vols. New Haven, CT: Yale University Press, 1966.

Hamilton, Alexander, James Madison, and John Jay. *The Federalist Papers.* Edited by Isaac Kramnick. New York: Viking, 1987.

Jensen, Merrill. *The Articles of Confederation.* Madison, WI: University of Wisconsin Press, 1963.

Lipset, Seymour M. *The First New Nation: The United States in Historical and Comparative Perspective.* New York: Basic Books, 1963.

McDonald, Forrest. *The Formation of the American Republic.* New York: Penguin, 1967.

Main, Jackson Turner. *The Social Structure of Revolutionary America.* Princeton, NJ: Princeton University Press, 1965.

Rossiter, Clinton. *1787: Grand Convention.* New York: Macmillan, 1966.

Storing, Herbert, ed. *The Complete Anti-Federalist.* 7 vols. Chicago: University of Chicago Press, 1981.

Wills, Gary. *A Necessary Evil.* New York: Simon and Schuster, 1999.

Wood, Gordon S. *The Creation of the American Republic.* New York: Norton, 1982.

Study Outline

Narrow Interests and Political Conflicts Shaped the First Founding

1. In an effort to alleviate financial problems, including considerable debt, the British government sought to raise revenue by taxing its North American colonies. This energized New England merchants and southern planters, who then organized colonial resistance.

2. Colonial resistance set into motion a cycle of provocation and reaction that resulted in the First Continental Congress and eventually the Declaration of Independence.

3. The Declaration of Independence was an attempt to identify and articulate a history and set of principles that might help to forge national unity.

4. The colonies established the Articles of Confederation and Perpetual Union. Under the Articles, the central government was based entirely in Congress, yet Congress had little power.

The Failure of the Articles Made the "Second Founding" Necessary

1. Concern over America's precarious position in the international community coupled with domestic concern that "radical forces" had too much influence in Congress and in state governments led to the Annapolis Convention in 1786.

2. Shays's Rebellion in Massachusetts provided critics of the Articles of Confederation with the evidence they needed to push for constitutional revision.

3. Recognizing fundamental flaws in the Articles, the delegates to the Philadelphia Convention abandoned the plan to revise the Articles and committed themselves to a second founding.

4. Conflict between large and small states over the issue of representation in Congress led to the Great Compromise, which created a bicameral legislature based on two different principles of representation.

5. The Three-fifths Compromise addressed the question of slavery by apportioning the seats in the House of Representatives according to a population in which five slaves would count as three persons.

The Constitution Created Both Bold Powers and Sharp Limits on Power

1. The new government was to be strong enough to defend the nation's interests internationally, promote commerce and protect property, and prevent the threat posed by "excessive democracy."

2. The House of Representatives was designed to be directly responsible to the people in order to encourage popular consent for the Constitution. The Senate was designed to guard against the potential for excessive democracy in the House.

3. The Constitution grants Congress important and influential powers, but any power not specifically enumerated in its text is reserved specifically to the states.

4. The framers hoped to create a presidency with energy—one that would be capable of timely and decisive action to deal with public issues and problems.

5. The establishment of the Supreme Court reflected the framers' preoccupations with nationalizing governmental power and checking radical democratic impulses while guarding against potential interference with liberty and property from the new national government itself.

6. Various provisions in the Constitution addressed the framers' concern with national unity and power. Such provisions included clauses promoting reciprocity among states.

7. Procedures for amending the Constitution are provided in Article V. These procedures are so difficult that amendments are quite rare in American history.

8. To guard against possible misuse of national government power, the framers incorporated the principles of the separation of powers and federalism, as well as a Bill of Rights, in the Constitution.

9. The separation of powers was based on the principle that power must be used to balance power.

10. Although the framers' move to federalism was a step toward greater centralization of national government power, they retained state power by devising a system of two sovereigns.

11. The Bill of Rights was adopted as the first ten amendments to the Constitution in 1791.

Ratification of the Constitution Was Difficult

1. The struggle for ratification was carried out in thirteen separate campaigns—one in each state.

2. The Federalists supported the Constitution and a stronger national government. The Antifederalists, on the other hand, preferred a more decentralized system of government and fought against ratification.

3. Federalists and Antifederalists had differing views regarding issues such as representation and the prevention of tyranny.

4. Antifederalist criticisms helped to shape the Constitution and the national government, but it was the Federalist vision of America that triumphed.

Constitutional Amendments Dramatically Changed the Relationship between Citizens and the Government

1. Provisions for amending the Constitution, incorporated into Article V, have proven to be difficult criteria to meet. Relatively few amendments have been made to the Constitution.

2. Most of the amendments to the Constitution deal with the structure or composition of the government.

Practice Quiz

1. In the Revolutionary struggles, which of the following groups was allied with the New England merchants?
   a) artisans
   b) southern planters
   c) western speculators
   d) laborers

2. How did the British attempt to raise revenue in the North American colonies?
   a) income tax
   b) taxes on commerce
   c) expropriation and government sale of land
   d) government asset sales

3. The first governing document in the United States was
   a) the Declaration of Independence.
   b) the Articles of Confederation and Perpetual Union.
   c) the Constitution.
   d) none of the above.

4. Which state's proposal embodied a principle of representing states in the Congress according to their size and wealth?
   a) Connecticut
   b) Maryland
   c) New Jersey
   d) Virginia

5. Where was the execution of laws conducted under the Articles of Confederation?
   a) the presidency
   b) the Congress
   c) the states
   d) the expanding federal bureaucracy

6. Which of the following was *not* a reason that the Articles of Confederation seemed too weak?
   a) the lack of a single voice in international affairs
   b) the power of radical forces in the Congress
   c) the impending "tyranny of the states"
   d) the power of radical forces in several states

7. What mechanism was instituted in the Congress to guard against "excessive democracy"?
   a) bicameralism
   b) staggered Senate terms
   c) appointment of senators for long terms
   d) all of the above

8. Which of the following best describes the Supreme Court as understood by the Founders?
   a) the highest court of the national government
   b) arbiter of disputes within the Congress

   c) a figurehead commission of elders
   d) a supreme court of the nation and its states

9. Which of the following were of greatest concern to the Antifederalists?
   a) interstate commerce
   b) the protection of property
   c) the distinction between principles and interests
   d) the potential for tyranny in the central government

10. The draft constitution that was introduced at the start of the Constitutional Convention was authored by
    a) Edmund Randolph.
    b) Thomas Jefferson.
    c) James Madison.
    d) George Clinton.

Critical Thinking Questions

1. In many ways, the framers of the Constitution created a central government much stronger than the government created by the Articles of Confederation. Still, the framers seem to have taken great care to limit the power of the central government in various ways. Describe the ways in which the central government under the Constitution was stronger than the central government under the Articles. Describe the ways in which the framers limited the national government's power under the Constitution. Why might the framers have placed such limits on the government they had just created?

2. Recount and explain the ideological, geographical, social, and political conflicts both at the time of the American Revolution and at the time of the writing of the United States Constitution. What experiences and interests informed the forces involved in each of these conflicts? How did the framers resolve these conflicts? Were there any conflicts left unresolved?

Key Terms

amendment (p. 41)
Antifederalists (p. 35)
Articles of Confederation (p. 22)
bicameral (p. 26)
Bill of Rights (p. 28)
checks and balances (p. 28)
confederation (p. 22)

elastic clause (p. 30)
electoral college (p. 28)
expressed powers (p. 30)
federalism (p. 28)
Federalist Papers (p. 38)
Federalists (p. 35)
Great Compromise (p. 26)
institutional racism (p. 27)
judicial review (p. 32)

limited government (p. 40)
New Jersey Plan (p. 25)
separation of powers (p. 28)
supremacy clause (p. 32)
Three-fifths Compromise (p. 27)
tyranny (p. 39)
Virginia Plan (p. 25)

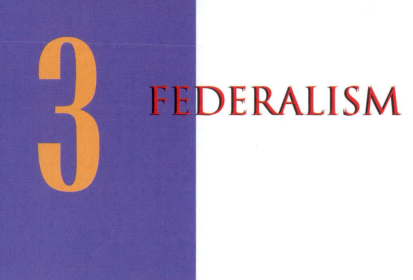

3 FEDERALISM

MAIN MESSAGE

Federalism is an enduring source of controversy between those who think that the national government should exercise more power and those who think it should have less power over people's lives.

Until the late 1980s, the legal drinking age varied from one state to another. In New York State, for example, the drinking age was eighteen. In neighboring Pennsylvania, however, it was twenty-one. But in 1984, the national government enacted legislation that pushed all the states to raise the age to twenty-one. The way it did this was by threatening to withhold federal highway construction and maintenance funds from any state that failed to raise the age to twenty-one. Within a few years, all fifty states complied. The last holdout, Louisiana, capitulated in 1996.

Key Concepts

1. Federalism has shaped American politics from the start of the country to the present.

2. The definition of federalism has changed radically in the last two centuries. The federal government has done far more since the 1930s than it did during the "traditional system" from 1789 to the 1930s.

3. The states continue to exert great power over citizens' everyday lives.

4. The "New Federalism" of recent years has turned more power back to the states.

5. Sometimes the federal government requires the states to do things but does not give the states the money to do them.

What is most interesting about the indirect method used to change drinking-age policy was that the federal government pressured the states by *threatening to withhold a benefit,* not by enacting a rule ordering the change. This is because drinking-age laws are part of state criminal codes, which each state regulates on its own. If Congress had passed a law simply ordering the states to change their drinking ages, the law would have certainly been declared unconstitutional on the grounds that the federal government was improperly infringing on state governmental power—in other words, as a violation of federalism. On the other hand, the federal government had every right to withhold highway funds, because it was not required to provide the money in the first place, nor were states required to accept the money.

This was not the first time the national government had used this method to influence the states. During the oil crisis of 1973, Congress enacted legislation to withhold federal highway funds from any state that did not reduce its maximum speed limit to fifty-five miles per hour (mph), at a time when most four-lane highways kept a sixty-five mph limit. This was done to reduce oil consumption, and all fifty states complied. In 1995, Congress repealed the law, allowing states to again set this limit for themselves.

Controversy over possible changes in the drinking age became a national issue in the 1980s because of outrage over alcohol-related deaths, and pressure from such interest groups as Mothers Against Drunk Driving (MADD). Similarly, national attention was focused on speed limits in the 1970s because of reported oil shortages and long lines for gasoline at service stations. But in most areas of daily life, state governments retain control over what citizens can and cannot do, meaning that where you live affects what you can and cannot do. A worker who loses a job in New Hampshire is entitled to a maximum unemployment insurance benefit payment of $301 per week; but a citizen thrown out of work in nearby Massachusetts could receive up to $646 per week. Welfare payments also fluctuate from one state to another. Public school curricula, local property tax rates, drivers license fees, and state university tuition all vary from one state to another. Most of the rules and regulations that Americans face in their daily lives are set by state and local governments.[1]

This chapter will examine the concept of federalism, demonstrating that state and local governments are vitally important to citizens in their everyday lives. Almost everyone agrees that governing powers should be divided between the national government and the states. The continuing controversy surrounding federalism lies with the question of exactly where the dividing line between national and state governmental power should be drawn.

Federalism Shapes American Politics

federalism a system of government in which power is divided, by a constitution, between a central government and regional governments

Even though the word "federalism" never appears in the Constitution, the concept arises directly from the document. **Federalism** can be defined with misleading ease as the division of powers and functions between the national government and the state governments. This simple definition causes confusion, however, as many assume that federalism means giving most power to the "federal" government, when in fact it does not. Aside from America, other nations with diverse ethnic or language groupings, such as Switzerland and Canada, also have federalist systems (although the specific ways in which power is shared in these nations varies, so that no two federal systems are exactly alike).

A governing system that does give most power to the federal or national government is called a **unitary system.** In this system, lower levels of government have little independent power. In France, for example, the central government was once so involved in the smallest details of local activity that the minister of education boasted that by looking at his watch he could tell what all French schoolchildren were learning at that time because the central government set the school curriculum. At the other end of the spectrum, a **confederation** is a system with a weak national government but strong states or provinces. America's first constitution, the Articles of Confederation, is such an example.

unitary system a centralized government system in which lower levels of government have little power independent of the national government

confederation a system of government in which states retain sovereign authority except for the powers expressly delegated to the national government

FEDERALISM COMES FROM THE CONSTITUTION

The United States was the first nation to adopt federalism as its governing framework. With federalism, the framers sought to limit the national government by creating a second layer of state governments. American federalism recognized two sovereigns in the original Constitution and reinforced the principle in the Bill of Rights by granting a few **"expressed powers"** to the national government and reserving all the rest to the states.

expressed powers specific powers granted to Congress under Article I, Section 8, of the Constitution

The Powers of the National Government   As we saw in Chapter 2, the "expressed powers" granted to the national government are found in Article I, Section 8, of the Constitution. These seventeen powers include the power to collect taxes, to coin money, to declare war, and to regulate commerce (which, as we will see, became a very important power for the national government). Article I, Section 8, also contains another important source of power for the national government: the **implied powers** that enable Congress "to make all Laws which shall be necessary and proper for carrying into Execution the foregoing Powers." Not until several decades after the founding did the Supreme Court allow Congress to exercise the power granted in this **necessary and proper clause,** but, as we shall see later in this chapter, this doctrine allowed the national government to expand considerably the scope of its authority, although the process was a slow one.

Aside from these powers, the federal government operates with one other advantage over the states: as mentioned in the last chapter, Article VI of the Constitution says that, whenever there is a conflict between a national law and a state law, the national law shall prevail. This doctrine of *national supremacy* says that "[t]his Constitution, and the Laws of the United States . . . and all Treaties made . . . shall be the supreme Law of the Land," even extending to state courts and constitutions.

implied powers powers derived from the "necessary and proper" clause of Article I, Section 8, of the Constitution. Such powers are not specifically expressed, but are implied through the expansive interpretation of delegated powers

necessary and proper clause from Article I, Section 8 of the Constitution, it provides Congress with the authority to make all laws "necessary and proper" to carry out its expressed powers

The Powers of State Government   One way in which the framers sought to preserve a strong role for the states was through the Tenth Amendment to the Constitution. The Tenth Amendment states that the powers that the Constitution does not delegate to the national government or prohibit to the states are "reserved to the States respectively, or to the people." The Antifederalists, who feared that a strong central government would encroach on individual liberty, repeatedly pressed for such an amendment as a way of limiting national power. Federalists agreed to the amendment because they did not think it would do much harm, given the powers of the Constitution already granted to the national government. The Tenth Amendment is also called the **reserved powers** amendment because it aims to reserve powers to the states.

reserved powers powers, derived from the Tenth Amendment to the Constitution, that are not specifically delegated to the national government or denied to the states

The most fundamental power that is retained by the states is that of coercion—the power to develop and enforce criminal codes, to administer health and safety rules, to regulate the family via marriage and divorce laws. The states have the power to regulate individuals' livelihoods; if you're a doctor or a lawyer or a plumber or a barber, you must be licensed by the state. Even more fundamentally, the states have the power to define private property—private property exists because state laws against trespass define who is and is not entitled to use a piece of property. If you own a car, your ownership isn't worth much unless the state is willing to enforce your right to possession by making it a crime for anyone else to drive your car. These are essential to citizens' everyday lives, and the powers of the states regarding these domestic issues are much greater than the powers of the national government, even today.

A state's authority to regulate these fundamental matters is commonly referred to as the **police power** of the state and encompasses the state's power to regulate the health, safety, welfare, and morals of its citizens. Policing is what states do—they coerce you in the name of the community in order to maintain public order. And this was exactly the type of power that the Founders intended the states to exercise.

police power power reserved to the government to regulate the health, safety, and morals of its citizens

In some areas, the states share **concurrent powers** with the national government, wherein they retain and share some power to regulate commerce and to affect the currency—for example, by being able to charter banks, grant or deny corporate charters, grant or deny licenses to engage in a business or practice a trade, and regulate the quality of products or the conditions of labor. This issue of concurrent versus exclusive power has come up from time to time in our history, but wherever there is a direct conflict of laws between the federal and the state levels, the issue will most likely be resolved in favor of national supremacy.

concurrent powers powers exercised by both the federal and the state governments

State Obligations to One Another   The Constitution also creates obligations among the states. These obligations, spelled out in Article IV, were intended to promote national unity. By requiring the states to recognize actions and decisions taken in other states as legal and proper, the framers aimed to make the states less like independent countries and more like parts of a single nation.

Article IV, Section I, calls for "Full Faith and Credit" among states, meaning that each state is normally expected to honor the "public Acts, Records, and judicial Proceedings" that take place in any other state. So, for example, if a couple is married in Texas—marriage being regulated by state law—Missouri must also recognize that marriage, even though they were not married under Missouri state law.

This **full faith and credit clause** has recently become embroiled in the controversy over gay and lesbian marriage. In 1999, the Vermont Supreme Court ruled that gay and lesbian couples should have the same rights as heterosexuals. The Vermont state legislature enacted legislation that allowed gays and lesbians to form "civil unions." Although not legally considered marriages, such unions allow gay and lesbian couples most of the benefits of marriage, such as eligibility for the partner's health insurance, inheritance rights, and the right to transfer property. As of 2003, thirty-seven states have passed "defense of marriage acts" that define marriage as a union between men and women only; whether these states would have to recognize Vermont's civil unions under the full faith and credit clause is still unclear. Anxious to show its disapproval of gay marriage, Congress passed the Defense of Marriage Act in 1996, which declared that states will *not* have to recognize a same-sex marriage, even if it is legal in one state. The act also said that the federal government will not recognize gay marriage—even if it is legal under state law—and that gay marriage partners will not be eligible for the federal benefits, such as Medicare and Social Security, normally available to spouses.[2]

In 2003, the gay marriage controversy was escalated to a new level when the Massachusetts Supreme Court struck down a state law that defined marriage as opposite-sex only, saying that that law violated the Massachusetts State Constitution. The court justified its decision by saying that its state constitution was even "more protective of individual liberty and equality than the federal Constitution"[3] After efforts began in that state to adopt a civil union measure similar to that of Vermont, the state supreme court said that such a measure would be inadequate and that the state must recognize gay marriage by May 2004. To avoid the full faith and credit problem of pushing other states to recognize a gay marriage performed in Massachusetts, the state's governor, Mitt Romney, said that his state would allow only state residents to receive marriage licenses, citing a 1913 state law that barred out-of-state residents from marrying in Massachusetts if the marriage would be void in their home state (the law was passed to support bans on interracial marriage in other states).[4] Yet numerous legal issues remain to be resolved, such as the status of people who could claim residency in more than one state (for example, college students), the legality of the 1913 state law, and the apparent contradiction between the full faith and credit clause and laws barring recognition of gay marriage.

Article IV, Section 2, known as the "comity clause," also seeks to promote national unity. It provides that citizens enjoying the **"Privileges and Immunities"** of one state should be entitled to similar treatment in other states. What this has come to mean is that a state cannot discriminate against someone from another state or give special privileges to its own residents. For example, in the 1970s, when Alaska passed a law that gave residents preference over nonresidents in

full faith and credit clause provision from Article IV, Section 1 of the Constitution, requiring that the states normally honor the public acts and judicial decisions that take place in another state

privileges and immunities clause provision from Article IV, Section 2 of the Constitution, that a state cannot discriminate against someone from another state or give its own residents special privileges

obtaining work on the state's oil and gas pipelines, the Supreme Court ruled the law illegal because it discriminated against citizens of other states.[5] This clause also regulates criminal justice among the states by requiring states to return fugitives to the states from which they have fled. Thus, in 1952, when an inmate escaped from an Alabama prison and sought to avoid being returned to Alabama on the grounds that he was being subjected to "cruel and unusual punishment" there, the Supreme Court ruled that he must be returned according to Article IV, Section 2.[6] This example highlights the difference between the obligations among states and those among different countries. Recently, France refused to return an American fugitive because he might be subject to the death penalty, which does not exist in France.[7] The Constitution clearly forbids states from doing something similar.

Local Government and the Constitution   Local government occupies a peculiar but very important place in the American system. In fact, the status of American local government is probably unique in world experience. First, it must be pointed out that local governments have no status in the American Constitution. *State* legislatures created local governments, and *state* constitutions and laws permit local governments to take on some of the responsibilities of the state governments. Most states amended their own constitutions to give their larger cities **home rule**—a guarantee of noninterference in various areas of local affairs. But local governments enjoy no such recognition in the Constitution. Local governments have always been mere conveniences of the states.[8]

Local governments became administratively important in the early years of the Republic because the states possessed little administrative capability. They relied on local governments—cities and counties—to implement the laws of the state. Local government was an alternative to a statewide bureaucracy (see Table 3.1).

home rule power delegated by the state to a local unit of government to manage its own affairs

Table 3.1	87,576 Governments in the United States

TYPE	NUMBER
National	1
State	50
County	3,034
Municipal	19,429
Townships	16,504
School districts	13,506
Other special districts	35,052

SOURCE: *Statistical Abstract of the United States, 2003* (Washington, DC: U.S. Government Printing Office, 2003), Table 431.

THE DEFINITION OF FEDERALISM HAS CHANGED RADICALLY

Many of the fiercest political controversies in American history have revolved around competing views of federalism. The best way to understand these disputes, and how federalism has been redefined throughout American history, is to examine how its conception has changed over time. During the "traditional system" in America, from 1789–1933, the political balance scales clearly favored the states over the federal government. From the New Deal period of the 1930s to the present, some important limits were placed on state governments, and the federal government exerted far more power than it had under the traditional system, despite efforts to roll back national government powers in recent decades.

FEDERALISM UNDER THE "TRADITIONAL SYSTEM" GAVE MOST POWERS TO THE STATES

The prevailing view of national government–state government relations under the traditional system was one of **dual federalism,** meaning that the powers of the national government were defined very narrowly and considered entirely separate from those of the states, whereas state powers were defined broadly but were also separate from national powers. Virtually all of the important policies affecting the lives of Americans were made by the state governments during this period. Remember that at the time of the country's founding, the states had existed as former colonies and then as virtually autonomous units for about thirteen years under the Articles of Confederation. The Constitution imposed a stronger national government upon the states, but the tradition of strong states continued. The novelty of this arrangement can be appreciated by noting that each of the major European countries at that time had a unitary government, composed of a single national government with national ministries, a national police force, and a national code of laws covering crime, commerce, public works, education, and all other areas.

dual federalism the system of government that prevailed in the United States from 1789 to the 1930s, in which the powers of the national government and the states were considered entirely separate and distinct from each other; during this time, the states possessed a vast amount of governing power

As we mentioned earlier, during the period of dual federalism, the states did most of the actual governing. For evidence, look at Table 3.2. It lists the major types of public policies by which Americans were governed for the first century and a half under the Constitution. We call it the "traditional system" because it prevailed for three-quarters of American history and because it closely approximates the intentions of the framers of the Constitution.

Under the traditional system, the national government was quite small by comparison both to the state governments and to the governments of other Western nations. Not only was it smaller than most governments of that time, it was actually very narrowly specialized in the functions it performed. The national government built or sponsored the construction of roads, canals, and bridges (internal improvements). It provided cash subsidies to shippers and shipbuilders and distributed free or low-priced public land to encourage western settlement and business ventures. It placed relatively heavy taxes on imported goods (tariffs), not only to raise revenues but to protect "infant industries" from competition from the more

Table 3.2 **The Federal System: Specialization of Governmental Functions in the Traditional System (1800–1933)**

NATIONAL GOVERNMENT POLICIES (DOMESTIC)	STATE GOVERNMENT POLICIES	LOCAL GOVERNMENT POLICIES
Internal improvements	Property laws (including slavery)	Adaptation of state laws to local conditions ("variances")
Subsidies	Estate and inheritance laws	Public works
Tariffs	Commerce laws	Contracts for public works
Public lands disposal	Banking and credit laws	Licensing of public accommodations
Patents	Corporate laws	Assessible improvements
Currency	Insurance laws	Basic public services
	Family laws	
	Morality laws	
	Public health laws	
	Education laws	
	General penal laws	
	Eminent domain laws	
	Construction codes	
	Land-use laws	
	Water and mineral laws	
	Criminal procedure laws	
	Electoral and political parties laws	
	Local government laws	
	Civil service laws	
	Occupations and professions laws	

Notice how few powers were exercised by the national government in the traditional system.

advanced European enterprises. It protected patents and provided for a common currency, also to encourage and facilitate enterprises and to expand markets.

What do these functions of the national government reveal? First, virtually all its functions were aimed at assisting commerce. It is quite appropriate to refer to the traditional American system as a "commercial republic." Second, virtually none of the national government's policies directly coerced citizens. The emphasis of governmental programs was on assistance, promotion, and encouragement—the allocation of land or capital where they were insufficiently available for economic development.

Meanwhile, state legislatures were actively involved in economic regulation during the nineteenth century. In the United States, then and now, private property exists only in state laws and state court decisions regarding property, trespass, and real estate. American capitalism took its form from state property and trespass laws, as well as from state laws and court decisions regarding contracts, markets, credit, banking, incorporation, and insurance. Laws concerning slavery were a subdivision of property law in states where slavery existed. The practice of important professions, such as law and medicine, was and is illegal except as provided for by state law. Marriage, divorce, and the birth or adoption of a child have always been regulated by state law. To educate or not to educate a child has been a decision governed more by state laws than by parents, and not at all by national law. It is important to note also that virtually all criminal laws—regarding everything from trespass to murder—have been state laws. Most of the criminal laws adopted by Congress are concerned with the District of Columbia and other federal territories.

All this (and more, as shown in the middle column of Table 3.2) demonstrates without any question that most of the fundamental governing in the United States was done by the states. The contrast between national and state policies, as shown by Table 3.2, demonstrates the difference in the power vested in each. The list of items in the middle column could actually have been made longer. Moreover, each item on the list is a category of law that fills many volumes of statutes and court decisions. This contrast between national and state governments is all the more impressive because it is basically what the framers of the Constitution intended.

Here lies the most important point of all: The fundamental impact of federalism on the way the United States is governed comes not from any particular provision of the Constitution but from the framework itself, which has determined the flow of government functions and, through that, the political development of the country. By allowing state governments to do most of the fundamental governing, the Constitution saved the national government from many policy decisions that might have proven too divisive for a large and very young country. There is no doubt that if the Constitution had provided for a unitary rather than a federal system, the war over slavery would have come in 1789 or 1809 rather than in 1860; and if it had come that early, the South might very well have seceded and established a separate and permanent slaveholding nation.

In helping the national government remain small and aloof from the most divisive issues of the day, federalism contributed significantly to the political stability of the young nation, even as the social, economic, and political systems of many of the states and regions of the country were undergoing tremendous, profound, and sometimes violent, change.[9] As we shall see, some important aspects of federalism have changed, but the federal framework has survived two centuries and a devastating civil war.

THE COURT PAVED THE WAY FOR THE END OF THE "TRADITIONAL SYSTEM"

Having created the national government, and recognizing the potential for abuse of power, the states sought through federalism to constrain the national government. The "traditional system" of a weak national government prevailed for over a century despite economic forces favoring its expansion and despite Supreme Court cases giving a pro-national interpretation to Article I, Section 8, of the Constitution.

That article delegates to Congress the power "to regulate commerce with foreign nations, and among the several States and with the Indian tribes." For most of the nineteenth century, the Supreme Court consistently interpreted this **commerce clause** *in favor* of national power. The first and most important case favoring national power over the economy was *McCulloch v. Maryland* (1819).[10] This case involved the question of whether Congress had the power to charter a national bank, since such an explicit grant of power was nowhere to be found in Article I, Section 8. Chief Justice John Marshall answered that the power could be "implied" from other powers that were expressly delegated to Congress, such as the "powers to lay and collect taxes; to borrow money; to regulate commerce; and to declare and conduct a war."

By allowing Congress to use the necessary and proper clause to interpret its delegated powers expansively, the Supreme Court created the potential for an unprecedented increase national government power. Marshall also concluded that whenever a state law conflicted with a federal law (as in the case of *McCulloch v. Maryland*), the state law would be deemed invalid since the Constitution states that "the Laws of the United States . . . shall be the supreme Law of the Land." Both parts of this great case are pro-national, yet Congress did not immediately seek to expand the policies of the national government.

Another major case, *Gibbons v. Ogden* in 1824, reinforced this nationalistic interpretation of the Constitution. The important but relatively narrow issue was whether the state of New York could grant a monopoly to Robert Fulton's steamboat company to operate an exclusive service between New York and New Jersey. Chief Justice Marshall argued that New York State did not have the power to grant this particular monopoly. In order to reach this decision, it was necessary for Marshall to define what Article I, Section 8, meant by "commerce among the several states." He insisted that the definition was "comprehensive," extending to "every species of commercial intercourse." He did say that this comprehensiveness was limited "to that commerce which concerns more states than one," giving rise to what later came to be called "interstate commerce." *Gibbons* is important because it established the supremacy of the national government in all matters affecting interstate commerce.[11] But what would remain uncertain during several decades of constitutional discourse was the precise meaning of interstate commerce.

Article I, Section 8, backed by the implied powers decision in *McCulloch* and by the broad definition of "interstate commerce" in *Gibbons,* was a

commerce clause Article 1, Section 8, of the Constitution, which delegates to Congress the power "to regulate Commerce with foreign Nations, and among the several States and with the Indian Tribes." The Supreme Court interpreted this clause in favor of national power over the economy

source of power for the national government as long as Congress sought to facilitate commerce through subsidies, services, and land grants. But later in the nineteenth century, when the national government sought to use those powers to *regulate* the economy rather than merely to promote economic development, federalism and the concept of interstate commerce began to operate as restraints on, rather than sources of, national power. This is why the Court rulings of *McCulloch* and *Gibbons* did not bring the "traditional system" to an end. The Supreme Court declared any effort of the national government to regulate commerce in such areas as fraud, the production of impure goods, the use of child labor, or the existence of dangerous working conditions or long hours to be unconstitutional as a violation of the concept of interstate commerce. Such legislation meant that the federal government was entering the factory and the workplace—local areas—and was attempting to regulate goods that had not passed into commerce. To enter these local workplaces was to exercise police power—the power reserved to the states for the protection of the health, safety, and morals of their citizens. No one questioned the power of the national government to regulate businesses that intrinsically involved interstate commerce, such as railroads, gas pipelines, and waterway transportation. But well into the twentieth century, the Supreme Court used the concept of interstate commerce as a barrier against most efforts by Congress to regulate local conditions.

This aspect of federalism was alive and well during an epoch of tremendous economic development, the period between the Civil War and the 1930s. It gave the American economy a freedom from federal government control that closely approximated the ideal of free enterprise. The economy was never entirely free, of course; in fact, entrepreneurs themselves did not want complete freedom from government. They needed law and order. They needed a stable currency. They needed courts and police to enforce contracts and prevent trespass. They needed roads, canals, and railroads. But federalism, as interpreted by the Supreme Court for seventy years after the Civil War, made it possible for business to have its cake and eat it, too. Entrepreneurs enjoyed the benefits of national policies facilitating commerce but were protected by the courts from policies regulating commerce.[12]

As we have seen, the Constitution contained the seeds of a very expansive national government—in the commerce clause. For much of the nineteenth century, federal power remained limited. The Tenth Amendment was used to bolster arguments about **states' rights,** which in their extreme version claimed that the states did not have to submit to national laws when they believed the national government had exceeded its authority. These arguments in favor of states' rights were voiced less often after the Civil War. But the Supreme Court continued to use the Tenth Amendment to strike down laws that it thought exceeded national power, including the Civil Rights Act passed in 1875.

In the early twentieth century, however, the Tenth Amendment appeared to lose its force. Reformers began to press for national regulations to limit the

states' rights the principle that the states should oppose the increasing authority of the national government. This principle was most popular in the period before the Civil War

power of large corporations and to preserve the health and welfare of citizens. The Supreme Court approved of some of these laws but it struck others down, including a law combating child labor. The Court stated that the law violated the Tenth Amendment because only states should have the power to regulate conditions of employment.

THE END OF THE "TRADITIONAL SYSTEM" GAVE WAY TO THE RISE OF COOPERATIVE FEDERALISM

The New Deal of the 1930s marked two key changes: the rise of a more active national government, and a major change in how the courts interpreted national power. The door to increase federal action opened when states proved unable to cope with the demands brought on by the Great Depression. Before the Depression, states and localities took responsibility for addressing the needs of the poor, usually through private charity. But the extent of the need created by the Depression quickly exhausted local and state capacities. By 1932, 25 percent of the workforce was unemployed. The jobless lost their homes and settled into camps all over the country, called "Hoovervilles" after President Herbert Hoover. Elected in 1928, the year before the Depression hit, Hoover steadfastly maintained that there was little the federal government could do to alleviate the misery caused by the Depression. It was a matter for state and local governments, he said.

Yet demands mounted for the federal government to take action. In Congress, some Democrats proposed that the federal government finance public works to aid the economy and put people back to work. Other members of Congress introduced legislation to provide federal grants to the states to assist them in their relief efforts. None of these measures passed while Hoover remained in the White House.

FDR'S NEW DEAL REMADE THE GOVERNMENT

When Franklin D. Roosevelt took office in 1933, he energetically threw the federal government into the business of fighting the Depression. He proposed a variety of temporary measures to provide federal relief and work programs. Most of the programs he proposed were to be financed by the federal government but administered by the states. In addition to these temporary measures, Roosevelt presided over the creation of several important federal programs designed to provide future economic security for Americans.

For the most part, the new national programs that the Roosevelt administration developed did not directly take power away from the states. Instead, Washington typically redirected states by offering them **grants-in-aid,** whereby Congress appropriated money to state and local governments on the condition that the money be spent for a particular purpose defined by Congress.

Franklin Roosevelt did not invent the idea of grants-in-aid, but his New Deal vastly expanded the range of grants-in-aid to include social programs, pro-

grants-in-aid programs through which Congress provides money to state and local governments on the condition that the funds be employed for purposes defined by the federal government

viding grants to the states for financial assistance to poor children. Congress added new grants after World War II, creating programs to help states fund activities such as providing school lunches and building highways. Sometimes the national government required state or local governments to match the national contribution dollar for dollar, but in some programs, such as the development of the interstate highway system, the congressional grants provided 90 percent of the cost of the program.

These newer types of federal grants-in-aid are called **categorical grants,** because the national government determines in more detail and with more rules the purposes, or categories, for which the money can be used. For the most part, the categorical grants created before the 1960s simply helped the states perform their traditional functions.[13] In the 1960s, however, the national role expanded and federal aid in the form of categorical grants increased dramatically (see Figure 3.1). For example, during the Eighty-ninth Congress (1965–66) alone, the number of categorical grant-in-aid programs grew from 221 to 379.[14] The grants authorized during the 1960s announced national purposes much more strongly than did earlier grants. Central to that national purpose was the need to provide opportunities to the poor.

categorical grants Congressional grants given to states and localities on the condition that expenditures be limited to a problem or group specified by law

The Rise, Decline, and Recovery of Federal Aid, 1960–2003   Figure 3.1

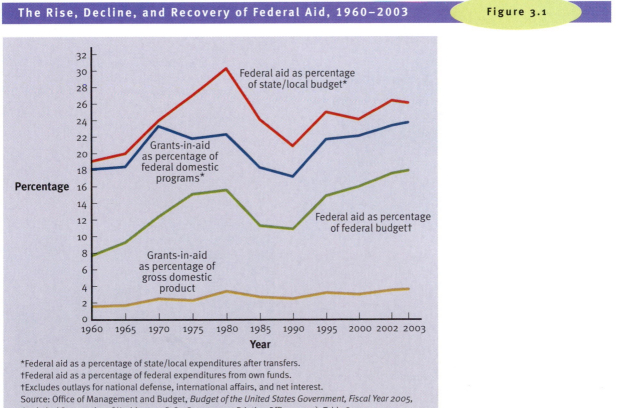

*Federal aid as a percentage of state/local expenditures after transfers.
†Federal aid as a percentage of federal expenditures from own funds.
†Excludes outlays for national defense, international affairs, and net interest.
Source: Office of Management and Budget, *Budget of the United States Government, Fiscal Year 2005, Analytical Perspectives* (Washington, D.C.: Government Printing Office, 2004), Table 8–3, p. 120.

Limiting Federal Power in Favor of States

During the Great Depression, the national government become more active in regulating the economy and supporting the poor, who lived in places like this Hooverville outside of Seattle.

In the 1950s the federal government covered 90 percent of the cost of building more than 42,500 miles of interstate highways. Since the highways would improve interstate commerce, the federal government took the lead in funding them.

Over the past fifty years, many politicians have embraced states' rights. Governor George Wallace of Alabama was a vocal supporter of states' rights and a segregationist. In 1963, he defied a federal mandate that allowed black students to enroll at the University of Alabama.

POLITICS

In the mid-1990s, Republican Party leaders contended that the national government had grown too powerful at the expense of the states and argued that the Tenth Amendment should restrict the growth of national power.

With the renewal of state autonomy in recent years, wide economic and social policy differences have emerged across the states. California, for example, is currently the only state with a paid family leave policy, which was passed by former governor Gray Davis in September 2002.

CHANGING COURT INTERPRETATIONS OF FEDERALISM HELPED ROOSEVELT'S NEW DEAL

In a dramatic change beginning in 1937, the Supreme Court threw out the old distinction between interstate and intrastate commerce on which it had relied in the late 1800s and early 1900s. It converted the commerce clause from a source of limitations to a source of power for the national government. The Court began to refuse to review appeals that challenged acts of Congress protecting the rights of employees to organize and engage in collective bargaining, regulating the amount of farmland in cultivation, extending low-interest credit to small businesses and farmers, and restricting the activities of corporations dealing in the stock market; it upheld many other laws that contributed to the construction of the modern "welfare state."[15]

The Court also reversed its position on the Tenth Amendment, which it had used to strike down national laws as violations of state power. Instead, the Court approved numerous expansions of national power, to such an extent that the Tenth Amendment appeared irrelevant. In fact, in 1941, Justice Harlan Fiske Stone declared that the Tenth Amendment was simply a "truism" that had no real meaning.[16]

Yet the idea that some powers should be reserved to the states did not go away. Indeed, in the 1950s, southern opponents of the civil rights movement revived the idea of states' rights. In 1956, ninety-six southern members of Congress issued a "Southern Manifesto" in which they declared that southern states were not constitutionally bound by Supreme Court decisions outlawing racial segregation. They believed that states' rights should override individual rights to liberty and formal equality. With the triumph of the civil rights movement, the slogan of "states' rights" became tarnished by its association with racial inequality.

Recent years have seen a revival of interest in the Tenth Amendment and important Supreme Court decisions limiting federal power. Much of the interest in the Tenth Amendment stems from conservatives who believe that a strong federal government encroaches on individual liberties. They believe such freedoms are better protected by returning more power to the states through the process of **devolution.** In 1996, Republican presidential candidate Robert Dole carried a copy of the Tenth Amendment in his pocket as he campaigned, pulling it out to read at rallies.[17] The Supreme Court's ruling in *United States v. Lopez* in 1995 fueled further interest in the Tenth Amendment. In that case, the Court, stating that Congress had exceeded its authority under the commerce clause, struck down a federal law that barred handguns near schools. This was the first time since the New Deal that the Court had limited congressional powers in this way. In 1997, the Court again relied on the Tenth Amendment to limit federal power in *Printz v. United States.*[18] The decision declared unconstitutional a provision of the Brady Handgun Violence Prevention Act that required state and local law enforcement officials to conduct background checks on handgun purchasers. The Court declared that this provision violated state sovereignty guaranteed in the Tenth Amendment because it required state and local officials to administer a federal regulatory program. The Court further limited the power of the federal government over the states in a 1996 ruling that prevented Native Americans from the Seminole tribe from suing the state of

devolution a policy to remove a program from one level of government by delegating it or passing it down to a lower level of government, such as from the national government to the state and local governments

Florida in federal court. A 1988 law had given Indian tribes the right to sue a state in federal court if the state did not negotiate in good faith over issues related to gambling casinos on tribal land. The Supreme Court's rulings appeared to signal a much broader limitation on national power by raising new questions about whether individuals can sue a state if it fails to uphold federal law.[19]

In 2002, the Court used the Eleventh Amendment, which grants the state immunity from private lawsuits, to limit federal government power. In the case of *Federal Maritime Commission v. South Carolina Ports Authority*, the Court expanded state sovereignty to protect states from having to respond to private complaints brought before federal government agencies.[20] In 2003, however, the Court ruled in favor of federal power in *Nevada Department of Human Resources v. Hibbs,* saying that state employees may sue states for violating a federal law that provides workers the right to take time off for family medical emergencies under the federal Family and Medical Leave Act.[21]

COOPERATIVE FEDERALISM PUSHES STATES TO ACHIEVE NATIONAL GOALS

The growth of categorical grants, along with favorable court rulings, created a new kind of federalism. If the traditional system of two sovereigns performing highly different functions could be called dual federalism, historians of federalism suggest that the system since the New Deal could be called **cooperative federalism.** The most important student of the history of American federalism, Morton Grozdins, characterized this as a move from "layer-cake federalism" to "marble-cake federalism,"[22] in which intergovernmental cooperation and sharing have blurred a once-clear distinguishing line, making it difficult to say where the national government ends and the state and local governments begin (see Figure 3.2).

cooperative federalism federalism existing since the New Deal era in which grants-in-aid have been used strategically to encourage states and localities to pursue nationally defined goals, with national and state governments sharing powers and resources via intergovernmental cooperation

Evolving Federalism

Figure 3.2

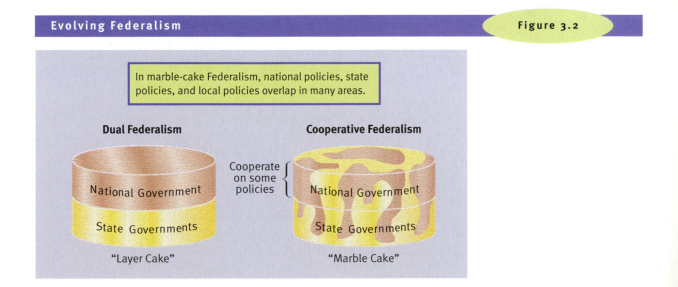

In marble-cake Federalism, national policies, state policies, and local policies overlap in many areas.

Dual Federalism

National Government

State Governments

"Layer Cake"

Cooperate on some policies

Cooperative Federalism

National Government

State Governments

"Marble Cake"

For a while in the 1960s, it appeared as if the state governments would become increasingly irrelevant to American federalism. Many of the new federal grants bypassed the states and instead sent money directly to local governments and even to local nonprofit organizations. The theme heard repeatedly in Washington was that the states simply could not be trusted to carry out national purposes.[23]

One of the reasons that Washington distrusted the states was because of the way African American citizens were treated in the South. The southern states' forthright defense of segregation, justified on the grounds of states' rights, helped to tarnish the image of the states as the civil rights movement took hold. The national officials who planned the War on Poverty in the 1960s pointed to the racial exclusion practiced in the southern states as a reason for bypassing state governments. Political scientist James Sundquist described how the "Alabama syndrome" affected the War on Poverty: "In the drafting of the Economic Opportunity Act, an 'Alabama syndrome' developed. Any suggestion within the poverty task force that the states be given a role in the administration of the act was met with the question, 'Do you want to give that kind of power to [Alabama governor] George Wallace?'"[24]

Yet, even though many national policies of the 1960s bypassed the states, other new programs, such as Medicaid—the health program for the poor—relied on state governments for their implementation. In addition, as the national government expanded existing programs run by the states, states had to take on more responsibility. These new responsibilities meant that the states were now playing a very important role in the federal system.

NATIONAL STANDARDS HAVE BEEN ADVANCED THROUGH FEDERAL PROGRAMS

Over time, the Supreme Court has pushed for greater uniformity in rules and procedures across the states. In addition to legal decisions, the national government uses two other tools to create similarities across the states: grants-in-aid and regulations.

Grants-in-aid, as we have seen, are a little like bribes: Congress give money to state and local governments if they agree to spend it for the purposes Congress specifies. But as Congress began to enact legislation in new areas, such as environmental policy, it also imposed additional *regulations* on states and localities. Some political scientists call this a move toward regulated federalism.[25] The national government began to set standards of conduct or required the states to set standards that met national guidelines. The effect of these national standards is that state and local policies in the areas of environmental protection, social services, and education are more uniform from coast to coast than are other nationally funded policies.

Some national standards require the federal government to take over areas of regulation formerly overseen by state or local governments. Such **preemption** occurs when state and local actions are found to be inconsistent with federal requirements. If this occurs, all regulations in the preempted area must

preemption the principle that allows the national government to override state or local actions in certain policy areas

henceforth come from the national government. In many cases, the courts determine the scope of the federal authority to preempt. For example, in 1973 the Supreme Court struck down a local ordinance prohibiting jets from taking off from the airport in Burbank, California, between 11 P.M. and 7 A.M. It ruled that the Federal Aeronautics Act granted the Federal Aviation Administration all authority over flight patterns, takeoffs, and landings and that local governments could not impose regulations in this area. As federal regulations increased after the 1970s, Washington increasingly preempted state and local action in many different policy areas. This preemption has escalated since 1995, when Republicans gained control of Congress. Although the Republicans came to power promising to grant more responsibility to the states, they have reduced state control in many areas by preemption. For example, in 1998 Congress passed a law that prohibits states and localities from taxing Internet commerce for the next three to six years. The 1996 Telecommunications Act reduced local control by giving broadcasters and digital companies broad discretion over where they could erect digital television and cellular phone towers even if local citizens objected.[26]

The growth of national standards has created some new problems and has raised questions about how far federal standardization should go. One problem that emerged in the 1980s was the increase in **unfunded mandates**—regulations or new conditions for receiving grants that impose costs on state and local governments for which they are not reimbursed by the national government. The growth of unfunded mandates was the product of a Democratic Congress, which wanted to achieve liberal social objectives, and a Republican president, who opposed increased social spending. Between 1983 and 1991, Congress mandated standards in many policy areas, including social services and environmental regulations, without providing additional funds to meet those standards. Altogether, Congress enacted twenty-seven laws that imposed new regulations or required states to expand existing programs.[27] For example, in the late 1980s, Congress ordered the states to extend the coverage provided by Medicaid, the medical insurance program for the poor. The aim was to make the program serve more people, particularly poor children, and to expand services. But Congress did not supply additional funding to help states meet these new requirements; the states had to shoulder the increased financial burden themselves.

States and localities quickly began to protest the cost of unfunded mandates. Although it is very hard to determine the exact cost of federal regulations, the Congressional Budget Office estimated that between 1983 and 1990, new federal regulations cost states and localities between \$8.9 and \$12.7 billion.[28] States complained that mandates took up so much of their budgets that they were not able to set their own priorities.

These burdens became part of a rallying cry to reduce the power of the federal government—a cry that took center stage when a Republican Congress was elected in 1994. One of the first measures the new Congress passed was an act to limit the cost of unfunded mandates, the Unfunded Mandate

unfunded mandates regulations or conditions for receiving grants that impose costs on state and local governments for which they are not reimbursed by the federal government

Reform Act (UMRA). Under this law, Congress must estimate the cost of any proposal it believes will cost more than $50 million. It must then vote to approve the regulation, acknowledging the expenditure. At most, UMRA represented an effort to move the national-state relationship a bit further to the state side. But it has had no significant impact on mandates. The act does not prevent congressional members from passing unfunded mandates, but only makes them think twice before they do. Moreover, the act exempts several areas of regulation. States must still enforce antidiscrimination laws and meet other requirements to receive federal assistance. New national problems inevitably raise the question of who pays. Since the terrorist attacks of 2001, state governments have grown deeply concerned about the costs of security. Although ensuring the common defense is traditionally a federal responsibility, where responsibility for homeland security lies is far less clear. This is not surprising since no one had ever used the term "homeland security" before the terror attacks. Since then, the costs of homeland security have fallen heavily on the states. In 2003, states, faced with their worst fiscal crises in sixty years, complained that the federal assistance provided for homeland security was far too little. At its annual meetings that year, the National Governors' Association declared homeland security an unfunded mandate for which the federal government should provide more assistance. The relationship between national security needs and state and local capabilities remains unsettled.

NEW FEDERALISM MEANS MORE STATE CONTROL

Since the 1970s, as states have become more capable of administering large-scale programs, the idea of devolution—transferring responsibility for policy from the federal government to the states and localities—has become popular.

block grants federal grants-in-aid that allow states considerable discretion in how the funds should be spent

Proponents of more state authority have looked to **block grants** as a way of reducing federal control. Block grants are federal grants that allow the states considerable leeway in spending federal money. President Richard Nixon led the first push for block grants in the early 1970s. Nixon's block grants consolidated programs in the areas of job training, community development, and social services into three large block grants. These grants imposed some conditions on states and localities for how the money should be spent, but not the narrow regulations contained in the categorical grants. In addition, Congress approved a fourth block grant called **revenue sharing.**

revenue sharing the process by which one unit of government yields a portion of its tax income to another unit of government, according to an established formula. Revenue sharing typically involves the national government providing money to state governments

Revenue sharing provided money to local governments and counties with no strings attached; localities could spend the money as they wished. Ronald Reagan's version of new federalism also looked to block grants. Like Nixon, Reagan wanted to reduce the national government's control and return power to the states. In all, Congress created twelve new block grants between 1981 and 1990.[29]

But these new approaches (summarized in Figure 3.3) have not provided magic solutions to the problems of federalism. For one thing, there is always a

Regulated versus New Federalism

Figure 3.3

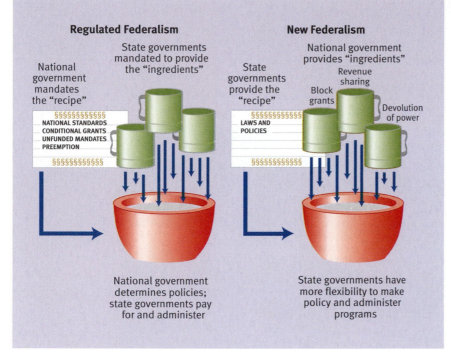

Regulated Federalism

National government mandates the "recipe"

State governments mandated to provide the "ingredients"

§§§§§§§§§§§§
NATIONAL STANDARDS
CONDITIONAL GRANTS
UNFUNDED MANDATES
PREEMPTION
§§§§§§§§§§§§

National government determines policies; state governments pay for and administer

New Federalism

National government provides "ingredients"

State governments provide the "recipe"

Revenue sharing
Block grants
Devolution of power

§§§§§§§§§§§§
LAWS AND POLICIES

§§§§§§§§§§§§

State governments have more flexibility to make policy and administer programs

trade-off between accountability, that is, whether the states are using funds for the purposes intended, and flexibility. Accountability and proper use of funds continue to be troublesome issues. Even after block grants were created, Congress reimposed regulations in order to increase the states' accountability. For example, the first major bipartisan legislation of the George W. Bush administration was an education bill that gave schools more discretion over how they used federal dollars but at the same time imposed educational standards by requiring annual reading and math tests. If the objective is to have accountable and efficient government, state bureaucracies are not necessarily any more efficient or more capable than national agencies. In Mississippi, for example, the state Department of Human Services spent money from the child care block grant for office furniture and designer salt and pepper shakers that cost $37.50 a pair. As one Mississippi state legislator said, "I've seen too many years of good ol' boy politics to know they shouldn't [transfer money to the states] without stricter controls and requirements."[30] Both liberals and conservatives have charged that block grants are a way for politicians to avoid

Should States Set the
Speed Limit?

The debate over national versus state control is illustrated by the question of speed limits. The issue arose in 1973, when gas supplies became scarce and gas prices skyrocketed. Drivers nationwide were forced to wait in long lines at gas stations.

The federal government responded to the gas crisis by instituting a national 55-mile-per-hour speed limit. The new limit was mandatory on all federal highways and was intended to reduce gas use.

POLITICS

In 1995 Congress lifted its speed limit restrictions and gave states the right to determine their own road speeds. As a result, speed limits went up on many highways.

Proponents of the states' right to set speed limits had insisted that raising them would not increase the number of accidents. However, car accidents like this fatal one—in which a truck carrying speed limit signs rolled over and caught fire—suggest that high speed limits may have dangerous consequences.

the big, controversial policy questions. Instead of facing problems head on, these critics say, the federal government uses block grants to kick the problem down to the states.[31]

THERE IS NO SIMPLE ANSWER TO FINDING THE RIGHT NATIONAL-STATE BALANCE

Some students of federalism say that states are best at doing some things and the national government is better at doing others. They argue that rather than share responsibility for funding, as many programs now do, each level of government should be fully responsible for the things that it does best.

Many economists and political scientists maintain that states and localities should not be in charge of programs that are primarily for the benefit of the poor. They argue that because states and local governments have to compete with one another, they do not have the incentive to spend their money on the needy people in their areas. Instead, they want to keep taxes low and spend money on things that promote economic development.[32] In this situation, states might engage in a "race to the bottom": If one state cuts assistance to the poor, neighboring states will institute similar or deeper cuts both to reduce expenditures and to discourage poorer people from moving into their states. As one New York legislator put it, "The concern we have is that unless we make our welfare system and our tax and regulatory system competitive with the states around us, we will have too many disincentives for business to move here. Welfare is a big part of that."[33]

In 1996, when Congress enacted a major welfare reform law, it followed a different logic. By changing welfare from a combined federal–state program into a block grant to the states, Congress gave the states more responsibility for programs that serve the poor. One argument in favor of this decision was that states can act as "laboratories of democracy," by experimenting with many different approaches to find one that best meet the needs of their citizens.[34] As states have altered their welfare programs in the wake of the new law, they have indeed designed diverse approaches. For example, Minnesota has adopted an incentive-based approach that offers extra assistance to families that take low-wage jobs. Other states, such as California, have more "sticks" than "carrots" in their new welfare programs. In the years since the passage of the law, welfare rolls have declined dramatically. On average they have declined by 47 percent from their peak in 1994; in six states the decline was 70 percent or higher. Politicians have cited these statistics to claim success for their programs, yet analysts caution that we do not yet know enough about the fate of those who have left welfare to judge the effect of welfare reform. Most studies have found that the majority of those leaving welfare remain in poverty. And even though many states have increased services to welfare recipients, they have also funneled savings on welfare expenditures into tax cuts for the nonpoor. Critics charge that by cutting taxes and limiting spending, states have missed a historic opportunity provided by reduced welfare rolls and budget surpluses to devise new ways to assist low-income residents.[35] As the case of welfare shows, assessments about "the right way" to divide responsibility in the federal system change over time.

Summary

In this chapter, we have examined one of the central principles of American government: federalism. The Constitution divides powers between the national government and the states, but over time national power has grown substantially. This expansion of national governmental power came from the changing needs of a vastly larger and more complex nation, and from the desire to extend liberty and equality to citizens who did not enjoy these benefits. While federalism today favors the national government far more than the Constitution's founders could have imagined, most agree that this change was necessary.

The aim of federalism in the Constitution was to limit national power by creating two sovereigns: the national government and the state governments. The Founders hoped that this system of dual federalism would ensure the liberty of citizens by preventing the national government from becoming too powerful. But during the 1930s, American citizens used the democratic system to change the balance between federal and state governments. The failure of the states to provide basic economic security for citizens during the Great Depression led to an expansion of the federal government. Most Americans were supportive of this growing federal power because they believed that economic power had become too concentrated in the hands of big corporations and the common person was the loser. Thus, the ideal of equality—in this case, the belief that working people should have a fighting chance to support themselves—overrode fears that a strong federal government would abridge liberties. Expanded federal powers first took the form of grants-in-aid to states. Later, federal regulations became more common.

In recent years, many Americans have come to believe that the pendulum has swung too far in the direction of expanded federal power. A common charge is that the federal government is too big and, as a result, has encroached on fundamental liberties. State and local governments complain that they cannot govern because their powers have been preempted or because they have to use their own funds to fulfill unfunded mandates imposed by the federal government. Advocates of devolving more power to the states to reduce federal power believe that states can protect liberty without creating unacceptable inequalities. Others continue to believe that a strong central government is essential to ensuring basic equalities. They argue that economic competition among the states means that states cannot ensure equality as well as the federal government can. Such questions about how federalism affects the relationship between citizens and their government are not easily settled and will remain a continuing task of American democracy.

For Further Reading

Anton, Thomas. *American Federalism and Public Policy.* Philadelphia: Temple University Press, 1989.

Bensel, Richard. *Sectionalism and American Political Development: 1880–1980.* Madison, WI: University of Wisconsin Press, 1984.

Bowman, Ann O'M., and Richard Kearny. *The Resurgence of the States.* Englewood Cliffs, NJ: Prentice Hall, 1986.

Dye, Thomas R. *American Federalism: Competition among Governments.* Lexington, MA: Lexington Books, 1990.

Elazar, Daniel. *American Federalism: A View from the States,* 3rd ed. New York: Harper & Row, 1984.

Grodzins, Morton. *The American System.* Chicago: Rand McNally, 1974.

Kelley, E. Wood. *Policy and Politics in the United States: The Limits of Localism.* Philadelphia: Temple University Press, 1987.

Kettl, Donald. *The Regulation of American Federalism.* Baltimore: Johns Hopkins University Press, 1987.

Peterson, Paul E. *The Price of Federalism.* Washington, DC: Brookings, 1995.

Study Outline

Federalism Shapes American Politics

1. In an effort to limit national power, the framers of the Constitution established a system of dual federalism, wherein both the national and state governments would have sovereignty.
2. Federalism and a restrictive definition of "interstate commerce" limited the national government's control over the economy.
3. Federalism allows a great deal of variation among states.

The Definition of Federalism Has Changed Radically

1. Under the traditional system of federalism, the national government was small and very narrowly specialized in its functions compared with other Western nations. Most of its functions were aimed at promoting commerce.
2. Under the traditional system, states rather than the national government did most of the fundamental governing in the country.

3. The system of federalism limited the expansion of the national government despite economic forces and expansive interpretations of the Constitution in cases such as *McCulloch v. Maryland* and *Gibbons v. Ogden.*
4. For most of U.S. history, the concept of interstate commerce kept the national government from regulating the economy. But in 1937, the Supreme Court converted the commerce clause from a source of limitations to a source of power for the national government.
5. The rise of national government activity after the New Deal did not necessarily mean that states lost power directly. Rather, the national government paid states through grants-in-aid to administer federal programs.
6. Some federal programs bypass the states by sending money directly to local governments or local organizations. The states are most important, however; they are integral to federal programs such as Medicaid.

Practice Quiz

1. Which term describes the sharing of powers between the national government and the state governments?
   a) separation of powers
   b) federalism
   c) checks and balances
   d) shared powers

2. The system of federalism that allowed states to do most of the fundamental governing from 1789 to 1937 was
   a) home rule.
   b) regulated federalism.
   c) dual federalism.
   d) cooperative federalism.

3. Which of the following resulted from the federal system?
   a) It limited the power of the national government in relation to the states.
   b) It restrained the power of the national government over the economy.
   c) It allowed variation among the states.
   d) all of the above

4. The overall effect of the growth of national policies has been
   a) to weaken state government.
   b) to strengthen state government.
   c) to provide uniform laws in the nation.
   d) to make the states more diverse culturally.

5. Which amendment to the Constitution stated that the powers not delegated to the national government or prohibited to the states were "reserved to the states"?
    a) First Amendment
    b) Fifth Amendment
    c) Tenth Amendment
    d) Twenty-sixth Amendment

6. The process of returning more of the responsibilities of governing from the national level to the state level is known as
    a) dual federalism.
    b) devolution.
    c) preemption.
    d) home rule.

7. One of the most powerful tools by which the federal government has attempted to get the states to act in ways that are desired by the federal government is by
    a) providing grants-in-aid.
    b) requiring licensing.
    c) granting home rule.
    d) defending states' rights.

8. The form of regulated federalism that allows the federal government to take over areas of regulation formerly overseen by states or local governments is called
    a) categorical grants.
    b) formula grants.
    c) project grants.
    d) preemption.

9. To what does the term "New Federalism" refer?
    a) the national government's regulation of state action through grants-in-aid
    b) the type of federalism relying on categorical grants
    c) efforts to return more policy-making discretion to the states through the use of block grants
    d) the recent emergence of local governments as important political actors

10. A recent notable example of the process of giving the states more responsibility for administering government programs is
    a) campaign finance reform.
    b) prison reform.
    c) trade reform.
    d) welfare reform.

Critical Thinking Questions

1. The role of the national government has changed significantly from the founding era to the present. In what ways and to what extent do you think the framers of the Constitution would recognize modern American federalism? Do you think they would be pleased by the current balance of power between the sovereign national government and the sovereign state governments? In what ways did the system of federalism perform its intended functions? In what ways did it not?

2. Should states be required to implement unfunded mandates? Are Americans better off or worse off as a result of devolution?

Key Terms

block grants (p. 70)
categorical grants (p. 63)
commerce clause (p. 60)
concurrent powers (p. 54)
confederation (p. 53)
cooperative federalism (p. 67)
devolution (p. 66)

dual federalism (p. 57)
expressed powers (p. 53)
federalism (p. 52)
full faith and credit clause (p. 55)
grants-in-aid (p. 62)
home rule (p. 56)
implied powers (p. 53)
necessary and proper clause (p. 53)
police power (p. 54)

preemption (p. 68)
privileges and immunities clause (p. 55)
reserved powers (p. 54)
revenue sharing (p. 70)
states' rights (p. 61)
unfunded mandates (p. 69)
unitary system (p. 53)

4 CIVIL LIBERTIES AND CIVIL RIGHTS

MAIN MESSAGE

The Fourteenth Amendment is the key to our rights.

One of the most widely known facts about our constitutional system is that the first ten amendments to the Constitution, called the **Bill of Rights,** are the basis for the freedoms we enjoy as American citizens. They are what we refer to as **civil liberties**—protections of individual rights of citizens *from* the government. Most citizens know that they are entitled to free speech, freedom of religious expression, protection from improper searches and seizures, the right to have a lawyer during a trial, and other basic protections.

But what most Americans do not know is that, for much of our history, Americans *could not* claim the specific civil liberties protections provided in the Bill of Rights under most circumstances. The fact that we can claim these protections today is because of another amendment, the Fourteenth. How the

> ## Key Concepts
> 1. Civil liberties are protections *from* the government; civil rights are protections *by* the government.
> 2. We can thank the opponents of the Constitution (the Antifederalists) for the fact that a Bill of Rights was added to the Constitution.
> 3. The Fourteenth Amendment made it possible for citizens to enjoy key Bill of Rights protections in their daily lives through the process of incorporation.
> 4. African Americans fought long and hard to win basic civil rights.
> 5. Other disadvantaged groups followed the trail blazed by the civil rights movement.
> 6. Affirmative action programs were designed to right past wrongs.

Bill of Rights the first ten amendments to the Constitution, which guarantee certain rights and liberties to the people

79

civil liberties areas of personal freedom with which governments are prevented from interfering

civil rights obligation imposed on government to take positive action to protect citizens from any illegal action of government agencies as well as other private citizens

Fourteenth Amendment achieved this will be discussed in this chapter. In addition, the Fourteenth Amendment played a critical role in the struggle to extend **civil rights**—protections of citizen equality provided by the government. The distinction between civil liberties and civil rights should be carefully noted. Civil liberties questions arise under the "due process" clause (mentioned in both the Fourteenth Amendment and in the original Bill of Rights), while civil rights questions arise under the "equal protection" clause of the Fourteenth Amendment. For this reason alone, the Fourteenth Amendment is perhaps the most important, if least understood, amendment in all of the Constitution. It is nothing less than the key to understanding, and providing, the rights we take for granted today.

In this chapter, we will examine the civil liberties found in the Bill of Rights. We will then examine civil rights, which will show how disadvantaged groups of Americans have won important protections. In both cases, we will see that the Fourteenth Amendment was the key to these liberties and rights. First, however, we will examine the basis for the creation of the Bill of Rights. Then, in order to understand how the Fourteenth Amendment was used to achieve the transformation of basic rights, we will examine two key ideas: dual citizenship—the principle behind the Supreme Court case of *Barron v. Baltimore*—and the doctrine of incorporation.

The Origin of the Bill of Rights Lies in Those Who Opposed the Constitution

When the first Congress under the newly ratified Constitution met in late April of 1789, the most important item of business was the consideration of a proposal to add a bill of rights to the Constitution. Such a proposal had been turned down with little debate in the waning days of the Philadelphia Constitutional Convention in 1787, not because the delegates were against rights, but because, as the Federalists, led by Alexander Hamilton, later argued, it was "not only unnecessary in the proposed Constitution but would even be dangerous."[1] First, according to Hamilton, a bill of rights would be irrelevant to a national government that was given only delegated powers in the first place. To put restraints on "powers which are not granted" could provide a pretext for governments to claim more powers than were in fact granted: "For why declare that things shall not be done which there is no power to do?"[2] Second, the Constitution was to Hamilton and the Federalists a bill of rights in itself, or contained provisions that amounted to a bill of rights without requiring additional amendments (see Table 4.1). For example, Article I, Section 9, included the right of **habeas corpus,** which prohibits the government from depriving a person of liberty without explaining the reason before a judge.

habeas corpus a court order demanding that an individual in custody be brought into court and shown the cause for detention

Despite the power of Hamilton's arguments, when the Constitution was submitted to the states for ratification, Antifederalists, most of whom had not been delegates in Philadelphia, picked up on the argument of Thomas Jefferson (who also had not been a delegate) that the omission of a bill of rights was a

Rights in the Original Constitution (Not in the Bill of Rights)

Table 4.1

CLAUSE	RIGHT ESTABLISHED
Article I, Sec. 9	guarantee of *habeas corpus*
Article I, Sec. 9	prohibition of **bills of attainder**
Article I, Sec. 9	prohibition of **ex post facto laws**
Article I, Sec. 9	prohibition against acceptance of titles of nobility, etc., from any foreign state
Article III	guarantee of trial by jury in state where crime was committed
Article III	treason defined and limited to the life of the person convicted, not to the person's heirs

bills of attainder laws that decree a person guilty of a crime without a trial

ex post facto laws laws that declare an action to be illegal after it has been committed

major imperfection of the new Constitution. The Federalists conceded that in order to gain ratification they would have to make an "unwritten but unequivocal pledge" to add a bill of rights.

The Bill of Rights might well have been entitled the "Bill of Liberties," because the provisions that were incorporated in the Bill of Rights were seen as defining a private sphere of personal liberty, free of governmental restrictions.[3] As Jefferson had put it, a bill of rights "is what people are entitled to against every government on earth. . . ." Note the emphasis—citizen *against* government. Civil liberties are *protections of citizens from* improper government action. Thus, the Bill of Rights is a series of "thou shalt nots"—restraints imposed upon government (see Table 4.2). Some of these restraints are **substantive liberties,** which put limits on *what* the government shall and shall not have power to do—such as establishing a religion, quartering troops in private homes without consent, or seizing private property without just compensation. Other restraints are **procedural liberties,** which deal with *how* the government is supposed to act. These procedural liberties are usually grouped under the general category of **due process of law,** which first appears in the Fifth Amendment provision that "no person shall be . . . deprived of life, liberty, or property, without due process of law." For example, even though the government has the substantive power to declare certain acts to be crimes and to arrest and imprison persons who violate criminal laws, it may not do so without meticulously observing procedures designed to protect the accused person. The best-known procedural rule is that an accused person is presumed innocent until proven guilty. This rule does not question the government's power to punish someone for committing a crime; it questions only the way the government determines who committed the crime. Substantive and procedural restraints together identify the realm of civil liberties.

In contrast, **civil rights** as a category refers to the obligations imposed on government to *take positive action* to protect citizens from any illegal actions of government agencies as well as of other private citizens. Civil rights did not

substantive liberties restraints on what the government shall and shall not have the power to do

procedural liberties restraints on how the government is supposed to act; for example, citizens are guaranteed the due process of law

due process of law the right of every citizen against arbitrary action by national or state governments

civil rights legal or moral claims that citizens are entitled to make upon government

Table 4.2 **Civil Liberties in the Bill of Rights**

AMENDMENT	EXAMPLE
I	"Congress shall make *no* law . . ."
II	"The right . . . to . . . bear Arms, shall *not* be infringed"
III	"*No* Soldier shall . . . be quartered . . ."
IV	"*No* Warrants shall issue, but upon probable cause . . ."
V	"*No* person shall be held to answer for a . . . crime, unless on a presentment or indictment of a Grand Jury . . ."
VIII	"Excessive bail shall *not* be required . . . *nor* cruel and unusual punishments inflicted."

The Bill of Rights accentuates the negative.

become part of the Constitution until 1868, with the adoption of the Fourteenth Amendment, which sought to provide for each citizen "the equal protection of the laws."

Dual Citizenship Was Defined by *Barron v. Baltimore*

dual citizenship the status of being governed concurrently by both the U.S. federal government and the individual's state government

To understand the vital role the Fourteenth Amendment has played in extending rights, we must begin with the concept of **dual citizenship,** and the story of a man named Barron. As the chapter on federalism explained, Americans are governed by two levels of government: the national government and state governments. Just as the national government makes laws and protects rights under the federal Constitution, so, too, does each state government make and carry out laws through its own three-branch system of government that includes the governor, state legislature, and state courts, all of which are created by each state's own constitution. Although each state constitution is different, they also protect individual rights. Thus, while most Americans do not realize it, they all possess "dual citizenship," in that they are simultaneously U.S. citizens *and* citizens of the state where they reside. Because of federalism, states may, within broad limits set by federal laws, treat their citizens differently.

The fact of dual citizenship (not to be confused with the "dual citizenship" of people who are citizens of more than one country at a time) takes us to the case of a businessman named John Barron, who owned a waterfront wharf in the city of Baltimore in the 1830s. While paving its streets, the city deposited gravel and sand into the water near Barron's wharf, making it impossible for ships to dock there, and thus ruining his business. Since Barron had received no compensation from the city, he sued, arguing that the city's lack of compensation violated the

U.S. Constitution's Fifth Amendment protection, referred to as the "takings clause," which protects citizens' private property from being "taken for a public use, without just compensation." In other words, Barron argued, Baltimore had the right to, in effect, "take" Barron's wharf (that is, render a formerly thriving business useless) only as long as it paid him for what the business had been worth. On appeal, the Supreme Court ruled in the case of *Barron v. Baltimore* in 1833 against Barron and for Baltimore, saying that "the fifth amendment must be understood as restraining the power of the General [i.e. national] Government, not as applicable to the States."[4] Had the *national* government filled in Barron's wharf, he could have recovered damages under the Fifth Amendment. But because Baltimore's actions were governed by the state of Maryland, and since the Maryland state constitution had no "takings clause," Barron was simply out of luck.

The key lesson here is that the Fifth Amendment as well as the other Bill of Rights protections were viewed as applying to citizens only insofar as their national citizenship came into play. So, for example, during this time in American history, a person accused of a state crime could not claim the Sixth Amendment right to counsel unless the individual was charged with a federal crime, such as treason or counterfeiting. On the other hand, if a person were accused of a state crime (remember that even today virtually all criminal activity is regulated by state laws), that person would have a right to counsel only if the state constitution provided that right. This same principle applied to free speech, free press, free assembly, and all of the other Bill of Rights protections we now enjoy.

Today, most Americans understand, even take for granted, the basic freedoms in the Bill of Rights. That we can do so is because of the adoption of the Fourteenth Amendment and the subsequent court rulings.

The Fourteenth Amendment Created the Doctrine of Incorporation

The Civil War cast new light on the large question of state versus national governmental power. After the war, the Fourteenth Amendment was added to the Constitution. Part of the amendment reads as though it were meant to tell the states that they must now adhere to the Bill of Rights:

> No *State* shall make or enforce any law which shall abridge the privileges or immunities of citizens of the United States; nor shall any *State* deprive any person of life, liberty, or property, without due process of law; nor deny to any person within its jurisdiction the equal protection of the laws [emphasis added].

This language sounds like an effort to extend the Bill of Rights to all citizens, wherever they might reside.[5] Yet this was not the Supreme Court's interpretation of the amendment for many decades. Within five years of ratification of the Fourteenth Amendment, the Court was making decisions as though the amendment had never been adopted.[6]

The first change in civil liberties following the adoption of the Fourteenth Amendment came in 1897, when the Supreme Court held that the due process clause of the Fourteenth Amendment did in fact prohibit states from taking property for a public use without just compensation, overruling the *Barron* case.[7] However, the Supreme Court had selectively "incorporated" under the Fourteenth Amendment only the property protection provision of the Fifth Amendment and no other clause of the Fifth or any other amendment of the Bill of Rights. In other words, although according to the Fifth Amendment "due process" applied to the taking of life and liberty as well as property, only property was incorporated into the Fourteenth Amendment as a limitation on state power.

No further expansion of civil liberties via the Fourteenth Amendment occurred until 1925, when the Supreme Court held that freedom of speech is "among the fundamental personal rights and 'liberties' protected by the due process clause of the Fourteenth Amendment from impairment by the states."[8] In 1931, the Court added freedom of the press to that short list protected by the Bill of Rights from state action; by 1937, it had added freedom of assembly and petitioning the government for redress of grievances.[9]

But that was as far as the Court was willing to go. As late as 1937, the Supreme Court was still unwilling to nationalize civil liberties beyond the First Amendment. The Constitution, as interpreted as late as 1937 by the Supreme Court in *Palko v. Connecticut* (discussed later in this chapter), left standing the framework in which the states had the power to determine their own law on a number of fundamental issues.

incorporation the process by which court decisions have required the states to follow parts of the Bill of Rights based on the use or application of the Fourteenth Amendment

As Table 4.3 shows, **incorporation**—the process by which court decisions have required the states to follow parts of the Bill of Rights based on the use or application of the Fourteenth Amendment—continued to occur gradually, up until the last incorporation case in 1969 (incorporation is also sometimes referred to as the "absorption" or the "nationalizing" of the Bill of Rights).

preferred freedoms certain protections in the Bill of Rights, such as free speech and free press, that are considered to be critically important and crucial to the process of incorporation

The pattern or sequence by which this process of incorporation occurred reveals that all Bill of Rights protections are not considered equally important. Some are clearly more important than others. These **preferred freedoms,** such as free speech and free press, are critically important because, according to Supreme Court justice Benjamin Cardozo, they are "the matrix, the indispensable condition, of nearly every other form of freedom."[10] By comparison, the Third Amendment prohibition against the quartering of troops in people's homes is a relic of the 1700s, in that it was included in the Bill of Rights as a reaction to British troops that engaged in this practice. Since the American Revolution, the practice has not been a problem or concern, unlike the First Amendment, which has spawned numerous legal disputes. The end result of the incorporation process is that, on the whole, the most important civil liberties in the Bill of Rights have now been applied to the states, so that the states must adhere to these protections of individual liberties.

The best way to examine the Bill of Rights today is the simplest way—to take each of the major provisions one at a time. Some of these provisions are settled areas of law, and others are not. The Court can reinterpret any one of them at any time.

Incorporation of the Bill of Rights under the Fourteenth Amendment

Table 4.3

SELECTED PROVISIONS AND AMENDMENTS	NOT "INCORPORATED" UNTIL	KEY CASE
Eminent domain (V)	1897	*Chicago, Burlington, and Quincy R.R. v. Chicago*
Freedom of speech (I)	1925	*Gitlow v. New York*
Freedom of press (I)	1931	*Near v. Minnesota*
Free exercise of religion (I)	1934	*Hamilton v. Regents of the University of California*
Freedom of assembly (I) and Freedom to petition the government for redress of grievances (I)	1937	*DeJonge v. Oregon*
Non-establishment of state religion (I)	1947	*Everson v. Board of Education*
Freedom from warrantless search and seizure (IV) ("exclusionary rule")	1961	*Mapp v. Ohio*
Freedom from cruel and unusual punishment (VIII)	1962	*Robinson v. California*
Right to counsel in any criminal trial (VI)	1963	*Gideon v. Wainwright*
Right against self-incrimination and forced confessions (V)	1964	*Mallory v. Hogan* *Escobedo v. Illinois*
Right to counsel and to remain silent (VI)	1966	*Miranda v. Arizona*
Right against double jeopardy (V)	1969	*Benton v. Maryland*

The First Amendment Guarantees Freedom of Religion

Congress shall make no law respecting an establishment of religion, or prohibiting the free exercise thereof; or abridging the freedom of speech, or of the press; or the right of the people peaceably to assemble, and to petition the Government for a redress of grievances.

The Bill of Rights begins by guaranteeing freedom, and the First Amendment provides for that freedom in two distinct clauses: "Congress shall make no law [1] respecting an establishment of religion, or [2] prohibiting the free exercise thereof." The first clause is called the "establishment clause," and the second is called the "free exercise clause."

SEPARATION BETWEEN CHURCH AND STATE COMES FROM THE FIRST AMENDMENT

establishment clause the First Amendment clause that says that "Congress shall make no law respecting an establishment of religion." This law means that a "wall of separation" exists between church and state

The **establishment clause** has been interpreted quite strictly to mean that a virtual "wall of separation" exists between church and state. The separation of church and state was especially important to the great numbers of American colonists who had sought refuge from persecution for having rejected membership in state-sponsored churches. The concept of a "wall of separation" was Jefferson's own formulation, and this concept has figured in all of the modern Supreme Court cases arising under the establishment clause.

Despite the absolute sound of the phrase "wall of separation," there is ample room to disagree on how high or strong this wall is. For example, the Court has been consistently strict in cases of school prayer, striking down such practices as Bible reading,[11] nondenominational prayer,[12] reading prayers over a public address system during a football game;[13] and even a moment of silence for meditation.[14] In each of these cases, the Court reasoned that school-sponsored observations, even of an apparently nondenominational character, are highly suggestive of school sponsorship and therefore violate the prohibition against establishment of religion. On the other hand, the Court has been quite permissive (and some would say inconsistent) about the public display of religious symbols, such as city-sponsored Nativity scenes in commercial or municipal areas.[15] And although the Court has consistently disapproved of government financial support for religious schools, even when the purpose has been purely educational and secular, the Court has permitted certain direct aid to students of such schools in the form of busing, for example. It also upheld a voucher system that allows the use of public money for religious school tuition.[16]

FREE EXERCISE OF RELIGION MEANS YOU HAVE A RIGHT TO WORSHIP

free exercise clause the First Amendment clause that protects a citizen's right to believe and practice whatever religion he or she chooses

The **free exercise clause** protects the right to believe and to practice whatever religion one chooses; it also protects the right to be a nonbeliever. The precedent-setting case involving free exercise is *West Virginia State Board of Education v. Barnette* (1943), which involved the children of a family of Jehovah's Witnesses who refused to salute and pledge allegiance to the American flag on the grounds that their religious faith did not permit it. Three years earlier, the Court had upheld such a requirement and had permitted schools to expel students for refusing to salute the flag. But the entry of the United States into a war to defend democracy coupled with the ugly treatment to which the Jehovah's Witnesses children had been subjected induced the Court to reverse itself and to endorse the free exercise of religion even when it may be offensive to the beliefs of the majority.[17]

Although the Supreme Court has been fairly consistent and strict in protecting the free exercise of religious belief, it has taken pains to distinguish between religious beliefs and *actions* based on those beliefs. In one case, for example, two Native Americans had been fired from their jobs for smoking peyote, an illegal drug. They claimed that they had been fired from their jobs illegally because smoking peyote was a religious sacrament protected by the free exercise clause. The Court disagreed with their claim in an important 1990 decision.[18]

In a different case, Amish parents refused to send their children to school beyond eighth grade because exposing their children to "modern values" would undermine their religious commitment. In this case, the Court decided in favor of the Amish and endorsed a very strong interpretation of the protection of free exercise.[19]

The First Amendment and Freedom of Speech and the Press Assure Free Exchange of Ideas

Congress shall make no law . . . abridging the freedom of speech, or of the press. . . .

Because democracy depends upon an open political process and because politics is basically talk, freedom of speech and freedom of the press are considered critical. For this reason, they were given a prominence in the Bill of Rights equal to that of freedom of religion. In 1938, freedom of speech (which in all important respects includes freedom of the press) was given extraordinary constitutional status when the Supreme Court established that any legislation that attempts to restrict these fundamental freedoms "is to be subjected to a more exacting judicial scrutiny . . . than are most other types of legislation."[20]

What the Court was saying is that the democratic political process must be protected at almost any cost. This higher standard of judicial review came to be called **strict scrutiny.** Strict scrutiny implies that speech—at least some kinds of speech—will be protected almost absolutely and any attempt to restrict speech or other critically important freedoms will be carefully "scrutinized" by the courts. But as it turns out, only some types of speech are fully protected against restrictions. As we shall see, many forms of speech are less than absolutely protected—even though they are entitled to strict scrutiny. This section will look at these two categories of speech: (1) absolutely protected speech, and (2) conditionally protected speech.

strict scrutiny test, used by the Supreme Court in racial discrimination cases and other cases involving civil liberties and civil rights, which places the burden of proof on the government rather than on the challengers to show that the law in question is constitutional

THE TRUTH IS ABSOLUTELY PROTECTED SPEECH

There is one and only one absolute defense against efforts to place limitations on speech, oral or in print: the truth. The truth is protected even when its expression damages the person to whom it applies. And of all forms of speech, political speech is the most consistently protected.

PICTURING

How the First Amendment Guarantees Freedom of Religion

Because of its ban on state-sanctioned religion, the Supreme Court ruled in 2000 that student-initiated public prayer at school is illegal and, likewise, that pregame prayer at public schools violates the establishment clause of the First Amendment.

Despite the establishment clause, the United States' motto remains "In God we trust." This South Carolina license plate was introduced in 2002.

POLITICS

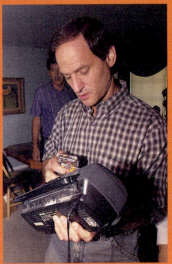

But such displays of religious patriotism are not accepted by all Americans. In 2002, Michael Newdow filed suit against his daughter's school district because the Pledge of Allegiance refers to God. The Supreme Court found that Newdow did not have a sufficient personal stake in the case, and so "under God" was left in.

At the time of the Newdow case, one public opinion poll found that 87 percent of Americans favored keeping the reference to God in the pledge.

Political Speech   Political speech was the activity of greatest concern to the framers of the Constitution, even though they found it the most difficult provision to observe. Within seven years of the ratification of the Bill of Rights in 1791, Congress adopted the infamous Alien and Sedition Acts, which, among other things, made it a crime to say or publish anything that might tend to defame or bring into disrepute the government of the United States. Quite clearly, the acts' intentions were to criminalize the very conduct given absolute protection by the First Amendment. Fifteen violators—including several newspaper editors—were indicted, and a few were actually convicted before the relevant portions of the acts were allowed to expire.

The first modern free speech case arose immediately after World War I. It involved persons who had been convicted under the federal Espionage Act of 1917 for opposing U.S. involvement in the war. The Supreme Court upheld the Espionage Act and refused to protect the speech rights of the defendants on the grounds that their activities—appeals to draftees to resist the draft— constituted a **"clear and present danger"** to security.[21] This is the first and most famous "test" for when government intervention or censorship could be permitted.

It was only after the 1920s that real progress toward a genuinely effective First Amendment was made. Since then, the courts have consistently protected political speech even when it has been deemed "insulting" or "outrageous."

Symbolic Speech, Speech Plus, and the Rights of Assembly and Petition   The First Amendment treats the freedoms of assembly and petition as equal to the freedoms of religion and political speech. Freedom of assembly and freedom of petition are closely associated with speech but go beyond it to speech associated with action. Since at least 1931, the Supreme Court has sought to protect actions that are designed to send a political message. (Usually the purpose of a symbolic act is not only to send a direct message but to draw a crowd—to do something spectacular in order to draw spectators to the action and thus strengthen the message.) Thus the Court held unconstitutional a California law making it a felony to display a red flag "as a sign, symbol or emblem of opposition to organized government."[22] Although today there are limits on how far one can go with actions that symbolically convey a message, the protection of such actions is very broad.

Another example is the burning of the American flag as a symbol of protest. In 1984, at a political rally held during the Republican National Convention in Dallas, Texas, a political protester burned an American flag in violation of a Texas statute that prohibited desecration of a venerated object. In a five-to-four decision, the Supreme Court declared the Texas law unconstitutional on the grounds that flag burning was expressive conduct protected by the First Amendment.[23] Congress reacted immediately with a proposal for a constitutional amendment reversing the Court's Texas decision, and when the amendment failed to receive the necessary two-thirds majority in the Senate, Congress passed the Flag Protection Act of 1989. Protesters promptly violated this act and their prosecution moved quickly into the federal district court, which declared

"clear and present danger" test
test to determine whether speech is protected or unprotected, based on its capacity to present a "clear and present danger" to society

the new law unconstitutional. The Supreme Court, in another five-to-four decision, affirmed the lower court decision[24] to strike down the law.

In 2003, the Supreme Court struck down a Virginia law that made it a crime to burn a cross. Even though the Court considered cross-burning a protected form of speech, it said in its decision that states could enact laws against cross-burning if such an action was intended as a threat and was not merely a form of symbolic expression. The Court noted that cross-burning is a "particularly virulent form of intimidation," but it nevertheless can be allowed as "a form of symbolic expression."[25]

Closer to the original intent of the assembly and petition clause is the category of **"speech plus"**—speech that is followed by physical activity such as picketing, distributing leaflets, and other forms of peaceful demonstration or assembly. Courts consistently protect such assemblies under the First Amendment; state and local laws regulating such activities are closely scrutinized and frequently overturned. But the same assembly on private property is quite another matter and can in many circumstances be regulated. For example, the directors of a shopping center can lawfully prohibit an assembly protesting a war or supporting a ban on abortion. Assemblies in public areas can also be restricted under some circumstances, especially when the assembly or demonstration jeopardizes the health, safety, or rights of others. This condition was the basis of the Supreme Court's decision to uphold a lower court order that restricted the access abortion protesters had to the entrances of abortion clinics.[26]

speech plus speech accompanied by conduct such as sit-ins, picketing, and demonstrations; protection of this form of speech under the First Amendment is conditional, and restrictions imposed by state or local authorities are acceptable if properly balanced by considerations of public order

FREEDOM OF THE PRESS IS BROAD

For all practical purposes, freedom of speech implies and includes freedom of the press. With the exception of the broadcast media, which are subject to federal regulation, the press is protected under the doctrine against prior restraint. Beginning with the landmark 1931 case of *Near v. Minnesota,* the U.S. Supreme Court has held that, except under the most extraordinary circumstances, the First Amendment of the Constitution prohibits government agencies from seeking to prevent newspapers or magazines from publishing whatever they wish.[27] In the case of *New York Times v. U.S.,* the so-called *Pentagon Papers* case, the Supreme Court ruled that the government could not even block publication of secret Defense Department documents furnished to the *New York Times* by an opponent of the Vietnam War who had obtained the documents illegally.[28]

By comparison, greater restrictions are allowed for the electronic media. In a 1990 case, the Supreme Court upheld a lower-court order restraining Cable News Network (CNN) from broadcasting tapes of conversations between former Panamanian dictator Manuel Noriega and his lawyer, supposedly recorded by the U.S. government. By a vote of seven to two, the Court held that CNN could be restrained from broadcasting the tapes until the trial court in the Noriega case had listened to the tapes and had decided whether their broadcast would violate Noriega's right to a fair trial.

SOME SPEECH HAS ONLY LIMITED PROTECTION

At least four forms of speech fall outside the absolute guarantees of the First Amendment and therefore outside the realm of absolute protection. Since they do enjoy some protection, they qualify as "conditionally protected" types of speech: (1) libel and slander, (2) obscenity and pornography, (3) fighting words, and (4) commercial speech. It should be emphasized once again that these four types of speech still enjoy considerable protection by the courts.

Libel and Slander Some speech is not protected at all. If a written statement is made in "reckless disregard of the truth" and is considered damaging to the victim because it is "malicious, scandalous, and defamatory," it can be punished as **libel**. If an oral statement of such nature is made, it can be punished as **slander**.

libel a written statement made in "Reckless disregard of the truth" that is considered damaging to a victim because it is "malicious, scandalous, and defamatory"

slander an oral statement, made in "reckless disregard of the truth," which is considered damaging to the victim because it is "malicious, scandalous, and defamatory"

Today, most libel suits involve freedom of the press, and the realm of free press is enormous. Historically, newspapers were subject to the law of libel, which provided that newspapers that printed false and malicious stories could be compelled to pay damages to those they defamed. In recent years, however, American courts have greatly narrowed the meaning of libel and made it extremely difficult, particularly for politicians or other public figures, to win a libel case against a newspaper. In the important 1964 case of *New York Times v. Sullivan,* the Court held that to be deemed libelous, a story about a public official not only had to be untrue but also had to result from "actual malice" or "reckless disregard" for the truth.[29] In other words, the newspaper had to print false and malicious material *deliberately.* In practice, it is nearly impossible to prove that a paper deliberately printed maliciously false information and it is especially difficult for a politician or other public figure to win a libel case.

Obscenity and Pornography If libel and slander cases can be difficult because of the problem of determining the truth of statements and whether those statements are malicious and damaging, cases involving pornography and obscenity can be even more sticky. It is easy to say that pornography and obscenity fall outside the realm of protected speech, but it is impossible to draw a clear line defining exactly where protection ends and unprotected speech begins. Not until 1957 did the Supreme Court confront this problem, and it did so with a definition of obscenity that may have caused more confusion than it cleared up. Justice William Brennan, in writing the Court's opinion, defined obscenity as speech or writing that appeals to the "prurient interest"—that is, books, magazines, films, and so on, whose purpose is to excite lust as this appears "to the average person, applying contemporary community standards. . . ." Even so, Brennan added, the work should be judged obscene only when it is "utterly without redeeming social importance."[30] Brennan's definition, instead of clarifying the Court's view, actually caused more confusion. In 1964, Justice Potter Stewart confessed that, although he found pornography impossible to define, "I know it when I see it."[31]

An effort was made to strengthen the restrictions in 1973, when the Supreme Court expressed its willingness to define pornography as a work which (1) as a whole, is deemed prurient by the "average person" according to "community standards"; (2) depicts sexual conduct "in a patently offensive way"; and (3) lacks "serious literary, artistic, political, or scientific value." This definition meant that pornography would be determined by local rather than national standards. Thus, a local bookseller might be prosecuted for selling a volume that was a best-seller nationally but that was deemed pornographic locally.[32] This new definition of standards did not help much either, and not long after 1973 the Court began again to review all such community antipornography laws, reversing most of them.

Consequently, today there is a widespread fear that Americans are free to publish any and all variety of intellectual expression, whether there is any "redeeming social value" or not. Yet this area of free speech is far from settled.

In recent years, the battle against obscene speech has been against "cyberporn"—pornography on the Internet. Opponents of this form of expression argue that it should be banned because of the easy access children have to the Internet. The first major effort to regulate the content of the Internet occurred in 1996, when Congress passed the Communications Decency Act (CDA), designed to regulate the on-line transmission of obscene material. The constitutionality of the CDA was immediately challenged in court by a coalition of interests led by the American Civil Liberties Union (ACLU). In the 1997 Supreme Court case of *Reno v. ACLU*, the Court struck down the CDA, ruling that it suppressed speech that "adults have a constitutional right to receive," saying that "the level of discourse reaching the mailbox simply cannot be limited to that which would be suitable for a sandbox." Supreme Court Justice John Paul Stevens described the Internet as the "town crier" of the modern age and said that the Internet was entitled to the greatest degree of First Amendment protection possible. By contrast, radio and television are subject to more control than the Internet.[33] In 2003, however, the Supreme Court upheld a federal law, the Children's Internet Protection Act, that requires public libraries to install antipornography filters on all Internet-accessible computers. Librarians are allowed to unblock some sites at the request of adult patrons.[34]

In 2000, the Supreme Court extended the highest degree of First Amendment protection to cable (not broadcast) television. In *U.S. v. Playboy Entertainment Group*, the Court struck down a portion of the Telecommunications Act of 1996 that required cable TV companies to limit the broadcast of sexually explicit programming to late-night hours. In its decision, the Court noted that the law already provided parents with the means to restrict access to sexually explicit cable channels through various blocking devices. Moreover, such programming could come into the home only if parents decided to purchase such channels in the first place.

Fighting Words   Speech can also lose its protected position when it moves toward the sphere of action. "Expressive speech," for example, is protected until it moves from the symbolic realm to the realm of actual conduct—to direct incitement of damaging conduct with the use of so-called **fighting words**. In 1942, the Supreme

fighting words speech that directly incites damaging conduct

Court upheld the arrest and conviction of a man who had violated a state law forbidding the use of offensive language in public. He had called the arresting officer a "goddamned racketeer" and "a damn Fascist." When his case reached the Supreme Court, the arrest was upheld on the grounds that the First Amendment provides no protection for such offensive language because such words "are no essential part of any exposition of ideas."[35] Since that time, however, the Supreme Court has reversed almost every conviction based on arguments that the speaker had used "fighting words."

Commercial Speech   Commercial speech, such as newspaper or television advertisements, does not have full First Amendment protection because it cannot be considered political speech. Initially considered to be entirely outside the protection of the First Amendment, commercial speech has made gains during the twentieth century. Some commercial speech is still unprotected and therefore regulated. For example, the regulation of false and misleading advertising by the Federal Trade Commission is an old and well-established power of the federal government. The Supreme Court long ago approved the constitutionality of laws prohibiting the electronic media from carrying cigarette advertising.[36] The Court has also upheld a state university ban on Tupperware parties in college dormitories.[37] It has also upheld city ordinances prohibiting the posting of all signs on public property (as long as the ban is total, so that there is no hint of censorship).[38] And the Court upheld Puerto Rico's statute restricting gambling advertising aimed at residents of Puerto Rico.[39]

The Second Amendment Protects the Right to Bear Arms in a Militia

> A well regulated Militia, being necessary to the security of a free State, the right of the people to keep and bear Arms, shall not be infringed.

The Second Amendment was included in the Bill of Rights to protect the right of citizens to keep and bear arms if called into militia service by the government. When the amendment was written, part-time citizen militias provided an important military force to supplement the small professional standing army at a time when the government possessed limited financial means to supply militiamen with weapons. Thus, the reference to the right of the people "to keep and bear Arms" meant that militia-eligible citizens (white males between the ages of eighteen and forty-five) were expected to keep their own firearms at the ready. As the Supreme Court ruled in 1939, the amendment has as its "obvious purpose" the protection of gun ownership only when related to "the preservation or efficiency of a well regulated militia."[40]

When the nation was governed under the Articles of Confederation, the states maintained exclusive control over militias, but the modern Constitution of 1787 gave control over militias to the national government in Article I, as well as the additional sweeping power to create a national standing army. Fearing both a loss of control over militias and the power of a new national army, Antifederalists insisted on reassurance that the states could continue to organize their own militias to meet their own military needs, resulting in the Second Amendment. The military inadequacies of the old militia system, seen especially in the disastrous performance of these part-time amateur soldiers during the War of 1812, rendered it obsolete, and militia call-ups were replaced with the military draft, which is used to expand the standing army in times of need.

Recent controversy has arisen concerning some citizens who have sought to form their own *private* militias, unconnected with the government. Yet the Supreme Court made clear that the Second Amendment does not allow citizens to form their own militias free from government control. When a private militia tried to assert such a right, the Supreme Court denied it.[41]

Thus, while much public controversy over the gun control issue holds up the banner of the Second Amendment, it is mostly irrelevant to the modern gun control controversy. This point is underscored by the fact that no gun control law has ever been declared unconstitutional as a violation of the Second Amendment, including a local law that banned the possession of working handguns except for those who used handguns for their jobs, such as police and security guards.[42] The gun control issue is one that will be settled through the political process, not by the courts.

Rights of the Criminally Accused Are Based on Due Process of Law

Except for the First Amendment, most of the battle to apply the Bill of Rights to the states was fought over the various protections granted to individuals who are accused of a crime, who are suspects in the commission of a crime, or who are brought before the court as a witness to a crime. The Fourth, Fifth, Sixth, and Eighth Amendments, taken together, are the essence of the due process of law, even though this fundamental concept does not appear until the very last words of the Fifth Amendment.

THE FOURTH AMENDMENT PROTECTS AGAINST UNLAWFUL SEARCHES AND SEIZURES

The right of the people to be secure in their persons, houses, papers, and effects, against unreasonable searches and seizures, shall not be violated, and no Warrants shall issue, but upon probable cause, supported by Oath or affirmation, and particularly describing the place to be searched, and the persons or things to be seized.

The purpose of the Fourth Amendment is to guarantee the security of citizens against unreasonable (i.e., improper) searches and seizures. In 1990 the Supreme

Court summarized its understanding of the Fourth Amendment brilliantly and succinctly: "A search compromises the individual interest in privacy; a seizure deprives the individual of dominion over his or her person or property."[43] But how are we to define what is reasonable and what is unreasonable?

The 1961 case of *Mapp v. Ohio* illustrates the beauty and the agony of one of the most important procedures that has grown out of the Fourth Amendment—the **exclusionary rule,** which prohibits evidence obtained during an illegal search from being introduced in a trial. Acting on a tip that Dolly Mapp was harboring a suspect in a bombing incident, several police officers forcibly entered Mapp's house claiming they had a warrant to look for the bombing suspect. The police did not find the bombing suspect but did find some materials connected to the local numbers racket (an illegal gambling operation) and a quantity of "obscene materials," in violation of an Ohio law banning possession of such materials. Although the warrant was never produced, the evidence that had been seized was admitted by a court, and Mapp was charged and convicted for illegal possession of obscene materials.

By the time Mapp's appeal reached the Supreme Court, the question was whether any evidence produced under the circumstances of the search of her home was admissible. The Court's opinion affirmed the exclusionary rule: Under the Fourth Amendment (applied to the states through the Fourteenth Amendment), "all evidence obtained by searches and seizures in violation of the Constitution . . . is inadmissible."[44] This means that even people who are clearly guilty of the crime of which they are accused must not be convicted if the only evidence for their conviction was obtained illegally. This idea was expressed by Supreme Court Justice Benjamin Cardozo nearly a century ago when he wrote that "the criminal is to go free because the constable has blundered."

The exclusionary rule is so dramatic a restriction because it rules out precisely the evidence that produces a conviction; it frees those people who are *known* to have committed the crime of which they have been accused. Because it works so dramatically in favor of persons known to have committed a crime, the Court has since softened the application of the rule. In recent years, the federal courts have relied upon a discretionary use of the exclusionary rule, whereby they make a judgment as to the "nature and quality of the intrusion." It is thus difficult to know ahead of time whether a defendant will or will not be protected from an illegal search under the Fourth Amendment.[45]

exclusionary rule the ability of courts to exclude evidence obtained in violation of the Fourth Amendment

THE FIFTH AMENDMENT COVERS COURT-RELATED RIGHTS

No person shall be held to answer for a capital, or otherwise infamous crime, unless on a presentment or indictment of a Grand Jury, except in cases arising in the land or naval forces, or in the Militia, when in actual service in time of War or public danger; nor shall any person be subject for the same offence to be twice put in jeopardy of life or limb; nor shall be compelled in any criminal case to be a witness against himself, nor be deprived of life, liberty, or property, without due process of law; nor shall private property be taken for public use, without just compensation.

Grand Juries   The first clause of the Fifth Amendment sets forth the right to a **grand jury** to determine whether a trial is warranted. Grand juries play an important role in federal criminal cases. However, the provision for a grand jury is the one important civil liberties provision of the Bill of Rights that was not incorporated by the Fourteenth Amendment to apply to state criminal prosecutions. Thus, some states operate without grand juries. In such states, the prosecuting attorney simply files a "bill of information" affirming that there is sufficient evidence available to justify a trial. If the accused person is to be held in custody, the prosecutor must take the available information before a judge to determine that the evidence shows probable cause.

> **grand jury** jury that determines whether sufficient evidence is available to justify a trial; grand juries do not rule on the accused's guilt or innocence

Double Jeopardy   "Nor shall any person be subject for the same offence to be twice put in jeopardy of life or limb" is the constitutional protection from **double jeopardy,** or being tried more than once for the same crime. The protection from double jeopardy was at the heart of the *Palko v. Connecticut* case in 1937. In that case, the state of Connecticut had indicted Frank Palko for first-degree murder, but a lower court had found him guilty of only second-degree murder and sentenced him to life in prison. Unhappy with the verdict, the state of Connecticut appealed the conviction to its highest state court, won the appeal, got a new trial, and then succeeded in getting Palko convicted of first-degree murder. Palko appealed to the Supreme Court on what seemed an open and shut case of double jeopardy. Yet, although the majority of the Court agreed that this could indeed be considered a case of double jeopardy, they decided that double jeopardy was not one of the provisions of the Bill of Rights incorporated in the Fourteenth Amendment as a restriction on the powers of the states. It took more than thirty years for the court to nationalize the constitutional protection against double jeopardy. Palko was eventually executed for the crime, because he lived in the state of Connecticut rather than in some state whose constitution included a guarantee against double jeopardy.

> **double jeopardy** the Fifth Amendment right providing that a person cannot be tried twice for the same crime

Self-Incrimination   Perhaps the most significant liberty found in the Fifth Amendment, and the one most familiar to many Americans who watch television crime shows, is the guarantee that no citizen "shall be compelled in any criminal case to be a witness against himself. . . ." The most famous case concerning self-incrimination involved twenty-three-year-old Ernesto Miranda, who was sentenced to between twenty and thirty years in prison for the kidnapping and rape of an eighteen-year-old woman. The woman had identified him in a police lineup, and, after two hours of questioning, Miranda confessed, subsequently signing a statement that his confession had been made voluntarily, without threats or promises of immunity. These confessions were admitted into evidence, served as the basis for Miranda's conviction, and also served as the basis of the appeal of his conviction all the way to the Supreme Court. In one of the most intensely and widely criticized decisions ever handed down by the Supreme Court, Miranda's case produced the rules the police must follow before questioning an arrested criminal suspect. The reading of a person's "Miranda rights" became a standard scene in every police station and on virtually every dramatization of police action on television and in the movies. *Miranda* advanced the civil liberties of accused persons by expanding not only the scope of the Fifth Amendment clause covering coerced confessions and self-incrimination, but also by confirming the right to counsel (discussed later). The Supreme Court under Warren Burger and William Rehnquist has considerably softened the *Miranda* restrictions, making the job of the police easier, but the **Miranda** **rule** still stands as a protection against egregious police abuses of arrested persons.

Miranda rule the requirement, articulated by the Supreme Court in *Miranda v. Arizona,* that persons under arrest must be informed prior to police interrogation of their rights to remain silent and to have the benefit of legal counsel

Eminent Domain   The other fundamental clause of the Fifth Amendment is the "takings clause," which extends to each citizen a protection against the "taking" of private property "without just compensation." Although this part of the Fifth Amendment is not specifically concerned with protecting persons accused of crimes, it is nevertheless a fundamentally important instance where the government and the citizen are adversaries. The power of any government to take private property for a public use is called **eminent domain.** The Fifth Amendment puts limits on that inherent power through procedures that require a showing of a public purpose and the provision of fair payment for the taking of someone's property.

eminent domain the right of government to take private property for public use

THE SIXTH AMENDMENT'S RIGHT TO COUNSEL IS CRUCIAL FOR A FAIR TRIAL

> In all criminal prosecutions, the accused shall enjoy the right to a speedy and public trial, by an impartial jury of the State and district wherein the crime shall have been committed, which district shall have been ascertained by law, and to be informed of the nature and the cause of the accusation; to be confronted with the witnesses against him; to have compulsory process for obtaining witnesses in his favor, and to have the Assistance of Counsel for his defence.

Like the exclusionary rule of the Fourth Amendment and the self-incrimination clause of the Fifth Amendment, the "right to counsel" provision of the Sixth Amendment is notable for freeing defendants who seem to the public to be guilty as charged. Other provisions of the Sixth Amendment, such as the right to a speedy trial and the right to confront witnesses before an impartial jury, are less controversial.

Gideon v. Wainwright (1963) is the perfect example because it involved a disreputable person who seemed patently guilty of the crime for which he was convicted. In and out of jails for most of fifty-one years, Clarence Earl Gideon received a five-year sentence for breaking and entering a poolroom in Panama City, Florida. While serving time in jail, Gideon became a fairly well-qualified "jailhouse lawyer," made his own appeal on a handwritten petition, and eventually won the landmark ruling on the right to counsel in all felony cases.[46]

The right to counsel has been expanded rather than contracted during the past few decades, even though the courts have become more conservative. The right to counsel extends beyond serious crimes to any trial, with or without jury, that holds the possibility of imprisonment.

THE EIGHTH AMENDMENT BARS CRUEL AND UNUSUAL PUNISHMENT

The Eighth Amendment prohibits "excessive bail," "excessive fines," and "cruel and unusual punishment." Virtually all the debate over Eighth Amendment issues focuses on the last clause of the amendment: the protection from "cruel and unusual punishment." One of the greatest challenges in interpreting this provision consistently arises over the death penalty. In 1972, the Supreme Court overturned several state death penalty laws, not because they were cruel and unusual, but because they were being applied in a capricious manner—that is, blacks were much more likely than whites to be sentenced to death, the poor more likely than the rich, and men more likely than women.[47] Very soon after that decision, a majority of states revised their capital punishment provisions to meet the Court's standards.[48] Since 1976, the Court has consistently upheld state laws providing for capital punishment, although the Court also continues to review numerous death penalty appeals each year.

Between 1976 and 2000, states executed 683 people. Most of those executions occurred in southern states, with Texas leading the way at 239. As of 2002, thirty-eight states had adopted some form of capital punishment, a move approved of by about three-quarters of all Americans.

Despite the seeming popularity of the death penalty, the debate has become, if anything, more intense. In 1997, for example, the American Bar Association passed a resolution calling for a halt to the death penalty until concerns about its fairness—that is, whether its application violates the principle of equality—and about ensuring due process are addressed. In 2000, the governor of Illinois imposed a moratorium on the death penalty and created a commission to review the capital punishment system. After a two-year study by the commission, Illinois adopted a number of reforms, including a ban on executions of the mentally retarded. In June 2002, the U.S. Supreme Court banned all executions of mentally retarded defendants, a decision that could move two hundred or more people off death row.

The Right to Privacy Is the Right to Be Left Alone

Although the word "privacy" never appears in the Bill of Rights, there is general agreement that a **"right to privacy"** emanates from the first ten amendments—even though judges and legal scholars continue to disagree about where the right comes from. The idea behind the right of privacy is simple: People have a right to be left alone from government or other persons' interference in certain personal areas, such as in a marriage (this does *not* mean that privacy protects the commission of crimes within marriage, such as spousal abuse; if the law is broken, the government may then intervene).

right to privacy the right to be let alone, which has been interpreted by the Supreme Court to entail free access to birth control and abortions

PICTURING

How the Constitution Protects Those Accused of a Crime

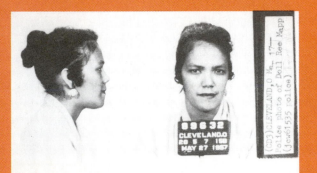

The Constitution provides several major protections for those accused of a crime. In the case of *Dollree Mapp v. Ohio*, the Supreme Court interpreted the Fourth Amendment to mean that incriminating material found through illegal search and seizure cannot be used as evidence in court. Mapp's case against the Cleveland Police Department resulted in the naturalization of the Fourth Amendment's exclusionary rule.

More recently, drug testing has raised concerns about the Fourth Amendment—is a drug test an unreasonable search? Though the Supreme Court initially upheld drug and alcohol tests, the Court indicated in a 1997 case that such tests illegally invade privacy if they are conducted randomly and without suspicion of guilt. However, the Court allowed tests on those engaged in risky activities, such as driving. Thus random alcohol tests at a police roadblock are valid.

POLITICS

SPECIFIC WARNING REGARDING INTERROGATIONS

DEFENDANT   LOCATION

1. YOU HAVE THE RIGHT TO REMAIN SILENT.

2. ANYTHING YOU SAY CAN AND WILL BE USED AGAINST YOU IN A COURT OF LAW.

3. YOU HAVE THE RIGHT TO TALK TO A LAWYER AND HAVE HIM PRESENT WITH YOU WHILE YOU ARE BEING QUESTIONED.

4. IF YOU CANNOT AFFORD TO HIRE A LAWYER ONE WILL BE APPOINTED TO REPRESENT YOU BEFORE ANY QUESTIONING, IF YOU WISH ONE.

SIGNATURE OF DEFENDANT   DATE

WITNESS   TIME

☐ REFUSED SIGNATURE   SAN FRANCISCO POLICE DEPARTMENT   PR.9.1.4

The modern interpretation of the Fifth Amendment was shaped by the 1966 case *Miranda v. Arizona*. Since Ernesto Miranda was never told that he was not required to answer police questions, his case was appealed on the grounds that his right against self-incrimination had been violated.

The trial resulted in the creation of the Miranda rights, which must be read to those arrested to make them aware of their constitutional rights.

In 1961, after being wrongly charged with burglary and sentenced to five years in prison, Clarence Earl Gideon, a fifty-two-year-old mechanic from Florida, filed an appeal to the Supreme Court arguing that his constitutional rights were denied when Florida refused him an attorney. The Court ruled in Gideon's favor, stating that the Sixth Amendment guarantees anyone accused of a crime the right to an attorney, whether or not he or she can afford one.

While the Eighth Amendment prohibits "cruel and unusual punishment," since 1976 this prohibition has not applied to the death penalty. Inmates on death row are able to appeal their convictions, but opponents of the death penalty have raised questions about whether the appeal process ensures due process. Death penalty supporters proclaim the punishment's deterrent effect and argue that it is a proper expression of retribution.

The sphere of privacy was drawn in earnest by the Supreme Court in 1965, when it ruled that a Connecticut statute forbidding the use of contraceptives violated the right of marital privacy. Estelle Griswold, the executive director of the Planned Parenthood League of Connecticut, was arrested by the state of Connecticut for providing information, instruction, and medical advice about contraception to married couples. She and her associates were found guilty as accessories to the crime and fined $100 each. The Supreme Court reversed the lower court decisions and declared the Connecticut law unconstitutional because it violated "a right of privacy older than the Bill of Rights—older than our political parties, older than our school system."[49] Justice William O. Douglas, author of the majority decision in the *Griswold* case, argued that this right of privacy is also grounded in the Constitution, because it fits into a "zone of privacy" created by a combination of the Third, Fourth, and Fifth Amendments. A concurring opinion, written by Justice Arthur Goldberg, attempted to strengthen Douglas's argument by adding that "the concept of liberty . . . embraces the right of marital privacy though that right is not mentioned explicitly in the Constitution [and] is supported by numerous decisions of this Court . . . and *by the language and history of the Ninth Amendment*" (emphasis added).[50]

The right to privacy was confirmed and extended in 1973 in the most important of all privacy decisions, and one of the most important and controversial Supreme Court decisions in American history: *Roe v. Wade.* This decision established a woman's right to seek an abortion and prohibited states from making abortion a criminal act.[51] It is important to emphasize that the preference for privacy rights and for their extension to include the rights of women to control their own bodies was not something invented by the Supreme Court in a vacuum. Most states did not regulate abortions in any fashion until the 1840s, at which time only six of the twenty-six existing states had any regulations governing abortion at all. In addition, many states had begun to ease their abortion restrictions well before the 1973 *Roe* decision, although in recent years a number of states have reinstated some restrictions on abortion.

Like any important principle, once privacy was established as an aspect of civil liberties protected by the Bill of Rights through the Fourteenth Amendment, it took on a life of its own. In a number of important decisions, the Supreme Court and the lower federal courts sought to protect rights that could not be found in the text of the Constitution but could be discovered through the study of the philosophic sources of fundamental rights. Increasingly in recent years, right-to-privacy claims have been made by those attempting to preserve the right to obtain legal abortions, as well as those seeking to obtain greater rights for homosexuals, and supporters of physician-assisted suicide (also known as the "right to die" movement). In the case of homosexuals, the Supreme Court extended privacy protections to them in 2003 when it ruled that they are "entitled to respect for their private lives" in the case of *Lawrence v. Texas.*[52] For the first time, gays and lesbians could claim right-to-privacy protection. These subjects are inherently controversial, which helps explain why the concept of privacy itself continues to spark controversy.

Civil Rights Are Protections by the Government

With the adoption of the Fourteenth Amendment in 1868, civil rights became part of the Constitution, guaranteed to each citizen through "equal protection of the laws." These words launched a century of political movements and legal efforts to press for racial equality. The African American quest for civil rights in turn inspired many other groups, including members of other racial and ethnic groups, women, the disabled, and gays and lesbians, to seek new laws and constitutional guarantees of their civil rights.

Congress passed the Fourteenth Amendment and the states ratified it in the aftermath of the Civil War. Together with the Thirteenth Amendment, which abolished slavery, and the Fifteenth Amendment, which guaranteed voting rights for black men, it seemed to provide a guarantee of civil rights for the newly freed black slaves. But the general language of the Fourteenth Amendment meant that its support for civil rights could be far-reaching. The very simplicity of the **equal protection clause** of the Fourteenth Amendment left it open to interpretation:

> No State shall make or enforce any law which shall . . . deny to any person within its jurisdiction the equal protection of the laws.

equal protection clause provision of the Fourteenth Amendment guaranteeing citizens "the equal protection of the laws." This clause has served as the basis for the civil rights of African Americans, women, and other groups

PLESSY V. FERGUSON ESTABLISHED "SEPARATE BUT EQUAL"

The Supreme Court was no more ready to enforce the civil rights aspects of the Fourteenth Amendment than it was to enforce the civil liberties provisions. The Court declared the Civil Rights Act of 1875 unconstitutional on the grounds that the act sought to protect blacks against discrimination by *private* businesses, while the Fourteenth Amendment, according to the Court's interpretation, was intended to protect individuals from discrimination only against actions by *public* officials of state and local governments.

In 1896, the Court went still further, in the infamous case of *Plessy v. Ferguson,* by upholding a Louisiana statute that *required* segregation of the races on trolleys and other public carriers (and by implication in all public facilities, including schools). Plessy, a man defined as "one-eighth black," had violated a Louisiana law that provided for "equal but separate accommodations" on trains and a $25 fine for any white passenger who sat in a car reserved for blacks or any black passenger who sat in a car reserved for whites. The Supreme Court held that the Fourteenth Amendment's "equal protection of the laws" was not violated by racial distinction as long as the facilities were equal, thus establishing the **"separate but equal" rule** that prevailed through the mid-twentieth century. People generally pretended that segregated accommodations were equal as long as some accommodation for blacks existed. Thus, racial inequality in the guise of the separate but equal doctrine persisted for decades.

separate but equal rule doctrine that public accommodations could be segregated by race but still be equal

RACIAL DISCRIMINATION BEGAN TO SUBSIDE AFTER WORLD WAR II

The Supreme Court had begun to change its position on racial discrimination before World War II by being stricter about the criterion of equal facilities in the "separate but equal" rule. In 1938, for example, the Court rejected Missouri's policy of paying the tuition of qualified blacks to out-of-state law schools rather than admitting them to the University of Missouri Law School.[53]

After the war, modest progress resumed. In 1950, the Court rejected Texas's claim that its new "law school for Negroes" afforded education equal to that of the all-white University of Texas Law School. Without confronting the "separate but equal" principle itself, the Court's decision anticipated its future civil rights rulings by opening the question of whether *any* segregated facility could be truly equal.[54]

The same was true in 1944, when the Supreme Court struck down the southern practice of "white primaries," which legally excluded blacks from participation in the nominating process. Here the Court simply recognized that primaries could no longer be regarded as the private affairs of the parties but were an integral aspect of the electoral process. This made parties "an agency of the State," and therefore any practice of discrimination against blacks was "state action within the meaning of the Fifteenth Amendment."[55] In *Shelley v. Kraemer,* the Court ruled against the widespread practice of "restrictive covenants," whereby the seller of a home added a clause to the sales contract requiring the buyer to agree not to sell the home later to any non-Caucasian, non-Christian, and so on. The Court ruled that although private persons could sign such restrictive covenants, they could not be judicially enforced since the Fourteenth Amendment prohibits any organ of the state, including the courts, from denying equal protection of its law.[56]

Although none of those pre-1954 cases confronted "separate but equal" and the principle of racial discrimination as such, they were extremely significant to black leaders in the 1940s and gave them encouragement enough to believe that there was at last an opportunity and enough legal precedent to change the constitutional framework itself. Much of this legal work was done by the Legal Defense and Educational Fund of the National Association for the Advancement of Colored People (NAACP). Formed in 1909 to fight discrimination against African Americans, the NAACP was the most important civil rights organization during the first half of the twentieth century.

In the fall of 1952, the Court had on its docket cases from Kansas, South Carolina, Virginia, Delaware, and the District of Columbia challenging the constitutionality of school segregation. Of these, the case filed in Kansas became the chosen one.

Oliver Brown, the father of three girls, lived "across the tracks" in a low-income, racially mixed Topeka neighborhood. Every school-day morning, Linda Brown took the school bus to the Monroe School for black children about a mile away. In September 1950, Oliver Brown took Linda to the all-white Sumner School, which was closer to home, to enter her into the third grade in defiance of state law and local segregation rules. When they were refused, Brown took his case to the NAACP, and soon thereafter *Brown v. Board of Education* was born.

In deciding the *Brown* case, the Court, to the surprise of many, basically rejected as inconclusive all the learned arguments about the intent and the history of the Fourteenth Amendment and committed itself to considering only the consequences of segregation:

> Does segregation of children in public schools solely on the basis of race, even though the physical facilities and other "tangible" factors may be equal, deprive the children of the minority group of equal educational opportunities? We believe that it does. . . . We conclude that in the field of public education the doctrine of "separate but equal" has no place. Separate educational facilities are inherently unequal.[57]

The *Brown* decision altered the constitutional framework in two fundamental respects. First, after *Brown,* the states no longer had the power to use race as a criterion of discrimination in law. Second, the national government from then on had the power (and eventually the obligation) to intervene with strict regulatory policies against the discriminatory actions of state or local governments, school boards, employers, and many others in the private sector.

THE CIVIL RIGHTS STRUGGLE ESCALATED AFTER *BROWN V. BOARD OF EDUCATION*

The historic decision in *Brown v. Board of Education* was merely a small opening move. First, most states refused to cooperate until sued, and many ingenious schemes were employed to delay obedience (such as paying the tuition for white students to attend newly created "private" academies). Second, even as southern school boards began to cooperate by eliminating their legally enforced (**de jure**) school segregation, there remained extensive actual (**de facto**) school segregation in the North as well as in the South, as a consequence of racially segregated housing that could not be reached by the 1954–55 *Brown* principles. Third, discrimination in employment, public accommodations, juries, voting, and other areas of social and economic activity were not directly touched by *Brown.*

Social Protest and Congressional Action   Ten years after *Brown,* fewer than 1 percent of black school-age children in the Deep South were attending schools with whites.[58] A decade of frustration made it fairly obvious to all observers that adjudication alone would not succeed. The goal of "equal protection" required positive, or affirmative, action by Congress and by federal agencies. And given massive southern resistance and a generally negative national public opinion toward racial integration, progress would not be made through courts, Congress, or federal agencies without intense, well-organized support. Table 4.4 shows the increase in civil rights demonstrations for voting rights and public accommodations during the fourteen years following *Brown.* It shows that organized civil rights demonstrations began to mount slowly but surely after

Brown v. Board of Education the 1954 Supreme Court decision that struck down the "separate but equal" doctrine as fundamentally unequal. This case eliminated state power to use race as a criterion of discrimination in law and provided the national government with the power to intervene by exercising strict regulatory policies against discriminatory actions

de jure literally, "by law"; legally enforced practices, such as school segregation in the South before the 1960s

de facto literally, "by fact"; practices that occur even when there is no legal enforcement, such as school segregation in much of the United States today

Table 4.4   **Peaceful Civil Rights Demonstrations, 1954–68**

YEAR	TOTAL	FOR PUBLIC ACCOMMODATIONS	FOR VOTING
1954	0	0	0
1955	0	0	0
1956	18	6	0
1957	44	9	0
1958	19	8	0
1959	7	11	0
1960	173	127	0
1961	198	122	0
1962	77	44	0
1963	272	140	1
1964	271	93	12
1965	387	21	128
1966	171	15	32
1967	93	3	3
1968	97	2	0

Note: This table is drawn from a search of the *New York Times Index* for all references to civil rights demonstrations during the years the table covers. The table should be taken simply as indicative, for the data—news stories in a single paper—are very crude. The classification of the incident as peaceful or violent and the subject area of the demonstration are inferred from the entry in the *Index,* usually the headline from the story. The two subcategories reported here—public accommodations and voting—do not sum to the total because demonstrations dealing with a variety of other issues (e.g., education, employment, police brutality) are included in the total.
SOURCE: Jonathan D. Casper, *The Politics of Civil Liberties* (New York: Harper & Row, 1972), p. 90. Demonstrations peaked just before and during enactment of major civil rights bills passed by Congress in 1964 and 1965.

Brown v. Board of Education. By the 1960s, the many organizations that made up the civil rights movement had accumulated experience and built networks capable of launching massive direct-action campaigns against southern segregationists. The Southern Christian Leadership Conference, the Student Nonviolent Coordinating Committee, and many other organizations had built a movement that stretched across the South. The movement used the media to attract nationwide attention and support. In the massive March on Washington in 1963, the Reverend Martin Luther King, Jr., staked out the movement's moral claims in his famous "I Have a Dream" speech. The image of protesters being beaten, attacked by police dogs, and set upon with fire hoses did much to win broad sympathy for the cause of black civil rights and to discredit state and local governments in the South. In this way, the movement created intense pressure for reluctant federal government to take more assertive steps to defend black civil rights.

THE CIVIL RIGHTS ACTS MADE EQUAL PROTECTION A REALITY

The right to equal protection of the laws could be established and, to a certain extent, implemented by the courts. But after a decade of very frustrating efforts, the courts and Congress ultimately came to the conclusion that the federal courts alone were not adequate to the task of changing the social rules, and that legislation and administrative action would be needed.

Congress used its legislative powers to help make equal protection of the laws a reality by passing the Civil Rights Act of 1964. The act seemed bold at the time, but it was enacted ten years after the Supreme Court had declared racial discrimination "inherently unequal" under the Fifth and Fourteenth Amendments. And it was enacted long after blacks had demonstrated that discrimination was no longer acceptable. The choice in 1964 was not between congressional action or inaction but between legal action and expanded violence.

Public Accommodations   After the passage of the 1964 Civil Rights Act, public accommodations quickly removed some of the most visible forms of racial discrimination. Signs defining "colored" and "white" restrooms, water fountains, waiting rooms, and seating arrangements were removed and a host of other practices that relegated black people to separate and inferior arrangements were ended. In addition, the federal government filed more than four hundred antidiscrimination suits in federal courts against hotels, restaurants, taverns, gas stations, and other "public accommodations."

Many aspects of legalized racial segregation—such as separate Bibles in the courtroom—seem like ancient history today. But the issue of racial discrimination in public settings is by no means over. In 1993, six African American Secret Service agents filed charges against the Denny's restaurant chain for failing to serve them; white Secret Service agents at a nearby table had received prompt service. Similar charges citing discriminatory service at Denny's restaurants surfaced across the country. Faced with evidence of a pattern of systematic discrimination and numerous lawsuits, Denny's paid $45 million in damages to plaintiffs in Maryland and California in what is said to be the largest settlement ever in a public accommodation case.[59] The Denny's case shows how effective the Civil Rights Act of 1964 can be in challenging racial discrimination. In addition to the settlement, the chain vowed to expand employment and management opportunities for minorities in Denny's restaurants. Other forms of racial discrimination in public accommodations are harder to challenge, however. For example, there is considerable evidence that taxicabs often refuse to pick up black passengers.[60] Such practices may be common, but they are difficult to prove and remedy through the law.

School Desegregation   The 1964 Civil Rights Act also declared discrimination by private employers and state governments (school boards, etc.) illegal, then went further to provide for administrative agencies to help the courts implement these laws. The act, for example, authorized the executive branch, through the Justice

Cause and Effect in the Civil Rights Movement

During the civil rights movement of the 1950s and '60s, political action and government action spurred each other to produce dramatic changes in American civil rights policies.

The *Brown v. Board of Education* decision of 1954 was a landmark victory against segregation. Flanked by the two other lawyers who argued the case is Thurgood Marshall, who was the lead lawyer and who would go on to become the first African American Supreme Court justice.

The South's slow response to *Brown's* desegregation mandate gave rise to political action. On December 1, 1955, in Montgomery, Alabama, Rosa Parks was arrested for refusing to give up her seat in the front of a bus, an act of protest that set off a year-long boycott of the city's buses. On December 21, 1956, the date of this famous photograph, a Supreme Court ruling banning segregation on public transportation went into effect.

A year after the successful conclusion of the Montgomery bus boycott, President Dwight D. Eisenhower signed the Civil Rights Act of 1957. One result of the act was renewed enforcement of desegregation in the South. Just weeks after Eisenhower signed the act into law, military troops escorted nine African American students to school in Little Rock, Arkansas.

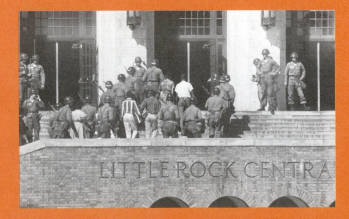

POLITICS

Nonviolent protests swept the country in the years following the passage of the Civil Rights Act of 1957. Groups such as the Student Nonviolent Coordinating Committee, formed in 1960, organized demonstrations, Freedom Rides, which tested the integration of public transportation across the South, and lunch counter sit-ins.

In many ways these political actions culminated in the summer of 1963 with the historic March on Washington for Jobs and Freedom. Hundreds of thousands of members of civil rights, labor, and religious groups gathered in the capital and marched from the Washington Monument to the Lincoln Memorial, where Martin Luther King Jr. delivered his famous "I Have a Dream" speech.

Less than a year after the march, Congress passed the Civil Rights Act of 1964, which covered voting, employment, public accommodations, and education. Here, after signing the act into law, President Lyndon B. Johnson shakes hands with Dr. King.

Department, to implement federal court orders to desegregate schools, and to do so without having to wait for individual parents to bring complaints. The act also vastly strengthened the role of the executive branch and the credibility of court orders by providing that federal grants-in-aid to state and local governments for education must be withheld from any school system practicing racial segregation.

Outlawing Discrimination in Employment   The federal courts and the Justice Department also fought employment discrimination through the Civil Rights Act of 1964, which outlawed job discrimination by all private and public employers, including governmental agencies (such as fire and police departments) that employed more than fifteen workers. We have already seen (in Chapter 3) that the Supreme Court gave "interstate commerce" such a broad definition that Congress had the constitutional authority to cover discrimination by virtually any local employers.[61] The 1964 act makes it unlawful to discriminate in employment on the basis of color, religion, sex, or national origin, as well as race.

In order to enforce fair employment practices, the national government could revoke public contracts for goods and services and refuse to engage in contracts for goods and services with any private company that could not guarantee that its rules for hiring, promotion, and firing were nondiscriminatory.

But one problem was that the complaining party had to show that deliberate discrimination was the cause of the failure to get a job or a training opportunity. Rarely does an employer explicitly admit discrimination on the basis of race, sex, or any other illegal reason. Recognizing the rarity of such an admission, the courts have allowed aggrieved parties (the plaintiffs) to make their case if they can show that an employer's hiring practices had the *effect* of exclusion, even if they cannot show the *intention* to discriminate.

Voting Rights   Although 1964 was the *most* important year for civil rights legislation, it was not the only important year. In 1965, Congress significantly strengthened legislation protecting voting rights by barring literacy and other tests as a condition for voting in six southern states,[62] by making it a crime to interfere with voting, and by providing for the replacement of local registrars with federally appointed registrars in counties designated by the attorney general as significantly resistant to registering eligible blacks to vote. The right to vote was further strengthened with ratification in 1964 of the Twenty-fourth Amendment, which abolished the poll tax, and later with legislation permanently outlawing literacy tests in all fifty states and mandating bilingual ballots or oral assistance for Spanish, Chinese, Japanese, Koreans, Native Americans, and Eskimos.

In the long run, the laws extending and protecting voting rights could prove to be the most effective of all the great civil rights legislation, because the progress in black political participation produced by these acts has altered the shape of American politics. In 1965, in the seven states of the Old Confederacy covered by the Voting Rights Act, 29.3 percent of the eligible black residents were registered to vote, compared to 73.4 percent of the white residents (see Table 4.5). Mississippi was the extreme case, with 6.7 percent black and 69.9

Registration by Race and State in Southern States Covered by the 1965 Voting Rights Act

Table 4.5

| | BEFORE THE ACT* | | | AFTER THE ACT* 1971–72 | | |
	WHITE	BLACK	GAP†	WHITE	BLACK	GAP†
Alabama	69.2%	19.3%	49.9%	80.7%	57.1%	23.6%
Georgia	62.6	27.4	35.2	70.6	67.8	2.8
Louisiana	80.5	31.6	48.9	80.0	59.1	20.9
Mississippi	69.9	6.7	63.2	71.6	62.2	9.4
North Carolina	96.8	46.8	50.0	62.2	46.3	15.9
South Carolina	75.7	37.3	38.4	51.2	48.0	3.2
Virginia	61.1	38.3	22.8	61.2	54.0	7.2
TOTAL	73.4	29.3	44.1	67.8	56.6	11.2

*Available registration data as of March 1965 and 1971–72.
†The gap is the percentage point difference between white and black registration rates.
SOURCE: U.S. Commission on Civil Rights, *Political Participation* (1968), Appendix VII: "Voter Education Project, Attachment to Press Release," October 3, 1972.
This 1965 law finally broke the back of voting segregation, meaning that it took almost one hundred years to carry out the Fifteenth Amendment.

percent white registration. In 1967, a mere two years after implementation of the voting rights laws, 52.1 percent of the eligible blacks in the seven states were registered, comparing favorably to 79.5 percent of the eligible whites, a gap of 27.4 points. By 1972, the gap between black and white registration in the seven states was only 11.2 points.

Housing The Civil Rights Act of 1964 did not address housing, but in 1968, Congress passed another civil rights act specifically to outlaw housing discrimination. Called the Fair Housing Act, the law prohibited discrimination in the sale or rental of most housing—eventually covering nearly all the nation's housing. Housing was among the most controversial of discrimination issues because of deeply entrenched patterns of residential segregation across the United States.

Although it pronounced sweeping goals, the Fair Housing Act had little effect on housing segregation because its enforcement mechanisms were so weak. Individuals believing they had been discriminated against had to file suit themselves. The burden was on the individual to prove that housing discrimination had occurred, even though such discrimination is often subtle and difficult to document. Although local fair-housing groups emerged to assist individuals in their court claims, the procedures for proving discrimination proved a formidable barrier to effective change. These procedures were not altered until 1988, when Congress passed the Fair Housing Amendments Acts. This new law put more teeth in the enforcement procedures and allowed the Department of Housing and Urban Development (HUD) to initiate legal action in cases of discrimination. With vigorous use, these provisions may prove more successful than past efforts at combating housing discrimination.[63]

The Civil Rights Struggle Was Extended to Other Disadvantaged Groups

Even before equal employment laws began to have a positive effect on the economic situation of blacks, something far more dramatic began to happen: the universalization of civil rights. The right not to be discriminated against was being successfully claimed by the other groups listed in the 1964 Civil Rights Act—those defined by sex, religion, or national origin—and eventually by still other groups defined by age or sexual preference. This universalization of civil rights has become the new frontier of the civil rights struggle, and women have emerged with the greatest prominence in this new struggle. The effort to define and end gender discrimination in employment has led to the historic joining of women's rights to the civil rights cause.

WOMEN FOUGHT GENDER DISCRIMINATION

In many ways the act fostered the growth of the women's movement. The first major campaign of the National Organization for Women (NOW) involved picketing the Equal Employment Opportunity Commission for its refusal to ban sex-segregated employment advertisements. NOW also sued the *New York Times* for continuing to publish such ads after the passage of the act. Another organization, the Women's Equity Action League (WEAL), pursued legal action on a wide range of sex discrimination issues, filing lawsuits against law schools and medical schools for discriminatory admission policies, for example.

Building on these victories and the growth of the women's movement, feminist activists sought an Equal Rights Amendment (ERA) to the Constitution. The proposed amendment was short; its substantive passage stated that "equality of rights under the law shall not be denied or abridged by the United States or by any State on account of sex." The amendment's supporters believed that such a sweeping guarantee of equal rights was a necessary tool for ending all discrimination against women and for making gender roles more equal. Opponents charged that it would be socially disruptive and would introduce changes—such as coed restrooms—that most Americans did not want. The amendment easily passed Congress in 1972 and won quick approval in many state legislatures, but it fell three states short of the thirty-eight needed to ratify the amendment by the 1982 deadline for its ratification.[64]

Despite the failure of the ERA, gender discrimination expanded dramatically as an area of civil rights law. In the 1970s, the conservative Burger Court (under Chief Justice Warren Burger) helped to establish gender discrimination as a major and highly visible civil rights issue. Although the Burger Court refused to treat gender discrimination as the equivalent of racial discrimination,[65] it did make it easier for plaintiffs to file and win suits on the basis of gender discrimination.

Courts began to find sexual harassment a form of sex discrimination during the late 1970s. Although sexual harassment law applies to education, most of the law of sexual harassment has been developed by courts through interpretation of Title VII of the Civil Rights Act of 1964. In 1986, the Supreme Court recognized two forms of sexual harassment: the quid pro quo type, which involves sexual extortion, and the hostile environment type, which involves sexual intimidation.[66] Employers and many employees have worried that hostile-environment sexual harassment is too ambiguous. When can an employee bring charges? When is the employer liable? In 1986, the Court said that sexual harassment may be legally actionable even if the employee did not suffer tangible economic or job-related losses in relation to it. In 1993, the Court added that sexual harassment may be legally actionable even if the employee did not suffer tangible psychological costs as a result of it.[67] In two 1998 cases, the Court further strengthened the law when it said that whether or not sexual harassment results in economic harm to the employee, an employer is liable for the harassment if it was committed by someone with authority over the employee—by a supervisor, for example. But the Court also said that an employer may defend itself by showing that it had a sexual harassment prevention and grievance policy in effect.[68]

Another major step was taken in 1992, when the Court decided in *Franklin v. Gwinnett County Public Schools* that violations of Title IX of the 1972 Education Act could be remedied with monetary damages.[69] Title IX forbade gender discrimination in education, but it initially sparked little litigation because of its weak enforcement provisions. The Court's 1992 ruling that monetary damages could be awarded for gender discrimination opened the door for more legal action in the area of education. The greatest impact has been in the areas of sexual harassment—the subject of the *Franklin* case—and in equal treatment of women's athletic programs. The potential for monetary damages has made universities and public schools take the problem of sexual harassment more seriously. Colleges and universities have also started to pay more attention to women's athletic programs.

In 1996, the Supreme Court made another important decision about gender and education by putting an end to all-male schools supported by public funds. It ruled that the policy of the Virginia Military Institute (VMI) not to admit women was unconstitutional.[70] Along with the Citadel, an all-male military college in South Carolina, VMI had never admitted women in its 157-year history. VMI argued that the unique educational experience it offered—including intense physical training and the harsh treatment of freshmen—would be destroyed if women students were admitted. The Court, however, ruled that the male-only policy denied "substantial equality" to women. Two days after the Court's ruling, the Citadel announced that it would accept women. VMI considered becoming a private institution in order to remain all-male, but in September 1996, the school board finally voted to admit women.

LATINOS AND ASIAN AMERICANS FIGHT FOR RIGHTS

Although the Civil Rights Act of 1964 outlawed discrimination on the basis of national origin, limited English proficiency barred many Asian Americans and Latinos from full participation in American life. Two developments in the 1970s, however, established rights for language minorities. In 1974, the Supreme Court ruled in *Lau v. Nichols,* a suit filed on behalf of Chinese students in San Francisco, that school districts have to provide education for students whose English is limited.[71] It did not mandate bilingual education but it established a duty to provide instruction that the students could understand. The 1970 amendments to the Voting Rights Act permanently outlawed literacy tests in all fifty states and mandated bilingual ballots or oral assistance for those who speak Spanish, Chinese, Japanese, Korean, Native American languages, or Eskimo languages.

Asian Americans and Latinos have also been concerned about the impact of immigration laws on their civil rights. Many Asian American and Latino organizations opposed the Immigration Reform and Control Act of 1986 because it imposed sanctions on employers who hire undocumented workers. Such sanctions, they feared, would lead employers to discriminate against Latinos and Asian Americans. These suspicions were confirmed in a 1990 report by the General Accounting Office that found employer sanctions had created a "widespread pattern of discrimination" against Latinos and others who appear foreign.[72] Latinos and Asian Americans have established organizations modeled on the NAACP's Legal Defense Fund, such as the Mexican-American Legal Defense Fund (MALDEF) and the Asian Law Caucus, to monitor and challenge such discrimination. These groups have turned their attention to the rights of legal and illegal immigrants, as anti-immigrant sentiment has grown in recent years.

NATIVE AMERICANS HAVE SOVEREIGNTY, BUT STILL LACK RIGHTS

As a language minority, Native Americans were affected by the 1975 amendments to the Voting Rights Act and the *Lau* decision. The *Lau* decision established the right of Native Americans to be taught in their own languages. This marked quite a change from the boarding schools once run by the Bureau of Indian Affairs, at which members of Indian tribes had been forbidden to speak their own languages. In addition to these language-related issues, Native Americans have sought to expand their rights on the basis of their sovereign status. Since the 1920s and 1930s, Native American tribes have sued the federal government for illegally seizing land, seeking monetary reparations and land as damages. Both types of damages have been awarded in such suits, but only in small amounts. Native American tribes have been more successful in winning federal recognition of their sovereignty. Sovereign status has, in turn, allowed them to exercise greater self-determination. Most significant economically was a 1987 Supreme Court decision that freed Native American tribes from most state regulations prohibiting gambling. The establishment of casino gambling on Native American lands has brought a substantial flow of new income into desperately poor reservations.

DISABLED AMERICANS WON A GREAT VICTORY IN 1990

The concept of rights for the disabled began to emerge in the 1970s as the civil rights model spread to other groups. The seed was planted in a little-noticed provision of the 1973 Rehabilitation Act, which outlawed discrimination against individuals on the basis of disabilities. As in many other cases, the law itself helped give rise to the movement demanding rights for the handicapped.[73] Modeling itself on the NAACP's legal Defense Fund, the disability movement founded a Disability Rights Education and Defense Fund to press its legal claims. The movement achieved its greatest success with the passage of the Americans with Disabilities Act (ADA) of 1990, which guarantees equal employment rights and access to public businesses for the disabled. The Equal Opportunities Commission considers claims of discrimination in violation of this act. The impact of the law has been far-reaching, as businesses and public facilities have installed ramps, elevators, and other devices to meet the act's requirements.[74] In 1998, the Supreme Court interpreted the ADA to apply to people with HIV. Until then, ADA was interpreted as covering people with AIDS but not people with HIV. The case arose out of the refusal of a dentist to fill a cavity of a woman with HIV except in a hospital setting. The woman sued, and her complaint was that HIV had already disabled her because it was discouraging her from having children. (The act prohibits discrimination in employment, housing, and health care.)

In 2001, professional golfer Casey Martin, who suffers from a degenerative circulatory disorder that causes great pain and leg deterioration, won the legal right to ride in a golf cart on the Professional Golfers Association (PGA) Tour under the ADA's provision that owners of public accommodations must make "reasonable modifications" for the disabled. Despite the PGA's argument that walking golf courses during tour events was a necessary part of the game, the Supreme Court ruled in *PGA Tour v. Martin* that walking was "at best peripheral" to the game, thus upholding Martin's right to use a motorized golf cart. Justice Stevens, himself an amateur golfer, wrote in the Court's opinion that "from early on, the essence of the game has been shot-making."

THE AGED ARE PROTECTED UNDER LAW

Age discrimination in employment is illegal. The 1967 federal Age Discrimination in Employment Act (ADEA) makes age discrimination illegal when practiced by employers with at least twenty employees. Many states have added to the federal provisions with their own age discrimination laws, and some such state laws are stronger than the federal provisions. Age discrimination—especially in hiring—is widespread, and it is all the more pressing a problem because of Americans' significantly increased life expectancy. We are a much older population than we used to be. The idea of reduced psychological and physical capacity at age fifty, once perhaps reasonable, seems ridiculous today; and forcible retirement at sixty-five is looking sillier every year. Reasonable people will continue to disagree over the merits of laws against age discrimination. But it is clear that the major lobbyist for seniors, the American Association of Retired Persons (AARP, see chapter 7), with its claim to over thirty million members, will maintain its vigilance and its influence to keep these laws on the books and to make sure that they are vigorously implemented.

GAYS AND LESBIANS GAINED SIGNIFICANT LEGAL GROUND

In less than thirty years, the gay and lesbian movement has become one of the largest civil rights movements in contemporary America. Beginning with street protests in the 1960s, the movement has grown into a well-financed and sophisticated lobby.

But until 1996, there was no Supreme Court ruling or national legislation explicitly protecting gays and lesbians from discrimination. The first gay rights case that the Court decided, *Bowers v. Hardwick* (1986), ruled against a right to privacy that would protect consensual homosexual activity.[75] After the *Bowers* decision, the gay and lesbian rights movement sought suitable legal cases to test the constitutionality of discrimination against gays and lesbians, much as the black Civil Rights movement did in the late 1940s and 1950s. As one advocate put it, "lesbians and gay men are looking for their *Brown v. Board of Education*."[76] Among the cases tested were those stemming from local ordinances restricting gay rights (including the right to marry), job discrimination, and family law issues such as adoption and parental rights. In 1996, the Supreme Court, in *Romer v. Evans,* explicitly extended fundamental civil rights protections to gays and lesbians, by declaring unconstitutional a 1992 amendment to the Colorado state constitution that prohibited local governments from passing ordinances to protect gay rights.[77] The decision's forceful language highlighted the connection between gay rights and civil rights as it declared discrimination against gay people unconstitutional.

In 2003, homosexuals won a major victory in the case of *Lawrence v. Texas,* in which the Supreme Court overturned *Bowers* and struck down a Texas law that made certain sexual conduct between consenting partners of the same sex illegal. Drawing lesbians and gay men under the right-to-privacy umbrella, the Court said that "petitioners are entitled to respect for their private lives. The State cannot demean their existence or control their destiny by making their private sexual conduct a crime."[78] While striking down laws that made homosexual acts a crime, the *Lawrence* ruling did not change various provisions in federal and state laws that deprive homosexuals of full civil rights, including the right to marry. The case did, however, embolden some local officials around the country, such as those in San Francisco and New Paltz, New York, to start performing gay marriages, despite state laws barring the practice. Most significantly, the Massachusetts State Supreme Court ordered the state to recognize gay marriage under its own state constitution beginning in May 2004. Fittingly, Massachusetts began performing gay marriages on May 17—the fifty-year anniversary of the *Brown* school desegregation decision.

Whatever the future of Court rulings in this area, gay and lesbian Americans will continue to press their cases against the many laws they view as discriminatory. In response to the legalization of gay and lesbian marriage in Massachusetts, they are likely to push for observance of the *full faith and credit clause,* as discussed in chapter 3. But because of the Defense of Marriage Act of 1996, declaring that states do not have to recognize same-sex marriage, and the efforts of many states to adopt state laws to put same-sex marriage off limits, the gay and lesbian struggle against discrimination will follow that of other minorities, using the federal equal protection clause.[79]

Affirmative Action Attempts to Right Past Wrongs

Not only has the politics of rights spread to increasing numbers of groups in American society since the 1960s, it has also expanded its goal. The relatively narrow goal of equalizing opportunity by eliminating discriminatory barriers developed toward the far broader goal of **affirmative action**—compensatory action to overcome the consequences of past discrimination. An affirmative action policy tends to involve two novel approaches: (1) positive or benign discrimination in which race or some other status is actually taken into account as a positive rather than negative factor; and (2) compensatory action to favor members of the disadvantaged group who themselves may never have been the victims of discrimination.

affirmative action government policies or programs that seek to address past injustices against specified groups by making special efforts to provide members of these groups with access to educational and employment opportunities

President Lyndon Johnson put the case emotionally in 1965: "You do not take a person who, for years, has been hobbled by chains . . . and then say you are free to compete with all the others, and still just believe that you have been completely fair."[80] Johnson attempted to inaugurate affirmative action through executive orders directing agency heads and personnel officers to pursue vigorously a policy of minority employment in the federal civil service and in companies doing business with the national government. But affirmative action did not become a prominent goal of the national government until the 1970s.

Affirmative action also took the form of efforts by the agencies in the Department of Health, Education, and Welfare to shift their focus from "desegregation" to "integration."[81] Federal agencies required school districts to present plans for busing children across district lines, for pairing schools, for closing certain schools, and for redistributing faculties as well as students, under pain of loss of grants-in-aid from the federal government. The guidelines issued for such plans literally constituted preferential treatment to compensate for past discrimination, and without this legislatively assisted approach to integration orders, there would certainly not have been the dramatic increase in black children attending integrated classes.

Affirmative action was also initiated in the area of employment opportunity. The Equal Employment Opportunity Commission often has required plans whereby employers must attempt to increase the number of their minority employees, and the office of Federal Contract Compliance in the Department of Labor has used the threat of contract revocation for the same purpose.

THE SUPREME COURT SHIFTS THE BURDEN OF PROOF IN AFFIRMATIVE ACTION

Efforts by the executive, legislative, and judicial branches to shape the meaning of affirmative action today tend to center on a key issue: What is the appropriate level of review in affirmative action cases—that is, on whom should the burden of proof be placed, the plaintiff or the defendant? The Supreme Court formally addressed the issue of qualification versus minority preference in the case of Allan Bakke. Bakke, a white male, brought suit against the University of California at Davis Medical School on the grounds that in denying him admission the school had discriminated against him on the basis of his race (that year the school had reserved sixteen of one hundred available slots for minority applicants). He argued that his grades and test scores had ranked him well above many students who had been accepted at the school and that the only possible explanation for his rejection was that those others accepted were black or Latino whereas he was white. In 1978, Bakke won his case before the Supreme Court and was admitted to the medical school, but he did not succeed in getting affirmative action declared unconstitutional. The Court rejected the procedures at the University of California because its medical school had used both a quota *and* a separate admissions system for minorities. The Court agreed with Bakke's argument that racial categorizations are suspect categories that place a severe burden of proof on those using them to show a "compelling public purpose." The Court went on to say that achieving "a diverse student body" was such a public purpose, but the method of a rigid quota of student slots assigned on the basis of race was incompatible with the equal protection clause. Thus, the Court permitted universities (and presumably other schools, training programs, and hiring authorities) to continue to take minority status into consideration, but limited severely the use of quotas to situations in which (1) previous discrimination had been shown, and (2) it was used more as a guideline for social diversity than as a mathematically defined ratio.[82]

In 1991, Congress enacted a piece of legislation designed to undo the effects of the decisions limiting affirmative action. The terms of the Civil Rights Act of 1991 shifted the burden of proof in employment discrimination cases back to employers. In addition, the act made it more difficult to mount later challenges to consent decrees in affirmative action cases. Despite Congress's actions, however, the federal judiciary will have the last word as cases under the new law reach the courts. In a five-to-four decision in 1993, the Supreme Court ruled that employees had to prove their employers intended discrimination, again placing the burden of proof on employees.[83]

In 1995, the Supreme Court's ruling in *Adarand Constructors v. Pena* further weakened affirmative action. This decision stated that race-based policies, such as preferences given by the government to minority contractors, must survive strict scrutiny, placing the burden on the government to show that such affirmative action programs serve a compelling government interest and are narrowly tailored to address identifiable past discrimination.[84]

In 2003, affirmative action again survived court challenge in two cases arising out of the University of Michigan. In *Grutter v. Bollinger,* the Court upheld the "holistic" and "individualized" affirmative action program used by Michigan's law school, finding it in keeping with the standard set in the *Bakke* case.[85] Michigan's undergraduate affirmative action program was declared unconstitutional, however, in *Gratz v. Bollinger* because it gave specific admissions points (20 out of 150) to African American, Hispanic, and Native American applicants.[86] This approach was barred for resembling too closely the specific numerical quota system struck down by *Bakke.*

Summary

The Fourteenth Amendment was the key to extending civil liberties and civil rights in America. The Bill of Rights was designed to protect citizens from improper actions by the federal government. During the country's first century, the Bill of Rights did not affect the states. After the adoption of the Fourteenth Amendment, however, and the passage of several decades, the Supreme Court began to hand down a series of decisions that used the Fourteenth (especially its due process clause) as the "tool" to incorporate the most important Bill of Rights protections by applying them to the states. It was this process that allows Americans today to claim the important Bill of Rights protections in their daily lives, regardless of what state they live in.

The Fourteenth Amendment's equal protection clause was similarly critical in defining and extending basic civil rights. The term "civil rights" refers to the expansion of government power so that the government can take an active, positive role in promoting equality. The centuries-long struggle by African Americans to win equality began with the abolition of slavery after the Civil War and the enactment of the Thirteenth, Fourteenth, and Fifteenth Amendments, but the process gained little momentum until after World War II. Landmark court decisions in the 1950s and 1960s and major congressional and administrative enactments in the 1960s outlawed long-standing discriminatory practices in such areas as state government action, education, employment, and public accommodations. The use of affirmative action programs to achieve these goals has sparked controversy, underscoring the fact that, while major gains have been made, discrimination and prejudice continue to plague American society.

For Further Reading

Abraham, Henry J. *Freedom and the Court: Civil Rights and Liberties in the United States,* 6th ed. New York: Oxford University Press, 1994.

Friendly, Fred W. *Minnesota Rag: The Dramatic Story of the Landmark Supreme Court Case that Gave New Meaning to Freedom of the Press.* New York: Vintage, 1982.

Garrow, David J. *Bearing the Cross: Martin Luther King and the Southern Christian Leadership Conference: A Personal Portrait.* New York: Morrow, 1986.

Glendon, Mary Ann. *Rights Talk: The Impoverishment of Political Discourse.* New York: Free Press. 1991.

Greenberg, Jack. *Crusades in the Courts: How a Dedicated Band of Lawyers Fought for the Civil Rights Revolution.* New York: Basic Books, 1994.

Hentoff, Nat. *The First Freedom: The Tumultuous History of Free Speech in America.* New York: Basic Books, 1994.

Lewis, Anthony. *Gideon's Trumpet.* New York: Random House, 1964.

Massey, Douglas S., and Nancy A. Denton. *American Apartheid: Segregation and the Making of the Underclass.* Cambridge, MA: Harvard University Press, 1993.

Minow, Martha. *Making All the Difference: Inclusion, Exclusion, and American Law.* Ithaca, NY: Cornell University Press, 1990.

Nava, Michael. *Created Equal: Why Gay Rights Matter to America.* New York: St. Martin's, 1994.

Rosenberg, Gerald N. *The Hollow Hope: Can Courts Bring about Social Change?* Chicago, University of Chicago Press, 1991.

Spitzer, Robert J. *The Right to Bear Arms.* Santa Barbara, CA: ABC-CLI0, 2001.

Stone, Geoffrey R., Richard A. Epstein, and Cass R. Sunstein, eds. *The Bill of Rights in the Modern State.* Chicago: University of Chicago Press, 1992.

Study Outline

The Origin of the Bill of Rights Lies in Those Who Opposed the Constitution

1. Despite the insistence of Alexander Hamilton that a bill of rights was both unnecessary and dangerous, adding a list of explicit rights was the most important item of business for the First Congress in 1789.

2. The Bill of Rights would have been more aptly named the "Bill of Liberties," because it is made up of provisions that protect citizens from improper government action.

3. Civil rights did not become part of the Constitution until 1868 with the adoption of the Fourteenth Amendment, which sought to provide for each citizen "the equal protection of the laws."

Dual Citizenship Was Defined by *Barron v. Baltimore*

1. In 1833, the Supreme Court found that the Bill of Rights limited only the national government and not state governments.

2. Although the language of the Fourteenth Amendment seems to indicate that the protections of the Bill of Rights apply to state governments as well as the national government, for the remainder of the nineteenth century the Supreme Court (with only one exception) made decisions as if the Fourteenth Amendment had never been adopted.

3. As of 1961, only the First Amendment and one clause of the Fifth Amendment had been "selectively incorporated" into the Fourteenth Amendment. After 1961, however, most of the provisions of the Bill of Rights were incorporated into the Fourteenth Amendment and applied to the states.

The First Amendment Guarantees Freedom of Religion

1. The religious movement of the 1980s, culminating in the judicial and congressional activities of the 1990s, identified or created unsettled areas involving the establishment clause and the free exercise clause.

The First Amendment and Freedom of Speech and the Press Assure Free Exchange of Ideas

1. Although freedom of speech and freedom of the press hold an important place in the Bill of Rights, the extent and nature of certain types of expression are subject to constitutional debate.

The Second Amendment Protects the Right to Bear Arms in a Militia

1. Constitutionally, the Second Amendment protects citizens' rights to bear arms when citizens are called into militia service by the government.

Rights of the Criminally Accused Are Based on Due Process of Law

1. The purpose of due process is to equalize the playing field between the accused individual and the all-powerful state.

The Right to Privacy Is the Right to Be Left Alone

1. In the case of *Griswold v. Connecticut,* the Supreme Court found a right of privacy in the Constitution. This right was confirmed and extended in 1973 in the case of *Roe v. Wade.*

Civil Rights Are Protections by the Government

1. From 1896 until the end of World War II, the Supreme Court held that the Fourteenth Amendment's equal protection clause was not violated by racial distinction as long as the facilities were equal.
2. After World War II, the Supreme Court began to undermine the separate but equal doctrine, eventually declaring it unconstitutional in *Brown v. Board of Education.*
3. The *Brown* decision marked the beginning of a difficult battle for equal protection in education, employment, housing, voting, and other areas of social and economic activity.
4. The first phase of school desegregation was met with such massive resistance in the South that, ten years after *Brown,* fewer than 1 percent of black children in the South were attending schools with whites.
5. Title VII of the civil Rights Act of 1964 outlawed job discrimination by all private and public employers, including governmental agencies, that employed more than fifteen workers.
6. In 1965, Congress significantly strengthened legislation protecting voting rights by barring literacy and other tests as a condition for voting in southern states. In the long run, the laws extending and protecting voting rights could prove to be the most effective of all civil rights legislation, because increased political participation by minorities has altered the shape of American politics.

The Civil Rights Struggle Was Extended to Other Disadvantaged Groups

1. The protections won by the African American civil rights movement spilled over to protect other groups as well, including women, Latinos, Asian Americans, Native Americans, disabled Americans, and gays and lesbians.

Affirmative Action Attempts to Right Past Wrongs

1. By seeking to provide compensatory action to overcome the consequences of past discrimination, affirmative action represents the expansion of the goals of groups championing minority rights.
2. Affirmative action has been a controversial policy. Opponents charge that affirmative action creates group rights and establishes quotas, both of which are inimical to the American tradition. Proponents of affirmative action argue that the long history of group discrimination makes affirmative action necessary and that efforts to compensate for some bad action in the past are well within the federal government's purview. Recent conflicts over affirmative action have raised questions about what is effective political action.

Practice Quiz

1. The amendment that provided the basis for the modern understanding of the government's obligation to protect civil rights was the
   a) First Amendment.
   b) Ninth Amendment.
   c) Fourteenth Amendment.
   d) Twenty-second Amendment.

2. The process by which some of the liberties in the Bill of Rights were applied to the states (or nationalized) is known as
   a) selective incorporation.
   b) judicial activism.
   c) civil liberties.
   d) establishment.

3. Which of the following protections are not contained in the First Amendment?
   a) the establishment clause
   b) the free exercise clause
   c) freedom of the press
   d) All of the above are First Amendment protections.

4. In what case was a right to privacy first found in the Constitution?
    a) *Griswold v. Connecticut*
    b) *Roe v. Wade*
    c) *Baker v. Carr*
    d) *Planned Parenthood v. Casey*

5. Which famous case deals with Sixth Amendment issues?
    a) *Miranda v. Arizona*
    b) *Mapp v. Ohio*
    c) *Gideon v. Wainwright*
    d) *Terry v. Ohio*

6. Which civil rights case established the "separate but equal" rule?
    a) *Plessy v. Ferguson*
    b) *Brown v. Board of Education*
    c) *Bakke v. Regents of the University of California*
    d) *Adarand Constructors v. Pena*

7. Which of the following organizations established a Legal Defense Fund to challenge segregation?
    a) the Association of American Trial Lawyers
    b) the National Association for the Advancement of Colored People
    c) the Student Nonviolent Coordinating Committee
    d) the Southern Christian Leadership Council

8. Which of the following made discrimination by private employers and state governments illegal?
    a) the Fourteenth Amendment
    b) *Brown v. Board of Education*
    c) the 1964 Civil Rights Act
    d) *Bakke v. Board of Regents*

9. Which of the following is *not* an example of an area in which women have made progress since the 1970s in guaranteeing certain civil rights?
    a) sexual harassment
    b) integration into all-male publicly supported universities
    c) more equal funding for college women's varsity athletic programs
    d) the passage of the Equal Rights amendment

10. In what case did the Supreme Court find that "rigid quotas" are incompatible with the equal protection clause of the Fourteenth Amendment?
    a) *Bakke v. Board of Regents*
    b) *Brown v. Board of Education*
    c) *United States v. Nixon*
    d) *Immigration and Naturalization Service v. Chadha*

Critical Thinking Questions

1. Recount the history of the constitutional "right to privacy." How has this right affected American politics since the 1960s? How has this right interacted with the other rights in the Bill of Rights? Read the Third, Fourth, Fifth, and Ninth Amendments. In your opinion, do American citizens have a right to privacy?

2. Supporters of affirmative action argue that it is intended not only to compensate for past discrimination, but also to level an uneven playing field in which discrimination still exists. What do you think? To what extent do we have a society free from discrimination? What is the impact of affirmative action on society today? What alternatives to affirmative action policies exist?

Key Terms

affirmative action (p. 117)
bills of attainder (p. 81)
Bill of Rights (p. 79)
Brown v. Board of Education (p. 105)
civil liberties (p. 80)
civil rights (p. 80, p. 81)
"clear and present danger" test (p. 90)
de facto (p. 105)
de jure (p. 105)
double jeopardy (p. 97)

dual citizenship (p. 82)
due process of law (p. 81)
eminent domain (p. 98)
equal protection clause (p. 103)
establishment clause (p. 86)
ex post facto laws (p. 81)
exclusionary rule (p. 96)
fighting words (p. 93)
free exercise clause (p. 86)
grand jury (p. 97)
habeas corpus (p. 80)
incorporation (p. 84)

libel (p. 92)
Miranda rule (p. 98)
preferred freedoms (p. 84)
procedural liberties (p. 81)
right to privacy (p. 99)
"separate but equal" rule (p. 103)
slander (p. 92)
speech plus (p. 91)
strict scrutiny (p. 87)
substantive liberties (p. 81)

5 PUBLIC OPINION AND THE MEDIA

MAIN MESSAGE

The political system shapes public opinion as much as public opinion shapes the political system.

Democratic governments are based on two big assumptions. The first is that the public is informed and interested in what the government does. The second assumption is that the government more or less does what the people want. While there is some validity to these assumptions, we will see in this chapter that the truth is much more complicated.

Take the example of gun control. Since the advent of modern public opinion polling in the late 1930s, large majorities of Americans have favored stronger gun laws. In a 1938 Gallup poll, 84 percent of Americans polled said that they favored mandatory registration of all handguns, one of the strictest gun measures ever discussed. In recent years, this number has fluctuated between 66 and 81 percent. Even at the

Key Concepts

1. Americans' opinions are shaped by fundamental values and demographic background.

2. Family, social groups, education, and political conditions all transmit political values and information.

3. The ability of public opinion to influence government decisions depends on specific conditions and events.

4. Electronic, print, and Internet media operate much like other large industries.

5. The First Amendment protection of free press protects print media more than electronic media.

6. Journalists, news sources, and consumers all influence the content of news.

low point of 66 percent, this represents a two-thirds majority in favor of the idea. In 2000, 73 percent of those polled favored handgun registration.[1] Yet from the 1970s through the 1990s, political leaders who supported tougher gun laws did not even dare to express public support for the idea of gun registration, because it was considered too far from anything the government might enact. Only in the 2000 presidential election did a major candidate openly support the idea, when former senator Bill Bradley pledged support for handgun registration during his unsuccessful race for the Democratic presidential nomination.

Here is an obvious example of a huge gap between what the public favors and what the government has, or has not, done. The explanation for this gap rests with several factors, including the power of the anti–gun control lobby (see chapter 7). But it also illustrates that the government does not necessarily follow public opinion. This does not mean that we are not a democracy, but it does mean that the link between the government and the public is complicated, especially when we include the influence of American mass media.

In this chapter, we will see that the political system shapes public opinion as much as public opinion shapes the political system. The term **public opinion** refers to the collective views and beliefs of people concerning events, issues, and personalities. These beliefs about politics are sometimes organized around a loose **political ideology**—that is, a coordinated and consistent set of beliefs about politics that provides some degree of order or general philosophy to the opinions people hold. In America, the dominant political ideologies are liberalism and conservatism, although most Americans do not think of themselves as being tied to a specific political ideology.

The public's ideas about politics constantly swirl around in the American media. But the media do more than report and discuss public opinion. By choosing what to report, how to report, and what *not* to report, the media also play a key role in shaping opinion. Yet the factors that shape opinions, including the media, are limited in part because most Americans share some fundamental values.

Fundamental Values Shape Our Opinions

Most Americans share a common set of values, including a belief in the principles—if not always the actual practice—of liberty, equality, and democracy. **Equality of opportunity** has always been an important theme in American society. Americans believe that all individuals should be allowed to seek personal and material success. Moreover, Americans generally believe that such success should be linked to personal effort and ability, rather than to family "connections" or other forms of special privilege. Similarly, Americans have always voiced strong support for the principle of individual **liberty.** They typically support the notion that governmental interference with individuals' lives and property should be kept to the minimum consistent with the general welfare, although in recent years Americans have grown accustomed to greater levels of governmental intervention. And most Americans also believe in **democracy.** They presume that

public opinion citizens' attitudes about political issues, leaders, institutions, and events

political ideology a cohesive set of beliefs that form a general philosophy about the role of government

equality of opportunity a widely shared American ideal that all people should have the freedom to use whatever talents and wealth they have to reach their fullest potential

liberty freedom from government control

democracy a system of rule that permits citizens to play a significant part in the governmental process, usually through the election of key public officials

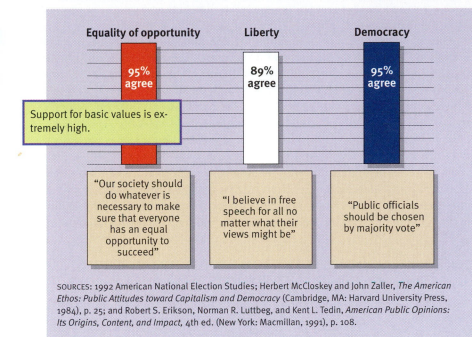

Americans' Support for Fundamental Values   Figure 5.1

SOURCES: 1992 American National Election Studies; Herbert McCloskey and John Zaller, *The American Ethos: Public Attitudes toward Capitalism and Democracy* (Cambridge, MA: Harvard University Press, 1984), p. 25; and Robert S. Erikson, Norman R. Luttbeg, and Kent L. Tedin, *American Public Opinions: Its Origins, Content, and Impact,* 4th ed. (New York: Macmillan, 1991), p. 108.

every person should have the opportunity to take part in the nation's governmental and policy-making processes and to have some "say" in determining how they are governed.[2] Figure 5.1 offers some indication of this American consensus on fundamental values: 95 percent of Americans who were polled believed in equal opportunity, 89 percent supported free speech without regard to the views being expressed, and 95 percent expressed support for majority rule.

Obviously, the principles that Americans espouse have not always been put into practice. For two hundred years, Americans were able to believe in the principles of equality of opportunity and individual liberty while denying them in practice to generations of African Americans. Yet it is important to note that the strength of the principles ultimately helped to overcome practices that deviated from those principles. Proponents of slavery and, later, of segregation were defeated in the arena of public opinion because their practices differed so sharply from the fundamental principles accepted by most Americans.

POLITICAL VALUES COME FROM POLITICAL SOCIALIZATION

The attitudes that individuals hold about political issues and personalities tend to be shaped by their underlying political beliefs and values. For example, an individual who has basically negative feelings about government intervention into America's economy and society would probably oppose the development of new health care and social programs. Similarly, someone who distrusts the military would likely be suspicious of any call for the use of American troops. The process through which these underlying political beliefs and values are formed is called **political socialization.**

political socialization the process by which people learn political attitudes and beliefs

The process of political socialization is important. Probably no nation, and certainly no democracy, could survive if its citizens did not share some fundamental beliefs. For example, most Americans grumble about paying taxes. If the typical American is asked why he or she pays taxes, the first response is usually fear that the government will punish nonpayers. Yet if millions of Americans stopped paying taxes, the government could not possibly prosecute all of the lawbreakers. In fact, most Americans, when asked more closely, will admit that they pay taxes at least in part because they believe that government has a *right* to take part of their income (even though they may wish that the percent the government takes were smaller). This fundamental belief helps explain how and why socialization is so important. Four of the most important agents of socialization are the family, membership in social groups, education, and prevailing political conditions.

OUR POLITICAL VALUES COME FROM FAMILY, SOCIAL GROUPS, EDUCATION, AND POLITICAL CONDITIONS

The Family Most people acquire their initial orientation to politics from their families. As might be expected, differences in family background tend to produce divergent political outlooks. Although relatively few parents spend much time teaching their children about politics, political conversations occur in many households and children tend to absorb the political views, perhaps without realizing it. Studies have suggested, for example, that party preferences are initially acquired at home. Children raised in households in which the primary caregivers are Democrats tend to become Democrats themselves, whereas children raised in homes where their caregivers are Republicans tend to favor the GOP (Grand Old Party, a traditional nickname for the Republican Party).[3] Obviously, not all children absorb their parents' political views. Two of former Republican president Ronald Reagan's three children, for instance, rejected their parents' conservative values. Moreover, even those children whose views are initially shaped by parental values may change their minds as they mature and experience political life for themselves. Nevertheless, the family is an important initial source of political orientation for everyone.

Social Groups Another group or important source of divergent political orientations and values is the social group or groups to which individuals belong. Social groups include those to which individuals belong involuntarily—gender and racial groups, for example—as well as those to which people belong voluntarily—such as political parties, labor unions, and educational and occupational groups. Some social groups have both voluntary and involuntary attributes. For example, individuals are born with a particular social-class background, but as a result of their own efforts people may move up—or down—the class structure.

Membership in a particular group can give individuals important experiences and perspectives that shape their view of political and social life. In American society, for example, the experiences of blacks and whites can differ significantly. Blacks have been victims of persecution and discrimination throughout American history. Blacks and whites also have different educational and occupational opportunities, often live in separate communities, and may attend separate schools. Such differences tend to produce distinctive political outlooks (see Figure 5.2). For example, nearly three-quarters of white Americans but only one-third of African Americans favored going to war against Iraq in 2003.

Men and women have important differences of opinion as well. Reflecting differences in social roles, political experience, and occupational patterns,

Disagreement Among Blacks and Whites   Figure 5.2

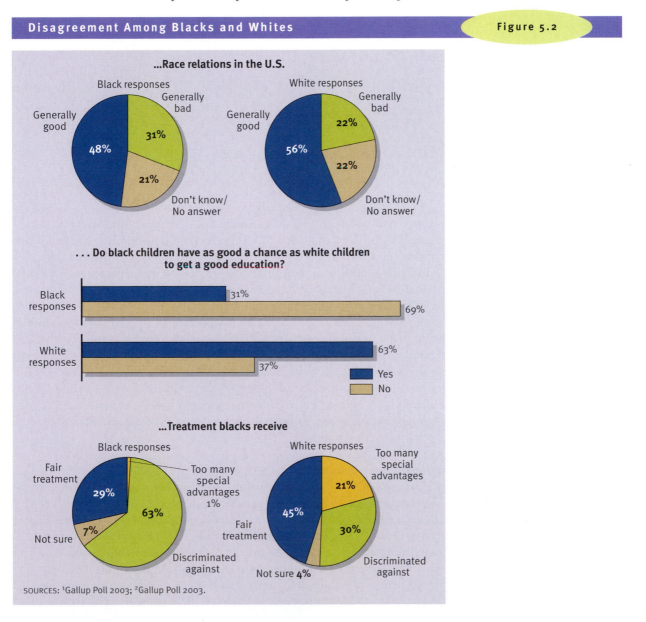

SOURCES: ¹Gallup Poll 2003; ²Gallup Poll 2003.

Table 5.1 Disagreements among Men and Women on Issues of War and Peace

	PERCENTAGE APPROVING OF ACTION	
GOVERNMENT ACTION	MEN	WOMEN
Go to war against Iraq (2003)	78	66
U.S. should mount long-term war in Afghanistan (2002)	64	42
Prefer cease-fire over NATO airstrikes on Yugoslavia (1999)	44	51
Favor unilateral military action against Iraq (1998)	55	35
Military operation against Somali warlord (1993)	72	60
Going to war against Iraq (1991)	72	53
Sending U.S. troops to Saudi Arabia in response to Iraqi invasion of Kuwait (1991)	78	54

The "gender gap" continued to be large throughout the 1990s.
SOURCE: Gallup Poll, 1991, 1993, 1998, 1999, 2002, 2003.

women tend to be less militaristic than men on issues of war and peace, more likely than men to favor measures to protect the environment, and more supportive than men of government social and health care programs (see Table 5.1). Perhaps because of these differences on issues, women are more likely than men to vote for Democratic candidates.[4] This tendency for men's and women's opinions to differ is called the *gender gap*.

In addition, social group membership can affect political beliefs through what might be called objective political interests. On many economic issues, for example, the interests of the rich and poor differ significantly. Struggles over tax policy, social security, medicare, welfare, and so forth are fueled by differences of interest between wealthier and poorer Americans. In a similar vein, objective differences of interest between "senior citizens" and younger Americans can lead to very different views on such diverse issues as health care policy, social security, and criminal justice.

Differences in Education A third important source of differences in political perspectives comes from a person's education. In some respects, of course, schooling is a great equalizer. Governments use public education to try to teach all children a common set of civic values. It is mainly in school that Americans acquire their basic belief in liberty, equality, and democracy. In history classes, students are taught that the Founders fought for the principle of liberty. Through participation in class elections and student government, students are taught the virtues of democracy. In the course of studying such topics as the Constitution, the Civil War, and the civil rights movement, students are taught the importance of equality. These lessons are repeated in every grade in a variety of contexts. No wonder they are such an important element in Americans' beliefs.

At the same time, however, differences in educational attainment are strongly associated with differences in political outlook. In particular, those who attend college are often exposed to philosophies and modes of thought that will forever distinguish them from their friends and neighbors who do not pursue college diplomas. Table 5.2 outlines some general differences of opinion that are found between college graduates and other Americans.

A college education helps convince students of the importance of political participation and of their own ability to have an impact on politics and policy. Thus, one of the major differences between college graduates and Americans with less education can be seen in levels of political participation. College graduates are more likely to vote, write "letters to the editor," join campaigns, take part in protests, and, generally, make their voices heard.

Political Conditions   A fourth set of factors that shapes political orientations and values is the conditions under which individuals and groups are recruited into and involved in political life. Although political beliefs are influenced by family background and group membership, the precise content and character of these views is, to a large extent, determined by political circumstances. For example,

Education and Public Opinion in 2000   Table 5.2

ISSUES	DROP-OUT	HIGH SCHOOL	SOME COLLEGE	COLLEGE GRAD.
1. Women and men should have equal roles.	45%	72%	84%	85%
2. Abortion should never be allowed.	31	16	11	5
3. The government should adopt national health insurance.	50	43	38	37
4. The U.S. should not concern itself with other nations' problems.	27	34	27	12
5. Government should see to fair treatment in jobs for African Americans.	24	33	32	43
6. Government should provide fewer services to reduce government spending.	18	13	19	31

The figures show the percentage of respondents in each category agreeing with the statement.
SOURCE The American National Election Studies, 2000 data, provided by the Inter-University Consortium for Political and Social Research, University of Michigan.

American white southerners were staunch members of the Democratic Party from the Civil War through the 1960s. As members of this political group, they became key supporters of liberal New Deal and post–New Deal social programs that greatly expanded the size and power of the American national government. Since the 1960s, however, southern whites have shifted in large numbers to the Republican Party. Now they provide a major base of support for efforts to scale back social programs and to reduce sharply the size and power of the national government. The South's move from the Democratic to the Republican camp took place because of white southern opposition to the Democratic Party's racial policies and because of determined Republican efforts to win white southern support. It was not a change in the character of white southerners but a change in the political circumstances in which they found themselves that induced this major shift in political allegiances and outlooks in the South.

THE TWO MAIN IDEOLOGIES IN AMERICA ARE LIBERALISM AND CONSERVATISM

As we have seen, people's beliefs about government can vary widely. But for some individuals, this set of beliefs can fit together into a coherent philosophy about government. This set of underlying orientations, ideas, and beliefs through which we come to understand and interpret politics is called a political ideology. Ideologies take many different forms. Some people may view politics primarily in religious terms. After its 1979 revolution, Iran was headed by the Ayatollah Khomeini, who was also the spiritual leader of this predominantly Muslim nation. In this and other nations, religion is indivisible from politics. In Israel, the religious beliefs of the Jewish faith dovetail closely with, and have a great effect on, national politics. Other people may see politics through racial lenses. Nazism was a political ideology that placed race at the center of political life and sought to interpret politics in terms of racial categories.

In America today, people often describe themselves as liberals or conservatives. Liberalism and conservatism are political ideologies that include beliefs about the role of the government, ideas about public policies, and notions about which groups in society should properly exercise power. These ideologies can be seen as the end result of the process of political socialization that was discussed in the preceding section.

liberal today, one who generally supports political and social reform; extensive governmental intervention in the economy; the expansion of federal social services; more vigorous efforts on behalf of the poor, minorities, and women; and greater concern for consumers and the environment

Today, the term **liberal** has come to imply support for political and social reform, extensive government intervention in the economy, support for federal social services, and more vigorous efforts on behalf of the poor, minorities, and women, as well as greater concern for consumers and the environment. In social and cultural areas, liberals generally support abortion rights and stronger gun laws, are concerned with the rights of persons accused of crime, and oppose state involvement with religious institutions and religious expression. In international affairs, liberal positions are usually seen as including support for arms control, opposition to the development and testing of nuclear weapons, support for aid to poor nations, opposition to the use of American troops to influence the domestic affairs of developing nations, and support for international organizations such as the United Nations. Of course, liberalism is not monolithic. For example, among individuals who view themselves as liberal, many support American military intervention when it is tied to a humanitarian purpose, as in the case of America's military action in Kosovo in 1998–99.

By contrast, the term **conservative** today is used to describe those who generally support the social and economic status quo and are suspicious of efforts to increase government control. Conservatives believe strongly that a large and powerful government poses a threat to citizens' freedom. Thus, in the domestic arena, conservatives generally oppose the expansion of governmental activity, asserting that solutions to social and economic problems can be developed in the private sector. Conservatives particularly oppose efforts to impose government regulation on business, pointing out that such regulation is frequently economically inefficient and costly and can ultimately lower the entire nation's standard of living. As to social and cultural positions, many conservatives oppose abortion and gun control, support school prayer, are more concerned for the victims than the perpetrators of crimes, oppose school busing, and support traditional family arrangements. In international affairs, conservatism has come to mean support for the maintenance of American military power.

Of course, it is important to note that many people who call themselves liberals or conservatives accept only part of the liberal or conservative ideology. Many individuals who are liberal on social issues are conservative on economic issues. There is nothing illogical about these mixed positions. They simply indicate the relatively open and fluid character of American political debate. As Figure 5.3 indicates, Americans are often apt to shift their ideological preferences.

conservative today this term refers to those who generally support the social and economic status quo and are suspicious of efforts to introduce new political formulae and economic arrangements. Conservatives believe that a large and powerful government poses a threat to citizens' freedom

Americans' Shifting Ideology, 1973–2002   **Figure 5.3**

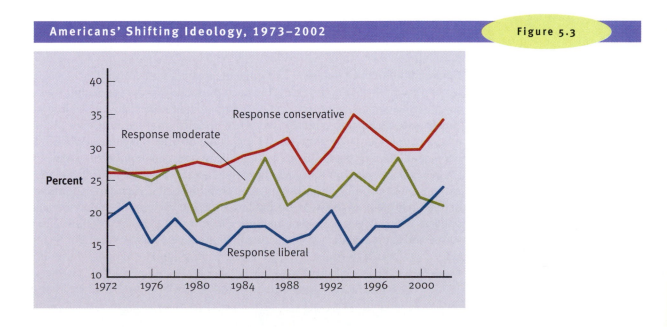

OPINION TRAITS EXPLAIN HOW PUBLIC OPINION INFLUENCES POLITICS

Several factors help explain how and why public opinion does or does not shape national politics. These include intensity of opinion, opinion stability and fluidity, political knowledge, the role of leaders in trying to direct or manipulate opinion, and the role of private groups attempting to alter opinion.

Intensity of Opinion   As discussed, the fact that Americans hold certain opinions does not mean that opinion will have an effect on the political system. Another, even more important factor, is opinion intensity—the depth or strength of feeling Americans hold about an issue. For example, former president George Bush pushed for a constitutional amendment in 1990 to outlaw flag burning, a position that was supported by a large majority of Americans. Yet Bush's effort to win enactment of the measure failed in large part because it was not an issue about which most Americans cared all that deeply. Without stronger public support, Bush suffered an embarrassing political failure in Congress.[5]

In 2004, national attention was drawn to the issue of gay marriage, when it became legal in Massachusetts. A national survey that year found that 46 percent of Americans favored adoption of a federal constitutional amendment barring homosexual marriage, while 45 percent said that the matter should be left to individual states to decide. Despite this even split, the intensity of feelings was not the same on each side. Among those opposed to gay marriage, 49 percent reported feeling "strongly" against same-sex marriage, compared to only 25 percent of supporters reporting "strong" feelings in favor of it.[6] This difference in intensity helps explain why efforts proceeded in Congress to enact a constitutional amendment barring gay marriage and why President George W. Bush changed his earlier position and endorsed the amendment: Even though the country was evenly split, it was an issue very important to the Republican Party's base (a "high-intensity" issue for them) and therefore would be a way to rally these supporters in an election year.

Opinion Stability and Fluidity   Related to the matter of intensity is that of stability and fluidity—that is, the extent to which opinions can change or shift over a short period of time. In general, public opinion tends to be relatively stable, with changes occurring only gradually over many months or years. Sometimes, however, a major shift in opinion over a short space of time is recorded. When this happens, it often prompts political leaders to pay attention to popular wishes.

When such shifts are observed, they are either the result of some highly dramatic event or of polling mistakes. An example of the first occurred in the summer of 1963. Throughout that year, the public's attention was riveted to the dramatic struggle of nonviolent protestors attempting to win civil rights in the South. News stories and television film footage repeatedly showed peaceful demonstrators being chased and beaten by police, suffering attacks by dogs, and being sprayed with fire hoses. These scenes filled Americans with shock and outrage. Then, in August 1963, civil rights leaders staged a massive march on Washington (when Martin

Luther King, Jr., delivered his famous "I Have a Dream" speech on the steps of the Lincoln Memorial). The impact on public opinion was dramatic: Between the spring and summer of that year, the percentage of Americans who considered civil rights to be "the most important issue" facing the country increased from 4 percent to 52 percent—the largest such increase ever recorded.[7] This is also an example of "agenda setting"—the ability of the media to turn the country's focus toward a particular issue (see discussion later in this chapter).

An example of polls falsely showing unstable or fluid opinion occurs during every presidential election year when pollsters conduct "trial heats"—hypothetical matchups between presidential contenders months before the election is held. Polling is done before and after each presidential nominating convention, held in the summer of the presidential election year, to see how much of a "bump" each candidate receives—that is, how much each candidate improves in the public's eyes as a result of favorable publicity received during the convention. These "bumps" are, however, of little or no importance in measuring the actual strength of each candidate, because the fluctuations are predictable reactions to the heavy and favorable publicity each candidate receives during the conventions. Moreover, the election is still months away, so as many as a third of likely voters indicate support that is "soft," meaning that they are likely to change their minds during the fall campaign.[8]

Opinion Consistency   As we have seen, general political beliefs can guide the formation of opinions on specific issues, but an individual's beliefs and opinions are not always consistent with one another. Studies of political opinion have shown that most people don't hold specific and clearly defined opinions on every political issue. As a result, they are easily influenced by others. The degree of consistency citizens show is shaped by knowledge and information about political issues. In general, knowledgeable citizens are better able to evaluate new information and determine whether it is relevant to and consistent with their beliefs and opinions. As a result, better-informed individuals can recognize their political interests and act consistently on behalf of them.

One of the most obvious and important examples of this proposition is voting. Despite the predisposition of voters to support their own party's candidates (see chapter 6 for a discussion of party identification), millions of voters are affected by the information they receive about candidates during a campaign. During the 1996 presidential campaign, for instance, voters weighed the arguments of Bill Clinton against those of Bob Dole about who was better fit to run the U.S. economy based on what they (the voters) knew about the country's economic health. Many Republican voters actually supported Clinton because they approved of the economic policies followed during his first term in office. Thus citizens can use information and judgment to overcome their predispositions.

Politicians Lead Opinion   Governmental leaders invariably attempt to influence, manipulate, or manage the opinions of the people. To some extent, this is the definition of a leader people admire. In the years leading up to World War II, for example, President Franklin Roosevelt came to believe that the United States should enter the war on the side of Britain and its allies against Nazi Germany and Imperial Japan, but there was strong sentiment in the United States that we should stay out of the war. Still, Roosevelt used his persuasive powers to move American opinion in favor of intervention. The debate came to an end when Japan attacked Pearl Harbor, which immediately rallied nearly all Americans to support going to war, showing also how a single dramatic event can sometimes help leaders move the country in a certain direction.

Political leaders pay close attention to public opinion even when the country does not face a crisis. For example, the Reagan and Clinton administrations regularly used techniques borrowed from election campaigns to bolster popular support for White House initiatives. President Clinton established a political "war room," similar to the one that operated in his campaign headquarters, where representatives from all departments met daily to discuss and coordinate the president's public relations efforts. Many of the same consultants and pollsters who directed the successful Clinton campaign were employed in the selling of the president's programs.[9]

Indeed, the Clinton White House made more sustained and systematic use of public opinion polling than any previous administration. For example, during his presidency Clinton relied heavily on the polling firm of Penn & Schoen to help him decide which issues to emphasize and what strategies to adopt. During the 1995–96 budget battle with Congress, the White House commissioned polls almost every night to chart changes in public perceptions about the struggle. Poll data suggested to Clinton that he should present himself as struggling to save Medicare from Republican cuts. Clinton responded by launching a media attack against what he claimed were GOP efforts to hurt the elderly. This proved to be a successful strategy and helped Clinton defeat the Republican budget.[10] The administration, however, asserted that it used polls only as a check on its communications strategy.[11]

The Bush administration's efforts to mold public opinion were manifested during the 2003 Iraq war. Prior to the war, the administration invited more than 100 news correspondents and photographers to accompany American forces into battle. These "embedded" journalists rode in tanks and armored personnel carriers with the troops, sharing their hardships and dangers. As the administration anticipated, the embedded journalists developed considerable rapport with the soldiers and provided generally sympathetic war coverage, often beginning their accounts of military actions with the pronoun *we*. Despite these and other ploys, public support for the president's military policies faltered when the occupation of Iraq produced a steady stream of U.S. casualties and the president was unable to prove his allegations that Iraq possessed weapons of mass destruction.

Politicians Manipulate Opinion   Sometimes governmental leaders succeed in manipulating opinion to serve their political image purposes by using public relations techniques. For example, early in the Reagan administration, public opinion polls showed that the public disapproved of Reagan's handling of education by a two-to-one margin, as a result of the administration's cuts in federal aid to education programs. In order to change this negative public perception, the White House launched a "public relations blitz" in 1983, in which President Reagan was sent out to make about twenty-five public appearances around the country to emphasize the themes of educational excellence, merit pay for teachers, and greater discipline in the classroom. After several months, new polling revealed that the public now *supported* Reagan's handling of education by the same two-to-one ratio. It is important to note two facts about this change: First, the three themes Reagan repeatedly emphasized were not under the control of the federal government, because such teacher and classroom policies are set by state and local education leaders; second, the public switch from opposition to support occurred even though the actual policy of cutting educational programs *did not change*.[12]

An example of a Bush administration effort to manipulate public opinion is a series of commercials it produced at taxpayer expense in 2004 to promote the new Medicare prescription drug program. The commercials, prominently featuring the president, were designed to look like actual news stories and were aired in English and Spanish on hundreds of local television stations. Called a "video news release," this type of commercial is designed to give viewers the impression that they are watching a real news story. The presumption is that viewers are more likely to believe news coverage than advertising. Democrats, of course, accused the administration of conducting a partisan propaganda campaign with public funds, but Republicans pointed out that the Clinton administration had engaged in similar practices. Manipulation of opinion can occur, but it is unlikely to succeed when Americans are more interested in, or informed about, an issue. And most efforts to manipulate opinion can be neutralized by sustained counterpublicity.

PRIVATE GROUPS SHAPE OPINION

As the discussion of opinion manipulation shows, the effort to sway public opinion sometimes goes beyond mere persuasion. Not surprisingly, private groups are very interested in shifting public opinion to their benefit. The ideas that become prominent in political life are often developed and spread by powerful economic and political groups searching for issues that will advance their causes. One example is the "right-to-life" issue that has inflamed American politics over the past thirty years.

The notion of right-to-life, whose proponents seek to outlaw abortion and overturn the Supreme Court's *Roe v. Wade* decision, was developed and heavily promoted by conservative politicians who saw the issue of abortion as a means of uniting Catholic and Protestant conservatives and linking both groups to the Republican Party. These politicians convinced Catholic and evangelical Protestant leaders that they shared similar views on the question of abortion, and they worked with religious leaders to focus public attention on the negative issues in the abortion debate. To advance their cause, leaders of the movement sponsored

How Presidents Shape Public Opinion

Because of the importance of public opinion, most presidents have made major efforts both to ascertain the public's views and to promote opinions favorable to themselves and their policies. Franklin Delano Roosevelt was the first president to employ professional pollsters and systematically use newspapers, newsreels, and the radio to attempt to shape public opinion on domestic and foreign policies. FDR's famous "fireside chats" brought him into every American home via the radio.

BOB GORRELL
Courtesy Richmond Times-Dispatch/
Copley News Service

America's two most recent presidents, Bill Clinton and George W. Bush, undertook elaborate White House communications efforts to convince the American people of the wisdom of their policies. As in this political cartoon, Clinton was often criticized for retaining pollsters to chart daily shifts in public opinion.

POLITICS

Though Bush established a communications office that tried to stay in front of the headlines by providing the media with stories and sound bites that would dominate coverage for days, his efforts to shape public opinion haven't always been successful. For example, on May 2, 2003, President Bush staged a large media event on board the *USS Abraham Lincoln* to declare "mission accomplished" and the end of "major combat" in Iraq. Though it was designed to show the president as the central figure in a decisive military victory, some suggest this image may have done the president more political harm than good, as fighting continued for months and then years after the declaration. (See also Chapter 13, Picturing Politics: "The War in Iraq.")

In 2003, Bush signed a ban on "partial birth" abortions while surrounded by a group of men. The controversial nature of the ban and the context within which it was presented to the public alienated moderate voters, particularly moderate women voters.

well-publicized Senate hearings, where testimony, photographs, and other exhibits were presented to illustrate the violent effects of abortion procedures. At the same time, publicists for the movement produced leaflets, articles, books, and films such as *The Silent Scream* to highlight the agony and pain ostensibly felt by the "unborn" when they were being aborted. All this underscored the movement's claim that abortion was nothing more or less than the murder of millions of innocent human beings. Finally, Catholic and evangelical Protestant religious leaders were organized to denounce abortion from their church pulpits and, increasingly, from their electronic pulpits on the Christian Broadcasting Network (CBN) and the various other television forums available for religious programming. Religious leaders also organized demonstrations, pickets, and disruptions at abortion clinics throughout the nation.[13] Abortion rights remains a potent issue; it even influenced the debate over health care reform.

Measuring Public Opinion Is Crucial to Understanding What It Is

public opinion polls scientific instruments for measuring public opinion

It is no secret that politicians and public officials make extensive use of **public opinion polls** to help them decide whether to run for office, what policies to support, how to vote on important legislation, and what types of appeals to make in their campaigns. President Lyndon Johnson was famous for carrying the latest Gallup and Roper poll results in his pocket, and it is widely believed that he began to withdraw from politics because the polls reported losses in public support. All recent presidents and other major political figures have worked closely with polls and pollsters.

PUBLIC OPINION SURVEYS ARE VERY ACCURATE IF DONE PROPERLY

sample a small group selected by researchers to represent the most important characteristics of an entire population

random sampling a method of measuring popular opinion whereby a small group of people, randomly selected from the population as a whole, may be considered representative, as long as every person had an equal chance of being picked

probability sampling a method used by pollsters to select a sample in which every individual in the population has an equal probability of being selected as a respondent so that the correct weight can be given to all segments of the population

The population in which pollsters are interested is usually quite large. To conduct their polls they first choose a **sample** of the total population. The selection of this sample is important. Above all, it must be representative. To be reliable, the views of those in the sample must accurately and proportionately reflect the views of the whole.

Modern polling is based on the principle of **random sampling,** meaning that, even though a national poll sample may consist of only 500 to 1,500 people, it *can* be considered representative of the population as a whole, even though the sample seems very small, as long as each person in the population has an equal chance of being picked.

The most common techniques for choosing such a sample are probability sampling and random digit dialing. In the case of **probability sampling,** the pollster begins with a listing of the population to be surveyed. This listing is called the *sampling frame.* After the members of the population are assigned a number, a table of random numbers or a computerized random selection process is used to select those to be surveyed. This technique is appropriate where the entire population can be identified. For example, all students registered at Texas colleges and universities can be identified from college records and a sample easily drawn. Where the pollster is interested in a national sample of Americans, however, this technique is not feasible, since no complete list of Americans exists.[14] National samples are usually drawn using a technique called **random digit dialing.** A computer random number generator is used to produce a list of as many ten-digit numbers as the pollster deems to be necessary. Since more than 95 percent of American households have telephones, this technique usually results in a random national sample.

The importance of sampling was brought home early in the history of political polling. A 1936 *Literary Digest* poll predicted that Republican presidential candidate Alf Landon would defeat Democrat Franklin D. Roosevelt in that year's presidential election. The actual election, of course, ended in a Roosevelt landslide. The main problem with the survey had been what is called **selection bias** in drawing the sample. The pollsters relied upon telephone directories and automobile registration rosters to produce a sampling frame. During the Great Depression, only wealthier Americans owned telephones and automobiles. Thus, the millions of working-class Americans who constituted Roosevelt's principal base of support were excluded from the sample.

In recent years, the issue of selection bias has been further complicated by the fact that growing numbers of individuals refuse to answer pollsters' questions or use such devices as answering machines and caller ID to screen unwanted callers. If pollsters could be certain that those who responded to their surveys simply reflected the views of those who refused to respond, there would be no problem. Some studies, however, suggest that the views of respondents and nonrespondents can differ, especially along social-class lines. Middle- and upper-middle-class individuals are more likely to be willing to respond to surveys than their working-class counterparts.[15] Adding further to pollsters' problems is the fact that increasing numbers of Americans rely solely on cellular phones, which pollsters are barred from calling. Thus far, nonresponse or other forms of bias have not undermined a major national survey, but the possibility of a future *Literary Digest* fiasco should not be ignored.

Even with reliable sampling procedures, **measurement error** can occur. One frequent source of measurement error is the wording of survey questions. The validity of survey results can be adversely affected by poor question format, faulty ordering of questions, inappropriate vocabulary, ambiguity of questions, or questions with built-in biases. Often, seemingly minor differences in the wording of a question can convey vastly different meanings to respondents and thus produce quite different response patterns. For example, for many years the University of Chicago's National Opinion Research Center has asked respondents whether they think the federal government is spending too much, too little, or about the right amount of money on "assistance for the poor." Answering the question posed this way, about two-thirds of all respondents seem to believe that the government is spending too little. However, the same survey also asks

random digit dialing polls in which respondents are selected at random from a list of ten-digit telephone numbers, with every effort made to avoid bias in the construction of the sample

selection bias polling error that arises when the sample is not representative of the population being studied which create errors in over-representing or underrepresenting some opinions

measurement error failure to identify the true distribution of opinion within a population because of errors such as ambiguous or poorly worded questions

whether the government spends too much, too little, or about the right amount for "welfare." When the word "welfare" is substituted for "assistance for the poor," about half of all respondents indicate that too much is being spent.[16]

In recent years, a new form of bias has been introduced into surveys by the use of a technique called **push polling.** This technique involves asking a respondent a loaded question about a political candidate designed to elicit the response sought by the pollster and, simultaneously, to build a negative image of the opponent. For example, in the 2000 election, the Bush campaign used push polling against opponent John McCain. During the South Carolina primary, the Bush campaign asked voters in a survey whether they approved of McCain's "legislation that proposed the largest tax increase in U.S. history" and McCain's plan to "increase taxes on charitable contributions to churches, colleges, and charities by $20 billion."[17] The purpose of such polling is not simply to solicit opinions but to spread the view that McCain favored these obviously unpopular ideas, in hopes of "pushing" McCain voters away from him. More than one hundred consulting firms across the nation now specialize in push polling.[18]

push polling a polling technique in which the questions are designed to shape the respondent's opinion

Public Opinion Must Matter in a Democracy

In democratic nations, leaders should pay attention to public opinion, and the evidence suggests that indeed they do. There are many instances in which public policy and public opinion do not coincide, but in general the government's actions are consistent with citizens' preferences. One recent study, for example, found that between 1935 and 1979, in about two-thirds of all cases, significant changes in public opinion were followed within one year by changes in government policy consistent with the shift in the popular mood.[19] Other studies have come to similar conclusions about public opinion and government policy at the state level.[20] Some recent studies, however, have suggested that the responsiveness of government to public opinion has been declining. These findings imply that, contrary to popular beliefs, elected leaders don't always pander to the results of public opinion polls, but instead use polling to sell their policy proposals and shape the public's views.[21]

Several factors can contribute to a lack of consistency between opinion and governmental policy. First, the numerical majority on a particular issue may not be as intensely committed to its preference as the adherents of the minority viewpoint. An intensely committed minority may often be more willing to commit its time, energy, efforts, and resources to the affirmation of its opinions than an apathetic, even if large, majority. In the case of firearms, for example, although the proponents of gun control are by a wide margin the majority, most do not regard the issue as one of critical importance to themselves and are not willing to commit much effort to advancing their cause. The opponents of gun control, by contrast, are intensely committed, well organized, and well financed, and as a result are usually able to carry the day.

A second important reason that public policy and public opinion may not coincide has to do with the character and structure of the American system of government. The framers of the American Constitution, as we saw in chapter 2, sought to create a system of government that was based upon popular consent but that did not invariably and automatically translate shifting popular sentiments into public policies. As a result, the American governmental process includes arrangements such as an appointed judiciary that can produce policy decisions that may run contrary to prevailing popular sentiment—at least for a time.

The Media Must Also Matter in a Democracy

It is impossible to imagine democratic politics without a vigorous media. The public, and therefore public opinion, depend on the news media to publicize and assess the claims of political candidates. We depend on the media to examine government policies and programs and to reveal wrongdoing on the part of government agencies and public officials. Without the information provided by the media, the public could not possibly know enough to play any role in national politics. Freedom of the press definitely belongs in the First Amendment as one of the first principles of democratic government.

Attempts to silence or discredit the opposition press have a long history in America. The infamous Alien and Sedition Acts of 1798 were enacted by the Federalists in an attempt to silence the Republican press. In more recent times, during the McCarthy era of the 1950s, right-wing politicians used charges of communist infiltration to intimidate the liberal news media. During President Richard Nixon's administration, the White House attacked its critics in the media by threatening to take action to bar the television networks from owning local affiliates, as well as by illegally wiretapping the phones of government officials suspected of leaking information to the press. In the early 1980s, conservative groups financed a series of libel suits against CBS News, *Time* magazine, and other media organizations in an attempt to discourage them from publicizing material critical of Reagan administration policies.[22] In 1998, President Clinton's political allies accused the national news media of engaging in tabloid journalism and invading the president's privacy in order to discredit him by publicizing the intimate details of Clinton's sexual relationship with former White House intern Monica Lewinsky. In a similar vein, in October 2003, President George W. Bush accused the media of failing to report American successes in the occupation of Iraq and dwelling on apparent failures of U.S. policy. In 2004, an article by investigative reporter Seymour Hersh in the *New Yorker* along with a story on *60 Minutes 2* revealed that American soldiers had abused Iraqi prisoners in their custody. The story prompted a televised apology from President Bush, congressional hearings, and calls for the resignation of Defense Secretary Donald Rumsfeld. As the abuse scandal widened, it became an issue in the 2004 presidential race. The Bush administration was furious but, as had been the case during previous presidencies, could do little to silence its media critics. In all these instances, attempts to browbeat and intimidate the press failed.

News Coverage Matters Because People Rely on It

Because of the important role the media can play in national politics, it is vitally important to understand the factors that affect media coverage.[23] What accounts for the media's agenda of issues and topics? What explains the character of coverage—why does a politician receive good or bad press? What factors determine the interpretation or "spin" that a particular story will receive? Although a host of minor factors plays a role, three major factors are important: (1) the journalists and others who produce the news; (2) the subjects or topics of the news; and (3) the audience for the news.

JOURNALISTS CAN SHAPE THE NEWS

Media content and news coverage are inevitably affected by the views, ideals, and interests of those who seek out, write, and produce news and other stories. At one time, newspaper publishers exercised a great deal of influence over their papers' news content. Publishers such as William Randolph Hearst and Joseph Pulitzer became political powers through their manipulation of news coverage. Hearst, for example, almost single-handedly pushed the United States into war with Spain in 1898 through his newspapers' relentless coverage of the alleged brutality employed by Spain in its efforts to suppress a rebellion in Cuba, at that time a Spanish colony. The sinking of the American battleship *Maine* in Havana harbor under mysterious circumstances gave Hearst the ammunition he needed to force a reluctant President McKinley to lead the nation into war. Today, few publishers have that kind of power. Most publishers are concerned more with the business operations of their newspapers than with editorial content, although a few continue to impose their interests and tastes on the news. For example, CNN owner Ted Turner was well known for his active promotion of environmental causes, and for pushing the all-news network to do pro-environment news stories. Media mogul Rupert Murdoch, head of the media company called the News Corporation, is widely known for his conservative views, which are reflected in Murdoch-owned media outlets including the *New York Post* and the Fox News channel. Although Fox News's slogan is "fair and balanced," few would disagree that it offers a conservative view of political events, led by such commentators as Bill O'Reilly and Sean Hannity. The head of Fox News is Roger Ailes, who formerly worked as a political media consultant for Republicans, including presidents Richard Nixon, Ronald Reagan, and George H. W. Bush (the father of President George W. Bush).

NEWS SUBJECTS CAN SHAPE THE NEWS

News coverage is also influenced by the individuals or groups who are subjects of the news or whose interests and activities are actual or potential news topics. All politicians, for example, seek to shape or manipulate their media images by cultivating good relations with reporters as well as through news leaks and staged news events. For example, during the lengthy investigation of President Clinton conducted by Special Counsel Kenneth Starr, both the Office of the Special Counsel and the White House frequently leaked information to the press designed to bolster their respective positions in the struggle. Starr admitted speaking to reporters on a not-for-attribution basis about aspects of his investigation of the president. One journalist, Steven Brill, accused a number of prominent reporters of serving as "lap dogs" for the Special Counsel by reporting as fact the information fed to them by Starr.[24] Some politicians become extremely adept image makers—or at least skilled at hiring publicists who are skillful image makers. Indeed, press releases drafted by skillful publicists often become the basis for reporters' stories. A substantial percentage of the news stories published every day were initially drafted by publicists and later rewritten only slightly, if at all, by busy reporters and editors.

Furthermore, political candidates often endeavor to tailor their images for specific audiences. For example, to cultivate a favorable image among younger voters during his 1992 campaign, Clinton made several appearances on MTV, and he continued to grant interviews to MTV after his election. His MTV forays came to an end, however, when he was severely criticized for discussing his preferred type of underwear with members of an MTV audience.

Occasionally, a politician proves incredibly adept at surviving repeated media attacks. Clinton, for example, was able to survive repeated revelations of sexual improprieties, financial irregularities, lying to the public, and illegal campaign fund-raising activities. Clinton and his advisors crafted what the *Washington Post* called a "toolkit" for dealing with potentially damaging media revelations. This toolkit includes techniques such as chiding the press, browbeating reporters, referring inquiries quickly to lawyers who will not comment, and acting quickly to change the agenda. These techniques helped Clinton maintain a favorable public image despite the Lewinsky scandal and even the humiliation of a formal impeachment and trial.

CONSUMERS CAN INFLUENCE NEWS CONTENT

The print and broadcast media are businesses that, in general, seek to show a profit. This means that like any other business, they must cater to the preferences of consumers. This has very important consequences for the content and character of the news media.

Catering to the Upscale Audience   The print and broadcast media and the publishing industry are not only responsive to the interests of consumers generally, but they are particularly responsive to the interests and views of the more "upscale" segments of their audience. The preferences of these audience segments have a profound effect on the content and orientation of the press, of radio and television programming, and of books, especially in the areas of news and public affairs.[25]

Newspapers, magazines, and the broadcast media depend primarily on advertising revenues for their profits. These revenues, in turn, depend on the character and size of the audience that they are able to provide to advertisers for their product displays and promotional efforts. From the perspective of most advertisers and especially those whose products are relatively expensive, the most desirable audiences for their ads and commercials consist of younger, upscale consumers. What makes these individuals an especially desirable consumer audience is, of course, their affluence and their spending habits. Although they represent only a small percentage of the population, individuals under the age of fifty whose family income is in the top 20 percent account for nearly 50 percent of the retail dollars spent on consumer goods in the United States. To reach this audience, advertisers are particularly anxious to promote their products in the periodicals and newspapers and on the radio and television broadcasts that are known or believed to attract upscale patronage.

The Media and Protest   While the media respond most to the upscale audience, groups who cannot afford the services of media consultants and issues managers can publicize their views and interests through protest. Frequently, the media are accused of encouraging protest and even violence as a result of the fact that they are instantly available to cover it, providing protesters with the publicity they crave. Clearly, protest and even violence can be important vehicles for attracting the attention and interest of the media, and thus may provide an opportunity for media attention to groups otherwise lacking the financial or organizational resources to broadcast their views. During the 1960s, for example, the media coverage given to civil rights demonstrators and particularly to the violence that southern law enforcement officers in cities such as Selma and Birmingham directed against peaceful black demonstrators dramatically increased white sympathy for the civil rights cause. This was, of course, one of the chief aims of Dr. Martin Luther King's strategy of nonviolence.[26] In subsequent years, the media turned their attention to antiwar demonstrations and, more recently, to anti-abortion demonstrations, antinuclear demonstrations, and even to acts of international terrorism designed specifically to induce the Western media to publicize the terrorists' causes.

The Media Affect Power Relations in American Politics

The content and character of news and public affairs programming—what the media choose to present and how they present it—can have far-reaching political consequences. Media disclosures can greatly enhance—or fatally damage—the careers of public officials. Media coverage can rally support for—or intensify opposition to—national policies. The media can shape and modify public perceptions of events, issues, and institutions.

THE MEDIA INFLUENCE PUBLIC OPINION THROUGH AGENDA SETTING, PRIMING, AND FRAMING

Many people wrongly assume that the American media has an almost dictatorial power over public opinion—that people believe anything and everything presented in the media. This is obviously false, not only because people get information from many sources, but because people are typically skeptical about what is portrayed in the media. The media do have an effect on opinion, but this occurs through agenda setting, priming, and framing.

Agenda Setting   The media almost never tell people what to think; however, they can shape what people think *about.* This is referred to as **agenda setting.** When the media focus primary attention on a single story, especially when it appears on the front pages of newspapers and as the lead story on network news broadcasts, the public turns more attention to it, thereby elevating its importance, and making it more likely that the government will act. For example, in October 1987, NBC News aired an extensive report on a devastating famine in Ethiopia. Suddenly, major relief efforts were launched, polls showed that African famine relief was now on the minds of many citizens, and political leaders urged that action be taken. As a news producer noted about this sudden outpouring of attention, "This famine has been going on for a long time and nobody cared. Now it's on TV and everybody cares. I guess a picture is worth many words."[27]

More recently, a sudden rise in gasoline prices in the spring of 2004 prompted extensive media scrutiny of oil supplies and national energy policy, causing this issue to become a prominent one in the opinions of many citizens. This example also underscores the fact that media agenda setting is an especially strong force when the stories in the news tie in with citizens' actual experiences—in this case, drivers noticing the sudden rise in the price of gasoline at the pump. In general, if the media are persuaded that an issue is important, this makes a policy response by the government more likely. On the other hand, if an idea or issue loses media appeal, the likelihood that the government will respond is reduced. National health insurance and health care reform received considerable media attention in the 1970s, all but disappeared during the 1980s, and then became a major topic again after 1992. Sometimes, political campaigns can elevate issues, prompting agenda setting in the media. For example, Ross Perot's 1992 presidential campaign focused heavily on deficit spending and the ballooning national debt. The media gave these topics extensive coverage, prompting more Americans to think of them as a top priority.

Priming   Priming refers to the criteria people rely on to make judgments or form opinions about events or people. If the criteria are positive, people are likely to have a positive view of the issue or person, but if negative, the result may be the opposite.

During Jimmy Carter's presidency, for example, Iranian revolutionaries took over the American embassy and held about fifty Americans hostage

agenda setting the power of the media to bring public attention to particular issues and problems

priming preparing the public to take a particular view of an event or political actor

throughout 1980. At first, America paid little attention to the takeover, but as the months wore on, and Carter failed to win release of the hostages, this event came to be tied closely to his presidency. By the time of the 1980 election, Carter's presidency had come to be defined by his inability to resolve the situation, because of the extensive and prolonged media coverage given to the hostage situation, and because of the close link established in the media between the crisis and Carter. Carter's defeat in 1980 to Ronald Reagan occurred at least in part because of this negative priming-induced link.

To take another example, during 1998 and 1999, a bitter struggle over priming played itself out in the news media over how citizens judged President Clinton during the Lewinsky scandal and ensuing impeachment attempt. Clinton's critics sought to portray and define Clinton in the media as an immoral person who had an affair with a young woman, who lied about it under oath, and who was therefore unfit to serve as president. Clinton's supporters urged the public to judge him by his performance as president, noting that Clinton had been an effective president, that the economy was in good shape, and unemployment and inflation were low; they also argued that Clinton's private behavior, though wrong, should not have been a basis for judging him politically. Ultimately, polls showed that most Americans agreed with the pro-Clinton priming and therefore opposed his removal from office. This lack of public support for impeachment was a key reason for Congress's failure to remove him.[28]

framing the power of the media to influence how events and issues are interpreted

Framing   A third source of media influence over opinion, known as **framing,** is their ability to influence how the American people interpret political events and issues. For example, during the 1995–96 struggle between President Clinton and congressional Republicans over the nation's budget—a struggle that led to several partial shutdowns of the federal government—the media's interpretation of events forced the Republicans to back down and agree to a budget on Clinton's terms. At the beginning of the crisis, congressional Republicans, led by then House Speaker Newt Gingrich, were confident that they could compel Clinton to accept their budget, which called for substantial cuts in domestic social programs. Republicans calculated that Clinton would fear being blamed for lengthy government shutdowns and would quickly accede to their demands, and that once Americans saw that life went on with government agencies closed, they would support the Republicans in asserting that the United States could get along with less government.

For the most part, however, the media did not cooperate with the GOP's plans. Gingrich, who was generally portrayed as the villain who caused the crisis, came to be called the "Gin*grinch*" who stole Christmas from the children of hundreds of thousands of federal workers. Rather than suggest that the shutdown demonstrated that America could carry on with less government, media accounts focused on the difficulties encountered by Washington tourists unable to visit the capital's monuments, museums, and galleries. The woes of American travelers whose passports were delayed were given considerable attention. Thus, the "dominant frame" became the hardship and disruption caused by the Republicans. The GOP's "competing frame" was dismissed.[29]

The media also have a good deal of power to shape popular perceptions of politicians and political leaders. Most citizens will never meet Bill Clinton or Al Gore or George W. Bush. Popular perceptions and evaluations of these individuals are often based solely on their media images. Obviously, through public relations and other techniques, politicians seek to cultivate favorable media images. But the media have a good deal of discretion over how individuals are portrayed or how they are allowed to portray themselves.

In the case of political candidates, the media have considerable influence over whether or not a particular individual will receive public attention, whether or not a particular individual will be taken seriously as a viable contender, and whether the public will perceive a candidate's performance favorably. Thus, if the media find a candidate interesting, they may treat him or her as a serious contender even though the facts of the matter seem to suggest otherwise. In a similar vein, the media may declare that a candidate has "momentum," a mythical property that the media confer on candidates they admire. Momentum has no substantive meaning—it is simply a media prediction that a particular candidate will do even better in the future than in the past. Such media prophecies can become self-fulfilling as contributors and supporters jump on the bandwagon of the candidate possessing this "momentum."

Media frames were quite important during the 2000 election. Early in the campaign, the national media presented Bush as lacking in intelligence and Gore as somewhat dishonest. Many stories reinforced these characterizations. For example, when Bush responded to a question about his favorite book by naming a well-known children's book, *The Very Hungry Caterpillar,* news accounts suggested that the book was one of his current favorites.[30] As for Gore, the media frequently played up what it deemed his tendency to exaggerate with stories poking fun at his claims of having worked on a farm in his youth and his contention that he played a role in the development of the Internet. These media frames helped to shape voters' perceptions of the two candidates. Strikingly, in one instance, a media frame shaped a candidate's perception of himself. After the first presidential debate, the news media presented Gore as overly aggressive. Not only did the public accept this characterization, but Gore himself responded to the image presented by the media by completely shifting his behavior in the second debate. While he had been extremely critical of Bush in their first encounter, Gore went out of his way to praise Bush during their second meeting.[31] In this case, a media frame affected the participants as much as the viewers.

The media's power to shape images is not absolute. Throughout the last decade, politicians implemented new techniques for communicating with the public and shaping their own images. For instance, Clinton pioneered the use of town meetings and television entertainment programs as means for communicating directly with voters in the 1992 election. During the 2000 presidential race between Bush and Gore, both candidates made use of town meetings, as well as talk shows and entertainment programs such as *The Oprah Winfrey Show, The Tonight Show with Jay Leno,* and *Saturday Night Live,* to reach mass audiences.

| Table 5.3 | Learning while Laughing |

LEARN ABOUT CAMPAIGN FROM . . .	18–29 %	30–49 %	50–64 %	65+ %
Comedy shows*				
Regularly	21	6	5	2
Sometimes	29	21	9	9
Late Night TV**				
Regularly	13	7	7	9
Sometimes	31	20	8	14
Number of cases	(276)	(596)	(343)	(278)

Comedy shows are becoming important sources of news, especially for the young
*Like *Saturday Night Live* or *The Daily Show*
**Like Jay Leno or David Letterman
SOURCE: Pew Research Center, *Cable and Internet Loom large in Fragmented Political News Universe*, January 11, 2004, p. 8.

During a town meeting, talk show, or entertainment program, politicians are free to craft their own images without interference from journalists.

As the information in Table 5.3 shows, exposure on TV comedy shows has taken on even greater importance, especially among young viewers. Among eighteen- to twenty-nine-year-olds, an astonishing 50 percent said in 2004 that they learned about political campaigns "regularly" or "sometimes" from comedy shows such as *Saturday Night Live* or *The Daily Show*.

THE INTERNET'S IMPACT ON POLITICS IS GROWING

In 2000, only 9 percent of Americans reported that they regularly learned information about political campaigns on the Internet. By 2004, that number had risen to 13 percent. Yet reliance on the Internet is higher for younger voters. Among those aged eighteen to twenty-nine, 20 percent reported regular reliance on the Internet, a figure that will only increase in the years to come.[32]

Political movements have increasingly used the Internet to advance their causes. In 1998, two liberal Silicon Valley entrepreneurs founded MoveOn.org, a Web site that worked to defend President Clinton from impeachment charges. In 2001, it organized a peace campaign to oppose military reactions to the 9/11 terrorist attacks. In 2003 and 2004, it criticized the American invasion of Iraq, opposed George W. Bush's reelection, and supported other liberal causes, using its site to raise money, organize letter-writing campaigns, gather petition signatures, and organize meetings around the country in support of its causes.

Among the most effective users of the Internet was the presidential campaign of former Vermont governor Howard Dean, a Democratic candidate who enlisted hundreds of friendly "bloggers" (people who maintain on-line Web logs) to organize pro-Dean meetings around the country, spread Dean campaign messages, coordinate nine hundred pro-Dean groups, and raise tens of millions of dollars—almost all of it in small donations, and more than any other Democratic presidential candidate at that early stage of the campaign season.[33] Even though Dean lost the presidential nomination to Massachusetts senator John Kerry, the Dean campaign's shrewd use of the Internet showed the effectiveness of this medium.

MEDIA BIAS CAN BE IDEOLOGICAL OR INSTITUTIONAL

Charges that the media are biased for or against public officials, candidates, or issues, are commonplace. While bias certainly exists, many of these claims disguise the simple fact that people do not like some of the news they hear. For example, many who oppose gun control argue that the media are pro–gun control. According to conservative media critic Jonah Goldberg, "there are few things they [reporters] hate more than guns." This attitude is "so prevalent and so obvious," according to Goldberg, that the media are simply incapable of being objective on the issue.[34] Yet another media critic, Jeff Cohen, has argued exactly the opposite—that the "gun lobby," dominated by the National Rifle Association, has "dominated the terms of the media debate on gun control." To Cohen, the media has shown "bias toward the NRA's view of the Second Amendment," even though the courts have never supported the NRA view that the "right to bear arms" supports individual gun ownership.[35]

Regardless of whether the media are biased for or against gun control, it is certainly true that much of the recent reporting on gun issues has resulted from sensational crimes involving guns, such as the shooting at Columbine High School in Colorado in April 1999, when fourteen students and one teacher died in a shooting spree. By the very nature of the story, it is inevitable that many will consider guns to be part of the problem, no matter what kind of "bias" the reporters do or do not have.

The Institutional Bias of the Media   Some analysts have argued that the biggest bias in reporting is not liberal or conservative at all, but rather is either for or against the institutions of government. The charge of bias in favor of the government argues that reporters rely for most of their information on government sources, which are naturally self-serving. During the Persian Gulf War of 1990–91, for example, most stories of the war came from the government's military sources, which gave a far more rosy and sanitized picture of the war than what emerged later. According to media expert Doris Graber, successful military actions were shown, but not the mistakes and failures, nor pictures of the dead and wounded.[36] The American military told the press that all Iraqi airfields had been destroyed; ten days later, it was revealed that 65 percent of them were still

PICTURING

Is the Media Biased?

Compared to the election of 2000, a higher percentage of both Republican and Democratic voters felt that campaign coverage leading up to the 2004 election was biased. Not surprisingly, Democrats felt that the news had a stronger Republican bias, while Republicans felt it had a stronger Democratic bias.

Fox News Channel, with its motto "Fair and Balanced," has constantly come under attack by Democrats who see it as a Republican propaganda machine. Bill O'Reilly, host of *The O'Reilly Factor*, is one of Fox News's most controversial personalities.

POLITICS

Some politicians believe that entertainment and "soft interview" programs give them excellent exposure without subjecting them to the difficult questions and commentary they often face in press conferences and news shows. During his 2000 presidential campaign, Vice President Al Gore appeared on *The Oprah Winfrey Show.*

Comedy Central's *The Daily Show with Jon Stewart* is a mock news program that has become one of the most popular shows on television, especially among younger voters. One of the show's main targets is the mainstream news media.

working. The military bragged that American Patriot missiles had shot down many Iraqi Scud missiles; ultimately, the Pentagon was unable to confirm a single instance when a Patriot actually hit a Scud.[37] This pattern has been true in every modern war, even Vietnam.

War aside, government reports, presidential and congressional statements, and other government actions compose the bulk of daily domestic and foreign policy reporting. This adds up to a bias in favor of whoever is running the government, as does the huge effort made by every modern president, and other top governmental leaders, to provide a positive public relations "spin" on what they do.[38] In addition, the broadcast media—radio and television—are regulated by the Federal Communications Commission (FCC), an independent regulatory agency established in 1934 to license and regulate all broadcasting. While the FCC is not a "Big Brother" agency monitoring every transmission, it does have the power to withdraw the operating licenses of broadcasters as a form of "performance control."[39]

In opposition to this is the view that the press is biased against the government. From the muckraking tradition during the Progressive Era in the early 1900s, to critical coverage of the Vietnam War in the late 1960s, to the *Washington Post*'s investigation of the Watergate scandal in the early 1970s, to the subsequent rise of more aggressive, **adversarial journalism** and investigative reporting, as seen in such popular investigative TV programs as *60 Minutes* and *20/20,* reporters seem to relish finding scandal and wrongdoing in government. To some, reporters are so anxious to report what is wrong in government and politics that they neglect telling positive stories about our political system, thereby contributing to the general cynicism many Americans feel toward their government today. Another element of this emerges from research which has shown that reporters have a strong bias against incumbent presidents, regardless of whether they are Republicans or Democrats, liberals or conservatives. According to such researchers as Michael Robinson, Margaret Sheehan, and Thomas Patterson, reporters will "go after" whoever is in charge, regardless of party or ideology. Reporters who land a big corruption story are rewarded in their profession, in the way *Washington Post* Watergate reporters Bob Woodward and Carl Bernstein became heroes for their early reporting of Watergate.[40]

Assessing these views, one can find some support for all of them. But in order for any charge of bias in reporting to stick, one must show that the bias actually produces biased reporting. That case has been made most strongly by those who say there is an institutional bias.

adversarial journalism an aggressive form of investigative journalism that attempts to expose and antagonize the status quo

Public Opinion, Media, and Democracy Are Closely Linked

We have seen throughout this chapter that the link between public opinion and the government is complicated. Yes, the government does follow the wishes of the public, but the public's opinions are also shaped by the government, and by the messages and information people receive from the media. If every citizen worked diligently to be fully informed about the issues of the day and the actions of our political leaders, and if everyone paid great attention to news from multiple media outlets, then the government would surely be highly responsive to the wishes of the people. But this is not very realistic, because many people simply take no interest in politics, even though political decisions directly affect virtually every aspect of their lives. This means that those people who do pay some attention to politics, who do follow the news in newspapers, on television, through magazines, and on the Internet, and who do express their views, are able to exert a considerable influence on the political system.

This is both the opportunity and the paradox of the relationship between the citizen and the government. People who are well informed, interested, and willing to act on their beliefs may be able to score political victories, even if the public at large holds a different view. On the other hand, when the public as a whole is aroused by a tragedy, a scandal, a crisis, or a national election, the government is much more likely to follow the public's will. The media's role in this process is vital because the information they provide, and the form in which they present it, may be decisive in shaping how people think about an issue or problem.

Summary

Americans disagree on many issues, based on their backgrounds, upbringing, and social circumstances, but they do share some fundamental values, including beliefs in liberty, equality, and democracy. Governmental leaders and private interest groups try to shape public opinion in order to advance their goals. While they may succeed at times in turning opinion a certain way, at other times the public will turns the course of governmental action.

Central to the interaction between public opinion and the government is the media. Thanks to the First Amendment's protection of freedom of press, the American media are among the most free of any nation. The media play a critical role in setting the national political agenda—that is, shaping the key issues and ideas that are the focus of American politics. Over the past century, the media have helped to nationalize American politics and to dramatize key issues and struggles between opposing political leaders. Factors of the news profession, including the impact of journalistic biases, continue to shape the content of news.

For Further Reading

Ansolabehere, Stephen, and Shanto Iyengar. *Going Negative: How Attack Ads Shrink and Polarize the Electorate.* New York: Free Press, 1995.

Bagdikian, Ben. *The Media Monopoly,* 4th ed. Boston: Beacon, 1992.

Erikson, Robert S., Norman Luttbeg, and Kent Tedin. *American Public Opinion: Its Origins, Content and Impact,* 5th ed. Boston: Allyn and Bacon, 1994.

Gallup, George. *The Pulse of Democracy.* New York: Simon and Schuster, 1940.

Ginsberg, Benjamin. *The Captive Public: How Mass Opinion Promotes State Power.* New York: Basic Books, 1986.

Graber, Doris. *Mass Media and American Politics,* 4th ed. Washington, DC: Congressional Quarterly Press, 1992.

Herbst, Susan. *Numbered Voices: How Opinion Polling Has Shaped American Politics.* Chicago: University of Chicago Press, 1993.

Key, V. O. *Public Opinion and American Democracy.* New York: Knopf, 1961.

Lippman, Walter. *Public Opinion.* New York: Harcourt, Brace, 1922.

Page, Benjamin I., and Robert Y. Shapiro. *The Rational Public: Fifty Years of Trends in Americans' Policy Preferences.* Chicago: University of Chicago Press, 1992.

Schuman, Howard, Charlotte Steeh, and Lawrence Bobo. *Racial Attitudes in America.* Cambridge, MA: Harvard University Press, 1990.

Spitzer, Robert J., ed. *Media and Public Policy.* Westport, CT: Praeger, 1993.

Study Outline

Fundamental Values Shape Our Opinions

1. Although Americans have many political differences, they share a common set of values, including liberty, equality of opportunity, and democracy.
2. Agreement on fundamental political values is probably more widespread in the United States than anywhere else in the Western world.
3. Often for reasons associated with demographics, Americans do differ widely with one another on a variety of issues.
4. Most people acquire their initial orientation to politics from their families.
5. Membership in both voluntary and involuntary social groups can affect an individual's political values through personal experience, the influence of group leaders, and recognition of political interests.
6. One's level of education is an important factor in shaping political beliefs.
7. Conditions under which individuals and groups are recruited into political life also shape political orientations.
8. Many Americans describe themselves as either liberal or conservative in political orientation.
9. Although ideologies shape political opinions, they seldom fully determine one's views.
10. Political opinions are influenced by an individual's underlying values, knowledge of political issues, and external forces such as the government, private groups, and the media.

Measuring Public Opinion Is Crucial to Understanding What It Is

1. In order to construct public opinion from surveys, a polling sample must be large and the views of those in the sample must accurately and proportionately reflect the views of the whole.

Public Opinion Must Matter in a Democracy

1. Government policies in the United States are generally consistent with popular preferences. There are, however, always some inconsistencies.
2. Disagreements between opinion and policy come about because on some issues, such as gun control, an intensely committed minority can defeat a more apathetic majority. Moreover, the American system of government is not designed to quickly transform changes in opinion into changes in government programs.

The Media Must Also Matter in a Democracy

1. Without the information provided by the media, the public could not possibly know enough to play any role in national politics.

News Coverage Matters Because People Rely on It

1. Media content and news coverage are inevitably affected by the views, ideals, and interests of the journalists who seek out, write, and produce news stories.

2. News coverage is also influenced by the individuals or groups who are subjects of the news or whose interests and activities are actual or potential news topics.

3. Because the print and broadcast media are businesses that generally seek a profit, they must cater to the preferences of consumers.

4. The print and broadcast media, as well as the publishing industry, are particularly responsive to the interests and views of the upscale segments of their audiences.

5. Protest is one way that groups who cannot afford the services of media consultants and issues managers can publicize their views and interests.

The Media Affect Power Relations in American Politics

1. The power of the media stems from several sources, all of which contribute to the media's great influence in setting the political agenda, shaping electoral outcomes, and interpreting events and political results.

2. The political power of the news media has greatly increased in recent years through the growing prominence of investigative reporting.

Public Opinion, Media, and Democracy Are Closely Linked

1. Because the media provide the information citizens need for meaningful participation in the political process, they are essential to democratic government.

Practice Quiz

1. The term *public opinion* is used to describe
   a) the collected speeches and writings made by a president during his term in office.
   b) the analysis of events broadcast by news reporters during the evening news.
   c) the beliefs and attitudes that people have about issues.
   d) decisions of the Supreme Court.

2. Variables such as income, education, race, gender, and ethnicity
   a) often create differences of political opinion in America.
   b) have consistently been a challenge to America's core political values.

   c) have little impact on political opinions.
   d) help explain why public opinion polls are so unreliable.

3. Which of the following is an agency of socialization?
   a) the family
   b) social groups
   c) education
   d) all of the above

4. When men and women respond differently to issues of public policy, they are demonstrating an example of
   a) liberalism.
   b) educational differences.
   c) the gender gap.
   d) party politics.

5. The process by which Americans learn political beliefs and values is called
   a) brainwashing.
   b) propaganda.
   c) indoctrination.
   d) political socialization.

6. In addition to one's basic political values, what other two factors influence one's political opinions?
   a) ideology and party identification
   b) political knowledge and the influence of political leaders, private groups, and the media
   c) the gender gap and the education gap
   d) sample size and the bandwagon effect

7. Which of the following is the term used in public opinion polling to denote the small group representing the opinions of the whole population?
   a) control group
   b) sample
   c) micropopulation
   d) respondent

8. Which of the following have an impact on the nature of media coverage of politics?
   a) reporters
   b) political actors
   c) news consumers
   d) all of the above

9. Which of the following is a strategy available to poor people to increase their coverage by the news media?
   a) protest
   b) media consultants
   c) television advertising
   d) newspaper advertising "time sharing"

10. The media's powers to determine what becomes a part of the political discussion and to shape how political events are interpreted by the American people are known as
    a) issue definition and protest power.
    b) agenda setting and framing.
    c) the illusion of saliency and the bandwagon effect.
    d) the equal time rule and the right of rebuttal.

Critical Thinking Questions

1. In the American system of government, public opinion seems to be an important factor in political and governmental decision making. In what ways does the public, through opinion, control its political leaders? In what ways do political leaders control public opinion? What are the positive and negative consequences of governing by popular opinion?

2. If the public receives most of its information about politics from the media, how accurate is its knowledge of government and politics? How does the media itself distort political reality? How do politicians use the media for their own purposes? What are the consequences for American democracy when the electorate is informed through such a filter? How might the quality of political information in America be improved?

Key Terms

adversarial journalism (p. 152)
agenda setting (p. 145)
conservative (p. 131)
democracy (p. 124)
equality of opportunity (p. 124)
framing (p. 146)

liberal (p. 130)
liberty (p. 124)
measurement error (p. 139)
political ideology (p. 124)
political socialization (p. 126)
priming (p. 145)
probability sampling (p. 138)
public opinion (p. 124)

public opinion polls (p. 138)
push polling (p. 140)
random digit dialing (p. 139)
random sampling (p. 138)
sample (p. 138)
selection bias (p. 139)

6 POLITICAL PARTIES AND ELECTIONS

MAIN MESSAGE

Political parties and elections play a key role in uniting citizens and the government, especially at critical moments in American politics.

In modern history, political parties have been the chief points of contact between governments, on the one side, and people in society, on the other. In organized political parties, social forces can gain some control over governmental policies and personnel. Simultaneously, governments often seek to organize and influence important groups in society through political parties. All political parties have this dual character: They are instruments through which citizens and governments attempt to influence one another. In some nations, such as the People's Republic of China, the leading political party serves primarily the interests of the government. In others, such as the United States, political parties force the government to concern itself with the needs of its citizens.

Key Concepts

1. America is one of the few nations in the world with a two-party system.
2. Electoral realignments define the important stages of American history.
3. While political parties are less important to citizens than they once were, they are more important to the organization and functioning of the government than ever.
4. The bases for voter decisions are party, issues, and candidate.
5. Money is the mother's milk of politics.

The idea of political parties was at first met with great suspicion and hostility. In the early years of the Republic, parties were seen as threats to the social order. In his 1796 "Farewell Address," President George Washington warned his countrymen to shun partisan politics:

> Let me warn you in the most solemn manner against the baneful effects of the spirit of party generally. This spirit exists under different shapes in all government, more or less stifled, controlled, or repressed, but in those of the popular form it is seen in its greater rankness and is truly their worst enemy.

Often, those in power viewed the formation of political parties by their opponents as acts of treason that merited severe punishment. Thus, in 1798, the Federalist Party, which controlled the national government, in effect sought to outlaw its Jeffersonian Republican opponents through the infamous Alien and Sedition Acts, which, among other things, made it a crime to publish or say anything critical that might tend to defame or bring into disrepute either the president or the Congress. Under this law, fifteen individuals—including several Republican newspaper editors—were arrested and convicted.[1]

In this chapter, we will see that political parties, operating mostly through elections, provide a vital link between the people and the government. This is especially true when key issues and crises have arisen. Yet the important role of parties and elections is minimized by two factors: First, even though political parties are not viewed with the same kind of hostility today as they were in George Washington's day, hostility toward the parties lingers, coloring the way many Americans view elections; and second, political parties have declined in power and importance in recent years, having been replaced, at least in part, by interest groups and the mass media.

Parties and Elections Have Been Vital to American Politics and Government

political parties organized groups that attempt to influence the government by electing their members to important government offices

Political parties, like interest groups, are organizations seeking influence over government. Ordinarily, they can be distinguished from interest groups on the basis of their orientation. A party seeks to control the entire government by electing its members to office and thereby controlling the government's personnel. Interest groups usually accept government and its personnel as a given and try to influence government policies through them.

POLITICAL PARTIES AROSE FROM THE ELECTORAL PROCESS

Political parties as they are known today developed along with the expansion of suffrage and can be understood only in the context of elections. The two are so intertwined that American parties actually take their structure from the electoral process. The shape of party organization in the United States has followed a simple rule: For every district where an election is held, there should be some kind of party unit. Republicans failed to maintain units in most counties of the southern states between 1900 and 1952; Democrats were similarly unsuccessful in many areas of New England. But for most of the history of the United States, two major parties have had enough of an organized presence to oppose each other in elections in most of the nation's towns, cities, and counties. This makes the American party system one of the oldest political institutions in the history of democracy.

Political parties play a traditionally important role in elections. They recruit candidates to run for office, get their loyal party members out to vote, and work in a variety of ways to promote the causes and issues of the party. In earlier times, the parties had near monopoly control over the electoral process. In recent decades, however, they have lost their monopoly to candidates who decide not to work within the party, to political action committees (PACs) that generate millions of dollars for candidates, and to direct appeals through the media.

PARTIES RECRUIT CANDIDATES

One of the most important but least noticed party activities is the recruitment of candidates for local, state, and national office. Each election year, candidates must be found for thousands of state and local offices as well as congressional seats. Where they do not have an incumbent running for reelection, party leaders attempt to identify strong candidates and to interest them in entering the campaign.

An ideal candidate will have an unblemished record and the capacity to raise enough money to mount a serious campaign. Party leaders are usually not willing to provide financial backing to candidates who are unable to raise substantial funds on their own. For a House seat, this can mean several hundred thousand dollars; for a Senate seat, a serious candidate must be able to raise several million dollars. Often, party leaders have difficulty finding attractive candidates and persuading them to run. Candidate recruitment has become particularly difficult in an era in which **incumbents** (those already in office) are so hard to beat, when political campaigns often involve mudslinging, and when candidates must assume that their personal lives will be intensely scrutinized in the press.[2]

incumbent a candidate running for a position that he or she already holds

PARTIES ORGANIZE NOMINATIONS

Article I, Section 4, of the Constitution makes only a few provisions for elections. It delegates to the states the power to set the "times, places, and manner" of holding elections, even for U.S. senators and representatives. It does, however, reserve to Congress the power to make such laws if it chooses to do so. The Constitution has been amended from time to time to expand the right to participate in elections. Congress has also occasionally passed laws about elections, congressional districting, and campaign practices. But the Constitution and the laws are almost completely silent on nominations, setting only citizenship and age requirements for candidates. The president must be at least thirty-five years of age, a natural-born citizen, and a resident of the United States for fourteen years. A senator must be at least thirty, a U.S. citizen for at least nine years, and a resident of the state he or she represents. A member of the House must be at least twenty-five, a U.S. citizen for seven years, and a resident of the state he or she represents.

nomination the process through which political parties select their candidates for election to public office

Nomination is the process by which a party selects a single candidate to run for each elective office. The nominating process can precede the election by many months, as it does when the many candidates for the presidency are eliminated from consideration through a grueling series of debates and state primaries until there is only one survivor in each party—the party's nominee.

Nomination is the parties' most serious and difficult business. When more than one person aspires to an office, the choice can divide friends and associates. In comparison to such an internal dispute, the electoral campaign against the opposition is almost fun, because there the fight is against the declared adversaries.

PARTIES HELP GET OUT THE VOTE

The actual election period begins immediately after the nominations. Historically, this has been a time of glory for the political parties, whose popular base of support is fully displayed. All the paraphernalia of party committees and all the committee members are activated into local party workforces.

The first step in the electoral process involves voter registration. This aspect of the process takes place all year round. There was a time when party workers were responsible for virtually all of this kind of electoral activity, but they have been supplemented (and in many states virtually supplanted) by civic groups such as the League of Women Voters, unions, and chambers of commerce.

Registered voters then have to decide on election day whether to go to the polling place, stand in line, and actually vote for the various candidates and referenda on the ballot. Political parties, candidates, and campaigning can make a big difference in convincing the voters to vote. In recent years, each of the two parties has developed extensive data files on hundreds of millions of potential voters. The GOP has called its archive "Voter Vault," while the Democratic file has been designated "Demzilla." Democrats claim their files contain the names, addresses, voting preferences, contribution history, ethnic background, and other information on some 165 million Americans. Republican files contain similar data on nearly 200 million individuals. These elaborate data files allow the two parties to bring their search for votes, contributions, and campaign help down to named individuals. Voter mobilization, once an art, has now become a science.

PARTIES FACILITATE VOTER CHOICE

On any general election ballot, there are likely to be only two or three candidacies where the nature of the office and the characteristics and positions of the candidates are well known to voters. But what about the choices for judges, the state comptroller, the state attorney general, and many other elective positions? And what about referenda? This method of making policy choices is being used more and more as a means of direct democracy. A referendum may ask: Should there be a new bond issue for financing the local schools? Should there be a constitutional amendment to increase the number of county judges? In 1996, Californians approved Proposition 201, a referendum that called for an end to most statewide affirmative action programs, including those employed for college admission. Another famous proposition on the 1978 California ballot was a referendum to reduce local property taxes. It started a taxpayer revolt that spread to many other states. By the time it had spread, most voters knew where they stood on the issue. But the typical referendum question is one on which few voters have clear and knowledgeable positions. Parties and campaigns help most by giving information when voters must choose among obscure candidates and vote on unclear referenda.

PARTIES ORGANIZE POWER IN CONGRESS

The ultimate test of the party system is its relationship to and influence on the institutions of government. Congress, in particular, depends more on the party system than is generally recognized. For one thing, power in Congress is organized along party lines. Specifically, the speakership of the House is essentially a party office. All the members of the House take part in the election of the speaker. But the actual selection is made by the **majority party,** that is, the party that holds a majority of seats in the House. (The other party is known as the **minority party.**) When the majority party caucus presents a nominee to the entire House, its choice is then invariably ratified in a straight vote along party lines.

majority party the party that holds the majority of legislative seats in either the House or the Senate

minority party the party that holds a minority of legislative seats in either the House or the Senate

The committee system of both houses of Congress is also a product of the two-party system. Although the rules organizing committees and the rules defining the jurisdiction of each are adopted like ordinary legislation by the whole membership, parties shape all other features of the committees.

The assignment of individual members to committees is a party decision. Each party has a "committee on committees" to make such decisions. Permission to transfer to another committee is also a party decision. Moreover, advancement up the committee ladder toward the chair is a party decision. Since the late nineteenth century, most advancements have been automatic—based upon the length of continual service on the committee. This seniority system has existed only because of the support of the two parties, however, and either party can depart from it by a simple vote.

PRESIDENTS NEED POLITICAL PARTIES

The party that wins the White House is always led, in title anyway, by the president. The president normally depends on fellow party members in Congress to support legislative initiatives. At the same time, members of the party in

PICTURING

The Role of Political Parties in Contemporary Politics

Political parties have traditionally played an important role in elections, although the near stranglehold they once held over the electoral process has diminished in the last four decades. One of the most important but least-noticed party activities is the recruitment of candidates for local, state, and national office.

During the nineteenth century, America's political parties worked hard to mobilize voters, using everything from barbecues to bribes to get out the vote. On a presidential Election Day, thousands of party workers handed out leaflets, knocked on doors, and even provided free transportation to those unable to get to the polls on their own. Today, political parties are not as strong as they were in the nineteenth century, but other groups and organizations endeavor to mobilize voters.

POLITICS

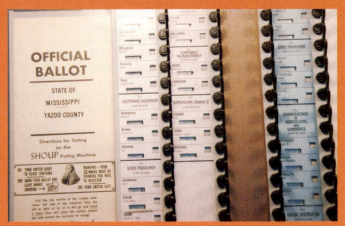

Once in the election booth, voters often face a bewildering array of choices. Parties can provide information to voters, who sometimes must choose among obscure candidates and vote on unclear referenda.

Political parties are essential to the process of making policy. Within the government, parties are coalitions of individuals with shared interests who support one another's programs. As a result, party leaders have tremendous agenda-setting power in Congress. For example, during the 104th Congress, House Speaker Newt Gingrich was able to maintain nearly unanimous support among Republican party members for the GOP's "Contract with America."

The president also depends on fellow party members in Congress to support legislative initiatives. Without the support of his party, the president would be compelled to undertake the daunting and probably impossible task of forming a new coalition for every individual policy proposal. During his presidency, George W. Bush has united his party around core Republican issues such as tax cuts and military strength.

Congress hope that the president's programs and personal prestige will help them raise campaign funds and secure reelection.

America Is One of the Few Nations with a Two-Party System

two-party system a political system in which only two parties have a realistic opportunity to compete effectively for control

Although George Washington and many other leaders of his time deplored partisan politics, the **two-party system** emerged early in the history of the new Republic. Beginning with the Federalists and the Jeffersonian Republicans in the 1790s, two major parties would dominate national politics, although which particular two parties they were would change with the times and issues. This two-party system has culminated, after a series of historical collisions, in today's Democrats and Republicans (see Figure 6.1). Each has had an important place in U.S. history.

The Democrats   When the Jeffersonian Party splintered in 1824, Andrew Jackson emerged as the leader of one of its four factions. In 1830, Jackson's group became the Democratic Party. This new party had the strongest national organization of its time and presented itself as the party of the common man. Jacksonians supported reductions in the price of public lands and a policy of cheaper money and credit. Laborers, immigrants, and settlers west of the Alleghenies were quickly attracted to this new party.

From 1828, when Jackson was elected president, to 1860, the Democratic Party was the dominant force in American politics. For all but eight of those years, the Democrats held the White House. In addition, a Democratic majority controlled the Senate for twenty-six years and the House for twenty-four years during the same time period. These nineteenth-century Democrats emphasized the importance of interpreting the Constitution literally, upholding states' rights, and limiting federal spending.

In 1860, the issue of slavery split the Democrats along geographic lines. In the South, many Democrats served in the Confederate government. In the North, one faction of the party (the Copperheads) opposed the war and advocated negotiating a peace with the South. Thus, for years after the war, Republicans denounced the Democrats as the "party of treason."

The Democratic Party was not fully able to regain its political strength until the Great Depression. In 1933, Democrat Franklin D. Roosevelt entered the White House and the Democrats won control of Congress as well. Roosevelt's New Deal coalition, composed of Catholics, Jews, blacks, farmers, residents of urban areas, intellectuals, and members of organized labor, dominated American politics until the 1970s and served as the basis for the party's expansion of federal power and efforts to remedy social problems.

The Democrats were never fully united. In Congress, southern Democrats often aligned with Republicans in the "conservative coalition" rather than with members of their own party. But the Democratic Party remained

How the Party System Evolved

Figure 6.1

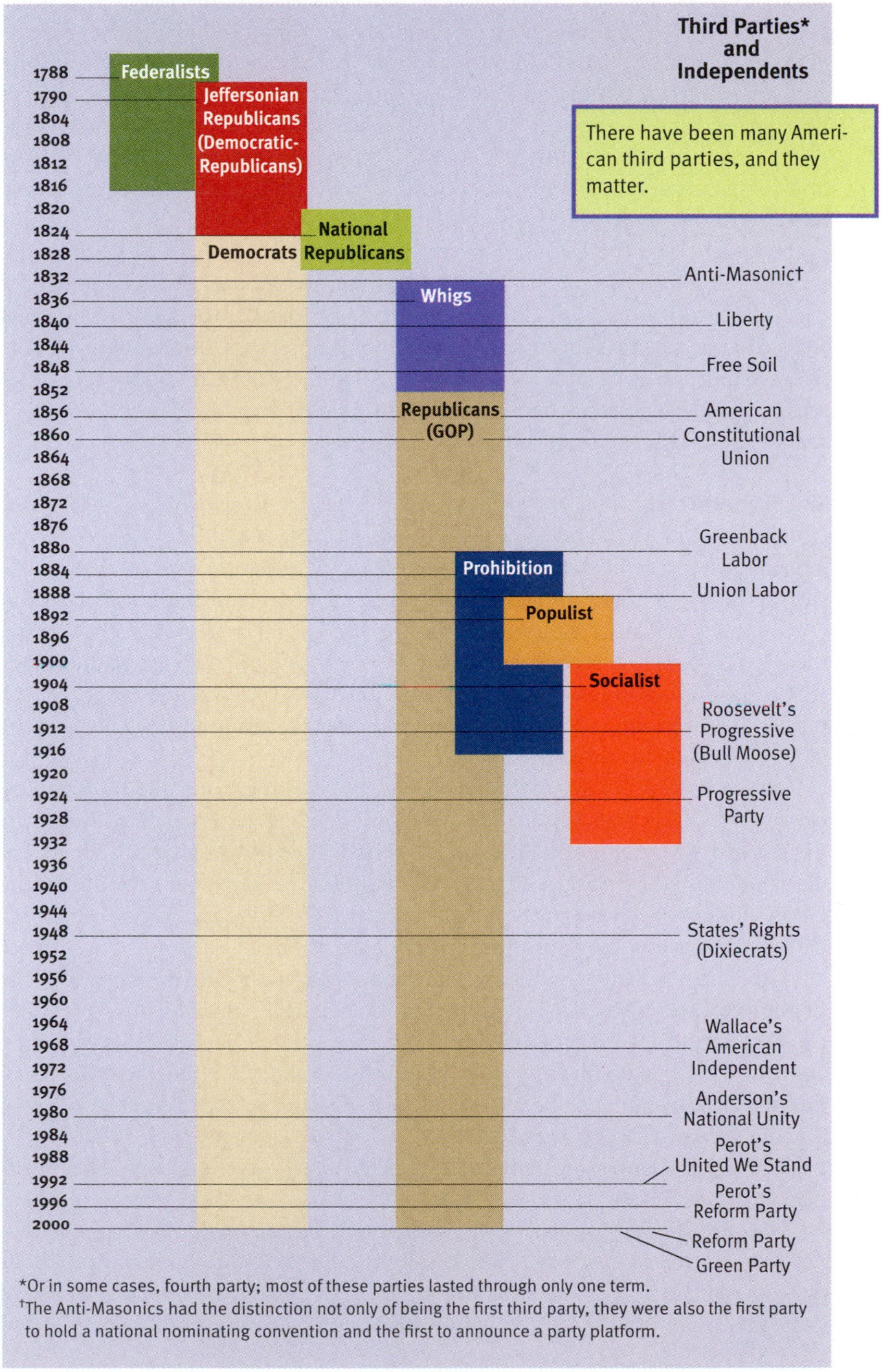

Third Parties*
and
Independents

> There have been many American third parties, and they matter.

1788	Federalists	
1790		
1804	Jeffersonian Republicans (Democratic-Republicans)	
1808		
1812		
1816		
1820		
1824		National Republicans
1828	Democrats	
1832		Anti-Masonic†
1836	Whigs	
1840		Liberty
1844		
1848		Free Soil
1852		
1856	Republicans (GOP)	American
1860		Constitutional Union
1864		
1868		
1872		
1876		
1880		Greenback Labor
1884	Prohibition	
1888		Union Labor
1892		Populist
1896		
1900		
1904		Socialist
1908		
1912		Roosevelt's Progressive (Bull Moose)
1916		
1920		
1924		Progressive Party
1928		
1932		
1936		
1940		
1944		
1948		States' Rights (Dixiecrats)
1952		
1956		
1960		
1964		Wallace's American Independent
1968		
1972		
1976		Anderson's National Unity
1980		
1984		Perot's United We Stand
1988		
1992		Perot's Reform Party
1996		Reform Party
2000		Green Party

*Or in some cases, fourth party; most of these parties lasted through only one term.
†The Anti-Masonics had the distinction not only of being the first third party, they were also the first party to hold a national nominating convention and the first to announce a party platform.

America's majority party, usually controlling both Congress and the White House, for nearly four decades after 1932. By the 1980s, the Democratic coalition faced serious problems. The once solidly Democratic South often voted for the Republicans, along with many white, blue-collar northern voters. On the other hand, the Democrats increased their strength among African American voters and women. The Democrats maintained a strong base in the bureaucracies of the federal government and the states, in labor unions, and in the not-for-profit sector of the economy. During the 1980s and 1990s, moderate Democrats were able to take control of the party nominating process and sought to broaden middle-class support for the Democrats. This helped the Democrats elect a president in 1992. In 1994, however, growing Republican strength in the South led to the loss of the Democrats' control of both houses of Congress for the first time since 1952. Democrats were unable to recapture control of either house of Congress until 2001, when Senator Jim Jeffords decided to leave the Republican party to become an Independent (caucusing with the Democrats), thereby giving the Democrats a slight (fifty to forty-nine) advantage.

The Republicans   The 1854 Kansas-Nebraska Act overturned the Missouri Compromise of 1820 and the Compromise of 1850, which had barred the expansion of slavery in the American territories. The Kansas-Nebraska Act gave each territory the right to decide whether or not to permit slavery. Opposition to this policy galvanized antislavery groups and led them to create a new party, the Republicans. It drew its membership from existing political groups—former Whigs, Know-Nothings, Free Soilers, and antislavery Democrats. In 1856, the party's first presidential candidate, John C. Fremont, won one-third of the popular vote and carried eleven states.

The early Republican platforms appealed to commercial as well as antislavery interests. The Republicans favored homesteading, internal improvements, the construction of a transcontinental railroad, and protective tariffs, as well as the containment of slavery. In 1858, the Republican Party won control of the House of Representatives; in 1860, the Republican presidential candidate, Abraham Lincoln, was victorious in a four-way race.

For almost seventy-five years after the North's victory in the Civil War, the Republicans were America's dominant political party, especially after 1896. Between 1860 and 1932, Republicans occupied the White House for fifty-six years, controlled the Senate for sixty years, and the House for fifty. During these years, the Republicans came to be closely associated with big business. The party of Lincoln became the party of Wall Street.

The Great Depression ended Republican hegemony, however. The voters held President Herbert Hoover responsible for the economic catastrophe, and by 1936 the party's popularity was so low that Republicans won only eighty-nine seats in the House and seventeen in the Senate. The Republican presidential candidate in 1936, Governor Alfred M. Landon of Kansas, carried only two states. The Republicans won only four presidential elections between 1932 and

1980, and they controlled Congress for only four of those years (1947–49 and 1953–55).

The Republican Party has widened its appeal over the last four decades. Groups previously associated with the Democratic Party—particularly white, blue-collar workers and white southern Democrats—have been increasingly attracted to Republican presidential candidates (for example, Dwight D. Eisenhower, Richard Nixon, Ronald Reagan, George H. W. Bush, and George W. Bush). Yet Republicans generally did not do as well at the state and local levels and, until recently, had little chance of capturing a majority in either the House or the Senate. In 1994, however, the Republican Party finally won a majority in both houses of Congress, in large part because of the party's growing strength in the South. By the end of the 1990s, most state governors were Republicans. The Republicans held a slim advantage in both the House and Senate until Jefford's defection in May 2001, noted previously. In 2002, the Republicans narrowly won control of both houses, giving them full control of both Congress and the presidency for the first time since 1955. The 2004 elections saw modest increases in Republican control of Congress, along with Republican President George W. Bush's re-election.

ELECTORAL ALIGNMENTS AND REALIGNMENTS DEFINE AMERICAN HISTORY

American party history has followed a fascinating and very regular pattern (see Figure 6.2). Typically, the national electoral arena has been dominated by one party for a period of roughly thirty years. At the conclusion of this period, the dominant party has been replaced by a new party in what political scientists call an **electoral realignment.** The realignment is typically followed by a long period in which the new party is the dominant political force in the United States—not necessarily winning every election but generally maintaining control of the Congress and usually of the White House as well.[3]

Although there are some disputes among scholars about the precise timing of these critical realignments, there is general agreement that at least five have occurred since the founding. The first took place around 1800 when the Jeffersonian Republicans defeated the Federalists and became the dominant force in American politics. The second realignment occurred in about 1828, when the Jacksonian Democrats took control of the White House and the Congress. The third period of realignment centered on 1860. During this period, the newly founded Republican Party led by Abraham Lincoln won power, in the process destroying the Whig Party, which had been one of the nation's two major parties since the 1830s. During the fourth critical period, centered on the election of 1896, the Republicans reasserted their dominance of the national government, which had been weakening since the 1880s. The fifth realignment took place during the period 1932–36, when the Democrats, led by Franklin Delano Roosevelt, took control of the White House and Congress and, despite sporadic interruptions, maintained control of both through the 1960s. Since that time, American party politics has been

electoral realignment the point in history when a new party supplants the ruling party, becoming in turn the dominant political force. In the United States, this has tended to occur roughly every thirty years

Figure 6.2   Electoral Realignments

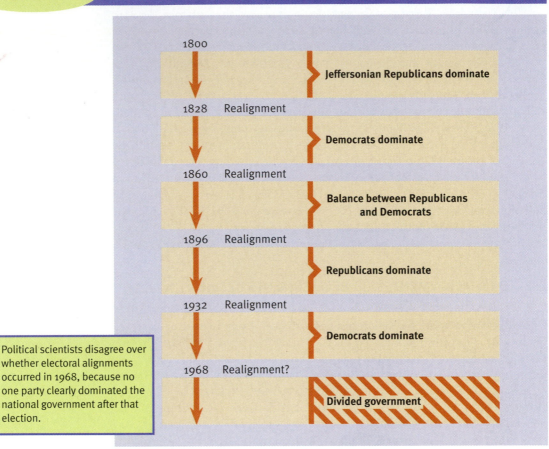

1800

→ Jeffersonian Republicans dominate

1828   Realignment

→ Democrats dominate

1860   Realignment

→ Balance between Republicans and Democrats

1896   Realignment

→ Republicans dominate

1932   Realignment

→ Democrats dominate

1968   Realignment?

→ Divided government

> Political scientists disagree over whether electoral alignments occurred in 1968, because no one party clearly dominated the national government after that election.

divided government the condition in American government wherein the presidency is controlled by one party while the opposing party controls one or both houses of Congress

characterized primarily by **divided government,** wherein the presidency is controlled by one party while the other party controls one or both houses of Congress.

Historically, realignments occur when new issues combined with economic or political crises mobilize new voters and persuade large numbers of voters to reexamine their traditional partisan loyalties and permanently shift their support from one party to another. For example, during the 1850s, the issues of slavery and sectionalism produced divisions within both the Democratic and the Whig parties, ultimately leading to the dissolution of the latter, and the rise of the new antislavery Republicans.

In the election of 1896, Republican candidate William McKinley, emphasizing business, industry, and urban interests, defeated Democrat William Jennings Bryan, who spoke for sectional interests, farmers, and fundamentalism. Republican dominance lasted until 1932.

Such periods of party realignment in American politics have had extremely important institutional and policy results. Realignments occur when new issue concerns coupled with economic or political crises weaken the established political elite and permit new groups of politicians to create coalitions of forces capable of capturing and holding the reins of governmental power. The construction of new governing coalitions during these realigning periods has effected major changes in American governmental institutions and policies. Each period of realignment represents a turning point in American politics. The choices made by the national electorate during these periods have helped shape the course of American political history for a generation.[4]

AMERICAN THIRD PARTIES HAVE ALTERED THE SHAPE OF THE MAJOR PARTIES

Although the United States is said to possess a two-party system, the country has always had more than two parties. Typically, **third parties** in the United States have represented social and economic interests that, for one reason or another, were not given voice by the two major parties.[5] Such parties have had a good deal of influence on ideas and elections in the United States. The Populists, a party centered in the rural areas of the West and Midwest, and the Progressives, spokespeople for the urban middle classes in the late nineteenth and early twentieth centuries, are the most important examples in the past hundred years. More recently, Ross Perot, who ran in 1992 as an independent and in 1996 as the Reform Party's nominee, impressed voters with his folksy style; he garnered almost 19 percent of the votes cast in the 1992 presidential election. Table 6.1 shows a listing of all the parties that offered candidates in one or more states in the presidential elections of 2004, as well as independent candidates who ran. With the exception of Ralph Nader, the third-party and independent candidates together polled only 1.05 million votes. They gained no electoral votes for president, and most of them disappeared immediately after the presidential election. The significance of Table 6.1 is that it demonstrates the large number of third parties running candidates and appealing to voters. Third-party candidacies also arise at the state and local levels. In New York, the Liberal and Conservative parties have been on the ballot for decades. In 1998, Minnesota elected a third-party governor, former professional wrestler Jesse Ventura.

Although the Republican Party was only the third American political party ever to make itself permanent (by replacing the Whigs), other third parties have enjoyed an influence far beyond their electoral size. This was because large parts of their programs were adopted by one or both of the major parties, who sought to appeal to the voters mobilized by the new party, and so to expand their own electoral strength. The Democratic Party, for example, became a great deal more liberal when it adopted most of the Progressive program early in the twentieth century. Many socialists felt that President Franklin Roosevelt's New Deal had

third parties   parties that organize to compete against the two major American political parties

Table 6.1

Parties and Candidates in 2004

In the 2004 presidential election, in addition to the Democratic and Republican nominees, at least fifteen candidates appeared on the ballot in one or more states.

CANDIDATE	PARTY	VOTE TOTAL*	PERCENTAGE OF VOTE
George W. Bush	Republican	58,978,616	51%
John F. Kerry	Democratic	55,384,497	48%
Ralph Nader	Independent	394,578	0%
Michael Badnarik	Libertarian	377,940	0%
Micheal A. Peroutka	Constitution	129,842	0%
David Cobb	Green	105,525	0%
Leonard Peltier	Peace and Freedom	21,616	0%
Walter F. Brown	Independent	10,258	0%
James Harris	Socialist Workers	6,699	0%
Roger Calero	Socialist Workers	5,274	0%
Thomas J. Harens	Other	2,395	0%
Bill Van Auken	Independent	2,078	0%
Gene Amondson	Libertarian	1,896	0%
John Parker	Liberty Union	1,159	0%
Charles Jay	Personal Choice	867	0%
Stanford "Andy" E. Andress	Unaffiliated	720	0%
Earl F. Dodge	Prohibition	122	0%
None of the above	—	3,646	0%

*With 99 percent of votes tallied.
SOURCE: www.washingtonpost.com/wp-srv/elections/2004/page/295001 (Accessed 11/8/04).

single-member district an electorate that is allowed to select only one representative from each district; the normal method of representation in the United States

multiple-member district an electorate that selects all candidates at large from the whole district; each voter is given the number of votes equivalent to the number of seats to be filled

plurality system a type of electoral system in which, to win a seat in the parliament or other representative body, a candidate need only receive the most votes in the election, not necessarily a majority of the votes cast

proportional representation a multiple-member district system that allows each political party representation in proportion to its percentage of the total vote

adopted most of their party's program, including old-age pensions, unemployment compensation, an agricultural marketing program, and laws guaranteeing workers the right to organize into unions.

As many scholars have pointed out, third-party prospects for winning elections are hampered by America's **single-member-district** plurality election system. In many other nations, several individuals can be elected to represent each legislative district. This is called a system of **multiple-member districts.** With this type of system, the candidates of weaker parties have a better chance of winning at least some seats. For their part, voters are less concerned about wasting ballots and usually more willing to support minor-party candidates.

Reinforcing the effects of the single-member district, the **plurality system** of voting generally has the effect of setting what could be called a high threshold for victory. To win a plurality race, candidates usually must secure many more votes than they would need under most European systems of **proportional representation.** For example, to win an American plurality election in a single-member district where there are only two candidates, a politician must win more than 50 percent of the votes cast. To win a seat from a European multiple-member district under proportional rules, a candidate may need to win only 15 or 20 percent of the votes cast. This high American threshold discourages minor parties and encourages the various political factions that might otherwise form minor parties to minimize their differences and remain within the major-party coalitions.[6]

GROUP AFFILIATIONS ARE BASED ON VOTERS' PSYCHOLOGICAL TIES TO ONE OF THE PARTIES

The Democratic and Republican parties are America's only national parties made up of millions of rank-and-file members who develop **party identification** with one of the political parties. Although the strength of partisan ties in the United States has declined in recent years, most Americans continue to identify with either the Republican Party or the Democratic Party (see Figure 6.3). The two parties do not draw equal support from members of every social stratum, however. When we refer to the Democratic or Republican "coalition," we mean the groups that generally support one or the other party. In the United States today, a variety of group characteristics are associated with party identification. These include race and ethnicity, gender, religion, class, ideology, and region.

party identification an individual voter's psychological ties to one party or another

---

Americans' Party Identification, 1952–2002

Figure 6.3

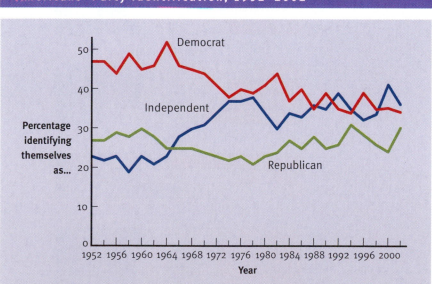

SOURCES: Harold W. Stanley and Richard G. Niemi, *Vital Statistics on American Politics, 1999–2000* [Washington, DC: Congressional Quarterly Press, 2000], p. 113, and *National Election Studies Guide to Public Opinion and Political Behavior,* at www.umich.edu/~nes/nesguilde/nesguide.htm.

Figure 6.4 indicates the relationship between party identification and a number of social criteria. Race, religion, and income seem to have the greatest influence on Americans' party affiliations. None of these social characteristics is inevitably linked to partisan identification, however. There are black Republicans, southern white Democrats, Jewish Republicans, and even an occasional conservative Democrat. The general party identifications just discussed are

---

Figure 6.4 — **Party Identification by Social Groups, 2004**

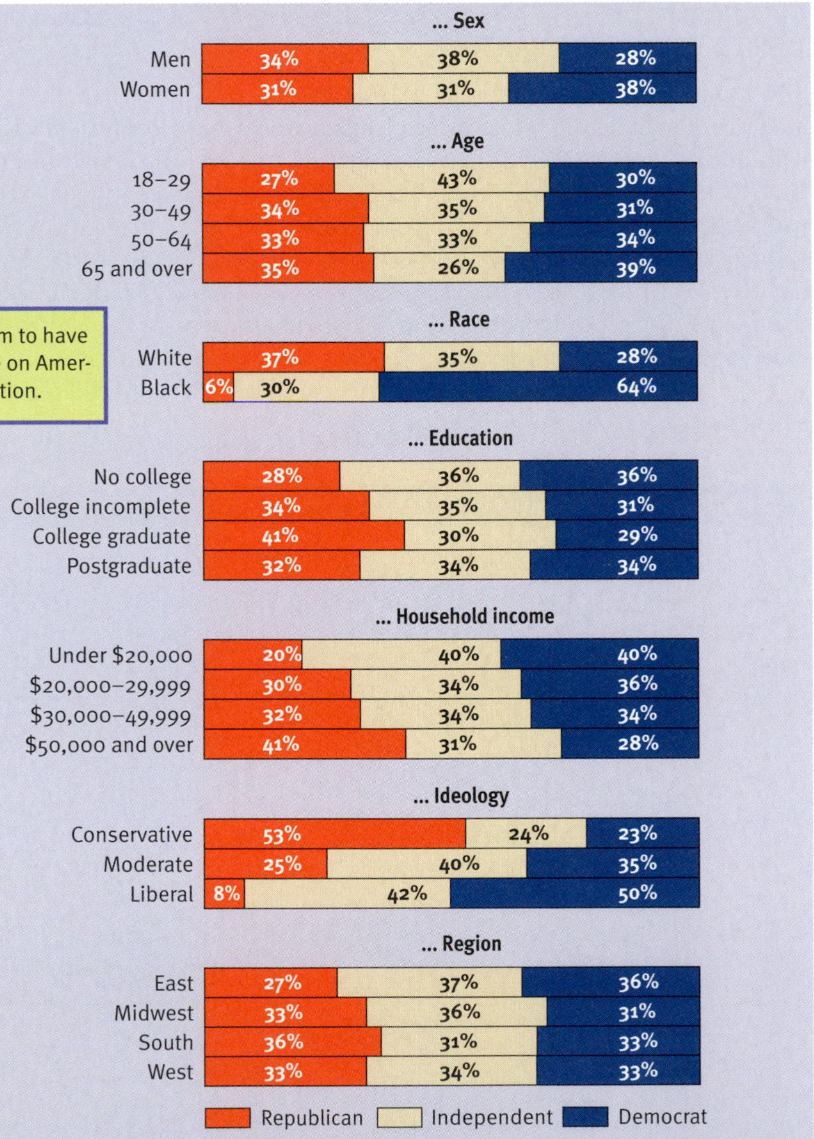

... Sex

	Republican	Independent	Democrat
Men	34%	38%	28%
Women	31%	31%	38%

... Age

	Republican	Independent	Democrat
18–29	27%	43%	30%
30–49	34%	35%	31%
50–64	33%	33%	34%
65 and over	35%	26%	39%

... Race

	Republican	Independent	Democrat
White	37%	35%	28%
Black	6%	30%	64%

> Race and income seem to have the greatest influence on Americans' party identification.

... Education

	Republican	Independent	Democrat
No college	28%	36%	36%
College incomplete	34%	35%	31%
College graduate	41%	30%	29%
Postgraduate	32%	34%	34%

... Household income

	Republican	Independent	Democrat
Under $20,000	20%	40%	40%
$20,000–29,999	30%	34%	36%
$30,000–49,999	32%	34%	34%
$50,000 and over	41%	31%	28%

... Ideology

	Republican	Independent	Democrat
Conservative	53%	24%	23%
Moderate	25%	40%	35%
Liberal	8%	42%	50%

... Region

	Republican	Independent	Democrat
East	27%	37%	36%
Midwest	33%	36%	31%
South	36%	31%	33%
West	33%	34%	33%

Republican Independent Democrat

SOURCE: Harold W. Stanley and Richard G. Niemi, *Vital Statistics on American Politics,* 5th ed. (Washington, DC: Congressional Quarterly Press, 1995), p. 149.

broad tendencies that both reflect and reinforce the issue and policy positions the two parties take in the national and local political arenas.

Voters Decide Based on Party, Issues, and Candidate

Three key factors influence voters' decisions at the polls: party loyalty, issue and policy concerns, and candidate characteristics.

PARTY LOYALTY IS STILL IMPORTANT

Party loyalty was considerably stronger during the 1940s and 1950s than it is today. But even now, most voters feel a certain sense of identification or kinship with the Democratic or Republican party. This sense of identification is often handed down from parents to children and is reinforced by social and cultural ties. Partisan identification predisposes voters in favor of their party's candidates and against those of the opposing party (see Figure 6.5). At the level of the presidential contest, issues and candidate personalities may become very important, although even here many Americans supported George W. Bush or John Kerry in the 2004 race only because of party loyalty. But partisanship is more likely to be a factor in the less-visible races, where issues and the candidates are not as well known. State legislative races, for example, are often decided by voters' party ties. Once formed, voters' partisan loyalties seldom change. Voters tend to keep their

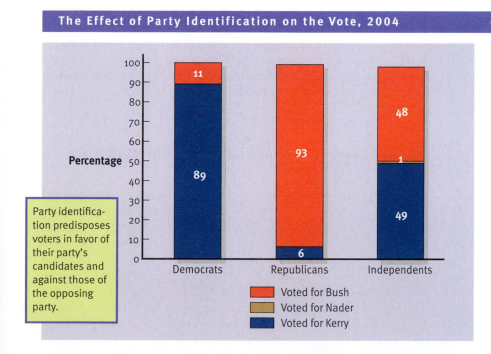

The Effect of Party Identification on the Vote, 2004　　Figure 6.5

Percentage

Democrats: 89, 11
Republicans: 6, 93
Independents: 49, 1, 48

Democrats Republicans Independents

■ Voted for Bush
■ Voted for Nader
■ Voted for Kerry

Party identification predisposes voters in favor of their party's candidates and against those of the opposing party.

party affiliations unless some crisis causes them to reexamine the bases of their loyalties and to conclude that they have not given their support to the appropriate party. During these relatively infrequent periods of electoral change, millions of voters can change their party ties. For example, at the beginning of the New Deal era, between 1932 and 1936, millions of former Republicans transferred their allegiance to Franklin Roosevelt and the Democrats.

ISSUES CAN SHAPE AN ELECTION

Issues and policy preferences are a second factor influencing voters' choices at the polls. Voters may cast their ballots for the candidate whose position on economic issues they believe to be closest to their own. Similarly, they may select the candidate who has what they believe to be the best record on foreign policy. Issues are more important in some races than others. If candidates actually "take issue" with one another—that is, articulate and publicize very different positions on important public questions—then voters are more likely to be able to identify and act on whatever policy preferences they may have. The 1992 election emphasized economic issues. Voters concerned with America's continuing economic recession and long-term economic prospects gave their support to Bill Clinton, who called for an end to "Reaganomics." Efforts by George H. W. Bush to inject other issues, such as "family values" and foreign policy, into the race proved generally unsuccessful. In 1996, Bob Dole's major issue was a pledge to cut federal income taxes. Clinton called for a "middle-class bill of rights" and tough measures to deal with crime, and also advocated the "family values" that Bush had unsuccessfully championed in 1992. In 2004, the state of the economy, terrorism, morality, and the war in Iraq were all key issues defining that year's elections.

The ability of voters to make choices on the basis of issue or policy preferences is diminished, however, if competing candidates do not differ substantially or do not focus their campaigns on policy matters. Very often, candidates deliberately take the safe course and emphasize issues that will not be offensive to any voters. Thus, candidates often trumpet their opposition to corruption, crime, and inflation. Presumably, few voters favor these things.

CANDIDATE CHARACTERISTICS ARE MORE IMPORTANT IN THE MEDIA AGE

Candidates' personal attributes always influence voters' decisions. The more important candidate characteristics that affect voters' choices include race, ethnicity, religion, gender, geography, and social background. In general, voters prefer candidates who are closer to themselves in terms of these categories; voters presume that such candidates are likely to have views and perspectives close to their own. Moreover, they may be proud to see someone of their ethnic, religious, or geographic background in a position of leadership. This is why, for many years, politicians sought to "balance the ticket," making certain that their party's ticket included members of as many important groups as possible.

Just as a candidate's personal characteristics may attract some voters, they may repel others. Many voters are prejudiced against candidates of certain ethnic, racial, or religious groups. In 1960, for example, John F. Kennedy's religion both won and lost him votes—but in a way that helped him get elected. As a Roman Catholic, Kennedy lost votes in the South because of lingering anti-Catholic sentiment there; on the other hand, he picked up additional votes in the Northeast because of the greater concentration of Catholic voters there. On the whole, this helped Kennedy, because northeastern Catholic voters provided him with a critical boost in this highly competitive and electoral-vote-rich area, whereas he could afford to lose votes in southern states he was likely to lose anyway, and which had fewer electoral votes (population increases in the South in the last few decades have given these states more electoral clout).

Voters also pay attention to candidates' personality characteristics, such as "decisiveness," "honesty," and "vigor." In the 2000 election, Republican Arizona senator John McCain won much support because people admired his heroic record during the Vietnam War. McCain, a former Navy pilot whose plane was shot down over North Vietnam, had spent several years as a prisoner of war (POW), during which time he was tortured by his captors. In 2004, Democratic presidential nominee John Kerry's campaign included frequent references to his military service in Vietnam, where he was wounded and received several decorations. President George W. Bush's reelection campaign emphasized his strong, decisive, and steady leadership in the post-9/11 war against terrorism.

Elections Are Important to Democracy, but the System Can Seem Complicated

The act that results in the election of members of Congress, presidents, and countless state and local leaders is, of course, voting. Its obvious purpose is the democratic selection of leaders, yet it also serves other, less obvious purposes.

Elections help insure that our leaders will be accountable to the people. When people vote, they are making choices between differing leaders and issues—and therefore, about the direction of the country. Leaders who fail to act as the people wish can be held accountable by being voted out of office.

The right to vote, or **suffrage,** can also serve as an important source of protection for groups in American society. The passage of the 1965 Voting Rights Act, for example, enfranchised millions of African Americans in the South, paving the way for election of thousands of new black public officials at the local, state, and national levels and ensuring that white politicians could no longer ignore the views and needs of African Americans.

suffrage the right to vote; also called franchise

VOTER TURNOUT IN AMERICA IS LOW

Although the United States has developed a system of universal suffrage, America's rate of voter participation, or **turnout,** is very low. For example, in the 1996

turnout the percentage of eligible individuals who actually vote

presidential election only 49 percent of eligible voters cast ballots, the lowest percentage in a presidential election in more than seventy years. In 2004, massive efforts to bring out the vote caused voter turnout to rise to over 59 percent. This is the first significant increase in years. (see Figure 6.6). Turnout in state and local races that do not coincide with national contests is typically even lower. In European countries, by contrast, national voter turnout is usually between 80 and 90 percent.[7]

The difference between American and European levels of turnout has much to do with registration rules and party strength. In the United States, individuals who are eligible to vote must register with the state election board before they are actually allowed to vote. Registration requirements particularly depress the participation of those with little education and low incomes because registration requires a greater degree of political involvement and interest than does the act of voting itself. To vote, a person need be concerned only with the particular election campaign at hand. Requiring individuals to register before the next election forces them to make a decision to participate on the basis of an abstract interest in the electoral

Figure 6.6   **Voter Turnout in Presidential and Midterm Elections, 1892–2004**

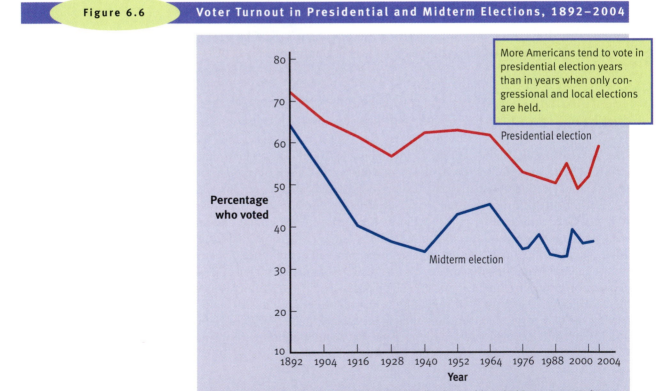

SOURCES: 1892–1958: Erik Austin and Jerome Clubb, *Political Facts of the United States since 1789* (New York: Columbia University Press, 1986), pp. 378–79; 1960–96. U.S. Bureau of the Census, *Statistical Abstract of the United States: 1997* (Washington, DC: Government Printing Office, 1997), p. 289.

process rather than a simple concern with a specific campaign. Such an abstract interest in electoral politics is largely a product of education and age. Those with relatively little education may become interested in political events once the issues of a particular campaign become salient, but by that time it may be too late to register. Young people tend to assign a low priority to registration even if they are well educated. As a result, personal registration requirements not only diminish the size of the electorate but also tend to create an electorate that is, on average, better educated, higher in income and social status, and composed of fewer young people, African Americans, and other minorities than the citizenry as a whole.

Over the years, voter registration restrictions have been relaxed some to make registration easier. In most states, an eligible individual may register to vote simply by mailing a postcard to the state election board. In 1993, Congress approved and President Clinton signed the Motor Voter bill to ease voter registration by allowing individuals to register when they apply for driver's licenses, as well as in public assistance and military recruitment offices.[8] In most democratic nations, there is typically no registration burden on the individual voter; the government handles voter registration automatically. This is one reason that voter turnout rates in these nations are higher than those in the United States.

The second factor explaining low rates of voter turnout in the United States is the weakness of the American party system. During the nineteenth century, American political party machines employed hundreds of thousands of workers to organize and mobilize voters and bring them to the polls. The result was an extremely high rate of turnout, typically more than 90 percent of eligible voters.[9] But political party machines began to decline in strength in the early twentieth century and have now largely disappeared. Without party workers to encourage them to go to the polls and even to bring them there if necessary, many eligible voters will not participate. In the absence of strong parties, participation rates drop the most among poorer and less-educated citizens.

THE TWO TYPES OF ELECTIONS ARE PRIMARIES AND GENERAL ELECTIONS

Two types of elections are held broadly in the United States: primary elections and general elections.

Primary elections are used to select each party's candidates for the general election. In the case of local and statewide offices, the winners of primary elections face one another as their parties' nominees in the general election. At the presidential level, however, primary elections are indirect because they are used to select state delegates to the national nominating conventions, at which the major party presidential candidates are chosen (see Figure 6.7 for a timeline of this process). America is one of the only nations in the world to use primary elections. In most countries, nominations are controlled by party officials, as they once were in the United States. The primary system was introduced at the turn of the century by Progressive reformers who hoped to weaken the power of party leaders by taking candidate nominations out of their hands.

primary elections elections used to select a party's candidate for the general election

Figure 6.7 The 2004 Presidential Election Season

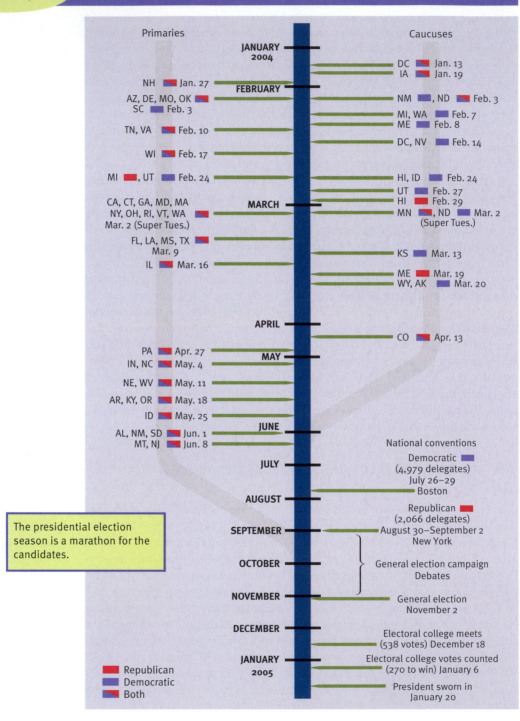

The presidential election season is a marathon for the candidates.

Under the law of most states, only registered members of a political party may vote in a primary election to select that party's candidates. This is called a **closed primary.** Other states allow all registered voters to decide on the day of the primary in which party's primary they will participate. This is called an **open primary.**

The primary is followed by the general election—the decisive electoral contest. The winner of the general election is elected to office for a specified term. In some states, however, mainly in the Southeast, if no candidate wins an absolute majority in the primary, a runoff election is held before the general election. This situation is most likely to arise if there are more than two candidates, none of whom receives a majority of the votes cast. A runoff election is held between the two candidates who received the largest number of votes.

Twenty-four states also provide for referendum voting. The **referendum** process allows citizens to vote directly on proposed laws or other governmental actions. In recent years, voters in several states have voted to set limits on tax rates, to block state and local spending proposals, and to prohibit social services for illegal immigrants. Although it involves voting, a referendum is not an election. The election is an institution of representative government. Through an election, voters choose officials to act for them. The referendum, by contrast, is an institution of direct democracy; it allows voters to govern directly without intervention by government officials. The validity of referenda results, however, is subject to judicial action. If a court finds that a referendum outcome violates the state or national constitution, it can overturn the result. This happened in the case of a 1995 California referendum curtailing social services to illegal aliens.[10]

Eighteen states also have legal provisions for **recall** elections. The recall is an electoral device introduced by turn-of-the-century Populists to allows voters to remove governors and other state officials from office prior to the expiration of their terms. Federal officials, such the president and members of Congress, are not subject to recall. Generally, a recall effort begins with a petition campaign. For example, in California, the site of a tumultuous recall battle in 2003, if 12 percent of those who voted in the last general election sign petitions demanding a special recall election, the state board of elections must schedule one. Such petition campaigns are relatively common, but most fail to garner enough signatures to bring the matter to a statewide vote. In the California case, however, a conservative Republican member of Congress, Derrell Issa, led a successful effort to recall Democratic governor Gary Davis. Voters were unhappy about the state's economy, dissatisfied with Davis's performance, and blamed Davis for the state's $38 billion budget deficit. Issa and his followers were able to secure enough signatures to force a vote, and in October 2003 Davis became only the second governor in American history to be recalled by his state's electorate. The first was North Dakota governor Lynn Frazier, who was recalled in 1921. Under California law, voters in a special recall election are also asked to choose a replacement for the official whom they dismiss. Californians in 2003 elected movie star Arnold Schwarzenegger to be their governor. Ironically, the new

closed primary a primary election in which voters can participate in the nomination of candidates, but only of the party in which they are enrolled for a period of time prior to primary day

open primary a primary election in which the voter can wait until the day of the primary to choose which party to enroll in to select candidates for the general election

referendum the practice of referring a measure proposed or passed by a legislature to the vote of the electorate for approval or rejection

recall removal of a public official by popular vote

Republican governor had starred in such films as *The Terminator, Running Man,* and *Total Recall.* While critics charged that the Davis recall had been a "political circus," the campaign had the effect of greatly increasing voter interest and involvement in the political process. More than four hundred thousand new voters registered in California in 2003, many drawn into the political arena by the opportunity to participate in the recall campaign.

THE ELECTORAL COLLEGE STILL ORGANIZES PRESIDENTIAL ELECTIONS

In the early history of popular voting, nations often made use of indirect elections. In these elections, voters would choose the members of an intermediate body. These members would, in turn, select public officials. The assumption underlying such processes was that ordinary citizens were not really qualified to choose their leaders and could not be trusted to do so directly. The last vestige of this procedure in America is the **electoral college,** the group of electors who, according to the Constitution (Article II, Section 1), formally select the president and vice president of the United States.

electoral college the presidential electors from each state who meet after the popular election to cast ballots for president and vice president

When Americans go to the polls on election day, they are technically not voting directly for presidential candidates. Instead, voters within each state are choosing among slates of electors selected by each state's party leadership and pledged, if elected, to support that party's presidential candidate. In each state, the slate that wins casts all the state's electoral votes for its party's candidate. Each state is entitled to a number of electoral votes equal to the number of the state's senators and representatives combined (although the members of Congress are barred from serving as electors), for a total of 538 electoral votes for the fifty states plus the District of Columbia. Occasionally, an elector will break his or her pledge and vote for the other party's candidate. For example, in 1976, when the Republicans carried the state of Washington, one Republican elector from that state refused to vote for Gerald Ford, the Republican presidential nominee. Many states have now enacted statutes formally binding electors to their pledges, but some constitutional authorities doubt whether such statutes are enforceable.

In each state, the electors whose slate has won proceed to the state's capital on the Monday following the second Wednesday in December and formally cast their ballots. These are sent to Washington, tallied by the Congress in January, and the name of the winner is formally announced. If no candidate were to receive a majority of all electoral votes, the names of the top three candidates would be submitted to the House, where each state would be able to cast one vote. Whether a state's vote would be decided by a majority, plurality, or some other fraction of the state's delegates would be determined under rules established by the House.

In 1800 and 1824, the electoral college failed to produce a majority for any candidate. In the election of 1800, Thomas Jefferson was chosen by the House. In 1824, John Quincy Adams was selected over Andrew Jackson. Four years later, Jackson came back and soundly defeated Adams.

On all but three occasions since 1824, the electoral vote has simply ratified the nationwide popular vote. Since electoral votes are won on a state-by-state basis, it is mathematically possible for a candidate who receives a nationwide popular plurality to fail to carry states whose electoral votes would add up to a majority. Thus, in 1876, Rutherford B. Hayes was the winner in the electoral college despite receiving fewer popular votes than his rival, Samuel Tilden. In 1888, Grover Cleveland received more popular votes than Benjamin Harrison, but received fewer electoral votes. And in 2000, Al Gore outpolled his opponent, George W. Bush, but narrowly lost the electoral college by a mere four electoral votes.

The 2004 Elections

In 2004, President George W. Bush led the Republican party to a solid electoral victory, winning 51 percent of the popular vote versus Senator John Kerry's 48 percent, a 286–252 majority in the Electoral College (see Figure 6.8), and helping to solidify what had been shaky Republican control of both houses of Congress. Republicans added four seats in the Senate, giving them a 55–44 majority (with one independent) and five seats in the House of Representatives to gain a 234–200 majority in the lower chamber (with one independent). To further embarrass the Democrats, Senate Democratic leader Tom Daschle was defeated by his Republican opponent in a hard-fought South Dakota campaign.

The roots of this GOP triumph go back nearly three years. In the wake of George W. Bush's disputed Electoral College victory in 2000, many pundits predicted that Bush would be a weak president. Bush had lost the popular vote to Democrat Al Gore and held office only because of a controversial Supreme Court decision that, in effect, awarded him Florida's electoral votes. The conventional wisdom held that, lacking a popular mandate, Bush would be unable to govern effectively and would have difficulty in a quest for a second term. The conventional wisdom, however, did not anticipate the events of September 11, 2001. On that day, Al Qaeda terrorists, under the direction of Osama bin Laden, inflicted serious damage upon the Pentagon and destroyed New York's World Trade Center, which incurred an enormous loss of American lives.

President Bush responded forcefully to the attack. In a series of speeches and dramatic visits to the sites of the strikes, Bush rallied the nation for what he warned would become a lengthy "war on terror." As the first campaign of that war, Bush ordered a massive American, air and ground assault on Afghanistan. That nation's Taliban regime was closely associated with bin Laden and provided sanctuary and support for Al Qaeda. After weeks of fierce fighting, American troops and their Afghan allies routed the Taliban, killed many of the most important Al Qaeda leaders, and installed a pro-American regime in Kabul, Afghanistan. The first American campaign of the war on terror appeared to result in a great triumph for the president.

By responding to Al Qaeda's attack on the United States with the successful Afghan campaign, Bush temporarily silenced all but the most intransigent of his

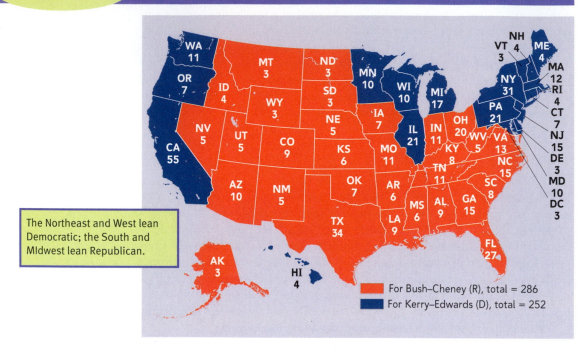

Figure 6.8 **Distribution of Electoral Votes in the 2004 Election**

The Northeast and West lean Democratic; the South and Midwest lean Republican.

For Bush–Cheney (R), total = 286
For Kerry–Edwards (D), total = 252

critics. The president's popular approval approached a stratospheric 90 percent, and pundits who had previously called him an ineffectual and illegitimate leader now praised Bush and proclaimed that his presidency had been transformed. The circumstances of George W. Bush's election were all but forgotten.

Despite this triumph, Bush and his advisers knew that his political future was far from assured. During the course of American history, military victory has been no guarantee of lasting political success. Indeed, popular gratitude to wartime leaders tends to be short-lived. When the danger has passed, the public usually returns to its mundane economic and social concerns and is as likely as not to send its wartime champions into political retirement. This was precisely the fate of Bush's father, President George H. W. Bush. The first Bush had been enormously popular after he led the nation in a victorious campaign against Iraq in 1991. He was, nevertheless, defeated by Bill Clinton in the 1992 presidential election when the public was more concerned with an ongoing economic recession than with the previous year's martial glory.

BUILDING BLOCKS OF REPUBLICAN SUCCESS

George W. Bush was determined not to fall victim to his father's fate. The administration's political strategists, led by senior adviser Karl Rove, believed that three ingredients would combine to solidify the president's political strength and ensure his reelection in 2004. The first of these was an expansive economic policy. The Bush administration pursued a program of tax cuts and low interest rates that it hoped would produce a booming economy by election time. Generally, presidents who preside during times of economic expansion are returned to office. The second ingredient was money. Early in his term, President Bush embarked upon an unprecedented fund-raising effort, building a $100 million campaign chest before the Democrats were even close to nominating a candidate.

The final ingredient was the war on terror. The war on terror entailed new risks but, politically speaking, also produced new opportunities. A war of indefinite duration would mean that on a permanent and ongoing basis the American public would look to its government, especially to its president, for protection and reassurance. So long as the public remained convinced that President Bush was making an effective effort to safeguard the nation, it would be unlikely to deprive him of office. And, precisely in order to convince the public that his administration stood between it and mortal danger, the president organized a massive "homeland security" program that included far-reaching government reorganization and sweeping new powers for law enforcement agencies. Many elements of this program, such as enhanced inspection of passengers and freight in the nation's transport system, were designed to thwart terrorists. Other elements of the homeland security program, including a color-coded national alert system, seemed designed to remind Americans of the ongoing threat and the efforts of the Bush administration to protect the nation. Coupled with fund-raising activities and economic expansion, the war on terror appeared to promise political success for President Bush.

DEMOCRATIC OPPORTUNITIES

In the aftermath of September 11, President Bush seemed virtually guaranteed of political success. A new set of political circumstances, however, emerged to diminish the president's political standing and to threaten his grip on power. The first of these was the economy. Despite the administrations' efforts, economic growth was slow and job growth anemic during Bush's first term in office. The sluggish economy allowed Democrats to declare that Bush was the only president in recent history to preside over a net loss of jobs during his administration. Ultimately more important then the economy was the Iraq war. In March, 2003, American military forces launched a full-scale invasion of Iraq aimed at occupying the country and toppling the government of President Saddam Hussein. The invasion followed months of demands by the United States that Iraq acknowledge possessing outlawed weapons of mass destruction (WMDs) and agree to destroy them. The administration also charged that Iraq had been conspiring with Al Qaeda against the United States. Iraq denied American claims and even though UN weapons inspectors failed to find WMDs in Iraq, the Bush administration was convinced that the Iraqis were lying and that the United Nations was inept. After a brief war in which American forces performed at their customarily high level, the Iraqis were overwhelmed and forced to surrender. A short time later Saddam Hussein was captured. Most Americans initially supported the war, and early battlefield success seemed to bolster President Bush's standing. It soon became apparent, however, that whatever Iraqi WMD program might once have existed had been largely abandoned by Saddam Hussein's regime. The Bush administration, moreover, failed to prove a connection between Saddam and terrorism. Thus the president's stated war aims seemed to have been mistaken. To make matters worse, armed resistance to the American occupation of Iraq gradually stiffened, producing a steady drumbeat of American casualties. The Iraq war, though militarily successful, appeared to have been pointless, and suddenly made Bush politically vulnerable.

Adding to the president's problems and to the Democrats' opportunities was the effort by rich liberal activists—George Soros, for example—to form new independent groups, known as 527 Committees, specifically to defeat President Bush (527 Committees are discussed in more detail later in the chapter). Beyond raising millions of dollars to defeat Bush, these groups also registered millions of new Democratic voters. This influx of registrants posed a substantial threat to the GOP, not only at the presidential level but in congressional and local races as well.

But Democrats still faced formidable obstacles in their effort to unseat Bush. The first problem, of course, was identifying a viable candidate. After months of candidate debates and primaries, Senator John Kerry of Massachusetts, a Senate veteran and Vietnam War hero, captured the party's nomination. Kerry named North Carolina senator John Edwards as his running mate. Edwards, a former trial lawyer, lacked a particularly distinguished record in the Senate but was seen as an excellent fund-raiser who might help the Democrats among Southern and rural voters.

Democrats understood that to have any serious chance of defeating President Bush, they must somehow undermine the president's strongest political claim—that he responded forcefully to the September 11 attacks and continued to protect the country from the threat of terrorism. As long as voters accepted the president's contentions, he could not be defeated. As far back as the winter of 2002, Congressional Democrats hoped that a probe of the Bush administration's failure to anticipate the September 11 attacks might embarrass the president in an election year and undermine public confidence in his ability to protect the nation's security. However, their party did not control either house of Congress and, therefore, lacked access to the House or Senate's formal investigative machinery. Nevertheless, Democrats demanded an investigation and, ultimately, through public pressure, forced Congressional Republicans to agree to the creation of an ad hoc, bipartisan investigative panel to be appointed by the leaders of the two parties in Congress. Recognizing the president's peril and seeking to limit any political damage from the 9/11 Commission's findings, the GOP insisted that an investigation be completed and its report released by July 2004, some four months before the 2004 election. The Commission hearings in March and April suggested that the Bush administration had not been sufficiently attentive to the terrorist threat prior to September 2001. Bush was now clearly vulnerable, and throughout the campaign, Democrats charged that the president had failed to heed warnings of a terrorist attack and had subsequently focused on an imaginary threat from Iraq rather than the real danger from Al Qaeda. This was a theme emphasized by Senator Kerry during all three presidential debates.

REPUBLICAN STRATEGY

Republicans were hardly idle while their Democratic foes enrolled new voters and castigated the president. To deal with the threat posed by newly registered Democratic voters, the GOP began its own voter registration effort. Armed with data on millions of voters and potential voters, GOP operatives in every state—especially in so-called battleground states such as Ohio, Florida, Iowa, and Pennsylvania—embarked upon an ambitious effort to register millions of conservative voters. Religious conservatives were a particular target of GOP efforts. The president had appealed to these voters for four years with his stand against abortion and stem-cell research, his support for religious education, and his "faith-based initiative" to allow church-affiliated organizations to win federal contracts to deliver social services. Bush also made much of his own religious faith in televised and personal appearances.

To ensure that the growing legion of religious conservatives actually went to the polls on November 2, Republican campaign materials emphasized moral themes and the president's religious and moral commitments and the GOP launched a series of ballot initiatives on such "hot button" issues as same-sex marriage and abortion. Republicans calculated that these initiatives in such battleground states as Ohio and Florida would bring religious conservatives to the polls. Once at their polling places, they would also vote for President Bush. This strategy seems to have been especially successful in Ohio, where religious conservatives mobilized furiously behind an initiative to ban same-sex marriage. Ohio turned out to be essential to Bush's reelection.

Ultimately, competitive Democratic and Republican registration efforts produced the highest level of voter turnout in nearly four decades. Slightly more than 59 percent of eligible Americans went to the polls in 2004, an increase of almost 5 percentage points over 2000. Ultimately, more new voters supported Kerry than Bush, but the margin was not overwhelming. The Democratic effort to overwhelm the GOP with new registrants had been blunted.

In addition to enrolling their own new voters and emphasizing the religious themes deemed to be important to these voters, Republicans worked to discredit Kerry as a plausible president. Bush and other Republican campaigners accused Kerry of continually "flip-flopping" on important issues. Republicans also sought to undermine one of Kerry's strongest moral claims, his record of heroism during the Vietnam war. Just as Democrats had raised questions about Bush's leadership during September 11, Republicans raised questions about Kerry's war record. The GOP organized a group of conservative veterans called "Swift Boat Veterans for Truth" who traveled around the country making appearances and seeking media attention. The "Swifties" succeeded in raising questions about Kerry's claims of wartime heroism and converting what had

PICTURING

The 2004 Presidential Campaign

The field of candidates vying for the 2004 Democratic presidential nomination was particularly wide and varied. Seen here before their October 9, 2003, debate in Phoenix, Arizona, from left to right, are former senator Carol Moseley Braun, former army general Wesley Clark, Reverend Al Sharpton, Senator John Edwards, Representative Dick Gephardt, Senator John Kerry, Representative Dennis Kucinich, former Vermont governor Howard Dean, and Senator Joe Lieberman.

Although most states use primary elections to choose delegates for the Democratic and Republican national conventions, a few, like Iowa, use the caucus system. Along with the New Hampshire primaries, which usually take place a week later, the Iowa caucuses are considered the most important of the early events, and candidates spend months courting voters in these two states. Seen here after his January 19, 2004, victory in Iowa is Senator John Kerry of Massachusetts, who would go on to dominate in the remaining primaries and eventually win his party's presidential nomination.

POLITICS

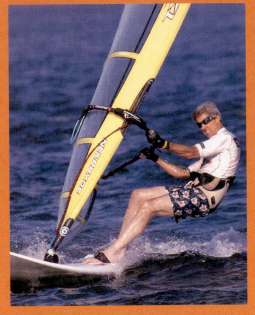

After the Democratic and Republican National Conventions, where each party's candidate was officially chosen, Senator Kerry and President George W. Bush embarked on their general election campaigns. An important component of presidential campaigns is the debates. Broadcast live on every major news network, the debates allow voters to see their candidates in action. Not surprisingly, viewer opinions as to who won the debates split along party lines.

Also important in the lead-up to the General Election are advertisements. These short television spots are designed not only to advance the platform of the candidates, but also to expose weaknesses in their opponents. In President Bush's ads, images of Senator Kerry windsurfing played into the negative stereotype of him as the out-of-touch, elitist Massachusetts liberal.

The General Election in early November is the culmination of rigorous campaigning. By this time, the candidates have had to endure, among other things, months of travel, speaking engagements, grassroots organizing, and television appearances. In the end, President Bush was declared the winner.

been a given into a "he said, she said" situation. The GOP's efforts seemed to bear fruit. Throughout the fall of 2004, President Bush maintained a solid lead in the polls despite months of Democratic attacks.

THE END GAME

In October, however, Bush's lead appeared to evaporate in the wake of the presidential debates. The two parties had agreed to engage in three nationally televised presidential debates and one vice-presidential debate, with the first set for September 30, 2004. In most national elections, the first debate is crucial. Usually, much of the nation watches or listens to the first debate, and the audience diminishes in size during the subsequent debates. In 2004, most observers agreed that President Bush's performance in the first debate was a political disaster. The president appeared ill-at-ease, some commentators described him as irritable, while Senator Kerry was articulate and quite presidential in demeanor. The national news media declared the debate to have been a major Kerry victory. Republicans were stunned and Democrats elated. Bush rallied in the subsequent debates, but most of the media continued to declare Kerry the victor and to award Edwards the victory in the vice-presidential clash. In the aftermath of the debates, the polls indicated that the two tickets were now running neck and neck.

As the election approached, each side realized that success would depend upon its ability to produce high levels of turnout among its most loyal partisans in the ten or so states that could swing to either party. Democrats relied upon their traditional allies such as labor unions and African-American churches, as well as seeking to ensure high levels of turnout among their new registrants. For example, to encourage newly registered college students to go to the polls, the Kerry campaign charged that President Bush was planning to reinstitute military conscription—a factually baseless but politically useful claim. For their part, Republicans relied heavily upon such conservative groups as the Home School Legal Defense Fund and a host of religious organizations to bring out their voters. In this so-called ground game, each party made use of enormous computer data banks to identify likely voters and volunteers.

In the end, the GOP's superior on-the-ground organization prevailed. Republicans registered and brought to the polls tens of millions of religious conservatives who gave President Bush the margin of victory in such key states as Florida, Ohio, and Missouri. The importance of religious conservatives is manifest in the exit poll data, which indicates that on a national basis 22 percent of all voters cited moral values as the issue that mattered most to them—more than cited the economy, terrorism, the Iraq war, or any other issue. Of these morally committed Americans, an astonishing 82 percent gave their votes to President Bush.

For the most part, each candidate ran well among voters who normally support his party. Kerry won the support of union members, Jews, African Americans, and women. Bush was successful among white males, upper-income wage earners, and southerners. Neither candidate reached much beyond his political base, though Bush was somewhat more successful in 2004 than in 2000 among women, Hispanics, and Catholics. After hundreds of millions of dollars in expenditures and years of planning and maneuvering, the key to victory was old-fashioned voter turnout. After the issues had been debated, charges made and answered, claims made and debunked, Bush and the GOP prevailed because a record number of Republicans went to the polls on November 2—a democratic conclusion to an untidy but thoroughly democratic process.

Money Is the Mother's Milk of Politics

Modern national political campaigns are fueled by enormous amounts of money. In a national race, millions of dollars are spent on media time, as well as on public opinion polls and media consultants. In 2000, political candidates spent a total of more than $3.0 billion on election campaigns. The average winning candidate that year in a campaign for a seat in the House of Representatives spent more than $630,000; the average winner in a senatorial campaign spent $5.6 million.[11] In 2004, Kerry and Bush raised nearly $500 million in private contributions during the presidential primary season. The 2004 Democratic and Republican presidential candidates received a total of $150 million in public funds to run their general campaigns.[12] Both presidential candidates were also helped by hundreds of millions of dollars in so-called independent expenditures by individuals and groups. As long as such political expenditures are not formally coordinated with a candidate's campaign, they are considered to be constitutionally protected free speech and are not subject to legal limitation or even reporting requirements.

CAMPAIGN FUNDS COME FROM DIRECT MAIL, THE RICH, PACS, AND PARTIES

Federal Election Commission (FEC) data suggest that approximately one-fourth of the private funds spent on political campaigns in the United States is raised through small, direct-mail contributions; about one-fourth is provided by large, individual gifts; and another fourth comes from contributions from PACs. The remaining fourth is drawn from the political parties and from candidates' personal or family resources.[13] Independent expenditures by independent groups and individuals, which are not required to be reported to the Federal Election Commission, are another source of campaign funds.

Individual Donors   Direct mail serves both as a vehicle for communicating with voters and as a mechanism for raising funds. Direct-mail fund-raising efforts begin with the purchase or rental of computerized mailing lists of voters deemed likely to support the candidate because of their partisan ties, interests, or ideology. Candidates send out pamphlets, letters, and brochures describing their views and appealing for funds. Tens of millions of dollars are raised by national, state, and local candidates through direct mail each year. These contributions usually consist of $25 and $50 donations,[14] although in 2000, Bush and Gore collected about three-quarters of their donor contributions from individuals giving the $1,000 maximum amount.

political action committee (PAC) a private group that raises and distributes funds for use in election campaigns

Political Action Committees Political action committees (PACs) are organizations established by corporations, labor unions, or interest groups to channel the contributions of their members into political campaigns. Under the terms of the 1971 Federal Election Campaign Act, which governs campaign finance in the United States, PACs are permitted to make larger contributions to any given candidate than individuals are allowed to make. Individuals may donate a maximum of $2,000 to any single candidate, but a PAC may donate as much as $5,000 to each candidate. Moreover, allied or related PACs often coordinate their campaign contributions, greatly increasing the amount of money a candidate actually receives from the same interest group. As a result, PACs have become central to campaign finance in the United States. Many critics assert that PACs corrupt the political process by allowing corporations and other interests to influence politicians with large contributions. It is by no means clear, however, that PACs corrupt the political process any more than large, individual contributions.

The Candidates On the basis of the Supreme Court's 1976 decision in *Buckley v. Valeo,* the right of individuals to spend their *own* money to campaign for office is a constitutionally protected matter of free speech and is not subject to limitation.[15] Thus, extremely wealthy candidates often contribute millions of dollars to their own campaigns. Jon Corzine, for example, spent approximately $60 million of his own funds in a successful New Jersey Senate bid in 2000.

issue advocacy independent spending by individuals or interest groups on a campaign issue but not directly tied to a particular candidate

Independent Spending As was noted previously, "independent" spending by individuals is also free from regulation; private groups and wealthy individuals, engaging in what is called **issue advocacy,** may spend as much as they wish to help elect one candidate or defeat another, as long as these expenditures are not coordinated with any political campaign. Many business and ideological groups engage in such activities. Some estimates suggest that groups and individuals spent as much as $400 million on issue advocacy—generally through television advertising—during the 2000 elections.[16] Issue advocacy and independent expenditures increased even more during the 2000 election cycle, to an estimated $400 million or more. The National Rifle Association, for example, spent $3 million dollars reminding voters of the importance of the right to bear arms, while the National Abortion and Reproductive Rights League spent nearly $5 million to express its support for Al Gore.

Public Funding The Federal Election Campaign Act also provides for public funding of presidential campaigns. As they seek a major party presidential nomination, candidates become eligible for public funds by raising at least

$5,000 in individual contributions of $250 or less in each of twenty states. Candidates who reach this threshold may apply for federal funds to match, on a dollar-for-dollar basis, all individual contributions of $250 or less they receive. The funds are drawn from the Presidential Election Campaign Fund. Taxpayers can contribute $3 to this fund, at no additional cost to themselves, by checking a box on the first page of their federal income tax returns. Major party presidential candidates receive a lump sum (currently nearly $75 million) during the summer prior to the general election. They must meet all their general expenses from this money. Third-party candidates are eligible for public funding only if they received at least 5 percent of the vote in the previous presidential race. This stipulation effectively blocks preelection funding for third-party or independent candidates, although a third party that wins more than 5 percent of the vote can receive public funding after the election. In 1980, John Anderson convinced banks to loan him money for an independent candidacy on the strength of poll data showing that he would receive more than 5 percent of the vote and thus would obtain public funds with which to repay the loans. Under current law, no candidate is required to accept public funding for either the nominating races or general presidential election. Candidates who do not accept public funding are not affected by any expenditure limits. Thus, in 1992 Ross Perot financed his own presidential bid and was not bound by the $55 million limit to which the Democratic and Republican candidates were held that year. Perot accepted public funding in 1996. In 2000, George W. Bush refused public funding and raised enough money to finance his own campaign. In 2004, both Bush and Democrat John Kerry declined to accept federal funding prior to receiving the Republican and Democratic presidential nominations. But both candidates later accepted public funding for their general election campaigns, each receiving approximately $75 million.

CAMPAIGN FINANCE REFORM WAS ENACTED IN 2002

In 2002, Congress enacted the most sweeping reform of the campaign finance process since the 1970s. Known as the Bipartisan Campaign Reform Act (BCRA) or McCain-Feingold, named after cosponsor senators John McCain (a Republican) and Russell Feingold (a Democrat), the law attempted to ban **soft money** (money contributed directly to political parties for voter registration and organization) by barring the national political parties from soliciting, receiving, or directing money contributions from corporations, unions, or individuals to their respective state parties, although state and local parties can continue to receive up to $10,000 a year in soft money donations. The law also prohibits issue ads (that is, ads that focus on specific issues rather than individual candidates) within sixty days of a national election. Yet both parties have found ways around the law. Democratic and Republican activists have formed their own organizations that are unaffiliated with the national parties, known as **"527" committees** (after their tax code designation). They are usually headed by long-time party officials who resign from their party jobs to take positions in

soft money money contributed directly to political parties for voter registration

527 committee nonprofit independent groups that receive and disburse funds to influence the nomination, election, or defeat of candidates. Named after Section 527 of the Internal Revenue Code, which defines and provides tax-exempt status for nonprofit advocacy groups

these new groups. These 527s are not subject to the BCRA provisions, so they can raise and spend millions of dollars on elections. For example, in 2004 liberal financier George Soros donated over $12 million to groups trying to defeat George W. Bush. Republican supporters formed groups like Americans for a Better Country to raise and spend money to help Republicans running for election. The law's constitutionality was challenged in court, but in 2003 the Supreme Court upheld the key portions of the law. In 2004, the FEC postponed a ruling on the legality of 527 group activities. In short, the law has failed to eliminate soft money, but has driven it farther away from the national parties, and it has put some limits on issue ads.

THE CURRENT SYSTEM HAS NEGATIVE IMPLICATIONS FOR DEMOCRACY

The important role played by private funds in American politics affects the balance of power among contending social groups. Politicians need large amounts of money to campaign successfully for major offices. This fact inevitably ties their interests to the interests of the groups and forces that can provide this money. In a nation as large and diverse as the United States, to be sure, campaign contributors represent many different groups and often represent clashing interests. Business groups, labor groups, environmental groups, and pro-choice and right-to-life forces all contribute millions of dollars to political campaigns. Through such PACs as EMILY's List, women's groups contribute millions of dollars to women running for political office. One set of trade associations may contribute millions to win politicians' support for telecommunications reform, while another set may contribute just as much to block the same reform efforts. Insurance companies may contribute millions of dollars to Democrats to win their support for changes in the health care system, while physicians may contribute equal amounts to prevent the same changes from becoming law.

Despite this diversity of contributors, however, not all interests play a role in financing political campaigns. Only those interests that have a good deal of money to spend can make their interests known in this way. These interests are not monolithic, but they do not completely reflect the diversity of American society. The poor, the destitute, and the downtrodden also live in America and have an interest in the outcome of political campaigns. Who is to speak for them?

Summary

Political parties and elections serve as an important link between citizens and the government, especially at key moments in our history. Parties seek to control the government by electing party leaders to office. Parties therefore revolve around, and are directly linked to, elections. America is one of the few nations that has maintained a two-party system, although third parties have, from time to time, exerted considerable influence over American elections. Party politics has followed a fairly regular cycle, whereby one party tends to dominate national politics for about thirty to thirty-five years. Such periods come to an end during an electoral realignment. Five such realignments have occurred in American political history (not including the current period since 1968).

Political parties are less important to voters than they once were, but they continue to affect the organization, operation, and policy direction of the national government. Three critical factors—party, issues, and candidates—explain how and why voters decide as they do. Because so many millions of Americans do not vote, candidates and parties focus campaign resources on key constituencies and voting blocks.

For Further Reading

Aldrich, John W. *Why Parties? The Origin and Transformation of Political Parties in America*. Chicago: University of Chicago Press, 1995.

Beck, Paul A., and Frank J. Sorauf. *Party Politics in America*, 7th ed. New York: HarperCollins, 1991.

Black, Earl, and Merle Black. *The Vital South: How Presidents Are Elected*. Cambridge, MA: Harvard University Press, 1992.

Edsall, Thomas Byrne, and Mary D. Edsall. *Chain Reaction: The Impact of Race, Rights, and Taxes on American Politics*. New York: Norton, 1993.

Ginsberg, Benjamin, and Martin Shefter. *Politics by Other Means: Institutional Conflict and the Declining Significance of Elections in America*. New York: Norton, 1999.

Lawson, Kay, and Peter Merkl. *When Parties Fail: Emerging Alternative Organizations*. Princeton, NJ: Princeton University Press, 1988.

Milkis, Sidney. *The President and the Parties: The Transformation of the American Party System since the New Deal*. New York: Oxford University Press, 1993.

Piven, Frances Fox, and Richard A. Cloward. *Why Americans Don't Vote*. New York: Pantheon, 1988.

Shefter, Martin. *Political Parties and the State: The American Historical Experience*. Princeton, NJ: Princeton University Press, 1994.

Tate, Katherine. *From Protest to Politics: The New Black Voters in American Elections*. Cambridge, MA: Harvard University Press, 1994.

Study Outline

1. In modern history, political parties have been the chief points of contact between governments and groups and forces in society. By organizing political parties, social forces attempt to gain some control over government policies and personnel.

Parties and Elections Have Been Vital to American Politics and Government

1. Political parties as they are known today developed along with the expansion of suffrage, and actually took their shape from the electoral process.
2. Parties are important in the electoral process for recruiting and nominating candidates for office.
3. Political parties help to organize Congress. Congressional leadership and the committee system are both products of the two-party system.
4. The president serves as an informal party head by seeking support from congressional members of the party and by supporting their bids for reelection.

America Is One of the Few Nations with a Two-Party System

1. The Democratic Party originated when the Jeffersonian party splintered into four factions in 1824, and Andrew Jackson emerged as the leader of one of these four groups.
2. The Republican Party grew as antislavery groups formed a new party to oppose the 1854 Kansas-Nebraska Act.

3. The United States has experienced five realigning eras, which occur when the established political elite weakens sufficiently to permit the creation of new coalitions of forces capable of capturing and holding the reins of government.

4. American third parties have always represented social and economic protests ignored by the other parties, despite the fact that the United States is said to have a two-party system.

5. Individuals tend to form psychological ties with parties; these ties are called party identification. This identification often follows demographic, ideological, and regional lines.

Voters Decide Based on Party, Issues, and Candidate

1. Three factors influence voters' decisions at the polls: party, issues, and candidate.

2. Party loyalty predisposes voters in favor of their party's candidates and against those of the opposing party.

3. The impact of issues and policy preferences on electoral choice is diminished if competing candidates do not differ substantially or do not focus their campaigns on policy matters.

4. Candidates' attributes and personality characteristics always influence voters' decisions.

5. The salience of these three bases of electoral choice varies from contest to contest and from voter to voter.

Elections Are Important to Democracy, but the System Can Seem Complicated

1. Throughout American history, there has been a progressive, if uneven, expansion of suffrage to groups such as African Americans, women, and youths.

2. Though the United States now has a system of universal suffrage, voter turnout continues to be low.

3. Americans do not vote directly for presidential candidates. Rather, they choose electors who are pledged to support a party's presidential candidate.

Money Is the Mother's Milk of Politics

1. Campaign funds in the United States are provided by small, direct-mail contributions, large gifts, PACs, political parties, candidates' personal resources, and public funding. In 2000, some candidates also benefited from issues advocacy.

2. Campaign finance is regulated by the Federal Elections Campaign Act of 1971. Following the 1996 elections, the role of soft money was scrutinized. The McCain-Feingold bill, a bipartisan attempt to restrict soft money contributions and issues advocacy, was passed by Congress in 2002.

3. The role played by private money in American politics affects the relative power of social groups. As a result, less affluent groups have considerably less power in the political system.

Practice Quiz

1. A political party is different from an interest group in that a political party
   a) seeks to control the entire government by electing its members to office and thereby controlling the government's personnel.
   b) seeks to control only limited, very specific functions of government.
   c) is entirely nonprofit.
   d) has a much smaller membership.

2. The periodic episodes in American history in which an "old" dominant political party is replaced by a "new" dominant political party are called
   a) constitutional revolutions.
   b) party turnovers.
   c) presidential elections.
   d) electoral realignments.

3. Which party was founded as a political expression of the antislavery movement?
   a) American Independent
   b) Prohibition
   c) Republican
   d) Democratic

4. Historically, when do realignments occur?
   a) typically, every twenty years
   b) whenever a minority party takes over Congress
   c) when large numbers of voters permanently shift their support from one party to another
   d) in odd-numbered years

5. Parties today are most important in the electoral process in
   a) recruiting and nominating candidates for office.
   b) financing all of the campaign's spending.
   c) providing millions of volunteers to mobilize voters.
   d) creating a responsible party government.

6. What role do parties play in Congress?
   a) They select leaders, such as the speaker of the House.
   b) They assign members to committees.
   c) Both a and b are correct.
   d) Parties play no role in Congress.

7. In general, parties are important in a democracy because they
   a) encourage electoral competition.
   b) promote voter turnout.
   c) make governance possible by organizing elected leaders into governing coalitions.
   d) all of the above.

8. What is the difference between an open and a closed primary?
   a) You must pay a poll tax to vote in a closed primary.
   b) Open primaries allow voters to split the ticket.
   c) In closed primaries, only registered members of a political party may vote to select that party's candidates.
   d) They are fundamentally the same thing.

9. In *Buckley v. Valeo*, the Supreme Court ruled that
   a) PAC donations to campaigns are constitutionally protected.
   b) The right of individuals to spend their own money to campaign is constitutionally protected.
   c) The political system is corrupt.
   d) The Federal Elections Campaign Act is unconstitutional.

10. Party loyalty
    a) is often handed down from parents to children.
    b) changes frequently.
    c) has little impact on electoral choice.
    d) is mandated in states with closed primaries.

Critical Thinking Questions

1. Historically, third parties have developed in American history when the existing parties have ignored certain issues or constituencies. Considering the similarities and differences between the Democratic and Republican parties, where might a budding third party find a constituency? What issues might it adopt? Finally, what structural and ideological obstacles might that third party face?

2. What are the sources of campaign money in American politics? Why do candidates for public office need to raise so much money? How has the government sought to balance the competing ideals of free expression and equal representation in regard to campaign financing? Is this yet another example of a conflict between liberty and democracy?

Key Terms

closed primary (p. 179)
divided government (p. 168)
electoral college (p. 180)
electoral realignment (p. 167)
"527" committees (p. 191)
incumbent (p. 159)
issue advocacy (p. 190)
majority party (p. 161)

minority party (p. 161)
multiple-member district (p. 170)
nomination (p. 160)
open primary (p. 179)
party identification (p. 171)
plurality system (p. 170)
political action committee (PAC) (p. 190)
political parties (p. 158)
primary elections (p. 177)

proportional representation (p. 170)
recall (p. 179)
referendum (p. 179)
single-member district (p. 170)
soft money (p. 191)
suffrage (p. 175)
third parties (p. 169)
turnout (p. 175)
two-party system (p. 164)

7 INTEREST GROUPS

MAIN MESSAGE

Group politics in America is both pluralist and elitist.

In the late 1980s, the New York State government announced that it was seeking a location within the state to bury low-level nuclear waste materials, including such items as contaminated protective clothing worn by workers at nuclear power facilities and waste by-products from medical research and treatments that used radiation. The choice of a site rapidly came down to two possible locations: one in western New York, and the other in Cortland County, located in the state's geographic center. Not surprisingly, Cortland County residents were extremely alarmed at the prospect of placing a permanent storage facility for nuclear waste—even "low-level" waste—in their backyards. Mobilized by this threat, local residents of this mostly rural area began to organize to express their political opposition and to try to reverse the decision of the commission chosen to select a site.

Key Concepts

1. Interest groups have become the most vital and effective form of political expression for citizens trying to shape government decisions.

2. Interest group activity does not necessarily equal democracy, since those with more time, information, and resources are more likely to succeed through group action.

3. The growth of government programs has spurred the growth of groups.

4. Interest groups follow many strategies aside from lobbying to shape government decisions.

The odds of success seemed slim, as the state already possessed the necessary legal authority to obtain land via eminent domain (the power of the government to take land for a public purpose, as long as it paid fair market value for the land) and Congress had passed a law requiring states to find in-state locations for nuclear waste. Nevertheless, local residents who had never taken an interest in politics, and who possessed little in the way of wealth or experience, mobilized their limited resources, set up a storefront office, and formed a group called Citizens Against Radioactive Dumping (CARD). The group organized, raised money, wrote letters, held protests, met with public officials, lobbied the government, and filed legal motions. They also garnered extensive media attention, eventually bringing Cortland County to national attention on several network evening news broadcasts and to the front pages of newspapers such as the *New York Times*. CARD and other similar grassroots groups succeeded in winning a halt to the nuclear dump siting process, and a later court challenge resulted in the Supreme Court striking down the federal law requiring states to find in-state dump sites. The local political amateurs had succeeded in beating the state government.

The actions of CARD provide an excellent example of pluralist, grassroots (that is, locally organized, locally based political action) interest group politics. Political action of this kind is hardly new to American politics. Writing in the 1830s, a French aristocrat named Alexis de Tocqueville noted that the genius of American democracy lay in "voluntary association." Even then, Americans were not particularly civic-minded most of the time, de Tocqueville noted. They were happy to go their individual ways most of the time. But, like the minutemen of the Revolution, when a threat to their community or way of life arose, Americans mobilized into "voluntary associations" to engage in politics long enough to put things right.[1]

In this chapter, we will see that interest group politics is the most vital link between citizens and governments, and that it has, in fact, become even more important in recent decades. We will also see that, at times, interest group politics can be strongly pluralist, as shown by the example of CARD, but at other times it can be highly elitist.

Pluralist and Elitist Views Both Explain the Group Process

The framers of the American Constitution feared the power that could be wielded by organized interests. Yet they believed that interest groups thrived because of liberty—the freedom that all Americans enjoyed to organize and express their views. If the government were given the power to regulate or in any way to forbid efforts by organized interests to interfere in the political process, the government would in effect have the power to suppress liberty. The solution to this dilemma was presented by James Madison:

> Take in a greater variety of parties and interest [and] you make it less probable that a majority of the whole will have a common motive to invade the rights of other citizens.... [Hence the advantage] enjoyed by a large over a small republic.[2]

According to the Madisonian theory, a good constitution encourages multitudes of interests so that no single interest, which he called a "faction," can ever tyrannize the others. The basic assumption is that competition among interests will produce balance, with all the interests regulating each other.[3] Today, this Madisonian principle of regulation is called **pluralism.** According to pluralist theory, all interests are and should be free to compete for influence in the United States. Moreover, according to a pluralist doctrine, the outcome of this competition is compromise and moderation, since no group is likely to be able to achieve any of its goals without accommodating itself to some of the views of its many competitors.[4]

> **pluralism** the theory that all interests are and should be free to compete for influence in the government. The outcome of this competition is compromise and moderation

Tens of thousands of organized groups have formed in the United States, ranging from civic associations to huge nationwide groups such as the National Rifle Association, whose chief cause is opposition to restrictions on gun ownership, or Common Cause, a public-interest group that advocates a variety of liberal political reforms. Despite the array of interest groups in American politics, however, we can be sure neither that all interests are represented equally nor that the results of this group competition are consistent with the common good. One criticism of interest-group politics is its class bias in favor of those with greater financial resources. As one critic put it, "The flaw in the pluralist heaven is that the heavenly chorus sings with a strong upper-class accent."[5] When interest group politics is dominated by the rich and the socially well-positioned, such as top business or government officials, it may take an elitist orientation.

Another assumption of pluralism is that all groups have equal access to the political process and that achieving an outcome favorable to a particular group depends only upon that group's strength and resources, not upon biases inherent in the political system. But, as we shall see, group politics is a political format that has worked and continues to work more to the advantage of some types of interests than others.

Interest Groups Represent Different Interests but Have Similar Organizations and Membership

An **interest group** is an organized group of people that makes policy-related appeals to government. This definition of interest groups includes membership organizations but also businesses, corporations, universities, and other institutions that do not accept members. The members of an interest group pursue a common interest (or interests), through political participation, toward the ultimate goal of getting favorable public policy decisions from government. Individuals form groups in order to increase the chance that their views will be heard and their interests treated favorably by the government. Interest groups are organized to influence governmental decisions.

> **interest group** a voluntary membership association organized to pursue a common interest (or interests), through political participation, toward the ultimate goal of getting favorable public policy decisions from government

Interest groups are sometimes referred to as "lobbies." They are also sometimes confused with political action committees. PACs are actually interest groups that focus on influencing elections rather than trying to influence the elected. One final distinction that we should make is that interest groups are also different from political parties: Interest groups tend to concern themselves with the *policies* of government; parties tend to concern themselves with the *personnel* of government.

WHAT INTERESTS ARE REPRESENTED?

Business and Agricultural Groups   Interest groups come in as many shapes and sizes as the interests they represent. When most people think about interest groups, they immediately think of groups with a direct economic interest in governmental actions. These groups are generally supported by groups of producers or manufacturers in a particular economic sector. Examples of this type of group include the National Petroleum Refiners Association and the American Farm Bureau Federation. At the same time that broadly representative groups such as these are active in Washington, specific companies, such as Shell Oil, IBM, and General Motors, may be active on certain issues that are of particular concern to them.

Labor Groups   Labor organizations are equally active lobbyists. The AFL-CIO, the United Mine Workers, and the Teamsters are all groups that lobby on behalf of organized labor. In recent years, groups have arisen to further the interests of public employees, the most significant among these being the American Federation of State, County, and Municipal Employees (AFSCME). Public school teachers, including faculty who teach at public colleges and universities, are today represented by two powerful unions. The National Education Association (NEA) and the American Federation of Teachers (AFT) wield considerable political clout.

Professional Associations   Professional lobbies like the American Bar Association and the American Medical Association have been particularly successful in furthering their members' interests in state and federal legislatures. Financial institutions, represented by organizations such as the American Bankers Association and the National Savings & Loan League, although often less visible than other lobbies, also play an important role in shaping legislative policy.

Public Interest Groups   Recent years have witnessed the growth of a powerful "public interest" lobby, purporting to represent interests whose concerns are not addressed by traditional lobbies. These groups have been most visible in the consumer protection and environmental policy areas, although public interest groups cover a broad range of issues. The National Resources Defense Council, the Sierra Club, the Union of Concerned Scientists, and Common Cause are all examples of public interest groups.

Ideological Groups   Closely related to and overlapping public interest groups are ideological groups, organized in support of a particular political or philosophical perspective. People for the American Way, for example, promotes liberal values, whereas the Christian Coalition focuses on conservative social goals and the National Taxpayers Union campaigns to reduce the size of the federal government.

Public-Sector Groups   The perceived need for representation on Capitol Hill has generated a public-sector lobby in the past several years, including the National League of Cities and the "research" lobby. The latter group comprises think tanks and universities that have an interest in obtaining government funds for research and support, and it includes such institutions as Harvard University, the Brookings Institution, and the American Enterprise Institute. Indeed, universities have expanded their lobbying efforts even as they have reduced faculty positions and course offerings.[6]

THE ORGANIZATIONAL COMPONENTS OF GROUPS INCLUDE MONEY, OFFICES, AND MEMBERS

Although there are many interest groups, most share certain key organizational components. These include leadership, money, an agency or office, and members.

First, every group must have a leadership and decision-making structure. For some groups, this structure is very simple. For others, it can be quite elaborate and involve hundreds of local chapters that are melded into a national apparatus. Interest group leadership is, in some respects, analogous to business leadership. Just as is true in the business world, successful groups often become bureaucratized; the initial entrepreneurial leadership is replaced by a paid professional staff. In the 1960s, for example, Ralph Nader led a loosely organized band of consumer advocates ("Nader's Raiders") in a crusade for product safety that resulted in the enactment of a number of pieces of legislation and numerous regulations, such as the requirement that all new cars be equipped with air bags. Today, Nader's ragtag band of raiders has been transformed into a well-organized and well-financed phalanx of interlocked groups, including Public Citizen, the Center for the Study of Responsive Law, and the Center for Science in the Public Interest, all led by professional staffs.

Second, every interest group must build a financial structure capable of sustaining an organization and funding the group's activities. Most interest groups rely on membership dues and voluntary contributions from sympathizers. Many also sell some ancillary services to members, such as insurance and vacation tours. Third, most groups establish an agency that carries out the group's tasks. This may be a research organization, a public relations office, or a lobbying office in Washington or a state capital.

Finally, all interest groups must attract and keep members. Somehow, groups must persuade individuals to invest the money, time, energy, or effort required to take part in the group's activities. Members play a larger role in some groups than in others. In membership associations, group members actually serve on committees and engage in projects. In the case of labor unions, members may march on picket lines, and in the case of political or ideological groups, members may participate in demonstrations and protests. In another set of groups, "staff organizations," a professional staff conducts most of the group's activities; members are called upon only to pay dues and make other contributions. Among the well-known public interest groups, some, such as the National Organization for Women (NOW), are membership groups, whereas others, such as Defenders of Wildlife and the Children's Defense Fund, are staff organizations.

The "Free Rider" Problem   Whether they need individuals to volunteer or merely to write checks, both types of groups need to recruit and retain members. Yet many groups find this task difficult, even when it comes to recruiting members who agree strongly with the group's goals. Why? As economist Mancur Olson explains, the benefits of a group's success are often broadly available and cannot be denied to nonmembers.[7] Such benefits can be called **collective goods.** Following Olson's own example, suppose a number of private property owners live near a mosquito-infested swamp. Each owner wants this swamp cleared. But if one or a few of the owners were to clear the swamp alone, their actions would benefit all the other owners as well, without any effort on the part of those other owners. Each of the inactive owners would be a **free rider** on the efforts of the ones who cleared the swamp. Thus, there is a disincentive for any of the owners to undertake the job alone.

  Since the number of concerned owners is small in this particular case, they might eventually be able to organize themselves to share the costs as well as enjoy the benefits of clearing the swamp. But suppose the number of interested people increases. Suppose the common concern is not the neighborhood swamp but polluted air or groundwater involving thousands of residents in a region, or in fact millions of residents in a whole nation. National defense is the most obvious collective good whose benefits are shared by every resident, regardless of the taxes they pay or the support they provide. As the number of involved persons increases, or as the size of the group increases, the free rider phenomenon becomes more of a problem. Individuals do not have much incentive to become active members and supporters of a group that is already working more or less on their behalf.

Why Join?   Despite the free rider problem, interest groups offer numerous incentives to join. Most importantly, they make various "selective benefits" available only to group members. These benefits can be information-related, material, solidary, or purposive. Table 7.1 gives some examples of the range of benefits in each of these categories.

  Informational benefits are the most widespread and important category of selective benefits offered to group members. Information is provided through conferences, training programs, and newsletters and other periodicals sent automatically to those who have paid membership dues.

collective goods benefits, sought by groups, that are broadly available and cannot be denied to nonmembers

free riders those who enjoy the benefits of collective goods but did not participate in acquiring them

Selective Benefits of Interest Group Membership

Table 7.1

CATEGORY	BENEFITS
Informational benefits	Conferences
	Professional contacts
	Training programs
	Publications
	Coordination among organizations
	Research
	Legal help
	Professional codes
	Collective bargaining
Material benefits	Travel packages
	Insurance
	Discounts on consumer goods
Solidary benefits	Friendship
	Networking opportunities
Purposive benefits	Advocacy
	Representation before government
	Participation in public affairs

SOURCE: Adapted from Jack Walker, Jr., *Mobilizing Interest Groups in America: Patrons, Professions, and Social Movements* (Ann Arbor, MI: University of Michigan Press, 1991), p. 86.

Material benefits include anything that can be measured monetarily, such as special services, goods, and even money. A broad range of material benefits can be offered by groups to attract members. These benefits often include discount purchasing, shared advertising, and, perhaps most valuable of all, health and retirement insurance.

Another option identified on Table 7.1 is that of **solidary benefits.** The most notable of this class of benefits are the friendship and "networking" opportunities that membership provides. Many businesspeople join their local chapters of Rotary International, a service organization, in order to meet and develop contacts with other businesspeople in their communities. Another benefit that has become extremely important to many of the newer nonprofit and citizen groups is what has come to be called "consciousness-raising." One example of this can be seen in the claims of many women's organizations that active participation conveys to each female member of the organization an enhanced sense of her own value and a stronger ability to advance individual as well as collective civil rights.

A fourth type of benefit involves the appeal of the purpose of an interest group. The benefits of religious interest groups provide us with the best examples of such **purposive benefits.** The Christian Right is a powerful movement made up of a number of interest groups that offer virtually no material benefits to their

material benefits special goods, services, or money provided to members of groups to entice others to join

solidary benefits selective benefits of a group membership that emphasize friendship, networking, and consciousness-raising

purposive benefits selective benefits of group membership that emphasize the purpose and accomplishments of the group members. The growth and success of these groups depend upon the deeply held religious beliefs of their members. Many such religion-based interest groups have arisen, especially at state and local levels, throughout American history. For example, both the abolition and the prohibition movements were driven by religious interest groups whose main attractions were nonmaterial benefits.

Ideology itself, or the sharing of a commonly developed ideology, is a similar nonmaterial benefit. Many of the most successful interest groups of the past twenty years have been citizen groups or public interest groups, whose members are brought together largely around shared ideological goals, including government reform, election and campaign reform, civil rights, economic equality, "family values," or even opposition to government itself.

GROUP MEMBERSHIP HAS AN UPPER-CLASS BIAS

Membership in interest groups is not randomly distributed in the population. People with higher incomes, higher levels of education, and management or professional occupations are much more likely to become members of groups than those who occupy the lower rungs on the socioeconomic ladder (see Figure 7.1).[8] Well-educated, upper-income business and professional people are more likely to have the time and the money and to have acquired through the

Figure 7.1 **Interest Group Membership by Income Level**

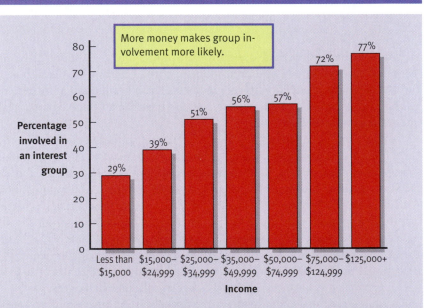

SOURCE: Kay Lehman Scholzman, "Voluntary Organizations in Politics: Who Gets Involved?" in *Representing Interests and Interest Group Representation*, ed. William Crotty, Mildred A. Schwartz, and John C. Green (Lanham, MD: University Press of America, 1994), p. 76.

educational process the concerns and skills needed to play a role in a group or association. Moreover, for business and professional people, group membership may provide personal contacts and access to information that can help advance their careers. At the same time, of course, corporate entities—businesses and the like—usually have ample resources to form or participate in groups that seek to advance their causes.

The result of this elitist tendency is that interest-group politics in the United States tends to have a very pronounced upper-class bias. Certainly, there are many interest groups and political associations that have a working-class or lower-class membership—labor organizations or welfare rights organizations, for example—but the great majority of interest groups and their members are drawn from the middle and upper-middle classes. In general, the "interests" served by interest groups are the interests of society's "haves." Even when interest groups take opposing positions on issues and policies, the conflicting positions they espouse usually reflect divisions among upper-income strata rather than conflicts between the upper and lower classes.

The Number of Groups Has Increased in the Last Thirty Years

Over the past thirty-five years, there has been an enormous increase both in the number of interest groups seeking to play a role in the American political process and in the extent of their influence over that process. This explosion of interest-group activity has three basic origins: first, the expansion of the role of government during this period; second, the coming of age of a new dynamic set of political forces in the United States—forces that have relied heavily on public interest groups to advance their causes; and third, an explosion in the number and political vitality of grassroots and conservative groups.

THE EXPANSION OF GOVERNMENT HAS SPURRED THE GROWTH OF GROUPS

Modern governments' extensive economic and social programs have powerful politicizing effects, often sparking the organization of new groups and interests. In other words, interest groups often form as the result of, or in response to, government actions, rather than groups pressing the government to take on new responsibilities. Even when national policies are initially responses to the appeals of pressure groups, government involvement in any area can be a powerful stimulus for political organization and action by those whose interests are affected. For example, during the 1970s, expanded federal regulation of the automobile, oil, gas, education, and health care industries impelled each of these interests to increase substantially its efforts to influence the government's behavior. These efforts, in turn, spurred the organization of other groups to either support or oppose the activities of the first.[9] Similarly, federal social programs have occasionally sparked political organization and action on the part of clientele groups seeking to influence the distribution of benefits and, in turn, the organization of groups opposed to the programs or their cost. For example, federal programs and court decisions in such areas as abortion and school prayer were the stimuli for new political action and organization by fundamentalist religious groups. Thus, the expansion of government in recent decades has also stimulated increased group activity and organization.

THE NEW POLITICS MOVEMENT FOCUSES ON PUBLIC INTEREST GROUPS

The second factor accounting for the explosion of interest-group activity in recent years has been the emergence of a new set of forces in American politics that can collectively be called the "New Politics" movement.

New Politics movement a political movement that began in the 1960s and 1970s, made up of professionals and intellectuals for whom the civil rights and antiwar movements were formative experiences. The New Politics movement strengthened public-interest groups

The **New Politics movement** is made up of upper-middle-class professionals and intellectuals for whom the civil rights and anti-Vietnam War movements of the 1960s were formative experiences, just as the Great Depression and World War II had been for their parents in the 1930s and 1940s. The crusade against racial discrimination and the Vietnam War led these young men and women to see themselves as a political force in opposition to the public policies and politicians associated with the nation's postwar regime. In recent years, the forces of New Politics have focused their attention on such issues as environmental protection, women's rights, and nuclear disarmament.

Members of the New Politics movement constructed or strengthened public interest groups such as Common Cause, the Sierra Club, the Environmental Defense Fund, Physicians for Social Responsibility, the National Organization for Women, and the various organizations formed by consumer activist Ralph Nader. Through these groups, New Politics forces were able to influence the media, Congress, and even the judiciary and enjoyed a remarkable degree of success during the late 1960s and early 1970s in securing the enactment of policies they favored. New Politics activists also played a major role in securing the enactment of environmental, consumer, and occupational health and safety legislation.

CONSERVATIVE INTEREST GROUPS GO GRASSROOTS

The third factor associated with the expansion of interest-group politics in contemporary America has been an explosion of grassroots conservative activity. For example, the Christian Coalition, whose major focus is opposition to abortion, has nearly two million active members organized in local chapters in every state. Twenty of its state chapters have full-time staff and fifteen have annual budgets of over $200,000.[10] The National Taxpayers Union has several hundred local chapters. The National Federation of Independent Business

(NFIB) has hundreds of active local chapters throughout the nation, particularly in the Midwest and Southeast. Associations dedicated to defending "property rights" exist at the local level throughout the West. Right-to-life groups are organized in virtually every U.S. congressional district. Even proponents of the rather exotic principle of "home schooling" are organized through the Home School Legal Defense Association (HSLDA), which has seventy-five regional chapters that, in turn, are linked to more than three thousand local support groups.

These local conservative organizations have been energized by the political struggles of the last decade. During the 2004 run for the presidency, President Bush's reelection campaign invested substantial effort to mobilize conservative religious congregations around the country to register new voters and distribute campaign literature, inspired by the fact that regular churchgoers voted heavily for Bush in 2000. In fact, the Bush campaign considered these efforts a "top priority" for victory in 2004. In Pennsylvania alone, Bush campaign coordinators asked state leaders to identify 1,600 friendly congregations to be contacted. Liberal critics complained that the effort violated the separation of church and state. Churches are normally exempted from paying taxes; openly political groups that take sides in elections are required to pay taxes, and in the 1990s some conservative churches lost their tax exempt status because they engaged in express political activity for the Republican Party.[11]

Interest Groups Use Different Strategies to Gain Influence

As we have seen, interest groups work to improve the probability that they and their interests will be heard and treated favorably by the government. The quest for political influence or power takes many forms, but among the most frequently used strategies are lobbying, gaining access to key decision makers, using the courts, mobilizing public opinion, and using electoral politics. These "tactics of influence" do not exhaust all the possibilities, but they paint a broad picture of groups competing for power through the maximum utilization of their resources (see Figure 7.2).

Many groups employ a mix of strategies. For example, environmental groups such as the Sierra Club lobby members of Congress and key congressional staff members, participate in bureaucratic rule making by offering comments and suggestions to agencies on new environmental rules, and bring lawsuits under various environmental acts such as the Endangered Species Act, which authorizes groups and citizens to come to court if they believe the act is being violated. At the same time, the Sierra Club attempts to influence public opinion through media campaigns and to influence electoral politics by supporting candidates who they believe share their environmental views and opposing candidates who they view as foes of environmentalism.

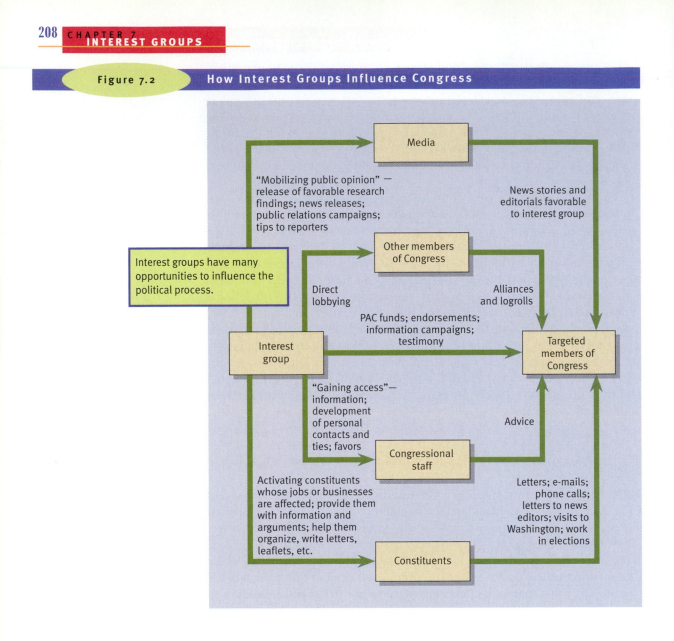

Figure 7.2 — How Interest Groups Influence Congress

Interest groups have many opportunities to influence the political process.

Media

"Mobilizing public opinion" — release of favorable research findings; news releases; public relations campaigns; tips to reporters

News stories and editorials favorable to interest group

Other members of Congress

Direct lobbying

Alliances and logrolls

PAC funds; endorsements; information campaigns; testimony

Interest group

Targeted members of Congress

"Gaining access" — information; development of personal contacts and ties; favors

Advice

Congressional staff

Activating constituents whose jobs or businesses are affected; provide them with information and arguments; help them organize, write letters, leaflets, etc.

Letters; e-mails; phone calls; letters to news editors; visits to Washington; work in elections

Constituents

DIRECT LOBBYING COMBINES EDUCATION, PERSUASION, AND PRESSURE

lobbying a strategy by which organized interests seek to influence the passage of legislation by exerting direct pressure on members of the legislature

Lobbying is an attempt by a group to influence the policy process through persuasion of government officials. Most Americans tend to think that interest groups exert their influence through direct contact with members of Congress, but lobbying encompasses a wide range of activities that groups engage in with all sorts of government officials and the public as a whole.

Lobbying involves a great deal of activity on the part of someone speaking for an interest. Lobbyists badger and buttonhole legislators, administrators, and committee staff members, bring to their attention facts about pertinent issues and facts or claims about public support of certain issues or facts.[12] Lobbyists can serve a useful purpose in the legislative and administrative processes by providing this kind of information. In 1978, during debate on a bill to expand the requirement for lobbying disclosures, Democratic senators Edward Kennedy of Massachusetts and Dick Clark of Iowa joined with Republican Senator Robert Stafford of Vermont to issue the following statement: "Government without lobbying could not function. The flow of information to Congress and to every federal agency is a vital part of our democratic system."[13]

Groups often select lobbyists with a considerable amount of Washington experience. In the days following the September 11, 2001, terrorist attacks, the airline industry mounted a furious lobbying effort to win a multibillion-dollar aid package to rescue the industry. Among the most important lobbyists was Linda Daschle, a lobbyist for American Airlines and wife of the Senate Democratic leader Tom Daschle. In less than two weeks after the attacks, Congress had given the airlines a $15 billion aid package, including $5 billion in direct grants and $10 billion in loan guarantees (to support airline loans from private banks, so that if any airline were unable to pay back a loan, the government would cover it). According to Illinois senator Peter Fitzgerald, the lobbying by the airlines "was masterful. The airline industry made a full-court press to convince Congress that giving them billions in taxpayer cash was the only way to save the republic."[14] A study by the Center for Responsive Politics concluded in 1999 that 129 former members of Congress lobbied the institution where they once worked. Some estimates run even higher. Many former members of the executive branch also pursue lobbying careers, underscoring the value of well-connected and well-financed efforts to influence public policy.

Even when an interest group is very successful at getting its bill passed by Congress and signed by the president, the prospect of full and faithful implementation of that law is not guaranteed. Often, a group and its allies do not pack up and go home as soon as the president turns their lobbied-for new law over to the appropriate agency. On average, 40 percent of interest-group representatives regularly contact both legislative and executive branch organizations, while 13 percent contact only the legislature and 16 percent only the executive branch.[15]

CULTIVATING ACCESS MEANS GETTING THE ATTENTION OF DECISION MAKERS

Exerting influence on Congress or government agencies by providing them with information about issues, support, and even threats of retaliation requires easy and constant access to decision makers.

Figure 7.3 illustrates one of the most important access patterns in recent American political history: that of the defense industry. Each such pattern, or **iron triangle,** is almost literally a triangular shape, with one point in an executive branch program, another point in a Senate or House legislative committee

iron triangle the stable, cooperative relationships that often develop between a congressional committee, an administrative agency, and one or more supportive interest groups. Similar relationships with more than three parties exist, but the iron triangle is the most typical

Figure 7.3   The Iron Triangle in the Defense Sector

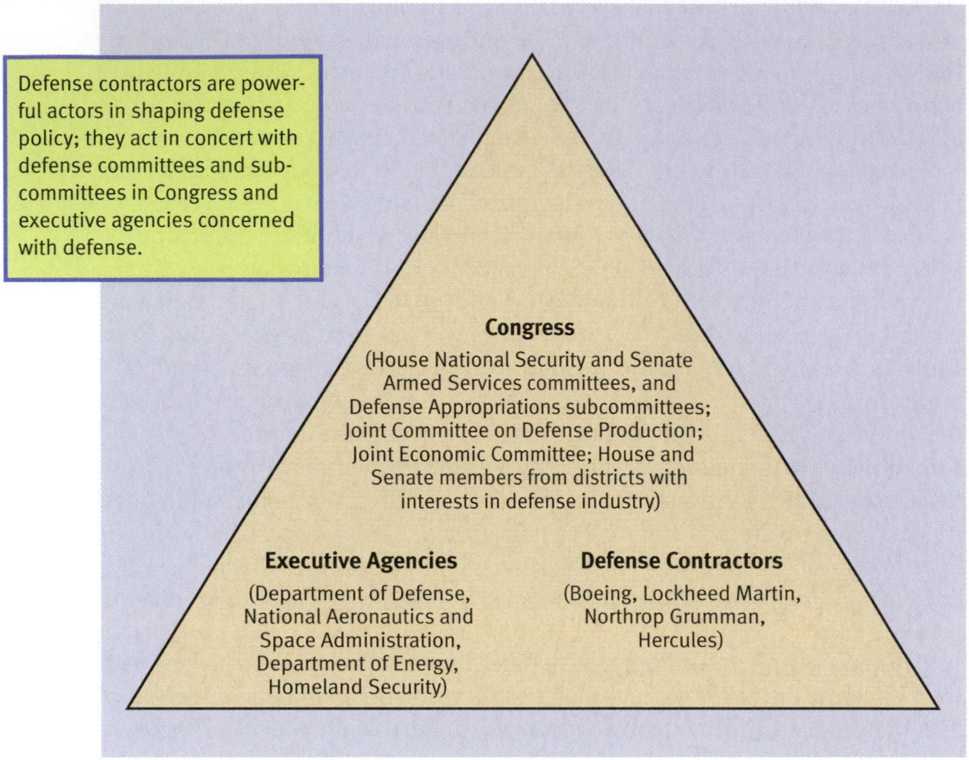

Defense contractors are powerful actors in shaping defense policy; they act in concert with defense committees and subcommittees in Congress and executive agencies concerned with defense.

Congress
(House National Security and Senate Armed Services committees, and Defense Appropriations subcommittees; Joint Committee on Defense Production; Joint Economic Committee; House and Senate members from districts with interests in defense industry)

Executive Agencies
(Department of Defense, National Aeronautics and Space Administration, Department of Energy, Homeland Security)

Defense Contractors
(Boeing, Lockheed Martin, Northrop Grumman, Hercules)

or subcommittee, and a third point in some highly stable and well-organized interest group. The points in the triangular relationship are mutually supporting; they count as access only if they last over a long period of time. For example, access to a legislative committee or subcommittee requires that at least one member of it support the interest group in question. This member also must have built up considerable seniority in Congress. An interest cannot feel comfortable about its access to Congress until it has one or more of its "own" people with ten or more years of continuous service on the relevant committee or subcommittee.[16]

USING THE COURTS (LITIGATION) CAN BE HIGHLY EFFECTIVE

Most people think of lobbying as the chief, or only, way interest groups attempt to influence politics. Yet interest groups often turn to lawsuits as a way to change policy, government agency behavior, and the actions of other groups they oppose. Interest groups can use the courts to affect public policy in at least three ways: (1) by bringing suit directly on behalf of the group itself, (2) by financing suits brought by individuals, or (3) by filing a companion brief as *"amicus curiae"* (literally "friend of the court") to an existing court case.

Among the most significant modern illustrations of the use of the courts as a strategy for political influence are those that accompanied the "sexual revolution" of the 1960s and the emergence of the movement for women's rights.

The 1973 Supreme Court case of *Roe v. Wade,* which made it illegal for states to ban abortions, sparked a controversy that brought conservatives to the fore on a national level.[17] These conservative groups made extensive use of the courts to whittle away the scope of the privacy doctrine. They obtained rulings, for example, that prohibit the use of federal funds to pay for voluntary abortions. And in 1989, right-to-life groups were able to use a strategy of litigation that significantly undermined the *Roe v. Wade* decision, namely in the case of *Webster v. Reproductive Health Services,* which restored the right of states to place restrictions on abortion.[18] The *Webster* case brought more than three hundred interest groups on both sides of the abortion issue to the Supreme Court's door.

Another extremely significant set of contemporary illustrations of the use of the courts as a strategy for political influence consists of those found in the history of the National Association for the Advancement of Colored People (NAACP). The most important of these court cases was, of course, *Brown v. Board of Education of Topeka, Kansas,* in which the U.S. Supreme Court held that legal segregation of the schools was unconstitutional.[19]

Business groups are also frequent users of the courts because of the number of government programs applied to them. Litigation involving large businesses is most mountainous in such areas as taxation, antitrust, interstate transportation, patents, and product quality and standardization. Often a business is brought to litigation against its will by virtue of initiatives taken against it by other businesses or by government agencies. But many individual businesses bring suit themselves in order to influence government policy.

New Politics forces made significant use of the courts during the 1970s and 1980s, and judicial decisions were instrumental in advancing their goals. Facilitated by changes in the rules governing access to the courts, the New Politics agenda was clearly visible in court decisions handed down in several key policy areas. In the environmental policy area, New Politics groups were able to force federal agencies to pay attention to environmental issues, even when the agency was not directly involved in activities related to environmental quality. For example, the Federal Trade Commission (FTC) became very responsive to the demands of New Politics activists during the 1970s and 1980s. The FTC stepped up its activities considerably, litigating a series of claims arising under regulations prohibiting deceptive advertising in cases ranging from false claims for over-the-counter drugs to inflated claims about the nutritional value of children's cereal.

And while feminists and equal rights activists enjoyed enormous success in litigating discrimination claims under the Civil Rights Act of 1964, antinuclear power activists succeeded in virtually shutting down the nuclear power industry.

How Lobbyists Help Interest Groups Gain Influence

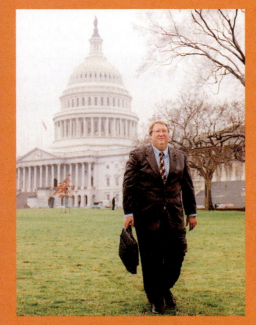

Lobbyists frequent the halls of power. Frank Gladics is a lobbyist for the U.S. timber industry.

Lobbyists represent not only thousands of private and public interests but also the different branches of government. For instance, President Bill Clinton employed John Hilley, pictured here, as his chief congressional lobbyist for matters concerning the federal budget.

While lobbyists most often meet with members of Congress, some do succeed in meeting with the president. Former President George H. W. Bush is seen here with lobbyists from Citizens for a Sound Economy.

POLITICS

In recent years, foreign interest and governments have employed lobbyists in Washington. Otilie English (left), a lobbyist for the Afghan Northern Alliance, is shown here shaking hands with Representative Juanita Millender-McDonald during a Congressional Women's Caucus briefing in 2001.

Lobbyists are likely to have professional experience in government, and government officials are sometimes hired from the lobbying industry. Howard Metzenbaum (left) is a former senator from Ohio now working as a lobbyist for the Consumer Federation of America. President George W. Bush's first Secretary of Agriculture, Ann Veneman, chose Dale Moore, former head lobbyist for the National Cattlemen's Beef Association, as her chief of staff. Secretary Veneman is shown here speaking at the NCBA convention in January 2003.

Despite significant defeats, challenges to power plant siting and licensing regulations were instrumental in discouraging energy companies from pursuing nuclear projects over the long term.[20]

MOBILIZING PUBLIC OPINION BRINGS WIDER ATTENTION TO AN ISSUE

going public a strategy that attempts to mobilize the widest and most favorable climate of opinion

Going public is a strategy that attempts to mobilize the widest and most favorable climate of opinion. Many groups consider it imperative to maintain this climate at all times, even when they have no issue to fight about. An increased use of this kind of strategy is usually associated with modern advertising. As early as the 1930s, political analysts were distinguishing between the "old lobby" of direct group representation before Congress and the "new lobby" of public relations professionals addressing the public at large to reach Congress.[21]

institutional advertising advertising designed to create a positive image of an organization

Institutional Advertising One of the best known ways of going public is the use of **institutional advertising.** A casual scanning of important mass circulation magazines and newspapers provides numerous examples of expensive and well-designed ads by the major oil companies, automobile and steel companies, other large corporations, and trade associations. The ads show how much these organizations are doing for the country, for the protection of the environment, or for the defense of the American way of life. Their purpose is to create and maintain a strongly positive association between the organization and the community at large, in the hope that these favorable feelings can be drawn on as needed for specific political campaigns later on.

Social Movements Going public is not limited to businesses or to groups of upper-income professionals. Many groups resort to it because they lack the resources, the contacts, or the experience to use other political strategies. The sponsorship of boycotts, sit-ins, mass rallies, and marches by Martin Luther King's Southern Christian Leadership Conference (SCLC) and related organizations in the 1950s and 1960s is one of the most significant and successful cases of going public to create a more favorable climate of opinion by calling attention to abuses. The success of these events inspired similar efforts on the part of women. Organizations such as the National Organization for Women (NOW) used public strategies in their drive for legislation and in their efforts to gain ratification of the Equal Rights Amendment. In 1993, gay rights groups organized a mass rally as part of their effort to eliminate restrictions on military service and other forms of discrimination based on individuals' sexual preferences. Gay rights leaders met with President Clinton in mid-April 1993 and were assured of his support for a demonstration in Washington to be held at the end of the month.[22] Although President Clinton had campaigned actively for gay and lesbian support during the election, he did not attend the march for fear of offending religious conservatives.

Grassroots Mobilization   Another form of going public is **grassroots lobby-ing.** In such a campaign, a lobby group mobilizes its members and their families throughout the country to write to their elected representatives in support of the group's position.

grassroots lobbying a lobbying campaign in which a group mobilizes its membership to contact government officials in support of the group's position

Among the most effective users of the grassroots lobby effort in contemporary American politics is the religious right. Networks of evangelical churches have the capacity to generate hundreds of thousands of letters and phone calls to Congress and the White House. For example, the religious right was outraged when President Clinton announced soon after taking office that he planned to end the military's ban on gay and lesbian soldiers. The Rev. Jerry Falwell, an evangelical leader, called upon viewers of his television program to dial a telephone number that would add their names to a petition urging Clinton to retain the ban on gays in the military. Within a few hours, twenty-four thousand people had called to support the petition.[23]

Has grassroots campaigning been cynically exploited? More and more people, including leading members of Congress, are becoming quite skeptical of such methods, charging that these are not genuine grassroots campaigns but instead represent "Astroturf lobbying" (a play on the name of an artificial grass used on many sports fields). Such Astroturf campaigns have increased in frequency in recent years as members of Congress have grown more and more skeptical of Washington lobbyists and far more concerned about demonstrations of support for a particular issue by their constituents.

GROUPS OFTEN USE ELECTORAL POLITICS

In addition to attempting to influence members of Congress and other government officials, interest groups also seek to use the electoral process to elect the right legislators in the first place and to ensure that those who are elected will owe them a debt of gratitude for their support. To put matters into perspective, groups invest far more resources in lobbying than in electoral politics. Nevertheless, financial support and campaign activism can be important tools for organized interests.

Political Action Committees   By far the most common electoral strategy employed by interest groups is that of giving financial support to the parties or to particular candidates. But such support can easily cross the threshold into outright bribery. Therefore, Congress has occasionally made an effort to regulate this strategy. Congress's most recent effort was the Federal Election Campaign Act of 1971 (amended in 1974). This act limits campaign contributions and requires that each candidate or campaign committee itemize the full name and address, occupation, and principal business of each person who contributes more than $100. These provisions have been effective up to a point, considering the rather large number of embarrassments, indictments, resignations, and criminal convictions in the aftermath of the Watergate scandal of the early 1970s.

Reaction to Watergate produced further legislation on campaign finance in 1974 and 1976, but the effect has been to restrict individual rather than interest-group campaign activity. Individuals may now contribute no more than $2,000 (as of 2002) to any candidate for federal office in any primary or general election. A **political action committee (PAC),** however, can contribute $5,000, provided it contributes to at least five different federal candidates each year. Beyond this, the laws permit corporations, unions, and other interest groups to form PACs and to pay the costs of soliciting funds from private citizens for the PACs. In other words, PACs are interest groups, trade associations, unions, corporations, and even some wealthy individuals operating in the electoral system rather than in the interest-group system.

political action committee (PAC)
a private group that raises and distributes funds for use in election campaigns

Electoral spending by interest groups has been increasing steadily despite the flurry of reform following Watergate. Table 7.2 presents a dramatic picture of the growth of PACs as the source of campaign contributions. The dollar amounts for each year reveal the growth in electoral spending. The number of PACs has also increased significantly—from 480 in 1972 to more than 4,000 in 2003 (see Figure 7.4). Although the reform legislation of the early and mid-1970s attempted to reduce the influence that special interests have over elections, the effect has been almost the exact opposite. Opportunities for legally influencing campaigns are now widespread.

Given the enormous costs of television commercials, polls, computers, and other elements of the new political technology, most politicians are eager to receive PAC contributions and are at least willing to give a friendly hearing to the

---

Table 7.2 | **PAC Spending, 1977–2002**

PAC spending has shot up.

YEARS	CONTRIBUTIONS
1977–78 (est.)	$ 77,800,000
1979–80	131,153,384
1981–82	190,173,539
1983–84	266,822,476
1985–86	339,954,416
1987–88	364,201,275
1989–90	357,648,557
1991–92	394,785,896
1993–94	388,102,643
1995–96	429,887,819
1997–98	470,830,847
1999–2000	579,358,330
2001–2002	685,305,553

SOURCE: Federal Election Commission.

Growth of POlitical Action Committees, 1980–2002   Figure 7.4

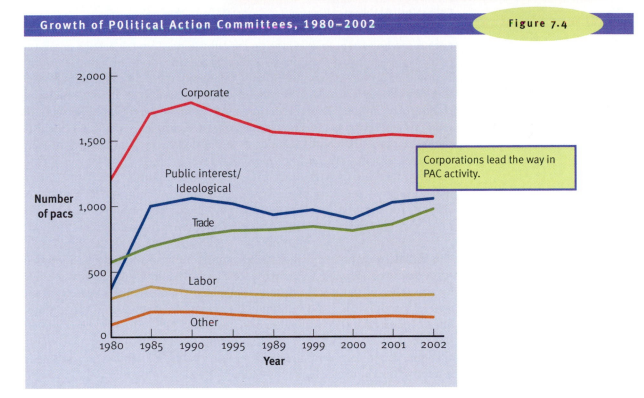

needs and interests of contributors. It is probably not the case that most politicians simply sell their votes to the interests that fund their campaigns. But there is considerable evidence to support the contention that interest groups' campaign contributions do influence the overall pattern of political behavior in Congress and in the state legislatures.

Indeed, PACs and campaign contributions provide organized interests with such a useful tool for gaining access to the political process that calls to abolish PACs have been quite frequent among political reformers. Concern about PACs grew through the 1980s and 1990s, creating a constant drumbeat for reform of federal election laws. Proposals were introduced in Congress on many occasions, perhaps the most celebrated being the McCain-Feingold bill. When it was originally proposed in 1996, the bill was aimed at reducing or eliminating PACs. But, in a stunning about-face, when campaign finance reform was adopted in 2002, it did not restrict PACs in any significant way. Rather, it eliminated unrestricted soft money donations to the national political parties. One consequence of this reform was the creation of a host of new organizations, often directed by former party officials but nominally unaffiliated with the two parties. These organizations are free to raise and spend as much money as they are able. Thus, contemporary reforms may have weakened political parties and strengthened interest groups.

Campaign Activism   Financial support is not the only way that organized groups seek influence through electoral politics. Sometimes, activism can be even more important than campaign contributions. Campaign activism on the part of conservative groups played a very important role in bringing about the Republican capture of both houses of Congress in the 1994 congressional elections. For example, Christian Coalition activists played a role in many races, including ones in which Republican candidates were not overly identified with the religious right. One postelection study suggested that more than 60 percent of the more than six hundred candidates supported by the Christian right were successful in state, local, and congressional races in 1994.[24] The efforts of conservative Republican activists to bring voters to the polls is one major reason that turnout among Republicans exceeded Democratic turnout in a midterm election for the first time since 1970. This increased turnout was especially marked in the South, where the Christian Coalition was most active.

The Initiative   Another political tactic sometimes used by interest groups is sponsorship of ballot initiatives at the state level. The initiative, a device adopted by a number of states around 1900, allows proposed laws to be placed on the general election ballot and submitted directly to the state's voters. This procedure bypasses the state legislature and governor. The initiative was originally promoted by late-nineteenth-century Populists as a mechanism that would allow the people to govern directly. Populists saw the initiative as an antidote to interest-group influence in the legislative process.

Ironically, many studies have suggested that most initiative campaigns today are actually sponsored by interest groups seeking to circumvent legislative opposition to their goals. In recent years, for example, initiative campaigns have been sponsored by the insurance industry, trial lawyers associations, and tobacco companies.[25] The role of interest groups in initiative campaigns should come as no surprise since such campaigns can cost millions of dollars.

Interest Groups Both Help and Hurt Democracy

There is considerable competition among organized groups in the United States. Although the weak and poor do occasionally become organized to assert their rights, interest-group politics is generally a form of political competition in which the wealthy and powerful are best able to engage. In the realm of group politics, liberty seems inconsistent with equality.

Moreover, although groups sometimes organize to promote broad public concerns, interest groups more often represent relatively narrow, selfish interests. Small, self-interested groups can be organized much more easily than large and more diffuse collectives. For one thing, the members of a relatively small group—say, bankers or hunting enthusiasts—are usually able to recognize their shared interests and the need to pursue them in the political arena. Members of large and more diffuse groups—say, consumers or potential victims of firearms—often find it difficult to recognize their shared interests or the need to engage in collective action to achieve their common goals.[26] This is why causes presented as public interests by their proponents often turn out, upon examination, to be private interests wrapped in a public mantle. Thus, the elitist quality of group politics often appears to be inconsistent with democracy.

Summary

Interest groups are perhaps the most vital link between citizens and government in today's political environment. While interest groups often have an upper-class or elite bias, average people seeking to protect their interests can use the group process in a classic pluralistic fashion. To be successful, groups need good leaders, money, and members. To overcome the free rider problem, groups offer various benefits to members. The expansion of government influence and intervention has in turn prompted an increase in the number and variety of interest groups, including economic-based groups, socially conservative groups, and "public interest" groups. Interest groups rely on a variety of techniques to influence government and policy. Lobbying is the most well-known tactic, but groups also seek access, pursue litigation through the courts, go public, and get involved in election politics.

For Further Reading

Cigler, Allan J., and Burdett A. Loomis, eds. *Interest Group Politics.* Washington, DC: Congressional Quarterly Press, 1983.

Clawson, Dan, Alan Neustadtl, and Denise Scott. *Money Talks: Corporate PACs and Political Influence.* New York: Basic Books, 1992.

Hansen, John Mark. *Gaining Access: Congress and the Farm Lobby, 1919–1981.* Chicago: University of Chicago Press, 1991.

Heinz, John P., Edward O. Laumann, Robert L. Nelson, and Robert H. Salisbury. *The Hollow Core: Private Interests in National Policy Making.* Cambridge, MA: Harvard University Press, 1993.

Lowi, Theodore J. *The End of Liberalism.* New York: Norton, 1979.

Moe, Terry M. *The Organization of Interests.* Chicago: University of Chicago Press, 1980.

Olson, Mancur, Jr. *The Logic of Collective Action: Public Goods and the Theory of Groups.* Cambridge, MA: Harvard University Press, 1971.

Petracca, Mark, ed. *The Politics of Interests: Interest Groups Transformed.* Boulder, CO: Westview, 1992.

Scholzman, Kay Lehman, and John T. Tierney. *Organized Interests and American Democracy.* New York: Harper & Row, 1986.

Spitzer, Robert J. *The Politics of Gun Control.* Washington, D.C.: CQ Press, 2004.

Truman, David. *The Governmental Process: Political Interests and Public Opinion.* New York: Knopf, 1951.

Study Outline

Interest Groups Represent Different Interests but Have Similar Organizations and Membership

1. An enormous number of diverse interest groups exist in the United States.
2. Most interest groups share key organizational components, such as mechanisms for member recruitment, financial and decision-making processes, and agencies that actually carry out group goals.

3. Interest-group politics in the United States tends to have a pronounced upper-class bias because of the characteristics of interest-group members.

4. Because of natural disincentives to join interest groups, groups offer material, solidary, and purposive benefits to entice people to join.

The Number of Groups Has Increased in the Last Thirty Years

1. The modern expansion of governmental economic and social programs has contributed to the enormous increase in the number of groups seeking to influence the American political system.

2. The second factor accounting for the explosion of interest-group activity in recent years was the emergence of a new set of forces in American politics: the New Politics movement.

Interest Groups Use Different Strategies to Gain Influence

1. Lobbying is an effort by outsiders to influence Congress or government agencies by providing them with information about issues, giving them support, and even threatening them with retaliation.

2. Access is actual involvement and influence in the decision-making process.

3. Interest groups often turn to litigation when they lack access or feel they have insufficient influence over the formulation and implementation of public policy.

4. Going public is a strategy that attempts to mobilize the widest and most favorable climate of opinion.

5. Many groups use a nonpartisan strategy in electoral politics to avoid giving up access to one party by embracing the other.

Interest Groups Both Help and Hurt Democracy

1. The organization of private interests into groups to advance their own views is a necessary and intrinsic element of the liberty of citizens to pursue their private lives, and to express their views, individually and collectively.

2. The organization of private interests into groups is biased in favor of the wealthy and the powerful, who have superior knowledge, opportunity, and resources with which to organize.

Practice Quiz

1. The theory that competition among organized interests will produce balance with all the interests regulating one another is
   a) pluralism.
   b) elite power politics.
   c) democracy.
   d) socialism.

2. To overcome the free rider problem, groups
   a) provide general benefits.
   b) litigate.
   c) go public.
   d) provide selective benefits.

3. Politically organized religious groups often make use of
   a) material benefits.
   b) solidary benefits.
   c) purposive benefits.
   d) none of the above.

4. Which of the following best describes the reputation of the AARP in the Washington community?
   a) It is respected and feared.
   b) It is supported and well liked by all political forces.
   c) It is believed to be ineffective.
   d) It wins the political battles it fights.

5. Which types of interest groups are most often associated with the New Politics movement?
   a) public interest groups
   b) professional associations
   c) government groups
   d) labor groups

6. Access politics, exemplified by defense contractors acting in concert with congressional committees and executive agencies, is an example of
   a) campaign activism.
   b) public interest politics.
   c) an iron triangle.
   d) the role of conservative interest groups.

7. "Corridoring" refers to
   a) lobbying the corridors of Congress.
   b) a litigation technique.
   c) lobbying the president and the White House staff.
   d) lobbying an executive agency.

8. In which of the following ways do interest groups use the courts to affect public policy?
   a) filing *amicus* briefs
   b) bringing lawsuits
   c) financing those bringing suit
   d) all of the above

9. According to this text, what is the limit a PAC can contribute to a primary or general election campaign?
   a) $1,000
   b) $5,000
   c) $10,000
   d) $50,000

10. Which of the following is not an activity in which interest groups frequently engage?
    a) starting their own political party
    b) litigation
    c) lobbying
    d) contributing to campaigns

Critical Thinking Questions

1. A dilemma is presented by the values of liberty and equality in regard to interest-group activity. On the one hand, individuals should have the liberty to organize themselves politically in order to express their views. On the other hand, there is a strong class bias in the politics of organized interests. How has the U.S. government sought to regulate group activity in order to balance these competing values? What else might government do to make group politics less biased? What are the potential consequences—both good and bad—of the actions you suggest?

2. Describe the different techniques of influence used by organized interests. When is one technique preferable to another? With the rise of the New Politics movement, different techniques are now used more frequently. Which ones? Why, do you think, are these techniques so well suited to New Politics?

Key Terms

collective goods (p. 202)
free riders (p. 202)
going public (p. 214)
grassroots lobbying (p. 215)

institutional advertising (p. 214)
interest group (p. 199)
iron triangle (p. 209)
lobbying (p. 208)
material benefits (p. 203)
New Politics movement (p. 206)

pluralism (p. 199)
political action committee (PAC) (p. 216)
purposive benefits (p. 203)
solidary benefits (p. 203)

8 CONGRESS

MAIN MESSAGE

Congress has gone from first branch to worst branch.

Of the three branches of government, Congress would seem to be the one closest to the people, and therefore the most popular. Yet it is not.

Consider a May 2004 public opinion poll that asked Americans how much "respect and confidence" they have for fourteen American institutions, including the military, the police, organized religion, schools, and the three branches of govern-

Key Concepts

1. Congress was designed to be the people's most direct voice in the national government, and the most powerful of the three branches.

2. Power in Congress is allocated by political party.

3. Most of Congress's important work is done in committees and by staff people.

4. Because of the lengthy process by which a bill becomes a law, most bills never become law.

5. The president, interest groups, and constituents all influence congressional actions.

ment. Of those surveyed, 52 percent reported having "a great deal or quite a lot of confidence" in the presidency; 46 percent reported the same for the Supreme Court. Congress came in third from last on the list, with only 30 percent.[1]

The low esteem in which Americans hold Congress generally reflects the common view that Congress is, according to Congress specialist Alan Clem, "slow, uncertain, contentious, undignified, unresponsive, secretive, unimaginative, dominated by special interests, and tolerant of unethical behavior among its members."[2] While there is much truth to these charges, they arise at least in part *because* Congress was designed to be the branch of government most responsive to the people.

Remember that the president is not directly elected by the people, but by the electoral college, while the Supreme Court is not elected at all; rather, its members are nominated by the president, confirmed by the Senate, and serve for life. The entire membership of the House of Representatives is reelected every two years from relatively small districts; members of the Senate serve for six years (with one-third elected every two years), and they represent states, not the entire nation, as does the president. This closeness to the people encourages the 535 individual members of Congress (435 in the House, 100 in the Senate) to think first and foremost about the people they represent, not the nation as a whole. But since Congress must make policy for the nation, it is little wonder that the public has less regard for Congress's need to balance representation with lawmaking.

In this chapter, we will examine the key factors that explain how and why Congress operates as it does. It may be something of an oversimplification to say that Congress has gone from first branch to worst branch, but it is true that the Constitution's framers expected Congress to be, literally, the first and most important branch of government. We know this because, first, the framers said so. As James Madison wrote in Federalist Paper 51, "In a republican government, the legislative authority necessarily predominates." Second, Congress's preeminence is confirmed by the Constitution itself. In the document, "Congress is granted a breathtaking array of powers . . . the bulk of governmental authority as the Founders understood it."[3]

That most people no longer consider Congress the first and most important branch of government is reflected in the poll numbers just discussed, and by the fact that most Americans think of the president as the most important national governing institution. Congress may not actually be the "worst" branch, but it certainly is the least regarded of the three branches. Yet Congress continues to be vital to modern governance, and it serves as a critical link between the citizen and Washington-based decisions.

Congressional Power Is Rooted in the Constitution

The very fact that Congress is discussed in the first article of the Constitution reflects the special importance accorded this branch by the framers. Writing in 1885, a then-obscure political science professor named Woodrow Wilson published a book titled *Congressional Government,* because at the time, American government was just that, "congressional government." This reflected the Founders' purpose of establishing *legislative supremacy* rather than three purely equal branches.[4]

This idea is clearly seen in Article I, where Congress has vast authority over the two most important powers given to any government: the power of force (control over the nation's military forces); and the power over money. Specifically, in Article I, Section 8, Congress can "lay and collect Taxes," deal with indebtedness and bankruptcy, impose duties, borrow and coin money, and generally control the nation's purse strings. It also may "provide for the common Defense and general Welfare," regulate interstate commerce, undertake public works, acquire and control federal lands, promote science and "useful Arts" (pertaining mostly to patents and copyrights), and regulate the militia.

In the realm of foreign policy, Congress has the power to declare war, deal with piracy, regulate foreign commerce, and raise and regulate the armed forces and military installations. These powers over war and the military are supreme—even the president, as commander-in-chief of the military, must obey the laws and orders of Congress *if* Congress chooses to assert its constitutional authority. (In the past century, Congress has usually surrendered this authority to the president.) Further, the Senate has the power to approve treaties (by a two-thirds vote) and to approve the appointment of ambassadors. Capping these powers, Congress is charged to make laws "which shall be necessary and proper for carrying into Execution the foregoing Powers, and all other Powers vested by this Constitution in the Government of the United States, or in any Department or Officer thereof." This last phrase is known as the elastic clause.

If it seems to the reader that many of these powers belong to the president, from war power to spending power, that is because modern presidents do exercise great authority in these areas. The modern presidency is a more powerful institution than it was two hundred years ago, and much of that power has come from Congress, either because Congress has delegated the power to the president by law, or because Congress has simply allowed, or even urged, presidents to be more active in these areas. This also helps explain why the executive branch seems like a more important branch of government today than Congress. Still, the constitutional powers of Congress remain intact in the document. This takes us to Congress's pivotal role as a representative institution.

Congress Represents the American People

Congress is the most important representative institution in American government. Each member's primary responsibility is to the district, to his or her **constituency,** not to the congressional leadership, a party, or even Congress itself. Yet the task of representation is not a simple one. Views about what constitutes fair and effective representation differ and constituents can make very different kinds of demands on their representatives. Members of Congress must consider these diverse views and demands as they represent their districts.

constituency the district comprising the area from which an official is elected

THE HOUSE AND SENATE OFFER DIFFERENCES IN REPRESENTATION

The framers of the Constitution provided for a **bicameral** legislature—that is, a legislative body consisting of two chambers. The 435 members of the House are elected from districts apportioned according to population; the 100 members of the Senate are elected by state, with 2 senators from each. Senators

bicameral having a legislative assembly composed of two chambers or houses; opposite of unicameral

| Table 8.1 | Differences between the House and the Senate | |

	HOUSE	**SENATE**
Minimum age of member	25 years	30 years
U.S. citizenship	At least 7 years	At least 9 years
Length of term	2 years	6 years
Number per state	Depends on population: 1 per 30,000 in 1789; now 1 per 600,000	2 per state
Constituency	Tends to be local	Both state and national

continue to have much longer terms in office and usually represent much larger and more diverse constituencies than do their counterparts in the House (see Table 8.1).

Both formal and informal factors contribute to differences between the two chambers of Congress. Differences in the length of terms and requirements for holding office specified by the Constitution in turn generate differences in how members of each body develop their constituencies and exercise their powers of office. The result is that members of the House most effectively and frequently serve as the agents of well-organized local interests with specific legislative agendas—for instance, used-car dealers seeking relief from regulation, labor unions seeking more favorable legislation, or farmers looking for higher subsidies. The small size and relative homogeneity of their constituencies and the frequency with which they must seek reelection make House members more attuned to the legislative needs of local interest groups.

Senators, on the other hand, serve larger and more heterogeneous constituencies. As a result, they are somewhat better able than members of the House to serve as the agents for groups and interests organized on a statewide or national basis. Moreover, with longer terms in office, senators have the luxury of considering "new ideas" or seeking to bring together new coalitions of interests rather than simply serving existing ones.

REPRESENTATION CAN BE SOCIOLOGICAL OR AGENCY

We have become so accustomed to the idea of representative government that we tend to forget what a peculiar concept representation really is. A representative claims to act or speak for some other person or group. But how can one person be trusted to speak for another? How do we know that those who call themselves our representatives are actually speaking on our behalf rather than simply pursuing their own interests?

There are two circumstances under which one person reasonably might be trusted to speak for another. The first of these occurs if the two individuals are so similar in background, character, interests, and perspectives that anything said by one would very likely reflect the views of the other as well. This principle is at the heart of what is sometimes called **sociological representation**—the sort of representation that takes place when representatives have the same racial, ethnic, religious, or educational backgrounds as their constituents. The assumption is that sociological similarity helps to promote good representation; thus, the composition of a properly constituted representative assembly should mirror the composition of society.

The second circumstance under which one person might be trusted to speak for another occurs if the two are formally bound together so that the representative is in some way accountable to those he or she purports to represent. If representatives can somehow be punished or held to account for failing to speak properly for their constituents, then they have incentive to provide good representation even if their own personal backgrounds, views, and interests differ from those of the people they represent. This principle is called **agency representation**—the sort of representation that takes place when constituents have the power to hire and fire their representatives.

Both sociological and agency representation play a role in the relationship between members of Congress and their constituencies.

The Social Composition of the U.S. Congress   The extent to which the U.S. Congress is representative of the American people in a sociological sense can be seen by examining the distribution of important social characteristics in the House and Senate today.

African Americans, women, Hispanic Americans, and Asian Americans have increased their congressional representation somewhat in the past two decades (see Figure 8.1). In 2003, sixty-three women served in the House of Representatives (up from only twenty-nine in 1990). Most notably, California Democrat Nancy Pelosi became the first woman to hold top House leadership positions, becoming Minority Leader in 2003 after having served as Democratic Whip. Thirteen women now serve in the Senate. However, the representation of women and minorities in Congress is still not comparable to their proportions in the general population. Since many important contemporary national issues do cut along racial and gender lines, a considerable amount of clamor for reform in the representative process is likely to continue until these groups are fully represented.

The occupational backgrounds of members of Congress have always been a matter of interest because so many issues cut along economic lines that are relevant to occupations and industries. The legal profession is the dominant career of most members of Congress prior to their election. Public service or politics is also a significant background. In addition, many members of Congress also have important ties to business and industry.[5] One composite portrait of a typical member of Congress has been that of "a middle-aged male lawyer whose

sociological representation a type of representation in which representatives have the same racial, ethnic, religious, or educational backgrounds as their constituents. It is based on the principle that if two individuals are similar in background, character, interests, and perspectives, then one could correctly represent the other's views

agency representation the type of representation by which representatives are held accountable to their constituency if they fail to represent that constituency properly. This is the incentive for good representation when the personal backgrounds, views, and interests of the representative differ from those of his or her constituency

Figure 8.1

Women, African Americans, and Latinos in the U.S. Congress, 1971–2001

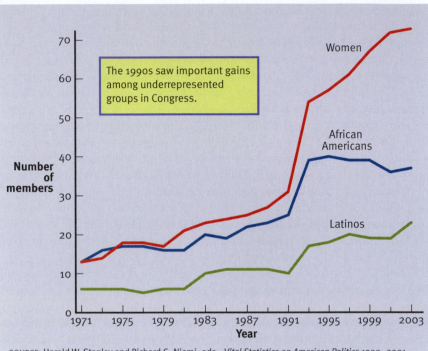

The 1990s saw important gains among underrepresented groups in Congress.

SOURCE: Harold W. Stanley and Richard G. Niemi, eds., *Vital Statistics on American Politics 1999–2001*, (Washington, DC: AEI Press, 2002), p. 201.

father was of the professional or managerial class; a native-born 'white,' or—if he cannot avoid being an immigrant—a product of northwestern or central Europe or Canada, rather than of eastern or southern Europe, Latin America, Africa or Asia."[6] This is not a portrait of the U.S. population.

Is Congress still able to legislate fairly or to take account of a diversity of views and interests if it is not a sociologically representative assembly? The task is certainly much more difficult. Yet there is reason to believe it can. Representatives can serve as the agents of their constituents, even if they do not precisely mirror their sociological attributes.

Representatives as Agents A good deal of evidence indicates that whether or not members of Congress share their constituents' sociological characteristics, they do work very hard to speak for their constituents' views and serve their constituents' interests in the governmental process. The idea of representative as agent is similar to the relationship of lawyer and client. True, the relationship between the member of Congress and as many as six hundred thousand "clients" in the district, or the senator and millions of "clients" in the state, is very different from that of the lawyer and client. But the criteria of performance are comparable. One expects at the very least that each representative will constantly be seeking to discover the interests of the constituency and will be speaking for those interests in Congress and in other centers of government.[7]

A good example of the representative as agent is the case of former First Lady Hillary Rodham Clinton. Even though she had never lived in New York State, she and her husband purchased a house in the state before the end of President Clinton's second term. State Democrats urged Mrs. Clinton to run for the U.S. Senate; opponents charged that she was an outsider who had no ties to the state. Yet she campaigned vigorously, arguing that she would work diligently for the interests of the state and its people as New Yorkers' "agent" in Congress. In 2000, she was elected to the Senate, defeating a lifelong state resident, Representative Rick Lazio.

There is constant communication between constituents and congressional offices. For example, each year the House and Senate post offices handle nearly one hundred million pieces of incoming mail, and in recent years, members of Congress have spent as much as $112 million annually to send out 458 million pieces of mail.[8]

The seriousness with which members of the House attempt to behave as representatives can be seen in the amount of time spent on behalf of their constituents. Well over a quarter of their time and nearly two-thirds of the time of their staff members is devoted to constituency service (called "case work"). This service is not merely a matter of writing and mailing letters. It includes talking to constituents, providing them with minor services, presenting special bills for them, and attempting to influence decisions by regulatory commissions on their behalf.[9]

Although no members of Congress are above constituency pressures (and they would not want to be), on many issues constituents do not have very strong views, so representatives are free to act as they think best. Foreign policy issues often fall into this category. But in many districts there are two or three issues on which constituents have such pronounced opinions that representatives feel they have little freedom of choice. For example, representatives from districts that grow wheat, cotton, or tobacco probably will not want to exercise a great deal of independence on relevant agricultural legislation. In the oil-rich states (such as Oklahoma, Texas, and California), senators and members of the House are likely to be leading advocates of oil interests. For one thing, representatives are probably fearful of voting against their district interests; for another, the districts are unlikely to have elected representatives who would *want* to vote against them.

The influence of constituencies is so pervasive that both parties have strongly embraced the informal rule that nothing should be done to endanger the reelection chances of any member. Party leaders obey this rule fairly consistently by not asking any member to vote in a way that might conflict with a district interest.

THE ELECTORAL CONNECTION HINGES ON INCUMBENCY

The sociological composition of Congress and the activities of representatives once they are in office are very much influenced by electoral considerations.

Two factors related to the U.S. electoral system affect who gets elected and what they do once in office. The first issue is that of incumbency advantage. Second, the way congressional district lines are drawn can greatly affect the outcome of an election. Let us examine more closely the impact that these considerations have on representation.

incumbency holding a political office for which one is running

Incumbency plays a very important role in the American electoral system and in the kind of representation citizens get in Washington. Once in office, members of Congress possess an array of tools that they can use to stack the deck in favor of their reelection. The most important of these is constituency service—taking care of the problems and requests of individual voters. Congressional offices will intervene on behalf of constituents when they have problems with federal programs or agencies, such as social security benefits, veterans benefits, obtaining passports, and so on. When congressional offices contact federal agencies dealing with such matters, the offices usually respond with extra speed, knowing that members of Congress can embarrass or penalize an agency that doesn't do its job properly. Through such services and through regular newsletter mailings, the incumbent seeks to establish a "personal" relationship with his or her constituents. The success of this strategy is evident in the high rates of reelection for congressional incumbents, which is as high as 98.5 percent for House members and 96 percent for members of the Senate in recent years (see Figure 8.2). It is also evident in what is called "sophomore surge"—the tendency for candidates to win a higher percentage of the vote when seeking future terms in office.

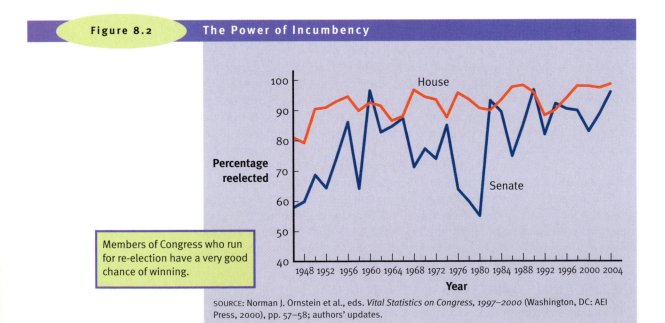

Figure 8.2 The Power of Incumbency

Percentage reelected

House

Senate

Members of Congress who run for re-election have a very good chance of winning.

SOURCE: Norman J. Ornstein et al., eds. *Vital Statistics on Congress, 1997–2000* (Washington, DC: AEI Press, 2000), pp. 57–58; authors' updates.

As in past elections, voters returned large numbers of congressional incumbents to office in 2004—specifically, 98.5 percent to the House and 96.0 percent to the Senate. There were several notable exceptions, however. Candidates who were associated with strong ideological positions were especially vulnerable. For example, some of the incumbents who lost their seats were closely connected to the controversial impeachment of Bill Clinton.

Incumbency can also help a candidate by scaring off potential challengers. In many races, potential candidates may decide not to run because they fear that the incumbent simply has too much money or is too well liked or too well known. Potentially strong challengers may also decide that a district's partisan leanings are too unfavorable. The efforts of incumbents to raise funds to ward off potential challengers start early. Kansas Democrat Dennis Moore, who was elected to the House in 1998, held his first fund-raiser for the 2000 campaign in December 1998—before he had even been sworn into office!

The advantage of incumbency thus tends to preserve the status quo in Congress. This fact has implications for the social composition of Congress. For example, incumbency advantage makes it harder for women to increase their numbers in Congress because most incumbents are men. Women who run for open seats (for which there are no incumbents) are just as likely to win as male candidates.[10] Supporters of **term limits** argue that such limits are the only way to get new faces into Congress. They believe that because of incumbency advantage and the tendency of many legislators to view politics as a career, very little turnover will occur in Congress unless limits are imposed on the number of terms a legislator can serve.

The final factor that affects who wins a seat in Congress is the way congressional districts are drawn. Every ten years, state legislatures must redraw congressional districts to reflect population changes. This is a highly political process: Districts are shaped to create an advantage for the majority party in the state legislature, which controls the **redistricting** process. In this complex process, those charged with drawing districts use sophisticated computer technologies to come up with the most favorable district boundaries. Redistricting can create open seats and pit incumbents of the same party against one another, ensuring that one of them will lose. Redistricting can also give an advantage to one party by clustering voters with some ideological or sociological characteristics in a single district, or by separating those voters into two or more districts. This process is known as **gerrymandering.**

Since the passage of the 1982 amendments to the 1964 Civil Rights Act, race has become a major—and controversial—consideration in drawing voting districts. These amendments, which encouraged the creation of districts in which members of racial minorities have decisive majorities, have greatly increased the number of minority representatives in Congress. After the 1991–92 redistricting, the number of predominantly minority districts doubled, rising from twenty-six to fifty-two. Among the most fervent supporters of the new minority districts were white Republicans, who used the opportunity to create more districts dominated by white Republican voters. These developments raise thorny

term limits legally prescribed limits on the number of terms an elected official can serve

redistricting the process of redrawing election districts and redistributing legislative representatives. This happens every ten years to reflect shifts in population or in response to legal challenges to existing districts

gerrymandering the process of redrawing legislative district boundary lines to provide political advantage or disadvantage

questions about representation. Some analysts argue that the system may grant minorities greater sociological representation, but it has made it more difficult for minorities to win substantive policy goals. This was a common argument after the sweeping Republican victories in the 1994 congressional elections. Others dispute this argument, noting that the strong surge of Republican voters was more significant than any losses due to racial redistricting.[11]

In 1995, the Supreme Court limited racial redistricting in *Miller v. Johnson,* in which the Court stated that race could not be the predominant factor in creating electoral districts.[12] Yet concerns about redistricting and representation have not disappeared. The distinction between race being a "predominant" factor and its being one factor among many is very hazy. Moreover, the practice of political redistricting has come under fire, as Democrats, angered by the aggressive Republican use of gerrymandering after the 2000 census, sought to challenge political gerrymandering. In 2002, Pennsylvania Democrats brought suit against the Republican remap of Pennsylvania, charging that the redistricting would cost Democrats an unconstitutional number of seats in the House. The justices upheld the Pennsylvania plan on the grounds that there were no clear standards for ruling against it. Because the drawing of district boundaries affects incumbents as well as the field of candidates who decide to run for office, it continues to be a key battleground on which political parties fight about the meaning of representation.

DIRECT PATRONAGE MEANS BRINGING HOME THE BACON

patronage the resources available to higher officials, usually opportunities to make partisan appointments to offices and to confer grants, licenses, or special favors to supporters

pork barrel appropriations made by legislative bodies for local projects that are often not needed but that are created to help local representatives win reelection in their home districts

Members of Congress often have an opportunity to provide direct benefits, or **patronage,** for their constituents. The most important of these opportunities for direct patronage is in legislation that has been described half-jokingly as the **pork barrel.** This type of legislation specifies a project to be funded, as well as the location of the project within a particular district. Many observers of Congress argue that pork-barrel bills are the only ones that some members are serious about moving toward actual passage, because they are seen as so important to members' reelection bids.

A common form of pork barreling is the "earmark," the practice through which members of Congress insert into otherwise pork-free bills language that provides special benefits for their own constituents. Highway bills are a favorite vehicle for congressional pork-barrel spending. The 2004 highway bill was full of such items, containing more than three thousand projects earmarked for specific congressional districts. Among them were such projects as $3.5 million for horse trails in Virginia and $5 million for a parking garage in downtown Bozeman, Montana. These measures often have little to do with transportation needs, instead serving as evidence that congressional members can bring federal dollars back home. Perhaps the most extravagant—and least needed for transportation—item in the 2004 bill was a bridge in Alaska designed to connect a barely populated island to the town of Ketchikan, whose population is just short of eight thousand. At a cost that could soar to $2 billion, the bridge would replace an existing five-minute ferry ride. Representative Don Young, an Alaska

Republican, proudly claimed credit for such pork-barrel projects. At the suggestion that Alaska's senior senator Ted Stevens, Republican chair of the Senate Appropriations Committee, might be the reason Alaska won these projects, Young pretended to be offended, saying, "If he's the chief porker, I'm upset."[13]

A limited amount of other direct patronage also exists (see Figure 8.3). One important form of constituency service is intervention with federal administrative agencies on behalf of constituents. Members of the House and Senate and their staff members spend a great deal of time on the telephone and in administrative offices seeking to secure favorable treatment for constituents and supporters. Among the kind of services that members of Congress offer to constituents is assistance for senior citizens who are having Social Security or Medicare benefit eligibility problems. They may also assist constituents in finding federal grants for which they may be eligible to apply. As Representative Pete Stark (D-Calif.) puts it on his Web site, "We cannot make the decision for a federal agency on such matters, but we can make sure that you get a fair shake."[14] A small but related form of patronage is getting an appointment to one of the military academies for the child of a constituent. Traditionally, these appointments are allocated one to a district.

How Members of Congress Represent Their Districts   Figure 8.3

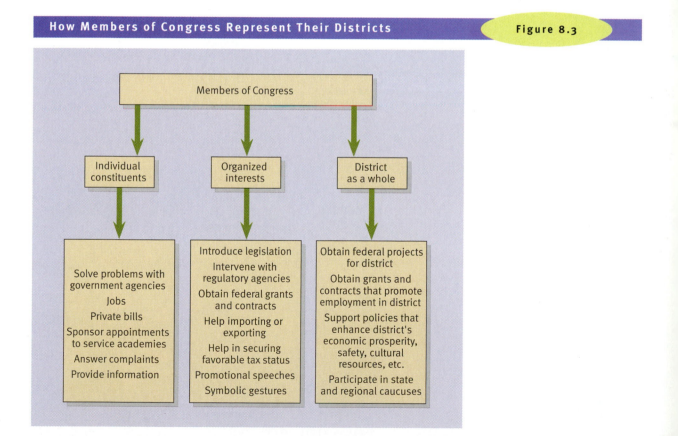

P I C T U R I N G

Pork Barrel Politics

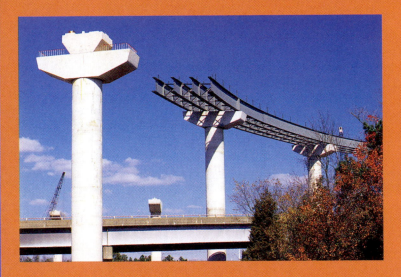

Funding for "pork barrel" projects—projects that are not needed but are created to help representatives win reelection in their home districts—is often buried inside massive appropriations bills. Highway bills are a favorite vehicle for congressional pork spending.

Homeland Security dollars have been used to achieve many valuable goals, but accusations of pork-barrel spending have been leveled at such "homeland security" projects as a new paging system for a state fair in South Dakota, courses in public speaking for sanitation workers in Washington, D.C., and a trailer to carry lawnmowers to lawnmower races in Texas.

POLITICS

The federal transportation bill passed by Congress in July of 2005 included $24 billion in special projects. Government watchdog groups have found that Representative Don Young of Alaska (pictured here) did particularly well for his constituents, bringing home hundreds of millions of dollars in federal money. One project, dubbed "the bridge to nowhere" by critics, is to be named "Don Young's Way."

An influx of government money can mean great benefits to the communities lucky enough to get it, and great hardship when the money eventually dries up. Several recent rounds of military base closings illustrate this point, and it is not surprising that politicians often fight to keep bases open in their home districts, regardless of those bases' actual military utility. Here a business owner in Clovis, New Mexico, expresses his opinion about the possible closure of nearby Cannon Air Force Base.

Various efforts have been made to limit pork-barrel spending. In 1996, for example, Congress gave the president the power to strike specific elements of appropriations bills with a line-item veto. Here, Representative Peter Blute illustrates the point by presenting a pig at a press conference to discuss the new power. In 1998 the Supreme Court eliminated the line-item veto, ruling it unconstitutional.

private bill a proposal in Congress to provide a specific person with some kind of relief, such as a special exemption from immigration quotas

A different form of patronage is the **private bill**—a proposal to grant some kind of relief, special privilege, or exemption to the person named in the bill. The private bill is a type of legislation, but it is distinguished from a public bill, which is supposed to deal with general rules and categories of behavior, people, and institutions. As many as 75 percent of all private bills introduced (and one-third of the ones that pass) are concerned with providing relief for foreign nationals who cannot get permanent visas to the United States because the immigration quota for their country is filled or because of something unusual about their particular situation.[15]

The Organization of Congress Is Shaped by Party

The United States Congress is not only a representative assembly. It is also a legislative body. For Americans, representation and legislation go hand in hand; however, many parliamentary bodies are representative without the power to legislate. It is no small achievement that the U.S. Congress both represents *and* governs.

Because of the many interests represented by the 535 members of Congress, it is typically difficult for Congress to get things done. For this reason, presidents have come to play a vital role in leading Congress. In fact, members of Congress often complain when the president fails to provide leadership on important issues, even when the party controlling Congress is different from that of the president.

conference/caucus a gathering every two years to elect House leaders. Democrats call their gathering a caucus; Republicans call theirs a conference

speaker of the House the chief presiding officer of the House of Representatives. The speaker is elected at the beginning of every Congress on a straight party vote. The speaker is the most important party and House leader, and can influence the legislative agenda, the fate of individual pieces of legislation, and members' positions within the House

majority leader the elected leader of the majority party in the House of Representatives or in the Senate. In the House, the majority leader is subordinate in the party hierarchy to the speaker of the House

minority leader the elected leader of the minority party in the House or Senate

PARTY LEADERSHIP IN THE HOUSE AND THE SENATE ORGANIZES POWER

Every two years, at the beginning of a new Congress, the members of each party in the House of Representatives gather to elect their leaders. This gathering is traditionally called the **conference** (House Democrats call theirs the **caucus**). The elected leader of the majority party is later proposed to the whole House and is automatically elected to the position of **speaker of the House,** with voting along straight party lines. The House majority conference or caucus then also elects a **majority leader.** The minority party goes through the same process and selects the **minority leader.** Both parties also elect assistants to their party leaders, called whips, who line up party members on important votes and relay voting information to the leaders.

Next in line of importance for each party after the speaker and majority or minority leader is its Committee on Committees (called the Steering and Policy Committee by the Democrats), whose tasks are to assign new legislators to committees and to deal with the requests of incumbent members for transfers from one committee to another.

Generally, members of Congress seek assignments that will allow them to influence decisions of special importance to their districts. Representatives from farm districts, for example, may request seats on the Agriculture Committee.[16] Seats on powerful committees such as Ways and Means, which is responsible for tax legislation, and Appropriations are especially popular.

Within the Senate, the president pro tempore exercises primarily ceremonial leadership. Usually, the majority party designates a member with the greatest seniority to serve in this capacity. Real power is in the hands of the majority leader and minority leader, each elected by party conference. Together they control the Senate's calendar, or agenda for legislation. In addition, the senators from each party elect a whip. Each party also elects a Policy Committee, which advises the leadership on legislative priorities.

The structure of majority party leadership in the House and the Senate is shown in Figures 8.4 and 8.5.

In addition to these tasks of organization, congressional party leaders may also seek to establish a legislative agenda. Since the New Deal, presidents have taken the lead in creating legislative agendas (this trend will be discussed in the next chapter). When congressional leaders have been faced with a White House controlled by the opposing party, they have attempted to devise their own agendas. Democratic leaders of Congress sought to create a common Democratic perspective in 1981 when Ronald Reagan became president. The Republican Congress elected in 1994 expanded on this idea, calling its agenda the "Contract with America." More recently,

Majority Party Structure in the House of Representatives

Figure 8.4

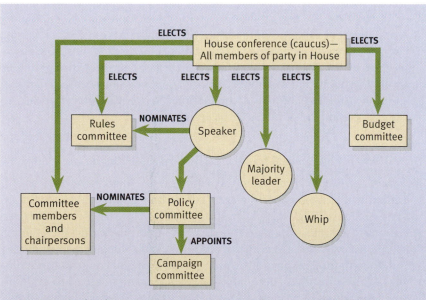

*Includes speaker (chair), majority leader, chief and deputy whips, caucus chair, four members appointed by the speaker, and twelve members elected by regional caucuses.

Figure 8.5 **Majority Party Structure in the Senate**

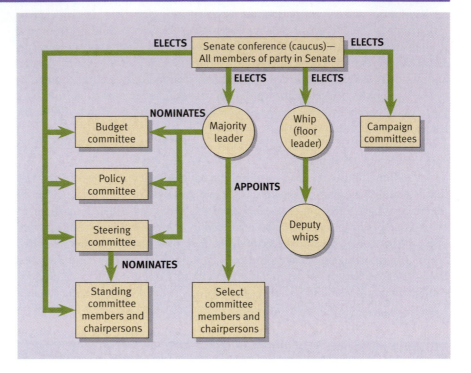

with both houses of Congress in the hands of Republicans, congressional leaders have worked closely with the White House. President George W. Bush's aggressive campaigning in the 2002 congressional elections helped to cement strong relationships with Republican representatives. Although minor tensions between Congress and the White House have emerged, congressional Republicans have been very responsive to the legislative priorities of the president.

THE COMMITTEE SYSTEM IS THE CORE OF CONGRESS

The committee system is central to the operation of Congress. At each stage of the legislative process, Congress relies on committees and subcommittees to do the hard work of sorting through alternatives and writing legislation. There are several different kinds of congressional committees; these include standing committees, select committees, joint committees, and conference committees.

standing committee a permanent committee with the power to propose and write legislation that covers a particular subject, such as finance or appropriations

Standing committees are the most important arenas of congressional policy making. These committees continue in existence from congress to congress; they have the power to propose and write legislation. The jurisdiction of each standing committee covers a particular subject matter, which in most cases parallels the major departments or agencies in the executive branch (see Table 8.2).

Permanent Committees of Congress

Table 8.2

HOUSE COMMITTEES

Agriculture	Resources
Appropriations	Rules
Armed Services	Science
Budget	Select Intelligence
Education and the Workforce	Small Business
Energy and Commerce	Standards of Official Conduct
Financial Services	Transportation and Infrastructure
Government Reform	Veterans' Affairs
House Administration	Ways and Means
International Relations	
Judiciary	

SENATE COMMITTEES

Agriculture, Nutrition, and Forestry	Foreign Relations
Appropriations	Governmental Affairs
Armed Services	Health, Education, Labor, and Pensions
Banking, Housing, and Urban Affairs	Judiciary
Budget	Rules and Administration
Commerce, Science, and Transportation	Select Intelligence
Energy and Natural Resources	Small Business
Environment and Public Works	Veterans' Affairs
Finance	

Among the most important standing committees are those in charge of finances. The House Ways and Means Committee and the Senate Finance Committee are powerful because of their jurisdiction over taxes, trade, and expensive entitlement programs such as Social Security and Medicare. The Senate and House Appropriations committees also play important ongoing roles because they decide how much funding various programs will actually receive; they also determine exactly how the money will be spent. A seat on the Appropriations Committee allows a member the opportunity to direct funds to a favored program—perhaps one in his or her home district.

Except for the House Rules Committee, all standing committees receive proposals for legislation and process them into official bills. The House Rules Committee decides the order in which bills come up for a vote on the House floor and determines the specific rules that govern the length of debate and opportunity for amendments. The Senate, which has less formal organization and fewer rules, does not have a rules committee.

select committee a (usually) temporary legislative committee set up to highlight or investigate a particular issue or address an issue not within the jurisdiction of existing committees

Select committees are usually not permanent and usually do not have the power to report legislation. (The House and Senate Select Intelligence committees are permanent, however, and do have the power to report legislation.) These committees may hold hearings and serve as focal points for the issues they are charged with considering. Congressional leaders form select committees when they want to take up issues that fall between the jurisdictions of existing committees, to highlight an issue, or to investigate a particular problem. Examples of select committees investigating political scandals include the Senate Watergate Committee of 1973, the committees set up in 1987 to investigate the Iran-Contra affair, and the Whitewater Committee of 1995–96. In 2003, Congress created the Select Homeland Security Committee to oversee the new cabinet department, Homeland Security. This committee also has the power to report legislation.

joint committee a legislative committee formed of members of both the House and the Senate

Joint committees involve members from both the Senate and the House. There are four such committees: economic, taxation, library, and printing. These joint committees are permanent, but they do not have the power to report legislation. The Joint Economic Committee and the Joint Taxation Committee have often played important roles in collecting information and holding hearings on economic and financial issues.

conference committee a joint committee created to work out a compromise on House and Senate versions of a piece of legislation

Finally, **conference committees** are temporary committees whose members are appointed by the speaker of the House and the presiding officer of the Senate. These committees are charged with reaching a compromise on legislation once it has been passed by the House and the Senate. Conference committees play an extremely important role in determining what laws are actually passed, because they must reconcile any differences in the legislation passed by the House and Senate.

seniority priority or status ranking given to an individual on the basis of length of continuous service on a committee in Congress

Within each committee, hierarchy is based on seniority. **Seniority** is determined by years of continuous service on a particular committee, not years of service in the House or Senate. In general, each committee is chaired by the most senior member of the majority party. But the principle of seniority is not absolute. Both Democrats and Republicans have violated it on occasion. But in 1995, when the Republicans won control of the House, then-speaker Newt Gingrich instituted a new practice of frequent seniority violations, often selecting committee chairs based on loyalty or fund-raising abilities, a practice that subsequent Republican leaders have maintained.

THE STAFF SYSTEM IS THE POWER BEHIND THE POWER

A congressional institution second in importance only to the committee system is the staff system. Every member of Congress employs a large number of staff members, whose tasks include handling constituency requests and, to a large and growing extent, dealing with legislative details and the activities of administrative agencies. Increasingly, staffers bear the primary responsibility for formulating and drafting proposals, organizing hearings, dealing with administrative agencies, and negotiating with lobbyists. Indeed, legislators typically deal with one another through staff rather than through direct, personal contact. Representatives and senators together employ nearly eleven thousand staffers in their Washington and home offices. Today, staffers develop policy ideas, draft legislation, and have a good deal of influence over the legislative process.

In addition to the personal staffs of individual senators and representatives, Congress also employs roughly two thousand committee staffers. These individuals make up the permanent staff, who stay attached to every House and Senate committee regardless of turnover in Congress and who are responsible for organizing and administering the committee's work, including researching, scheduling, organizing hearings, and drafting legislation. Committee staffers also play key roles in the legislative process.

The number of congressional staff members grew rapidly during the 1960s and 1970s, leveled off in the 1980s, and decreased dramatically in 1995. This sudden drop fulfilled the Republican congressional candidates' campaign promise to reduce the size of committee staffs.

Rules of Lawmaking Explain How a Bill Becomes a Law

The institutional structure of Congress is one key factor that helps to shape the legislative process. A second and equally important set of factors is the rules of congressional procedure. These rules govern everything from the introduction of a **bill** through its submission to the president for signing (see Figure 8.6). Not only do these regulations influence the fate of each and every bill, they also help to determine the distribution of power in the Congress.

bill a proposed law that has been sponsored by a member of Congress and submitted to the clerk of the House or Senate

THE FIRST STEP IS COMMITTEE DELIBERATION

Even if a member of Congress, the White House, or a federal agency has spent months developing and drafting a piece of legislation, it does not become a bill until it is submitted officially by a senator or representative to the clerk of the House or Senate and referred to the appropriate committee for deliberation. No floor action on any bill can take place until the committee with jurisdiction over it has taken all the time it needs to deliberate. During the course of its deliberations, the committee typically refers the bill to one of its subcommittees, which may hold hearings, listen to expert testimony, and amend the proposed legislation before referring it to the full committee for consideration. The full committee may accept the recommendation of the subcommittee or hold its own hearings and prepare its own amendments. Or, even more frequently, the committee and subcommittee may do little or nothing with a bill that has been submitted to them. Many bills are simply allowed to "die in committee" with little or no serious consideration given to them. In a typical congressional session, 95 percent of the roughly eight thousand bills introduced die in committee—an indication of the power of the congressional committee system.

Figure 8.6 How a Bill Becomes a Law

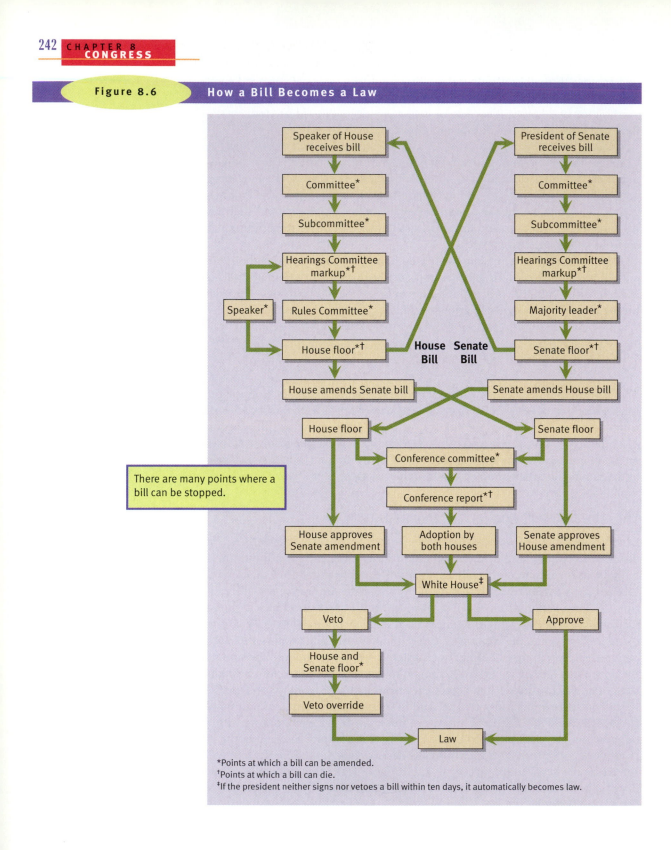

There are many points where a bill can be stopped.

*Points at which a bill can be amended.
†Points at which a bill can die.
‡If the president neither signs nor vetoes a bill within ten days, it automatically becomes law.

The relative handful of bills that are reported out of committee must, in the House, pass one additional hurdle within the committee system: the Rules Committee. This powerful committee determines the rules that will govern action on the bill on the House floor. In particular, the Rules Committee allots the time for debate and decides to what extent amendments to the bill can be proposed from the floor.

DEBATE IS LESS RESTRICTED IN THE SENATE THAN IN THE HOUSE

In the House, virtually all of the time allotted for debate on a given bill is controlled by the bill's sponsor and by its leading opponent. In almost every case, these two people are the committee chair and the ranking minority member of the committee that processed the bill—or those they designate. These two participants are, by rule and tradition, granted the power to allocate most of the debate time in small amounts to members who are seeking to speak for or against the measure. Preference in the allocation of time goes to the members of the committee whose jurisdiction covers the bill.

In the Senate, the leadership has much less control over floor debate. Indeed, the Senate is unique among the world's legislative bodies for its commitment to unlimited debate. Once given the floor, a senator may speak as long as he or she wishes. On a number of memorable occasions, senators have used the right to talk without interruption for as long as they want to prevent action on legislation that they opposed. Through this tactic, called the **filibuster,** small minorities or even one individual in the Senate can attempt to force the majority to give in. During the 1950s and 1960s, for example, opponents of civil rights legislation often sought to block its passage by staging a filibuster. Democrats have used the threat of a filibuster to block some of President George W. Bush's judicial nominees, much as Republicans used the same tactic to derail Clinton nominees. In 2003, Senate Republicans staged a thirty-hour marathon, bringing cots and sleeping bags into the Senate to protest Democratic use of the tactic. The votes of three-fifths of the Senate, or sixty votes, are needed to end a filibuster. This procedure is called **cloture.** Whereas the filibuster was once an extraordinary tactic used only on rare occasions, in recent years it has been used increasingly often.

Once debate is concluded on the floor of the House and the Senate, the leaders schedule it for a vote on the floor of each chamber. By this time, congressional leaders know what the vote will be; leaders do not bring legislation to the floor unless they are fairly certain it is going to pass. As a consequence, it is unusual for the leadership to lose a bill on the floor. On rare occasions, the last moments of the floor vote can be very dramatic, as each party's leadership puts its whip organization into action to make sure that wavering members vote with the party. The passage of Medicare reform in 2003 was one such occasion. Republican party leaders took the unprecedented step of keeping the vote open for two hours and fifty-one minutes while they looked high and low for the remaining votes they needed to pass the law. It was nearly 6 A.M. by the time the bill passed.

filibuster a tactic used by members of the Senate to prevent action on legislation they oppose by continuously holding the floor and speaking until the majority backs down. Once given the floor, senators have unlimited time to speak, and it requires a vote of three-fifths of the Senate to end a filibuster

cloture a rule allowing a majority of two-thirds or three-fifths of the members in a legislative body to set a time limit on debate over a given bill

CONFERENCE COMMITTEES RECONCILE HOUSE AND SENATE VERSIONS OF LEGISLATION

Getting a bill out of committee and through one of the houses of Congress is no guarantee that a bill will be enacted into law. Before a bill can be sent to the president, both houses must pass it in the same identical form. Frequently, bills that began with similar provisions in both chambers emerge with little resemblance to each other. Alternatively, a bill may be passed by one chamber but undergo substantial revision in the other chamber. In such cases, a conference committee composed of the senior members of the committees or subcommittees that initiated the bills may be convened to iron out differences between the two pieces of legislation.

When a bill comes out of conference, it faces one more hurdle. Before a bill can be sent to the president for signing, the House-Senate conference committee's version of the bill must be approved on the floor of each chamber. Usually such approval is given quickly. Occasionally, however, a bill's opponents use this round of approval as one last opportunity to defeat a piece of legislation.

THE PRESIDENT'S VETO CONTROLS THE FLOW OF LEGISLATION

veto the president's constitutional power to turn down acts of Congress. A presidential veto may be overridden by a two-thirds vote of each house of Congress

pocket veto a presidential veto that is automatically triggered if the president does not act on a given piece of legislation passed during the final ten days of a legislative session if Congress, by its adjournment, prevents the bill from being returned to it by the president

Once adopted by the House and Senate, a bill goes to the president, who may choose to sign the bill into law or **veto** it. The veto is the president's constitutional power to reject a piece of legislation. To veto a bill, the president returns it unsigned within ten days to the house of Congress in which it originated. If Congress adjourns during the ten-day period, such that congressional adjournment prevents the president from returning the bill to Congress, the bill is also considered to be vetoed. This latter method is known as the **pocket veto.** The possibility of a presidential veto affects how willing members of Congress are to push for different pieces of legislation at different times. If they think a proposal is likely to be vetoed, they might shelve it for a later time.

A presidential veto may be overridden by a two-thirds vote in both the House and Senate. A veto override says much about the support that a president can expect from Congress, and it can deliver a stinging blow to the executive branch.

Several Factors Influence How Congress Decides

What determines the kinds of legislation that Congress ultimately produces? According to the most simple theories of representation, members of Congress would respond to the views of their constituents. In fact, the process of creating a legislative agenda, drawing up a list of possible measures, and deciding among them is a very complex process, in which a variety of influences from inside and outside government play important roles. External influences include a legislator's constituency and various interest groups. Influences from inside government include party leadership, congressional colleagues, and the president. Let us examine each of these influences individually and then consider how they interact to produce congressional policy decisions.

CONSTITUENTS MATTER

Because members of Congress, for the most part, want to be reelected, we would expect the views of their constituents to be a primary influence on the decisions that legislators make. Yet most constituents do not even know what policies their representatives support. The number of citizens who *do* pay attention to such matters—the attentive public—is usually very small. Nonetheless, members of Congress spend a lot of time worrying about what their constituents think, because these representatives realize that the choices they make may be scrutinized in a future election and used as ammunition by an opposing candidate. Because of this possibility, members of Congress try to anticipate their constituents' policy views.[17]

INTEREST GROUPS SHAPE CONSTITUENTS AND CONGRESS

Interest groups are another important external influence on the policies that Congress produces. When members of Congress are making voting decisions, those interest groups that have some connection to constituents in particular members' districts are most likely to be influential. For this reason, interest groups with the ability to mobilize followers in many congressional districts may be especially influential in Congress.

Interest groups also have substantial influence in setting the legislative agenda and in helping to craft specific language in legislation. Today, sophisticated lobbyists win influence by providing information about policies to busy members of Congress. As one lobbyist noted, "You can't get access without knowledge. . . . I can go in to see [former Energy and Commerce Committee chair] John Dingell, but if I have nothing to offer or nothing to say, he's not going to want to see me."[18] In recent years, interest groups have also begun to build broader coalitions and comprehensive campaigns around particular policy issues. In 1995, the Republican congressional leadership worked so closely with lobbyists that critics charged that the boundaries between lobbyists and legislators had been erased, and that lobbyists had become "adjunct staff to the Republican leadership."[19]

PARTY LEADERS RELY ON PARTY DISCIPLINE

In both the House and Senate, party leaders have a good deal of influence over the behavior of their party members. This influence, sometimes called "party discipline," was once so powerful that it dominated the lawmaking process. At the turn of the century, party leaders could often command the allegiance of more than 90 percent of their members. A vote on which 50 percent or more of

party vote a roll-call vote in the House or Senate in which at least 50 percent of the members of one party take a particular position and are opposed by at least 50 percent of the members of the other party. Party votes are rare today, although they were fairly common in the nineteenth century

roll-call vote a vote in which each legislator's yes or no vote is recorded as the clerk calls the names of the members alphabetically

the members of one party take one position while at least 50 percent of the members of the other party take the opposing position is called a **party vote.** At the beginning of the twentieth century, nearly half of all **roll-call votes** in the House of Representatives were party votes. While party voting is more rare today than a century ago, in the last decade it has been fairly common to find at least a majority of the Democrats opposing a majority of the Republicans on any given issue.

Typically, party unity is greater in the House than in the Senate. House rules give more power to the majority party leaders, which gives them more influence over House members. In the Senate, however, the leadership has few controls over its members. Senate majority leader Tom Daschle once observed that a Senate leader seeking to influence other senators has as incentives "a bushel full of carrots and a few twigs."[20]

Party unity has been on the rise in the last decade because the divisions between the parties have deepened on many high-profile issues such as abortion, affirmative action, the minimum wage, and school vouchers (see Figure 8.7), and because the majority-minority party difference has been small in recent years. Party unity scores rise when congressional leaders try to put a partisan stamp on legislation. For example, in 1995, then-speaker Newt Gingrich sought to enact a Republican Contract with America that few Democrats supported. The result was more party unity in the House than in any year since 1954. In 1998, party unity scores rose as bitter divisions between Democrats and Republicans over impeachment reduced either party's willingness to compromise on legislation.

Although party organization has weakened since the turn of the century, today's party leaders still have some resources at their disposal: (1) committee

Figure 8.7   **Party Unity Scores by Chamber**

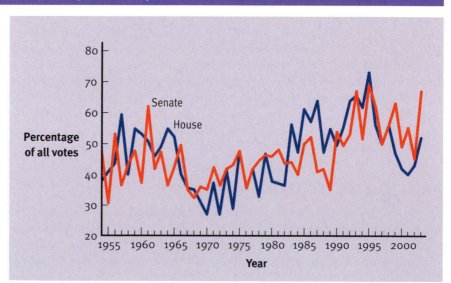

assignments, (2) access to the floor, (3) the whip system, (4) logrolling, and (5) the presidency. These resources are regularly used and are often effective in securing the support of party members.

Committee Assignments   Leaders can create debts among members by helping them get favorable committee assignments. These assignments are made early in the congressional careers of most members and cannot be taken from them if they later go against party discipline. Nevertheless, if the leadership goes out of its way to get the right assignment for a member, this effort is likely to create a bond of obligation that can be called upon without any other payments or favors. This is one reason the Republican leadership gave freshmen favorable assignments when the Republicans took over Congress in 1995.

Access to the Floor   The most important everyday resource available to the parties is control over access to the floor. With thousands of bills awaiting passage and most members clamoring for access in order to influence a bill or to publicize themselves, floor time is precious. In the Senate, the leadership allows ranking committee members to influence the allocation of floor time—who will speak for how long; in the House, the speaker, as head of the majority party (in consultation with the minority leader), allocates large blocks of floor time. Thus, floor time is allocated in both houses in Congress by the majority and minority leaders. More importantly, the speaker of the House and the majority leader in the Senate possess the power of recognition—that is, they decide who may and may not speak on the floor. Although this power may not appear to be substantial, it is a formidable authority and can be used to stymie a piece of legislation completely or to frustrate a member's attempts to speak on a particular issue. Because the power is significant, members of Congress usually attempt to stay on good terms with the speaker and the majority leader in order to ensure that they will continue to be recognized.

The Whip System   Some influence accrues to party leaders through the **whip system** within each party in Congress, which is primarily a communications network. Between twelve and twenty assistant and regional whips are selected to operate at the direction of the majority or minority leader and the whip. They take polls of all the members in order to learn their intentions on specific bills. This enables the leaders to know if they have enough support to allow a vote as well as whether the vote is so close that they need to put pressure on a few undecided members. Leaders also use the whip system to convey their wishes and plans to the members, but only in very close votes do they actually exert pressure on a member.

The whip system helps maintain party unity in both houses of Congress, but it is particularly critical in the House of Representatives because of the large number of legislators whose positions and votes must be accounted for. The majority and minority whips and their assistants must be adept at inducing compromise among legislators who hold widely differing viewpoints.

whip system a communications network in each house of Congress; whips take polls of the membership in order to learn their intentions on specific legislative issues and to assist the majority and minority leaders in various tasks

PICTURING

How Congress Decides

The typical day in the life of a member of Congress is hectic. The complex process of creating legislation is subject to a variety of influences from inside and outside government. Committee meetings, such as this conference committee's attempt to reconcile the differences between House and Senate versions of a bill, are a major component of a member's day.

Before a vote, members of Congress are pressed by outside influences. Here, Congressman Tom Barrett of Michigan meets with lobbyists from the auto industry.

Sometimes the president influences congressional decision-making. President Bush meets here with members of Congress to discuss Medicare reform.

POLITICS

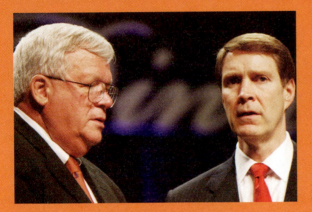

In both the House and the Senate, party leaders have a good deal of influence over the behavior of their party members. This influence, sometimes called "party discipline," has increased in recent years due in part to partisan polarization. Here, House Speaker Dennis Hastert confers with Senate Majority Leader Bill Frist.

Members of Congress want to be accessible to their constituents and often genuinely want to know what their constituents think about important issues. Pennsylvania representative Paul McHale established regular "Open Till Midnight" evenings, during which constituents could call him directly at his Washington office.

Members of Congress also spend time at home in their electoral districts. Congressman Rick Renzi of Arizona is shown here meeting with some constituents in his Navajo Nation office.

As Republican House whip from 1995 to 2002, Tom DeLay (R-Tex.) established a reputation as an effective vote counter and a tough leader, earning the nickname "the hammer." DeLay also expanded the reach of the whip, building alliances with Republican allies outside of Congress in ideological and business-oriented groups. Under DeLay's leadership, these lobbyists effectively worked as part of the whip operation. As whip, DeLay also began a campaign to pressure trade associations to hire Republicans as their lobbyists, which has since been continued by his successor, Roy Blunt (R-Mo.).

Logrolling   An agreement between two or more members of Congress who have nothing in common except the need for support is called **logrolling.** The agreement states, in effect, "You support me on bill X and I'll support you on bill Y." Since party leaders are the center of the communications networks in the two chambers, they can help members create large logrolling coalitions. Hundreds of logrolling deals are made each year, and although there are no official record-keeping books, it would be a poor party leader whose whips did not know who owed what to whom.

The Presidency   Of all the influences that maintain the clarity of party lines in Congress, the influence of the presidency is probably the most important. Indeed, the office is a touchstone of party discipline in Congress. Since the late 1940s, under President Harry Truman, presidents each year have identified a number of bills to be considered part of their administration's program. By the mid-1950s, both parties in Congress began to look to the president for these proposals, which became the most significant part of Congress's agenda. The president's support is a criterion for party loyalty, and party leaders are able to use it to rally some members.

Much Congressional Energy Goes to Tasks Other Than Lawmaking

In addition to the power to make the law, Congress has at its disposal an array of other instruments through which to influence the process of government. The Constitution gives the Senate the power to approve treaties and appointments. And Congress has a number of other powers through which it can influence the other branches of government.

CONGRESS OVERSEES HOW LEGISLATION IS IMPLEMENTED

Oversight refers to the effort by Congress to oversee or to supervise how legislation is carried out by the executive branch. Oversight is carried out by committees or subcommittees of the Senate or the House, which conduct hearings and investigations in order to analyze and evaluate bureaucratic agencies and the ef-

logrolling a legislative practice wherein agreements are made between legislators in voting for or against a bill. Unlike bargaining, parties to logrolling have nothing in common but their desire to exchange support

oversight the effort by Congress, through hearings, investigations, and other techniques, to exercise control over the activities of executive agencies

fectiveness of their programs. Their purpose may be to locate inefficiencies or abuses of power, to explore the relationship between what an agency does and what a law intended, or to change or abolish a program. Most programs and agencies are subject to some oversight every year during the course of hearings on **appropriations,** that is, the funding of agencies and government programs.

Committees or subcommittees have the power to subpoena witnesses, take oaths, cross-examine, compel testimony, and bring criminal charges for contempt (refusing to cooperate) and perjury (lying). Hearings and investigations resemble each other in many ways, but they differ on one fundamental point. A hearing is usually held on a specific bill, and the questions asked there are usually intended to build a record with regard to that bill. In an investigation, the committee or subcommittee does not begin with a particular bill, but examines a broad area or problem and then concludes its investigation with one or more proposed bills. One example of an investigation is the Senate hearings on the abuse of prisoners in Iraq's Abu Ghraib prison. Many Democrats and some Republicans complained that congressional oversight of the entire Iraq war had been lax. Reflecting on the prison abuse scandal, Representative Christopher Shays (R-Conn.) stated, "I believe our failure to do proper oversight has hurt our country and the administration. Maybe they wouldn't have gotten into some of this trouble if our oversight had been better."[21]

appropriations the amounts of money approved by Congress in statutes (bills) that each unit or agency of government can spend

SPECIAL SENATE POWERS INCLUDE ADVICE AND CONSENT

The Constitution has given the Senate a special power, one that is not based on lawmaking. The president has the power to make treaties and to appoint top executive officers, ambassadors, and federal judges—but only "with the Advice and Consent of the Senate" (Article II, Section 2). For treaties, two-thirds of those present must concur; for appointments, a simple majority is required.

The power to approve or reject presidential requests also involves the power to set conditions. The Senate only occasionally exercises its power to reject treaties and appointments, and usually that is when opposite parties control the Senate and the White House. For example, only nine judicial nominees have been rejected by the Senate during the past century, whereas hundreds have been approved.

IMPEACHMENT IS THE POWER TO REMOVE TOP OFFICIALS

The Constitution also grants Congress the power of **impeachment** over the president, vice president, and judicial officials. To impeach means to charge a government official (president or otherwise) with "Treason, Bribery, or other high Crimes and Misdemeanors" and bring them before Congress to determine their guilt. Impeachment is thus like a criminal indictment in which the House of Representatives acts like a grand jury, voting (by simple majority) on whether the accused ought to be impeached. If a majority of the House votes to impeach, the impeachment trial moves to the Senate, which acts like a trial jury by voting

impeachment the formal charge by the House of Representatives that a government official has committed "Treason, Bribery, or other high Crimes and Misdemeanors"

whether to convict and forcibly remove the person from office (this vote requires a two-thirds majority of the Senate).

Controversy over Congress's impeachment power has arisen over the grounds for impeachment, especially the meaning of "high Crimes and Misdemeanors." The most widely accepted legal view says that an impeachable offense would include a serious crime committed by the president, such as murder, but not all crimes. Obviously, no one would impeach a president for, say, a traffic violation. In addition, an impeachable offense could include an action that is legal, such as a president deserting his office and presidential responsibilities to, say, lie on a beach in Brazil for six months. Any serious abuse of presidential powers and responsibilities would also be impeachable.[22] Politically speaking, the ambiguity of the definition of impeachment also means that "an impeachable offense is whatever the majority of the House of Representatives considers it to be at a given moment in history."[23] In other words, impeachment, especially impeachment of a president, is a political decision.

Two presidents have been subjected to impeachment trials. In 1867, President Andrew Johnson, a southern Democrat who had battled a congressional Republican majority over Reconstruction, was impeached by the House but saved from conviction by one vote in the Senate. On December 19, 1998, the House of Representatives approved two articles of impeachment against President Bill Clinton, accusing him of lying under oath and obstructing justice in the investigation of his affair with White House intern Monica Lewinsky. The articles were approved on a nearly straight line party vote, and Clinton's defenders argued that the impeachment effort was politically motivated and that while Clinton had made mistakes in attempting to hide his affair with Lewinsky, nothing he did constituted an impeachable offense. After a Senate trial, Clinton was acquitted on February 12, 1999. Neither of the two articles of impeachment garnered even a majority of Senate votes. Within days of the end of the impeachment saga, Clinton moved to resume constructive relations with Congress.

Summary

The U.S. Congress plays a vital role in American democracy. It is both the key national representative body and the focal point for decision making in Washington, D.C. Throughout American history, Congress has sought to combine representation and power as it made policy. Congress was designed to be the first and most important branch of government, and this was how it behaved throughout most of the nineteenth century. Since then, however, the other two branches of government have assumed a more prominent and active role. In recent years, many Americans have become disillusioned with the ability of Congress to represent the people fairly and to exercise power responsibly.

Both sociological and agency representation play a role in the relationship between members of Congress and their constituencies. However, Congress is not fully representative because it is not a sociological microcosm of the United

States. Members of Congress do seek to act as agents for their constituents by representing their views and interests.

The activities of members of Congress are strongly influenced by electoral considerations, including the power of incumbency, and the way congressional districts are drawn. In order to assist their chances of reelection, members of Congress provide services and patronage to their constituents.

The political parties play a major role in the organization and functioning of Congress, and in the shaping of Congress's relations with the president.

The committee system surpasses the party system in its importance in Congress, even though power within committees is based on party as well as seniority. Congress also establishes rules of procedure to guide policy making.

Many different factors affect how Congress ultimately decides on legislation. Among the most important influences are constituency preferences, interest-group pressures, and party discipline. Typically party discipline is stronger in the House than in the Senate.

In addition to the power to make law, Congress possesses other formidable powers in its relationship with the executive branch. Among these are oversight, advice and consent on treaties and appointments, and the power to impeach executive officials. In spite of its array of powers, Congress is often accused of being ineffective and out of touch with the American people.

For Further Reading

Berg, John C. *Class, Gender, Race, and Power in the U.S. Congress.* Boulder, CO: Westview, 1994.

Burrell, Barbara C. *A Woman's Place Is in the House: Campaigning for Congress in the Feminist Era.* Ann Arbor, MI: University of Michigan Press, 1994.

Davidson, Roger H., ed. *The Postreform Congress.* New York: St. Martin's, 1991.

Dodd, Lawrence, and Bruce I. Oppenheimer, eds. *Congress Reconsidered.* 5th ed. Washington, DC: Congressional Quarterly Press, 1993.

Fenno, Richard F. *Congressmen in Committees.* Boston: Little, Brown, 1973.

Fenno, Richard F. *Homestyle: House Members in Their Districts.* Boston: Little, Brown, 1978.

Fiorina, Morris. *Congress: Keystone of the Washington Establishment.* 2nd ed. New Haven, CT: Yale University Press, 1989.

Fowler, Linda, and Robert McClure. *Political Ambition: Who Decides to Run for Congress?* New Haven, CT: Yale University Press, 1989.

Mayhew, David R. *Congress: The Electoral Connection.* New Haven, CT: Yale University Press, 1974.

Sinclair, Barbara. *The Transformation of the U.S. Senate.* Baltimore: Johns Hopkins University Press, 1989.

Smith, Steven S., and Christopher Deering. *Committees in Congress.* 2nd ed. Washington, DC: Congressional Quarterly Press, 1990.

Spitzer, Robert J. *President and Congress.* New York: McGraw-Hill, 1993.

Thomas, Sue. *How Women Legislate.* New York: Oxford University Press, 1994.

Study Outline

Congress Represents the American People

1. House members are more attuned to localized narrow interests in society, whereas senators are better able than House members to represent statewide or national interests.

2. In recent years, the House has exhibited more partisanship and ideological division than the Senate.

3. Congress is not fully representative because it is not a sociological microcosm of American society.

4. Members of Congress frequently communicate with constituents and devote a great deal of staff time to constituency service.
5. Electoral motivations have a strong impact on both sociological and agency representation in Congress.
6. Incumbency affords members of Congress resources such as constituency service and mailing to help secure re-election.
7. In recent years, turnover rates in Congress have increased, although this is due more to incumbent retirement than to the defeat of incumbents in elections.
8. Members of Congress can supply benefits to constituents by passing pork-barrel legislation. Pork-barrel votes are exchanged by members of Congress for votes on others issues.

The Organization of Congress Is Shaped by Party

1. At the beginning of each Congress, Democrats and Republicans gather to select their leaders. The leader of the majority party in the House of Representatives is elected speaker of the House by a strict party-line vote.
2. In the Senate, the president pro tempore serves as the presiding officer, although the majority and minority leaders control the calendar and agenda of the Senate.
3. The committee system provides Congress with a second organizational structure that is more a division of labor than the party-based hierarchies of power.
4. With specific jurisdiction over certain policy areas and the task of processing proposals of legislation into bills for floor consideration, standing committees are the most important arenas of congressional policy making.
5. Power within committees is based on seniority, although the seniority principle is not absolute.
6. Each member of Congress has a personal staff that deals with constituency requests and, increasingly, with the details of legislative and administrative oversight.

Rules of Lawmaking Explain How a Bill Becomes a Law

1. Committee deliberation is necessary before floor action on any bill.
2. Many bills receive little or no committee or subcommittee action; they are allowed to "die in committee."

3. Bills reported out of committee in the House must be through the House Rules Committee before they can be debated on the floor. The Rules Committee allots the time for floor debate on a bill and the conditions under which a bill may (or may not) be amended.
4. In the Senate, rules of debate are much less rigid. In fact, senators may delay Senate action on legislation by refusing to yield the floor; this is known as a filibuster.
5. Conference committees are often required to reconcile House and Senate versions of bills that began with similar provisions but emerged with significant differences.
6. After being adopted by the House and the Senate, a bill is sent to the president, who may choose to sign the bill or veto it. Congress can override a president's veto by a two-thirds vote in both the House and the Senate.

Several Factors Influence How Congress Decides

1. Creating a legislative agenda, drawing up a list of possible measures, and deciding among them is a complex process in which a variety of influences from inside and outside government play important roles.
2. Interest groups can influence congressional decision making by mobilizing followers in congressional districts, setting the agenda, or writing legislative language.
3. Party discipline is still an important factor in congressional voting, despite its decline throughout the twentieth century.
4. Party unity is typically greater in the House than in the Senate. Party unity on roll-call votes has increased in recent sessions of Congress.
5. Party unity is a result of a combination of the ideology and background of individual members and the resources party leaders have at their disposal.
6. The influence of the presidency is probably the most important of all the resources that maintain party discipline in Congress.

Much Congressional Energy Goes to Tasks Other Than Lawmaking

1. Congress has increasingly relied on legislative oversight of administrators.
2. The Senate also has the power of approving or rejecting presidential treaties and appointments.
3. Congress has the power to impeach executive officials.

Practice Quiz

1. Members of Congress can work as agents of their constituents by
    a) providing direct patronage.
    b) taking part in a party vote.
    c) joining a caucus.
    d) supporting term limits.

2. Because they have larger and more heterogeneous constituencies, senators
    a) are more attuned to the needs of localized interest groups.
    b) care more about reelection than House members.
    c) can better represent the national interest.
    d) face less competition in elections than House members.

3. What type of representation is described when constituents have the power to hire and fire their representative?
    a) agency representation
    b) sociological representation
    c) democratic representation
    d) trustee representation

4. Incumbency is an important factor in deciding who is elected to Congress because
    a) incumbents have tools they can use to help ensure reelection.
    b) potentially strong challengers may be dissuaded from running because of the strength of the incumbent.
    c) Both a and b are true.
    d) Neither a nor b is true.

5. Some have argued that the creation of minority congressional districts has
    a) lessened the sociological representation of minorities in Congress.
    b) made it more difficult for minorities to win substantive policy goals.
    c) been a result of the media's impact on state legislative politics.
    d) lessened the problem of "pork-barrel" politics.

6. Which of the following is *not* an important influence on how members of Congress vote on legislation?
    a) the media
    b) constituency
    c) interest groups
    d) party leaders

7. Which of the following types of committees does *not* include members of both the House and the Senate?
    a) standing committee
    b) joint committee
    c) conference committee
    d) No committees include both House members and senators.

8. An agreement between members of Congress to trade support for each other's bill is known as
    a) oversight.
    b) filibuster.
    c) logrolling.
    d) patronage.

Critical Thinking Questions

1. Two of Congress's chief responsibilities are representation and lawmaking. Describe the ways in which these two responsibilities might conflict with one another. How do these responsibilities support and reinforce one another? What would Congress be like if its sole function were representative? What would it be like if it were solely legislative?

2. Describe the process by which a bill becomes a law. At the various stages of this process, assess who—both within government and outside of government—makes and influences decisions. Are there stages at which the process is more democratic than it is at others? Are there stages at which the people have less influence? In your judgment, is the overall process democratic?

Key Terms

agency representation (p. 227)
appropriations (p. 251)
bicameral (p. 225)
bill (p. 241)
cloture (p. 243)
conference/caucus (p. 236)
conference committee (p. 240)
constituency (p. 225)
filibuster (p. 243)
gerrymandering (p. 231)

impeachment (p. 251)
incumbency (p. 230)
joint committee (p. 240)
logrolling (p. 250)
majority leader (p. 236)
minority leader (p. 236)
oversight (p. 250)
party vote (p. 246)
patronage (p. 232)
pocket veto (p. 244)
pork barrel (p. 232)
private bill (p. 236)

redistricting (p. 231)
roll-call vote (p. 246)
select committee (p. 240)
seniority (p. 240)
sociological representation (p. 227)
speaker of the House (p. 236)
standing committee (p. 238)
term limits (p. 231)
veto (p. 244)
whip system (p. 247)

9 THE PRESIDENCY

MAIN MESSAGE

The rise of the modern strong presidency occurred during the twentieth century.

Key Concepts

1. Presidential power is rooted in the Constitution.
2. The powers exercised by modern presidents far outstrip what the Constitution provides.
3. The modern president is served by numerous offices and departments.
4. To get things done, presidents rely on a variety of political resources, including elections, political parties, interest groups, the media, and public opinion.

President Bill Clinton didn't have much going for him, it seemed, when the U.S. Senate failed to remove him from office at the conclusion of his impeachment trial in early 1999. As only the second president in history to be put on trial for impeachable offenses (the first was the hapless Andrew Johnson in 1868), Clinton avoided defeat at the hands of his opponents when the Senate failed to muster the necessary two-thirds vote to remove him from office. Still, how could he hope to govern in the final two years of his presidency when more Americans blamed Clinton for the impeachment mess than blamed his opponents in Congress,[1] when Clinton's personal reputation was caked with mud following his admission of having had an affair with White House intern Monica Lewinsky (after having denied the affair for months), and when the Republicans in Congress who tried to remove him from office were still furious at the Democratic president?

To the surprise of many, Clinton wasted no time getting back to work. Within days of the impeachment vote, Clinton had proposed moving ahead on such domestic policy ideas as raising pay for the military, fixing the Y2K computer problem, providing financial security for the Medicare and Social Security programs, allowing the states flexibility in their education policy, and developing an antimissile system. In foreign policy, Clinton engaged the United States in a full-scale daily air war over Iraq, followed shortly thereafter by a large-scale military intervention in Kosovo (the former Yugoslavia). Even more surprising than Clinton's flurry of activity was Congress's response: House and Senate Republican leaders said they were anxious to "pick up the pieces" and "move forward on the people's business."[2]

What is most important about Congress's response is this: The modern American government cannot operate without the active involvement of the president. Even though the Constitution's Founders created a system in which Congress was to be the first and most important branch (as we discussed in the last chapter), the political relationship between Congress and the presidency has changed dramatically since the start of the twentieth century, such that the presidency is viewed by most as the center of the national government. That is, we have witnessed the rise of the modern strong presidency. Even though congressional leaders despised Clinton, they knew that they could not govern without active presidential involvement.

For his part, Clinton realized that his presidency would be forever tarred by the stigma of impeachment, but that the power of his office meant that he still had the opportunity to move ahead with the business of the country. Indeed, the fact that Clinton continued to govern effectively during and after the impeachment ordeal helps explain why Clinton's job approval rating stood at an impressive 68 percent at the end of the impeachment trial—8 percentage points *higher* than Clinton's approval rating when the impeachment crisis began![3] This underscores the critical link between presidential power and citizen support.

The modern presidency is indeed a powerful office. But the Clinton example reveals two other facts about the presidency. First, what we expect of presidents is almost always greater than what they can deliver. In Clinton's case, for example, he continued to have little success to the end of his presidency in getting Congress to set aside money to cover the rising costs of Medicare and Social Security, or to pass new, tougher gun laws. And second, not all presidents are equally skilled at using the powers of their office. Even Clinton's opponents agreed that he was one of the most skillful politicians ever to occupy the White House. A less skillful president might not have been able to avoid removal from office, or may have been unable to pick up the pieces after the impeachment effort failed.

In short, (1) the modern strong presidency is a powerful office, but (2) most Americans expect more than any president can deliver, and (3) the most successful presidents are those who know how to best exploit the formal and informal powers available to them. In this chapter, we will see how these themes fit together. We begin with the Constitution.

Presidential Power Is Rooted in the Constitution

The presidency was established by Article II of the Constitution. Article II begins by asserting, "The executive power shall be vested in a President of the United States of America." It goes on to describe the manner in which the president is to be chosen and defines the basic powers of the presidency. By vesting the executive power in a single president, the framers were emphatically rejecting proposals for various forms of collective leadership.

Immediately following the first sentence of Section 1, Article II defines the manner in which the president is to be chosen. This is a very odd sequence, but it does say something about the struggle the delegates were having over how to provide great power of action or energy to the executive and at the same time to balance that power with limitations. The struggle was between those delegates who wanted the president to be selected by, and thus responsible to, Congress and those delegates who preferred that the president be elected directly by the people. Direct popular election would create a more independent and more powerful presidency. With the adoption of a scheme of indirect election through an electoral college in which the electors would be selected by the state legislatures (and close elections would be resolved in the House of Representatives), the framers hoped to achieve a "republican" solution: a strong president responsible to state and national legislators rather than directly to the electorate. This indirect method of electing the president probably did dampen the power of most presidents in the nineteenth century. This conclusion is supported by the fact that, as we shall see later in this chapter, presidential power increased as the president developed a closer and more direct relationship to a mass electorate.

While Section 1 of Article II explains how the president is to be chosen, Sections 2 and 3 outline the powers and duties of the president. These two sections identify two sources of presidential power. Some presidential powers are specifically established by the language of the Constitution. For example, the Constitution authorizes the president to make treaties, grant pardons, and nominate judges and other public officials. These specifically defined powers are called the **expressed powers** of the office and cannot be revoked by the Congress or any other agency without an amendment to the Constitution. Other expressed powers include the power to receive ambassadors and command of the military forces of the United States.

expressed powers specific powers granted to Congress under Article I, Section 8, of the Constitution

In addition to the president's expressed powers, Article II declares that the president "shall take Care that the Laws be faithfully executed." Since the laws are enacted by Congress, this language implies that Congress is to delegate to the president the power to implement or execute its will. Powers given to the president by Congress are called **delegated powers.** In principle, Congress delegates to the president only the power to identify or develop the means through which to carry out its decisions. So, for example, if Congress determines that air quality should be improved, it might delegate to the executive the power to identify the best means of bringing about such an improvement as well as the power to implement the cleanup process. In practice, of course, decisions about how to clean the air are

delegated powers constitutional powers that are assigned to one governmental agency but that are exercised by another agency with the express permission of the first

likely to have an enormous impact on businesses, organizations, and individuals throughout the nation. As it delegates power to the executive, Congress substantially enhances the importance of the presidency and the executive branch. In most cases, Congress delegates power to executive agencies rather than to the president. As we shall see, however, contemporary presidents have found ways to capture a good deal of this delegated power for themselves.

Presidents have claimed a third source of power beyond expressed and delegated powers. These are powers not specified in the Constitution or the law but said to stem from "the rights, duties and obligations of the presidency."[4] They are referred to as the **inherent powers** of the presidency and are most often asserted by presidents in times of war or national emergency. For example, after the fall of Fort Sumter and the outbreak of the Civil War, President Abraham Lincoln issued a series of executive orders for which he had no clear legal basis. Without even calling Congress into session, Lincoln combined the state militias into a ninety-day national volunteer force, called for forty thousand new volunteers, enlarged the regular army and navy, diverted $2 million in unspent appropriations to military needs, instituted censorship of the U.S. mails, ordered a blockade of southern ports, suspended the writ of *habeas corpus* in the border states, and ordered the arrest by military police of individuals whom he deemed to be guilty of engaging in or even contemplating treasonous actions.[5] Lincoln asserted that these extraordinary measures were justified by the president's inherent power to protect the nation.[6] Subsequent presidents, including Franklin D. Roosevelt and George W. Bush, have had similar views.

inherent powers powers claimed by a president that are not expressed in the Constitution, but are inferred from it

EXPRESSED POWERS COME DIRECTLY FROM THE WORDS OF THE CONSTITUTION

The president's expressed powers, as defined by Sections 2 and 3 of Article II, fall into several categories:

1. *Military.* Article II, Section 2, provides for the power as "Commander in Chief of the Army and Navy of the United States, and of the Militia of the several States, when called into the actual Service of the United States."
2. *Judicial.* Article II, Section 2, also provides the power to "grant Reprieves and Pardons for Offenses against the United States, except in Cases of Impeachment."
3. *Diplomatic.* Article II, Section 2, also provides the power "by and with the Advice and Consent of the Senate, to make Treaties." Article II, Section 3, provides the power to "receive Ambassadors and other public Ministers."
4. *Executive.* Article II, Section 3, authorizes the president to see to it that all the laws are faithfully executed; Section 2 gives the chief executive the power to appoint, remove, and supervise all executive officers and to appoint all federal judges.
5. *Legislative.* Article I, Section 7, and Article II, Section 3, give the president the power to participate authoritatively in the legislative process.

Military   The president's military powers are among the most important exercised by the chief executive. The position of **commander in chief** makes the president the highest military authority in the executive branch. Final authority over military matters rests with Congress, which may direct the commander in chief as it chooses. In the nineteenth century, Congress normally directed the president's military actions and decisions. In the twentieth century, however, presidents have engaged the country in many military campaigns abroad without congressional approval. Congress has not declared war since December 1941, and yet since then American military forces have engaged in numerous campaigns throughout the world under orders of the president. When North Korean forces invaded South Korea in June 1950, Congress was actually prepared to declare war but President Harry S. Truman decided not to ask for congressional action. Instead, Truman asserted the principle that the president and not Congress could decide when and where to deploy America's military might. Truman dispatched American forces to Korea without a congressional declaration, and in the face of the emergency, Congress felt it had to acquiesce. Congress passed a resolution approving the president's actions, and this became the pattern for future congressional-executive relations in the military realm. The wars in Vietnam, Bosnia, Afghanistan, Iraq, and a host of lesser conflicts, were all fought without declarations of war.

> **commander in chief** the power of the president as commander of the national military and the state national guard units (when called into service)

In 1973, Congress responded to presidential unilateralism by passing the **War Powers Resolution** over President Richard Nixon's veto. This resolution reasserted the principle of congressional war power, required the president to inform Congress of any planned military campaign, and stipulated that forces must be withdrawn within sixty days in the absence of a specific congressional authorization for their continued deployment. Presidents, however, have generally ignored the War Powers Resolution, claiming inherent executive power to defend the nation.

> **War Powers Resolution** a resolution of Congress that the president can send troops into action abroad only by authorization of Congress, or if American troops are already under attack or serious threat

Presidential war powers took on new dimensions during George W. Bush's presidency. Yet both of the major military efforts launched by the Bush administration—the "war on terrorism" beginning after the attacks against America on September 11, 2001, and the invasion and occupation of Iraq begun in 2003—were authorized by Congress. Three days after the 9/11 attacks, Congress passed a "Use of Force" resolution authorizing Bush to "use all necessary and appropriate force against those nations, organizations, or persons he determines planned, authorized, committed, or aided the terrorists attacks that occurred on September 11, or harbored such organizations or persons, in order to prevent any future acts of international terrorism against the United States." Some objected that this resolution gave too much power and discretion to the president, but the nation's shock and anger over the terrorist attacks called for immediate and broad action.

In October 2002, Congress passed a similar "Use of Force" resolution authorizing the president to use American military forces "as he determines to be necessary and appropriate" to respond to "the continuing threat posed by Iraq." Bush implemented the terms of the act when he directed the U.S. military invasion of Iraq in March 2003, arguing that Iraq's leader, Saddam Hussein, possessed weapons of mass destruction (WMDs, including chemical, biological, and nuclear weapons), had links to terrorism, and was an evil leader who needed to be removed for the good of the Middle East and America. After overthrowing the Hussein regime and occupying the country, it became clear that Hussein possessed no WMDs and had no active nuclear program, and that his regime maintained no significant links to terrorist groups outside of his country. These revelations undercut the legitimacy of Bush's actions, but faced with the task of rebuilding Iraq, most in Congress and the country supported a continued U.S. presence. In both of these cases, Congress provided legal authority for Bush, even though he claimed that he did not need such authority, and in neither case did Congress pass a formal declaration of war. Both measures also specifically cited the terms of the War Powers Resolution, indicating its continued legal import. Without question, the American mood after 9/11 was much more supportive of aggressive use of force, a fact that Bush used to galvanize public support for controversial military actions.

Within the executive branch, the president directs the secretary of defense, who heads the vast Defense Department, encompassing all the military branches of service. The president also directs the nation's intelligence network, which includes not only the Central Intelligence Agency (CIA) but also the National Security Council (NSC), the National Security Agency (NSA), the Federal Bureau of Investigation (FBI), and a host of less well-known but very powerful international and domestic security agencies.

Military Sources of Domestic Power   The president's military powers extend into the domestic sphere. Article IV, Section 4, provides that the "United States shall [protect] every State . . . against Invasion . . . and . . . domestic Violence," and Congress has made this an explicit presidential power through statutes directing the president as commander in chief to discharge these obligations.[7] The Constitution restrains the president's use of domestic force by providing that a state legislature (or governor when the legislature is not in session) must request federal troops before the president can send them into the state to provide public order. Yet this proviso is not absolute. First, presidents are not obligated to deploy national troops merely because the state legislature or governor makes such a request. And more important, the president may deploy troops in a state or city without a specific request from the state legislature or governor if the president considers it necessary to maintain an essential national service during an emergency, to enforce a federal judicial order, or to protect federally guaranteed civil rights.

One historic example of the unilateral use of presidential emergency power to protect the states against domestic disorder, even when the states don't request it, was the decision by President Dwight Eisenhower in 1957 to send troops into Little Rock, Arkansas, literally against the wishes of the state of Arkansas, to enforce court orders to integrate Little Rock's Central High School. The governor of Arkansas, Orval Faubus, had actually posted the Arkansas National Guard at the entrance of Central High School to prevent the court-ordered admission of nine black students. After an effort to negotiate with Governor Faubus failed, President Eisenhower reluctantly sent a thousand paratroopers to Little Rock, who stood watch while the black students took their places in the all-white classrooms. This case makes quite clear that the president does not have to wait for a request by a state legislature or governor before acting as a domestic commander in chief.[8]

Military emergencies have typically also led to expansion of the domestic powers of the executive branch. This was true during the First and Second World Wars and has been true in the wake of the war on terrorism as well. Within a month of the 9/11 attacks, the White House had drafted and Congress had enacted the USA Patriot Act, expanding the power of government agencies to engage in domestic surveillance activities, including electronic surveillance, and restricting judicial review of such efforts. The act also gave the attorney general greater authority to detain and deport aliens suspected of having terrorist affiliations. The following year, Congress created the Department of Homeland Security, combining offices from twenty-two federal agencies into one huge new cabinet department that would be responsible for protecting the nation from attack. The new agency, with a tentative budget of $40 billion, was to include the Coast Guard, Transportation Safety Administration, Federal Emergency Management Administration, Immigration and Naturalization Service, and offices from the departments of Agriculture, Energy, Transportation, Justice, Health and Human Services, Commerce, and the General Services Administration. The White House drafted the actual reorganization plan, but Congress weighed in to make certain that the new agency's workers had civil service and union protections.

Judicial   The presidential power to grant reprieves, pardons, and amnesties involves the power of life and death over all individuals who may be a threat to the security of the United States. Presidents may use this power on behalf of a particular individual, as did Gerald Ford when he pardoned Richard Nixon in 1974 "for all offenses against the United States which he . . . has committed or may have committed." Or they may use it on a large scale, as did President Andrew Johnson in 1868, when he gave full amnesty to all southerners who had participated in the "Late Rebellion," and President Carter in 1977, when he declared an amnesty for all the draft evaders of the Vietnam War. President Clinton created great controversy with a large number of last-minute pardons issued in the final days of his presidency in 2000. This power of life and death over others helped elevate the president to the level of earlier conquerors and kings by establishing him as the person before whom supplicants might come to make their pleas for mercy.

Diplomatic   The president is America's "head of state"—its chief representative in dealings with other nations. As head of state, the president has the power to make treaties for the United States (with the advice and consent of the Senate). And when President Washington received Edmond Genêt ("Citizen Genêt") as the formal emissary of the revolutionary government of France in 1793 and had his cabinet officers and Congress back his decision, he established a greatly expanded interpretation of the power to "receive Ambassadors and other public Ministers," extending it to the power to "recognize" other countries. That power gives the president the almost unconditional authority to review the claims of any new ruling groups to determine if they indeed control the territory and population of their country, so that they can commit it to treaties and other agreements.

In recent years, presidents have expanded the practice of using executive agreements instead of treaties to establish relations with other countries.[9] An **executive agreement** is exactly like a treaty because it is a contract between two countries, but an executive agreement does not require a two-thirds vote of approval by the Senate. Ordinarily, executive agreements are used to carry out commitments already made in treaties, or to arrange for matters well below the level of policy. But when presidents have found it expedient to use an executive agreement in place of a treaty, Congress has typically acquiesced.

executive agreement an agreement, made between the president and another country, that has the force of a treaty but does not require the Senate's "advice and consent"

Executive Power The most important basis of the president's power as chief executive is to be found in Article II, Section 3, which stipulates that the president must see that all the laws are faithfully executed, and Section 2, which provides that the president will appoint, remove, and supervise all executive officers, and appoint all federal judges (with Senate approval). The power to appoint the principal executive officers and to require each of them to report to the president on subjects relating to the duties of their departments makes the president the true chief executive officer (CEO) of the nation. In this manner, the Constitution focuses executive power and legal responsibility on the president. The famous sign on President Truman's desk, "The buck stops here," was not merely an assertion of Truman's personal sense of responsibility but was in fact recognition by him of the legal and constitutional responsibility of the president. The president is subject to some limitations, because the appointment of all such officers, including ambassadors, ministers, and federal judges, is subject to a majority approval by the Senate. But these appointments are at the discretion of the president, and the loyalty and the responsibility of each appointee are presumed to be directed toward the president.

The President's Legislative Power The president plays a role not only in the administration of government but also in the legislative process. Two constitutional provisions are the primary sources of the president's power in the legislative arena. The first of these is the provision in Article II, Section 3, providing that the president "shall from time to time give to the Congress Information of the State of the Union, and recommend to their Consideration such Measures as he shall judge necessary and expedient." The second of the president's legislative powers is of course the veto power assigned by Article I, Section 7.[10]

Delivering a "State of the Union" address does not at first appear to be of any great import. It is a mere obligation on the part of the president to make recommendations for Congress's consideration. But as political and social conditions began to favor an increasingly prominent role for presidents, each president, especially since Franklin Delano Roosevelt, began to rely on this provision to become the primary initiator of proposals for legislative action in Congress and the principal source for public awareness of national issues, as well as the most important single individual participant in legislative decisions. Few today doubt that the president and the executive branch together are the primary source for many important congressional actions.[11]

The **veto** power is the president's constitutional power to turn down acts of Congress (see Figure 9.1). This power alone makes the president the most

veto the president's constitutional power to turn down acts of Congress. A presidential veto may be overridden by a two-thirds vote of each house of Congress

The Veto Process

Figure 9.1

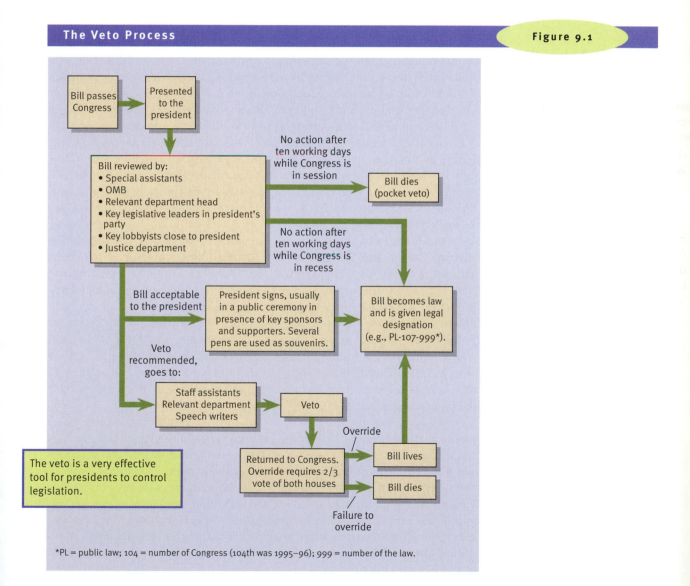

The veto is a very effective tool for presidents to control legislation.

*PL = public law; 104 = number of Congress (104th was 1995–96); 999 = number of the law.

pocket veto a presidential veto that is automatically triggered if the president does not act on a given piece of legislation passed during the final ten days of a legislative session if Congress, by its adjournment, prevents the bill from being returned to Congress

important single legislative leader.[12] No bill vetoed by the president can become law unless both the House and Senate override the veto by a two-thirds vote. Only about 7 percent of all vetoes have been overridden by Congress. In the case of a **pocket veto,** Congress does not even have the option of overriding the veto, but must reintroduce the bill in the next session. A pocket veto can occur when the president is presented with a bill during the last ten days of a legislative session and congressional adjournment prevents return of the bill. Usually, if a president does not sign a bill within ten days, it automatically becomes law. But this is true only while Congress is in session. If a president chooses not to sign a bill presented within the last ten days that Congress is in session, then the ten-day limit does not expire until Congress is out of session, and instead of becoming law, the bill is vetoed.

Use of the veto varies according to the political situation that each president confronts. During Bill Clinton's first two years in office, when Democrats controlled both houses of Congress, he vetoed no bills. Following the congressional elections of 1994, however, Clinton confronted a Republican-controlled Congress with a definite agenda, and he too began to use his veto power more vigorously. In the final six years of his term, as Congress continued under Republican control, Clinton vetoed thirty-seven bills. Only two of the vetoes were overridden. In his first three years and ten months as president, George W. Bush vetoed no bills. Except for an eighteen-month period when Democrats controlled the Senate by a slim one vote, Congress was controlled by fellow Republicans, making veto use less likely and less necessary than if both houses of Congress were controlled by the opposition party.

Clinton also recaptured some of his leadership by finding the path of legislative initiative that he had lost with the Republican takeover of the House and Senate after the 1994 congressional elections. Although not explicitly stated, the Constitution implies that the president has the power of **legislative initiative.** To "initiate" means to originate, and in government that can mean power. Initiative obviously implies the ability to formulate proposals for important policies, and the president, as an individual with a great deal of staff assistance, is able to initiate decisive action more frequently than Congress, with its large assemblies that have to deliberate and debate before taking action. With some important exceptions, Congress banks on the president to set the agenda of public policy.

legislative initiative the president's inherent power to bring a legislative agenda before Congress

The president's initiative does not end with policy making involving Congress and the making of laws in the ordinary sense of the term. The president has still another legislative role (in all but name) within the executive branch. This is designated as the power to issue **executive orders.** The executive order is first and foremost simply a normal tool of management, a power possessed by virtually any CEO to make rules setting procedures, etiquette, chains of command, functional responsibilities, and so on—"company policy." But evolving out of this normal management practice is a recognized presidential power to promulgate rules that have the effect and the formal status of legislation. Most of the executive orders of the president provide for the reorganization of struc-

executive order a rule or regulation issued by the president that has the effect and formal status of legislation

tures and procedures or otherwise direct the affairs of the executive branch—either to be applied across the board to all agencies or applied in some important respect to a single agency or department. One of the most important examples is Executive Order No. 8248, September 8, 1939, establishing the divisions of the Executive Office of the President. Another one of equal importance is President Nixon's executive order establishing the Environmental Protection Agency in 1970–71.

DELEGATED POWERS COME FROM CONGRESS

Many of the powers exercised by the president and the executive branch are not found in the Constitution but are the products of congressional statutes and resolutions. Over the past three-quarters of a century, Congress has voluntarily delegated a great deal of its own legislative authority to the executive branch. To some extent, this delegation of power has been an almost inescapable consequence of the expansion of government activity in the United States since the New Deal. Given the vast range of the federal government's responsibilities, Congress cannot execute and administer all the programs it creates and the laws it enacts. Inevitably, Congress must turn to the hundreds of departments and agencies in the executive branch or, when necessary, create new agencies to implement its goals. Thus, for example, in 2002, when Congress sought to protect America from terrorist attacks, it established a Department of Homeland Security and gave it broad powers in the realms of law enforcement, public health, and immigration. Similarly, in 1970, when Congress enacted legislation designed to improve the nation's air and water quality, it assigned the task of implementing its goals to the Environmental Protection Agency (EPA), which President Nixon created by an executive order. Congress gave the EPA substantial power to set and enforce air and water quality standards.

Institutional Resources of Presidential Power Are Numerous

Constitutional sources of power are not the only resources available to the president. Presidents have at their disposal a variety of other formal and informal resources that have important implications for their ability to govern (see Figure 9.2). Indeed, without these other resources, presidents would lack the ability—the tools of management and public mobilization—to make much use of the power and responsibility given to them by Congress. Let us first consider the president's formal institutional resources and then, in the section following, turn to the more informal political resources that affect a president's capacity to govern, in particular the president's base of popular support.

Figure 9.2   The Institutional Presidency

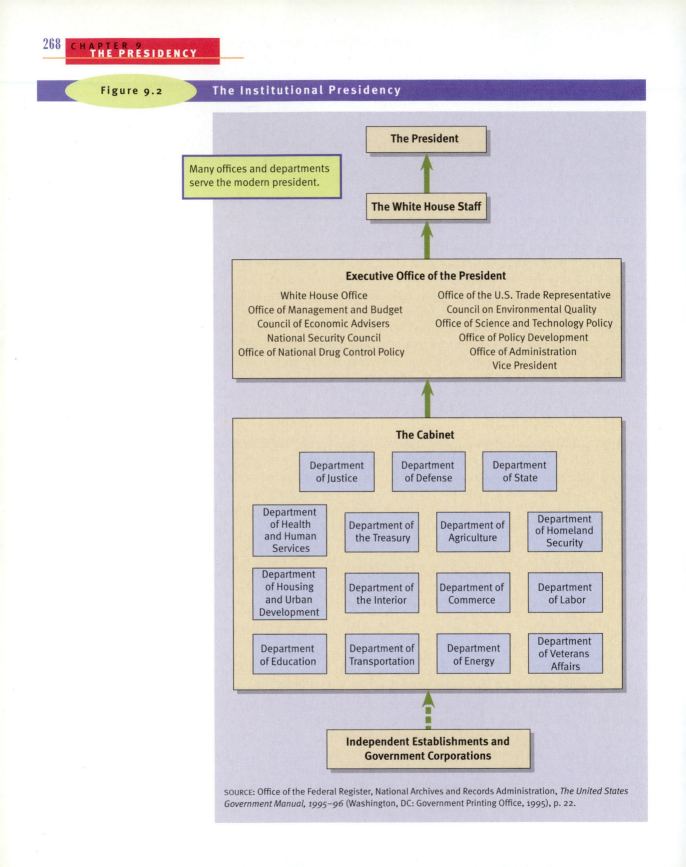

Many offices and departments serve the modern president.

The President

The White House Staff

Executive Office of the President

White House Office
Office of Management and Budget
Council of Economic Advisers
National Security Council
Office of National Drug Control Policy

Office of the U.S. Trade Representative
Council on Environmental Quality
Office of Science and Technology Policy
Office of Policy Development
Office of Administration
Vice President

The Cabinet

Department of Justice

Department of Defense

Department of State

Department of Health and Human Services

Department of the Treasury

Department of Agriculture

Department of Homeland Security

Department of Housing and Urban Development

Department of the Interior

Department of Commerce

Department of Labor

Department of Education

Department of Transportation

Department of Energy

Department of Veterans Affairs

Independent Establishments and Government Corporations

SOURCE: Office of the Federal Register, National Archives and Records Administration, *The United States Government Manual, 1995–96* (Washington, DC: Government Printing Office, 1995), p. 22.

POLITICAL APPOINTMENTS ARE AN IMPORTANT TOOL OF MANAGEMENT

The first management tool available to most presidents is a form of **patronage**—the choice of high-level political appointees. These appointments allow the president to fill top management positions with individuals who will attempt to carry out the president's agenda. But the president must appoint individuals who have experience and interest in the programs that they are to administer and who share the president's goals with respect to these programs. At the same time, presidents use the appointment process to build links to powerful political and economic constituencies by giving representation to important state political party organizations, the business community, organized labor, the scientific and university communities, organized agriculture, and certain large and well-organized religious groups.

patronage the resources available to higher officials, usually opportunities to make partisan appointments to offices and to confer grants, licenses, or special favors to supporters

THE WHITE HOUSE STAFF CONSTITUTES THE PRESIDENT'S EYES AND EARS

The **White House staff** is composed mainly of analysts and advisers who are closest to, and most responsive to, the president's needs and preferences.[13] Although many of the top White House staff members are given the title "special assistant" for a particular task or sector, the types of judgments they are expected to make and the kinds of advice they are supposed to give are a good deal broader and more generally political than those coming from the Executive Office of the President or from the cabinet departments. The members of the White House staff also tend to be more closely associated with the president than other presidentially appointed officials.

From an informal group of fewer than a dozen people (popularly called the **Kitchen Cabinet**), and no more than four dozen domestic advisors at the height of the Roosevelt presidency in 1937, the White House staff has grown substantially with each successive president.[14] Nixon employed 550 people in 1972. President Carter, who found so many of the requirements of presidential power distasteful, and who publicly vowed to keep his staff small and decentralized, built an even larger and more centralized staff. President Clinton promised during the campaign to reduce the White House staff by 25 percent, but the reduction was a modest one. A large White House staff has become essential.

White House staff analysts and advisers to the president, often given the title "special assistant"

Kitchen Cabinet an informal group of advisers to whom the president turns for counsel and guidance. Members of the official Cabinet may or may not also be members of the Kitchen Cabinet

THE EXECUTIVE OFFICE OF THE PRESIDENT IS A VISIBLE SIGN OF THE MODERN STRONG PRESIDENCY

The development of the White House staff can be appreciated only in its relation to the still-larger **Executive Office of the President** (EOP). Created in 1939, the EOP is a major part of what is often called the "institutional presidency"—the permanent agencies that perform defined management tasks for the president. The most important and the largest EOP agency is the Office of

Executive Office of the President the permanent agencies that perform defined management tasks for the president. Created in 1939, the EOP includes the Office of Management and Budget, the Council of Economic Advisers, the National Security Council, and other agencies

Management and Budget (OMB). Its roles in preparing the national budget, designing the president's program, reporting on agency activities, and overseeing regulatory proposals make OMB personnel part of virtually every conceivable presidential responsibility. The status and power of the OMB have grown in importance with each successive president. The process of budgeting at one time was a "bottom-up" procedure, with expenditure and program requests passing from the lowest bureaus through the departments to "clearance" in OMB and hence to Congress, where each agency could be called in to reveal what its "original request" had been before OMB revised it. Now the budgeting process is "top-down"; OMB sets priorities for agencies as well as for Congress. The director of OMB is now one of the most powerful officials in Washington.

THE CABINET IS OFTEN DISTANT FROM THE PRESIDENT

Cabinet the secretaries, or chief administrators, of the major departments of the federal government. Cabinet secretaries are appointed by the president with the consent of the Senate

In the American system of government, the **Cabinet** is the traditional but informal designation for the heads of all the major federal government departments. The Cabinet has no constitutional status. Unlike in England and many other parliamentary countries, where the cabinet *is* the government, the American Cabinet is not a collective body when it meets because it makes no decisions as a group. The Senate must approve each appointment, but Cabinet members are not responsible to the Senate or to Congress at large. Cabinet appointments help build party and popular support, but the Cabinet is not a party organ. The Cabinet is made up of directors, but is not a true board of directors.

Aware of this fact, the president tends to (1) develop a burning impatience with and a mild distrust of Cabinet members; (2) make the Cabinet a rubber stamp for actions already decided on; and (3) demand results, or the appearance of results, more immediately and more frequently than most department heads can provide them. Since Cabinet appointees generally have not shared political careers with the president or with each other, and since they may meet literally for the first time after their selection, the formation of an effective governing group out of this motley collection of appointments is unlikely.

THE VICE PRESIDENCY HAS BECOME MORE IMPORTANT SINCE THE 1970S

The vice presidency is a constitutional anomaly even though the Constitution created the office along with the presidency. The vice president exists for two purposes only: to succeed the president in case of death, resignation, or incapacitation and to preside over the Senate, casting a tie-breaking vote when necessary.[15]

The main value of the vice presidency as a political resource for the president is electoral. Traditionally, a presidential candidate's most important rule for the choice of a running mate is that he or she bring the support of at least one state (preferably a large one) not otherwise likely to support the ticket. Another rule holds that the vice presidential nominee should provide some regional balance and, wherever possible, some balance among various ideological or ethnic subsections of the party. It is very doubtful that John Kennedy would have won in 1960 without his vice presidential candidate, Lyndon Johnson, and the contribution Johnson made to winning in Texas. Bill Clinton combined considerations of region and ideology in his selection of a vice presidential running mate. The choice of Tennessee senator Al Gore signaled that Bill Clinton was solidly in the right wing of the Democratic Party and would also remain steadfastly a southerner. Democratic strategists had become convinced that Clinton could not win without carrying a substantial number of southern states.

Presidents have often promised to give their vice presidents more responsibility, but this has only happened with recent presidents. Jimmy Carter involved his vice president, Walter Mondale, in important administrative decisions. Under President Reagan, Vice President George Bush was "kept within the loop" of decision making because Reagan delegated much of his power. Copies of virtually everything made for Reagan were made for Bush, especially during Reagan's first term, when Bush's close friend James Baker was Reagan's chief of staff. During Bush's presidency, Vice President Dan Quayle sat in on top decision-making meetings during the Persian Gulf Crisis. President Clinton gave Vice President Al Gore major responsibility over such areas as administrative reform, technology, and environmental issues. Gore also became one of Clinton's closest, and most trusted, advisors.[16] The presidency of George W. Bush has resulted in unprecedented power and responsibility for his vice president, Dick Cheney.

THE FIRST LADY HAS BECOME IMPORTANT TO POLICY

The president serves as both chief executive and chief of state—the equivalent of Great Britain's prime minister and monarch rolled into one, simultaneously leading the government and serving as a symbol of the nation at official ceremonies and functions. For their part, most first ladies (all presidents so far have been men) limit their activities to the ceremonial portion of the presidency. First ladies greet foreign dignitaries, visit other countries, attend important national ceremonies, and otherwise act as America's "queen" when the president is called upon to serve in a kingly capacity.

Because the first lady is usually associated with the head-of-state aspect of America's presidency, she has not been subject to the same degree of media scrutiny or partisan attack as the president. Yet this has changed in recent times as first ladies have begun to exert more influence over policy. Franklin Roosevelt's wife, Eleanor, was widely popular, but also widely criticized, for her active role in many elements of her husband's presidency. She was a tireless advocate for the poor, the working class, and African Americans. She was also the first first lady to hold a former government post—assistant director of the Office of Civil Defense. Lyndon Johnson's wife, Lady Bird, headed the national campaign to beautify America. Jimmy Carter's wife, Rosalynn, sat in on cabinet meetings, and was considered a close advisor to her husband on policy matters. President Reagan's wife, Nancy, exercised great control over her husband's schedule and over who could and could not see the president. Hillary Clinton played a major political and policy role in Bill Clinton's presidency. During the 1992 campaign, Bill Clinton often implied that she would be active in the administration by joking that voters would get "two for the price of one." After the election, Hillary took a leading role in many policy areas, most notably heading the administration's health care reform effort. Like Eleanor Roosevelt, Hillary Clinton was fiercely criticized for exercising too much influence over her husband's administration. She also became the first first lady to seek public office on her own when she ran for and won a seat in the U.S. Senate from New York in 2000. While Laura Bush's role in the George W. Bush presidency has not been as prominent as Hillary Clinton's was in her husband's presidency, she has been an important spokesperson for the administration and played a major role in political advertisements for her husband's 2004 reelection. Laura's positive ratings in the polls were significantly higher than her husband's, making her an appealing representative for the administration.

The President Has Numerous Political Resources

All presidents come to office with great strength. The Constitution and the institutional resources of presidential power that presidents accrue make this certain. Yet as Richard Neustadt argued in his book *Presidential Power,* a president's formal powers are not the most important ones. Other political institutions such as Congress also possess formidable powers. As Neustadt put it simply, "presidential power is the power to persuade."[17] But presidents have varied in their abilities to "persuade" and thus exercise the powers of the office. The capacity to exercise these powers and govern effectively is affected by a number of political resources that presidents have grown to rely on, foremost among them the American people. These resources are a source of great strength but also, as we shall see, limited; they are, therefore, a potential source of weakness. This helps explain why presidents are normally unable to perform up to the high expectations people impose on them.

ELECTIONS PROVIDE A RESOURCE BOOST

mandate a claim by a victorious candidate that the electorate has given him or her special authority to carry out promises made during the campaign

A decisive presidential election translates into a more effective presidency. Some presidents claim that a landslide election gives them a **mandate,** by which they mean that the electorate approved the programs offered in the campaign and that Congress therefore ought to go along. And Congress is not unmoved by such an appeal. The electoral landslides of 1964 and 1980 gave Presidents Johnson and Reagan real strength during their "honeymoon" years. In contrast, the close elections of Kennedy in 1960, Nixon in 1968, and Carter in 1976 seriously hampered those presidents' effectiveness.

President Clinton, an action-oriented president, was hampered by having been elected in 1992 by a minority of the popular vote, a mere 43 percent. Clinton was reelected in 1996 with 49 percent of the vote, a larger percentage of the electorate, but still a minority. His appeals to bipartisanship in 1997 reflected his lack of a mandate from the electorate. President George W. Bush faced an even more difficult beginning, since he won the presidency in 2000 despite receiving 540,000 fewer popular votes nationwide than his opponent, Al Gore. This cast a shadow over his presidency that hampered his ability to rally public support and achieve his policy objectives. Immediately after the 9/11 terrorist attacks, however, Bush's popularity shot up to the highest ever recorded for a president, which had the effect of wiping away his lack of electoral mandate.

PARTY IS A KEY PRESIDENTIAL RESOURCE

Although on the decline, the president's party is far from insignificant as a political resource. Figure 9.3 dramatically demonstrates the point with a forty-three-year history of the presidential "batting average" in Congress—the percentage of winning roll-call votes in Congress on bills publicly supported by the president. Clinton, in his first two years in office, enjoyed high averages of legislative success—86 percent in both 1993 and 1994—but that figure dropped dramatically to 35 percent in 1995 following the Republican takeover of Congress in the 1994 elections.

The relatively low batting averages for Republican presidents such as Nixon, Ford, Reagan, and Bush, and for Democrat Clinton after 1994, reflect the fact that the opposing party controlled Congress during these presidencies, thus emphasizing the importance of party as a link between the legislative and executive branches. When party control of the two branches is the same, the president's batting average is normally much higher, as was true for Kennedy, Johnson, Carter, and Clinton from 1993–94 (see Figure 9.3).

At the same time, party has its limitations as a resource. The more unified the president's party is behind legislative requests from the White House, the more unified the opposition party is also likely to be. Unless the president's party majority is very large, appeals must also be made to the opposition to make up for the inevitable defectors within the ranks of the president's own party. Consequently, the president often poses as being above partisanship in order to win "bipartisan" support in Congress. But in pursuing a bipartisan strategy, a president cannot concentrate solely on building the party loyalty and party discipline that would maximize the value of the party's support in Congress. This is a dilemma for all presidents, particularly those faced with an opposition-controlled Congress.

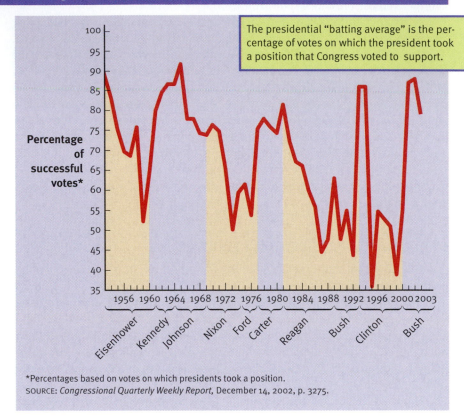

Figure 9.3

The Presidential Batting Average: Presidential Success on Congressional Votes, (1953–2003)

The presidential "batting average" is the percentage of votes on which the president took a position that Congress voted to support.

Percentage of successful votes*

Eisenhower · Kennedy · Johnson · Nixon · Ford · Carter · Reagan · Bush · Clinton · Bush

*Percentages based on votes on which presidents took a position.
SOURCE: *Congressional Quarterly Weekly Report,* December 14, 2002, p. 3275.

GROUPS ARE A LITTLE RECOGNIZED PRESIDENTIAL RESOURCE

New Deal coalition the coalition of northern urban liberals, southern white conservatives, organized labor, and blacks that dominated national politics until the 1960s

The classic case in modern times of groups as a resource for the presidency is the Roosevelt or **New Deal coalition.** The New Deal coalition was composed of a diverse set of interests. Some of these interests were not organized interest groups, but were regional interests, such as southern whites, residents of large cities in the industrial Northeast and Midwest, or blacks, who later succeeded in organizing as an interest group. In addition, the coalition included several large, self-consciously organized interest groups. The most important in the New Deal coalition were organized labor, agriculture, and the financial community.[18] All of the parts were held together by a judicious use of patronage—not merely patronage in jobs but patronage in policies. Many of the groups were permitted virtually to write their own legislation. In exchange, the groups supported President Roosevelt and his successors in their battles with opposing politicians.

Republican presidents have had their group coalition base also. The most important segments of organized business have tended to support Republican presidents. They have most often been joined by upper-income groups, as well as by some ethnic groups. In recent years, Republican presidents have expanded their interest coalition base. President Reagan, for example, won the support of traditionally Democratic southern white and northern blue-collar voters and fundamentalist Christian conservatives.

In 2000, Al Gore's campaign strategy was to mobilize the mass base of the Democratic Party with a populist appeal to working families, African Americans, the poor, and the elderly. He was able to win the endorsement of all the major trade unions, despite some of their misgivings about his views on international trade. In a sense, Gore sought to return to the class politics of the New Deal coalition, but without the support of southern whites.

In contrast, George W. Bush attempted to rebuild the GOP base that had been shattered during the 1998 fall of former House Speaker Newt Gingrich. In July 1999, at a meeting of Republican governors in St. Louis, twenty-three of twenty-nine governors, along with nineteen Republican senators and 136 Republican House members, endorsed Bush for president. They did so because Bush appeared to them to be the only Republican candidate who could pull the party together and win the presidency. Consequently, Bush's strategy was not to challenge Gore head on, but instead to consolidate the GOP base. To do so, Bush promised (and delivered) a massive tax cut to appeal to upper-income groups and espoused family values to appeal to rural and small-town conservatives.

The interest bases of the two parties have remained largely unchanged since 1980, when the GOP completed its absorption of most white southerners and religious conservatives. But whether these coalitions will last remains to be seen.

SUCCESSFUL PRESIDENTS ARE MEDIA-SAVVY

While the media have grown increasingly important during presidential campaigns, their importance is even greater during a president's term in office. Twentieth-century presidents sought a more direct relationship with the public and used the media to achieve this end. Modern presidents have learned that they can use their relationship with the media to mobilize popular support for their programs and to attempt to force Congress to follow their lead.

The president is able to take full advantage of access to the communications media mainly because virtually all newspapers and television networks habitually look to the White House as the chief source of news about public policy. They tend to assign one of their most skillful reporters to the White House "beat." And since news is money, they need the president as much as the president needs them in order to meet their mutual need to make news.

Presidential personalities make a difference in how these informal factors are used. Different presidents use the media in quite different ways. One of the first presidents to use the media was Theodore Roosevelt, who referred to the presidency as a "bully pulpit" because its visibility allowed him to preach to the nation and bring popular pressure to bear against his opponents in Congress. But the first president to try to reach the public directly through the media was Franklin Roosevelt. During the 1930s, FDR used radio broadcasts known as "fireside chats," press conferences, speeches, and movie newsreels to rally support for his

New Deal programs and, later, to build popular support for American rearmament in the face of the growing danger in Europe and the Far East. FDR also cultivated strong relationships with national news correspondents to ensure favorable publicity for his programs. FDR's efforts to reach out to the American people and mobilize their support were among the factors that made him one of the strongest presidents in American history. His appeals to the American people allowed FDR to "reach over the heads" of congressional opponents and force them to follow his lead because their constituents demanded it. Modern presidents have learned from FDR's example, although some presidents have been more adept at promoting a positive media image than others. Presidents Kennedy, Reagan, and Clinton were all considered highly skilled at promoting strong media images. On the other hand, President Nixon never felt comfortable with the press, and he blamed them for many of his troubles.

PUBLIC OPINION SHAPES PRESIDENTIAL POWER

Most Americans feel that presidents should follow public opinion. Interestingly, however, many of the must successful presidents have been public opinion leaders rather than followers.

In 1963, President Kennedy signed a nuclear test ban treaty with the Soviet Union, even though public opinion polls seemed to show that most Americans thought the treaty was a bad idea. Kennedy believed that the treaty served the national interest and that most Americans did not know enough about the issue at stake to have fixed views on the topic. He assured his nervous advisers that, since most Americans lacked strong views on the topic, they would assume that the president's actions were correct. Kennedy was right: After he signed the treaty, polls showed that most Americans supported his decision.

President George H. W. Bush used the same logic during the Persian Gulf crisis of 1990–91 that followed the Iraqi invasion of Kuwait. At the time, opinion was divided both within Congress and among the broader public. Congressional leaders tried to constrain the president's ability to use forces in combat, urging him instead to rely on diplomacy and economic sanctions to compel Iraq's withdrawal. Congressional criticism, especially televised Senate hearings, helped erode Bush's popular standing and almost undermined his power to act. In January 1991, however, Bush sought and narrowly received congressional approval to use force against Iraq. The overwhelming success of the American military effort produced a surge of popular support for Bush; his approval rating rose to over 90 percent.

The second President Bush followed a pattern similar to that of his father. Throughout the first nine months of the presidency, Bush's popularity was lower than that of his predecessors at the same point in their presidencies, and this severely hampered his ability to achieve his policy goals. Yet within days of the 2001 terrorist attacks in New York and Washington, Bush's popularity soared to over 90 percent. That popularity gave Bush's administration new political life. Within weeks, at the request of the White House, Congress enacted the Patriot Act, giving sweeping new powers to the government; in 2002, Congress approved Bush's request to create the first new cabinet department in more than a decade, the Department of Homeland Security, which created the second largest department in the government. This $40 billion department combined offices from twenty-two federal agencies in order to place under one departmental "roof" the job of protecting the nation from terrorism. Congress also approved Bush proposals to cut taxes and to enact the "No Child Left Behind" education bill, a Medicare prescription drug benefits program, and a faith-based aid program for the poor. Most importantly, Bush's popularity, and the continued terrorist threat, provided the political basis of support for Bush's 2003 invasion of Iraq and toppling of Saddam Hussein's regime (plans had been in the works for such a move before 9/11). Had there been no 9/11 attack, it is highly unlikely that Bush could have rallied popular support for the invasion of Iraq.

Presidents also read and study polls to try to adapt their priorities to what the people want. During 1995–96, a majority of Americans indicated support for welfare reform, which included cutting social welfare spending and turning more control over to the states. After vetoing welfare reform, Clinton came to support the idea, sensing the public's support of the issue. In 1996, he signed the welfare reform bill into law and claimed it as an achievement of his presidency.

MASS POPULARITY IS BOTH A RESOURCE AND A LIABILITY

In addition to utilizing the media and public opinion polls, recent presidents, particularly Bill Clinton, have reached out directly to the American public to gain its approval. President Clinton's enormously high public profile, as indicated by the number of public appearances he made (see Figure 9.4), was only the most recent dramatic expression of the presidency as a **"permanent campaign"** for reelection. A study by political scientist Charles O. Jones showed that President Clinton engaged in campaignlike activity throughout his presidency and became the most-traveled American president in history. In his first twenty months in office, he made 203 appearances outside of Washington, compared with 178 for George H. W. Bush and 58 for Ronald Reagan. Clinton's tendency to go around rather than through party organizations is reflected in the fact that while presidents Bush and Reagan devoted about 25 percent of their appearances to party functions, Clinton's comparable figure is only 8 percent.[19]

permanent campaign description of presidential politics in which all presidential actions are taken with reelection in mind

Even with the help of all other institutional and political resources, successful presidents have to be able to mobilize mass opinion in their favor in order to keep Congress in line. But as we shall see, each president tends to *use up* mass resources. Virtually everyone is aware that presidents are constantly making appeals to the public over the heads of Congress and the Washington community. But the mass public does not turn out to be made up of fools. The American people react to presidential actions rather than mere speeches or other image-making devices.

PICTURING
The President's Permanent Campaign

Theodore Roosevelt was the model for the twentieth-century president through his cultivation of a direct relationship with the American public. Roosevelt saw the presidency as a "bully pulpit," a terrific platform from which to advocate his agenda.

Three decades later, President Franklin D. Roosevelt's direct appeals to the American people allowed FDR to "reach over the heads" of congressional opponents and force them to follow his lead because their constituents demanded it.

POLITICS

President Bill Clinton was a master of the televised town meeting, in which he gave the appearance of consulting average citizens on important policy issues. Clinton's technique illustrated how campaign-style events could become tools to shape and sell national policy.

President George W. Bush has also made direct appeals to the public in cozy voter forums. One Bush innovation was to distribute tickets to these forums in advance so that the audience was comprised of his supporters.

Figure 9.4

Figure 9.4   Public Appearances by Presidents, 1929–95

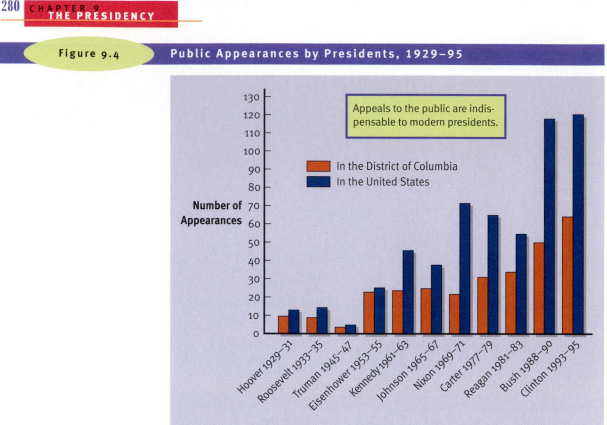

SOURCE: Samuel Kernell, *Going Public,* 3rd ed. (Washington DC: Congressional Quarterly Press, 1998), p. 118.

The public's sensitivity to presidential actions can be seen in the tendency of all presidents to lose popular support. Despite the twists and turns shown on Figure 9.5, the percentage of positive responses to "Do you approve of the way the president is handling his job?" starts out at a level significantly higher than the percentage of votes the president got in the previous national election and then declines over the next four years. Though the shape of the line differs, the destination is the same.

This general downward tendency is to be expected if American voters are rational, inasmuch as almost any action taken by the president can be divisive, with some voters approving and other voters disapproving. Public disapproval of specific actions has a cumulative effect on the president's overall performance rating. Thus all presidents are faced with the problem of boosting their approval ratings. And the public generally reacts favorably to presidential actions in foreign policy or, more precisely, to international events associated with the president. Analysts call this the **rallying effect.** Nevertheless the rallying effect turns out to be only a momentary reversal of the more general tendency of presidents to lose popular support.

rallying effect the generally favorable reaction of the public to presidential actions in foreign policy, or more precisely, to decisions made during international crises

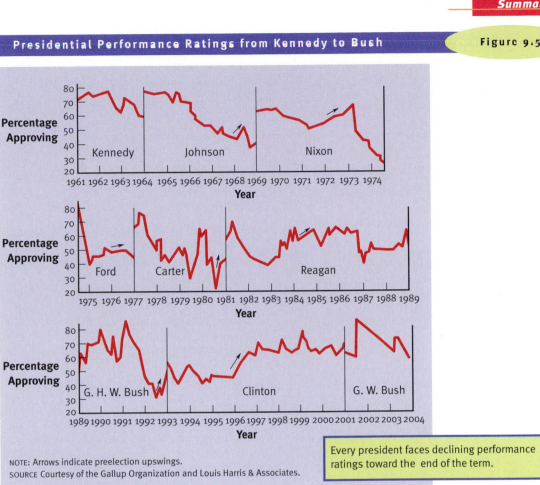

Presidential Performance Ratings from Kennedy to Bush — Figure 9.5

NOTE: Arrows indicate preelection upswings.
SOURCE Courtesy of the Gallup Organization and Louis Harris & Associates.

Every president faces declining performance ratings toward the end of the term.

Summary

The twentieth century witnessed the rise of the modern strong presidency. This growth of presidential power has been exceeded by public expectations, so that virtually no president can meet them. Thus, the people often wind up feeling disappointed with whomever happens to be president at the time. The presidents considered most effective are those who are able to use the formal (constitutional) and informal (political) powers of the office effectively in order to log achievements and stay popular with the people.

The modern president's institutional and political resources include the White House staff, the Executive Office of the President, and the Cabinet. The president's political party, supportive group coalitions, and access to the media (and, through that, access to millions of Americans) are formidable political resources that can be used to bolster a president's power. But these resources are not cost- or risk-free. A direct relationship with the mass public is the president's most potent modern resource, but it is also the most problematic.

For Further Reading

Barber, James David. *The Presidential Character.* Englewood Cliffs, NJ: Prentice Hall, 1985.

Fisher, Louis. *Presidential War Power.* Lawrence, KS: University Press of Kansas, 1995.

Genovese, Michael, and Robert J. Spitzer. *The Presidency and the Law.* New York: Palgrave/Macmillan, 2005.

Hinckley, Barbara, and Paul Brace. *Follow the Leader: Opinion Polls and Modern Presidents.* New York: Basic Books, 1992.

Kernell, Samuel. *Going Public: New Strategies of Presidential Leadership.* Washington, DC: Congressional Quarterly Press, 1998.

Lowi, Theodore J. *The Personal President: Power Invested, Promise Unfulfilled.* Ithaca, NY: Cornell University Press, 1985.

Neustadt, Richard E. *Presidential Power: The Politics of Leadership from Roosevelt to Reagan.* Rev. ed. New York: Free Press, 1990.

Pfiffner, James P. *The Modern Presidency.* New York: St. Martin's, 1994.

Rozell, Mark J., and Clyde Wilcox, eds. *The Clinton Scandal.* Washington, DC: Georgetown University Press, 2000.

Skowronek, Stephen. *The Politics Presidents Make: Presidential Leadership from John Adams to George Bush.* Cambridge, MA: Harvard University Press, 1993.

Spitzer, Robert J. *President and Congress.* McGraw-Hill, 1993.

Spitzer, Robert. *The Presidential Veto: Touchstone of the American Presidency.* Albany, NY: SUNY Press, 1988.

Tulis, Jeffrey. *The Rhetorical Presidency.* Princeton, NJ: Princeton University Press, 1987.

Study Outline

Presidential Power Is Rooted in the Constitution

1. The president as head of state is defined by three constitutional provisions—military, judicial, and diplomatic—that are the source of some of the most important powers on which the president can draw.
2. The position of commander in chief makes the president the highest military authority in the executive branch, with control of the entire military establishment.
3. The presidential power to grant reprieves, pardons, and amnesties allows the president to choose freedom or confinement, and even life or death for all individuals who have violated, or are suspected of having violated, federal laws, including people who directly threaten the security of the United States.
4. The power to receive representatives of foreign countries allows the president almost unconditional authority to determine whether a new ruling group can indeed commit its country to treaties and other agreements.
5. The president's role as head of government rests on a constitutional foundation consisting of three principal sources: executive power, domestic military authority, and legislative power.
6. The Constitution delegates to the president, as commander in chief, the obligation to protect every state against invasion and domestic violence.
7. The president's legislative power consists of the obligation to make recommendations for consideration by Congress and the ability to veto legislation.

Institutional Resources of Presidential Power Are Numerous

1. Presidents have at their disposal a variety of institutional resources—such as the power to fill high-level political positions—that directly affect a president's ability to govern.

2. Presidents increasingly have preferred the White House staff to the Cabinet as a tool for managing the gigantic executive branch.
3. The White House staff, which is composed primarily of analysts and advisers, has grown from an informal group of fewer than a dozen people to a new presidential bureaucracy.
4. The Executive Office of the President, often called the institutional presidency, is larger than the White House staff, and comprises the president's permanent management agencies.

The President Has Numerous Political Resources

1. The president also has political resources on which to draw in exercising the powers of office.
2. Presidents often use their electoral victories to increase their power by claiming the election was a mandate for a certain course of action.
3. Although its traditional influence is on the decline, the president's party is still significant as a means of achieving legislative success.
4. Interest groups and coalitions supportive of the president's agenda are also a dependable resource for presidential government.
5. Over the past half-century, the American executive branch has harnessed mass popularity successfully as a political resource.

Practice Quiz

1. Which article of the Constitution established the presidency?
   a) Article I
   b) Article II
   c) Article III
   d) none of the above

2. Which of the following does not represent a classification of a constitutional provision designating the president as head of state?
   a) legislative
   b) military
   c) judicial
   d) diplomatic

3. Which of the following does not require the advice and consent of the Senate?
   a) an executive agreement
   b) a treaty
   c) Supreme Court nominations
   d) All of the above require the advice and consent of the Senate.

4. Which of the following terms has been used to describe the presidency as it has used constitutional and other powers to make itself more powerful?
   a) "the delegated presidency"
   b) "the imperial presidency"
   c) "the personal presidency"
   d) "the preemptive presidency"

5. By what process can Congress reject a presidential veto?
   a) veto override
   b) pocket veto
   c) executive delegation
   d) impeachment

6. The Office of Management and Budget is part of
   a) the Executive Office of the President.
   b) the White House staff.
   c) the Kitchen Cabinet.
   d) both a and b.

7. Which twentieth-century presidency transformed the American system of government from a Congress-centered to a president-centered system?
   a) Woodrow Wilson's
   b) Franklin Roosevelt's
   c) Richard Nixon's
   d) Jimmy Carter's

8. How many people work for agencies within the Executive Office of the President?
   a) 25 to 50
   b) 700 to 1,000
   c) 1,500 to 2,000
   d) 4,500 to 5,000

Critical Thinking Questions

1. At times, the Congress has been the dominant branch of government. At other times, the presidency has predominated. Describe the changes in the relationship between the presidency and the Congress throughout American history. What factors contributed to the dominance of Congress? What factors contributed to the resurgence of the presidency? Which branch of government dominates now? Why do you think so?

2. Presidents have constitutional, institutional, and political sources of power. Which of the three do you think most accounts for the powers of the presidency? Is it, in fact, possible to discern among these the true source of presidential power? Select a president and discuss the ways in which that particular president used each source of power to succeed in the presidency.

Key Terms

Cabinet (p. 270)
commander in chief (p. 261)
delegated powers (p. 259)
executive agreement (p. 264)
Executive Office of the President
 (EOP) (p. 269)

executive order (p. 266)
expressed powers (p. 259)
inherent powers (p. 260)
Kitchen Cabinet (p. 269)
legislative initiative (p. 266)
mandate (p. 272)
New Deal coalition (p. 274)
patronage (p. 269)

permanent campaign (p. 277)
pocket veto (p. 266)
rallying effect (p. 280)
veto (p. 265)
War Powers Resolution (p. 261)
White House staff (p. 269)

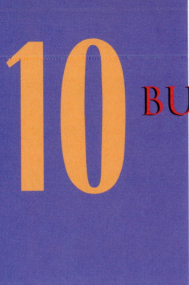

10 BUREAUCRACY

MAIN MESSAGE

Bureaucracy is necessary to the functioning of modern government and society.

I f there is a common attitude among college students about the government, it is that the government has little or nothing to do with their daily lives. Nothing could be further from the truth.

Imagine a typical day. You are awakened by a clock radio tuned in to your favorite radio station, whose license to operate and broadcasting standards are regulated by the Federal Communications Commission (as is true for television stations as well). The commercial ads on the radio must follow truth-in-advertising standards set by the Federal Trade Commission. The mattress you sleep on must be made of fire-resistant materials, as determined by the Consumer Product Safety Commission (CPSC). After struggling out of bed and taking a quick shower, you dry your hair using a hair dryer that is produced by a company that has stopped using asbestos for insulating material because the government's CPSC determined that asbestos poses a health risk. The aspirin you

Key Concepts

1. Bureaucratic structures exist to improve efficiency in large organizations.

2. The bureaucracy of the federal government is smaller than it used to be, and it is composed of people whose job is to serve the public.

3. Different types of government agencies perform different tasks.

4. Bureaucracy is controlled by the president, Congress, and federal rules.

take to relieve your headache has a child-proof safety cap, as per the Food and Drug Administration's (FDA) rule. Your breakfast orange juice must be manufactured under standards set by the FDA. Your bacon and eggs are inspected by the Department of Agriculture's Consumer and Marketing Service. The coffee you drink arrived in the United States under the scrutiny of both the FDA and the Bureau of Customs of the Treasury Department, and it was prepared by a coffee pot that meets federal standards to protect the user from electric shock, as per CPSC guidelines. You climb into your car to go to work or school, protected from injury within the vehicle by a collapsible steering column, padded dashboards, safety glass, air bags, and other safety features set by the Highway Traffic Safety Administration. Your car's exhaust is cleaned by a catalytic converter designed to reduce air pollution, as determined by the Environmental Protection Agency. The price you pay for gasoline is partly affected by policies set by the Department of Energy. When you arrive at your destination, the stairs you climb must meet government regulations as to the height and depth of each tread, as determined by the Occupational Safety and Health Administration. And so on.

In point of fact, the government plays a role in most facets of people's lives. And most of this involvement occurs through government agencies, also referred to as *bureaucracy*. In this chapter, we will examine the key role bureaucratic agencies play in keeping the government running, in maintaining rules and controls that most people agree with, and in linking citizens with their government. When most people have any contact with the government, it is with or through a government agency.

But if bureaucracy is so common in the workplace, why have "bureaucracy" and "bureaucrat" become such negative words? Why has "bureaucracy" come to mean only government, when in fact it is equally as common in the private sector? Why do we call government activity we don't like "bureaucracy" and government activity we approve of "administration"? Why do we reserve the term "bureaucrat" for people whose work we don't like when as a matter of fact most of us are or will be bureaucrats ourselves?

Bureaucracy Exists to Improve Efficiency

Bureaucracy is simply a form of organization. Whether found in a national, state, or local government, or in a private corporation, bureaucracies have six characteristics: a division of labor, meaning that workers specialize in particular tasks; allocation of functions, meaning that each task is assigned so that no one person makes the entire product; allocation of responsibility, meaning that each task is assigned to a particular individual or group of individuals; supervision, meaning that some workers have the job of watching over other workers; full-time employment, meaning that at least some of the workers devote their full work time to the organization; and worker careers within the organization, meaning that some workers maintain a long-term attachment to the organization, so that seniority, pensions, and promotions are part of their service in the organization.

To gain some objectivity, and to appreciate the universality of bureaucracy, let us take the word and break it into its two main parts—*bureau* and *cracy*. *Bureau,* a French word, can mean either "office" or "desk." *Cracy* is the Greek word for "rule" or "form of rule." For example, "democracy" means rule by the people *(demos),* a form of government in which the people prevail. "Theocracy" refers to rule by clergy or churches. "Gerontocracy" would describe a system ruled by the elders of the community. Putting *bureau* and *cracy* back together produces a very interesting definition: **bureaucracy** is a form of rule by offices and desks. Each member of an organization has an office, meaning a place as well as a set of responsibilities. That is, each "office" comprises a set of tasks that are specialized to the needs of the organization, and the person holding that office (or position) performs those specialized tasks. Specialization and repetition are essential to the efficiency of any organization. Therefore, when an organization is inefficient, it is almost certainly because it is not bureaucratized enough!

Americans depend on government bureaucracies to accomplish the most spectacular achievements as well as the most mundane. Yet, they often do not realize that public bureaucracies are essential for providing the services they use every day and rely on in emergencies. On a typical day, a college student might check the weather forecast, drive on an interstate highway, mail the rent check, drink from a public water fountain, check the calories on the side of a yogurt container, attend a class, log on to the Internet, and meet a relative at the airport. Each of these activities is possible because of a government bureaucracy: the U.S. Weather Service, the U.S. Department of Transportation, the U.S. Postal Service, the Environmental Protection Agency, the Food and Drug Administration, the student loan programs of the U.S. Department of Education, the Advanced Research Projects Agency (which developed the Internet in the 1960s), and the Federal Aviation Administration. Without the ongoing work of these agencies, many of these common activities would be impossible, unreliable, or more expensive.

In emergencies, government bureaucracies are often the main source of organizational expertise that can address urgent needs. The Federal Emergency Management Agency (FEMA) has long experience in providing assistance after national disasters such as hurricanes, floods, and earthquakes. FEMA's services range from cleanup to emergency housing to loans for reconstruction. Government bureaucracies also provide protection from less visible but equally deadly dangers. The federal Centers for Disease Control (CDC) tracks disease outbreaks around the country, often uncovering patterns of illness that would otherwise be missed. For example, the CDC conducted studies showing that freshmen dormitory residents were at a higher risk for infection with the deadly meningitis bacteria and recommended vaccination.

The overriding importance of bureaucracy as the means by which the government serves the American people is aptly illustrated by the newest cabinet

bureaucracy the complex structure of offices, tasks, rules, and principles of organization that are employed by all large-scale institutions to coordinate effectively the work of their personnel

department, Homeland Security. The new department was recommended by a conservative president and frequent critic of big government, George W. Bush, who proclaimed during the 2000 elections that "Big government is not the answer!" Approved by Congress in 2002, Homeland Security encompasses nearly 170,000 employees and a $40 billion budget, combining twenty-two existing and new agencies drawn from all over the government. It was formed to unify and coordinate American defense against terrorism after the terrorist attacks of September 11, 2001. Among the diverse offices now under Homeland Security are the Coast Guard, the Secret Service, elements of the Immigration and Naturalization Service, the Transportation Security Agency (a new office created after 9/11), the Customs Service, the Office of Domestic Preparedness, and the Federal Emergency Management Agency.[1] Despite many differences between Bush and Congress, nearly all representatives agreed that a new bureaucratic agency was the right way to confront the post-9/11 terrorist threat against America.

These routine and exceptional tasks require the organization, specialization, and expertise found in bureaucracies. To provide these services, government bureaucracies employ specialists such as meteorologists, doctors, and scientists. To do their job effectively, these specialists require resources and tools (ranging from paper to blood samples); they have to coordinate their work with others (for example, the traffic engineers must communicate with construction engineers); and there must be effective outreach to the public (for example, private doctors must be made aware of health warnings). Bureaucracy provides a way to coordinate the many different parts that must work together in order to provide good services.

THE SIZE OF THE FEDERAL SERVICE HAS ACTUALLY DECLINED

Despite fears of bureaucratic growth getting out of hand, the federal service has hardly grown at all during the past twenty-five years; it reached its peak postwar level in 1968 with 3.0 million civilian employees plus an additional 3.6 million military personnel (a figure swollen by Vietnam). The number of civilian federal employees has since fallen to approximately 2.8 million in 2003; the number of military personnel totals only 1.5 million.[2]

The growth of the federal service is even less imposing when placed in the context of the total workforce and when compared to the size of state and local public employment. Figure 10.1 indicates that, since 1950, the ratio of federal employment to the total workforce has been steady, and in fact as *declined* slightly in the past thirty years. In 1950, there were 4.3 million state and local civil service employees (about 6.5 percent of the country's workforce). In 2000, there were almost 18 million (nearly 13 percent of the workforce). Federal employment, in contrast, exceeded 5 percent of the workforce only during World War II (not shown), and almost all of that momentary growth was military. After the demobilization, which continued until 1950 (as shown in Figure 10.1), the federal service has tended to grow at a rate that keeps pace with the economy

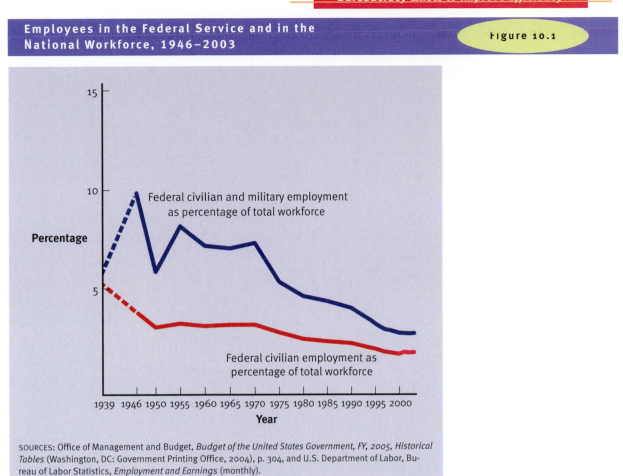

Employees in the Federal Service and in the National Workforce, 1946–2003

Figure 10.1

SOURCES: Office of Management and Budget, *Budget of the United States Government, FY, 2005, Historical Tables* (Washington, DC: Government Printing Office, 2004), p. 304, and U.S. Department of Labor, Bureau of Labor Statistics, *Employment and Earnings* (monthly).

and society. That is demonstrated by the lower line on Figure 10.1, which shows a constant relation between federal civilian employment and the size of the U.S. workforce. Variations in federal employment since 1946 have been in the military and are directly related to war and the cold war (as shown by the top line on Figure 10.1).

Another useful comparison is to be found in Figure 10.2. Although the dollar increase in federal spending shown by the bars looks impressive, the trend line indicating the relation of federal spending to the Gross Domestic Product (GDP) shows that in 2002, this percentage was barely higher than in 1960.

In sum, the national government is indeed "very large," but it has not been growing any faster than the economy or the society. The same is roughly true of the growth pattern of state and local public personnel.

Figure 10.2 | **Annual Federal Outlays, 1960–2005**

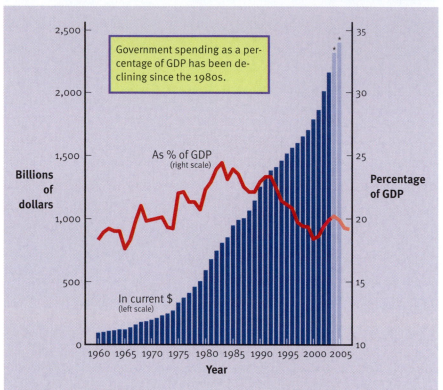

Government spending as a percentage of GDP has been declining since the 1980s.

As % of GDP (right scale)

Billions of dollars

Percentage of GDP

In current $ (left scale)

Year

*Data from 2004–2005 are estimated.
SOURCE: Office of Management and Budget, *Historical Tables, Budget of the United States Government, Fiscal Year 2005* (Washington, DC: Government Printing Office, 2004.); Office of Management and Budget, *Budget of the United States Government, FY 2005, Historical Tables* (Washington, DC: Government Printing Office, 2004) www.whitehouse.gov/omb/budget/fy2005/pdf/hist.pdf; Executive Office of the President, *Economic Report of the President.* (Washington, DC: Government Printing Office, 2004) a257.g.akamaitech.net/7/257/2422/09feb20040900/www.gpoaccess.gov/usbudget/fy05/pdf/2004_erp.pdf

BUREAUCRATS FULFILL IMPORTANT ROLES

Bureaucrats, whether in public or in private organizations, communicate with each other to coordinate all the specializations within their organization. This coordination is necessary to carry out the primary task of bureaucracy, which is **implementation**, that is, implementing the objectives of the organization as laid down by its board of directors (if a private company) or by law (if a public agency). In government, the "bosses" are ultimately the legislature and the elected chief executive.

When the bosses—Congress, in particular, when it is making the law—are clear in their instructions to bureaucrats, implementation is a fairly straightforward process. Bureaucrats translate the law into specific routines for each of the employees of an agency. But what happens to routine administrative implementation

implementation the efforts of departments and agencies to translate laws into specific bureaucratic routines

when several bosses disagree as to what the instructions ought to be? This requires yet another job for bureaucrats: interpretation. Interpretation is a form of implementation, in that the bureaucrats still have to carry out what they believe to be the intentions of their superiors. But when bureaucrats have to interpret a law before implementing it, they are in effect engaging in *lawmaking*. Congress often deliberately delegates to an administrative agency the responsibility of lawmaking. Members of Congress often conclude that some area of industry needs regulation or some area of the environment needs protection, but they are unwilling or unable to specify just how that should be done. In such situations, Congress delegates to the appropriate agency a broad authority within which the bureaucrats have to make law, through the procedures of rulemaking and administrative adjudication.

Rulemaking is exactly the same as legislation; in fact, it is often referred to as "quasi-legislation." The rules issued by government agencies provide more detailed and specific indications of what the policy actually will mean. For example, the Occupational Safety and Health Administration (OSHA) is charged with ensuring that our workplaces are safe. OSHA has regulated the use of chemicals and other well-known health hazards. In recent years, the widespread use of computers in the workplace has been associated with a growing number of cases of repetitive stress injury, which hurts the hands, arms, and neck. To respond to this new threat to workplace health, OSHA issued a new set of ergonomic rules in November 1999 that tell employers what they must do to prevent and address such injuries among their workers. Such rules take force only after a period of public comment. Reaction from the people or businesses that will be subject to the rules may cause an agency to modify the rules they first issue. The rules about ergonomic safety in the workplace, for example, were strongly contested by many businesses, which viewed their implementation as too costly. Two months into his presidency, George W. Bush signed a bill repealing the ergonomic regulations that had been scheduled to go into effect later in 2001. The rulemaking process is thus a highly political one. Once rules are approved, they are published in the *Federal Register* and have the force of law.

rulemaking a quasi-legislative administrative process that produces regulations by government agencies

Administrative adjudication is very similar to what the judiciary ordinarily does: applying rules and precedents to specific cases in order to settle disputes. In administrative adjudication, the agency charges the person or business suspected of violating the law. The ruling in an adjudication dispute applies only to the specific case being considered. Many regulatory agencies use administrative adjudication to make decisions about specific products or practices. For example, in December 1999, the Consumer Product Safety Commission held hearings on the safety of bleachers, sparked by concern over the death of children after falls from bleachers. It then issued guidelines about bleacher construction designed to prevent falls. These guidelines have the force of law. Likewise, product recalls are often the result of adjudication.

administrative adjudication the application of rules and precedents to specific cases to settle disputes with regulated parties

The Merit System: How to Become a Bureaucrat   Public bureaucrats are rewarded with greater job security than employees of most private organizations. More than a century ago, the federal government attempted to imitate business

by passing the Civil Service Act of 1883, which was followed by almost universal adoption of equivalent laws in state and local governments. These laws required that appointees to public office be qualified, as measured by competitive examinations, for the job to which they are appointed. This policy came to be called the **merit system;** its purpose was to put an end to political appointments under the **"spoils system."** Under the old spoils system, presidents filled up to two hundred thousand federal jobs with political friends and supporters. In 1881, President James A. Garfield wrote, "My day is frittered away with the personal seeking of people when it ought to be given to the great problems which concern the whole country."[3] Ironically, the final push to enact civil service reform occurred when a frustrated office-seeker shot and killed President Garfield in 1881.

As a further safeguard against political interference (and to compensate for the lower-than-average pay given to public employees), merit system employees—genuine civil servants—were given a form of tenure: legal protection against being fired without a show of cause. Reasonable people may disagree about the value of job tenure and how far it should extend in the civil service, but the justifiable objective of tenure—cleansing bureaucracy of political interference while upgrading performance—cannot be disputed.

The Executive Branch Is Organized Hierarchically

Cabinet departments, agencies, and bureaus are the operating parts of the bureaucratic whole. Figure 10.3 is an organizational chart of one of the largest and most important of the fourteen **departments,** the Department of Agriculture. At the top is the head of the department, who in the United States is called the "secretary" of the department.[4] Below the secretary and the deputy secretary is a second tier of "undersecretaries" who have management responsibilities for one or more operating agencies, shown in the smaller print directly below each undersecretary. Those operating agencies are the third tier of the department, yet they are the highest level of responsibility for the actual programs around which the entire department is organized. This third tier is generally called the "bureau level." Each bureau-level agency usually operates under a statute, adopted by Congress, that set up the agency and gave it its authority and jurisdiction. The names of these bureau-level agencies are often quite well known to the public— the Forest Service and the Agricultural Research Service, for example. These are the so-called line agencies, or agencies that deal directly with the public. Sometimes these agencies are officially called "bureaus," as in the Federal Bureau of Investigation (FBI), which is a part of the third tier of the Department of Justice. But "bureau" is also the conventional term for this level of administrative agency, even though many agencies or their supporters have preferred over the years to adopt a more palatable designation, such as "service" or "administration." Each bureau is, of course, subdivided into still other units, known as divisions, offices, or units—all are parts of the bureaucratic hierarchy.

merit system a product of civil service reform, in which appointees to positions in public bureaucracies must objectively be deemed qualified for the position

spoils system government jobs given out based on political connections rather than merit

department the largest subunit of the executive branch. The secretaries of the fourteen departments form the Cabinet

Organizational Chart of the Department of Agriculture, 1998

Figure 10.3

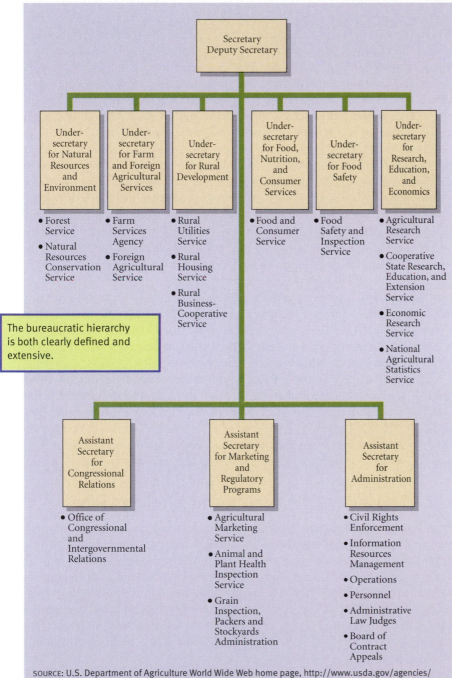

The bureaucratic hierarchy is both clearly defined and extensive.

Secretary
Deputy Secretary

Under-secretary for Natural Resources and Environment
- Forest Service
- Natural Resources Conservation Service

Under-secretary for Farm and Foreign Agricultural Services
- Farm Services Agency
- Foreign Agricultural Service

Under-secretary for Rural Development
- Rural Utilities Service
- Rural Housing Service
- Rural Business-Cooperative Service

Under-secretary for Food, Nutrition, and Consumer Services
- Food and Consumer Service

Under-secretary for Food Safety
- Food Safety and Inspection Service

Under-secretary for Research, Education, and Economics
- Agricultural Research Service
- Cooperative State Research, Education, and Extension Service
- Economic Research Service
- National Agricultural Statistics Service

Assistant Secretary for Congressional Relations
- Office of Congressional and Intergovernmental Relations

Assistant Secretary for Marketing and Regulatory Programs
- Agricultural Marketing Service
- Animal and Plant Health Inspection Service
- Grain Inspection, Packers and Stockyards Administration

Assistant Secretary for Administration
- Civil Rights Enforcement
- Information Resources Management
- Operations
- Personnel
- Administrative Law Judges
- Board of Contract Appeals

SOURCE: U.S. Department of Agriculture World Wide Web home page, http://www.usda.gov/agencies/agchart.htm (accessed May 11, 1998).

independent agency an agency that is not part of a Cabinet department

government corporation a government agency that performs a service normally provided by the private sector

Not all government agencies are part of Cabinet departments. Some **independent agencies** are set up by Congress outside the departmental structure altogether, even though the president appoints and directs the heads of these agencies. Independent agencies usually have broad powers to provide public services that are either too expensive or too important to be left to private initiatives. Some examples of independent agencies are the National Aeronautics and Space Administration (NASA), the Central Intelligence Agency (CIA), and the Environmental Protection Agency (EPA). **Government corporations** are a third type of government agency, but are more like private businesses performing and charging for a market service, such as delivering the mail (the United States Postal Service) or transporting railroad passengers (Amtrak).

Yet a fourth type of agency is the independent regulatory commission, given broad discretion to make rules. The first regulatory agencies established by Congress, beginning with the Interstate Commerce Commission in 1887, were set up as independent regulatory commissions because Congress recognized that regulatory agencies are "minilegislatures," whose rules are exactly the same as legislation but require the kind of expertise and full-time attention that is beyond the capacity of Congress. Until the 1960s, most of the regulatory agencies that were set up by Congress, such as the Federal Trade Commission (1914) and the Federal Communications Commission (1934), were independent regulatory commissions. But beginning in the late 1960s and the early 1970s, all new regulatory programs, with two or three exceptions (such as the Federal Election Commission), were placed within existing departments and made directly responsible to the president. Since the 1970s, no major new regulatory programs have been established, independent or otherwise.

The different agencies of the executive branch can be classified into three main groups based on the services that they provide to the American public. The first category of agencies provides services and products that seek to promote the public welfare. The second group of agencies works to promote national security. The third group provides services that help to maintain a strong economy. Let us look more closely at what each set of agencies offers to the American public.

FEDERAL BUREAUCRACIES PROMOTE THE PUBLIC WELFARE

One of the most important activities of the federal bureaucracy is to promote the public welfare. Americans often think of government welfare as a single program that goes only to the very poor, but a number of federal agencies provide services, build infrastructure, and enact regulations designed to enhance the well-being of the vast majority of citizens. Take, for example, the National Institutes of Health (NIH), an agency of the Department of Health and Human Services (HHS). Responsible for cutting-edge biomedical research, the NIH occupies a large campuslike complex with seventy-five buildings outside of Washington, D.C. In its own labs and in the grants it provides to outside researchers, the NIH's central aim is to advance knowledge about health and diseases. Five of the scientists working in NIH labs have been awarded Nobel prizes for their research. The NIH is one of the leaders in experimenting with gene therapy, which is expected to open new possibilities for curing diseases.

HHS is also responsible for the two major health programs provided by the federal government: Medicaid, which provides health care for low-income families and for many elderly and disabled people in nursing homes; and Medicare, which is the health insurance available to all elderly people in the United States. The Administration on Aging is another agency under HHS; it provides services to the elderly such as "meals on wheels," which is designed to help keep the elderly independent. Also under HHS auspices is the Centers for Disease Control and Prevention (CDC), which is responsible for fighting bioterrorism. The CDC is charged with identifying the causes of outbreaks of sickness and assembling a national pharmaceutical stockpile to respond to major health emergencies. Departments that have important responsibilities for promoting the public welfare in this sense include the Department of Housing and Urban Development, the Department of Health and Human Services, the Department of Veterans Affairs, the Department of the Interior, the Department of Education, and the Department of Labor. Ensuring the public welfare is also the main activity of agencies in other departments, such as the Department of Agriculture's Food and Nutrition Service, which administers the federal school lunch program and food stamps.

In addition, a variety of **regulatory agencies** enforce regulations that aim to safeguard the public health and welfare. Some of these are bureaus within departments, such as the Food and Drug Administration (FDA) within the Department of Health and Human Services, the Occupational Safety and Health Administration (OSHA) in the Department of Labor, and the Animal and Plant Health Inspection Service in the Department of Agriculture. As we saw earlier, other regulatory agencies are independent regulatory commissions, such as the Federal Communications Commission (FCC) and the Environmental Protection Agency (EPA). But whether departmental or independent, an agency or commission is regulatory if Congress delegates to it relatively broad powers over a sector of the economy or a type of commercial activity and authorizes it to make rules restricting the conduct of people and businesses within that jurisdiction. Rules made by regulatory agencies have the force and effect of law.

regulatory agencies agencies whose main job is to control some specific conduct in society through the issuance of rules and penalties if those rules are violated

The activities of these agencies seek to promote the welfare of all Americans, often working behind the scenes. The FDA, for example, works to protect public health by setting standards for food processing and inspecting plants to ensure that those standards are met. The EPA sets standards to limit polluting emissions from automobiles. The regulations required automobile manufacturers to change the way they design cars, and the result has been cleaner air in many metropolitan areas.

FEDERAL AGENCIES ALSO HELP MAINTAIN A STRONG ECONOMY AND PROVIDE NATIONAL SECURITY

One of the remarkable features of American federalism is that the most vital agencies for the maintenance of the Union are located in state and local governments—

namely, the police. But some agencies vital to maintaining national order and security do exist in the national government, and they can be grouped for convenience into three categories: (1) agencies for control of the sources of federal government revenue, (2) agencies for control of conduct defined as a threat to internal national security, and (3) agencies for defending American security from external threats. The departments of greatest concern in these three areas include Treasury, Justice, Homeland Security, Defense, and State.

In our capitalist economic system, the government does not directly run the economy. Yet many federal government activities are critical to maintaining a strong economy. Foremost among these are the agencies that are responsible for fiscal and monetary policy. Other agencies, such as the Internal Revenue Service (IRS), transform private resources into federal funds for public purposes. Tax policy may also strengthen the economy through decisions about whom to tax, how much, and when. Finally, the federal government, through such agencies as the Department of Transportation, the Commerce Department, and the Energy Department, may directly provide services or goods that bolster the economy.

Fiscal and Monetary Agencies   The best term for government activity affecting or relating to money is **fiscal policy.** The *fisc* was the Roman imperial treasury; "fiscal" can refer to anything and everything having to do with public finance. However, we in the United States choose to make a further distinction, reserving "fiscal" for taxing and spending policies and using "monetary" for policies having to do with banks, credit, and currency. Yet a third term, "welfare," deserves to be treated as an equal member of this category.[5]

The administration of fiscal policy occurs primarily in the Treasury Department. It is no contradiction to include the Treasury here as well as with the agencies for maintenance of the Union. This duplication indicates two things: first, that the Treasury is a complex department that performs more than one function of government; and second, that traditional controls have had to adapt to modern economic conditions and new technologies.

Today, in addition to collecting income, corporate, and other taxes, the Treasury is also responsible for managing the enormous national debt—$3.9 trillion in 2003. (The national debt was less than one trillion dollars in 1980.[6]) Debt is not simply something the country owes; it is something a country has to manage and administer. The debt is also a fiscal instrument in the hands of the federal government that can be used—through manipulation of interest rates and through the buying and selling of government bonds—to slow down or to speed up the activity of the entire national economy, as well as to defend the value of the dollar in international trade.

The Treasury Department is also responsible for printing the U.S. currency, but currency represents only a tiny proportion of the entire money economy. Most of the trillions of dollars used in the transactions of the private and public sectors of the U.S. economy exist in computerized accounts, not in currency.

Another important fiscal agency (although for technical reasons it is called an agency of monetary policy) is the **Federal Reserve System,** which is headed by

fiscal policy the use of taxing, monetary, and spending powers to manipulate the economy

Federal Reserve System a system of twelve Federal Reserve Banks that facilitates exchanges of cash, checks, and credit; regulates member banks; and uses monetary policies to fight inflation and deflation

the Federal Reserve Board. The Federal Reserve System (called simply the Fed) has authority over the interest rates and lending activities of the nation's most important banks. Congress established the Fed in 1913 as a clearinghouse responsible for adjusting the supply of money and credit to the needs of commerce and industry in different regions of the country. The Fed is also responsible for ensuring that banks do not overextend themselves, a policy that guards against a chain of bank failures during a sudden economic scare, such as occurred in 1929. The Federal Reserve Board directs the operations of the twelve district Federal Reserve Banks, which are essentially "bankers' banks," serving the monetary needs of the hundreds of member banks in the national banking system.[7]

Revenue Agencies   One of the first actions of Congress under President George Washington was to create the Department of the Treasury, and probably its oldest function is the collection of taxes on imports, called tariffs. Now housed in the United States Customs Service, federal customs agents are located at every U.S. seaport and international airport to oversee the collection of tariffs. But far and away the most important of the **revenue agencies** is the Internal Revenue Service (IRS). The Customs Service and the IRS are two of at least twelve bureaus within the Treasury Department. The IRS will be our single case study in this section.

> **revenue agencies** agencies responsible for collecting taxes. Examples include the Internal Revenue Service for income taxes, the U.S. Customs Service for tariffs and other taxes on imported goods, and the Bureau of Alcohol, Tobacco, and Firearms for collection of taxes on the sales of those particular products

The IRS is responsive to political influences, especially given the fact that it must maintain cooperative relationships with the two oldest and most important congressional committees, the House Ways and Means Committee and the Senate Finance Committee. Nevertheless, the political patterns of the IRS are virtually the opposite of those of a clientele agency (an agency that serves or provides benefits to some specific group or "clientele" in society). As one expert put it, "probably no organization in the country, public or private, creates as much clientele *dis*favor as the Internal Revenue Service. The very nature of its work brings it into an adversary relationship with vast numbers of Americans every year."[8] Yet few scandals have soiled its record. Complaints against the IRS have increased during the past few years, particularly since 1996 presidential candidate Steve Forbes staged his entire campaign on the need to abolish the IRS and the income tax itself. But aside from the principle of the income tax, all the other complaints against the IRS are against its needless complexity, its lack of sensitivity and responsiveness to individual taxpayers, and its overall lack of efficiency. As one of its critics put it, "Imagine a company that's owed $216 billion plus interest, a company with a 22-percent error rate. A company that spent $4 billion to update a computer system—with little success. It all describes the Internal Revenue Service."[9] Again leaving aside the issue of the income tax itself, all the other complaints amount to just one big complaint: The IRS is not bureaucratic enough; it needs *more* bureaucratization. It needs to succeed with its new computer processing system; it needs vast improvement in its "customer services"; it needs long-term budgeting and other management control; and it needs to borrow more management and technology expertise from the private sector.

Agencies for Internal Security As long as the country is not in a state of insurrection, most of the task of maintaining the Union takes the form of legal work, and the primary responsibility for that lies in the Department of Justice. It is indeed a luxury, and rare in the world, when national unity can be maintained by routines of civil law with an army of lawyers, instead of martial law imposed by a real army with guns.

The largest and most important unit of the Justice Department is the Criminal Division. Lawyers in the Criminal Division represent the United States government when it is the plaintiff enforcing the federal criminal laws, except for those cases (about 25 percent) specifically assigned to other divisions or agencies. Criminal litigation is handled by U.S. attorneys, who are appointed by the president. There is one U.S. attorney in each of the ninety-four federal judicial districts; he or she supervises the work of a number of assistant U.S. attorneys.

The Civil Division of the Justice Department deals with litigation in which the United States is the defendant being sued for injury and damages allegedly inflicted by a government official. The missions of the other divisions of the Justice Department—Antitrust, Civil Rights, Environment and Natural Resources, and Tax—are described by their names.

The best-known bureau of the Justice Department is the Federal Bureau of Investigation (FBI). The FBI handles no litigation but instead serves as the principal information-gathering agency for the department and for the president. Established in 1908, the FBI expanded and advanced in stature during the 1920s and 1930s under the direction of J. Edgar Hoover. Although it is only one of the many bureaus and divisions in the Department of Justice, and although it officially has no higher status than any of the others, it is politically the most significant.

Despite its professionalism and its fierce pride in its autonomy, the FBI has not been unresponsive to the partisan commitments of Democratic and Republican administrations. The FBI has always achieved its best publicity from the spectacular apprehension of famous criminals, such as John Dillinger, George "Machine Gun" Kelly, and Bonnie and Clyde.[10] It has followed the president's direction in focusing on particular crime problems. Thus it has infiltrated Nazi and Mafia organizations; it operates the vast loyalty and security investigation programs covering all federal employees since the Truman presidency; it monitored and infiltrated the Ku Klux Klan and the civil rights movement in the 1950s and 1960s; and it has infiltrated radical political groups and extreme religious cults and survivalist militias in the 1980s and 1990s. The FBI has played an active role in the war on terrorism. Its counterintelligence and counterterrorism activities were increased, and it now works more closely with the military and intelligence agencies. It also is now more involved in international investigations, playing an important role in investigating terrorist bombings of American embassies in Kenya and Tanzania in 1998 and bombings in Saudi Arabia in 2002 and 2003.

Since its creation in 2002, the Department of Homeland Security has also assumed a large role in domestic security, bringing under its umbrella such responsibilities as border safety and security (including immigration and customs); emergency preparedness; science-related concerns pertaining in particular to chemical, biological, and nuclear threats; and information and intelligence analysis and assessment. This new department has also faced competition from the FBI, and this competition has resulted in some confusion and delay—problems that should be ironed out over time.

Agencies for External National Security   Two departments occupy center stage in maintaining national security: the departments of State and Defense.

Although diplomacy is generally considered the primary task of the State Department, diplomatic missions are only one of its organizational dimensions. As of 2004, the State Department comprised twenty-seven bureau-level units, each under the direction of an assistant secretary. Six of these are geographic or regional bureaus concerned with all problems within a defined region of the world; thirteen are "functional" bureaus, handling such things as economic and business affairs, intelligence and research, and international organizations. Four are bureaus of internal affairs, which handle such areas as security, finance and management, and legal issues.

These bureaus support the responsibilities of the elite of foreign affairs, the foreign service officers (FSOs), who staff U.S. embassies around the world and who hold almost all of the most powerful positions in the department below the rank of ambassador.[11] The ambassadorial positions, especially the plum positions in the major capitals of the world, are filled by presidential appointees, many of whom get their positions by having been important donors to the victorious political campaign.

Despite the importance of the State Department in foreign affairs, fewer than 20 percent of all U.S. government employees working abroad are directly under its authority. By far the largest number of career government professionals working abroad are under the authority of the Defense Department.

The creation of the Department of Defense by legislation between 1947 and 1949 was an effort to unify the two historic military departments, the War Department and the Navy Department, and to integrate them with a new department, the Air Force. Real unification, however, did not occur. The Defense Department simply added more pluralism to an already pluralistic national security establishment.

The American military, following worldwide military tradition, is organized according to a "chain of command"—a tight hierarchy of clear responsibility and rank, made clearer by uniforms, special insignia, and detailed organizational charts and rules of order and etiquette. The "line agencies" in the Department of Defense are the military commands, distributed geographically by divisions and fleets to deal with current or potential enemies. The "staff agencies," such as logistics, intelligence, personnel, research and development, quartermaster, and engineering, exist to serve the "line agencies." At the top of the military chain of command are chiefs of staff (called chief of naval operations in the Navy, and commandant in the Marines). These chiefs of staff also constitute the membership of the Joint Chiefs of Staff—the center of military policy and management.

America's primary political problem with its military has not been the historic one of how to keep the military out of politics (which is a perennial problem in many of the world's countries), but how to keep politics out of the military. In 2004, President George W. Bush and Congress came into sharp conflict over a

Creating the Department of Homeland Security

After the attacks of September 11, 2001, the federal government's role in providing domestic security changed dramatically. In 2002 the Department of Homeland Security (DHS) was established, with Tom Ridge (pictured here) as its first head. This massive new bureaucracy consolidated twenty-two existing agencies and departments, some of which are described below.

The Federal Emergency Management Agency (FEMA) prepares for and responds to all kinds of domestic disasters. FEMA coordinated cleanup at the sites of the September 11 terrorist attacks and also assisted after four separate hurricanes struck Florida in September 2004. Here, former FEMA director Joe Allbaugh meets with urban search-and-rescue teams at the Pentagon.

With the passage of the Aviation and Transportation Security Act, the federal government took over the screening of airline passengers and their baggage. The Transportation Security Administration, formerly a part of the Transportation Department, is the branch of DHS in charge of airport screening.

POLITICS

DHS also oversees important scientific and technological research that was previously conducted by the Health and Human Services Department, the Agriculture Department, the Energy Department, and others. Here, a scientist examines anthrax samples as part of the investigation into anthrax-tainted mail sent to politicians and the news media in 2001.

Port and border security are seen as central to the prevention of future terrorist attacks. Both the Coast Guard and the U.S. Customs and Border Protection agency are now part of DHS.

$447 billion appropriations bill to cover military spending. Bush and the military supported the bill, but Congress inserted a provision to the bill that would have imposed a two-year delay in Bush's plans to close some military bases around the country. The Pentagon (the office building in Washington that serves as the head-quarters for the American military, and which has become synonymous with the military services) also favored the closings. Bush threatened to veto the entire bill if the base-closing extension was kept in, and the Pentagon supported the closings by saying that they would help the military by saving tens of billions of dollars on unnecessary bases. Congress wanted the bases to stay open for a political reason—because representatives feared that closing bases in an election year would result in unpopular job losses for which they would take the blame.[12]

The war on terrorism has given the Defense Department more control over policy decisions. For example, it took the lead in organizing the war against the Taliban in Afghanistan in 2001 and in the invasion of Iraq in 2003. In fact, some critics of the Iraq war argued that the postwar situation devolved into chaos at least partly because the State Department and the U.S. Agency for International Development (USAID, a civilian agency in charge of foreign aid and economic and social development in other nations) were kept out of American govern-ment decision making concerning the running of Iraq after the war. Even within American borders, the military now plays a greater role, as military planes now patrol airspace over major cities, and the National Guard has patrolled airports and subways—jobs traditionally reserved for civilian police forces.

The 9/11 Commission's Proposal to Reorganize Security   In 2004, the National Commission on Terrorist Attacks upon the United States (the 9/11 Commission) issued a widely read report that called for a major reorganization of bureaucratic responsibilities for internal and external security. The report revealed that different departments of the American government had information that, if handled prop-erly, might have prevented the attacks of September 11, 2001. The commission found that the federal government's attempts to improve security after September 11 still did not address the critical problems with duplication, prioritization, and coordination in the current system. To correct this, the commission made major recommendations designed to promote unity of effort across the bureaucracy.

Topping the list were proposals designed to bridge the divide between domestic and foreign security efforts. Prior to September 11, the FBI, which collects domes-tic information, did not talk to the CIA, and the Defense Department collected mountains of information that was not shared with either the FBI or the CIA. The commission recommended the creation of a National Counterterrorism Center. The NCTC would function like a superbrain that would analyze all sources of in-telligence and plan appropriate operational responses that could be carried out by existing agencies, such as the State Department, the CIA, the FBI, the Department of Homeland Security, and others. The commission also recommended that the President create a new position: National Intelligence Director. The director would oversee all intelligence activities in the federal government and advise the president about intelligence issues. Under this new reorganization, the new director would have the budgetary authority to shift money between different intelligence agencies, as necessary. This was sure to displease the Department of Defense, which controls 80 percent of the intelligence budget. It was also sure to be opposed by the CIA, whose director would no longer have overall responsibility for intelligence.

Even with President Bush's backing, the road to such a major bureaucratic reorganization was politically difficult. Many interests, including the Department of Defense and the CIA, lobbied fiercely to retain their autonomy and control over funds. However, the strong political momentum behind the report and its visibility in an election year where national security issues were front and center meant that the recommendations stood a good chance of becoming law.

Several Forces Control Bureaucracy

Many people assume that bureaucracy and democracy are contradictory.[13] Americans cannot live with bureaucracy, they sometimes say, but as this chapter shows, but they also cannot live without it. The task is neither to retreat from bureaucracy nor to attack it, but to take advantage of its strengths while making it more accountable to the demands of democratic politics and representative government. This task will be the focus of the remainder of this chapter.

Two hundred years, millions of employees, and trillions of dollars after America's founding, we must return to James Madison's observation, "You must first enable the government to control the governed; and in the next place oblige it to control itself."[14] Today the problem is the same, only now the process has a name: administrative accountability. Accountability implies that some higher authority will guide and judge the actions of the bureaucracy. The highest authority in a democracy is *demos*—the people—and the guidance for bureaucratic action is the popular will. But the president and Congress must translate that ideal of accountability into practical terms.

THE PRESIDENT AS CHIEF EXECUTIVE CAN DIRECT AGENCIES

In 1937, President Franklin Roosevelt's Committee on Administrative Management gave official sanction to an idea that had been growing increasingly urgent: "The president needs help." The national government had grown rapidly during the preceding twenty-five years, but the structures and procedures necessary to manage the burgeoning executive branch had not yet been established. The response to the call for "help" for the president initially took the form of three management policies: (1) All communications and decisions that related to executive policy decisions must pass through the White House; (2) In order to cope with such a flow, the White House must have adequate staffs of specialists in research, analysis, legislative and legal writing, and public affairs; and (3) The White House must have additional staff to follow through on presidential decisions—to ensure that those decisions are made, communicated to Congress, and carried out by the appropriate agency.

Making the Managerial Presidency   Establishing a management capacity for the presidency began in earnest with FDR, but it did not stop there.[15] The story of the modern presidency can be told largely as a series of responses to the plea for managerial help. Indeed, each expansion of the national government into new policies and programs in the twentieth century has been accompanied by a parallel expansion of the president's management authority.

Presidents John Kennedy and Lyndon Johnson were committed both to government expansion and to management expansion, in the spirit of their party's hero, FDR. President Nixon also strengthened and enlarged the managerial presidency, but for somewhat different reasons. He sought the strongest possible managerial hand because he had to assume that the overwhelming majority of federal employees had sympathies with the Democratic Party, which had controlled the White House and had sponsored governmental growth for twenty-eight of the previous thirty-six years.[16]

President Jimmy Carter was probably more preoccupied with administrative reform and reorganization than any other president in the twentieth century. His reorganization of the civil service will long be recognized as one of the most significant contributions of his presidency. The Civil Service Reform Act of 1978 was the first major revamping of the federal civil service since its creation in 1883. The 1978 act abolished the century-old Civil Service Commission (CSC) and replaced it with three agencies, each designed to handle one of the CSC's functions on the theory that the competing demands of these functions had given the CSC an "identity crisis." The Merit Systems Protection Board (MSPB) was created to defend competitive merit recruitment and promotion from political encroachment. A separate Federal Labor Relations Authority (FLRA) was set up to administer collective bargaining and individual personnel grievances. The third new agency, the Office of Personnel Management (OPM), was created to manage recruiting, testing, training, and the retirement system. The Senior Executive Service was also created at this time to recognize and foster "public management" as a profession and to facilitate the movement of top, "supergrade" career officials across agencies and departments.[17]

Carter also tried to impose a stringent budgetary process on all executive agencies. Called "zero-base budgeting," it was a method of budgeting from the bottom up, wherein each agency was required to rejustify its entire mission rather than merely its increase for the next year. Zero-base budgeting did not succeed, but the effort was not lost on President Reagan. Although Reagan gave the impression of being a laid-back president, he actually centralized management to an unprecedented degree. From Carter's "bottom-up" approach, Reagan went to a "top-down" approach, whereby the initial budgetary decisions would be made in the White House and the agencies would be required to fit within those decisions. This process converted the Office of Management and Budget (OMB) into an agency of policy determination and presidential management.[18] President George H. W. Bush took Reagan's centralization strategy even further in using the White House staff instead of Cabinet secretaries for managing the executive branch.[19]

President Clinton engaged in the most systematic effort to "change the way the government does business," a phrase he used often to describe the goal of his National Performance Review (NPR), one of the most important administrative reform efforts of the twentieth century. In September 1993, he launched the NPR, based on a set of 384 proposals drafted by a panel headed by Vice President Al Gore. The avowed goal of the NPR was to "reinvent government"—to make the federal bureaucracy more efficient, accountable, and effective. But this was little more than new language for the same management goal held by each of his predecessors. The NPR's original goal was to save more than $100 billion over five years, in large part by cutting the federal workforce by 12 percent (more than 270,000 jobs) by the end of 1999. Yet by the end of 1999, $136 billion in savings was achieved, and the federal workforce had been cut by 377,000.[20]

The NPR also focused on cutting red tape, streamlining procurement (how the government purchases goods and services), improving the coordination of federal management, and simplifying federal rules. For instance, the Defense Department's method for reimbursing its employees' travel expenses used to take seventeen steps and two months; an employee-designed reform encouraged by the NPR streamlined this to a four-step, computer-based procedure taking less than fifteen minutes, with an anticipated savings of $1 billion over five years.

Like his predecessors, George W. Bush pursued a strategy different from those of previous presidents. Bush dismantled Clinton's NPR and favored privatization—taking government programs out of the hands of the public sector and giving them to private companies under government supervision. Bush defended this approach by arguing that it saved the government money and placed work in the hands of more efficient private organizations. Yet privatization also came under criticism during the Iraq war, when the giant oil company Halliburton was given $9 billion in government contracts. Halliburton performed tasks ranging from supplying fuel for the military to providing cafeteria meals. Critics charged that Halliburton's costs were exorbitant: Pentagon auditors found that it overcharged the government by $61 million for the gas; Halliburton charged the government for forty-two thousand meals when it delivered only fourteen thousand. By the middle of 2004, the company had been accused of more than $250 million in overcharges to the government. These findings undercut claims of efficiency. Adding to charges of favoritism was the fact that Bush's vice president, Dick Cheney, had served as Halliburton's CEO in the 1990s.[21] Privatization aside, the Bush administration's effort to limit the size of government ran headlong into the terrorist attacks on America in 2001, which impelled the administration to expand government, mostly in areas related to law enforcement, security, research, and intelligence.

CONGRESS PROMOTES RESPONSIBLE BUREAUCRACY

Congress is constitutionally essential to responsible bureaucracy because ultimately the key to bureaucratic responsibility is legislation. When a law is passed and its intent is clear, the accountability for implementation of that law is also clear. Then the president knows what to "faithfully execute," and the responsible agency understands what is expected of it. But when Congress enacts vague legislation, agencies must resort to their own interpretations. The president and the federal courts often step in to tell agencies what the legislation intended. And so do the most intensely interested groups. Yet when everybody, from president to courts to interest groups, gets involved in the actual interpretation of legislative intent, to whom and to what is the agency accountable? Even when the agency wants to behave responsibly, how shall accountability be accomplished?

oversight the effort by Congress, through hearings, investigations, and other techniques, to exercise control over the activities of executive agencies

Congress's answer is **oversight.** The more power Congress has delegated to the executive, the more it has sought to reinvolve itself in directing the interpretation of laws through committee and subcommittee oversight of each agency. The standing committee system in Congress is well suited for oversight, inasmuch as most of the congressional committees and subcommittees have jurisdictions roughly parallel to one or more departments and agencies, and members of Congress who sit on these committees can develop expertise equal to that of the bureaucrats. Appropriations committees as well as authorization committees have oversight powers—as do their respective subcommittees. In addition to these, the Government Reform and Oversight Committee in the House and the Governmental Affairs Committee in the Senate have oversight powers not limited by departmental jurisdiction.

The best indication of Congress's oversight efforts is the use of public hearings, before which bureaucrats and other witnesses are summoned to discuss and defend agency budgets and past decisions. The data drawn from systematic studies of congressional committee and subcommittee hearings and meetings show quite dramatically that Congress has tried through oversight to keep pace with the expansion of the executive branch. Between 1950 and 1980, for example, the annual number of committee and subcommittee meetings in the House of Representatives rose steadily from 3,210 to 7,022; in the Senate, the number of such meetings rose from 2,607 to 4,265 (in 1975–76). Beginning in 1980 in the House and 1978 in the Senate, the number of committee and subcommittee hearings and meetings slowly began to decline, reaching 4,222 in the House and 2,597 in the Senate by the mid-1980s. New questions about the ability of Congress to exercise oversight arose when the Republicans took over Congress in 1995. Reductions in committee staffing and an emphasis on using investigative oversight to uncover scandal meant much less time spent on programmatic oversight. Moreover, congressional Republicans complained that they could not get sufficient information about programs from the White House to conduct effective oversight. Congressional records show that in 1991–92, when Democrats controlled the House, they issued reports on fifty-five federal programs, while in 1997–98 the Republican Congress issued only fourteen.[22] On issues of major national importance, multiple committees may initiate oversight hearings simultaneously.

In the months after the terror attacks in 2001, Congress exercised little of its oversight powers around issues of national security. At the time it seemed more important to support the president. Since then, however, many congressional committees have convened hearings related to the war on terrorism. These investigations cover a broad range of issues, including intelligence failures prior to the September 11 terrorism attacks, the financial war on terrorism, the implementation of the Patriot Act, and the reconstruction of Iraq after the war.

The report of the 9/11 Commission drew attention to the problems with congressional oversight of the intelligence community. Noting that "congressional oversight may be among the most difficult and important" of all its recommendations, the Commission declared that current arrangements were "dysfunctional." It found that the existing intelligence committees in Congress had insufficient power and expertise to provide adequate oversight. The Commission recommended the creation of a joint congressional committee or a single committee in either house with the ability to authorize and appropriate expenditures. The committees would be small and have a balanced partisan membership that would serve for an indefinite period of time, in order to develop the expertise and political credibility to oversee intelligence activities.

The Commission also recommended reorganizing congressional oversight of homeland security. Given that "the leaders of the Department of Homeland Security now appear before 88 committees and subcommittees of Congress," responsibility was spread so thinly that it was impossible to achieve accountability. The Commission advised that Congress create a single permanent standing committee in the House and in the Senate to provide a "principal point of oversight and review for homeland security."

Although congressional oversight is potent because of Congress's power to make, and therefore to change, the law, often the most effective and influential lever over bureaucratic accountability is "the power of the purse"—the ability of the House and Senate committees and subcommittees on appropriations to increase or decrease funding of agencies, as well as to investigate agency activities, to control agency performance.

Oversight can also be carried out by individual members of Congress. Such inquiries addressed to bureaucrats are considered standard congressional "case work" and can turn up significant questions of public responsibility even when the motivation is only to meet the demand of an individual constituent. Oversight also takes place through communications between congressional staff and agency staff. The number of congressional staff has increased tremendously since the Legislative Reorganization Act of 1946, and the legislative staff, especially the staff of the committees, is just as professionalized and specialized as the staff of executive agencies. In addition, Congress has created for itself three large agencies whose obligations are to engage in constant research on problems taking place in or confronted by the executive branch. These are the General Accounting Office (GAO), the Congressional Research Service (CRS), and the Congressional Budget Office (CBO). Each of these agencies is designed to give Congress information independent of the information it can get directly from the executive branch through hearings and other communications.[23] Another source of information for oversight is direct from citizens through the Freedom of Information Act (FOIA), which gives ordinary citizens the right of access to agency files and agency data to determine whether derogatory information exists in the file about the citizens themselves and to learn about what the agency is doing in general.

The effort of the George W. Bush administration to expand greatly the scope of privatization raises new questions about democratic accountability. When government work is contracted out, federal monitoring is essential to ensure that funds are spent in accordance with the public will and to confirm that the costs are fair. Yet, even with monitoring, accountability may be hard to achieve. Many of the mechanisms of democratic accountability do not apply to private firms that contract to perform public work. For example, private corporations can resist FOIA requests, and they are not constrained by the same ethics rules as public employees. Moreover, because private firms do not have to disclose information about their operations in the same way as public bureaucracies, Congress has much more limited oversight. The move to contracting out government work clearly will present major challenges to democratic accountability.

Democracy Can Control Bureaucracy

In the final analysis, the best approach for reconciling bureaucracy and democracy is to insist on clear rules and laws, maximum openness in agency decisions, clear rationales for those decisions, and accessible means for questioning and appealing those decisions. These methods are equally applicable to Congress as to the bureaucracy. The very best approach for Congress to ensure accountability of the bureaucracy is for Congress to spend more time clarifying its legislative intent and less time on oversight. Bureaucrats are more responsive to clear legislative guidance than to anything else, and when Congress and the president are at odds about the interpretation of laws, bureaucrats can evade responsibility by playing off one branch against another. If Congress's intent in its laws is made more clear, it could then defer far more to presidential management and presidential maintenance of bureaucratic accountability. Moreover, clearer laws from Congress and clearer rules and decisions made by administrative agencies would reduce the need for courts to review those laws and decisions; judicial approaches to administrative accountability are the most expensive and time consuming, and therefore the least available to individual citizens.

Bureaucracy and democracy can be more comfortable allies rather than warring adversaries. Make no mistake about it, however: Bureaucracy is here to stay. No reinvention of government, or radical decentralization of power, or substantial budget-cutting, or reductions in personnel can alter the necessity of bureaucracy or resolve the problem of reconciling bureaucracy with democracy.

Summary

Bureaucracy is a universal form of organization, found in businesses, churches, foundations, and universities, as well as in the public sphere. All essential government services and regulations are carried out by bureaucracies—specifically, by administrative agencies. Bureaucrats are appointed to their offices based on the "merit system." Federal bureaucrats are generally better educated than the U.S. population as a whole. Women and African Americans are also well represented, although they tend to be concentrated at the lower pay levels.

The agencies of the executive branch can be grouped into four categories: (1) clientele agencies, (2) agencies for maintaining the Union, (3) regulatory agencies, and (4) agencies for redistribution. All of these agencies are alike in that they are all bureaucratic. These agencies differ in the way they are organized, in the way they participate in the political process, and in their levels of responsiveness to political authority. In recent years, attempts have been made to reduce or "downsize" the bureaucracy. Although these efforts are popular with the American people, they cannot reduce the size of the federal bureaucracy by much.

The executive and the legislative branches do the toughest job any government is called on to do: making the bureaucracy accountable to the people. Democratizing bureaucracy is the unending task of politics in a democracy.

For Further Reading

Arnold, Peri E. *Making the Managerial Presidency: Comprehensive Organization Planning.* Princeton, NJ: Princeton University Press, 1986.

Fesler, James W., and Donald F. Kettl. *The Politics of the Administrative Process.* Chatham, NJ: Chatham House, 1991.

Skowronek, Stephen. *Building a New American State: The Expansion of National Administrative Capacities, 1877–1920.* New York: Cambridge University Press, 1982.

Wildavsky, Aaron. *The New Politics of the Budget Process.* 2nd ed. New York: HarperCollins, 1992.

Wilson, James Q. *Bureaucracy: What Government Agencies Do and Why They Do It.* New York: Basic Books, 1989.

Wood, B. Dan *Bureaucratic Dynamics: The Role of Bureaucracy in a Democracy.* Boulder, CO: Westview, 1994.

Study Outline

Bureaucracy Exists to Improve Efficiency

1. Bureaucracy is simply a form of organization. Specialization and repetition are essential to the efficiency of any organization.
2. Despite fears of bureaucratic growth, the federal service has grown little during the past twenty-five years. The national government is large, but the federal service has not been growing any faster than the economy or the society.
3. Through civil service reform, national and state governments have attempted to reduce political interference in public bureaucracies by granting certain public bureaucrats legal protection from being fired without a show of cause.
4. In terms of the hiring of various demographic groups, the federal civil service—like the rest of society—has problems, but it has been improving.

The Executive Branch Is Organized Hierarchically

1. One type of executive agency—the clientele agency—exists to foster the interests of a specific group in society. In turn, that group works to support its agency when it is in jeopardy.
2. America's chief revenue agency, the Internal Revenue Service, engenders hostility rather than clientele support among groups and individual citizens.
3. Political considerations have frequently had an impact both on agencies for internal security and on agencies for external national security.
4. Regulatory agencies in the United States are given the authority to regulate various industries; these agencies often act like courts when making decisions or settling disputes.
5. Agencies of redistribution influence the amount of money in the economy and directly influence who has money, who has credit, and whether people will want to invest or spend.

Several Forces Control Bureaucracy

1. Each expansion of the national government in the twentieth century has been accompanied by a parallel expansion of presidential management authority, but the expansion of presidential power cannot guarantee responsible bureaucracy.

2. Although Congress attempts to control the bureaucracy through oversight, a more effective way to ensure accountability may be to clarify legislative intent.

Practice Quiz

1. Which of the following best describes the growth of the federal service in the past twenty-five years?
   a) rampant, exponential growth
   b) little growth at all
   c) decrease in the total number of federal employees
   d) vast, compared to the growth of the economy and the society

2. Which of the following terms best characterizes the representation of African Americans in the federal workforce?
   a) overrepresentation
   b) underrepresentation
   c) nonexistent
   d) bifurcated

3. Which of the following is *not* an example of a clientele agency?
   a) Department of Justice
   b) Department of Commerce
   c) Department of Agriculture
   d) Department of Housing and Urban Development

4. What explains the FBI's political significance as compared to the other divisions and bureaus within the Department of Justice?
   a) the FBI's higher legal status
   b) the leadership of J. Edgar Hoover in the 1920s and 1930s
   c) the FBI's clientele nature
   d) the FBI's relationship to the CIA

5. The concept of oversight refers to the effort made by
   a) Congress to make executive agencies accountable for their actions.
   b) the president to make Congress accountable for its actions.
   c) the courts to make executive agencies responsible for their actions.
   d) the states to make the executive branch accountable for its actions.

Critical Thinking Questions

1. Often the efficiency of public bureaucracies is judged in terms of the efficiency of private business and other organizations. In many instances, government has been expected to do things that businesses in the marketplace have chosen not to do or have found unprofitable. Might the tasks that government is asked to perform be more prone to inefficiency? Think about the ways in which business might be able to perform some tasks that government currently performs. Would business necessarily perform these tasks more efficiently? Should efficiency be the only priority in the public enterprise?

2. Describe the ways in which the public controls its bureaucracy. How much and what kind of control should the public exercise? Through elected officials—i.e., the president and the Congress—the public can achieve some control over the bureaucracy. What are the relative advantages and disadvantages of presidential and congressional control of the bureaucracy?

Key Terms

administrative adjudication (p. 291)
bureaucracy (p. 287)
department (p. 292)
Federal Reserve System (p. 296)

fiscal policy (p. 296)
government corporation (p. 294)
implementation (p. 290)
independent agency (p. 294)
merit system (p. 292)
oversight (p. 306)

regulatory agencies (p. 295)
revenue agencies (p. 297)
rulemaking (p. 291)
spoils system (p. 292)

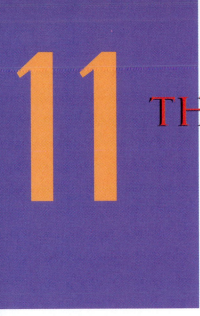

THE FEDERAL COURTS

MAIN MESSAGE

The courts have evolved from being the "least dangerous branch" to playing an ever more important role in people's lives.

Key Concepts

1. **Americans use the courts more than ever to resolve disputes and change policy.**
2. **State courts handle the vast majority of court cases in America.**
3. **The key power of the courts is judicial review.**
4. **Only a tiny percentage of cases get to the Supreme Court, which tightly controls the flow of cases it hears.**
5. **Court decisions are shaped by the justices' activism and ideology.**

It is often said that America is becoming an ever more "litigious" society, meaning that Americans file suits and pursue actions in courts more than ever. Tobacco companies and gun manufacturers have been recent targets of this new and vigorous action in courts.

For many years, people whose health was adversely affected by cigarette use sued the tobacco companies to recover damages for the harm caused by cigarettes. These suits usually failed, or were settled out of court. In the mid-1990s, however, such lawsuits began to gain momentum when it was discovered that tobacco companies engaged in a variety of deceptive practices, including manipulating the amount of nicotine in cigarettes to make them more addictive; falsely claiming that cigarettes were not addictive; and marketing cigarettes to those under the legal smoking age. (The "Joe Camel" cartoon ad campaign was ended after revelations that more young children could identify Joe Camel than Mickey Mouse, and that Camel cigarette use vastly increased among underage users after the Joe Camel campaign began.) To head off the prospect of unfavorable court rulings and jury verdicts, tobacco companies reached an agreement with state governments and trial lawyers, which required the companies to pay $368 billion over twenty-five years to the states as compensation for the health care money they spend (through Medicaid) for tobacco-related illnesses. In return, the states agreed to limit their legal actions against the companies. The large amount of money that the tobacco companies agreed to pay out as a settlement to avoid further costly lawsuits underscores the degree to which the companies feared further legal action. In a further court-related development, the Supreme Court ruled in 2000 that the Food and Drug Administration (FDA) did not have the authority to categorize cigarettes as a drug, thereby avoiding the prospect that the FDA would be able to regulate cigarettes the way it regulates other drugs. (Even the cigarette companies referred to their product as a "nicotine delivery system.")

The tobacco lawsuits inspired similar legal action against another industry: gun manufacturers. In early 1999, a Brooklyn jury found that several firearms manufacturers were legally liable for three shootings that occurred in New York City, based on the argument that the gun manufacturers engaged in irresponsible gun marketing and distribution practices, and because many guns were sold without safety locks. The jury levied damages of about a half-million dollars. The verdict was overturned on appeal, but within a year over thirty cities and counties around the country had filed similar suits against gun manufacturers. Many gun owners and users cried foul over the suits, charging that the courts had gone too far in permitting suits that were simply a back-door effort to regulate guns because such efforts had failed in Congress. The same criticism was made concerning the cigarette lawsuits.

Compared to legal action against tobacco, the suits against gun manufacturers could indeed be more devastating, as the cigarette companies posted total sales of $48 billion in 1997, while the gun industry's total sales the same year amounted to only $1.4 billion. In both cases, simmering political disputes over cigarettes and guns found their way to the courts, where future rulings might well reshape these industries. These cases also illustrate how the courts have come to play a key role in shaping national policy, serving as a forum for citizen complaints, and affecting citizens in their everyday lives.

Every year nearly twenty-five million cases are tried in American courts and one American in every nine is directly involved in litigation. Cases can arise from disputes between citizens, from efforts by government agencies to punish wrongdoing, or from citizens' efforts to prove that a right provided them by law has been infringed upon as a result of government action—or inaction. The heavy use that Americans make of the courts is an indication of the importance of courts as a forum to resolve conflict. All things considered, it is far better that Americans seek to settle their differences through the courts rather than by fighting or feuding.

The framers of the American Constitution called the Supreme Court the "least dangerous branch" of American government. Today, it is not unusual to hear friends *and* foes of the Court refer to it as the "imperial judiciary."[1] Before we can understand this transformation and its consequences, however, we must look in some detail at America's judicial process.

The Legal System Settles Disputes

Originally, a "court" was the place where a sovereign ruled—where the king and his entourage governed. Settling disputes between citizens was part of governing. According to the Bible, King Solomon had to settle the dispute between two women over which of them was the mother of the child both claimed. Judging is the settling of disputes, a function that was slowly separated from the king and the king's court and made into a separate institution of government. Courts have taken over from kings the power to settle controversies by hearing the facts on both sides and deciding which side possesses the greater merit. But since judges are not kings, they must have a basis for their authority. That basis in the United States is the Constitution and the law. Courts decide cases by hearing the facts on both sides of a dispute and applying the relevant law or principle to the facts.

COURT CASES PROCEED UNDER CRIMINAL, CIVIL, OR PUBLIC LAW

Court cases in the United States proceed under three broad categories of law: criminal law, civil law, and public law.

Cases of **criminal law** are those in which the government charges an individual with violating a statute (a law) that has been enacted to protect the public health, safety, morals, or welfare. In criminal cases, the government is always the **plaintiff** (the party that brings charges) and alleges that a criminal violation has been committed by a named **defendant.** Most criminal cases arise in state and municipal courts and involve matters from traffic offenses to robbery and murder. While the great bulk of criminal law is still a state matter, a large and growing body of federal criminal law deals with such matters as tax evasion, mail fraud, and the sale of narcotics. Defendants found guilty of criminal violations may be fined or sent to prison.

Cases of **civil law** involve disputes among individuals or between individuals and the government in which no criminal violation is charged. Unlike criminal cases, the losers in civil cases cannot be fined or sent to prison, although they may be required to pay monetary damages for their actions. In a civil case, the one who brings a complaint is the plaintiff and the one against whom the complaint is brought is the defendant. The two most common types of civil cases involve contracts and torts. In a typical contract case, an individual or corporation charges that it has suffered because of another's violation of a specific agreement between the two. For example, the Smith Manufacturing Corporation may charge that Jones Distributors failed to honor an agreement to deliver

criminal law the branch of law that deals with disputes or actions involving criminal penalties (as opposed to civil law); it regulates the conduct of individuals, defines crimes, and provides punishment for criminal acts

plaintiff the individual or organization that brings a complaint in court

defendant the one against whom a complaint is brought in a criminal or civil case

civil law a system of jurisprudence, including private law and governmental actions, to settle disputes that do not involve criminal penalties

raw materials at a specified time, causing Smith to lose business. Smith asks the court to order Jones to compensate it for the damage allegedly suffered. In a typical tort case, one individual charges that he or she has been injured by another's negligence or malfeasance. Medical malpractice suits are one example of tort cases.

In deciding cases, courts apply statutes (laws) and legal **precedents** (prior decisions). State and federal statutes, for example, often govern the conditions under which contracts are and are not legally binding. Jones Distributors might argue that it was not obliged to fulfill its contract with the Smith Corporation because actions by Smith, such as the failure to make promised payments, constituted fraud under state law. Attorneys for a physician being sued for malpractice, on the other hand, may search for prior instances in which courts ruled that actions similar to those of their client did not constitute negligence. Such precedents are applied under the doctrine of *stare decisis,* a Latin phrase meaning "let the decision stand."

A case becomes a matter of the third category, **public law,** when a plaintiff or defendant in a civil or criminal case seeks to show that the case involves the powers of government or rights of citizens as defined under the Constitution or by statute. One major form of public law is constitutional law, under which a court will examine the government's actions to see if they conform to the Constitution as it has been interpreted by the judiciary. Thus, what began as an ordinary criminal case may enter the realm of public law if a defendant claims that the police violated his or her constitutional rights. Another important arena of public law is administrative law, which involves disputes over the jurisdiction, procedures, or authority of administrative agencies. Under this type of law, civil litigation between an individual and the government may become a matter of public law if the individual asserts that the government is violating a statute or abusing its power under the Constitution. For example, landowners have asserted that federal and state restrictions on land use constitute violations of the Fifth Amendment's restrictions on the government's ability to confiscate private property. Recently, the Supreme Court has been very sympathetic to such claims, which effectively transform an ordinary civil dispute into a major issue of public law.

Most of the important Supreme Court cases we will examine in this chapter involve judgments concerning the constitutional or statutory basis of the actions of government agencies. As we shall see, it is in this arena of public law that the Supreme Court's decisions can have significant consequences for American politics and society.

TYPES OF COURTS INCLUDE TRIAL, APPELLATE, AND SUPREME

In the United States, systems of courts have been established both by the federal government and by the governments of the individual states. Both systems have several levels, as shown in Figure 11.1. More than 99 percent of all court cases in the United States are heard in state courts. The overwhelming majority of crimi-

precedent prior case whose principles are used by judges as the basis for their decisions in present cases

stare decisis literally, "let the decision stand." The doctrine that a previous decision by a court applies as a precedent in similar cases until that decision is overruled

public law cases in private law, civil law, or criminal law in which one party to the dispute argues that a license is unfair, a law is inequitable or unconstitutional, or an agency has acted unfairly, violated a procedure, or gone beyond its jurisdiction

nal cases, for example, involves violations of state laws prohibiting such actions as murder, robbery, fraud, theft, and assault. If such a case is brought to trial, it will be heard in a state **trial court,** in front of a judge and sometimes a jury, who will determine whether the defendant violated state law. If the defendant is convicted, he or she may appeal the conviction to a higher court, such as a state **appellate court,** and from there to a state's **supreme court.** Similarly, in civil cases, most litigation is brought in the courts established by the state in which the activity in question took place. For example, a patient bringing suit against a physician for malpractice would file the suit in the appropriate court in the state where the alleged malpractice occurred. The judge hearing the case would apply state law and state precedent to the matter at hand. (It should be noted that most criminal and civil cases are settled before trial through negotiated agreements between the parties. In criminal cases, these agreements are called **plea bargains**.)

Although each state has its own set of laws, these laws have much in common from state to state. Murder and robbery, obviously, are illegal in all states, although the range of possible punishments for those crimes varies from state to state. Some states, for example, provide for capital punishment (the death penalty) for murder and other serious offenses; other states do not. Some acts that are criminal offenses in one state may be legal in another state. Prostitution, for example, is legal in some Nevada counties, although it is outlawed in all other states. Considerable similarity among the states is also found in the realm

trial court the first court to hear a criminal or civil case

appellate court a court that hears the appeals of trial court decisions

supreme court the highest court in a particular state or in the United States. This court primarily serves an appellate function

plea bargains negotiated agreements in criminal cases in which a defendant agrees to plead guilty in return for the state's agreement to reduce the severity of the criminal charge the defendent is facing

The U.S. Court System

Figure 11.1

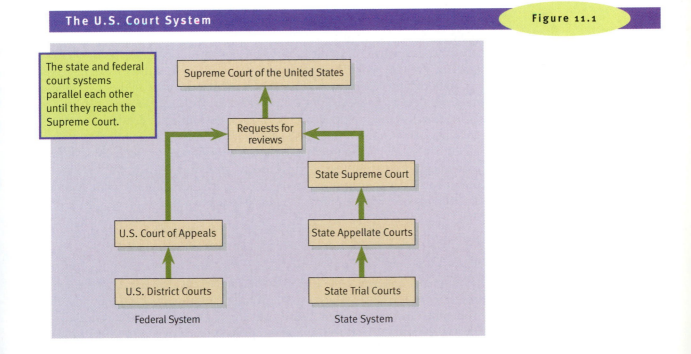

The state and federal court systems parallel each other until they reach the Supreme Court.

Uniform Commercial Code code used in many states in the area of contract law to reduce interstate differences in judicial decisions

jurisdiction the sphere of a court's power and authority

due process of law the right of every citizen against arbitrary action by national or state governments

of civil law. In the case of contract law, most states have adopted the **Uniform Commercial Code** in order to reduce interstate differences. In areas such as family law, however, which covers such matters as divorce and child custody arrangements, state laws vary greatly.

Cases are heard in the federal courts if they involve federal laws, treaties with other nations, or the U.S. Constitution; these areas are the official **jurisdiction** of the federal courts. In addition, any case in which the U.S. government is a party is heard in the federal courts. If, for example, an individual is charged with violating a federal criminal statute, such as evading the payment of income taxes, a federal prosecutor would bring charges before a federal judge. Civil cases involving the citizens of more than one state and in which more than $50,000 is at stake may be heard in either the federal or the state courts, usually depending on the preference of the plaintiff.

Federal courts serve another purpose in addition to trying cases within their jurisdiction: that of hearing appeals from state-level courts. Individuals found guilty of breaking a state criminal law, for example, can appeal their convictions to a federal court by raising a constitutional issue and asking a federal court to determine whether the state's actions were consistent with the requirements of the U.S. Constitution. An appellant might assert, for example, that the state court denied him or her the right to counsel, imposed excessive bail, or otherwise denied the appellant **due process.** Under such circumstances, an appellant can ask the federal court to overturn his or her conviction. Federal courts are not obligated to accept such appeals and will do so only if they feel that the issues raised have considerable merit and if the appellant has exhausted all possible remedies within the state courts. (This procedure is discussed in more detail later in this chapter.) The decisions of state supreme courts may also be appealed to the U.S. Supreme Court if the state court's decision has conflicted with prior U.S. Supreme Court rulings or has raised some important question of federal law. The U.S. Supreme Court accepts such appeals at its discretion.

Although the federal courts hear only a small fraction of all the civil criminal cases decided each year in the United States, their decisions are extremely important. It is in the federal courts that the Constitution and federal laws that govern all Americans are interpreted and their meaning and significance established. Moreover, it is in the federal courts that the powers and limitations of the increasingly powerful national government are tested. Finally, through their power to review the decisions of the state courts, it is ultimately the federal courts that dominate the American judicial system.

The Federal Courts Hear a Small Percentage of All Cases

Of all the cases heard in the United States in 2001, federal district courts (the lowest federal level) received 253,354. Although this number is up substantially from the 87,000 cases heard in 1961, it still constitutes about 1 percent of the judiciary's business. The federal courts of appeal listened to 56,823 cases in 2001, and the U.S. Supreme Court reviewed 7,852 in its 2000–2001 term. Most of the cases filed with the Supreme Court are dismissed without a ruling on their merits. The Court has broad latitude to decide what cases it will hear and generally listens to only those cases it deems to raise the most important issues. Only 86 cases were given full-dress Supreme Court review (the nine justices actually sitting *en banc*—in full court—and hearing the lawyers argue the case.)[2]

THE LOWER FEDERAL COURTS HANDLE MOST CASES

Most of the cases of original federal jurisdiction are handled by the federal district courts. Courts of **original jurisdiction** are the courts that are responsible for discovering the facts in a controversy and creating the record on which a judgment is based. Although the Constitution gives the Supreme Court original jurisdiction in several types of cases, such as those affecting ambassadors and those in which a state is one of the parties, most original jurisdiction goes to the lowest courts—the trial courts. (In courts that have appellate jurisdiction, judges receive cases after the factual record is established by the trial court. Ordinarily, new facts cannot be presented before appellate courts.)

There are eighty-nine district courts in the fifty states, plus one in the District of Columbia and one in Puerto Rico, and three territorial courts. These courts are staffed by 664 federal district judges. District judges are assigned to district courts according to the workload; the busiest of these courts may have as many as twenty-eight judges. Only one judge is assigned to each case, except where statutes provide for three-judge courts to deal with special issues. The routines and procedures of the federal district courts are essentially the same as those of the lower state courts, except that federal procedural requirements tend to be stricter. States, for example, do not have to provide a grand jury, a twelve-member trial jury, or a unanimous jury verdict. Federal courts must provide all these things.

original jurisdiction the authority to initially consider a case. Distinguished from appellate jurisdiction, which is the authority to hear the appeals from a lower court's decision

THE APPELLATE COURTS HEAR 10 PERCENT OF LOWER COURT CASES

Roughly 10 percent of all lower court and federal agency cases are accepted for review by the federal appeals courts and by the Supreme Court in its capacity as an appellate court. There are thirteen U.S. Court of Appeals judicial districts, or circuits (with a total of 179 judges). Those districts consist of eleven that divide up the nation geographically, plus one for the District of Columbia, and one federal circuit (this court deals with patents, trademarks, international trade, and claims against the federal government). So, for example, the Second Circuit includes New York, Connecticut, and Vermont; the Ninth Circuit includes California, Oregon, Washington State, Idaho, Montana, Nevada, and Arizona.

Except for cases selected for review by the Supreme Court, decisions made by the appeals courts are final. Because of this finality, certain safeguards have been built into the system. The most important is the provision of more than one judge for every appeals case. Each court of appeals has from six to twenty-eight permanent judgeships, depending on the workload of the circuit. Although normally three judges hear appealed cases, in some instances a larger number of judges sit together *en banc.*

Another safeguard is provided by the assignment of a Supreme Court justice as the circuit justice for each of the circuits. Since the creation of the appeals court in 1891, the circuit justice's primary duty has been to review appeals arising in the circuit in order to expedite Supreme Court action. The most frequent and best-known action of circuit justices is that of reviewing requests for stays of execution when the full Court is unable to do so—primarily during the summer, when the Court is in recess.

THE SUPREME COURT IS THE COURT OF FINAL APPEAL

chief justice justice on the Supreme Court who presides over the Court's public sessions

The Supreme Court is America's highest court. Article III of the Constitution vests "the judicial power of the United States" in the Supreme Court, and this court is supreme in fact as well as form. The Supreme Court is made up of a chief justice and eight associate justices (see Table 11.1). The **chief justice** presides over the Court's public sessions and conferences. In the Court's actual deliberations and decisions, however, the chief justice has no more authority than his colleagues. Each justice casts one vote. To some extent, the influence of the chief justice is a function of his or her own leadership ability. Some chief justices, such as the late Earl Warren, have been able to lead the court in a new direction. In other instances, forceful associate justices, such as the late Felix Frankfurter, are the dominant figures on the Court.

Table 11.1   **Supreme Court Justices, 2005 (as of October*)**

NAME	YEAR OF BIRTH	PRIOR EXPERIENCE	APPOINTED BY	YEAR OF APPOINTMENT
John G. Roberts, Jr. *Chief Justice*	1955	Federal judge	George W. Bush	2005
John Paul Stevens	1920	Federal judge	Ford	1975
Sandra Day O'Connor	1930	State judge	Reagan	1981
Antonin Scalia	1936	Law professor, federal judge	Reagan	1986
Anthony Kennedy	1936	Federal judge	Reagan	1988
David Souter	1939	Federal judge	George H. W. Bush	1990
Clarence Thomas	1948	Federal judge	George H. W. Bush	1991
Ruth Bader Ginsburg	1933	Federal judge	Clinton	1993
Stephen Breyer	1938	Federal judge	Clinton	1994

*On July 1, 2005, Sandra Day O'Connor announced her retirement from the Court, effective upon the confirmation of her successor. As this book went to press, Samuel Alito had been nominated but not yet confirmed to replace O'Connor.

The Constitution does not specify the number of justices who should sit on the Supreme Court; Congress has the authority to change the Court's size. In the early nineteenth century, there were six Supreme Court justices; later there were seven. Congress set the number of justices at nine in 1869, and the Court has remained that size ever since. In 1937, President Franklin Roosevelt, infuriated by several Supreme Court decisions that struck down New Deal programs, asked Congress to enlarge the Court so that he could add a few sympathetic justices to the bench. Although Congress balked at Roosevelt's "court packing" plan, the Court gave in to FDR's pressure and began to take a more favorable view of his policy initiatives. The president, in turn, dropped his efforts to enlarge the Court. The Court's surrender to FDR came to be known as "the switch in time that saved nine."

JUDGES ARE APPOINTED BY THE PRESIDENT AND APPROVED BY THE SENATE

Federal judges are appointed by the president and are generally selected from among the more prominent or politically active members of the legal profession. Many federal judges previously served as state court judges or state or local prosecutors. Candidates for vacancies on the U.S. District Court are generally suggested to the president by a U.S. senator from the president's own party who represents the state in which the vacancy has occurred. Senators often see such a nomination as a way to reward important allies and contributors in their states. If the state has no senator from the president's party, the governor or members of the state's House delegation may make suggestions. In general, presidents endeavor to appoint judges who possess legal experience and good character and whose partisan and ideological views are similar to the president's own. During the presidencies of Ronald Reagan and George H. W. Bush, most federal judicial appointees were conservative Republicans. Bush established an advisory committee to screen judicial nominees in order to make certain that their legal and political philosophies were sufficiently conservative. Bill Clinton's appointees to the federal bench, on the other hand, have tended to be liberal Democrats. Clinton also made a major effort to appoint women and African Americans to the federal courts. Nearly half of his nominees were drawn from these groups.

Once the president has formally nominated an individual, the nominee must be considered by the Senate Judiciary Committee and confirmed by a majority vote in the full Senate. Before the president makes a formal nomination, however, the senators from the candidate's own state must indicate that they support the nominee. This is an informal but seldom violated practice called **senatorial courtesy.** Because the Senate will rarely approve a nominee opposed by a senator from his or her own state, the president will usually not bother to present such a nomination to the Senate. Through this arrangement, senators are able to exercise veto power over appointments to the federal bench in their own states. In recent years, the Senate Judiciary Committee has also sought to signal the president when it has had qualms about a judicial nomination. After the Republicans won control of the Senate in 1994, for example, Judiciary

senatorial courtesy the practice whereby the president, before formally nominating a person for a federal judgeship, seeks the indication that senators from the candidate's own state support the nomination

Committee chair Orrin Hatch of Utah let President Clinton know that he considered many of Clinton's nominees to be too liberal. Hatch's committee succeeded in blocking dozens of Clinton's federal court nominees.

In the first three years of George W. Bush's presidency, Democrats succeeded in blocking a total of seven Bush nominees to the federal Court of Appeals by using the filibuster (the ability to block all action in the Senate). In the case of two of these—Charles Pickering and William Pryor—Bush then appointed them directly to the Court of Appeals by means of an unusual process called a "recess appointment," whereby the president can, under the Constitution, fill positions temporarily until the end of the next session of Congress. If the Senate fails to confirm the nominations at that time, both appointees lose their positions. Presidents rarely use recess appointments, and these actions enraged Democrats (Clinton never used recess appointments to fill judicial posts). Senate Democrats and the White House finally came to a compromise in 2004 when the Democrats agreed to approve a total of twenty-five Bush federal court nominees in exchange for a promise by Bush not to use the recess appointment power again through the end of 2004. But the Democratic block on the original seven nominees remained in place.[3]

In recent years, Supreme Court nominations have come to involve intense partisan struggle. Typically, after the president has named a nominee, interest groups opposed to the nomination have mobilized opposition in the media, the public, and the Senate. When President George H. W. Bush proposed conservative judge Clarence Thomas for the Court, for example, liberal groups launched a campaign to discredit Thomas. After extensive research into his background, opponents of the nomination were able to produce evidence suggesting that Thomas had sexually harassed a former subordinate, Anita Hill. Thomas denied the charge. After contentious Senate Judiciary Committee hearings, highlighted by testimony from both Thomas and Hill, Thomas narrowly won confirmation. Likewise, conservative interest groups carefully scrutinized Clinton's liberal nominees, hoping to find information about them that would sabotage their appointments.

These fierce struggles over judicial appointments indicate the growing intensity of partisan struggle in the United States today. They also indicate how much importance competing political forces attach to Supreme Court appointments.

THE SOLICITOR GENERAL AND LAW CLERKS ALSO CONTROL THE FLOW OF CASES

In addition to the judges themselves, two other entities play an important role in shaping the flow of cases through the federal courts: the solicitor general and federal law clerks.

The Solicitor General If any single person has greater influence than individual judges over the federal courts, it is the **solicitor general** of the United States. The solicitor general is the third-ranking official in the Justice Department (below the attorney general and the deputy attorney general) but is the top government lawyer in virtually all cases before the Supreme Court in which the government is

solicitor general the top government lawyer in all cases before the Supreme Court in which the government is a party a party. The solicitor general has the greatest control over the flow of cases by screening them before any agency of the federal government can appeal them to the Supreme Court; indeed, the justices rely on the solicitor general to "screen out undeserving litigation and furnish them with an agenda to government cases that deserve serious consideration."[4] Typically, more requests for appeals are rejected than are accepted by the solicitor general. Agency heads may lobby the president or otherwise try to circumvent the solicitor general, and a few of the independent agencies have a legal right to make direct appeals, but these are almost inevitably doomed to *per curiam* rejection—rejection through a brief, unsigned opinion by the whole Court—if the solicitor general refuses to participate. Congress has given only a few agencies, including the Federal Communications Commission, the Federal Maritime Commission, and in some cases the Department of Agriculture (even though it is not an independent agency), the right to appeal directly to the Supreme Court without going through the solicitor general.

The solicitor general can enter a case even when the federal government is not a direct litigant by writing an *amicus curiae* ("friend of the court") brief. A "friend of the court" is not a direct party to a case but has a vital interest in its outcome. Thus, when the government has such an interest, the solicitor general can file as *amicus curiae,* or a federal court can invite such a brief because it wants an opinion in writing. The solicitor general also has the power to invite others to enter cases as *amici curiae.*

In addition to exercising substantial control over the flow of cases, the solicitor general can shape the arguments used before the federal courts. Indeed, the Supreme Court tends to give special attention to the way the solicitor general characterizes the issues.

Law Clerks Every federal judge employs law clerks to research legal issues and assist with the preparation of opinions. Each Supreme Court justice is assigned four clerks. The clerks are almost always honors graduates of the nation's most prestigious law schools. A clerkship with a Supreme Court justice is a great honor and generally indicates that the fortunate individual is likely to reach the very top of the legal profession. The work of the Supreme Court clerks is a closely guarded secret, but some justices rely heavily on their clerks for advice in writing opinions and in deciding whether an individual case ought to be heard by the Court. In a recent book, a former law clerk to retired justice Harry Blackmun charged that Supreme Court justices yielded "excessive power to immature, ideologically driven clerks, who in turn use that power to manipulate their bosses."[5]

The Power of the Supreme Court Is Judicial Review

One of the most important powers of the Supreme Court is the power of **judicial review**—the authority and the obligation to review any lower court decision where a substantial issue of public law is involved. The disputes can be over the constitutionality of federal or state laws, over the propriety or constitutionality of

per curiam decision by an appellate court, without a written opinion, that refuses to review the decision of a lower court; amounts to reaffirmation of the lower court's opinion

amicus curiae literally, "friend of the court"; individuals or groups who are not parties to a lawsuit but who seek to assist the Supreme Court in reaching a decision by presenting additional briefs

judicial review the power of the courts to declare actions of the legislative and executive branches invalid or unconstitutional. The Supreme Court asserted this power in *Marbury v. Madison*

PICTURING

How Judges Are Appointed

Once a president formally nominates a candidate to the Supreme Court, the nominee must be considered by the Senate Judiciary Committee and then confirmed by a majority vote in the Senate. Seen here in a photo from June 1986, from left to right, are nominee Antonin Scalia, former president Reagan, newly promoted chief justice William Rehnquist, and retiring chief Warren Burger.

Appointing a Supreme Court justice often involves much scrutiny of the nominee's personal, educational, and occupational background, as happened with the nomination of Clarence Thomas in 1991, during which Anita Hill alleged that Thomas had sexually harassed her earlier in their careers. It is not uncommon for a nominee's college papers or family history to be used as evidence against an appointment.

POLITICS

Recent struggles over judicial appointments indicate the growing intensity of partisan politics in the United States today. In 2001 President George W. Bush saw eight of his first eleven candidates for federal judgeships face opposition from the narrow Democratic majority in the Senate. While Bush has had 201 nominees approved to the federal bench, several prominent judges that he nominated were not approved.

Because the Supreme Court wields so much influence over American law and politics and because justices' terms last far beyond those of the presidents who appoint them, virtually all presidents have tried to select justices who share their political philosophies. Following the 2005 retirement announcement of Sandra Day O'Connor, President George W. Bush nominated as her replacement U.S. Court of Appeals judge John Roberts, pictured here with Senator Patrick Leahy of Vermont, the ranking Democrat on the Senate Judiciary Committee. Roberts went on to be approved and, William Rehnquist having died, was named Chief Justice in September '05. Bush's strong conservative ideology has made many Democrats wary of whomever he nominates to the Court.

the court procedures followed, or over whether public officers are exceeding their authority. The Supreme Court's power of judicial review has come to mean review not only of lower court decisions but also of state legislation and acts of Congress. For this reason, the Supreme Court's decisions may alter the law of the land.

The Supreme Court's power of judicial review over lower court decisions has never been at issue. Nor has there been any serious quibble over the power of the federal courts to review administrative agencies in order to determine whether their actions and decisions are within the powers delegated to them by Congress. There has, however, been a great deal of controversy occasioned by the Supreme Court's efforts to review acts of Congress and the decisions of state courts and legislatures.

JUDICIAL REVIEW COVERS ACTS OF CONGRESS

The Constitution does not expressly grant the Supreme Court the power of judicial review over congressional or other enactments, so some people have argued that the court's later exercise of judicial review was improper. However, the Constitution's framers did discuss the matter, and according to historian Max Farrand, "it was generally assumed by the leading men in the convention that this power [judicial review] existed."[6] This question aside, the matter of judicial review was settled when the Supreme Court asserted the right in the 1803 case of *Marbury v. Madison.* Even then, the court's assertion of the power was generally accepted, even by people who were not happy with the decision itself.[7] Since then, the president and Congress have often found reasons to criticize the court, but the idea of judicial review has never been seriously challenged. Still, the Supreme Court has been careful in using this power; since 1789, it has struck down only about 160 laws passed by Congress.

JUDICIAL REVIEW ALSO APPLIES TO STATE ACTIONS

supremacy clause Article VI of the Constitution, which states that laws passed by the national government and all treaties are the supreme law of the land and superior to all laws adopted by any state or any subdivision

The logic of the **supremacy clause** of Article VI of the Constitution, which declares the Constitution and laws made under its authority to be the supreme law of the land, implies that the Court may review the constitutionality of state laws. Furthermore, in the Judiciary Act of 1789, Congress conferred on the Supreme Court the power to reverse state constitutions and laws whenever they are clearly in conflict with the U.S. Constitution, federal laws, or treaties.[8] This power gives the Supreme Court appellate jurisdiction over all of the millions of cases handled by American courts each year.

The supremacy clause of the Constitution not only established the federal Constitution, statutes, and treaties as the "supreme Law of the Land," but also provided that "the Judges in every State shall be bound thereby, any Thing in the Constitution or Laws of any State to the Contrary notwithstanding." Under this authority, the Supreme Court has frequently overturned state constitutional provisions or statutes and state court decisions it deems contrary to the federal Constitution or federal statutes.

The civil rights area abounds with examples of state laws that were overturned because the statutes violated guarantees of due process and equal protection contained in the Fourteenth Amendment to the Constitution. For example, in the 1954 case of *Brown v. Board of Education,* the Court overturned statutes from Kansas, South Carolina, Virginia, and Delaware that either required or permitted segregated public schools, on the basis that such statutes denied black schoolchildren equal protection of the law. In 1967, in *Loving v. Virginia,* the Court invalidated a Virginia statute prohibiting interracial marriages.[9]

State statutes in other subject matter areas are equally subject to challenge. In *Griswold v. Connecticut* (1965), the Court invalidated a Connecticut statute prohibiting the general distribution of contraceptives to married couples on the basis that the statute violated the couples' rights to marital privacy.[10]

Sometimes, court decisions are so broad and sweeping that they have the effect of changing the law, and legal practices, across the country. In the 1973 Supreme Court case of *Roe v. Wade,* for example, the Court ruled that a safe, legal abortion was a constitutionally protected right for women under most circumstances. This decision had the effect of striking down restrictive abortion laws in over forty states.

The 1963 case *Gideon v. Wainwright* extends the point. When the Supreme Court ordered a new trial for Clarence Earl Gideon because he had been denied the right to legal counsel,[11] it said to all trial judges and prosecutors that henceforth they would be wasting their time if they cut corners in trials of indigent defendants. It also invited thousands of prisoners to appeal their convictions. (See chapter 4 for a further discussion of this case.)

In redressing wrongs, the courts sometimes call for a radical change in legal principle. Changes in race relations, for example, would probably have taken a great deal longer if the Supreme Court had not rendered the 1954 decision *Brown v. Board of Education* that redefined the rights of African Americans, striking down "separate but equal."

Similarly, the Supreme Court interpreted the doctrine of the separation of church and state so as to alter significantly the practice of religion in public institutions. For example, in a 1962 case, *Engel v. Vitale,* the Court declared that a once widely observed ritual—the recitation of a prayer by students in a public school—was unconstitutional under the establishment clause of the First Amendment. Almost all the dramatic changes in the treatment of criminals and of persons accused of crimes have been made by the courts. The Supreme Court brought about a veritable revolution in the criminal process with three cases over less than five years: *Gideon v. Wainwright,* in 1963, was just discussed. *Escobedo v. Illinois,* in 1964, gave suspects the right to remain silent and the right to have counsel present during questioning. But the *Escobedo* decision left confusions that allowed differing decisions to be made by lower courts. In *Miranda v. Arizona,* in 1966, the Supreme Court cleared up these confusions by setting forth what is known as the **Miranda** rule: Arrested people have the right to remain silent, the right to be informed that anything they say can be held against them, and the right to counsel before and during police interrogation (see chapter 4).[12]

Miranda rule the requirement, articulated by the Supreme Court in *Miranda v. Arizona,* that persons under arrest must be informed prior to police interrogation of their rights to remain silent and to have the benefit of legal counsel

One of the most significant changes brought about by the Supreme Court was the revolution in legislative representation unleashed by the 1962 case of *Baker v. Carr*.[13] In this landmark case, the Supreme Court held that it could no longer avoid reviewing complaints about the apportionment of seats in state legislatures. Following that decision, the federal courts went on to force reapportionment of all state, county, and local legislatures in the country based on the principle of one person, one vote.

MOST CASES REACH THE SUPREME COURT BY APPEAL

Given the millions of disputes that arise every year, the job of the Supreme Court would be impossible if it were not able to control the flow of cases and its own caseload. Cases that come first to the Supreme Court are few in number. Original jurisdiction cases for the Supreme Court include (1) cases between the United States and one of the fifty states, (2) cases between two or more states, (3) cases involving foreign ambassadors or other ministers, and (4) cases brought by one state against citizens of another state or against a foreign country. The most important of these cases are disputes between states over land, water, or old debts. For example, New York and New Jersey have disagreed for years about who owns the small island on which the Statue of Liberty sits. This dispute was settled by the Supreme Court in 1999, when it ruled in favor of New Jersey's ownership. Generally, the Supreme Court deals with these cases by appointing a "special master," usually a retired judge, to actually hear the case and present a report. The Supreme Court then allows the states involved in the dispute to present arguments for or against the master's opinion.[14]

writ of *certiorari* a decision of at least four of the nine Supreme Court justices to review a decision of a lower court; from the Latin "to make more certain"

Writs Most cases reach the Supreme Court through the **writ of *certiorari*,** which is granted whenever four of the nine justices agree to review a case. The Supreme Court was once so inundated with appeals that in 1925 Congress enacted laws giving it some control over its caseload with the power to issue writs of *certiorari*. Rule 10 of the Supreme Court's own rules of procedure defines *certiorari* as "not a matter of right, but of sound judicial discretion . . . granted only where there are special and important reasons therefor." The reasons provided for in Rule 10 are:

1. Where a state has made a decision that conflicts with previous Supreme Court decisions;
2. Where a state court has come up with an entirely new federal question;
3. Where one court of appeals has rendered a decision in conflict with another;
4. Where there are other inconsistent rulings between two or more courts or states;
5. Where a single court of appeals has sanctioned too great a departure by a lower court from normal judicial proceedings [a reason rarely given].

The **writ of *habeas corpus*** is a fundamental safeguard of individual rights. Its historical purpose is to enable an accused person to challenge arbitrary detention and to force an open trial before a judge. But in 1867, Congress's distrust of southern courts led it to confer on federal courts the authority to issue writs of *habeas corpus* to prisoners already tried or being tried in state courts of proper jurisdiction where the constitutional rights of the prisoner were possibly being violated. This writ gives state prisoners a second channel toward Supreme Court review in case their direct appeal from the highest state court fails (see Figure 11.2). The writ of *habeas corpus* is discretionary; that is, the Court can decide which cases to review.

writ of *habeas corpus* a court order that the individual in custody be brought into court and shown the cause for detention. *Habeas corpus* is guaranteed by the Constitution and can be suspended only in cases of rebellion or invasion

How Cases Reach the Supreme Court

Figure 11.2

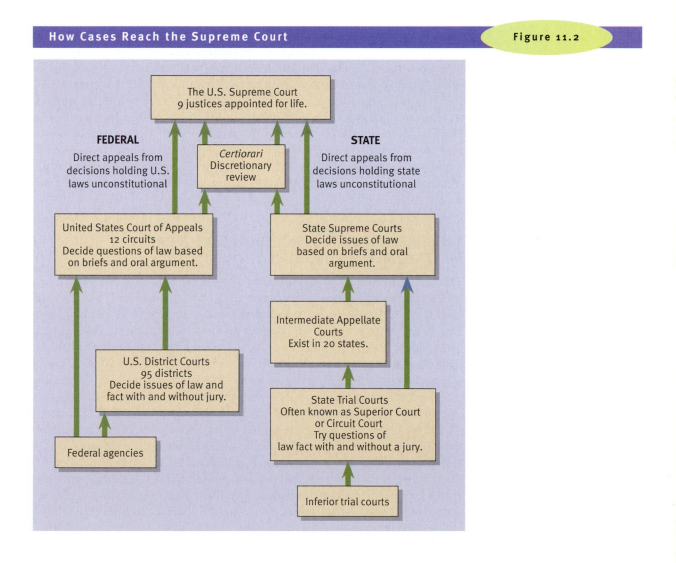

Lobbying for Access: Interests and the Court   At the same time that the Court exercises discretion over which cases it will review, groups and forces in society often seek to persuade the justices to listen to their problems. Interest groups use several different strategies to get the Court's attention. Lawyers representing these groups try to choose the proper client and the proper case, so that the issues in question are most dramatically and appropriately portrayed. They also have to pick the right district or jurisdiction in which to bring the case. Sometimes they even have to wait for an appropriate political climate.

Congress will sometimes provide interest groups with legislation designed to facilitate their use of litigation. One important recent example is the 1990 Americans with Disabilities Act (ADA), enacted after intense lobbying by public interest and advocacy groups. The ADA, in conjunction with the 1991 Civil Rights Act, opened the way for disabled individuals to make effective use of the courts to press their interests.

The two most notable users of the pattern of cases strategy in recent years have been the National Association for the Advancement of Colored People (NAACP) and the American Civil Liberties Union (ACLU). For many years, the NAACP (and its Defense Fund—now a separate group) has worked through local chapters and with many individuals to encourage litigation on issues of racial discrimination and segregation. Sometimes it distributes petitions to be signed by parents and filed with local school boards and courts, deliberately sowing the seeds of future litigation. The NAACP and the ACLU often encourage private parties to bring suit and then join the suit as *amici curiae*.

THE SUPREME COURT'S PROCEDURES MEAN CASES MAY TAKE MONTHS OR YEARS

The Supreme Court's decision to accept a case is the beginning of what can be a lengthy and complex process (see Figure 11.3). First, the attorneys on both sides must prepare **briefs**—written documents that may be several hundred pages long in which the attorneys explain why the Court should rule in favor of their client. Briefs are filled with referrals to precedents specifically chosen to show that other courts have frequently ruled in the same way that the Supreme Court is being asked to rule. The attorneys for both sides muster the most compelling precedents they can in support of their arguments.

As the attorneys prepare their briefs, they often ask sympathetic interest groups for their help. Groups are asked to file *amicus curiae* briefs that support the claims of one or the other litigant. In a case involving separation of church and state, for example, liberal groups such as the ACLU and Citizens for the American Way are likely to be asked to file *amicus* briefs in support of strict separation, whereas conservative religious groups are likely to file *amicus* briefs advocating increased public support for religious ideas. Often, dozens of briefs will be filed on each side of a major case. *Amicus* filings are a primary method used by interest groups to lobby the Court. By filing these briefs, groups indicate

briefs written documents in which attorneys explain, using case precedents, why the court should find in favor of their client

The Supreme Court's Decision-Making Process

Figure 11.3

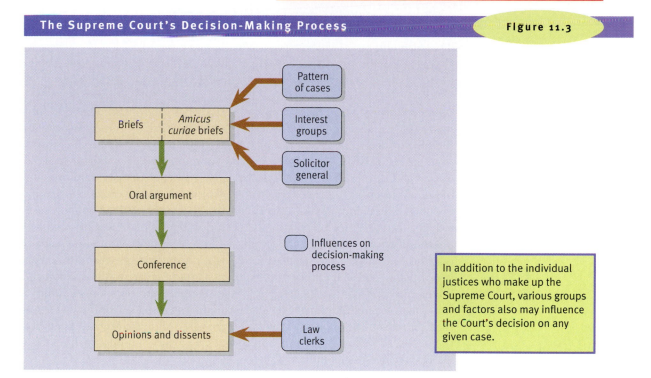

In addition to the individual justices who make up the Supreme Court, various groups and factors also may influence the Court's decision on any given case.

to the Court where their group stands and signal to the justices that they believe the case to be an important one.

The next stage of a case is **oral argument,** in which attorneys for both sides appear before the Court to present their positions and answer the justices' questions. Each attorney has only a half hour to present his or her case, and this time includes interruptions for questions. Certain members of the Court, such as Justice Antonin Scalia, are known to interrupt attorneys dozens of times. Others, such as Justice Clarence Thomas, seldom ask questions. For an attorney, the opportunity to argue a case before the Supreme Court is a singular honor and a mark of professional distinction. It can also be a harrowing experience, as justices interrupt a carefully prepared presentation to ask pointed questions. Oral argument can be very important to the outcome of a case. It allows justices to better understand the heart of the case and to raise questions that might not have been addressed in the opposing side's briefs. It is not uncommon for justices to go beyond the strictly legal issues and ask opposing counsel to discuss the implications of the case for the Court and the nation at large.

Following oral argument, the Court discusses the case in its Wednesday or Friday conference. The chief justice presides over the conference and speaks first; the other justices follow in order of seniority. The Court's conference is

oral argument stage in Supreme Court procedure in which attorneys for both sides appear before the Court to present their positions and answer questions posed by justices

secret, and no outsiders are permitted to attend. The justices discuss the case and eventually reach a decision on the basis of a majority vote. If the Court is divided, a number of votes may be taken before a final decision is reached. As the case is discussed, justices may try to influence or change one another's opinions. At times, this may result in compromise decisions.

opinion the written explanation of the Supreme Court's decision in a particular case

Opinion Writing   After a decision has been reached, one of the members of the majority is assigned to write the majority **opinion.** This assignment is made by the chief justice, or by the most senior justice in the majority if the chief justice is on the losing side. The assignment of the opinion can make a significant difference to the interpretation of a decision, because the majority opinion states the court's legal conclusion or result, and whoever writes this opinion is shaping the law. Lawyers and judges in the lower courts will examine the opinion carefully to ascertain the Supreme Court's meaning. Differences in wording and emphasis can have important implications for future litigation. Once the majority opinion is drafted, it is circulated to the other justices. Some members of the majority may decide that they cannot accept all the language of the opinion and therefore write "concurring" opinions that support the decision but offer a somewhat different rationale or emphasis. In assigning an opinion, serious thought must be given to the impression the case will make on lawyers and on the public, as well as to the probability that one justice's opinion will be more widely accepted than another's.

One of the more dramatic instances of this tactical consideration occurred in 1944, when Chief Justice Harlan F. Stone chose Justice Felix Frankfurter to write the opinion in the "white primary" case *Smith v. Allwright.* The chief justice believed that this sensitive case, which overturned the southern practice of prohibiting black participation in nominating primaries, required the efforts of the most brilliant and scholarly jurist on the Court. But the day after Stone made the assignment, Justice Robert H. Jackson wrote a letter to Stone urging a change of assignment. In his letter, Jackson argued that Frankfurter, a foreign-born Jew from New England, would not win the South with his opinion, regardless of its brilliance. Stone accepted the advice and substituted Justice Stanley Reed, an American-born Protestant from Kentucky and a southern Democrat in good standing.[15]

dissenting opinion a decision written by a justice in the minority in a particular case in which the justice wishes to express his or her reasoning in the case

Dissent   Justices who disagree with the majority decision of the Court may choose to publicize their disagreement in the form of a **dissenting opinion.** Dissents can be used to express opposition to an outcome or to signal to defeated political forces in the nation that their position is supported by at least some members of the Court. Because there is no need to please a majority, dissenting opinions can be more eloquent and less guarded than majority opinions. Some of the greatest writing in the history of the Court is found in dissents, and some of the most famous justices, such as Oliver Wendell Holmes, Louis D. Brandeis, and William O. Douglas, were notable dissenters. In the single 1952–53 Court term, Douglas wrote thirty-five dissenting opinions. In the

1958–59 term, he wrote eleven dissents. During the latter term, justices Frankfurter and Harlan wrote thirteen and nine dissents, respectively.

Dissent plays a special role in the work and impact of the Court because it amounts to an appeal to lawyers all over the country to keep bringing cases of the sort at issue. Therefore, an effective dissent influences the flow of cases through the Court as well as the arguments that will be used by lawyers in later cases. Even more important, dissent emphasizes the fact that, although the Court speaks with a single opinion, it is the opinion only of the majority—and one day the majority might go the other way.

SUPREME COURT DECISIONS ARE INFLUENCED BY ACTIVISM AND IDEOLOGY

The Supreme Court explains its decisions in terms of law and precedent. But although law and precedent do have an effect on the Court's deliberations and eventual decisions, it is the Supreme Court that decides what laws actually mean and what importance precedent will actually have. Throughout its history, the Court has shaped and reshaped the law. In the late nineteenth and early twentieth centuries, for example, the Supreme Court held that the Constitution, law, and precedent permitted racial segregation in the United States. Beginning in the late 1950s, however, the Court found that the Constitution prohibited segregation on the basis of race and indicated that the use of racial categories in legislation was always suspect. By the 1970s and 1980s, the Court once again held that the Constitution permitted the use of racial categories—when such categories were needed to help members of minority groups achieve full participation in American society. In the 1990s, the Court began to retreat from this position, too, indicating that governmental efforts to provide extra help to racial minorities could represent an unconstitutional infringement on the rights of the majority.

Although it is not the only relevant factor, the prime explanation for these movements is shifts in judicial philosophy. These shifts, in turn, result from changes in the Court's composition as justices retire and are replaced by new justices who, as we saw earlier, tend to share the philosophical outlook of the president who appointed them.

Activism and Restraint   One element of judicial philosophy is the issue of activism versus restraint. Over the years, some justices have believed that courts should narrowly interpret the Constitution according to the stated intentions of its framers and defer to the views of Congress when interpreting federal statutes. Justice Frankfurter, for example, advocated judicial deference to legislative bodies and avoidance of the "political thicket," in which the Court would entangle itself by deciding questions that were essentially political rather than legal in character. Advocates of **judicial restraint** are sometimes called "strict constructionists," because they look strictly to the words of the Constitution in interpreting its meaning.

judicial restraint judicial philosophy whose adherents refuse to go beyond the clear words of the Constitution in interpreting its meaning

PICTURING

The Supreme Court in Action

On September 17, 1998, a gay couple, John Lawrence (left) and Tyron Garner, were arrested and charged with violating Texas's anti-sodomy law. They took their case to the Texas Court of Criminal Appeals, where their request to have the case reviewed, based on Fourteenth Amendment equal protection grounds, was denied and the constitutionality of the law was upheld.

Almost four years after the arrest, the case was granted a hearing before the U.S. Supreme Court. Pictured here outside the Court are Ruth Harlow (left) and Kevin Cathcart of Lambda Legal, the firm that represented Lawrence and Garner. Harlow was the lead attorney on the case.

Amicus curiae briefs were filed in support of either side. Focus on the Family (left), a conservative Christian group based in Colorado, was among the groups that filed *amicus* briefs in support of the Texas law, citing the decay of the sanctity of marriage. The American Civil Liberties Union, led by Executive Director Anthony Romero, filed an *amicus* brief in support of the plaintiffs, challenging the constitutionality of the law.

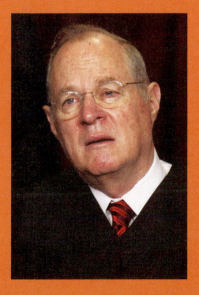

In what was seen as a historic step forward for gay rights, the Supreme Court voted 6–3 in favor of striking down the Texas law. Justice Anthony Kennedy wrote the majority opinion.

The Court's landmark decision against sodomy laws inspired gay rights advocates across the nation, and especially in Texas (above), where the case originated, to hit the streets in celebration.

judicial activism judicial philosophy that posits that the court should go beyond the words of the Constitution or a statute to consider the broader societal implications of its decisions

The alternative to restraint is **judicial activism.** Activist judges such as the former chief justice Earl Warren believed that the Court should go beyond the words of the Constitution or a statute to consider the broader societal implications of its decisions. Activist judges sometimes strike out in new directions, promulgating new interpretations or inventing new legal and constitutional concepts when they believe these to be socially desirable. For example, Justice Harry Blackmun's decision in *Roe v. Wade* was based on a constitutional right to privacy that is not found in the words of the Constitution. Blackmun and the other members of the majority in the *Roe* case argued that the right to privacy was implied by other constitutional provisions. The idea of privacy is in fact an old one, extending back to the nineteenth century (see chapter 4, on "Civil Liberties and Civil Rights"). However, its extension to abortion carved a new legal path, making it an example of judicial activism.

Activism and restraint are sometimes confused with liberalism and conservatism. For example, conservative politicians often castigate "liberal activist" judges and call for the appointment of conservative jurists who will refrain from reinterpreting the law. To be sure, some liberal jurists are activists and some conservatives have been advocates of restraint, but the relationship is by no means one to one. Indeed, the Rehnquist Court, dominated by conservatives, has been among the most activist courts in American history, striking out in new directions in such areas as federalism and election law.

Political Ideology   The second component of judicial philosophy is political ideology. The liberal or conservative outlooks of justices play an important role in their decisions. Indeed, the philosophy of activism versus restraint is, to a large extent, a smokescreen for political ideology. For the most part, liberal judges have been activists, willing to use the law to achieve social and political change, whereas conservatives have been associated with judicial restraint. Interestingly, however, in recent years some conservative justices who have long called for restraint have actually become activists in seeking to undo some of the work of liberal jurists over the past three decades.

From the 1950s to the 1980s, the Supreme Court took an activist role in such areas as civil rights, civil liberties, abortion, voting rights, and police procedures. For example, the Supreme Court was more responsible than any other governmental institution for breaking down America's system of racial segregation. The Supreme Court virtually prohibited states from interfering with the right of a woman to seek an abortion and sharply curtailed state restrictions on voting rights. And it was the Supreme Court that placed restrictions on the behavior of local police and prosecutors in criminal cases. In a series of decisions between 1989 and 2004, however, the conservative justices appointed by Reagan and George H. W. Bush were able to swing the Court to a more conservative position on civil rights, affirmative action, abortion rights, property rights, criminal procedure, voting rights, desegregation, and the power of the national government.

Unpredictability   Despite predictions about how active a new member of the Court is likely to be, or his or her ideological point of view, justices often behave differently on the Court than the presidents who nominate them expect. By one estimate, about a quarter of all justices appointed to the Court have behaved differently from what the presidents who appointed them predicted. Two of Republican president Dwight Eisenhower's appointees to the Court, William Brennan and Earl Warren, turned out to be far more liberal and activist than Eisenhower anticipated. (Eisenhower was once quoted as saying that these two appointees were the biggest mistakes of his presidency.) One of Democratic President John F. Kennedy's Court nominees, Byron White, proved to be a leading conservative on the court. Former Republican president George H. W. Bush's nominee David Souter has often sided with the liberal members of the Court.

All in all, presidents Reagan and Bush were relatively successful in pushing the federal courts, including the Supreme Court, in a more conservative direction, by virtue of appointing more conservative justices. Taking the twelve years of the Reagan and Bush presidencies together, the two appointed about two-thirds of all federal judges. The impact of these more conservative judges will be felt for years to come, especially when combined with President George W. Bush's conservative court appointees. However, an element of unpredictability remains in the appointment process, because it is difficult to know how a court nominee will actually vote in the wide range of cases that the courts consider, and because, protected by lifetime tenure, each justice is free to follow his or her conscience and interpret the law accordingly.

THE JUDICIARY WAS DESIGNED TO PROTECT LIBERTY

In the original conception of the framers, the judiciary was to be the institution that would protect individual liberty from the government. As we saw in chapter 2, the framers believed that in a democracy the great danger was what they termed "tyranny of the majority"—the possibility that a popular majority, "united or actuated by some common impulse or passion," would "trample on the rules of justice."[16] The framers hoped that the courts would protect liberty from the potential excesses of democracy. And for most of American history, this was precisely the role played by the federal courts. The courts' most important decisions were those that protected the freedoms—to speak, worship, publish, vote, and attend school—of groups and individuals whose political views, religious beliefs, or racial or ethnic backgrounds made them unpopular.

In recent years, however, the courts have been changing their role in the political process. Rather than serve simply as a bastion of individual liberty against the excessive power of the majority, the judiciary has tried to plan an active role in helping groups and forces in American society bring about social and political change in the fight for equality. In a sense, the judiciary has entered the political process and has begun to behave more like the democratic institutions whose sometimes misdirected impulses toward tyranny the courts were supposed to keep in check. Thus, the courts today play a more important role in linking citizens with their government, because more Americans than ever are affected by court rulings, and because more Americans than ever use the courts to defend and protect their rights and freedoms.

Summary

Millions of cases come to trial every year in the United States. The great majority —nearly 99 percent—are tried in state and local courts. The types of law are civil law, criminal law, and public law.

Three kinds of cases fall under federal jurisdiction: (1) civil cases involving citizens from different states, (2) civil cases where a federal agency is seeking to enforce federal laws that provide for civil penalties, and (3) cases involving federal criminal statutes or where state criminal cases have been made issues of public law. Judicial power extends only to cases and controversies. Litigants must have standing to sue, and courts neither hand down opinions on hypothetical issues nor take the initiative.

Federal judges are appointed by the president, subject to confirmation by the Senate. Presidents generally attempt to select judges whose political philosophy is similar to their own. Over time, presidents have been able to exert a great deal of influence over the federal courts through their appointments.

There is no explicit constitutional authority for the Supreme Court to review acts of Congress. Nonetheless, the 1803 case of *Marbury v. Madison* established the Court's right to review congressional acts. The supremacy clause of Article VI and the Judiciary Act of 1789 give the Court the power to review state constitutions and laws.

Both appellate and Supreme Court decisions, including the decision not to review a case, make law. Sometimes, the courts make rulings that have sweeping effects on society.

Once the Supreme Court has accepted a case, attorneys for both sides prepare briefs and seek *amicus curiae* briefs from sympathetic groups. Cases are presented to the Court in oral argument, are discussed by the justices during the Court's conference, and are decided by a majority vote of the justices. The Court's opinion is written by a member of the majority. Members of the minority may write dissenting opinions, while other members of the majority may write concurring opinions.

Writing the majority opinion for a case is an opportunity for a justice to influence the judiciary. But the need to frame an opinion in such a way as to develop majority support on the Court may limit such opportunities. Dissenting opinions can have an impact by stimulating a continued flow of cases around an issue. The solicitor general is the most important single influence outside the Court itself because he or she controls the flow of cases brought by the Justice Department and also shapes the argument in those cases. Social problems give rise to similar cases that ultimately must be adjudicated and appealed. Some interest groups try to develop such case patterns as a means of gaining power through the courts.

In recent years, the importance of the federal judiciary—the supreme Court in particular—has increased substantially as the courts have developed new tools of judicial power and forged alliances with important forces in American society.

For Further Reading

Abraham, Henry. *The Judicial Process.* 6th ed. New York: Oxford University Press, 1993.

Fisher, Louis. *Constitutional Dialogues.* Princeton: Princeton University Press, 1988.

Johnson, Timothy R. *Oral Arguments and Decision Making on the U.S. Supreme Court.* Albany, NY: SUNY Press, 2004.

Kahn, Ronald. *The Supreme Court and Constitutional Theory, 1953–1993.* Lawrence, KS: University Press of Kansas, 1994.

McCann, Michael W. *Rights at Work.* Chicago: University of Chicago Press, 1994.

O'Brien, David M. *Storm Center: The Supreme Court in American Politics.* 5th ed. New York: Norton, 2000.

Rosenberg, Gerald. *The Hollow Hope: Can Courts Bring about Social Change?* Chicago: University of Chicago Press, 1991.

Silverstein, Mark. *Judicious Choices: The New Politics of Supreme Court Confirmations.* New York: Norton, 1994.

Spitzer, Robert J., ed. *Politics and Constitutionalism.* Albany, NY: SUNY Press, 2000.

Ward, Artemus. *Deciding to Leave: The Politics of Retirement from the U.S. Supreme Court.* Albany, NY: SUNY Press, 2003.

Study Outline

The Legal System Settles Disputes

1. Court cases in the United States proceed under three categories of law: criminal, civil, and public.
2. In the area of criminal law, either a state government or the federal government is the plaintiff who alleges that someone has committed a crime.
3. Civil cases are those between individuals or between individuals and the government in which no criminal violation is charged. In deciding these cases, courts apply statutes and legal precedent.
4. Public law involves questions of whether the government has the constitutional or statutory authority to take action.
5. By far, most cases are heard by state courts.

6. Cases are heard in federal courts if the U.S. government is a party in the case or the case involves federal statutes, treaties with other nations, or the U.S. Constitution.
7. Although the federal courts hear only a fraction of all the cases decided every year in the United States, federal court decisions are extremely important.

The Federal Courts Hear a Small Percentage of All Cases

1. The eighty-nine federal district courts are trial courts of original jurisdiction and their cases are, in form, indistinguishable from cases in the state trial courts.
2. The thirteen U.S. courts of appeals review and render decisions in approximately 10 percent of all lower-court and agency cases.
3. Federal judges are appointed by the president and confirmed by a majority vote of the full Senate.
4. The Supreme Court is the highest court in the country and has the power and the obligation to review any lower court decision involving a substantial issue of public law, state legislation, or act of Congress.
5. The Constitution does not specify the number of justices that should sit on the Supreme Court, although since 1869 there have been nine—one chief justice and eight associate justices.
6. The solicitor general can influence the Supreme Court by screening cases before they reach the Court, submitting *amicus* briefs, and shaping the arguments used before the Court.

The Power of the Supreme Court Is Judicial Review

1. The Supreme Court's power to review acts of Congress, although accepted as natural and rarely challenged, is not specifically granted by the Constitution.
2. The Supreme Court's power to review state action or legislation derives from the Constitution's supremacy clause, although it is neither granted specifically by the Constitution nor inherent in the federal system.

3. Appeals of lower court decisions can reach the Supreme Court in one of two ways: through a writ of *certiorari,* or, in the case of convicted stage prisoners, through a writ of *habeas corpus.*

4. Groups and forces in society attempt to influence justices' rulings on particular issues.

5. After filing written arguments, or briefs, attorneys present oral argument to the Supreme Court. After oral argument, the justices discuss the case and vote on a final decision.

6. The Supreme Court always explains its decisions in terms of law and precedent.

7. Despite the rule of precedent, the Court often reshapes law. Such changes in the interpretation of law can be explained, in part, by changes in the judicial philosophy of activism versus restraint and by changes in political ideology.

Practice Quiz

1. Which of the following is a brief submitted to the Supreme Court by someone other than one of the parties in the case?
   a) *amicus curiae*
   b) *habeas corpus*
   c) solicitor general
   d) *ex post* brief

2. By what term is the practice of the courts to uphold precedent known?
   a) *certiorari*
   b) *stare decisis*
   c) rule of four
   d) senatorial courtesy

3. Which government official is responsible for arguing the federal government's position in cases before the Supreme Court?
   a) the vice president
   b) the attorney general
   c) the U.S. district attorney
   d) the solicitor general

4. What is the name for the body of law that involves disputes between private parties?
   a) civil law
   b) privacy law
   c) household law
   d) common law

5. Under what authority is the number of Supreme Court justices decided?
   a) the president
   b) the chief justice
   c) Congress
   d) the Constitution

6. Which of the following does not influence the flow of cases heard by the Supreme Court?
   a) the Supreme Court itself
   b) the solicitor general
   c) the attorney general
   d) the FBI

7. Which of the following cases involved the "right to privacy"?
   a) *Griswold v. Connecticut*
   b) *Brown v. Board of Education*
   c) *Schneckloth v. Bustamante*
   d) *Marbury v. Madison*

8. Which of the following Supreme Court cases from the 1960s involved the rights of criminal suspects?
   a) *Gideon v. Wainwright*
   b) *Miranda v. Arizona*
   c) *Escobedo v. Illinois*
   d) all of the above

9. Where do most trials in America take place?
   a) state and local courts
   b) appellate courts
   c) federal courts
   d) the Supreme Court

Critical Thinking Questions

1. Judicial philosophies of activism and restraint are often confused with the political ideologies of liberalism and conservatism in the courts. What do you think the roots of this confusion are? To what extent is the common understanding correct? To what extent is it incorrect? Are there ways in which conservatives have been or could be activists in the courts? Are there ways in which liberals have exercised or could exercise judicial restraint?

2. In many ways, courts are expected to be apolitical institutions of government. In what ways are courts, judges, and justices shielded from politics and political pressure? In what ways are they vulnerable to political pressure? Are the courts an appropriate place for politics? What is the danger of having too much or too little political accountability in judicial decision making?

Key Terms

amicus curiae (p. 321)
appellate court (p. 315)
briefs (p. 328)
chief justice (p. 318)
civil law (p. 313)
criminal law (p. 313)
defendant (p. 313)
dissenting opinion (p. 330)
due process of law (p. 316)

judicial activism (p. 334)
judicial restraint (p. 331)
judicial review (p. 321)
jurisdiction (p. 316)
Miranda rule (p. 325)
opinion (p. 330)
oral argument (p. 329)
original jurisdiction (p. 317)
per curiam (p. 321)
plaintiff (p. 313)
plea bargains (p. 315)

precedent (p. 314)
public law (p. 314)
senatorial courtesy (p. 319)
solicitor general (p. 320)
stare decisis (p. 314)
supremacy clause (p. 324)
supreme court (p. 315)
trial court (p. 315)
Uniform Commercial Code (p. 316)
writ of *certiorari* (p. 326)
writ of *habeas corpus* (p. 327)

12 DOMESTIC POLICY

MAIN MESSAGE

Public policy is based on the use of coercion by the government.

M ost of this book has focused on how government gets things done. This chapter, and the next, will focus on what the government produces, called **public policy**. Public policy can be defined simply as a purpose or goal expressed by the government that is backed by a sanction (a reward or punishment). Public policy can be a law, a rule, a regulation, or an order. It can include a law passed by Congress, a presidential directive, a Supreme Court ruling, or a rule issued by a bureaucratic agency.

In trying to achieve some purpose, public policy is inherently coercive, even when motivated by the best and most benign intentions. Note that the word "policy" shares a common origin with the word "police." Both terms come from the Greek words *polis* and *politeia,* which refer to the political community and the sources of public authority. Thus, the coercion that is the basis of public policy is necessary in order for the policy to be carried out, regardless of

Key Concepts

1. **Public policy is made through the use of various techniques of control exercised by the government, including promotional techniques, regulation, and redistribution.**

2. **The modern welfare state, dating from the 1930s, supports the idea of equality.**

3. **Government spending on social programs for the poor has declined in recent years.**

4. **Most social policy spending goes to the middle class.**

5. **Government policies, including education, employment, housing, and health, can break the cycle of poverty.**

public policy a law, rule, statute, or edict that expresses the government's goals and provides for rewards and punishments to promote their attainment whether one agrees or disagrees with the particular policy in question. So it is important to remember that, although the idea of coercion seems inherently negative, it is in fact a vital and necessary part of governing. (If overused or misused, coercion can obviously be harmful.)

To illustrate, let us take the example of abortion. Suppose, for the sake of argument, that the government wishes to enact a policy to prevent women from obtaining legal abortions. There are at least three different policy techniques that the government could use to achieve this end. The first and most obvious way this could be done would be by enacting a "regulation" making it a crime for women to obtain abortions. (This was the situation in most states before abortions were legalized by the Supreme Court ruling of *Roe v. Wade* in 1973.) Those violating such a law would face fines and time in prison if found guilty.

A different way the government might decide to discourage abortions is by paying pregnant women money to continue a pregnancy through to the birth of the child. A woman who obtained an abortion under these circumstances would not be breaking the law, but she would be missing out on the opportunity to receive money from the government. Even though the payment of money is less harsh than a criminal law, it is nevertheless a way the government might get more women to avoid abortions. This is referred to as a "promotional" policy technique.

A third technique would be to focus on a particular class or category of people. In this case, the government might provide a tax break for women whose annual income falls below a certain level if they choose not to get an abortion. This technique is an example of a "redistributive" policy. All three types of policy approaches—regulatory, promotional, and redistributive—will be discussed in this chapter. All three also represent different ways in which the government might try to accomplish a policy goal. Obviously, one might disagree with the policy goal itself, as most Americans today believe that abortions should continue to remain legal under most circumstances. Yet people might object less to a cash payment than to a harsh criminal regulation.

In this chapter, we will examine the different approaches to achieving policy goals. We will then examine one broad area of domestic public policy, called social policy. We focus on social policy because much of the government's annual budget goes to social programs, because such spending is often controversial, and because it illustrates the different ways in which the government tries to accomplish its goals.

The Tools for Making Policy Are Techniques of Control

Techniques of control are to policy makers what tools are to a carpenter. There is a limited number of techniques that the government can use, each with its own logic and limitations. An accumulation of experience helps us to understand when a certain technique is likely to work. There is no unanimous agreement on techniques, just as carpenters will disagree about the best tool for a task. But we offer here a workable elementary handbook of techniques that will be useful for analyzing policy.

Table 12.1 lists some important techniques of control available to policy makers. These techniques can be grouped into three categories: promotional, regulatory, and redistributive techniques.

Techniques of Public Control		Table 12.1

TYPE OF TECHNIQUE	TECHNIQUES	DEFINITIONS AND EXAMPLES
Promotional	Subsidies and grants of cash, land, etc.	"Patronage" is the promotion of private activity through what recipients consider "benefits" (example: in the nineteenth century the government encouraged westward settlement by granting land to those who went west)
	Contracts	Agreements with individuals or firms in the "private sector" to purchase goods or services
	Licenses	Unconditional permission to do something that is otherwise illegal (franchise, permit)
Regulatory	Criminal penalties	Heavy fines or imprisonment, loss of citizenship
	Civil penalties	Less onerous fines, probation, public exposure, restitution
	Administrative regulations	Setting interest rates, maintaining standards of health and safety, investigating and publicizing wrongdoing
	Subsidies and contracts	Can be considered regulatory when certain conditions are attached (example: the government refuses to award a contract to firms that show no evidence of affirmative action in hiring)
	Regulatory taxes	Taxes that keep consumption or production down (liquor, gas, cigarette taxes)
	Expropriation	"Eminent domain"—the power to take private property for public use
Redistributive	Taxes	Altering the redistribution of money by changing taxes or tax rules
	Budgeting and spending through subsidies and contracts	Deficit spending to pump money into the economy when it needs a boost; creating a budget surplus by cutting spending or increasing taxes to discourage consumption in inflationary times
	Fiscal use of credit and interest (monetary techniques)	Changing interest rates to affect both demand or money and consumption (example: the Federal Reserve Board raises interest rates to slow economic growth and ward off inflation)

PROMOTIONAL TECHNIQUES GET PEOPLE TO DO THINGS BY GIVING THEM REWARDS

Promotional techniques are the carrots of public policy. Their purpose is to encourage people to do something they might not otherwise do or to get people to do more of what they are already doing. Sometimes the purpose is merely to compensate people for something done in the past. Promotional techniques can be classified into at least two separate types: subsidies and contracts.

subsidies government grants of cash or other valuable commodities such as land to individuals or organizations; used to promote activities desired by the government, to reward political support, or to buy off political opposition

Subsidies Subsidies are simply government grants of cash or other valuable commodities, such as land. Subsidies were the dominant form of public policy of the national government and the state and local governments throughout the nineteenth century. They continue to be an important category of public policy at all levels of government.

During the nineteenth century, subsidies in the form of land grants were given to farmers and to railroad companies to encourage western settlement. Substantial cash subsidies have traditionally been given to shipbuilders to help build the commercial fleet and to guarantee the use of their ships as military personnel carriers in time of war. Policies using the subsidy technique have continued to be plentiful in the twentieth century, even during the 1990s when there was widespread public and official hostility toward subsidies. For example, through 1994, the total annual value of subsidies to industry alone was estimated at $53 billion, based on relatively conservative Congressional Budget Office (CBO) figures.[1] Crop subsidies alone, implemented by the Department of Agriculture, amounted to about $9 billion in 2002.

Subsidies have always been a technique favored by politicians because subsidies can be treated as "benefits" that can be spread widely in response to many demands that might otherwise produce profound political conflict. Subsidies can, in other words, be used to buy off the opposition. And once subsidies exist, the threat of their removal becomes a very significant technique of control.

contracting power the power of government to set conditions on companies seeking to sell goods or services to government agencies

Contracting Like any corporation, a government agency must purchase goods and services by contract. The law requires open bidding for a substantial proportion of these contracts because government contracts are extremely valuable to businesses in the private sector and because the opportunities and incentives for abuse are very great. But contracting is more than a method of buying goods and services. Contracting is also an important technique of policy because government agencies are often authorized to use their **contracting power** as a means of encouraging corporations to improve themselves, as a means of helping to build up whole sectors of the economy, and as a means of encouraging certain desirable goals or behavior, such as equal employment opportunity. For example, the infant airline industry of the 1930s was nurtured by the national government's lucrative contracts to carry airmail.

Government-by-contract has been around for a long time, and has always been seen by business as a major source of economic opportunity. In the Pentagon alone, nearly $94 billion was spent in 1994 on contracts with the twenty top defense companies in the United States and abroad. The top company, in terms of the value of its defense contracts, was Lockheed Martin, whose revenues from those defense contracts amounted to $14.4 billion. This represented nearly 63 percent of Lockheed Martin's total annual revenues. McDonnell Douglas came in second with slightly over $9 billion. Revenues from defense contracts represented nearly 64 percent of these companies' total annual revenues.[2]

REGULATORY TECHNIQUES ARE RULES BACKED BY PENALTIES

If promotional techniques are the carrots of public policy, regulatory techniques can be considered the sticks. **Regulation** comes in several forms, but every regulatory technique shares a common trait: direct government control of conduct. The conduct may be regulated because people feel it is harmful to others, or threatens to be, such as drunk driving or false advertising. Or the conduct may be regulated because people think it's immoral, whether it is harming anybody or not, such as prostitution, gambling, or drinking. Because there are many forms of regulation, we have subdivided them here: (1) police regulation, through civil and criminal penalties, (2) administrative regulation, and (3) regulatory taxation.

regulation a technique of control in which the government adopts rules imposing restrictions on the conduct of private citizens

Police Regulation "Police regulation" comes closest to the traditional exercise of **police power**—a power traditionally reserved to the states. After a person's arrest and conviction, these techniques are administered by courts and, where necessary, penal institutions. They are regulatory techniques.

Civil penalties usually refer to fines or some other form of material restitution (such as public service) as a sanction for violating civil laws or committing negligence. Civil penalties can range from a five-dollar fine for a parking violation to a more onerous penalty for late payment of income taxes to the much more onerous penalties for violating antitrust laws against unfair competition or environmental protection laws against pollution. **Criminal penalties** usually refer to imprisonment but can also involve heavy fines and the loss of certain civil rights and liberties, such as the right to vote.

police power power reserved to the government to regulate the health, safety, and morals of its citizens

civil penalties regulatory techniques in which fines or another form of material restitution is imposed for violating civil laws or common law principles, for example through negligence

criminal penalties regulatory techniques in which imprisonment or heavy fines and the loss of certain civil rights and liberties are imposed

Administrative Regulation Police regulation addresses conduct considered immoral. In order to eliminate such conduct, strict laws have been passed and severe sanctions enacted. But what about conduct that is not considered morally wrong but that may have harmful consequences? For example, there is nothing morally wrong with radio or television broadcasting. But government regulates broadcasting on a particular frequency or channel because there would be virtual chaos if everybody could broadcast on any frequency at any time.

This kind of conduct is thought of less as *policed* conduct and more as *regulated* conduct. When conduct is said to be regulated, the purpose is rarely to eliminate the conduct but rather to influence it toward more appropriate channels, toward more appropriate locations, or toward certain qualified types of persons,

administrative regulation rules made by regulatory agencies and commissions

all for the purpose of minimizing injuries or inconveniences. This type of regulation is sometimes called **administrative regulation** because the controls are given over to civilian agencies rather than to the police. Each regulatory agency has extensive powers to keep a sector of the economy under surveillance and also has powers to make rules dealing with the behavior of individual companies and people. But these administrative agencies have fewer powers of punishment than the police and the courts have, and the administrative agencies generally rely on the courts to issue orders enforcing the rules and decisions made by the agencies.

Table 12.1 listed subsidies and contracting as examples of both promotional and regulatory policies; although these techniques might normally be thought of as strictly promotional policies, they can also be used as techniques of administrative regulation. It all depends on whether the law sets serious conditions on eligibility for the subsidy or contract. To put it another way, the government can use the threat of losing a valuable subsidy or contract to improve compliance with the goals of regulation. For example, the threat of removal of the subsidies called "federal aid to education" has had a very significant influence on the willingness of schools to cooperate in the desegregation of their student bodies and faculties. For another example, social welfare subsidies (benefits) can be lowered to encourage or force people to take low-paying jobs, or they can be increased to placate people when they are engaging in political protest.[3]

regulatory tax a tax whose primary purpose is not to raise revenue but to influence conduct; for example, a heavy tax on gasoline to discourage recreational driving

Regulatory Taxation   In many instances, the primary purpose of a tax is not to raise revenue but to discourage or eliminate an activity altogether by making it too expensive for most people. Such taxes are called **regulatory taxes.** For example, since the end of Prohibition, although there has been no penalty for the production or sale of alcoholic beverages, the alcohol industry has not been free from regulation. First, all alcoholic beverages have to be licensed, allowing only those companies that are "bonded" to put their product on the market. Beyond that, federal and state taxes on alcohol are made disproportionately high, on the theory that, in addition to the revenue gained, less alcohol will be consumed. The same is true of cigarette taxes.

expropriation confiscation of property with or without compensation

Expropriation   Seizing private property for a public use, or **expropriation,** is a widely used technique of control in the United States, especially in land-use regulation. Almost all public works, from highways to parks to government office buildings, involve the forceful taking of some private property in order to assemble sufficient land and the correct distribution of land for the necessary construction. The vast Interstate Highway Program required expropriation of thousands of narrow strips of private land. Urban redevelopment projects often require city governments to use the powers of seizure in the service of private developers, who actually build the urban projects on the land that would be far too expensive if purchased on the open market. Private utilities that supply electricity and gas to individual subscribers are given powers to take private property whenever a new facility or a right-of-way is needed.

We generally call the power to expropriate **eminent domain,** a power that is recognized as inherent in any government. The Fifth Amendment of the U.S. Constitution surrounds this expropriation power with important safeguards against abuse, so that government agencies in the United States are not permitted to use that power except through a strict due process, and they must offer "fair market value" for the land sought.[4]

Forcing individuals to work for a public purpose is another form of expropriation. The draft of young men for the armed forces, court orders to strikers to return to work, and sentences for convicted felons to do community service are examples of the regular use of expropriation in the United States.

REDISTRIBUTIVE TECHNIQUES AFFECT BROAD CLASSES OF PEOPLE

Redistributive techniques (also called macroeconomic techniques) are usually of two types—fiscal and monetary—but they have a common purpose: to control people by manipulating the entire economy rather than by regulating people directly. (*Macroeconomic* refers to the economy as a whole.) Whereas regulatory techniques focus on individual conduct—"Walking on the grass is not permitted," or "Membership in a union may not be used to deny employment, nor may a worker be fired for promoting union membership"—redistributive techniques seek to control conduct more indirectly by altering the conditions of conduct or manipulating the environment of conduct.

Fiscal Techniques   Fiscal techniques of control are the government's taxing and spending powers. Personal and corporate income taxes, which raise most of the U.S. government's revenues, are the most prominent examples. While the direct purpose of an income tax is to raise revenue, each tax has a different impact on the economy, and government can plan for that impact. For example, although the main reason favoring a significant increase in the Social Security tax (which is an income tax) under President Jimmy Carter was to keep Social Security solvent, a big reason for it in the minds of many legislators was that it would reduce **inflation** by shrinking the amount of money people had in their hands to buy more goods and services.

Monetary Techniques   Government also seeks to influence conduct by manipulating the entire economy through the supply or availability of credit. The **Federal Reserve Board** (the Fed) can adopt what is called a "hard money policy" by increasing the interest rate it charges member banks (called the **discount rate**). In 1980, when inflation was at a historic high, the Fed permitted interest rates to reach a high of nearly 20 percent, in an attempt to rein in inflation. During the 1991 recession, however, the Fed permitted interest rates to drop well below 10 percent, hoping this would encourage people to borrow more to buy houses, and so on.

Spending Power as Fiscal Policy   Perhaps the most important redistributive technique of all is the most familiar one: the "spending power," which is a

eminent domain the right of government to take private property for public use

inflation a consistent increase in the general level of prices

Federal Reserve Board (Fed) the governing board of the Federal Reserve System, comprising a chair and six other members, all appointed by the president with the consent of the Senate

discount rate the interest rate charged by the Federal Reserve System when commercial banks borrow in order to expand their lending operations; an effective tool of monetary policy

combination of subsidies and contracts. Government can use these techniques to achieve policy goals far beyond buying goods and services and regulating individual conduct. This is why subsidies and contracting show up yet again in Table 12.1 as redistributive techniques.

Agricultural subsidies are one example of the national government's use of its purchasing power as a fiscal or redistributive technique. And since the 1930s, the federal government has attempted to raise and to stabilize the prices of several important agricultural products, such as corn and wheat, by authorizing the Department of Agriculture to buy enormous amounts of these commodities if prices on the market fall below a fixed level.

Social Policy and the Welfare System Buttress Equality

For much of American history, local governments and private charities were in charge of caring for the poor. During the 1930s, when this largely private system of charity collapsed in the face of widespread economic destitution, the federal government created the beginnings of an American welfare state. The idea of the welfare system was new; it meant that the national government would oversee programs designed to promote economic security for all Americans—not just for the poor. The American system of social welfare comprises many different policies enacted over the years since the Great Depression. Because each program is governed by distinct rules, the kind and level of assistance available varies widely.

THE HISTORY OF THE GOVERNMENT WELFARE SYSTEM DATES ONLY TO THE 1930s

There has always been a welfare system in America. But until 1935, it was almost entirely private, composed of an extensive system of voluntary philanthropy through churches and other religious groups, ethnic and fraternal societies, communities and neighborhoods, and philanthropically inclined rich individuals. Most often it was called "charity," and although it was private and voluntary, it was thought of as a public obligation.

The traditional approach of charity crumbled in 1929 before the stark reality of the Great Depression. During the Depression, misfortune became so widespread and private wealth shrank so drastically that private charity was out of the question and the distinction between deserving and undeserving became impossible to draw. Around 20 percent of the workforce immediately became unemployed; this figure grew as the Depression stretched into years. Moreover, few of these individuals had any monetary resources or any family farm on which to fall back. Banks failed, wiping out the savings of millions who had been prudent enough or fortunate enough to have any savings at all. Thousands of businesses failed as well, throwing middle-class Americans onto the bread lines along with unemployed laborers, dispossessed farmers, and those who had never worked in any capacity whatsoever. The Great Depression proved to

Americans that poverty could be a result of imperfections in the economic system as well as of individual irresponsibility. It also forced Americans to alter drastically their standards regarding who was deserving and who was not.

Once poverty and dependency were accepted as problems inherent in the economic system, a large-scale public policy approach was not far away. By the time President Franklin D. Roosevelt took office in 1933, the question was not whether there was to be a public welfare system, but how generous or restrictive that system would be.

The Social Security Act of 1935 Was the Foundation of the Welfare System

If the welfare state were truly a state, its founding would be the Social Security Act of 1935. This act created two separate categories of welfare: contributory and noncontributory. Table 12.2 lists the key programs in each of these categories, with the year of their enactment and recent figures on the number of Americans they benefit and their cost to the federal government.

Public Welfare Programs   Table 12.2

TYPE OF PROGRAM	YEAR ENACTED	NUMBER OF RECIPIENTS IN 2000 (IN MILLIONS)	FEDERAL OUTLAYS IN 2000 (IN BILLIONS)
Contributory (Insurance) System			
Old Age, Survivors, and Disability Insurance	1935	45.2	$407.4
Medicare	1965	39.6	$219.3
Unemployment Compensation	1935	7.0	$20.5
Noncontributory (Public Assistance) System			
Medicaid	1965	28.4	$117.7
Food Stamps	1964	17.2	$18.3
Supplemental Security Income (cash assistance for aged, blind, disabled)	1974	6.6	$30.7
Housing Assistance to low-income families	1937	4.69[†]	$22.5
School Lunch Program	1946	27.2	$5.6
Temporary Assistance to Needy Families	1996	5.8	$6.86

SOURCES: All data is from U.S. Census Bureau, *Statistical Abstract of the United States 2003* (Washington, D.C.: Government Printing Office, 2003).

contributory programs social programs financed in whole or in part by taxation or other mandatory contributions by their present or future recipients. The most important example is Social Security, which is financed by a payroll tax

Social Security a contributory welfare program into which working Americans contribute a percentage of their wages, and from which they receive cash benefits after retirement

Medicare a form of national health insurance for the elderly and the disabled

indexing periodic process of adjusting social benefits or wages to account for increases in the cost of living

cost-of-living adjustments (COLAs) changes made to the level of benefits of a government program based on the rate of inflation

noncontributory programs social programs that provide assistance to people based on demonstrated need rather than any contribution they have made

Aid to Families with Dependent Children (AFDC) federal funds, administered by the states, for children living with parents or relatives who fall below state standards of need. Replaced in 1996 by Temporary Assistance to Needy Families (TANF)

Temporary Assistance to Needy Families (TANF) a federal block grant that replaced the AFDC program in 1996

means testing a procedure by which potential beneficiaries of a public assistance program establish their eligibility by demonstrating a genuine need for the assistance

Medicaid a federally financed, state-operated program providing medical services to low-income people

Contributory Programs   The category of welfare programs that are financed by taxation can justifiably be called "forced savings"; these programs force working Americans to set aside a portion of their current earnings to provide income and benefits during their retirement years. These **contributory programs** are what most people have in mind when they refer to **Social Security** or social insurance. Under the original contributory program, old-age insurance, the employer and the employee were each required to pay equal amounts, which in 1937 were set at 1 percent of the first $3,000 of wages, to be deducted from the paycheck of each employee and matched by the same amount from the employer. This percentage has increased over the years; the contribution is now 7.65 percent subdivided as follows: 6.20 percent on the first $87,900 of income for Social Security benefits, plus 1.45 percent on all earnings for Medicare.[5] Social Security mildly redistributes wealth from higher- to lower-income people, and it quite significantly redistributes wealth from younger workers to older retirees.

Congress increased Social Security benefits every two or three years during the 1950s and 1960s. The biggest single expansion in contributory programs since 1935 was the establishment in 1965 of **Medicare,** which provides substantial medical services to elderly persons who are already eligible to receive old-age, survivors', and disability insurance under the original Social Security system. In 2003, Congress added a prescription drug benefit to the package of health benefits for the elderly. Social Security benefits and costs are adjusted through **indexing,** whereby benefits paid out under contributory programs are modified annually by **cost-of-living adjustments** (COLAs) designed to increase benefits to keep up with the rate of inflation. But, of course, Social Security taxes (contributions) also increased after almost every benefit increase.

Noncontributory Programs   Programs to which beneficiaries do not have to contribute—**noncontributory programs**—are also known as "public assistance programs," or, derisively, as "welfare." Until 1996, the most important noncontributory program was **Aid to Families with Dependent Children** (AFDC, originally called Aid to Dependent Children, or ADC), which was founded in 1935 by the original Social Security Act. In 1996, Congress abolished AFDC and replaced it with the **Temporary Assistance to Needy Families** (TANF) block grant. Eligibility for public assistance is determined by **means testing,** a procedure that requires applicants to show a financial need for assistance. Between 1935 and 1965, the government created programs to provide housing assistance, school lunches, and food stamps to other needy Americans.

As with contributory programs, the noncontributory public assistance programs also made their most significant advances in the 1960s and 1970s. The largest single category of expansion was the establishment in 1965 of **Medicaid,** a program that provides extended medical services to all low-income persons who have already established eligibility through means testing under AFDC or TANF. Noncontributory programs underwent another major transformation in the 1970s in the level of benefits they provide. Besides being means tested, noncontributory programs are provided by the national government to the states as incentives to establish the programs (see chapter 3). Thus, from the beginning there were considerable disparities in benefits from state to state. The national government sought to rectify the disparities in levels of old-age benefits in 1974 by creating the **Supplemental Security Income** (SSI) program to augment benefits for the aged, the blind, and the disabled. SSI provides uniform minimum benefits across the entire nation and includes mandatory COLAs. States are allowed to be more generous if they wish, but no state is permitted to provide benefits below the minimum level set by the national government. As a result, twenty-five states increased their own SSI benefits to the mandated level.

The new TANF program is also administered by the states and, as with the old-age benefits just discussed, benefit levels vary widely from state to state (see Figure 12.1). In 2001, the states' monthly TANF benefits varied from $164 in Alabama to $923 in Alaska.[6] In 2001, the nationally defined poverty level for a family of three was $14,824 a year, or $1,235 a month.

The number of people receiving AFDC benefits expanded in the 1970s, in part because new welfare programs had been established in the mid-1960s: Medicaid (discussed earlier) and **food stamps,** which are coupons that can be exchanged for food at most grocery stores. These programs provide what are

Supplemental Security Income (SSI) a program providing a minimum monthly income to people who pass a "means test" and who are sixty-five or older, blind, or disabled. Financed from general revenues rather than from Social Security contributions

food stamps coupons that can be exchanged for food at most grocery stores; the largest in-kind benefits program

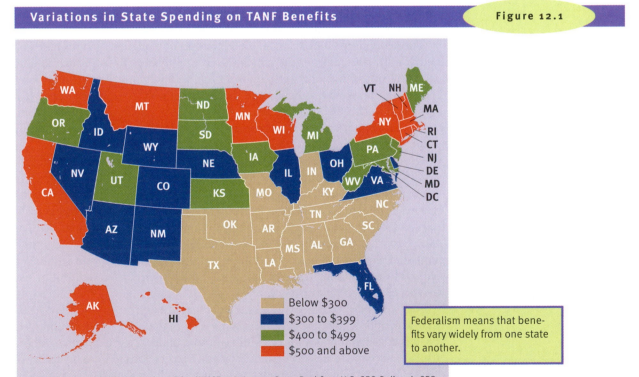

Variations in State Spending on TANF Benefits

Figure 12.1

Below $300
$300 to $399
$400 to $499
$500 and above

Federalism means that benefits vary widely from one state to another.

SOURCE: Ways and Means Committee Print, WMCP:108-6, *2003 Green Book* from U.S. GPO Online via GPO Access at waysandmeans.house.gov/media/pdf/greenbook2003/section7.pdf

in-kind benefits goods and services provided to needy individuals and families by the federal government

called **in-kind benefits**—noncash goods and services that the beneficiary would otherwise have to pay for in cash. In addition to simply adding on the cost of medical services and food to the level of benefits given to AFDC recipients, the possibility of receiving Medicaid benefits provided an incentive for poor Americans to establish their eligibility for AFDC, which would also establish their eligibility to receive Medicaid. At the same time, the government significantly expanded its publicity efforts to encourage the dependent unemployed to establish their eligibility for these various programs.

WELFARE REFORM HAS DOMINATED THE WELFARE AGENDA IN RECENT YEARS

The Republicans controlling the White House and the Senate in the 1980s initially had welfare reform very high on their agenda. They proceeded immediately, with the cooperation of many Democrats, to cut the rate of increase of all the major social welfare programs, including the contributory social insurance programs and the noncontributory, "need-based" programs. However, very little was actually cut in either type of program, and the welfare system quickly began to expand again. After 1984, expenditures for public assistance programs began to increase at a rate about equal to the rate of general economic growth (called the Gross Domestic Product, or GDP). Moreover, no public assistance programs were terminated, despite Republican criticisms of them.

The Republicans took control of both houses of Congress in 1995, based on their "Contract with America," which included a promise to introduce a bill to "reduce illegitimacy, control welfare spending, and reduce welfare dependence." The Republican welfare bill removed the federal guarantee of assistance, forced 1.5 million welfare recipients to work by 2000, denied public aid to legal immigrants who are not citizens, and granted states wide discretion in administering welfare programs.

During the 104th Congress (1995–96), President Clinton twice vetoed proposals for welfare reform, arguing that they would harm children. However, in August 1996, the president signed a third bill similar to the previous proposals. This major reform of welfare abolished AFDC and replaced the federal guarantee of assistance to the poor with block grants to the states through the new TANF program. This program allows states to deny assistance to legal immigrants and requires the head of each family receiving welfare to work within two years or lose assistance. The legislation also establishes a lifetime limit of five years on the receipt of assistance.

Since this new welfare law was enacted, the number of families receiving assistance dropped by 60 percent nationwide (see Figure 12.2).[7] Some observers take this as a sign that welfare reform is working; indeed, former welfare recipients have been more successful at finding and keeping jobs than many critics of the new law predicted. One important indicator of how welfare has changed is the proportion of funds it provides in cash assistance. Before the 1996 reform, assistance was largely provided in the form of a cash grant. By 2002, 56 percent of welfare funds were allocated for noncash assistance, and 44 percent for cash

AFDC/TANF Caseload, 1976–2002

Figure 12.2

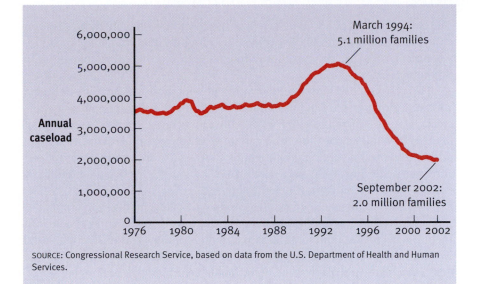

SOURCE: Congressional Research Service, based on data from the U.S. Department of Health and Human Services.

assistance. Thus an increasing proportion of welfare funds is spent on such costs as providing assistance with transportation to work, temporary shelter, or one-time payments for emergencies so that people do not go on the welfare rolls. The orientation of assistance has shifted away from subsidizing people who are not in the labor force toward addressing temporary problems that low-income people face and providing assistance that facilitates work.[8] Other evidence suggests more caution in declaring welfare reform a success. Early studies show that welfare recipients are not paid enough to pull their families out of poverty and that child care and transportation continue to cause many problems for people seeking to leave welfare.[9] Other evidence suggests more caution in declaring welfare reform a success. Early studies show that welfare recipients are not paid enough to pull their families out of poverty.[10]

Since 1996, two different perspectives on TANF reform have emerged. Democrats have proposed changes that would make the welfare law "an an-tipoverty weapon."[11] They hope to increase spending on child care, allow more education and training, and relax time limits for those working and receiving welfare benefits. Republicans, by contrast, have proposed stricter work requirements and advocated programs designed to promote marriage among welfare recipients.[12]

In his 2004 State of the Union address, President George W. Bush proposed expanding the government role in promoting marriage. These disagreements about the future direction of welfare prevented Congress from reauthorizing the TANF legislature in 2002 and 2003. Instead, Congress enacted temporary extensions of the 1996 legislation. Despite these disagreements, neither party has challenged the fundamental features—especially the work orientation—of the 1996 welfare reform.

Social Policy Spending Benefits the Middle Class More Than the Poor

The two categories of social policy—contributory and noncontributory—generally serve different groups of people. We can understand much about the development of social policy by examining which constituencies benefit from different policies.

The strongest and most generous programs are those in which the beneficiaries are widely perceived as deserving of assistance and also are politically powerful. Because Americans prize work, constituencies who have "earned" their benefits in some way or those who cannot work because of a disability are usually seen as most deserving of government assistance. Politically powerful constituencies are those who vote as a group, lobby effectively, and mobilize to protect the programs from which they benefit.

When we study social policies from a group perspective, we can see that senior citizens and the middle class receive the most benefits from the government's social policies and that children and the working poor receive the fewest. In addition, America's social policies do little to change the fact that minorities and women are more likely to be poor than white Americans and men.

SENIOR CITIZENS NOW RECEIVE OVER A THIRD OF ALL FEDERAL DOLLARS

The elderly are the beneficiaries of the two strongest and most generous social policies: old-age pensions (what we call Social Security) and Medicare (medical care for the elderly). As these programs have grown, they have provided most elderly Americans with economic security and have dramatically reduced the poverty rate among the elderly. In 1959, before very many people over the age of sixty-five received social insurance, the poverty rate for the elderly was 35 percent; by 2002, it had dropped to 10.4 percent.[13] Because of this progress, many people call Social Security the most effective antipoverty program in the United States.[14] This does not mean that the elderly are rich, however; in 2001, the median income of elderly households was $23,118, well below the national median income. The aim of these programs is to provide security and prevent poverty rather than to assist people once they have become poor. And they succeeded in preventing poverty among most of the aged.

One reason that Social Security and Medicare are politically strong is that the elderly are widely seen as a deserving population. They are not expected to work, because of their age. Moreover, both programs are contributory, and a work history is a requirement for receiving a Social Security pension. But these programs are also strong because they serve a constituency that has become quite powerful. The elderly are a very large group: in 2004, there were 36 million Americans over the age of sixty-five. Because Social Security and Medicare are not means tested, they are available to all former workers and their spouses over the age of sixty-five, whether they are poor or not. The size of this group is of such political importance because the elderly turn out to vote in higher numbers than the rest of the population.

In addition, the elderly have developed strong and sophisticated lobbying organizations that can influence policy making and mobilize elderly Americans to defend these programs against proposals to cut them. One important and influential organization that defends the interests of old people in Washington is the American Association of Retired Persons (AARP). The AARP had 35 million members in 2004, amounting to one-fifth of all voters. It also has a sophisticated lobbying organization in Washington that employs 28 lobbyists and a staff of 165 policy analysts.[15] Although the AARP is the largest and the strongest organization of the elderly, other groups, such as the National Council of Senior Citizens, to which many retired union members belong, also lobby Congress on behalf of the elderly.

These lobbying groups are among the most powerful in America. They mobilize their supporters and work with legislators to block changes they believe will hurt the elderly. Because of the tremendous political strength of the elderly, Social Security has been nicknamed the "third rail of American politics: touch it and you die."[16] In the case of Medicare reform, for example, the AARP had long opposed any reform that allowed private health care firms to provide Medicaid benefits. But in 2003, the AARP switched its position and endorsed the Bush administration's bill to provide prescription drug benefits through the involvement of private firms. The AARP's endorsement of the plan was decisive to its passage.

THE MIDDLE CLASS BENEFITS FROM SOCIAL POLICIES

Americans don't usually think of the middle class as benefiting from social policies, but government action promotes the social welfare of the middle class in a variety of ways. First, medical care and pensions for the elderly help the middle class by relieving them of the burden of caring for elderly relatives. Before these programs existed, old people were more likely to live with and depend financially on their adult children. Many middle-class families whose parents and grandparents are in nursing homes rely on Medicaid to pay nursing-home bills.

In addition, the middle class benefits from what some analysts call the **"shadow welfare state."**[17] These are the social benefits that private employers offer to their workers—medical insurance and pensions, for example. The federal government subsidizes such benefits by not taxing the payments that employers and employees make for health insurance and pensions. These **tax expenditures,** as they are called, are an important way in which the federal government helps ensure the social welfare of the middle class. (Such programs are called "tax expenditures" because the federal government helps finance them through the tax system rather than by direct spending.) Another key tax expenditure that helps the middle class is the tax exemption on mortgage interest payments: Taxpayers can

shadow welfare state social benefits that private employers offer to their workers, such as medical insurance and pensions

tax expenditures government subsidies provided to employers and employees through tax deductions for amounts spent on health insurance and other benefits; these represent one way the government helps to ensure the social welfare of the middle class

deduct the amount they have paid in interest on a mortgage from the income they report on their tax return. By not taxing these payments, the government makes homeownership less expensive.

People often don't think of these tax expenditures as part of social policy because they are not as visible as the programs that provide direct payments or services to beneficiaries. But tax expenditures represent a significant federal investment: They cost the national treasury some $300 billion a year and make it easier and less expensive for working Americans to obtain health care, save for retirement, and buy homes. These programs are very popular with the middle class, so Congress rarely considers reducing them. On the few occasions when public officials have tried to limit these programs—with proposals to limit the amount of mortgage interest that can be deducted, for example—they have quickly retreated. These programs are simply too popular among Americans whose power comes from their numbers at the polling booth.

THE WORKING POOR RECEIVE FEWER BENEFITS

People who are working but are poor or are just above the poverty line receive only limited assistance from government social programs. This is somewhat surprising, given that Americans value work so highly. But the working poor are typically employed in jobs that do not provide pensions or health care; often they are renters because they cannot afford to buy homes. This means they cannot benefit from the shadow welfare state that subsidizes the social benefits enjoyed by most middle-class Americans. At the same time, however, they cannot get assistance through programs such as Medicaid and TANF, which are largely restricted to the nonworking poor.

Two government programs do assist the working poor: the Earned Income Tax Credit (EITC) and food stamps. The EITC was implemented in 1976 to provide poor workers some relief from increases in the taxes that pay for Social Security. As it has expanded, the EITC has provided a modest wage supplement for the working poor, allowing them to catch up on utility bills or pay for children's clothing. Poor workers can also receive food stamps. These two programs help supplement the income of poor workers, but they offer only modest support. Because the wages of less-educated workers have declined significantly over the past fifteen years and minimum wages have not kept pace with inflation, the problems of the working poor remain acute.

Even though the working poor may be seen as deserving, they are not politically powerful because they are not organized. There is no equivalent to the AARP for the poor. Nonetheless, because work is highly valued in American society, politicians find it difficult to cut the few social programs that help the working poor. In 1995, efforts to cut the EITC were defeated by coalitions of Democrats and moderate Republicans, although Congress did place new restrictions on food stamps and reduced the level of spending.

SPENDING FOR THE NONWORKING POOR IS DECLINING

The only nonworking, able-bodied poor people who receive federal cash assistance are parents who are caring for children. The primary source of cash assistance for these families was AFDC and now is the state-run TANF program, but they also rely on food stamps and Medicaid. Able-bodied adults who are not caring for children are not eligible for federal assistance other than food stamps. Many states provide small amounts of cash assistance to such individuals through programs called "general assistance," but in the past decade, many states have abolished or greatly reduced their general assistance programs in an effort to encourage these adults to work. Thus, the primary reason the federal government provides any assistance to able-bodied adults is because they are caring for children. Although Americans don't like to subsidize adults who are not working, they do not want to harm children.

AFDC was the most unpopular social spending program, and as a result, spending on it declined after 1980. Under TANF, states receive a fixed amount of federal funds, whether the welfare rolls rise or fall. Because the number of people on welfare has declined so dramatically since 1994—by nearly 50 percent—states have had generous levels of federal resources for the remaining welfare recipients. Many states, however, have used the windfall of federal dollars to cut taxes and indirectly support programs that benefit the middle class, not the poor.[18] Welfare recipients have little political power to resist cuts in their benefits.

MINORITIES, WOMEN, AND CHILDREN ARE MOST LIKELY TO FACE POVERTY

Minorities, women, and children are disproportionately poor. Much of this poverty is the result of disadvantages rooted in the position of these groups in the labor market. African Americans and Latinos tend to be economically less well off than the rest of the American population. Much of this economic inequality stems from the fact that minority workers tend to have low-wage jobs. Minorities are also more likely to become unemployed and to remain unemployed for longer periods of time than are white Americans. African Americans, for example, typically have experienced twice as much unemployment than other Americans have. The combination of low-wage jobs and unemployment often means that minorities are less likely to have jobs that give them access to the shadow welfare state. They are more likely to fall into the precarious categories of the working poor or the nonworking poor.

In the past several decades, policy analysts have begun to talk about the "feminization of poverty," or the fact that women are more likely to be poor than men are. This problem is particularly acute for single mothers, who are more than twice as likely to fall below the poverty line than the average American (see Figure 12.3). When the Social Security Act was passed in 1935, the main programs for poor women were ADC and survivors' insurance for widows. The framers of the act believed that ADC would gradually disappear as more women became

Who Gets What from Social Policy

The poor and working poor, as well as the young, receive the fewest government benefits. Single mothers with children, for example, have little influence on policymaking and are often short-changed by social policy initiatives.

Though organized protests representing the interests of the poor and working poor occasionally occur, they fail to have the impact of similar protests by other groups, such as senior citizens. The elderly have developed strong and sophisticated lobbying organizations like AARP that can influence policy.

Political influence is as important a factor as need in determining which groups will benefit from social policy. The more organized and powerful the group, the more likely its chances that policymakers will meet its demands. In 1995, the Republican-led Congress proposed cuts in Medicare spending, prompting vigorous protests from senior citizens.

POLITICS

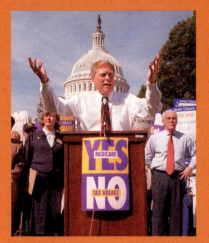

The political influence of the elderly was demonstrated by the immediate defense of Medicare spending by Democratic leaders in Congress, such as House minority leader Dick Gephardt, shown here speaking at a senior citizens' rally in Washington, D.C. Fearing negative political repercussions in the 1996 elections, Congressional Republicans ultimately retreated from their efforts to overhaul the Medicare system.

The middle class benefits a great deal from social policies, primarily from tax expenditures, which help ensure their social welfare. The rapid growth of the suburbs around major metropolitan areas is a prime example of government actions accommodating the interests of the middle class.

eligible for survivors' insurance. The social model behind the Social Security Act was that of a male breadwinner with a wife and children. Women were not expected to work, and if a woman's husband died, ADC or survivors' insurance would help her stay at home and raise her children. The framers of Social Security did not envision today's large number of single women heading families. At the same time, they did not envision that so many women with children would also be working. This combination of changes helped make AFDC (the successor program to ADC) more controversial. Many people ask, why shouldn't welfare recipients work, if the majority of women who are not on welfare work?

One of the most troubling issues related to American social policy is the number of American children who live in poverty. The rate of child poverty in 2002 was 16.7 percent—4.6 percent higher than that of the population as a whole. These high rates of poverty stem in part from the design of American social policies. Because these policies do not generously assist able-bodied adults who aren't working, and because these policies offer little help to the working poor, the children of these adults are likely to be poor as well.

Figure 12.3   **Poverty Level in the United States, 1960–2002**

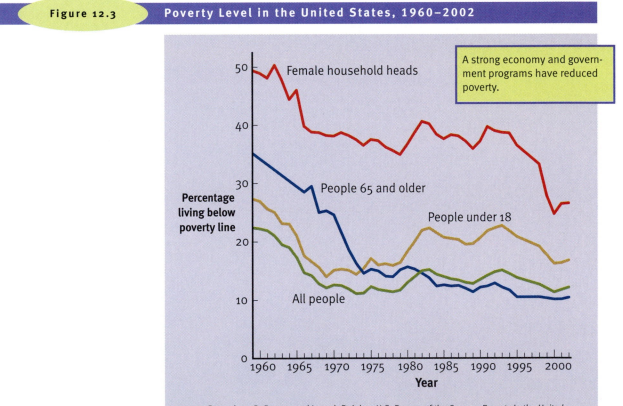

SOURCE: Bernadette D. Proctor and Joseph Dalakar, U.S. Bureau of the Census, *Poverty in the United States, 2002,* at www.census.gov/prod/2003pubs/p60-222.pdf (accessed February 10, 2004).

The Cycle of Poverty Can Be Broken by Education, Employment, Health, and Housing Policies

Poverty is a cycle. Many individuals break out of it, but they have to overcome heavy odds. Although many policies may aim at breaking the cycle and others have a beneficial effect on the redistribution of opportunities, four types of policies stand out as most significant: education policies, employment policies, health policies, and housing policies.

EDUCATION POLICIES PROVIDE LIFE TOOLS

Education is highly valued in America, a belief reflected in the fact that the vast majority of the education provided to Americans comes from public educational institutions financed through state, local, and (to a lesser extent) national government education policy. Less well appreciated is the fact that education is an extremely important factor in shaping the distribution and redistribution of wealth and opportunity in America. This assertion is supported by the fact that a person's lifelong income is directly correlated with his or her level of education. In other words, people with more education earn more in their lifetimes than people with less education.

Compared to state and local efforts, the role of national government education policy is limited. Moreover, the most important national education policies have come only since World War II: the GI Bill of Rights of 1944, the National Defense Education Act (NDEA) of 1958, the Elementary and Secondary Education Act of 1965 (ESEA), and various youth and adult vocational training acts since 1958. Note, however, that since the GI Bill was aimed almost entirely at postsecondary schooling, the national government did not really enter the field of elementary education until after 1957.[19]

What finally brought the national government into elementary education was embarrassment over the fact that the Soviet Union had beaten the United States into space with the launching of Sputnik. The national policy under NDEA was aimed specifically at improving education in science and mathematics. General federal aid for education did not come until ESEA in 1965, which allocated funds to school districts with substantial numbers of children from families who were unemployed or earning very little.

President Clinton's education program included more federal aid for preschool programs for needy children, national education standards coupled with teachers' incentives, and, at the postsecondary level, scholarships for minorities and an ambitious national service program available to all students to earn credit toward college tuition. Clinton's most concrete achievement in education policy was the Improving America's Schools Act of 1994, also known as Goals 2000, which aimed to reverse federal policies dating back to the 1960s that set lower academic standards for schools in poorer school districts than for those in wealthier ones. Goals 2000 set uniform national standards for educational achievement from the wealthiest to the poorest school districts, and committed $400 million in federal funds to help establish these standards. The logic of the old system was that it was unfair to expect disadvantaged children to have to perform at the same level as children from wealthier backgrounds. But the result, not surprisingly, was to discourage children in poor school districts from achieving academic excellence.

President George W. Bush's most prominent policy achievement in education was the No Child Left Behind Act of 2001, which enacted stronger federal requirements for student testing and school accountability. It required every child in grades three through eight to be tested yearly for proficiency in math and reading, with the scores to serve as a basis for judging schools. Parents with children in schools whose scores are poor have the right to transfer their children to a better school or to get funds for tutoring and summer programs. Since enactment, some states have rebelled against what they considered an "unfunded mandate," meaning that the government failed to provide the funds necessary to comply with the law. By 2004, the federal government decided to relax some of the law's requirements.

EMPLOYMENT AND TRAINING PROGRAMS MEAN STEADY INCOMES

Considering the importance that Americans attach to work and the high value they place on education, it is somewhat surprising that the United States does not have a strong system for employment and job training. Such programs have two goals. One is to prepare entry-level workers for new jobs or to retrain workers whose jobs have disappeared. A second goal is to provide public jobs during economic downturns when sufficient private employment is not available. Since the 1930s, the American employment and training systems have fared poorly in terms of expenditures, stability, and results.[20]

The first public employment programs were launched during Roosevelt's New Deal. These programs were created to use the power of the federal government to get people back to work again. But by the end of the 1930s, questions about corruption and inefficiency in employment programs reduced support for them.

Not until the 1960s did the federal government try again. This time, as part of the War on Poverty, government programs were designed to train and retrain workers, primarily the poor, rather than to provide them with public employment. For the most part, the results of these programs were disappointing. It proved very difficult to design effective training policies in the federal system; lack of coordination and poor administration plagued the Great Society training programs.

In 1982, Congress created a new program that supported local efforts at job training. The Job Training Partnership Act (JTPA) became the primary federal program supporting job training. In addition to retraining adult workers, JTPA provides funding for summer jobs for youth. President Clinton placed an especially high value on creating a strong system of job training. Clinton's program made use of tax credits and direct subsidies to employers to set up apprentice-training jobs for young people and was to be part of a more ambitious national system that was called "lifelong learning." It was inspired by training programs that exist in some European countries, and it coupled national initiatives with community organizations and administration. Yet Clinton's initiatives in job training remained small, as budgetary pressures and congressional skepticism limited his legislative achievements.

HEALTH POLICIES MEAN FEWER SICK DAYS

Until recent decades, no government in the United States—national, state, or local—concerned itself directly with individual health. But public responsibility was always accepted for *public* health. After New York City's newly created Board of Health was credited with holding down a cholera epidemic in 1867, most states followed with the creation of statewide public health agencies. Within a decade, the results were obvious. Between 1884 and 1894, for example, Massachusetts's rate of infant mortality dropped from 161.3 per 1,000 to 141.4 per 1,000.[21] Reductions in mortality rates during the late nineteenth century may be the most significant contribution ever made by government to human welfare.

The U.S. Public Health Service (USPHS) has been in existence since 1798 but was a small part of public health policy until after World War II. Established in 1937, but little noticed for twenty years, was the National Institutes of Health (NIH), an agency within the USPHS created to do biomedical research. Between 1950 and 2003, NIH expenditures by the national government increased from $160 million to $27 billion. NIH research on the link between smoking and disease led to one of the most visible public-health campaigns in American history. Today, NIH's focus has turned to cancer and acquired immunodeficiency syndrome (AIDS). As with smoking, this work on AIDS has resulted in massive public-health education as well as new products and regulations.

Other, more recent commitments to the improvement of public health are the numerous laws aimed at cleaning up and defending the environment (including the creation in 1970 of the Environmental Protection Agency) and laws attempting to improve the health and safety of consumer products (regulated by the Consumer Product Safety Commission, created in 1972). Health policies aimed directly at the poor include Medicaid and nutritional programs, particularly food stamps and the school lunch program.

HOUSING POLICIES PROVIDE RESIDENTIAL STABILITY

The United States has one of the highest rates of homeownership in the world, and the central thrust of federal housing policy has been to promote homeownership. The federal government has traditionally done much less to provide housing for low-income Americans who cannot afford to buy homes. Federal housing programs were first created in the 1930s depression period when many

Americans found themselves unable to afford housing. Through public housing for low-income families, which originated in 1937 with the Wagner-Steagall National Housing Act, and subsidized private housing after 1950, the percentage of American families living in overcrowded conditions was reduced from 20 percent in 1940 to 9 percent in 1970. Federal policies made an even greater contribution to reducing "substandard" housing, defined by the U.S. Census Bureau as dilapidated houses without hot running water and without some other plumbing. In 1940, almost 50 percent of American households lived in substandard housing. By 1950, this had been reduced to 35 percent; by 1975, the figure was reduced further to 8 percent.[22] Despite these improvements in housing standards, federal housing policy until the 1970s was largely seen as a failure. Restricted to the poorest of the poor, marked by racial segregation and inadequate spending, public housing contributed to the problems of the poor by isolating them from shopping, jobs, and urban amenities. Dilapidated high-rise housing projects stood as a symbol of the failed American policy of "warehousing the poor." By the 1980s, the orientation of housing policy had changed: Most federal housing policy for low-income Americans came in the form of housing vouchers (called Section 8 vouchers) that provided recipients with support to rent in the private market. While this program did not promote the same isolation of the poor, it was often useless in expensive housing markets where the vouchers provided too little money to cover rental costs.

Summary

The study of public policy is the study of how the government attempts to get people to do things through various forms of coercion. In order for policy to be effective, it must include rewards or penalties, and the government must have some way to carry these out. There are three general categories or types of control techniques: promotional techniques, regulatory techniques, and redistributive techniques. Promotional techniques are incentives, or "carrots," such as government subsidies and contracts. Regulatory techniques are penalties imposed directly on individuals or other entities such as corporations. Redistributive techniques aim to influence broad classes of people, or even the economy as a whole. They include fiscal and monetary policy, and social welfare programs.

Social policy, known as the modern welfare state, encompasses a variety of policies that try to minimize poverty and boost opportunities for equality. Modern national welfare policies date from the 1930s and are composed of two broad types: contributory and noncontributory. Contributory programs are those where the recipients contribute to the program, such as Social Security. The elderly and the middle class tend to benefit most from these programs. Noncontributory programs, also known as "public assistance," benefit those considered in need of assistance. Public policies aimed at helping people out of poverty include education, employment, health, and housing policies.

For Further Reading

Gutman, Amy. *Democratic Education.* Princeton, NJ: Princeton University Press, 1987.

Katz, Michael. *In the Shadow of the Poorhouse: A Social History of Welfare in America.* New York: Basic Books, 1986.

Katznelson, Ira, and Margaret Weir. *Schooling for All: Race, Class, and the Democratic Ideal.* New York: Basic Books, 1985.

Krugman, Paul. *Peddling Prosperity: Economic Sense and Nonsense in the Age of Diminished Expectations.* New York: Norton, 1994.

Light, Paul. *Artful Work: The Politics of Social Security Reform.* New York: Random House, 1985.

Marmor, Theodore R., Jerry L. Mashaw, and Phillip L. Harvey. *America's Misunderstood Welfare State.* New York: Basic Books, 1990.

Murray, Charles. *Losing Ground: American Social Policy, 1950–1980.* New York: Basic Books, 1984.

Patterson, James T. *America's Struggle against Poverty, 1900–1994.* Cambridge, MA: Harvard University Press, 1994.

Piven, Frances, Fox, and Richard A. Cloward. *Regulating the Poor.* New York: Pantheon, 1971.

Schwarz, John E. *America's Hidden Success: A Reassessment of Twenty Years of Public Policy.* New York: Norton, 1988.

Spitzer, Robert J. *The Politics of Gun Control.* Washington, D.C.: CQ Press, 2004.

Weir, Margaret, Ann Orloff, and Theda Skocpol. *The Politics of Social Policy in the United States.* Princeton, NJ: Princeton University Press, 1988.

Study Outline

1. Public policy is an officially expressed intention backed by a sanction, which can be a reward or a punishment.

The Tools for Making Policy Are Techniques of Control

1. Promotional techniques, which can promote private activity through unconditional benefits, are the carrots of public policy. Promotional techniques can be classified into two categories: subsidies and contracts.
2. Regulatory techniques come in several forms—police regulation, administrative regulation, regulatory taxation, and expropriation—but share the common trait of direct government control of conduct.
3. Redistributive techniques usually take one of two forms, but their common purpose is to control people by manipulating the entire economy rather than by regulating people directly. Redistributive techniques include both fiscal and monetary techniques.
4. The government's spending power may be the most important fiscal technique since it can be used for policy goals beyond buying goods and services and regulating individual conduct.

Social Policy and the Welfare System Buttress Equality

1. Prior to 1935, the welfare system in America was composed of private groups rather than government. State governments gradually assumed some of the obligation to relieve the poor.
2. The founding of the welfare state can be dated to the Social Security Act of 1935; this act provided for both contributory and noncontributory welfare programs.
3. Contributory programs—such as Social Security and unemployment compensation—provide "forced savings" for individuals who, as a consequence of making a contribution, can receive program benefits at a later time.
4. Noncontributory programs—such as food stamps and Temporary Assistance to Needy Families (TANF)—provide assistance to people based on demonstrated need rather than any contribution they may have made.
5. Spending on social policies, especially Social Security and Medicare, has increased dramatically in recent decades, raising concerns about how entitlement programs will be paid for in future decades.

Social Policy Spending Benefits the Middle Class More Than the Poor

1. The elderly are the beneficiaries of generous social policies in part because they are perceived as being a deserving population and because they have become a strong interest group.
2. The middle class benefits from social policies in many ways; one way is through the use of tax expenditures, which provide that certain payments made by employers and employees are not taxed by the government.
3. People who are working but are still poor receive limited assistance from government social programs. Although they may be seen as deserving, they receive only limited assistance because they lack organization and political power.
4. Medicaid and TANF are programs aimed at the able-bodied, nonworking poor, but they only receive assistance

if they are supporting children. The unpopularity of such programs has prompted efforts to decrease spending in recent years.

The Cycle of Poverty Can Be Broken by Education, Employment, Health, and Housing Policies

1. Education, employment, health, and housing policies are four ways to break the cycle of poverty and redistribute opportunities.
2. The education policies of state and local governments are the most important single force in the distribution and redistribution of opportunity in America.
3. Employment and job training programs have not been a consistent goal of the modern welfare state.
4. Although states also took the early lead in the arena of public health policy, the federal government began to adopt policies in the early 1900s to protect citizens from the effects of pollution and other health hazards.

Practice Quiz

1. Which of the following is not a category of the techniques of public control?
   a) promotional
   b) apportioning
   c) regulatory
   d) redistributive

2. A situation in which the government attempts to affect the economy through taxing and spending is an example of
   a) an expropriation policy.
   b) a monetary policy.
   c) a fiscal policy.
   d) eminent domain.

3. Which of the following is not an example of a contributory program?
   a) Social Security
   b) Medicare
   c) food stamps
   d) All of the above are examples of contributory programs.

4. America's welfare state was constructed initially in response to
   a) World War II.
   b) political reforms of the Progressive era.

   c) the Great Depression.
   d) the growth of the military-industrial complex.

5. Which of the following are examples of in-kind benefits?
   a) Medicaid and food stamps
   b) Social Security payments and cost-of-living adjustments
   c) Medicare and unemployment compensation
   d) None of the above are examples of in-kind benefits.

6. Means testing requires that applicants for welfare benefits show
   a) that they are capable of getting to and from their workplace.
   b) that they have the ability to store and prepare food.
   c) some definite need for assistance plus an inability to provide for it.
   d) that they have the time and resources to take full advantage of federal educational opportunities.

7. In 1996, as part of welfare reform, Aid to Families with Dependent Children was abolished and replaced by
   a) the Earned Income Tax Credit.
   b) Aid to Dependent Children.
   c) Supplemental Security Income.
   d) Temporary Assistance to Needy Families.

8. In terms of receiving benefits of social policies, what distinguishes the elderly from the working poor?
   a) The elderly are perceived as deserving, whereas the working poor are not.
   b) There is no significant difference between these two groups.
   c) The elderly are more organized and more politically powerful than are the working poor.
   d) The elderly are less organized and less politically powerful than are the working poor.

9. Who are the chief beneficiaries of the "shadow welfare state"?
   a) the rich
   b) the nonworking poor
   c) the working poor
   d) the middle class

10. Which of the following is *not* aimed at breaking the cycle of poverty?
    a) drug policies
    b) education policies
    c) employment training programs
    d) health policies

Critical Thinking Questions

1. Two factors that seem to influence a particular group's ability to get what it wants from social policy are (a) the perception that the group is deserving, and (b) the political organization and power of the group. In some ways, it is easy to take each of these factors as an independent ingredient of social policy success. But each factor could be seen as having an impact on the other. Select a group and discuss its relative success or failure in social policy. How might the perception of a group as deserving of assistance (and the assistance it receives) help that group become organized and politically powerful? How might organization and political power help shape public opinion favorably toward the group you selected?

2. Describe the changes over time in the welfare state in the United States. What factors led to the expansion of governmental power (both state and national) over social policy? What factors might lead to a decrease of governmental activity in social policy? How do you think social policy in the United States will change in the future? Which of today's political forces and debates will be important in shaping the social policies of the future?

Key Terms

administrative regulation (p. 346)
Aid to Families with Dependent Children (AFDC) (p. 350)
civil penalties (p. 345)
contracting power (p. 344)
contributory programs (p. 350)
cost-of-living adjustments (COLAs) (p. 350)
criminal penalties (p. 345)
discount rate (p. 347)

eminent domain (p. 347)
expropriation (p. 346)
Federal Reserve Board (Fed) (p. 347)
food stamps (p. 351)
indexing (p. 350)
inflation (p. 347)
in-kind benefits (p. 352)
means testing (p. 350)
Medicaid (p. 350)
Medicare (p. 350)
noncontributory programs (p. 350)
police power (p. 345)

public policy (p. 341)
regulation (p. 345)
regulatory tax (p. 346)
shadow welfare state (p. 355)
Social Security (p. 350)
subsidies (p. 344)
Supplemental Security Income (SSI) (p. 351)
tax expenditures (p. 355)
Temporary Assistance to Needy Families (TANF) (p. 350)

13 FOREIGN POLICY

MAIN MESSAGE

Since the end of World War II, America has been the dominant force on the world stage, even though Americans continue to have mixed feelings about this active role.

Ever since George Washington, in his farewell address, warned the American people "to have . . . as little political connection as possible" with foreign nations and to "steer clear of permanent alliances," Americans have been distrustful of foreign policy. For most of America's history, this distrust has largely kept America out of world affairs. Yet since the end of World War II, the U.S. has become the dominant nation on the world stage, and it has pursued its national interests throughout the world. This has included economic as well as military intervention. Even with America's emergence as an interventionist world power, Americans continue to have doubts about this active foreign policy. As Alexis de Tocqueville noted in the 1830s, democracies lack the best qualities for the successful pursuit of foreign policy goals:

> ## Key Concepts
>
> 1. American foreign policy is shaped by the president, the bureaucracy, and Congress, as well as interest groups and the media.
>
> 2. Americans have a long history of suspicion toward involvement in world affairs.
>
> 3. America has been actively involved in world affairs only since World War II.
>
> 4. The instruments through which America shapes foreign policy include diplomacy, international organizations such as the United Nations, economic aid, and military force.

Foreign policies demand scarcely any of those qualities which are peculiar to a democracy; they require, on the contrary, the perfect use of almost all those in which it is deficient. . . . A democracy can only with great difficulty regulate the details of an important undertaking, persevere in a fixed design, and work out its execution in spite of serious obstacles. It cannot combine its measures with secrecy or await their consequences with patience.[1]

The fear of foreign entanglements and the secrecy necessary to make foreign policy work formed the basis of American distrust. In some cases involving national security or fighting certain evils in the world, intervention and even cooperation with other nations was justified in the eyes of the public. Americans even learned to tolerate secrecy in the conduct of diplomacy to prevent war. But the Vietnam War shifted American sentiments back toward distrust.

When citizens pay attention to foreign policy, they can indeed influence its direction. But except for a major foreign policy crisis, Americans usually pay little attention to America's relations with other nations. Yet foreign policy decisions can be momentous. A bad decision in domestic policy might result in wasteful spending, the collapse of a bridge, or the demolition of a housing project built only a few years earlier, but a mistake in foreign policy could mean war, and the deaths of thousands. And in the nuclear age, military miscalculation could result in the destruction of millions of people.

In this chapter, we will examine the making of American foreign policy, noting that America was little involved in world affairs from the country's founding until World War II. Since that time, the United States has been a dominant factor in the shaping of world events. Even so, many Americans continue to have reservations about this active international role.

The Makers and Shapers of Foreign Policy Include the President, the Bureaucracy, and Congress

American foreign policy is shaped by a number of competing forces. First there are the official players, those who comprise the "foreign policy establishment"; these players and the agencies they head can be called the actual "makers" of foreign policy. But there are other major players, less official but still influential. We call these the "shapers."

FOREIGN POLICY IS OFTEN MADE IN THE NAME OF THE PRESIDENT

The President   Although many foreign policy decisions can be made without so much as the president's fingerprint on them, these decisions are often made and implemented in the name of the president. Of course, much of the action in foreign policy takes place far from the White House and the president. Nevertheless, foreign policy tends to center around the president and his or her priorities, as reflected in the key persons appointed to head agencies that control foreign policy, as well as in the president's own stated foreign policy goals (fighting communism during the cold war, or improving relations with nations still under communist control in the post–cold war era, such as China and Cuba).

The ability of a president to shape, or reshape, the outlines of American foreign policy is clearly seen in George W. Bush's actions after 9/11. In 2002, Bush articulated a new and more military-reliant approach to foreign policy, a doctrine of preemptive use of force. This so-called Bush Doctrine says that America has the right to strike at an opponent if there is credible evidence that the adversary is likely to attack America first. The policy seemed a logical consequence of the 9/11 terrorist attacks, but its first major use came in a different case: the invasion of Iraq in 2003. That invasion revealed two problems with the Bush Doctrine. One is that it places even greater emphasis on military, as opposed to diplomatic, action. The fear is that an America more willing to initiate military action without being attacked might in turn encourage other nations to do the same. The second problem is that, in the case of Iraq, the primary reasons offered to support the charge of Iraq posing an imminent threat to the United States have not panned out. Specifically, Bush's arguments that invasion was necessary because of ties between Iraq leader Saddam Hussein and international terrorists, and because Iraq possessed weapons of mass destruction (WMDs) including chemical, biological, and perhaps nuclear, have turned out to be false.

The Bureaucracy The major foreign policy players in the bureaucracy, appointed by the president, are the secretaries of the departments of State, Defense, and the Treasury; the Joint Chiefs of Staff (JCOS), especially the chair of the JCOS; and the director of the Central Intelligence Agency (CIA). A separate unit in the bureaucracy comprising these people and a few others is the National Security Council (NSC), whose main purpose is to iron out the differences among the key players and to integrate their positions in order to confirm or reinforce a decision the president wants to make in foreign policy or military policy. In the Clinton administration, the secretary of the Department of Commerce also became an increasingly important foreign policy maker, with the rise and spread of economic globalization. Clinton's first secretary of commerce, Ron Brown, was not the first to be active in promoting world trade, but he may well have been the most vigorous and successful.

To this group another has been added: the Department of Homeland Security, currently headed by former Pennsylvania governor Tom Ridge. The department has four main divisions: Border and Transportation Security; Emergency Preparedness and Response; Chemical, Biological, Radiological, and Nuclear Countermeasures; and Information Analysis and Infrastructure Protection. Although each of the twenty-two agencies within the four main divisions has an expertise in homeland security, their missions are more wide-ranging, such as providing relief to victims of natural disasters and stopping counterfeiters.

In addition to these top cabinet-level officials, key lower-level staff members have policy-making influence as strong as that of the Cabinet secretaries—some may occasionally exceed Cabinet influence. These include the two or three specialized national security advisers in the White House, the staff of the NSC (headed by the national security adviser), and a few other career bureaucrats in the departments of State and Defense whose influence varies according to their specialty and to the foreign policy issue at hand.

Congress   While the Constitution gives Congress the power to declare war, Congress has exercised this power on only five occasions: the War of 1812, the Mexican War (1846), the Spanish–American War (1898), World War I, and World War II. For the first 150 years of American history, Congress's role was limited because, as we will see, the United States' role in world affairs was limited. During this time, the Senate was the only important congressional foreign policy player because of its constitutional role in reviewing and approving treaties and approving the appointment of ambassadors. The treaty power is still the primary entrée of the Senate into foreign policy making. But since World War II and the continual involvement of the United States in international security and foreign aid, both houses of Congress have become a major foreign policy maker because most modern foreign policies require financing,

Table 13.1	Principal Foreign Policy Provisions of the Constitution

| | POWER GRANTED TO | |
	PRESIDENT	CONGRESS
War power	Serves as commander in chief of armed forces	Provide for the common defense; declare war; raise, finance, and regulate the military
Treaties	Negotiate treaties	Ratify treaties, by two-thirds majority (Senate)
Appointments	Nominate high-level government officials	Confirm presidents appointments (Senate)
Foreign commerce	No explicit powers, but treaty negotiations and appointment powers pertain	Explicit power "to regulate foreign commerce"
General powers	Executive power; veto	Legislative power; power of the purse; oversight and investigation

which requires approval from both the House of Representatives and the Senate. For example, Congress's first action after September 11 was to authorize the president to use "all necessary and appropriate force," coupled with a $40 billion emergency appropriations bill for homeland defense. And while Bush believed he possessed the constitutional authority to invade Iraq, he still first sought congressional approval, which he received in October 2002. Another opening for congressional involvement is in rejecting **executive agreements** made by the president. Executive agreements have the force of treaties but do not require prior approval by the Senate. They can, however, be revoked by action of both chambers of Congress.

Another congressional player is the foreign policy and military policy committees. In the Senate, these are the Foreign Relations Committee and the Armed Services Committee; in the House, they are the International Affairs Committee and the Armed Services Committee. Usually, a few members of these committees who have spent years specializing in foreign affairs become trusted members of the foreign policy establishment and are actually makers rather than mere shapers of foreign policy. In fact, several members of Congress have left to become key foreign affairs Cabinet members.[2]

executive agreement an agreement, made between the president and another country, that has the force of a treaty but does not require the Senate's "advice and consent"

NON-GOVERNMENT ACTORS ALSO SHAPE FOREIGN POLICY

The "shapers of foreign policy" are the nonofficial, informal players who are typically people or groups that have great influence in the making of foreign policy. Of course, the influence of any given group varies according to the party and the ideology that is dominant at a given moment.

Interest Groups   Far and away the most important category of nonofficial player is the interest group—that is, the interest groups to whom one or more foreign policy issues are of long-standing and vital relevance. The type of interest group with the reputation for the most influence is the economic interest group. Yet the actual influence of organized economic interest groups in foreign policy varies enormously from issue to issue and year to year. Most of these groups are "single-issue" groups and are therefore most active when their particular issue is on the agenda. On many of the broader and more sustained policy issues, such as the **North American Free Trade Agreement** (NAFTA) or the general question of American involvement in international trade, the larger interest groups find it difficult to maintain tight enough control of their many members to speak with a single voice. The most systematic study of international trade policies and their interest groups concluded that the leaders of these large, economic interest groups spend more time maintaining consensus among their members than they do actually lobbying Congress or pressuring major players in the executive branch.[3] The more successful economic interest groups, in terms of influencing foreign policy, are the narrower, single-issue groups, such as the tobacco industry, which over the years has successfully kept American foreign policy

North American Free Trade Agreement (NAFTA) trade treaty between the United States, Canada, and Mexico to lower and eliminate tariffs between the three countries

from putting heavy restrictions on international trade in and advertising of tobacco products, and the computer hardware and software industries, which have successfully hardened the American attitude toward Chinese piracy of intellectual property rights.

Another type of interest group with a well-founded reputation for influence in foreign policy is made up of people with strong attachments and identifications to their country of national origin. The interest group with the reputation for greatest influence is American Jews, whose family and emotional ties to Israel make them one of the most alert and potentially one of the most active foreign policy interest groups. But note once again how narrowly specialized that interest is—it focuses almost entirely and exclusively on policies toward Israel. Similarly, Americans of Irish heritage, despite having resided in the United States for two, three, or four generations, still maintain a vigilance about American policies toward Ireland and Northern Ireland; some even contribute to the terrorist activities of the Irish Republican Army. Many other ethnic and national interest groups wield similar influence over American foreign policy.

A third type of interest group, one with a reputation that has been growing in the past two decades, is the human rights interest group. Such groups are made up of people who, instead of having self-serving economic or ethnic interests in foreign policy, are genuinely concerned for the welfare and treatment of people throughout the world—particularly those who suffer under harsh political regimes. A relatively small but often quite influential example is Amnesty International, whose exposés of human rights abuses have altered the practices of many regimes around the world. In recent years, the Christian Right has also been a vocal advocate for the human rights of Christians who are persecuted in other parts of the world, most notably in China, for their religious beliefs.

A related type of group with a fast-growing influence is the ecological or environmental group, sometimes called the "greens." Groups of this nature often depend more on demonstrations than on the usual forms and strategies of influence in Washington—lobbying and using electoral politics, for example. Demonstrations in strategically located areas can have significant influence on American foreign policy. One good example of this is the opposition that relatively small environmental protection groups in the United States raised against American contracts to buy electrical power from the Canadian province of Quebec: The group opposed the ecological effect of the enlarged hydroelectric power dams that were going to have to be built in order to accommodate American demands.[4]

The Media   The most important element of the policy influence of the media is the speed and scale with which the media can spread political communications. In that factor alone, the media's influence is growing—more news reaches more people faster, and people's reaction times are therefore shorter. For instance, media coverage of the 2003 Iraq war by about six hundred embedded journalists was the most intensive and instantaneous military coverage in history. When we combine this ability to communicate faster with the "feedback" medium of public opinion polling, it becomes clear how the media have become so influential—they enable the American people to reach the president and other official makers of foreign policy.[5]

FOREIGN POLICY EVOLVES IN SMALL STEPS

We can observe three trends about the shaping of American foreign policy. First, as we noted earlier, foreign policy tends to revolve around the president. This is especially true when the nation is faced with an international crisis and when that crisis requires a quick response. Thus, for example, when President John F. Kennedy learned in October 1962 that the Soviet Union was secretly building missiles in Cuba, he realized that he had to decide quickly how to respond, since American action would be even more complicated and risky once the missiles were operational. The final decision to impose a naval blockade around Cuba, instead of launching a military attack, was made by a handful of top presidential advisors and the president himself.

Second, key foreign policy decisions often involve a small number of decision makers, such as the president's national security advisor, the secretary of state, the secretary of defense, and the chair of the Joint Chiefs of Staff, and perhaps a few members of Congress who specialize in foreign policy. In such circumstances, decision making follows an "elitist" pattern. When foreign policy concerns involve long-term public debate, such as whether to join in NAFTA, decision making is more open, public, and pluralist.

Third, America's options in foreign policy may be severely limited by the actions and decisions of other nations. With all its influence, America can often do little to change other nations' decisions. For example, American leaders were dismayed, but helpless, when India and Pakistan engaged in a series of nuclear weapons tests in 1998. Many in the United States and elsewhere feared that such testing might result in a new war between the two nations that might even include a nuclear exchange. These factors lead us to a consideration of the values that underlie American foreign policy.

America Is Historically Suspicious of Foreign Entanglements

When President Washington was preparing to leave office in 1796, he crafted with great care, and with the help of Alexander Hamilton and James Madison, a farewell address that is one of the most memorable documents in American history. We have already had occasion to look at a portion of Washington's farewell address, because in it he gave some stern warnings against political parties (see

PICTURING

Making and Shaping Foreign Policy

Like many of his predecessors, when George W. Bush took office he was well versed in matters of domestic policy but somewhat unfamiliar with foreign policy issues. To make up for that weakness, the president stacked his Cabinet with veteran foreign and defense policy experts like Donald Rumsfeld.

Besides the president, the Pentagon, home to the Department of Defense, is the most visible part of the foreign policy establishment. In September 2002 Secretary of Defense Donald Rumsfeld, shown here with the Vice Chairman of the Joint Chiefs of Staff, General Peter Pace, made the case to invade Iraq by arguing that waiting for Saddam Hussein to use chemical, biological, or nuclear weapons would be a mistake. This preemptive strategy is at the heart of the "Bush Doctrine."

Though Congress has rarely exercised its constitutional authority to declare war, it still plays an important part in foreign policy making. After September 11, for example, Congress authorized the president's use of force, and congressional leaders regularly conferred with Bush on the war on terrorism. This photo from October 2001 shows Bush meeting with (from lower left) then-Senate Minority leader Trent Lott, House Speaker Dennis Hastert, then-Senate Majority Leader Tom Daschle, and then-House Minority Leader Richard Gephardt.

Among the unofficial, informal shapers of foreign policy, interest groups are the most influential. For example, pro-Israel Jewish groups are quite strong in the United States. Here, pro-Israeli demonstrators rally in front of the United Nations building in April 2002.

chapter 6). But Washington's greater concern was to warn the nation against foreign influence:

> History and experience prove that foreign influence is one of the most baneful foes of republican government. . . . The great rule of conduct for us in regard to foreign nations is, in extending our commercial relations to have with them as little *political* connection as possible. So far as we have already formed engagements let them be fulfilled with perfect good faith. Here let us stop. . . . [emphasis in original.][6]

With the exception of a few leaders such as Thomas Jefferson and Thomas Paine, who were eager to take sides with the French against all others, Washington was probably expressing sentiments shared by most Americans. In fact, during most of the nineteenth century, American foreign policy was to a large extent no foreign policy. This avoidance of foreign policy relationships is often referred to as isolationism, a term that, strictly speaking, did not fit American behavior, because America was eager to increase trade with other nations (isolationism means that a nation cuts itself off entirely from the other nations of the world). The United States was also sharply expansionist, as it occupied the vast western territories stretching to the Pacific Ocean (see Figure 13.1). In addition, the United States intervened militarily in the affairs of nations in Central America and elsewhere in this hemisphere

Figure 13.1   **Territorial Expansion by the United States, 1803–53**

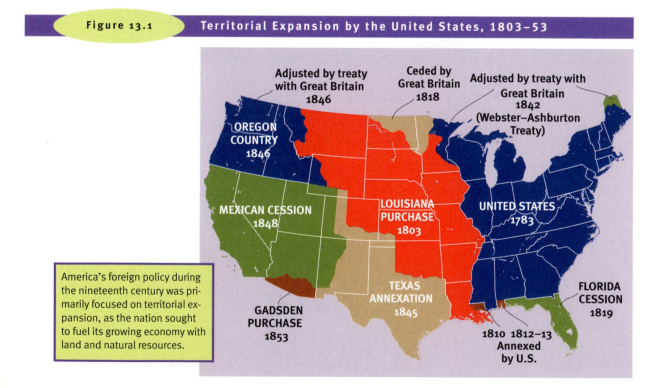

America's foreign policy during the nineteenth century was primarily focused on territorial expansion, as the nation sought to fuel its growing economy with land and natural resources.

throughout the late nineteenth and early twentieth centuries. The term that best describes American behavior in its first 150 years is **unilateralism,** meaning that America preferred to "go it alone."

AMERICA'S GREAT LEAP TO WORLD POWER OCCURRED AFTER WORLD WAR II

America's involvement in World War I represented a major departure from its long-standing avoidance of Europe's diplomatic alliances and military problems. America's late entry into the war in 1917, three years after the war had started, showed the country's initial reluctance to meddle in European problems. The U.S. decision to enter the war was decisive in the Allied victory, yet American refusal to join the new League of Nations reflected a return to unilateralism. As one analyst noted, "[T]he United States withdrew once more into its insularity. Since America was unwilling to use its power, that power, for purposes of foreign policy, did not really exist."[7]

America's "great leap" into foreign policy occurred following World War II (1941–45), when pressure for a new tradition came into direct conflict with the old. The new tradition required foreign entanglements; the old tradition feared them deeply. The new tradition required diplomacy; the old distrusted it. The new tradition required acceptance of antagonistic political systems; the old embraced democracy and was aloof from all else.

The values of the new tradition were all apparent during the **cold war.** Instead of unilateralism, the United States pursued **multilateralism,** entering into treaties with other nations to achieve its foreign policy goals (see Figure 13.2). The most notable of these treaties is that which formed the **North Atlantic Treaty Organization** (NATO) in 1948, which allied the United States, Canada, and most of Western Europe. With its NATO allies, the United States practiced a two-pronged policy in dealing with its cold war rival, the Soviet Union: **containment** and deterrence. Fearing that the Soviet Union was bent on world domination, the United States fought wars in Korea and Vietnam to "contain" Soviet power. And in order to deter a direct attack against itself or its NATO allies, the United States developed a multi-billion-dollar nuclear arsenal capable of destroying the Soviet Union many times over. An arms race between the United States and the Soviet Union was extremely difficult if not impossible to resist because there was no way for either side to know when they had enough deterrent to continue preventing aggression by the other side. The cold war ended abruptly in 1989, after the Soviet Union had spent itself into oblivion and allowed its empire to collapse. Many observers called the end of the cold war a victory for democracy. But more importantly, it was a victory for capitalism over communism, a vindication of the free market as the best way to produce the greatest wealth of nations. Furthering capitalism has long been one of the values guiding American foreign policy and this might be more true at the end of the twentieth century than at any time before.

unilateralism a foreign policy that seeks to avoid international alliances, entanglements, and permanent commitments in favor of independence, neutrality, and freedom of action

cold war the period of hostilities, but no direct war, between the United States and the former Soviet Union between the late 1940s and about 1990

multilateralism a foreign policy that seeks to encourage the involvement of several nation-states in coordinated action, usually in relation to a common adversary, with terms and conditions usually specified in a multicounty treaty

North Atlantic Treaty Organization (NATO) a treaty organization, comprising the United States, Canada, and most of Western Europe, formed in 1948 to counter the perceived threat from the Soviet Union

containment the policy used by the United States during the cold war to restrict the expansion of communism and limit the influence of the Soviet Union

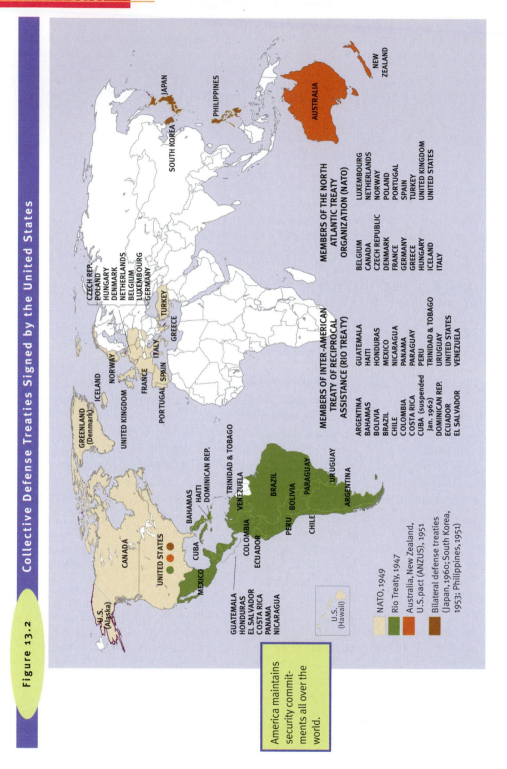

Figure 13.2   Collective Defense Treaties Signed by the United States

America maintains security commitments all over the world.

MEMBERS OF THE NORTH ATLANTIC TREATY ORGANIZATION (NATO)

BELGIUM
CANADA
CZECH REPUBLIC
DENMARK
FRANCE
GERMANY
GREECE
HUNGARY
ICELAND
ITALY

LUXEMBOURG
NETHERLANDS
NORWAY
POLAND
PORTUGAL
SPAIN
TURKEY
UNITED KINGDOM
UNITED STATES

MEMBERS OF INTER-AMERICAN TREATY OF RECIPROCAL ASSISTANCE (RIO TREATY)

ARGENTINA
BAHAMAS
BOLIVIA
BRAZIL
CHILE
COLOMBIA
COSTA RICA
CUBA (suspended Jan. 1962)
DOMINICAN REP.
ECUADOR
EL SALVADOR

GUATEMALA
HAITI
HONDURAS
MEXICO
NICARAGUA
PANAMA
PARAGUAY
PERU
TRINIDAD & TOBAGO
URUGUAY
UNITED STATES
VENEZUELA

NATO, 1949
Rio Treaty, 1947
Australia, New Zealand, U.S. pact (ANZUS), 1951
Bilateral defense treaties (Japan, 1960; South Korea, 1953; Philippines, 1951)

The Instruments of Modern American Foreign Policy Include Diplomacy, Money, and Military Force

Any **nation-state** has at hand certain instruments, or tools, to use in implementing its foreign policy. An instrument is neutral, capable of serving many goals. We deal here with those instruments most important in the modern era: diplomacy, the United Nations, the international monetary structure, economic aid, collective security, and military deterrence. In this section, we will evaluate each of these instruments for its utility in the conduct of American foreign policy, and in the promotion of American values.

nation-state a political entity consisting of people with some common cultural experience (nation) who also share a common political authority (state), recognized by the sovereignties (nation-states)

DIPLOMACY PROMOTES NATIONAL VALUES THROUGH PEACEFUL MEANS

We begin this treatment of instruments with diplomacy because it is the instrument to which all other instruments should be subordinated, although they seldom are. **Diplomacy** is the representation of a government to other foreign governments. Its purpose is to promote national values or interests by peaceful means. According to Hans Morgenthau, "a diplomacy that ends in war has failed in its primary objective."[8]

diplomacy the representation of a government to other foreign governments

The first effort to create a modern diplomatic service in the United States was made through the Rogers Act of 1924, which established the initial framework for a professional foreign service staff. But it took World War II and the Foreign Service Act of 1946 to forge the foreign service into a fully professional diplomatic corps.

Diplomacy, by its very nature, is overshadowed by spectacular international events, dramatic initiatives, and meetings among heads of state or their direct personal representatives. The traditional American distrust of diplomacy continues today, albeit in weaker form. Impatience with or downright distrust of diplomacy has been built not only into all the other instruments of foreign policy but also into the modern presidential system itself.[9] So much personal responsibility has been heaped upon the presidency that it is difficult for presidents to entrust any of their authority or responsibility in foreign policy to professional diplomats in the State Department and other bureaucracies.

Distrust of diplomacy has also produced a tendency among all recent presidents to turn frequently to military and civilian personnel outside the State Department to take on a special diplomatic role as direct personal representatives of the president. As discouraging as it is to those who have dedicated their careers to foreign service to have personal appointees chosen over their heads, it is probably even more discouraging when they are displaced from a foreign policy issue as soon as relations with the country they are posted in begin to heat up. When a special personal representative is sent abroad to represent the president, the envoy holds a status higher than that of the local ambassador, and the embassy becomes the envoy's temporary residence and base of operation. Despite the impressive professionalization of the American foreign service—with advanced training, competitive exams, language requirements, and career commitment—this practice of displacing career ambassadors with political appointees and with special personal presidential representatives continues. For instance, when President Clinton sought in 1994 to make a final diplomatic attempt to persuade Haiti's military dictator to relinquish power to the country's freely elected president before dispatching U.S. military forces to the island, he sent a team of three personal representatives—former president Jimmy Carter, Senator Sam Nunn, and former chair of the Joint Chiefs of Staff Colin Powell.

Diplomacy continues to be vital to American foreign policy after the terrorist attacks of September 11, 2001. While much emphasis has been placed on American military actions—most notably, the invasion of Afghanistan aimed at overthrowing the Taliban regime that had sponsored al Qaeda terrorist camps—diplomacy has also been important. Many nations around the world have publicly or secretly aided America by turning over arrested terrorist suspects, providing intelligence, and offering other forms of cooperation. George W. Bush's secretary of state, Colin Powell, made calls to the leaders of over eighty nations to obtain dozens of promises of assistance in the weeks after 9/11.

The significance of diplomacy and its vulnerability to domestic politics may be better appreciated as we proceed to the other instruments. The other instruments to be identified and assessed in the following sections are more reflective of American culture and values than is diplomacy.

THE UNITED NATIONS CONTINUES TO SUPPORT AMERICAN INTERESTS

United Nations (UN) an organization of nations founded in 1945 to serve as a channel for negotiation and a means of settling international disputes peaceably. The UN has had frequent successes in providing a forum for negotiation and on some occasions a means of preventing international conflicts from spreading. On a number of occasions, the UN has been a convenient cover for U.S. foreign policy goals

The utility of the **United Nations** (**UN**) to the United States as an instrument of foreign policy can be too easily underestimated, because the United Nations is a very large and unwieldy institution with few powers and no armed forces to implement its rules and resolutions. Its supreme body is the UN General Assembly, comprised of one representative of each of the 191 member states. Each member representative has one vote, regardless of the size of the country. Important issues require a two-thirds majority vote, and the annual session of the General Assembly runs only from September to December (although it can call extra sessions). It has little organization that can make it an effective decision-making body, with only six standing committees, few tight rules of procedure, and no political parties to provide priorities and discipline. Its defenders are quick to add that although it lacks armed forces, it relies on power of world opinion, and this is not to be taken lightly. The powers of the United Nations devolve mainly to its "executive committee," the UN Security Council, which alone has the real power to make decisions and rulings that member states are obligated by the UN Charter to implement. The Security Council may be called into session at any time, and each member (or a designated alternate) must be present at UN Headquarters in New York at all times. It is composed of fifteen members: Five are permanent, and ten are elected by the General Assembly for two-year, nonrepeatable terms. The five permanent members are China, France, Russia, the United Kingdom, and the United States. Each of the fifteen members has only one vote, and a nine-vote majority of the fifteen is required on all substantive matters. But each of the five permanent members also has a negative vote, a "veto," and one veto is sufficient to reject any substantive proposal.

During the first decade or more after its founding in 1945, the United Nations was a direct servant of American interests. The most spectacular example of this was the official UN authorization and sponsorship of intervention in Korea with an international "peacekeeping force" in 1950.

The United States provided 40 percent of the UN budget in 1946 (its first full year of operation) and 25 percent of the $2.4 billion UN budget in 2001–02.[10] Many Americans feel that the United Nations does not give good value for the investment. But any evaluation of the United Nations must take into account the purpose for which the United States sought its creation: to achieve power without diplomacy. After World War II, when the United States could no longer remain aloof from foreign policy, the nation's leaders sought to use our power to create an international structure that could be run with a minimum of regular diplomatic involvement—so that Americans could return to their normal domestic pursuits.

The UN gained a new lease on life in the post–cold war era, with its performance in the 1991 Gulf War. Although President George H. W. Bush's immediate reaction to Iraq's invasion of Kuwait was unilateral, he quickly turned to the UN for sponsorship. The UN General Assembly initially adopted resolutions condemning the invasion and approving the full blockade of Iraq. Once the blockade was seen as having failed to achieve the unconditional withdrawal demanded by the UN, the General Assembly adopted further resolutions authorizing the twenty-nine nation coalition to use force if, by January 15, 1991, the resolutions were not observed. The Gulf War victory was a genuine UN victory. The cost of the operation was estimated at $61.1 billion. First authorized by the U.S. Congress, actual U.S. outlays were offset by pledges from the other participants—the largest shares coming from Saudi Arabia ($15.6 billion), Kuwait ($16 billion), Japan ($10 billion), and Germany ($6.5 billion). The final U.S. costs were estimated at a maximum of $8 billion.[11]

Of course, not all UN-sponsored actions are clear-cut victories. When Yugoslavia's communist regime collapsed in the early 1990s, the country broke apart into historically ethnically distinct regions. In one of these, Bosnia, a fierce war broke out between Muslims, Croatians, and Serbians. From the outset, all outside parties urged peace, and United Nations troops were deployed to create "safe havens" in several Bosnian cities and towns. Yet the international community failed to prevent Serbs from waging a war of aggression and "ethnic cleansing." Only in 1999 did a multinational air campaign, led by the United States, force Serbs out of nearby Muslim-dominated Kosovo, where Serbian ethnic cleansing exacted a heavy toll in death and misery. After the war, multinational forces served as peacekeepers between the hostile factions and supervised Kosovo's rebuilding.

The UN continued to be important after 9/11. Within weeks of the attacks on America, the UN Security Council adopted an American-backed resolution requiring all countries to deny safe haven to anyone supporting or engaging in terrorism. In the case of the 2003 invasion of Iraq, President George W. Bush maintained doubts about the necessity of seeking UN approval. Even so, Bush and Secretary of State Colin Powell went to the UN to justify American actions and to seek international support. Ultimately, Bush decided against seeking UN approval of an invasion after France, Russia, and other nations expressed reservations. The Bush administration's decision to go it alone (with some limited military assistance from a few allies, such as Britain) reflected its unilateralist approach to foreign policy. Recent UN actions show the promise and the limits of the UN as an instrument of foreign policy in the post–cold war era. Although the United States can no longer control UN decisions, as it could in the UN's early days, the UN continues to function as a useful instrument of American foreign policy.[12]

THE INTERNATIONAL MONETARY STRUCTURE HELPS PROVIDE ECONOMIC STABILITY

Fear of a repeat of the economic devastation that followed World War I brought the United States together with its allies (except the USSR) to Bretton Woods, New Hampshire, in 1944 to create a new international economic structure for the postwar world. The result was two institutions: the International Bank for Reconstruction and Development (commonly called the World Bank) and the International Monetary Fund.

The World Bank was set up to finance long-term capital. Leading nations took on the obligation of contributing funds to enable the World Bank to make loans to capital-hungry countries. (The U.S. quota has been about one-third of the total.)

International Monetary Fund (IMF) an institution—established in 1944 at Bretton Woods, New Hampshire—that provides loans and facilitates international monetary exchange

The **International Monetary Fund (IMF)** was set up to provide for the short-term flow of money. After the war, the dollar, instead of gold, was the chief means by which the currencies of one country would be "changed into" currencies of another country for purposes of making international transactions. To permit debtor countries with no international balances to make purchases and investments, the IMF was set up to lend dollars or other appropriate currencies to needy member countries to help them overcome temporary trade deficits. For many years after World War II, the IMF, along with U.S. foreign aid, in effect constituted the only international medium of exchange.

During the past decade, the IMF has returned to a position of enhanced importance through its efforts to reform some of the largest debtor nations and formerly communist countries, to bring them more fully into the global capitalist economy. In the early 1990s, Russia and thirteen other former Soviet republics were invited to join the IMF and the World Bank with the expectation of receiving $10.5 billion from these two agencies, primarily for a ruble-stabilization fund. Each republic was to get a permanent IMF representative, and the IMF increased its staff by at least 10 percent to provide the expertise necessary to cope with the problems of these emerging capitalist economies.[13]

These activities of the IMF indicate just how effectively it is committed to the extension of the capitalist victory over communism. The reforms imposed on poorer countries—imposed as conditions to be met before receiving IMF loans—are reforms that commit a troubled country to joining or maintaining membership in the system of global capital exchange that allows investment to seek the highest profits, without restraint. This goal can ignite a boom—as it did in South Korea, Indonesia, Singapore, and Thailand—but that boom can terminate just as abruptly, leaving the economy in question defenseless.

ECONOMIC AID HELPS DIPLOMACY

Commitment to rebuilding war-torn countries came as early as commitment to the basic postwar international monetary structure. This is the way President Franklin Roosevelt put the case in a press conference in November 1942, less than one year after the United States entered World War II:

> Sure, we are going to rehabilitate [other nations after the war]. Why? . . . Not only from the humanitarian point of view . . . but from the viewpoint of our own pocket-books, and our safety from future war.[14]

America's decision to help war-torn Europe rebuild was heavily influenced by Great Britain's sudden decision in 1947 to reverse its commitments to Greece and Turkey. Within three weeks of Britain's announcement, President Harry Truman recommended a $400 million direct aid program for Greece and Turkey, which was then approved by Congress in May 1947. This aid program was quickly followed by the historically unprecedented program to rebuild all of Europe. The program, known as the **Marshall Plan,** was named in honor of Secretary of State (and former five-star general) George C. Marshall. This program had two main motivations. One was humanitarian, to help the millions of people who suffered from the effects of the Nazi era. The second motivation was more selfish—by providing such massive aid, America was making sure that it would have European allies that would be both strong and loyal to America in the coming cold war struggle against the Soviet Union and its allies in eastern Europe.

By 1952, the United States had spent over $34 billion for the relief, reconstruction, and recovery of Western Europe. The program's emphasis shifted in 1951, with the passage of the Mutual Security Act, which was designed to rebuild the military capabilities of America's European allies. Of the $48 billion appropriated between 1952 and 1961, over half went for military assistance, the rest for continuing economic aid. Over those years, the geographic emphasis of U.S. aid also shifted, toward South Korea, Taiwan, the Philippines, Vietnam, Iran, Greece, and Turkey—that is, toward the rim of communism. In the 1960s, the emphasis shifted once again, toward what became known as the Third

Marshall Plan the U.S. European Recovery Plan, in which over $34 billion was spent for the relief, reconstruction, and economic recovery of Western Europe after World War II

World, or the Developing World. From 1962 to 1975, over $100 billion was sent, mainly to Latin America for economic assistance. Other countries of Africa and Asia were also brought in.[15] Promises of American aid to Afghanistan and Pakistan were vital in obtaining support from the rulers of these two countries in the war on terrorism, as was the extension of economic aid to Iraq after the United States deposed Saddam Hussein.

Many critics have argued that foreign aid is really aid for political and economic elites, not for the people. Although this is to a large extent true, it needs to be understood in a broader context. If a country's leaders oppose distributing food or any other form of assistance to its people, there is little the United States, or any aid organization, can do, short of terminating the assistance. Goods have to be exchanged across national borders before they can reach the people who need them. Needy people would probably be worse off if the United States cut off aid altogether. The lines of international communication must be kept open. That is why diplomacy exists, and foreign aid can facilitate diplomacy, just as diplomacy is necessary to help get foreign aid where it is most needed.

COLLECTIVE SECURITY IS DESIGNED TO DETER WAR

In 1947, most Americans hoped that the United States could meet its world obligations through the United Nations and economic structures alone. But most foreign policy makers recognized that it was a vain hope even as they were permitting and encouraging Americans to believe it. They had anticipated the need for military entanglements at the time of drafting the original UN Charter by insisting upon language that recognized the right of all nations to provide for their mutual defense independently of the United Nations.

At first quite reluctant to approve treaties providing for national security alliances, the Senate ultimately agreed with the executive branch. The first collective security agreement was the Rio Treaty (ratified by the Senate in September 1947), which created the Organization of American States (OAS). This was the model treaty, anticipating all succeeding collective security treaties by providing that an armed attack against any of its members "shall be considered as an attack against all the American States," including the United States. A more significant break with U.S. tradition against peacetime entanglements came with the North Atlantic Treaty (signed in April 1949), which created the North Atlantic Treaty Organization (NATO). ANZUS, a treaty tying Australia and New Zealand to the United States, was signed in September 1951. Three years later, the Southeast Asia Treaty created the Southeast Asia Treaty Organization (SEATO).

bilateral treaties treaties made between two nations

In addition to these multilateral treaties, the United States entered into a number of **bilateral treaties**—treaties between two countries. As one author has observed, the United States has been a *producer* of security while most of its allies have been *consumers* of security.[16] For example, the United States has consistently devoted a greater percentage of its Gross Domestic Product (GDP) to defense than have its NATO allies and Japan.

This pattern has continued in the post–cold war era, and its best illustration is in the 1991 Persian Gulf War, where the United States provided the initiative, the leadership, and most of the armed forces, even though its allies were obliged to reimburse over 90 percent of the cost.

It is difficult to evaluate collective security and its treaties, because the purpose of collective security as an instrument of foreign policy is prevention, and success of this kind has to be measured according to what did *not* happen. The critics have argued that U.S. collective security treaties posed a threat of encirclement to the Soviet Union, forcing it to produce its own collective security, particularly the Warsaw Pact.[17] Nevertheless, no one can deny the counterargument that the world has enjoyed sixty years without world war.

MILITARY DETERRENCE IS BASED ON PERMANENT MILITARY MOBILIZATION

For the first century and a half of its existence as an independent republic, the United States held strongly to a "Minuteman" theory of defense: Maintain a small corps of professional officers, a few flagships, and a small contingent of marines; leave the rest of defense to the state militias. In case of war, mobilize as quickly as possible, taking advantage of the country's immense size and its separation from Europe to gain time to mobilize.

The United States applied this policy as recently as the post–World War I years and was beginning to apply it after World War II, until the new policy of preparedness won out. The cycle of demobilization-remobilization was broken, and in its place the United States adopted a new policy of constant mobilization and preparedness: **deterrence,** or the development and maintenance of military strength as a means of discouraging attack. After World War II, military deterrence against the Soviet Union became the fundamental American foreign policy objective, requiring a vast commitment of national resources. With preparedness as the goal, peacetime defense expenditures grew steadily over the course of the cold war.

deterrence the development and maintenance of military strength as a means of discouraging attack

The end of the cold war raised public expectations for a "peace dividend"—surplus federal money resulting from reductions in the defense budget—after nearly a decade of the largest peacetime defense budget increases in U.S. history. Many defense experts, liberal and conservative, countered that deterrence was still needed, and that severe and abrupt cuts could endanger private industry in many friendly foreign countries as well as in the United States.

The Persian Gulf War brought both points dramatically into focus. First, the 1990 Iraqi invasion of Kuwait revealed the size, strength, and advanced modern technological base not only of the Iraqi armed forces but of other countries, Arab and non-Arab, including the capability, then or soon, to make atomic weapons and other weapons of massive destructive power, including chemical and biological weapons. Second, the demand for advanced weaponry was intensifying. The decisive victory of the United States and its allies in the Gulf War, far from discouraging the international arms trade, gave it fresh impetus. Following the Gulf War victory, *Newsweek* reported that "industry reps quickly realized that foreign

The War with Iraq

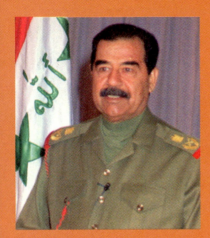

As part of his rationale for declaring war in March 2003, George W. Bush declared that it was necessary to depose the authoritarian regime of Saddam Hussein and institute democracy. President Bush cited as the determining factors Saddam's ties to terrorist organizations like Al Qaeda and the "imminent threat" posed by Hussein's stockpiling of weapons of mass destruction (WMD). Bush reasoned that the removal of Saddam and the replacement of his regime with a democracy would begin the process of peacefully reconfiguring the entire Middle East.

In preparing for a potential war against Iraq, the United States fell back on a unilateral approach. While President Bush went before the United Nations and ultimately received the approval of its Security Council, among the world's leaders only Britain's prime minister Tony Blair explicitly endorsed the United States' preemptive intervention in Iraq. During the fighting, the United States contributed a large majority of the troops.

Though initially somewhat popular at home, America's unilateral approach to the war on Iraq alienated members of the international community. During the first months of 2003, millions of people—from Australia to Peru—rallied to condemn America's potential invasion of Iraq.

POLITICS

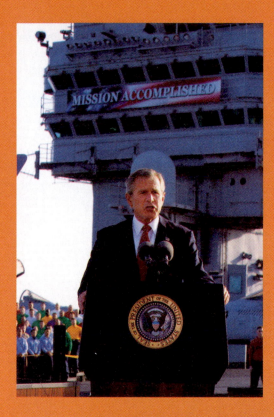

In what has become a rather infamous moment in the Iraq war, Bush addressed a crowd of American military personnel on the *USS Abraham Lincoln*. Although the president hailed the end of major combat in Iraq, as emphasized by the "Mission Accomplished" banner in the background, the number of American dead continued to rise and fighting went on. As of late 2005, America has yet to withdraw its forces from Iraq.

customers would now be beating a path to their doors, seeking to buy the winning weaponry." The Soviet Union at one time led the list of major world arms sellers, and Russia and several other republics of the former Soviet Union have continued to make international arms sales, particularly since now there are "no ideological limitations" in the competition for customers.[18] The United States now leads the list of military weapons exporters, followed by Great Britain, France, and Russia. Thus, some shrinkage of defense expenditure has been desirable, but Democrats and Republicans alike agree that this reduction must be guided by the continuing need to maintain U.S. and allied credibility as a deterrent to post–cold war arms races.

As to the second point, domestic pressures join international demands to fuel post–cold war defense spending. Each cut in military production and each closing of a military base or plant translates into a significant loss of jobs. Moreover, the conversion of defense industries to domestic uses is not a problem faced by the United States alone. Figure 13.3 conveys a dramatic picture of the "international relations" of the production of one single weapons system, the F-16 fighter airplane.

Figure 13.3 How the F-16 Is Produced: The International Relations of Defense

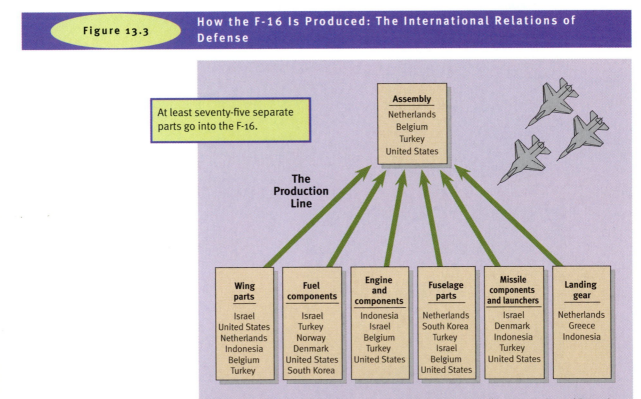

At least seventy-five separate parts go into the F-16.

Assembly
Netherlands
Belgium
Turkey
United States

The Production Line

Wing parts	Fuel components	Engine and components	Fuselage parts	Missile components and launchers	Landing gear
Israel	Israel	Indonesia	Netherlands	Israel	Netherlands
United States	Turkey	Israel	South Korea	Denmark	Greece
Netherlands	Norway	Belgium	Turkey	Indonesia	Indonesia
Indonesia	Denmark	Turkey	Israel	Turkey	
Belgium	United States	United States	Belgium	United States	
Turkey	South Korea		United States		

SOURCE: U.S. Congress, Office of Technology Assessment, *Arming Our Allies: Cooperation and Competition in Defense Technology*, Series OTA-ICS-449 (Washington, DC: Government Printing Office, May 1990), pp. 42–43. Information provided by the primary manufacturer, General Dynamics Corporation.

The threat of the arms race and international conflict persists even in the post–cold war era. Although the United States is an important part of the problem, it is also the most essential part of the solution. The only real hope for a significant reduction in the international demand for arms will come from changes in the general political and economic environment. But such changes do not happen spontaneously. On the international level, genuine reduction in the demand for arms will require diplomacy; try as we might, power without diplomacy can never be a permanent solution.

Foreign Policy Values for America Today Emphasize Economic Relationships

Although "making the world safe for democracy" was used to justify the U.S. entry into World War I, it was taken more seriously after World War II, when at last the United States was willing to play a more sustained part in world affairs. To create the world's ruling regimes in the American image would indeed give Americans the opportunity to return to their private pursuits, for if all or even most of the world's countries were governed by democratic constitutions, there would be no more war, since no democracy would ever attack another democracy—or so it has been assumed.

MAKING THE WORLD SAFE FOR DEMOCRACY MAY NOT PRODUCE PEACE

The emergence of the Soviet Union as a superpower was the overwhelming influence on American foreign policy thinking in the post–World War II era. The distribution of power in the world was "bipolar," and Americans saw the world separated in two, with an "iron curtain" dividing the communist world from the free world. The "containment" of communism became the driving force behind American foreign policy.[19] According to foreign policy expert Richard Barnet, during the 1950s and 1960s, "the United States used its military or paramilitary power on an average of once every eighteen months either to prevent a government deemed undesirable from coming to power or to overthrow a revolutionary or reformist government considered inimical to America's interests."[20]

During the 1970s, the United States began to de-emphasize containment, not so much because of the outcome of the Vietnam War as because of the emergence of a multipolar world. In 1972, the United States accepted (and later recognized) the communist government of the People's Republic of China and broke forever its pure bipolar, cold war view of world power distribution. Other powers became politically important as well, including Japan, the European Economic Community (now the European Union), India, and, depending on their own resolve, the countries making up the Organization of Petroleum Exporting Countries (OPEC).

This multipolar phase ended after 1989, with the collapse of the Soviet Union and the end of the cold war. Soon thereafter the Warsaw Pact collapsed too, ending armed confrontation in Europe. With almost equal suddenness, the popular demand for "self-determination" produced several new nation-states and the demand for still more. On the one hand, it was indeed good to witness the reemergence of some twenty-five major nationalities after decades of suppression. On the other hand, policy makers with a sense of history are aware that this new world order bears a strong resemblance to the world of 1914. Then, the trend was known as "Balkanization." Balkanization meant nationhood and self-determination, but it also meant war. The Soviet Union after World War I and Yugoslavia after World War II kept more than twenty nationalities from making war against each other for several decades. In 1989 and the years that followed, the world was caught unprepared for the dangers of a new disorder that the reemergence of these nationalities produced. Some argue that the international threat of terrorism is also a product of the post–cold war Balkanization process.

MAKING THE WORLD SAFE FOR DEMOCRACY AND MARKETS MEANS GLOBAL CAPITALISM

The abrupt end of the cold war unleashed another dynamic factor, the globalization of markets; one could call it the globalization of capitalism. This is good news, but it has its problematic side because the free market can disrupt nationhood. Although the globalization of markets is enormously productive, countries like to enjoy its benefits while attempting at the same time to prevent international economic influences from affecting local jobs, local families, and established class and tribal relationships.

Approval of the NAFTA in 1993 serves as a good example of how such agreements cause political conflicts *within* nations. A majority of Democrats and Republicans supported NAFTA on the grounds that a freer, global market was in America's national interest. But even as large bipartisan majorities in Congress were embracing NAFTA, three important factions were rising to fight it. Former presidential candidate Pat Buchanan led a large segment of conservative Americans to fight NAFTA because, he argued, communities and families would be threatened by job losses and by competition from legal and illegal immigrant workers. Another large faction, led by Ross Perot, opposed NAFTA largely on the theory that American companies would move their operations to Mexico, where labor costs are lower. Organized labor and many farmers joined the fight against NAFTA.

As *New York Times* foreign affairs columnist Thomas Friedman put it, ". . . now that the free market is triumphing on a global basis, the most interesting conflicts are between the winners and losers within countries. It is these internal battles that will increasingly shape international affairs."[21]

Similar issues arose when the United States joined in the General Agreement on Tariffs and Trade, or GATT. GATT began in 1948 when 23 nations agreed to free trade among themselves. By the time the United States joined in 1994, 123 nations had signed off on the agreement, which among other things called for reduced border taxes, cuts in government subsidies to protected industries, and an increase in duty-free imports. In 1995, GATT became the World Trade Organization (WTO). In the United States, labor unions and farmers continued to voice concerns about American involvement in this agreement, as did environmentalists, who feared that enhanced trade was occurring at the cost of environmental protection and humane labor practices. These conflicts came to a head when the WTO met in Seattle, Washington, in 1999. Pro-environment and pro-labor protestors successfully disrupted the WTO meeting, focusing national and international attention on the WTO's apparent lack of concern for environmental and labor practices in some member nations.

The global market is here to stay and American values have changed enough to incorporate it, despite the toll it may take on community and family tradition. Meanwhile, many of the elements of foreign policy created during the cold war still exist because they turned out to be good adjustments to the modern era.

Summary

The skepticism of American citizens about foreign entanglements was reflected in the policy of most American leaders from America's founding to the end of the nineteenth century—unilateralism. In the twentieth century, especially after World War II, America became the most influential nation on the world stage. Yet even in the last half of the twentieth century, many Americans continued to doubt the wisdom of America's active foreign policy role.

The first section of this chapter looked at the players in foreign policy—the makers and the shapers. Since the president is central to foreign policy, it is best to assess how other actors interact with the president. In most instances, this interaction involves only the narrowest element of the foreign policy establishment. The American people have an opportunity to influence foreign policy, but primarily through Congress or interest groups. The values that have shaped American foreign policy emphasize the continuing tension between America's active role and Americans' continue suspicion of that active role.

Modern American foreign policy is conducted through the use of diplomacy, the United Nations, the international monetary structure, economic aid, collective security, and military deterrence. The containment of communism and the expansion of capitalism have been major goals of American foreign policy.

For Further Reading

Crabb, Cecil V., and Kevin V. Mulcahy. *Presidents and Foreign Policymaking: From FDR to Reagan.* Baton Rouge, LA: Louisiana State University Press, 1986.

Doremus, Paul N., William W. Keller, Louis Pauly, and Simon Reich. *The Myth of the Global Corporation.* Princeton, NJ: Princeton University Press, 1998.

Gilpin, Robert. *The Political Economy of International Relations.* Princeton, NJ: Princeton University Press, 1987.

Graubard, Stephen, ed. "The Exit from Communism." *Daedalus* 121, no. 2 (spring 1992).

____. "The Quest for World Order." *Daedalus* 124, no. 3 (summer 1995).

Greenfield, Liah. *Nationalism: Five Roads to Modernity.* Cambridge, MA: Harvard University Press, 1993.

Keller, William W. *Arm in Arm: The Political Economy of the Global Arms Race.* New York: Basic Books, 1995.

Kennan, George F. *Around the Cragged Hill: A Personal and Political Philosophy.* New York: Norton, 1993.

Kennedy, Paul M. *The Rise and Fall of the Great Powers: Economic Change and Military Conflict from 1500 to 2000.* New York: Random House, 1987.

LaFeber, Walter. *The American Age: United States Foreign Policy at Home and Abroad since 1750.* New York: Norton, 1989.

____. *The Clash: U.S.–Japanese Relations throughout History.* New York: Norton, 1997.

Wirls, Daniel. *Buildup: The Politics of Defense in the Reagan Era.* Ithaca, NY: Cornell University Press, 1992.

Study Outline

1. Traditionally, Americans have been skeptical and distrustful of foreign policy.
2. Public opinion can have a determinative impact on the success or failure of foreign policy. Consequently, politicians often engage in deceit in order to curry the public's favor.

The Makers and Shapers of Foreign Policy Include the President, the Bureaucracy, and Congress

1. All foreign policy decisions must be made and implemented in the name of the president.
2. The key players in foreign policy in the bureaucracy are the secretaries of State, Defense, and Treasury; the Joint Chiefs of Staff (especially the chair); and the director of the Central Intelligence Agency.
3. Although the Senate traditionally has more foreign policy power than the House, since World War II, the House and the Senate have both been important players in foreign policy.
4. Many types of interest groups help shape American foreign policy. These groups include economic interest groups, ethnic or national interest groups, and human rights interest groups.
5. The media serve to communicate issues and policies to the American people, and to communicate the public's opinions back to the president. One definite influence of television on foreign policy has been to make the American people more cynical and skeptical than they otherwise would have been.
6. Individual or group influence in foreign policy varies from case to case and from situation to situation.

America Is Historically Suspicious of Foreign Entanglements

1. Traditionally, unilateralism, the desire to go it alone, was the American posture toward the world.
2. Although the traditional era of American foreign policy came to an end with World War I, there was no discernible change in approach to such policy until after World War II.

The Instruments of Modern American Foreign Policy Include Diplomacy, Money, and Military Forces

1. Diplomacy is the representation of a government to other foreign governments, and it is the foreign policy instrument to which other instruments must be subordinated.
2. The United Nations is an instrument whose usefulness to American foreign policy can too easily be underestimated.
3. The international monetary structure, which consists of the World Bank and the International Monetary Fund, was created to avoid the economic devastation that followed World War I.
4. After World War II, the United States recognized the importance of collective security, and subsequently entered into multilateral collective security treaties and other bilateral treaties.

5. World War II broke the American cycle of demobilization-remobilization and led to a new policy of military preparedness.

Practice Quiz

1. Who noted that a democracy such as the United States lacked the qualities best suited for successful foreign policies?
   a) George Washington
   b) Alexis de Tocqueville
   c) Woodrow Wilson
   d) Ronald Reagan

2. The making of American foreign policy is
   a) dominated entirely by the president.
   b) dominated entirely by Congress.
   c) dominated entirely by interest groups.
   d) highly pluralistic, involving a large mix of both official and unofficial players.

3. The term "unilateralism" describes
   a) an approach to foreign policy that involves complex and time-consuming negotiations between multiple powers.
   b) a "go-it-alone" approach to foreign policy.
   c) episodes in American foreign policy during which the president dominates Congress.
   d) instances when the U.S. Supreme Court refuses to approve a treaty negotiated by the president.

4. The term "cold war" refers to the
   a) competition between the United States and Canada over Alaska.
   b) the years between World War I and World War II when the United States and Germany were hostile to one another.
   c) the period of struggle between the United States and the Soviet Union between the late 1940s and the late 1980s.
   d) the economic competition between the United States and Japan today.

5. The North Atlantic Treaty Organization was formed in 1948 by the United States,
   a) Canada, and most of Eastern Europe.
   b) Canada, and Mexico.
   c) Canada, and most of Western Europe.
   d) Canada, and the United Kingdom.

6. Which of the following terms best describes the American posture toward the world prior to the middle of the twentieth century?
   a) interventionist
   b) isolationist
   c) unilateralist
   d) none of the above

7. The United Nations' activity in which country points to a new humanitarian role for the UN?
   a) Pakistan
   b) Russia
   c) the former Yugoslavia
   d) the United States

8. Which of the following are important international economic institutions created after World War II?
   a) the Federal Reserve
   b) the World Bank
   c) the International Monetary Fund
   d) Both b and c are correct.

9. Which of the following terms describes the idea that the development and maintenance of military strength discourages attack?
   a) deterrence
   b) containment
   c) "minuteman" theory of defense
   d) detente

10. Which of the following was dedicated to the relief, reconstruction, and economic recovery of Western Europe?
    a) the Marshall Plan
    b) the Lend-Lease Act
    c) the General Agreement on Tariffs and Trade
    d) the North American Free Trade Agreement

Critical Thinking Questions

1. In previous chapters we have learned about the political nature of most of the key players in American foreign policy. How might politics (in addition to democracy) impede the effectiveness of the United States in the international arena? Can you think of an instance in which the United States was hampered by domestic politics?

2. What is the proper balance between governmental effectiveness in international politics and the public's "right to know"? Surely, for tactical reasons the government should be able to keep some activities secret. But given the potential for abuse of governmental secrecy, how might the public hold the government accountable while preserving for the United States the tactical advantage of secrecy?

Key Terms

bilateral treaties (p. 386)
cold war (p. 379)
containment (p. 379)
deterrence (p. 387)
diplomacy (p. 381)

executive agreement (p. 373)
International Monetary Fund (IMF) (p. 384)
Marshall Plan (p. 385)
multilateralism (p. 379)
nation-state (p. 381)

North American Free Trade Agreement (NAFTA) (p. 373)
North Atlantic Treaty Organization (NATO) (p. 379)
unilateralism (p. 379)
United Nations (p. 382)

APPENDIX

THE DECLARATION OF INDEPENDENCE

In Congress, July 4, 1776

The unanimous Declaration of the thirteen united States of America,

When in the Course of human events, it becomes necessary for one people to dissolve the political bands which have connected them with another, and to assume among the powers of the earth, the separate and equal station to which the Laws of Nature and of Nature's God entitle them, a decent respect to the opinions of mankind requires that they should declare the causes which impel them to the separation.

We hold these truths to be self-evident, that all men are created equal, that they are endowed by their Creator with certain unalienable Rights, that among these are Life, Liberty and the pursuit of Happiness.—That to secure these rights, Governments are instituted among Men, deriving their just powers from the consent of the governed.—That whenever any Form of Government becomes destructive of these ends, it is the Right of the People to alter or to abolish it, and to institute new Government, laying its foundation on such principles and organizing its powers in such form, as to them shall seem most likely to effect their Safety and Happiness. Prudence, indeed, will dictate that Governments long established should not be changed for light and transient causes; and accordingly all experience hath shewn, that mankind are more disposed to suffer, while evils are sufferable, than to right themselves by abolishing the forms to which they are accustomed. But when a long train of abuses and usurpations, pursuing invariably the same Object evinces a design to reduce them under absolute Despotism, it is their right, it is their duty, to throw off such Government, and to provide new Guards for their future security.—Such has been the patient sufferance of these Colonies; and such is now the necessity which constrains them to alter their former Systems of Government. The history of the present King of Great Britain is a history of repeated injuries and usurpations, all having in direct object the establishment of an absolute Tyranny over these States. To prove this, let Facts be submitted to a candid world.

He has refused his Assent to Laws, the most wholesome and necessary for the public good.

He has forbidden his Governors to pass Laws of immediate and pressing importance, unless suspended in their operation till his Assent should be obtained; and when so suspended, he has utterly neglected to attend to them.

He has refused to pass other Laws for the accommodation of large districts of people, unless those people would relinquish the right of Representation in the Legislature, a right inestimable to them and formidable to tyrants only.

He has called together legislative bodies at places unusual, uncomfortable, and distant from the depository of their public Records, for the sole purpose of fatiguing them into compliance with his measures.

He has dissolved Representative Houses repeatedly, for opposing with manly firmness his invasions on the rights of the people.

He has refused for a long time, after such dissolutions, to cause others to be elected; whereby the Legislative powers, incapable of Annihilation, have returned to the People at large for their exercise; the State remaining in the mean time exposed to all the dangers of invasion from without, and convulsions within.

He has endeavoured to prevent the population of these States; for that purpose obstructing the Laws for Naturalization of Foreigners; refusing to pass others to encourage their migrations hither, and raising the conditions of new Appropriations of Lands.

He has obstructed the Administration of Justice, by refusing his Assent to Laws for establishing Judiciary powers.

He has made Judges dependent on his Will alone, for the tenure of their offices, and the amount and payment of their salaries.

He has erected a multitude of New Offices, and sent hither swarms of Officers to harrass our people, and eat out their substance.

He has kept among us, in times of peace, Standing Armies without the Consent of our legislatures.

He has affected to render the Military independent of and superior to the Civil power.

He has combined with others to subject us to a jurisdiction foreign to our constitution, and unacknowledged by our laws; giving his Assent to their Acts of pretended Legislation:

For Quartering large bodies of armed troops among us:

For protecting them, by a mock Trial, from punishment for any Murders which they should commit on the Inhabitants of these States:

For cutting off our Trade with all parts of the world:

For imposing Taxes on us without our Consent:

For depriving us in many cases, of the benefits of Trial by Jury:

For transporting us beyond Seas to be tried for pretended offences:

For abolishing the free System of English Laws in a neighboring Province, establishing therein an Arbitrary government, and enlarging its Boundaries so as to render it at once an example and fit instrument for introducing the same absolute rule into these Colonies:

For taking away our Charters, abolishing our most valuable Laws, and altering fundamentally the Forms of our Governments:

For suspending our own Legislatures, and declaring themselves invested with power to legislate for us in all cases whatsoever.

He has abdicated Government here, by declaring us out of his Protection and waging War against us.

He has plundered our seas, ravaged our Coasts, burnt our towns, and destroyed the lives of our people.

He is at this time transporting large Armies of foreign Mercenaries to compleat the works of death, desolation and tyranny, already begun with circumstances of Cruelty & perfidy scarcely paralleled in the most barbarous ages, and totally unworthy the Head of a civilized nation.

He has constrained our fellow Citizens taken Captive on the high Seas to bear Arms against their Country, to become the executioners of their friends and Brethren, or to fall themselves by their Hands.

He has excited domestic insurrections amongst us, and has endeavoured to bring on the inhabitants of our frontiers, the merciless Indian Savages, whose known rule of warfare, is an undistinguished destruction of all ages, sexes and conditions.

In every stage of these Oppressions We have Petitioned for Redress in the most humble terms: Our repeated Petitions have been answered only by repeated injury. A Prince whose character is thus marked by every act which may define a Tyrant, is unfit to be the ruler of a free people.

Nor have We been wanting in attentions to our British brethren. We have warned them from time to time of attempts by their legislature to extend an unwarrantable jurisdiction over us. We have reminded them of the circumstances of our emigration and settlement here. We have appealed to their native justice and magnanimity, and we have conjured them by the ties of our common kindred to disavow these usurpations, which, would inevitably interrupt our connections and correspondence. They too have been deaf to the voice of justice and of consanguinity. We must, therefore, acquiesce in the necessity, which denounces our Separation, and hold them, as we hold the rest of mankind, Enemies in War, in Peace Friends.

We, Therefore, the Representatives of the United States of America, in General Congress, Assembled, appealing to the Supreme Judge of the world for the rectitude of our intentions, do, in the Name, and by Authority of the good People of these Colonies, solemnly publish and declare, That these United Colonies are, and of Right ought to be Free and Independent States; that they are Absolved from all Allegiance to the British Crown, and that all political connection between them and the State of Great Britain, is and ought to be totally dissolved; and that as Free and Independent States, they have full Power to levy War, conclude Peace, contract Alliances, establish Commerce, and to do all other Acts and Things which Independent States may of right do. And for the support of this Declaration, with a firm reliance on the protection of divine Providence, we mutually pledge to each other our Lives, our Fortunes and our sacred Honor.

The foregoing Declaration was, by order of Congress, engrossed, and signed by the following members:

John Hancock

NEW HAMPSHIRE

Josiah Bartlett

William Whipple

Matthew Thornton

MASSACHUSETTS BAY

Samuel Adams

John Adams

Robert Treat Paine

Elbridge Gerry

RHODE ISLAND

Stephen Hopkins

William Ellery

CONNECTICUT

Roger Sherman

Samuel Huntington

William Williams

Oliver Wolcott

NEW YORK

William Floyd

Philip Livingston

Francis Lewis

Lewis Morris

NEW JERSEY

Richard Stockton

John Witherspoon

Francis Hopkinson

John Hart

Abraham Clark

PENNSYLVANIA

Robert Morris

Benjamin Rush

Benjamin Franklin

John Morton

George Clymer

James Smith

George Taylor

James Wilson

George Ross

DELAWARE

Caesar Rodney

George Read

Thomas M'Kean

MARYLAND

Samuel Chase

William Paca

Thomas Stone

Charles Carroll, of Carrollton

VIRGINIA

George Wythe

Richard Henry Lee

Thomas Jefferson

Benjamin Harrison

Thomas Nelson, Jr.

Francis Lightfoot Lee

Carter Braxton

NORTH CAROLINA

William Hooper

Joseph Hewes

John Penn

SOUTH CAROLINA

Edward Rutledge

Thomas Heyward, Jr.

Thomas Lynch, Jr.

Arthur Middleton

GEORGIA

Button Gwinnett

Lyman Hall

George Walton

Resolved, That copies of the Declaration be sent to the several assemblies, conventions, and committees, or councils of safety, and to the several commanding officers of the continental troops; that it be proclaimed in each of the United States, at the head of the army.

THE ARTICLES OF CONFEDERATION

Agreed to by Congress November 15, 1777;
RATIFIED AND IN FORCE MARCH 1, 1781

To all whom these Presents shall come, we the undersigned Delegates of the States affixed to our Names, send greeting. Whereas the Delegates of the United States of America, in Congress assembled, did, on the fifteenth day of November, in the Year of Our Lord One thousand Seven Hundred and Seventy seven, and in the Second Year of the Independence of America, agree to certain articles of Confederation and perpetual Union between the States of Newhampshire, Massachusetts-bay, Rhodeisland and Providence Plantations, Connecticut, New-York, New-Jersey, Pennsylvania, Delaware, Maryland, Virginia, North-Carolina, South-Carolina and Georgia in the words following, viz. Articles of Confederation and perpetual Union between the states of Newhampshire, Massachusetts-bay, Rhodeisland and Providence Plantations, Connecticut, New-York, New-Jersey, Pennsylvania, Delaware, Maryland, Virginia, North-Carolina, South-Carolina and Georgia.

Art. I. The Stile of this confederacy shall be "The United States of America."

Art. II. Each state retains its sovereignty, freedom and independence, and every Power, Jurisdiction and right, which is not by this confederation expressly delegated to the United States, in Congress assembled.

Art. III. The said states hereby severally enter into a firm league of friendship with each other, for their common defence, the security of their Liberties, and their mutual and general welfare, binding themselves to assist each other, against all force offered to, or attacks made upon them, or any of them, on account of religion, sovereignty, trade, or any other pretence whatever.

Art. IV. The better to secure and perpetuate mutual friendship and intercourse among the people of the different states in this union, the free inhabitants of each of these states, paupers, vagabonds and fugitives from Justice excepted, shall be entitled to all privileges and immunities of free citizens in the several states; and the people of each state shall have free ingress and regress to and from any other state, and shall enjoy therein all the privileges of trade and commerce, subject to the same duties, impositions and restrictions as the inhabitants thereof respectively, provided that such restriction shall not extend so far as to prevent the removal of property imported into any state, to any other state, of which the Owner is an inhabitant; provided also that no imposition, duties or restriction shall be laid by any state, on the property of the united states, or either of them.

If any Person guilty of, or charged with treason, felony, or other high misdemeanor in any state, shall flee from Justice, and be found in any of the united states, he shall, upon demand of the Governor or executive power, of the state from which he fled, be delivered up and removed to the state having jurisdiction of his offence.

Full faith and credit shall be given in each of these states to the records, acts and judicial proceedings of the courts and magistrates of every other state.

Art. V. For the more convenient management of the general interests of the united states, delegates shall be annually appointed in such manner as the legislature of each state shall direct, to meet in Congress on the first Monday in November, in every year, with a power reserved to each state, to recall its delegates, or any of them, at any time within the year, and to send others in their stead, for the remainder of the Year.

No state shall be represented in Congress by less than two, nor by more than seven Members; and no person shall be capable of being a delegate for more than three years in any term of six years; nor shall any person, being a delegate, be capable of holding any office under the united states, for which he, or another for his benefit receives any salary, fees or emolument of any kind.

Each state shall maintain its own delegates in a meeting of the states, and while they act as members of the committee of the states.

In determining questions in the united states, in Congress assembled, each state shall have one vote.

Freedom of speech and debate in Congress shall not be impeached or questioned in any Court, or place out of Congress, and the members of congress shall be protected in their persons from arrests and imprisonments, during the time of their going to and from, and attendance on congress, except for treason, felony, or breach of the peace.

Art. VI. No state without the Consent of the united states in congress assembled, shall send any embassy to, or receive any embassy from, or enter into any conference, agreement, or alliance or treaty with any King, prince or state; nor shall any person holding any office or profit or trust under the united states, or any of them, accept of any present, emolument, office or title of any kind whatever from any king, prince or foreign state; nor shall the united states in congress assembled, or any of them, grant any title of nobility.

No two or more states shall enter into any treaty, confederation or alliance whatever between them, without the consent of the united states in congress assembled, specifying accurately the purposes for which the same is to be entered into, and how long it shall continue.

No state shall lay any imposts or duties, which may interfere with any stipulations in treaties, entered into by the united states in congress assembled, with any king, prince or state, in pursuance of any treaties already proposed by congress, to the courts of France and Spain.

No vessels of war shall be kept up in time of peace by any state, except such number only, as shall be deemed necessary by the united states in congress assembled, for the defence of such state, or its trade; nor shall any body of forces be kept up by any state, in time of peace, except such number only, as in the judgment of the united states, in congress assembled, shall be deemed requisite to garrison the forts necessary for the defence of such state; but every state shall always keep up a well regulated and disciplined militia, sufficiently armed and accoutred, and shall provide and constantly have ready for use, in public stores, a due number of field pieces and tents, and a proper quantity of arms, ammunition and camp equipage.

No state shall engage in any war without the consent of the united states in congress assembled, unless such state be actually invaded by enemies, or shall have received certain advice of a resolution being formed by some nation of Indians to invade such state, and the danger is so imminent as not to admit of a delay, till the united states in congress asssembled can be consulted; nor shall any state grant commissions to any ships or vessels of war, nor letters of marque or reprisal, except it be after a declaration of war by the united states in congress assembled, and then only against the kingdom or state and the subjects thereof, against which war has been so declared, and under such regulations as shall be established by the united states in congress assembled, unless such state be infested by pirates; in which case vessels of war may be fitted out for that occasion, and kept so long as the danger shall continue, or until the united states in congress assembled shall determine otherwise.

Art. VII. When land-forces are raised by any state for the common defence, all officers of or under the rank of colonel, shall be appointed by the legislature of each state respectively, by whom such forces shall be raised, or in such manner as such state shall direct, and all vacancies shall be filled up by the state which first made the appointment.

Art. VIII. All charges of war, and all other expences that shall be incurred for the common defence or general welfare, and allowed by the united states in congress assembled, shall be defrayed out of a common treasury, which shall be supplied by the several states in proportion to the value of all land within each state, granted to or surveyed for any Person, as such land and the buildings and improvements thereon shall be estimated according to such mode as the united states in congress assembled, shall from time to time direct and appoint.

The taxes for paying that proportion shall be laid and levied by the authority and direction of the legislatures of the several states within the time agreed upon by the united states in congress assembled.

Art. IX. The united states in congress assembled, shall have the sole and exclusive right and power of determining on peace and war, except in the cases mentioned in the sixth article—of sending and receiving ambassadors—entering into treaties and alliances, provided that no treaty of commerce shall be made whereby the legislative power of the respective states shall be restrained from imposing such imposts and duties on foreigners, as their own people are subjected to, or from prohibiting the exportation of any species of goods or commodities whatsoever—of establishing rules for deciding in all cases, what captures on land or water shall be legal, and in what manner prizes taken by land or naval forces in the service of the united states shall be divided or appropriated—of granting letters of marque and reprisal in times of peace—appointing courts for the trial of piracies and felonies committed on the high seas and establishing courts for receiving and determining finally appeals in all cases of captures, provided that no member of congress shall be appointed a judge of any of the said courts.

The united states in congress assembled shall also be the last resort on appeal in all disputes and differences now subsisting or that hereafter may arise between two or more states concerning boundary, jurisdiction or any other cause whatever; which authority shall always be exercised in the manner following. Whenever the legislative or executive authority or lawful agent of any state in controversy with another shall present a petition to congress stating the matter in question and praying for a hearing, notice thereof shall be given by order of congress to the legislative or executive authority of the other state in controversy, and a day assigned for the appearance of the parties by their lawful agents, who shall then be directed to appoint by joint consent, commissioners or judges to constitute a court for hearing and determining the matter in question: but if they cannot agree, congress shall name three persons out of each of the united states, and from the list of such persons each party shall alternately strike out one, the petitioners beginning, until the number shall be reduced to thirteen; and from that number not less than seven, nor more than nine names as congress shall direct, shall in the presence of congress be drawn out by lot, and the persons whose names shall be so drawn or any five of them, shall be commissioners or judges, to hear and finally determine the controversy, so always as a major part of the judges who shall hear the cause shall agree in the determination: and if either party shall neglect to attend at the day appointed, without shewing reasons, which congress shall judge sufficient, or being present shall refuse to strike, the congress shall proceed to nominate three persons out of each state, and the secretary of congress shall strike in behalf of such party absent or refusing; and the judgment and sentence of the court to be appointed, in the manner before prescribed, shall be final and conclusive; and if any of the parties shall refuse to submit to the authority of such court, or to appear to defend their claim or cause, the court shall nevertheless proceed to pronounce sentence, or judgment, which shall in like manner be final and decisive, the judgment or sentence and other proceedings being in either case transmitted to congress, and lodged among the acts of congress for the security of the parties concerned: provided that every commissioner, before he sits in judgment, shall take an oath to be administered by one of the judges of the supreme or superior court of the state, where the cause shall be tried, "well and truly to hear and determine the matter in question, according to the best of his judgment, without favour, affection or hope of reward:" provided also, that no state shall be deprived of territory for the benefit of the united states.

All controversies concerning the private right of soil claimed under different grants of two or more states, whose jurisdictions as they may respect such lands, and the states which passed such grants are adjusted, the said grants or either of them being at the same time claimed to have originated antecedent to such settlement of jurisdiction, shall on the petition of either party to the congress of the united states, be finally determined as near as may be in the same manner as is before prescribed for deciding disputes respecting territorial jurisdiction between different states.

The united states in congress assembled shall also have the sole and exclusive right and power of regulating the alloy and value of coin struck by their own authority, or by that of the respective states—fixing the standard of weights and measures throughout the united states—regulating the trade and managing all affairs with the Indians, not members of any of the states, provided that the legislative right of any state within its own limits be not infringed or violated—establishing and regulating post-offices from one state to another, throughout all the united states, and exacting such postage on the papers passing thro' the same as may be requisite to defray the expences of the said office—appointing all officers of the land forces, in the service of the united states, excepting regimental officers—appointing all the officers of the naval forces, and commissioning all officers whatever in the service of the united states—making rules for the government and regulation of the said land and naval forces, and directing their operations.

The united states in congress assembled shall have authority to appoint a committee, to sit in the recess of congress, to be denominated "A Committee of the States," and to consist of one delegate from each state; and to appoint such other committees and civil officers as may be necessary for managing the general affairs of the united states under their direction—to appoint one of their number to preside, provided that no person be allowed to serve in the office of president more than one year in any term of three years; to ascertain the necessary sums of Money to be raised for the service of the united states, and to appropriate and apply the same for defraying the public expenses—to borrow money, or emit bills on the credit of the united states, transmitting every half year to the respective states an account of the sums of money so borrowed or emitted,—to build and equip a navy—to agree upon the number of land forces, and to make requisitions from each state for its quota, in proportion to the number of white inhabitants in such state; which requisition shall be binding, and thereupon the legislature of each state shall appoint the regimental officers, raise the men and cloath, arm and equip then in a sol-dier like manner, at the expense of the united states; and the officers and men so cloathed, armed and equipped shall march to the place appointed, and within the time agreed on by the united states in congress assembled: But if the united states in congress assembled shall, on consideration of circumstances judge proper that any state should not raise men, or should raise a smaller number than its quota, and that any other state should raise a greater number of men than the quota thereof, such extra number shall be raised, officered, cloathed, armed and equipped in the same manner as the quota of such state, unless the legislature of such state shall judge that such extra number cannot be safely spared out of the same, in which case they shall raise officer, cloath, arm and equip as many of such extra number as they judge can be safely spared. And the officers and men so cloathed, armed and equipped, shall march to the place appointed, and within the time agreed on by the united states in congress assembled.

The united states in congress assembled shall never engage in a war, nor grant letters of marque and reprisal in time of peace, nor enter into any treaties or alliances, nor coin money, nor regulate the value thereof, nor ascertain the sums and expenses necessary for the defence and welfare of the united states, or any of them, nor emit bills, nor borrow money on the credit of the united states, nor appropriate money, nor agree upon the number of vessels of war, to be built or purchased, or the number of land or sea forces to be raised, nor appoint a commander in chief of the army or navy, unless nine states as-sent to the same: nor shall a question on any other point, except for adjourning from day to day be determined, unless by the votes of a majority of the united states in congress assembled.

The congress of the united states shall have power to adjourn to any time within the year, and to any place within the united states, so that no period of adjournment be for a longer duration than the space of six Months, and shall publish the Journal of their pro-ceedings monthly, except such parts thereof relating to treaties, alliances or military op-erations, as in their judgment require secrecy; and the yeas and nays of the delegates of each state on any question shall be entered on the Journal, when it is desired by any dele-gate; and the delegates of a state, or any of them, at his or their request shall be furnished with a transcript of the said Journal, except such parts as are above excepted, to lay be-fore the legislatures of the several states.

Art. X. The committee of the states, or any nine of them, shall be authorised to exe-cute, in the recess of congress, such of the powers of congress as the united states in con-gress assembled, by the consent of nine states, shall from time to time think expedient to vest them with; provided that no power be delegated to the said committee, for the exer-cise of which, by the articles of confederation, the voice of nine states in the congress of the united states assembled is requisite.

Art. XI. Canada acceding to this confederation, and joining in the measures of the united states, shall be admitted into, and entitled to all the advantages of this union: but no other colony shall be admitted into the same, unless such admission be agreed to by nine states.

Art. XII. All bills of credit emitted, monies borrowed and debts contracted by, or under the authority of congress, before the assembling of the united states, in pursuance of the present confederation, shall be deemed and considered as a charge against the united states, for payment and satisfaction whereof the said united states and the public faith are hereby solemnly pledged.

Art. XIII. Every state shall abide by the determinations of the united states in congress assembled, on all questions which by this confederation are submitted to them. And the Articles of this confederation shall be inviolably observed by every state, and the union shall be perpetual; nor shall any alteration at any time hereafter be made in any of them; unless such alteration be agreed to in a congress of the united states, and be afterwards confirmed by the legislatures of every state.

And Whereas it hath pleased the Great Governor of the World to incline the hearts of the legislatures we respectively represent in congress, to approve of, and to authorize us to ratify the said articles of confederation and perpetual union. Know Ye that we the undersigned delegates, by virtue of the power and authority to us given for that purpose, do by these presents, in the name and in behalf of our respective constituents, fully and entirely ratify and confirm each and every of the said articles of confederation and perpetual union, and all and singular the matters and things therein contained: And we do further solemnly plight and engage the faith of our respective constituents, that they shall abide by the determinations of the united states in congress assembled, on all questions, which by the said confederation are submitted to them. And that the articles thereof shall be inviolably observed by the states we respectively represent, and that the union shall be perpetual. In Witness whereof we have hereunto set our hands in Congress. Done at Philadelphia in the state of Pennsylvania the ninth day of July, in the Year of our Lord one Thousand seven Hundred and Seventy-eight, and in the third year of the independence of America.

THE CONSTITUTION OF THE UNITED STATES OF AMERICA

We the People of the United States, in Order to form a more perfect Union, establish Justice, insure domestic Tranquility, provide for the common defence, promote the general Welfare, and secure the Blessings of Liberty to ourselves and our Posterity, do ordain and establish this Constitution for the United States of America.

Article I

Section 1

[LEGISLATIVE POWERS]

All legislative Powers herein granted shall be vested in a Congress of the United States, which shall consist of a Senate and House of Representatives.

Section 2

[HOUSE OF REPRESENTATIVES, HOW CONSTITUTED, POWER OF IMPEACHMENT]

The House of Representatives shall be composed of Members chosen every second Year by the People of the several States, and the Electors in each State shall have the Qualifications requisite for Electors of the most numerous Branch of the State Legislature.

No Person shall be a Representative who shall not have attained to the Age of twenty five Years, and been seven Years a Citizen of the United States, and who shall not, when elected, be an Inhabitant of that State in which he shall be chosen.

Representatives and *direct Taxes*[1] shall be apportioned among the several States which may be included within this Union, according to their respective Numbers, *which shall be determined by adding to the whole Number of free Persons, including those bound to Service for a Term of Years,* and excluding Indians not taxed, *three fifths of all other Persons.*[2] The actual Enumeration shall be made within three Years after the first Meeting of the Congress of the United States, and within every subsequent Term of ten Years, in

---

[1]Modified by Sixteenth Amendment.
[2]Modified by Fourteenth Amendment.

such Manner as they shall by Law direct. The Number of Representatives shall not exceed one for every thirty Thousand, but each State shall have at Least one Representative; *and until such enumeration shall be made, the State of New Hampshire shall be entitled to chuse three, Massachusetts eight, Rhode-Island and Providence Plantations one, Connecticut five, New-York six, New Jersey four, Pennsylvania eight, Delaware one, Maryland six, Virginia ten, North Carolina five, South Carolina five, and Georgia three.*[3]

When vacancies happen in the Representation from any State, the Executive Authority thereof shall issue Writs of Election to fill such Vacancies.

The House of Representatives shall chuse their Speaker and other Officers; and shall have the sole Power of Impeachment.

Section 3

[THE SENATE, HOW CONSTITUTED, IMPEACHMENT TRIALS]

The Senate of the United States shall be composed of two Senators from each State, *chosen by the Legislature thereof,*[4] for six Years; and each Senator shall have one Vote.

Immediately after they shall be assembled in Consequence of the first Election, they shall be divided as equally as may be into three Classes. The Seats of the Senators of the first Class shall be vacated at the Expiration of the second Year, of the second Class at the Expiration of the fourth Year, and of the third Class at the Expiration of the sixth Year, so that one third may be chosen every second Year; *and if Vacancies happen by Resignation, or otherwise, during the Recess of the Legislature of any State, the Executive thereof may make temporary Appointments until the next Meeting of the Legislature, which shall then fill such Vacancies.*[5]

No Person shall be a Senator who shall not have attained to the Age of thirty Years, and been nine Years a Citizen of the United States, and who shall not, when elected, be an Inhabitant of that State for which he shall be chosen.

The Vice President of the United States shall be President of the Senate, but shall have no Vote, unless they be equally divided.

The Senate shall chuse their other Officers, and also a President pro tempore, in the Absence of the Vice President, or when he shall exercise the Office of President of the United States.

The Senate shall have the sole Power to try all Impeachments. When sitting for that Purpose, they shall be on Oath or Affirmation. When the President of the United States is tried, the Chief Justice shall preside: And no Person shall be convicted without the Concurrence of two thirds of the Members present.

Judgment in Cases of Impeachment shall not extend further than to removal from Office, and disqualification to hold and enjoy any Office of honor, Trust or Profit under the United States: but the Party convicted shall nevertheless be liable and subject to Indictment, Trial, Judgment and Punishment, according to Law.

Section 4

[ELECTION OF SENATORS AND REPRESENTATIVES]

The Times, Places and Manner of holding Elections for Senators and Representatives, shall be prescribed in each State by the Legislature thereof; but the Congress may at any time by Law make or alter such Regulations, except as to the Places of chusing Senators.

[3]Temporary provision.
[4]Modified by Seventeenth Amendment.
[5]Modified by Seventeenth Amendment.

The Congress shall assemble at least once in every Year, and such Meeting shall be on the first Monday in December, unless they shall by Law appoint a different Day.[6]

Section 5

[QUORUM, JOURNALS, MEETINGS, ADJOURNMENTS]

Each House shall be the Judge of the Elections, Returns and Qualifications of its own Members, and a Majority of each shall constitute a Quorum to do Business; but a smaller Number may adjourn from day to day, and may be authorized to compel the Attendance of absent Members, in such Manner, and under such Penalties as each House may provide.

Each House may determine the Rules of its Proceedings, punish its Members for disorderly Behaviour, and, with the Concurrence of two thirds, expel a Member.

Each House shall keep a Journal of its Proceedings, and from time to time publish the same, excepting such Parts as may in their Judgment require Secrecy; and the Yeas and Nays of the Members of either House on any questions shall, at the Desire of one fifth of those Present, be entered on the Journal.

Neither House, during the Session of Congress, shall, without the Consent of the other, adjourn for more than three days, nor to any other Place than that in which the two Houses shall be sitting.

Section 6

[COMPENSATION, PRIVILEGES, DISABILITIES]

The Senators and Representatives shall receive a Compensation for their Services, to be ascertained by Law, and paid out of the Treasury of the United States. They shall in all Cases, except Treason, Felony and Breach of the Peace, be privileged from Arrest during their Attendance at the Session of their respective Houses, and in going to and returning from the same; and for any Speech or Debate in either House, they shall not be questioned in any other Place.

No Senator or Representative shall, during the Time for which he was elected, be appointed to any civil Office under the Authority of the United States, which shall have been created, or the Emoluments whereof shall have been encreased during such time; and no Person holding any Office under the United States, shall be a Member of either House during his Continuance in Office.

Section 7

[PROCEDURE IN PASSING BILLS AND RESOLUTIONS]

All Bills for raising Revenue shall originate in the House of Representatives; but the Senate may propose or concur with Amendments as on other Bills.

Every Bill which shall have passed the House of Representatives and the Senate, shall, before it become a Law, be presented to the President of the United States: If he approve he shall sign it, but if not he shall return it, with his Objections to that House in which it shall have originated, who shall enter the Objections at large on their Journal, and proceed to reconsider it. If after such Reconsideration two thirds of that House shall agree to pass the Bill, it shall be sent, together with the Objections, to the other House, by which it shall likewise be reconsidered, and if approved by two thirds of that House, it shall become a Law. But in all such Cases the Votes of both Houses shall be determined by yeas and Nays, and the Names of the Persons voting for and against the Bill shall be entered

[6]Modified by Twentieth Amendment.

on the Journal of each House respectively. If any Bill shall not be returned by the President within ten Days (Sundays excepted) after it shall have been presented to him, the Same shall be a Law, in like Manner as if he had signed it, unless the Congress by their Adjournment prevent its Return, in which Case it shall not be a Law.

Every Order, Resolution, or Vote to which the Concurrence of the Senate and House of Representatives may be necessary (except on a question of Adjournment) shall be presented to the President of the United States; and before the Same shall take Effect, shall be approved by him, or being disapproved by him, shall be repassed by two thirds of the Senate and House of Representatives, according to the Rules and Limitations prescribed in the Case of a Bill.

Section 8

[POWERS OF CONGRESS]

The Congress shall have Power

To lay and collect Taxes, Duties, Imposts and Excises, to pay the Debts and provide for the common Defence and general Welfare of the United States; but all Duties, Imposts and Excises shall be uniform throughout the United States;

To borrow Money on the credit of the United States;

To regulate Commerce with foreign Nations, and among the several States, and with the Indian Tribes;

To establish an uniform Rule of Naturalization, and uniform Laws on the subject of Bankruptcies throughout the United States;

To coin Money, regulate the Value thereof, and of foreign Coin, and fix the Standard of Weights and Measures;

To provide for the Punishment of counterfeiting the Securities and current Coin of the United States;

To establish Post Offices and post Roads;

To promote the Progress of Science and useful Arts, by securing for limited Times to Authors and Inventors the exclusive Right to their respective Writings and Discoveries;

To constitute Tribunals inferior to the supreme Court;

To define and punish Piracies and Felonies committed on the high Seas, and Offences against the Law of Nations;

To declare War, grant Letters of Marque and Reprisal, and make Rules concerning Captures on Land and Water;

To raise and support Armies, but no Appropriation of Money to that Use shall be for a longer Term than two Years;

To provide and maintain a Navy;

To make Rules for the Government and Regulation of the land and naval Forces;

To provide for calling forth the Militia to execute the Laws of the Union, suppress Insurrections and repel Invasions;

To provide for organizing, arming, and disciplining, the Militia, and for governing such Part of them as may be employed in the Service of the United States, reserving to the States respectively, the Appointment of the Officers, and the Authority of training the Militia according to the discipline prescribed by Congress;

To exercise exclusive Legislation in all Cases whatsoever, over such District (not exceeding ten Miles square) as may, by Cession of particular States, and the Acceptance of Congress, become the Seat of the Government of the United States, and to exercise like Authority over all Places purchased by the Consent of the Legislature of the State in which the Same shall be, for the Erection of Forts, Magazines, Arsenals, dock-Yards, and other needful Buildings;—And

To make all Laws which shall be necessary and proper for carrying into Execution the foregoing Powers, and all other Powers vested by this Constitution in the Government of the United States, or in any Department or Officer thereof.

Section 9

[SOME RESTRICTIONS ON FEDERAL POWER]

The Migration or Importation of such Persons as any of the States now existing shall think proper to admit, shall not be prohibited by the Congress prior to the Year one thousand eight hundred and eight, but a Tax or duty may be imposed on such Importation, not exceeding ten dollars for each Person.[7]

The Privilege of the Writ of Habeas Corpus shall not be suspended, unless when in Cases of Rebellion or Invasion the public Safety may require it.

No Bill of Attainder or ex post facto Law shall be passed.

No Capitation, or other direct, Tax shall be laid, unless in Proportion to the Census or Enumeration herein before directed to be taken.[8]

No Tax or Duty shall be laid on Articles exported from any State.

No Preference shall be given by any Regulation of Commerce or Revenue to the Ports of one State over those of another; nor shall Vessels bound to, or from, one State, be obliged to enter, clear, or pay Duties in another.

No Money shall be drawn from the Treasury, but in Consequence of Appropriations made by Law; and a regular Statement and Account of the Receipts and Expenditures of all public Money shall be published from time to time.

No Title of Nobility shall be granted by the United States: And no Person holding any Office of Profit or Trust under them, shall, without the Consent of the Congress, accept of any present, Emolument, Office, or Title, of any kind whatever, from any King, Prince, or foreign State.

Section 10

[RESTRICTIONS UPON POWERS OF STATES]

No State shall enter into any Treaty, Alliance, or Confederation; grant Letters of Marque and Reprisal; coin Money; emit Bills of Credit; make any Thing but gold and silver Coin a Tender in Payment of Debts; pass any Bill of Attainder, ex post facto Law, or Law impairing the Obligation of Contracts, or grant any Title of Nobility.

No State shall, without the Consent of the Congress, lay any Imposts or Duties on Imports or Exports, except what may be absolutely necessary for executing it's inspection Laws: and the net Produce of all Duties and Imposts, laid by any State on Imports or Exports, shall be for the Use of the Treasury of the United States; and all such Laws shall be subject to the Revision and Control of the Congress.

No State shall, without the Consent of Congress, lay any Duty of Tonnage, keep Troops, or Ships of War in time of Peace, enter into any Agreement or Compact with another State, or with a foreign Power, or engage in War, unless actually invaded, or in such imminent Danger as will not admit of delay.

---

[7]Temporary provision.
[8]Modified by Sixteenth Amendment.

Article II

Section 1

[EXECUTIVE POWER, ELECTION, QUALIFICATIONS OF THE PRESIDENT]

The executive Power shall be vested in a President of the United States of America. *He shall hold his Office during the Term of four Years, and, together with the Vice President, chosen for the same Term, be elected, as follows*[9]

Each State shall appoint, in such Manner as the Legislature thereof may direct, a Number of Electors, equal to the whole Number of Senators and Representatives to which the State may be entitled in the Congress: but no Senator or Representative, or Person holding an Office of Trust or Profit under the United States, shall be appointed an Elector.

The electors shall meet in their respective States, and vote by ballot for two Persons, of whom one at least shall not be an Inhabitant of the same State with themselves. And they shall make a List of all the Persons voted for, and of the Number of Votes for each; which List they shall sign and certify, and transmit sealed to the Seat of the Government of the United States, directed to the President of the Senate. The President of the Senate shall, in the Presence of the Senate and House of Representatives, open all the Certificates, and the Votes shall then be counted. The Person having the greatest Number of Votes shall be the President, if such Number be a Majority of the whole Number of Electors appointed; and if there be more than one who have such Majority, and have an equal Number of Votes, then the House of Representatives shall immediately chuse by Ballot one of them for President; and if no Person have a Majority, then from the five highest on the List the said House shall in like Manner chuse the President. But in chusing the President, the Votes shall be taken by States, the Representation from each State having one Vote; A quorum for this Purpose shall consist of a Member or Members from two thirds of the States, and a Majority of all the States shall be necessary to a Choice. In every Case, after the Choice of the President, the person having the greatest Number of Votes of the Electors shall be the Vice President. But if there should remain two or more who have equal Votes, the Senate shall chuse from them by Ballot the Vice President.[10]

The Congress may determine the Time of chusing the Electors, and the Day on which they shall give their Votes; which Day shall be the same throughout the United States.

No Person except a natural born Citizen, or a Citizen of the United States, at the time of the Adoption of this Constitution, shall be eligible to the Office of President; neither shall any Person be eligible to that Office who shall not have attained to the Age of thirty five Years, and been fourteen Years a Resident within the United States.

In Case of the Removal of the President from Office, or his Death, Resignation, or Inability to discharge the Powers and Duties of the said Office, the Same shall devolve on the Vice President, and the Congress may by Law provide for the Case of Removal, Death, Resignation or Inability, both of the President and Vice President, declaring what Officer shall then act as President, and such Officer shall act accordingly, until the Disability be removed, or a President shall be elected.

The President shall, at stated Times, receive for his Services, a Compensation, which shall neither be increased nor diminished during the Period for which he shall have been elected, and he shall not receive within that Period any other Emolument from the United States, or any of them.

Before he enter on the Execution of his Office, he shall take the following Oath or Af-

[9]Number of terms limited to two by Twenty-second Amendment.
[10]Modified by Twelfth and Twentieth Amendments.

firmation:—"I do solemnly swear (or affirm) that I will faithfully execute the Office of President of the United States, and will to the best of my Ability, preserve, protect and defend the Constitution of the United States."

Section 2

[POWERS OF THE PRESIDENT]

The President shall be Commander in Chief of the Army and Navy of the United States, and of the Militia of the several States, when called into the actual Service of the United States; he may require the Opinion, in writing, of the principal Officer in each of the executive Departments, upon any Subject relating to the Duties of their respective Offices, and he shall have Power to grant Reprieves and Pardons for Offences against the United States, except in Cases of Impeachment.

He shall have Power, by and with the Advice and Consent of the Senate, to make Treaties, provided two thirds of the Senators present concur; and he shall nominate, and by and with the Advice and Consent of the Senate, shall appoint Ambassadors, other public Ministers and Consuls, Judges of the supreme Court, and all other Officers of the United States, whose Appointments are not herein otherwise provided for, and which shall be established by Law: but the Congress may by Law vest the Appointment of such inferior Officers, as they think proper, in the President alone, in the Courts of Law, or in the Heads of Departments.

The President shall have Power to fill up all Vacancies that may happen during the Recess of the Senate, by granting Commissions which shall expire at the End of their next Session.

Section 3

[POWERS AND DUTIES OF THE PRESIDENT]

He shall from time to time give to the Congress Information of the State of the Union, and recommend to their Consideration such Measures as he shall judge necessary and expedient; he may, on extraordinary Occasions, convene both Houses, or either of them, and in Case of Disagreement between them, with Respect to the Time of Adjournment, he may adjourn them to such Time as he shall think proper; he shall receive Ambassadors and other public Ministers; he shall take Care that the Laws be faithfully executed, and shall Commission all the Officers of the United States.

Section 4

[IMPEACHMENT]

The President, Vice President and all civil Officers of the United States, shall be removed from Office on Impeachment for, and Conviction of, Treason, Bribery, or other high Crimes and Misdemeanors.

Article III

Section 1

[JUDICIAL POWER, TENURE OF OFFICE]

The judicial Power of the United States, shall be vested in one supreme Court, and in such inferior Courts as the Congress may from time to time ordain and establish. The Judges, both of the supreme and inferior Courts, shall hold their Offices during good Behaviour, and shall, at stated Times, receive for their Services, a Compensation, which shall not be diminished during their Continuance in Office.

Section 2

[JURISDICTION]

The judicial Power shall extend to all Cases, in Law and Equity, arising under this Constitution, the Laws of the United States, and Treaties made, or which shall be made, under their Authority;—to all Cases affecting Ambassadors, other public Ministers and Consuls;—to all Cases of admiralty and maritime Jurisdiction;—to Controversies to which the United States shall be a Party;—to Controversies between two or more States;—*between a State and Citizens of another State;*—between Citizens of different States,—between Citizens of the same State claiming Lands under Grants of different States, *and between a State,* or the Citizens thereof, *and foreign States, Citizens or Subjects.*[11]

In all Cases affecting Ambassadors, other public Ministers and Consuls, and those in which a State shall be Party, the supreme Court shall have original Jurisdiction. In all the other Cases before mentioned, the supreme Court shall have appellate Jurisdiction, both as to Law and Fact, with such Exceptions, and under such Regulations as the Congress shall make.

The Trial of all Crimes, except in Cases of Impeachment, shall be by Jury; and such Trial shall be held in the State where the said Crimes shall have been committed; but when not committed within any State, the Trial shall be at such Place or Places as the Congress may by Law have directed.

Section 3

[TREASON, PROOF, AND PUNISHMENT]

Treason against the United States, shall consist only in levying War against them, or in adhering to their Enemies, giving them Aid and Comfort. No Person shall be convicted of Treason unless on the Testimony of two Witnesses to the same overt Act, or on Confession in open Court.

The Congress shall have Power to declare the Punishment of Treason, but no Attainder of Treason shall work Corruption of Blood, or Forfeiture except during the Life of the Person attainted.

Article IV

Section 1

[FAITH AND CREDIT AMONG STATES]

Full Faith and Credit shall be given in each State to the public Acts, Records, and judicial Proceedings of every other State. And the Congress may by general Laws prescribe the Manner in which such Acts, Records and Proceedings shall be proved, and the Effect thereof.

Section 2

[PRIVILEGES AND IMMUNITIES, FUGITIVES]

The Citizens of each State shall be entitled to all Privileges and Immunities of Citizens in the several States.

A Person charged in any State with Treason, Felony or other Crime, who shall flee from Justice, and be found in another State, shall on Demand of the executive Authority

---

[11]Modified by Eleventh Amendment.

of the State from which he fled, be delivered up, to be removed to the State having Jurisdiction of the Crime.

No person held to Service or Labour in one State, under the Laws thereof, escaping into another, shall, in Consequence of any Law or Regulation therein, be discharged from such Service or Labour, but shall be delivered up on Claim of the Party to whom such Service or Labour may be due.[12]

Section 3

[ADMISSION OF NEW STATES]

New States may be admitted by the Congress into this Union; but no new State shall be formed or erected within the Jurisdiction of any other State; nor any State be formed by the Junction of two or more States, or Parts of States, without the Consent of the Legislatures of the States concerned as well as of the Congress.

The Congress shall have Power to dispose of and make all needful Rules and Regulations respecting the Territory or other Property belonging to the United States; and nothing in this Constitution shall be so construed as to Prejudice any Claims of the United States, or of any particular State.

Section 4

[GUARANTEE OF REPUBLICAN GOVERNMENT]

The United States shall guarantee to every State in this Union a Republican Form of Government, and shall protect each of them against Invasion; and on Application of the Legislature, or of the Executive (when the Legislature cannot be convened), against domestic Violence.

Article V

[AMENDMENT OF THE CONSTITUTION]

The Congress, whenever two thirds of both Houses shall deem it necessary, shall propose Amendments to this Constitution, or, on the Application of the Legislatures of two thirds of the several States, shall call a Convention for proposing Amendments, which, in either Case, shall be valid to all Intents and Purposes, as Part of this Constitution, when ratified by the Legislatures of three fourths of the several States, or by Conventions in three fourths thereof, as the one or the other Mode of Ratification may be proposed by the Congress; *Provided that no Amendment which may be made prior to the Year One thousand eight hundred and eight shall in any Manner affect the first and fourth Clauses in the Ninth Section of the first Article;*[13] and that no State, without its Consent, shall be deprived of its equal Suffrage in the Senate.

Article VI

[DEBTS, SUPREMACY, OATH]

All Debts contracted and Engagements entered into, before the Adoption of this Constitution, shall be as valid against the United States under this Constitution, as under the Confederation.

---

[12]Repealed by Thirteenth Amendment.
[13]Temporary provision.

This Constitution, and the Laws of the United States which shall be made in Pursuance thereof; and all Treaties made, or which shall be made, under the Authority of the United States, shall be the supreme Law of the Land; and the Judges in every State shall be bound thereby, any Thing in the Constitution or Laws of any State to the Contrary notwithstanding.

The Senators and Representatives before mentioned, and the Members of the several State Legislatures, and all executive and judicial Officers, both of the United States and of the several States, shall be bound by Oath or Affirmation, to support this Constitution; but no religious Test shall be required as a Qualification to any Office or public Trust under the United States.

Article VII

[RATIFICATION AND ESTABLISHMENT]

The Ratification of the Conventions of nine States, shall be sufficient for the Establishment of this Constitution between the States so ratifying the Same.[14]

Done in Convention by the Unanimous Consent of the States present the Seventeenth Day of September in the Year of our Lord one thousand seven hundred and Eighty seven and of the Independence of the United States of America the Twelfth. *In Witness* whereof We have hereunto subscribed our Names,

G:⁰ WASHINGTON—
Presidt. and deputy from Virginia

NEW HAMPSHIRE

John Langdon

Nicholas Gilman

MASSACHUSETTS

Nathaniel Gorham

Rufus King

CONNECTICUT

Wm. Saml. Johnson

Roger Sherman

NEW YORK

Alexander Hamilton

NEW JERSEY

Wil: Livingston

David Brearley

Wm. Paterson

Jona: Dayton

PENNSYLVANIA

B Franklin

Thomas Mifflin

Robt. Morris

Geo. Clymer

Thos. FitzSimons

Jared Ingersoll

James Wilson

Gouv Morris

DELAWARE

Geo: Read

Gunning Bedford jun

John Dickinson

Richard Bassett

Jaco: Broom

[14]The Constitution was submitted on September 17, 1787, by the Constitutional Convention, was ratified by the conventions of several states at various dates up to May 29, 1790, and became effective on March 4, 1789.

MARYLAND

James McHenry

Dan of St Thos. Jenifer

Danl. Carroll

VIRGINIA

John Blair—

James Madison Jr.

NORTH CAROLINA

Wm. Blount

Richd. Dobbs Spaight

Hu Williamson

SOUTH CAROLINA

J. Rutledge

Charles Cotesworth Pinckney

Charles Pinckney

Pierce Butler

GEORGIA

William Few

Abr Baldwin

AMENDMENTS TO THE CONSTITUTION

Proposed by Congress and Ratified by the Legislatures of the Several States, Pursuant to Article V of the Original Constitution.

Amendments I–X, known as the Bill of Rights, were proposed by Congress on September 25, 1789, and ratified on December 15, 1791.

Amendment I

[FREEDOM OF RELIGION, OF SPEECH, AND OF THE PRESS]

Congress shall make no law respecting an establishment of religion, or prohibiting the free exercise thereof; or abridging the freedom of speech, or of the press; or the right of the people peaceably to assemble, and to petition the Government for a redress of grievances.

Amendment II

[RIGHT TO KEEP AND BEAR ARMS]

A well regulated Militia, being necessary to the security of a free State, the right of the people to keep and bear Arms, shall not be infringed.

Amendment III

[QUARTERING OF SOLDIERS]

No Soldier shall, in time of peace be quartered in any house, without the consent of the Owner, nor in time of war, but in a manner to be prescribed by law.

Amendment IV

[SECURITY FROM UNWARRANTABLE SEARCH AND SEIZURE]

The right of the people to be secure in their persons, houses, papers, and effects, against unreasonable searches and seizures, shall not be violated, and no Warrants shall issue, but upon probable cause, supported by Oath or affirmation, and particularly describing the place to be searched, and the persons or things to be seized.

Amendment V

[RIGHTS OF ACCUSED PERSONS IN CRIMINAL PROCEEDINGS]

No person shall be held to answer for a capital, or otherwise infamous crime, unless on a presentment or indictment of a Grand Jury, except in cases arising in the land or naval forces, or in the Militia, when in actual service in time of War or in public danger; nor shall any person be subject for the same offence to be twice put in jeopardy of life or limb; nor shall be compelled in any criminal case to be a witness against himself, nor be deprived of life, liberty, or property, without due process of law; nor shall private property be taken for public use, without just compensation.

Amendment VI

[RIGHT TO SPEEDY TRIAL, WITNESSES, ETC.]

In all criminal prosecutions, the accused shall enjoy the right to a speedy and public trial, by an impartial jury of the State and district wherein the crime shall have been committed, which district shall have been previously ascertained by law, and to be informed of the nature and cause of the accusation; to be confronted with the witnesses against him; to have compulsory process for obtaining witnesses in his favor, and to have the Assistance of Counsel for his defence.

Amendment VII

[TRIAL BY JURY IN CIVIL CASES]

In suits at common law, where the value in controversy shall exceed twenty dollars, the right of trial by jury shall be preserved, and no fact tried by a jury, shall be otherwise reexamined in any Court of the United States, than according to the rules of the common law.

Amendment VIII

[BAILS, FINES, PUNISHMENTS]

Excessive bail shall not be required, nor excessive fines imposed, nor cruel and unusual punishments inflicted.

Amendment IX

[RESERVATION OF RIGHTS OF PEOPLE]

The enumeration in the Constitution, of certain rights, shall not be construed to deny or disparage others retained by the people.

Amendment X

[POWERS RESERVED TO STATES OR PEOPLE]

 The powers not delegated to the United States by the Constitution, nor prohibited by it to the States, are reserved to the States respectively, or to the people.

Amendment XI

[PROPOSED BY CONGRESS ON MARCH 4, 1794; DECLARED RATIFIED ON JANUARY 8, 1798.]
[RESTRICTION OF JUDICIAL POWER]

 The Judicial power of the United States shall not be construed to extend to any suit in law or equity, commenced or prosecuted against one of the United States by Citizens of another State, or by Citizens or Subjects of any Foreign State.

Amendment XII

[PROPOSED BY CONGRESS ON DECEMBER 9, 1803; DECLARED RATIFIED ON SEPTEMBER 25, 1804.]
[ELECTION OF PRESIDENT AND VICE PRESIDENT]

 The Electors shall meet in their respective states and vote by ballot for President and Vice-President, one of whom, at least, shall not be an inhabitant of the same state with themselves; they shall name in their ballots the person voted for as President, and in distinct ballots the person voted for as Vice-President, and they shall make distinct lists of all persons voted for as President, and of all persons voted for as Vice-President, and of the number of votes for each, which lists they shall sign and certify, and transmit sealed to the seat of the government of the United States, directed to the President of the Senate;—the President of the Senate shall, in presence of the Senate and House of Representatives, open all the certificates and the votes shall then be counted;—The person having the greatest number of votes for President, shall be the President, if such number be a majority of the whole number of Electors appointed; and if no person have such majority, then from the persons having the highest numbers not exceeding three on the list of those voted for as President, the House of Representatives shall choose immediately, by ballot, the President. But in choosing the President, the votes shall be taken by states, the representation from each state having one vote; a quorum for this purpose shall consist of a member or members from two-thirds of the states, and a majority of all the states shall be necessary to a choice. And if the House of Representatives shall not choose a President whenever the right of choice shall devolve upon them, before the fourth day of March next following, then the Vice-President shall act as President, as in the case of the death or other constitutional disability of the President.—The person having the greatest number of votes as Vice-President, shall be the Vice-President, if such number be a majority of the whole number of Electors appointed, and if no person have a majority, then from the two highest numbers on the list, the Senate shall choose the Vice-President; a quorum for the purpose shall consist of two-thirds of the whole number of Senators, and a majority of the whole number shall be necessary to a choice. But no person constitutionally ineligible to the office of President shall be eligible to that of Vice-President of the United States.

Amendment XIII

[PROPOSED BY CONGRESS ON JANUARY 31, 1865; DECLARED RATIFIED ON DECEMBER 18, 1865.]

Section 1

[ABOLITION OF SLAVERY]

Neither slavery nor involuntary servitude, except as a punishment for crime whereof the party shall have been duly convicted, shall exist within the United States, or any place subject to their jurisdiction.

Section 2

[POWER TO ENFORCE THIS ARTICLE]

Congress shall have power to enforce this article by appropriate legislation.

Amendment XIV

[PROPOSED BY CONGRESS ON JUNE 13, 1866, DECLARED RATIFIED ON JULY 28, 1868.]

Section 1

[CITIZENSHIP RIGHTS NOT TO BE ABRIDGED BY STATES]

All persons born or naturalized in the United States, and subject to the jurisdiction thereof, are citizens of the United States and of the State wherein they reside. No State shall make or enforce any law which shall abridge the privileges or immunities of citizens of the United States; nor shall any State deprive any person of life, liberty, or property, without due process of law; nor deny to any person within its jurisdiction the equal protection of the laws.

Section 2

[APPORTIONMENT OF REPRESENTATIVES IN CONGRESS]

Representatives shall be apportioned among the several States according to their respective numbers, counting the whole number of persons in each State, excluding Indians not taxed. But when the right to vote at any election for the choice of electors for President and Vice-President of the United States, Representatives in Congress, the Executive and Judicial officers of a State, or the members of the Legislature thereof, is denied to any of the male inhabitants of such State, being twenty-one years of age, and citizens of the United States, or in any way abridged, except for participation in rebellion, or other crime, the basis of representation therein shall be reduced in the proportion which the number of such male citizens shall bear to the whole number of male citizens twenty-one years of age in such State.

Section 3

[PERSONS DISQUALIFIED FROM HOLDING OFFICE]

No person shall be a Senator or Representative in Congress, or elector of President and Vice-President, or hold any office, civil or military, under the United States, or under any State, who, having previously taken an oath, as a member of Congress, or as an officer of the United States, or as a member of any State legislature, or as an executive or judicial officer of any State, to support the Constitution of the United States, shall have engaged in insurrection or rebellion against the same, or given aid or comfort to the enemies thereof. But Congress may by a vote of two-thirds of each House, remove such disability.

Section 4

[WHAT PUBLIC DEBTS ARE VALID]

The validity of the public debt of the United States, authorized by law, including debts incurred for payment of pensions and bounties for services in suppressing insurrection or rebellion, shall not be questioned. But neither the United States nor any State shall assume or pay any debt or obligation incurred in aid of insurrection or rebellion against the United States, or any claim for the loss or emancipation of any slave; but all such debts, obligations and claims shall be held illegal and void.

Section 5

[POWER TO ENFORCE THIS ARTICLE]

The Congress shall have power to enforce, by appropriate legislation, the provisions of this article.

Amendment XV

[PROPOSED BY CONGRESS ON FEBRUARY 26, 1869; DECLARED RATIFIED ON MARCH 30, 1870.]

Section 1

[NEGRO SUFFRAGE]

The right of citizens of the United States to vote shall not be denied or abridged by the United States or by any State on account of race, color, or previous condition of servitude.

Section 2

[POWER TO ENFORCE THIS ARTICLE]

The Congress shall have power to enforce this article by appropriate legislation.

Amendment XVI

[PROPOSED BY CONGRESS ON JULY 2, 1909; DECLARED RATIFIED ON FEBRUARY 25, 1913.]
[AUTHORIZING INCOME TAXES]

The Congress shall have power to lay and collect taxes on incomes, from whatever source derived, without apportionment among the several States, and without regard to any census or enumeration.

Amendment XVII

[PROPOSED BY CONGRESS ON MAY 13, 1912; DECLARED RATIFIED ON MAY 31, 1913.]
[POPULAR ELECTION OF SENATORS]

The Senate of the United States shall be composed of two Senators from each State, elected by the people thereof, for six years; and each Senator shall have one vote. The electors in each State shall have the qualifications requisite for electors of the most numerous branch of the State legislatures.

When vacancies happen in the representation of any State in the Senate, the executive authority of such State shall issue writs of election to fill such vacancies: *Provided,* That the legislature of any State may empower the executive thereof to make temporary appointments until the people fill the vacancies by election as the legislature may direct.

This amendment shall not be so construed as to affect the election or term of any Senator chosen before it becomes valid as part of the Constitution.

Amendment XVIII

[PROPOSED BY CONGRESS DECEMBER 18, 1917; DECLARED RATIFIED ON JANUARY 29, 1919.]

Section 1

[NATIONAL LIQUOR PROHIBITION]

After one year from the ratification of this article the manufacture, sale, or transportation of intoxicating liquors within, the importation thereof into, or the exportation thereof from the United States and all territory subject to the jurisdiction thereof for beverage purposes is hereby prohibited.

Section 2

[POWER TO ENFORCE THIS ARTICLE]

The Congress and the several States shall have concurrent power to enforce this article by appropriate legislation.

Section 3

[RATIFICATION WITHIN SEVEN YEARS]

This article shall be inoperative unless it shall have been ratified as an amendment to the Constitution by the legislatures of the several States, as provided in the Constitution, within seven years from the date of the submission hereof to the States by the Congress.[1]

Amendment XIX

[PROPOSED BY CONGRESS ON JUNE 4, 1919; DECLARED RATIFIED ON AUGUST 26, 1920.]

[WOMAN SUFFRAGE]

The right of citizens of the United States to vote shall not be denied or abridged by the United States or by any State on account of sex.

Congress shall have power to enforce this article by appropriate legislation.

Amendment XX

[PROPOSED BY CONGRESS ON MARCH 2, 1932; DECLARED RATIFIED ON FEBRUARY 6, 1933.]

Section 1

[TERMS OF OFFICE]

The terms of the President and Vice President shall end at noon on the 20th day of January, and the terms of Senators and Representatives at noon on the 3d day of January,

---

[1]Repealed by Twenty-first Amendment.

of the years in which such terms would have ended if this article had not been ratified; and the terms of their successors shall then begin.

Section 2

[TIME OF CONVENING CONGRESS]

The Congress shall assemble at least once in every year, and such meeting shall begin at noon on the 3d day of January, unless they shall by law appoint a different day.

Section 3

[DEATH OF PRESIDENT-ELECT]

If, at the time fixed for the beginning of the term of the President, the President elect shall have died, the Vice President elect shall become President. If a President shall not have been chosen before the time fixed for the beginning of his term, or if the President elect shall have failed to qualify, then the Vice President elect shall act as President until a President shall have qualified; and the Congress may by law provide for the case wherein neither a President elect nor a Vice President elect shall have qualified, declaring who shall then act as President, or the manner in which one who is to act shall be selected, and such person shall act accordingly until a President or Vice President shall have qualified.

Section 4

[ELECTION OF THE PRESIDENT]

The Congress may by law provide for the case of the death of any of the persons from whom the House of Representatives may choose a President whenever the right of choice shall have devolved upon them, and for the case of the death of any of the persons from whom the Senate may choose a Vice President whenever the right of choice shall have devolved upon them.

Section 5

[AMENDMENT TAKES EFFECT]

Sections 1 and 2 shall take effect on the 15th day of October following the ratification of this article.

Section 6

[RATIFICATION WITHIN SEVEN YEARS]

This article shall be inoperative unless it shall have been ratified as an amendment to the Constitution by the legislatures of three-fourths of the several States within seven years from the date of its submission.

Amendment XXI

[PROPOSED BY CONGRESS ON FEBRUARY 20, 1933; DECLARED RATIFIED ON DECEMBER 5, 1933.]

Section 1

[NATIONAL LIQUOR PROHIBITION REPEALED]

The eighteenth article of amendment to the Constitution of the United States is hereby repealed.

Section 2

[TRANSPORTATION OF LIQUOR INTO "DRY" STATES]

The transportation or importation into any State, Territory, or Possession of the United States for delivery or use therein of intoxicating liquors, in violation of the laws thereof, is hereby prohibited.

Section 3

[RATIFICATION WITHIN SEVEN YEARS]

This article shall be inoperative unless it shall have been ratified as an amendment to the Constitution by conventions in the several States, as provided in the Constitution, within seven years from the date of the submission hereof to the States by the Congress.

Amendment XXII

[PROPOSED BY CONGRESS ON MARCH 21, 1947; DECLARED RATIFIED ON FEBRUARY 27, 1951.]

Section 1

[TENURE OF PRESIDENT LIMITED]

No person shall be elected to the office of President more than twice, and no person who has held the office of President or acted as President, for more than two years of a term to which some other person was elected President shall be elected to the office of the President more than once. But this Article shall not apply to any person holding the office of President when this Article was proposed by the Congress, and shall not prevent any person who may be holding the office of President, or acting as President, during the term within which this Article becomes operative from holding the office of President or acting as President during the remainder of such term.

Section 2

[RATIFICATION WITHIN SEVEN YEARS]

This article shall be inoperative unless it shall have been ratified as an amendment to the Constitution by the legislatures of three-fourths of the several States within seven years from the date of its submission to the States by the Congress.

Amendment XXIII

[PROPOSED BY CONGRESS ON JUNE 16, 1960; DECLARED RATIFIED ON MARCH 29, 1961.]

Section 1

[ELECTORAL COLLEGE VOTES FOR THE DISTRICT OF COLUMBIA]

The District constituting the seat of Government of the United States shall appoint in such manner as the Congress may direct:

A number of electors of President and Vice President equal to the whole number of Senators and Representatives in Congress to which the District would be entitled if it were a State, but in no event more than the least populous State; they shall be in addition to those appointed by the States, but they shall be considered, for the purposes of the election of President and Vice President, to be electors appointed by a State; and they shall meet in the District and perform such duties as provided by the twelfth article of amendment.

Section 2

[POWER TO ENFORCE THIS ARTICLE]
    The Congress shall have power to enforce this article by appropriate legislation.

Amendment XXIV

[PROPOSED BY CONGRESS ON AUGUST 27, 1962; DECLARED RATIFIED ON JANUARY 23, 1964.]

Section 1

[ANTI-POLL TAX]
    The right of citizens of the United States to vote in any primary or other election for President or Vice President, for electors for President or Vice President, or for Senator or Representative of Congress, shall not be denied or abridged by the United States or any State by reason of failure to pay any poll tax or other tax.

Section 2

[POWER TO ENFORCE THIS ARTICLE]
    The Congress shall have power to enforce this article by appropriate legislation.

Amendment XXV

[PROPOSED BY CONGRESS ON JULY 6, 1965; DECLARED RATIFIED ON FEBRUARY 10, 1967.]

Section 1

[VICE PRESIDENT TO BECOME PRESIDENT]
    In case of the removal of the President from office or his death or resignation, the Vice President shall become President.

Section 2

[CHOICE OF A NEW VICE PRESIDENT]
    Whenever there is a vacancy in the office of the Vice President, the President shall nominate a Vice President who shall take the office upon confirmation by a majority vote of both houses of Congress.

Section 3

[PRESIDENT MAY DECLARE OWN DISABILITY]
    Whenever the President transmits to the President pro tempore of the Senate and the Speaker of the House of Representatives his written declaration that he is unable to discharge the powers and duties of his office, and until he transmits to them a written declaration to the contrary, such powers and duties shall be discharged by the Vice President as Acting President.

Section 4

[ALTERNATE PROCEDURES TO DECLARE AND TO END PRESIDENTIAL DISABILITY]

Whenever the Vice President and a majority of either the principal officers of the executive departments, or of such other body as Congress may by law provide, transmit to the President pro tempore of the Senate and the Speaker of the House of Representatives their written declaration that the President is unable to discharge the powers and duties of his office, the Vice President shall immediately assume the powers and duties of the office as Acting President.

Thereafter, when the President transmits to the President pro tempore of the Senate and the Speaker of the House of Representatives his written declaration that no inability exists, he shall resume the powers and duties of his office unless the Vice President and a majority of either the principal officers of the executive department, or of such other body as Congress may by law provide, transmit within four days to the President pro tempore of the Senate and the Speaker of the House of Representatives their written declaration that the President is unable to discharge the powers and duties of his office. Thereupon Congress shall decide the issue, assembling within forty eight hours for that purpose if not in session. If the Congress, within twenty one days after receipt of the latter written declaration, or, if Congress is not in session, within twenty one days after Congress is required to assemble, determines by two-thirds vote of both Houses that the President is unable to discharge the powers and duties of his office, the Vice President shall continue to discharge the same as Acting President; otherwise, the President shall resume the powers and duties of his office.

Amendment XXVI

[PROPOSED BY CONGRESS ON MARCH 23, 1971; DECLARED RATIFIED ON JULY 1, 1971.]

Section 1

[EIGHTEEN-YEAR-OLD VOTE]

The right of citizens of the United States, who are eighteen years of age or older, to vote shall not be denied or abridged by the United States or by any State on account of age.

Section 2

[POWER TO ENFORCE THIS ARTICLE]

The Congress shall have power to enforce this article by appropriate legislation.

Amendment XXVII

[PROPOSED BY CONGRESS ON SEPTEMBER 25, 1789; DECLARED RATIFIED ON MAY 8, 1992.]
[CONGRESS CANNOT RAISE ITS OWN PAY]

No law varying the compensation for the services of the Senators and Representatives, shall take effect, until an election of representatives shall have intervened.

THE FEDERALIST PAPERS

No. 10: Madison

Among the numerous advantages promised by a well constructed Union, none deserves to be more accurately developed than its tendency to break and control the violence of faction. The friend of popular governments never finds himself so much alarmed for their character and fate, as when he contemplates their propensity to this dangerous vice. He will not fail therefore to set a due value on any plan which, without violating the principles to which he is attached, provides a proper cure for it. The instability, injustice, and confusion introduced into the public councils have, in truth, been the mortal diseases under which popular governments have everywhere perished, as they continue to be the favorite and fruitful topics from which the adversaries to liberty derive their most specious declamations. The valuable improvements made by the American constitutions on the popular models, both ancient and modern, cannot certainly be too much admired; but it would be an unwarrantable partiality to contend that they have as effectually obviated the danger on this side, as was wished and expected. Complaints are everywhere heard from our most considerate and virtuous citizens, equally the friends of public and private faith and of public and personal liberty, that our governments are too unstable, that the public good is disregarded in the conflicts of rival parties, and that measures are too often decided, not according to the rules of justice and the rights of the minor party, but by the superior force of an interested and overbearing majority. However anxiously we may wish that these complaints had no foundation, the evidence of known facts will not permit us to deny that they are in some degree true. It will be found, indeed, on a candid review of our situation, that some of the distresses under which we labor have been erroneously charged on the operation of our governments; but it will be found, at the same time, that other causes will not alone account for many of our heaviest misfortunes; and, particularly, for that prevailing and increasing distrust of public engagements and alarm for private rights which are echoed from one end of the continent to the other. These must be chiefly, if not wholly, effects of the unsteadiness and injustice with which a factious spirit has tainted our public administration.

By a faction I understand a number of citizens, whether amounting to a majority or minority of the whole, who are united and actuated by some common impulse of passion, or of interest, adverse to the rights of other citizens, or to the permanent and aggregate interests of the community.

There are two methods of curing the mischiefs of faction: the one, by removing its causes; the other, by controlling its effects.

There are again two methods of removing the causes of faction: the one, by destroying the liberty which is essential to its existence; the other, by giving to every citizen the same opinions, the same passions, and the same interests.

It could never be more truly said than of the first remedy, that it is worse than the disease. Liberty is to faction what air is to fire, an aliment without which it instantly expires. But it could not be a less folly to abolish liberty, which is essential to political life, because it nourishes faction, than it would be to wish the annihilation of air, which is essential to animal life, because it imparts to fire its destructive agency.

The second expedient is as impracticable, as the first would be unwise. As long as the reason of man continues fallible, and he is at liberty to exercise it, different opinions will be formed. As long as the connection subsists between his reason and his self-love, his opinions and his passions will have a reciprocal influence on each other; and the former will be objects to which the latter will attach themselves. The diversity in the faculties of men, from which the rights of property originate, is not less an insuperable obstacle to a uniformity of interests. The protection of these faculties is the first object of Government. From the protection of different and unequal faculties of acquiring property, the possession of different degrees and kinds of property immediately results; and from the influence of these on the sentiments and views of the respective proprietors, ensues a division of the society into different interests and parties.

The latent causes of faction are thus sown in the nature of man; and we see them everywhere brought into different degrees of activity, according to the different circumstances of civil society. A zeal for different opinions concerning religion, concerning Government, and many other points, as well of speculation as of practice; an attachment to different leaders ambitiously contending for pre-eminence and power; or to persons of other descriptions whose fortunes have been interesting to the human passions, have in turn divided mankind into parties, inflamed them with mutual animosity, and rendered them much more disposed to vex and oppress each other, than to co-operate for their common good. So strong is this propensity of mankind to fall into mutual animosities, that where no substantial occasion presents itself, the most frivolous and fanciful distinctions have been sufficient to kindle their unfriendly passions, and excite their most violent conflicts. But the most common and durable source of factions has been the various and unequal distribution of property. Those who hold and those who are without property have ever formed distinct interests in society. Those who are creditors, and those who are debtors, fall under a like discrimination. A landed interest, a manufacturing interest, a mercantile interest, a moneyed interest, with many lesser interests, grow up of necessity in civilized nations, and divide them into different classes, actuated by different sentiments and views. The regulation of these various and interfering interests forms the principal task of modern Legislation, and involves the spirit of party and faction in the necessary and ordinary operations of Government.

No man is allowed to be judge in his own cause, because his interest would certainly bias his judgment and, not improbably, corrupt his integrity. With equal, nay with greater reason, a body of men are unfit to be both judges and parties at the same time; yet what are many of the most important acts of legislation but so many judicial determinations, not indeed concerning the rights of single persons, but concerning the rights of large bodies of citizens; and what are the different classes of legislators but advocates and parties to the causes which they determine? Is a law proposed concerning private debts? It is a question to which the creditors are parties on one side and the debtors on the other. Justice ought to hold the balance between them. Yet the parties are, and must be, themselves the judges; and the most numerous party, or in other words, the most powerful faction must be expected to prevail. Shall domestic manufacturers be encouraged, and in what degree, by restrictions on foreign manufacturers? are questions which would be differently decided by the landed and the manufacturing classes, and probably by neither with a sole regard to justice and the public good. The apportionment of taxes on the various descriptions of property is an act which seems to require the most exact impartiality; yet there is, perhaps, no legislative act in which greater opportunity and temptation are given to a predominant party to trample on the rules of justice. Every shilling with which they overburden the inferior number is a shilling saved to their own pockets.

It is in vain to say that enlightened statesmen will be able to adjust these clashing interests and render them all subservient to the public good. Enlightened statesmen will not always be at the helm. Nor, in many cases, can such an adjustment be made at all without taking into view indirect and remote considerations, which will rarely prevail over the immediate interest which one party may find in disregarding the rights of another or the good of the whole.

The inference to which we are brought is that the *causes* of faction cannot be removed and that relief is only to be sought in the means of controlling its *effects*.

If a faction consists of less than a majority, relief is supplied by the republican principle, which enables the majority to defeat its sinister views by regular vote. It may clog the administration, it may convulse the society; but it will be unable to execute and mask its violence under the forms of the Constitution. When a majority is included in a faction, the form of popular government, on the other hand, enables it to sacrifice to its ruling passion or interest both the public good and the rights of other citizens. To secure the public good and private rights against the danger of such a faction, and at the same time to preserve the spirit and the form of popular government, is then the great object to which our enquiries are directed. Let me add that it is the great desideratum by which alone this form of government can be rescued from the opprobrium under which it has so long labored and be recommended to the esteem and adoption of mankind.

By what means is this object attainable? Evidently by one of two only. Either the existence of the same passion or interest in a majority at the same time must be prevented, or the majority, having such co-existent passion or interest, must be rendered, by their number and local situation, unable to concert and carry into effect schemes of oppression. If the impulse and the opportunity be suffered to coincide, we well know that neither moral nor religious motives can be relied on as an adequate control. They are not found to be such on the injustice and violence of individuals, and lose their efficacy in proportion to the number combined together, that is, in proportion as their efficacy becomes needful.

From this view of the subject it may be concluded that a pure Democracy, by which I mean a Society consisting of a small number of citizens, who assemble and administer the Government in person, can admit of no cure for the mischiefs of faction. A common passion or interest will, in almost every case, be felt by a majority of the whole; a communication and concert results from the form of Government itself; and there is nothing to check the inducements to sacrifice the weaker party or an obnoxious individual.

Hence it is that such Democracies have ever been spectacles of turbulence and contention; have ever been found incompatible with personal security or the rights of property; and have in general been as short in their lives as they have been violent in their deaths. Theoretic politicians, who have patronized this species of Government, have erroneously supposed that by reducing mankind to a perfect equality in their political rights, they would at the same time be perfectly equalized and assimilated in their possessions, their opinions, and their passions.

A Republic, by which I mean a Government in which the scheme of representation takes place, opens a different prospect and promises the cure for which we are seeking. Let us examine the points in which it varies from pure Democracy, and we shall comprehend both the nature of the cure and the efficacy which it must derive from the Union.

The two great points of difference between a Democracy and a Republic are: first, the delegation of the Government, in the latter, to a small number of citizens elected by the rest; secondly, the greater number of citizens and greater sphere of country over which the latter may be extended.

The effect of the first difference is, on the one hand, to refine and enlarge the public views by passing them through the medium of a chosen body of citizens, whose wisdom may best discern the true interest of their country and whose patriotism and love of justice will be least likely to sacrifice it to temporary or partial considerations. Under such a regulation it may well happen that the public voice, pronounced by the representatives of the people, will be more consonant to the public good than if pronounced by the people themselves, convened for the purpose. On the other hand, the effect may be inverted. Men of factious tempers, of local prejudices, or of sinister designs, may, by intrigue, by corruption, or by other means, first obtain the suffrages, and then betray the interests of the people. The question resulting is, whether small or extensive Republics are most favorable to the election of proper guardians of the public weal; and it is clearly decided in favor of the latter by two obvious considerations.

In the first place it is to be remarked that however small the Republic may be, the Representatives must be raised to a certain number in order to guard against the cabals of a few; and that however large it may be they must be limited to a certain number in order to guard against the confusion of a multitude. Hence, the number of Representatives in the two cases not being in proportion to that of the Constituents, and being proportionally greatest in the small Republic, it follows that if the proportion of fit characters be not less in the large than in the small Republic, the former will present a greater option, and consequently a greater probability of a fit choice.

In the next place, as each Representative will be chosen by a greater number of citizens in the large than in the small Republic, it will be more difficult for unworthy candidates to practise with success the vicious arts by which elections are too often carried; and the suffrages of the people being more free, will be more likely to centre on men who possess the most attractive merit and the most diffusive and established characters.

It must be confessed that in this, as in most other cases, there is a mean, on both sides of which inconveniencies will be found to lie. By enlarging too much the number of electors, you render the representative too little acquainted with all their local circumstances and lesser interests; as by reducing it too much, you render him unduly attached to these, and too little fit to comprehend and pursue great and national objects. The Federal Constitution forms a happy combination in this respect; the great and aggregate interests being referred to the national, the local and particular to the State legislatures.

The other point of difference is the greater number of citizens and extent of territory which may be brought within the compass of Republican than of Democratic Government; and it is this circumstance principally which renders factious combinations less to be dreaded in the former than in the latter. The smaller the society, the fewer probably will be the distinct parties and interests composing it; the fewer the distinct parties and interests, the more frequently will a majority be found of the same party; and the smaller the number of individuals composing a majority, and the smaller the compass within which they are placed, the more easily will they concert and execute their plans of oppression. Extend the sphere and you take in a greater variety of parties and interests; you make it less probable that a majority of the whole will have a common motive to invade the rights of other citizens; or if such a common motive exists, it will be more difficult for all who feel it to discover their own strength and to act in unison with each other. Besides other impediments, it may be remarked, that where there is a consciousness of unjust or dishonorable purposes, communication is always checked by distrust in proportion to the number whose concurrence is necessary.

Hence, it clearly appears that the same advantage which a Republic has over a Democracy in controlling the effects of faction is enjoyed by a large over a small republic—is enjoyed by the Union over the States composing it. Does this advantage consist in the substitution of representatives whose enlightened views and virtuous sentiments render them superior to local prejudices and to schemes of injustice? It will not be denied that the representation of the Union will be most likely to possess these requisite endowments. Does it consist in the greater security afforded by a greater variety of parties, against the event of any one party being able to outnumber and oppress the rest? In an equal degree does the increased variety of parties comprised within the Union increase this security? Does it, in fine, consist in the greater obstacles opposed to the concert and accomplishment of the secret wishes of an unjust and interested majority? Here again the extent of the Union gives it the most palpable advantage.

The influence of factious leaders may kindle a flame within their particular States but will be unable to spread a general conflagration through the other States: a religious sect may degenerate into a political faction in a part of the Confederacy; but the variety of sects dispersed over the entire face of it must secure the national Councils against any danger from that source: a rage for paper money, for an abolition of debts, for an equal division of property, or for any other improper or wicked project, will be less apt to pervade the whole body of the Union than a particular member of it; in the same proportion as such a malady is more likely to taint a particular county or district than an entire State.

In the extent and proper structure of the Union, therefore, we behold a republican remedy for the diseases most incident to Republican Government. And according to the degree of pleasure and pride we feel in being republicans ought to be our zeal in cherishing the spirit and supporting the character of federalist.

PUBLIUS

No. 51: Madison

To what expedient, then, shall we finally resort, for maintaining in practice the necessary partition of power among the several departments as laid down in the constitution? The only answer that can be given is that as all these exterior provisions are found to be inadequate the defect must be supplied, by so contriving the interior structure of the government as that its several constituent parts may, by their mutual relations, be the means of keeping each other in their proper places. Without presuming to undertake a full development of this important idea I will hazard a few general observations which may perhaps place it in a clearer light, and enable us to form a more correct judgment of the principles and structure of the government planned by the convention.

In order to lay a due foundation for that separate and distinct exercise of the different powers of government, which to a certain extent is admitted on all hands to be essential to the preservation of liberty, it is evident that each department should have a will of its own; and consequently should be so constituted that the members of each should have as little agency as possible in the appointment of the members of the others. Were this principle rigorously adhered to, it would require that all the appointments for the supreme executive, legislative, and judiciary magistracies should be drawn from the same fountain of authority, the people, through channels having no communication whatever with one another. Perhaps such a plan of constructing the several departments would be less difficult in practice than it may in contemplation appear. Some difficulties, however, and some additional expense would attend the execution of it. Some deviations, therefore, from the principle must be admitted. In the constitution of the judiciary department in particular, it might be inexpedient to insist rigorously on the principle: first, because peculiar qualifications being essential in the members, the primary consideration ought to be to select that mode of choice which best secures these qualifications; second, because the permanent tenure by which the appointments are held in that department must soon destroy all sense of dependence on the authority conferring them.

It is equally evident that the members of each department should be as little dependent as possible on those of the others for the emoluments annexed to their offices. Were the executive magistrate, or the judges, not independent of the legislature in this particular, their independence in every other would be merely nominal.

But the great security against a gradual concentration of the several powers in the same department consists in giving to those who administer each department the necessary constitutional means and personal motives to resist encroachments of the others. The provision for defence must in this, as in all other cases, be made commensurate to the danger of attack. Ambition must be made to counteract ambition. The interest of the man must be connected with the constitutional rights of the place. It may be a reflection on human nature that such devices should be necessary to control the abuses of government. But what is government itself but the greatest of all reflections on human nature? If men were angels, no government would be necessary. If angels were to govern men, neither external nor internal controls on government would be necessary. In framing a government which is to be administered by men over men, the great difficulty lies in this: You must first enable the government to control the governed; and in the next place oblige it to control itself. A dependence on the people is, no doubt, the primary control on the government; but experience has taught mankind the necessity of auxiliary precautions.

This policy of supplying, by opposite and rival interests, the defect of better motives, might be traced through the whole system of human affairs, private as well as public. We see it particularly displayed in all the subordinate distributions of power, where the constant aim is to divide and arrange the several offices in such a manner as that each may be a check on the other; that the private interest of every individual may be a sentinel over the public rights. These inventions of prudence cannot be less requisite in the distribution of the supreme powers of the State.

But it is not possible to give to each department an equal power of self-defense. In republican government, the legislative authority necessarily predominates. The remedy for this inconveniency is to divide the legislature into different branches; and to render them, by different modes of election and different principles of action, as little connected with each other as the nature of their common functions and their common dependence on the society will admit. It may even be necessary to guard against dangerous encroachments by still further precautions. As the weight of the legislative authority requires that it should be thus divided, the weakness of the executive may require, on the other hand, that it should be fortified. An absolute negative on the legislature appears, at first view, to be the natural defense with which the executive magistrate should be armed. But perhaps it would be neither altogether safe nor alone sufficient. On ordinary occasions it might not be exerted with the requisite firmness, and on extraordinary occasions it might be perfidiously abused. May not this defect of an absolute negative be supplied by some qualified connection between this weaker branch of the stronger department, by which the latter may be led to support the constitutional rights of the former, without being too much detached from the rights of its own department?

If the principles on which these observations are founded be just, as I persuade myself they are, and they be applied as a criterion to the several State constitutions, and to the federal Constitution, it will be found that if the latter does not perfectly correspond with them, the former are infinitely less able to bear such a test.

There are, moreover, two considerations particularly applicable to the federal system of America, which place that system in a very interesting point of view.

First. In a single republic, all the power surrendered by the people is submitted to the administration of a single government; and usurpations are guarded against by a division of the government into distinct and separate departments. In the compound republic of America, the power surrendered by the people is first divided between two distinct governments, and then the portion allotted to each subdivided among distinct and separate departments. Hence a double security arises to the rights of the people. The different governments will control each other, at the same time that each will be controlled by itself.

Second. It is of great importance in a republic not only to guard the society against the oppression of its rulers, but to guard one part of the society against the injustice of the other part. Different interests necessarily exist in different classes of citizens. If a majority be united by a common interest, the rights of the minority will be insecure. There are but two methods of providing against this evil: The one by creating a will in the community independent of the majority—that is, of the society itself; the other, by comprehending in the society so many separate descriptions of citizens as will render an unjust combination of a majority of the whole very improbable, if not impracticable. The first method prevails in all governments possessing an hereditary or self-appointed authority. This, at best, is but a precarious security; because a power independent of the society may as well espouse the unjust views of the major as the rightful interests of the minor party, and may possibly be turned against both parties. The second method will be exemplified in the federal republic of the United States. Whilst all authority in it will be derived from and dependent on the society, the society itself will be broken into so many parts, interests and classes of citizens, that the rights of individuals, or of the minority, will be in little danger from interested combinations of the majority. In a free government the security for civil rights must be the same as that for religious rights. It consists in the one case in the multiplicity of interests, and in the other in the multiplicity of sects. The degree of security in both cases will depend on the number of interests and sects; and this may be presumed to depend on the extent of country and number of people comprehended under the same government. This view of the subject must particularly recommend a proper federal system to all the sincere and considerate friends of republican government: Since it shows that in exact proportion as the territory of the Union may be formed into more circumscribed Confederacies, or States, oppressive combinations of a majority will be facilitated; the best security, under the republican form, for the rights of every class of citizens, will be diminished; and consequently the stability and independence of some member of the government, the only other security, must be proportionally increased. Justice is the end of government. It is the end of civil society. It ever has been and ever will be pursued until it be obtained, or until liberty be lost in the pursuit. In a society under the forms of which the stronger faction can readily unite and oppress the weaker, anarchy may as truly be said to reign as in a state of nature, where the weaker individual is not secured against the violence of the stronger: And as, in the latter state, even the stronger individuals are prompted, by the uncertainty of their condition, to submit to a government which may protect the weak as well as themselves: So, in the former state, will the more powerful factions or parties be gradually induced, by a like motive, to wish for a government which will protect all parties, the weaker as well as the more powerful. It can be little doubted that if the State of Rhode Island was separated from the Confederacy and left to itself, the insecurity of rights under the popular form of government within such narrow limits would be displayed by such reiterated oppressions of factious majorities that some power altogether independent of the people would soon be called for by the voice of the very factions whose misrule had proved the necessity of it. In the extended republic of the United States, and among the great variety of interests, parties, and sects which it embraces, a coalition of a majority of the whole society could seldom take place on any other principles than those of justice and the general good; and there being thus less danger to a minor from the will of the major party, there must be less pretext, also, to provide for the security of the former, by introducing into the government a will not dependent on the latter, or, in other words, a will independent of the society itself. It is no less certain than it is important, notwithstanding the contrary opinions which have been entertained, that the larger the society, provided it lie within a practicable sphere, the more duly capable it will be of self-government. And happily for the *republican cause,* the practicable sphere may be carried to a very great extent by a judicious modification and mixture of the *federal principle.*

PUBLIUS

PRESIDENTS AND VICE PRESIDENTS

PRESIDENT	VICE PRESIDENT
1 George Washington (Federalist 1789)	John Adams (Federalist 1789)
2 John Adams (Federalist 1797)	Thomas Jefferson (Dem.-Rep. 1797)
3 Thomas Jefferson (Dem.-Rep. 1801)	Aaron Burr (Dem.-Rep. 1801) George Clinton (Dem.-Rep. 1805)
4 James Madison (Dem.-Rep. 1809)	George Clinton (Dem.-Rep. 1809) Elbridge Gerry (Dem.-Rep. 1813)
5 James Monroe (Dem.-Rep. 1817)	Daniel D. Tompkins (Dem.-Rep. 1817)
6 John Quincy Adams (Dem.-Rep. 1825)	John C. Calhoun (Dem.-Rep. 1825)
7 Andrew Jackson (Democratic 1829)	John C. Calhoun (Democratic 1829) Martin Van Buren (Democratic 1833)
8 Martin Van Buren (Democratic 1837)	Richard M. Johnson (Democratic 1837)
9 William H. Harrison (Whig 1841)	John Tyler (Whig 1841)
10 John Tyler (Whig and Democratic 1841)	

PRESIDENT	VICE PRESIDENT
11 James K. Polk (Democratic 1845)	George M. Dallas (Democratic 1845)
12 Zachary Taylor (Whig 1849)	Millard Fillmore (Whig 1849)
13 Millard Fillmore (Whig 1850)	
14 Franklin Pierce (Democratic 1853)	William R. D. King (Democratic 1853)
15 James Buchanan (Democrat 1857)	John C. Breckinridge (Democrat 1857)
16 Abraham Lincoln (Republican 1861)	Hannibal Hamlin (Republican 1861) Andrew Johnson (Unionist 1865)
17 Andrew Johnson (Unionist 1865)	
18 Ulysses S. Grant (Republican 1869)	Schuyler Colfax (Republican 1869) Henry Wilson (Republican 1873)
19 Rutherford B. Hayes (Republican 1877)	William A. Wheeler (Republican 1877)
20 James A. Garfield (Republican 1881)	Chester A. Arthur (Republican 1881)
21 Chester A. Arthur (Republican 1881)	
22 Grover Cleveland (Democratic 1885)	Thomas A. Hendricks (Democratic 1885)
23 Benjamin Harrison (Republican 1889)	Levi P. Morton (Republican 1889)
24 Grover Cleveland (Democratic 1893)	Adlai E. Stevenson (Democratic 1893)
25 William McKinley (Republican 1897)	Garret A. Hobart (Republican 1897) Theodore Roosevelt (Republican 1901)
26 Theodore Roosevelt (Republican 1901)	Charles W. Fairbanks (Republican 1905)
27 William H. Taft (Republican 1909)	James S. Sherman (Republican 1909)
28 Woodrow Wilson (Democratic 1913)	Thomas R. Marshall (Democratic 1913)
29 Warren G. Harding (Republican 1921)	Calvin Coolidge (Republican 1921)
30 Calvin Coolidge (Republican 1923)	Charles G. Dawes (Republican 1925)

PRESIDENT	VICE PRESIDENT
31 Herbert Hoover (Republican 1929)	Charles Curtis (Republican 1929)
32 Franklin D. Roosevelt (Democratic 1933)	John Nance Garner (Democratic 1933) Henry A. Wallace (Democratic 1941) Harry S. Truman (Democratic 1945)
33 Harry S. Truman (Democratic 1945)	Alben W. Barkley (Democratic 1949)
34 Dwight D. Eisenhower (Republican 1953)	Richard M. Nixon (Republican 1953)
35 John F. Kennedy (Democratic 1961)	Lyndon B. Johnson (Democratic 1961)
36 Lyndon B. Johnson (Democratic 1963)	Hubert H. Humphrey (Democratic 1965)
37 Richard M. Nixon (Republican 1969)	Spiro T. Agnew (Republican 1969) Gerald R. Ford (Republican 1973)
38 Gerald R. Ford (Republican 1974)	Nelson Rockefeller (Republican 1974)
39 James E. Carter (Democratic 1977)	Walter Mondale (Democratic 1977)
40 Ronald Reagan (Republican 1981)	George H. W. Bush (Republican 1981)
41 George H. W. Bush (Republican 1989)	J. Danforth Quayle (Republican 1989)
42 William J. Clinton (Democrat 1993)	Albert Gore, Jr. (Democrat 1993)
43 George W. Bush (Republican 2001)	Richard B. Cheney (Republican 2001)

GLOSSARY

administrative adjudication the application of rules and precedents to specific cases to settle disputes with regulated parties

administrative regulation rules made by regulatory agencies and commissions

adversarial journalism an aggressive form of investigative journalism that attempts to expose and antagonize the status quo

affirmative action government policies or programs that seek to address past injustices against specified groups by making special efforts to provide members of these groups with access to educational and employment opportunities

agency representation the type of representation by which representatives are held accountable to their constituency if they fail to represent that constituency properly. This is the incentive for good representation when the personal backgrounds, views, and interests of the representative differ from those of his or her constituency

agenda setting the power of the media to bring public attention to particular issues and problems

agents of socialization social institutions, including families and schools, that help to shape individuals' basic political beliefs and values

Aid to Families with Dependent Children (AFDC) federal funds, administered by the states, for children living with parents or relatives who fall below state standards of need. Replaced in 1996 by Temporary Assistance to Needy Families (TANF)

amendment a change added to a bill, law, or constitution

amicus curiae literally, "friend of the court"; individuals or groups who are not parties to a lawsuit but who seek to assist the Supreme Court in reaching a decision by presenting additional briefs

Antifederalists those who favored strong state governments and a weak national government and who were opponents of the constitution proposed at the American Constitutional Convention of 1787

appellate court a court that hears the appeals of trial court decisions

appropriations the amounts of money approved by Congress in statutes (bills) that each unit or agency of government can spend

Articles of Confederation America's first written constitution; served as the basis for America's national government until 1789

authoritarian government a system of rule in which the government recognizes no formal limits but may nevertheless be restrained by the power of other social institutions

bicameral having a legislative assembly composed of two chambers or houses; opposite of unicameral

bilateral treaties treaties made between two nations

bill a proposed law that has been sponsored by a member of Congress and submitted to the clerk of the House or Senate

Bill of Rights the first ten amendments to the Constitution, which guarantee certain rights and liberties to the people

bills of attainder laws that decree a person guilty of a crime without a trial

block grants federal grants-in-aid that allow states considerable discretion in how the funds should be spent

briefs written documents in which attorneys explain, using case precedents, why the court should find in favor of their client

Brown v. Board of Education the 1954 Supreme Court decision that struck down the "separate but equal" doctrine as fundamentally unequal. This case eliminated state power to use race as a criterion of discrimination in law and provided the national government with the power to intervene by exercising strict regulatory policies against discriminatory actions

bureaucracy the complex structure of offices, tasks, rules, and principles of organization that are employed by all large-scale institutions to coordinate effectively the work of their personnel

Cabinet the secretaries, or chief administrators, of the major departments of the federal government. Cabinet secretaries are appointed by the president with the consent of the Senate

categorical grants congressional grants given to states and localities on the condition that expenditures be limited to a problem or group specified by law

checks and balances mechanisms through which each branch of government is able to participate in and influence the activities of the other branches. Major examples include the presidential veto power over congressional legislation, the power of the Senate to approve presidential appointments, and judicial review of congressional enactments

chief justice justice on the Supreme Court who presides over the Court's public sessions

citizenship informed and active membership in a political community

civil law a system of jurisprudence, including private law and governmental actions, to settle disputes that do not involve criminal penalties

civil liberties areas of personal freedom with which governments are constrained from interfering

civil penalties regulatory techniques in which fines or another form of material restitution is imposed for violating civil laws or common law principles, for example through negligence

civil rights legal or moral claims that citizens are entitled to make upon government

"clear and present danger" test test to determine whether speech is protected or unprotected, based on its capacity to present a "clear and present danger" to society

closed primary a primary election in which voters can participate in the nomination of candidates, but only of the party in which they are enrolled for a period of time prior to primary day

cloture a rule allowing a majority of two-thirds or three-fifths of the members in a legislative body to set a time limit on debate over a given bill

cold war the period of hostilities, but no direct war, between the United States and the former Soviet Union between the late 1940s and about 1990

collective goods benefits, sought by groups, that are broadly available and cannot be denied to nonmembers

commander in chief the power of the president as commander of the national military and the state national guard units (when called into service)

commerce clause Article 1, Section 8, of the Constitution, which delegates to Congress the power "to regulate Commerce with foreign Nations, and among the several States and with the Indian Tribes." The Supreme Court interpreted this clause in favor of national power over the economy

confederation a system of government in which states retain sovereign authority except for the powers expressly delegated to the national government

conference/caucus a gathering every two years to elect House leaders. Democrats call their gathering a caucus; Republicans call theirs a conference

conference committee a joint committee created to work out a compromise on House and Senate versions of a piece of legislation

conservative today this term refers to those who generally support the social and economic status quo and are suspicious of efforts to introduce new political formulae and economic arrangements. Conservatives believe that a large and powerful government poses a threat to citizens' freedom

constituency the district comprising the area from which an official is elected

constitutional government a system of rule in which formal and effective limits are placed on the powers of the government

containment the policy used by the United States during the cold war to restrict the expansion of communism and limit the influence of the Soviet Union

contracting power the power of government to set conditions on companies seeking to sell goods or services to government agencies

contributory programs social programs financed in whole or in part by taxation or other mandatory contributions by their present or future recipients. The most important example is Social Security, which is financed by a payroll tax

cooperative federalism federalism existing since the New Deal era in which grants-in-aid have been used strategically to encourage states and localities to pursue nationally defined goals, with national and state governments sharing powers and resources via intergovernmental cooperation

cost-of-living adjustments (COLAs) changes made to the level of benefits of a government program based on the rate of inflation

criminal law the branch of law that deals with disputes or actions involving criminal penalties (as opposed to civil law); it regulates the conduct of individuals, defines crimes, and provides punishment for criminal acts

criminal penalties regulatory techniques in which imprisonment or heavy fines and the loss of certain civil rights and liberties are imposed

de facto literally, "by fact"; practices that occur even when there is no legal enforcement, such as school segregation in much of the United States today

de jure literally, "by law"; legally enforced practices, such as school segregation in the South before the 1960s

defendant the one against whom a complaint is brought in a criminal or civil case

delegated powers constitutional powers that are assigned to one governmental agency but that are exercised by another agency with the express permission of the first

democracy a system of rule that permits citizens to play a significant part in the governmental process, usually through the election of key public officials

department the largest subunit of the executive branch. The secretaries of the fourteen departments form the Cabinet

deterrence the development and maintenance of military strength as a means of discouraging attack

devolution a policy to remove a program from one level of government by delegating it or passing it down to a lower level of government, such as from the national government to the state and local governments

diplomacy the representation of a government to other foreign governments

direct democracy a system of rule that permits citizens to vote directly on laws and policies

discount rate the interest rate charged by the Federal Reserve System when commercial banks borrow in order to expand their lending operations; an effective tool of monetary policy

dissenting opinion a decision written by a justice in the minority in a particular case in which the justice wishes to express his or her reasoning in the case

divided government the condition in American government wherein the presidency is controlled by one party while the opposing party controls one or both houses of Congress

double jeopardy the Fifth Amendment right providing that a person cannot be tried twice for the same crime

dual citizenship the status of being governed concurrently by both the U.S. federal government and the individual's state government

dual federalism the system of government that prevailed in the United States from 1789 to the 1930s, in which the powers of the national government and the states were considered entirely separate and distinct from each other; during this time, the states possessed a vast amount of governing power

due process of law the right of every citizen against arbitrary action by national or state governments

elastic clause Article 1, Section 8, of the Constitution (also known as the necessary and proper clause), which enumerates the powers of Congress and provides Congress with the authority to make all laws "necessary and proper" to carry them out

electoral college the presidential electors from each state who meet after the popular election to cast ballots for president and vice president

electoral realignment the point in history when a new party supplants the ruling party, becoming in turn the dominant political force. In the United States, this has tended to occur roughly every thirty years

eminent domain the right of government to take private property for public use

equal protection clause provision of the Fourteenth Amendment guaranteeing citizens "the equal protection of the laws." This clause has served as the basis for the civil rights of African Americans, women, and other groups

equality of opportunity a widely shared American ideal that all people should have the freedom to use whatever talents and wealth they have to reach their fullest potential

establishment clause the First Amendment clause that says that "Congress shall make no law respecting an establishment of religion." This law means that a "wall of separation" exists between church and state

ex post facto laws laws that declare an action to be illegal after it has been committed

exclusionary rule the ability of courts to exclude evidence obtained in violation of the Fourth Amendment

executive agreement an agreement, made between the president and another country, that has the force of a treaty but does not require the Senate's "advice and consent"

Executive Office of the President the permanent agencies that perform defined management tasks for the president. Created in 1939, the EOP includes the Office of Management and Budget, the Council of Economic Advisers, the National Security Council, and other agencies

executive order a rule or regulation issued by the president that has the effect and formal status of legislation

expressed powers specific powers granted to Congress under Article I, Section 8, of the Constitution

expropriation confiscation of property with or without compensation

Federal Reserve Board (Fed) the governing board of the Federal Reserve System, comprising a chair and six other members, all appointed by the president with the consent of the Senate

Federal Reserve System a system of twelve Federal Reserve Banks that facilitates exchanges of cash, checks, and credit; regulates member banks; and uses monetary policies to fight inflation and deflation

federalism a system of government in which power is divided, by a constitution, between a central government and regional governments

Federalist Papers a series of essays written by James Madison, Alexander Hamilton, and John Jay supporting the ratification of the Constitution

Federalists those who favored a strong national government and supported the constitution proposed at the American Constitutional Convention of 1787

fighting words speech that directly incites damaging conduct

filibuster a tactic used by members of the Senate to prevent action on legislation they oppose by continuously holding the floor and speaking until the majority backs down. Once given the floor, senators have unlimited time to speak, and it requires a vote of three-fifths of the Senate to end a filibuster

fiscal policy the use of taxing, monetary, and spending powers to manipulate the economy

527 committee nonprofit independent groups that receive and disburse funds to influence the nomination, election, or defeat of candidates. Named after Section 527 of the Internal Revenue Code, which defines and provides tax-exempt status for nonprofit advocacy groups

food stamps coupons that can be exchanged for food at most grocery stores; the largest in-kind benefits program

framing the power of the media to influence how events and issues are interpreted

free exercise clause the First Amendment clause that protects a citizen's right to believe and practice whatever religion he or she chooses

free riders those who enjoy the benefits of collective goods but did not participate in acquiring them

full faith and credit clause provision from Article IV, Section 1 of the Constitution, requiring that the states normally honor the public acts and judicial decisions that take place in another state

going public a strategy that attempts to mobilize the widest and most favorable climate of public opinion

government institutions and procedures through which a territory and its people are ruled

government corporation a government agency that performs a service normally provided by the private sector

grand jury jury that determines whether sufficient evidence is available to justify a trial; grand juries do not rule on the accused's guilt or innocence

grants-in-aid programs through which Congress provides money to state and local governments on the condition that the funds be employed for purposes defined by the federal government

grassroots lobbying a lobbying campaign in which a group mobilizes its membership to contact government officials in support of the group's position

Great Compromise the agreement reached at the Constitutional Convention of 1787 that gave each state an equal number of senators regardless of its population, but linked representation in the House of Representatives to population

habeas corpus a court order demanding that an individual in custody be brought into court and shown the cause for detention

home rule power delegated by the state to a local unit of government to manage its own affairs

impeachment the formal charge by the House of Representatives that a government official has committed "Treason, Bribery, or other high Crimes and Misdemeanors"

implementation the efforts of departments and agencies to translate laws into specific bureaucratic routines

implied powers powers derived from the "necessary and proper" clause of Article I, Section 8, of the Constitution. Such powers are not specifically expressed, but are implied through the expansive interpretation of delegated powers

in-kind benefits goods and services provided to needy individuals and families by the federal government

incorporation the process by which court decisions have required the states to follow parts of the Bill of Rights based on the use or application of the Fourteenth Amendment

incumbency holding a political office for which one is running

incumbent a candidate running for a position that he or she already holds

independent agency an agency that is not part of a Cabinet department

indexing periodic process of adjusting social benefits or wages to account for increases in the cost of living

inflation a consistent increase in the general level of prices

inherent powers powers claimed by a president that are not expressed in the Constitution, but are inferred from it

institutional advertising advertising designed to create a positive image of an organization

institutional racism rules or laws that protect or perpetuate the oppression of racial groups

interest group a voluntary membership association organized to pursue a common interest (or interests), through political participation, toward the ultimate goal of getting favorable public policy decisions from government

International Monetary Fund (IMF) an institution—established in 1944 at Bretton Woods, New Hampshire—that provides loans and facilitates international monetary exchange

iron triangle the stable, cooperative relationships that often develop between a congressional committee, an administrative agency, and one or more supportive interest groups. Similar relationships with more than three parties exist, but the iron triangle is the most typical

issue advocacy independent spending by individuals or interest groups on a campaign issue but not directly tied to a particular candidate

joint committee a legislative committee formed of members of both the House and the Senate

judicial activism judicial philosophy that posits that the court should go beyond the words of the Constitution or a statute to consider the broader societal implications of its decisions

judicial restraint judicial philosophy whose adherents refuse to go beyond the clear words of the Constitution in interpreting its meaning

judicial review the power of the courts to declare actions of the legislative and executive branches invalid or unconstitutional. The Supreme Court asserted this power in *Marbury v. Madison*

jurisdiction the sphere of a court's power and authority

Kitchen Cabinet an informal group of advisers to whom the president turns for counsel and guidance. Members of the official Cabinet may or may not also be members of the Kitchen Cabinet

laissez-faire capitalism an economic system in which the means of production and distribution are privately owned and operated for profit with minimal or no government interference

legislative initiative the president's inherent power to bring a legislative agenda before Congress

libel a written statement made in "Reckless disregard of the truth" that is considered damaging to a victim because it is "malicious, scandalous, and defamatory"

liberal today, one who generally supports political and social reform; extensive governmental intervention in the economy; the expansion of federal social services; more vigorous efforts on behalf of the poor, minorities, and women; and greater concern for consumers and the environment

liberty freedom from government control

limited government a government whose powers are defined and limited by a constitution

line-item veto the power of the executive to veto specific provisions (lines) of a bill passed by the legislature

lobbying a strategy by which organized interests seek to influence the passage of legislation by exerting direct pressure on members of the legislature

logrolling a legislative practice wherein agreements are made between legislators in voting for or against a bill. Unlike bargaining, parties to logrolling have nothing in common but their desire to exchange support

majority leader the elected leader of the majority party in the House of Representatives or in the Senate. In the House, the majority leader is subordinate in the party hierarchy to the speaker of the House

majority party the party that holds the majority of legislative seats in either the House or the Senate

majority rule/minority rights the democratic principle that a government follows the preferences of the majority of voters but protects the interests of the minority

mandate a claim by a victorious candidate that the electorate has given him or her special authority to carry out promises made during the campaign

Marshall Plan the U.S. European Recovery Plan, in which over $34 billion was spent for the relief, reconstruction, and economic recovery of Western Europe after World War II

material benefits special goods, services, or money provided to members of groups to entice others to join

means testing a procedure by which potential beneficiaries of a public assistance program establish their eligibility by demonstrating a genuine need for the assistance

measurement error failure to identify the true distribution of opinion within a population because of errors such as ambiguous or poorly worded questions

Medicaid a federally financed, state-operated program providing medical services to low-income people

Medicare a form of national health insurance for the elderly and the disabled

merit system a product of civil service reform, in which appointees to positions in public bureaucracies must objectively be deemed qualified for the position

minority leader the elected leader of the minority party in the House or Senate

minority party the party that holds a minority of legislative seats in either the House or the Senate

***Miranda* rule** the requirement, articulated by the Supreme Court in *Miranda v. Arizona,* that persons under arrest must be informed prior to police interrogation of their rights to remain silent and to have the benefit of legal counsel

multilateralism a foreign policy that seeks to encourage the involvement of several nation-states in coordinated action, usually in relation to a common adversary, with terms and conditions usually specified in a multicounty treaty

multiple-member district an electorate that selects all candidates at large from the whole district; each voter is given the number of votes equivalent to the number of seats to be filled

nation-state a political entity consisting of people with some common cultural experience (nation) who also share a common political authority (state), recognized by the sovereignties (nation-states)

necessary and proper clause from Article I, Section 8 of the Constitution, it provides Congress with the authority to make all laws "necessary and proper" to carry out its expressed powers

New Deal coalition the coalition of northern urban liberals, southern white conservatives, organized labor, and blacks that dominated national politics until the 1960s

New Jersey Plan a framework for the Constitution, introduced by William Paterson, which called for equal state representation in the national legislature regardless of population

New Politics movement a political movement that began in the 1960s and 1970s, made up of professionals and intellectuals for whom the civil rights and antiwar movements were formative experiences. The New Politics movement strengthened public-interest groups

nomination the process through which political parties select their candidates for election to public office

noncontributory programs social programs that provide assistance to people based on demonstrated need rather than any contribution they have made

North American Free Trade Agreement (NAFTA) trade treaty between the United States, Canada, and Mexico to lower and eliminate tariffs between the three countries

North Atlantic Treaty Organization (NATO) a treaty organization, comprising the United States, Canada, and most of Western Europe, formed in 1948 to counter the perceived threat from the Soviet Union

open primary a primary election in which the voter can wait until the day of the primary to choose which party to enroll in to select candidates for the general election

opinion the written explanation of the Supreme Court's decision in a particular case

oral argument stage in Supreme Court procedure in which attorneys for both sides appear before the Court to present their positions and answer questions posed by justices

original jurisdiction the authority to initially consider a case. Distinguished from appellate jurisdiction, which is the authority to hear the appeals from a lower court's decision

oversight the effort by Congress, through hearings, investigations, and other techniques, to exercise control over the activities of executive agencies

party identification an individual voter's psychological ties to one party or another

party vote a roll-call vote in the House or Senate in which at least 50 percent of the members of one party take a particular position and are opposed by at least 50 percent of the members of the other party. Party votes are rare today, although they were fairly common in the nineteenth century

patronage the resources available to higher officials, usually opportunities to make partisan appointments to offices and to confer grants, licenses, or special favors to supporters

per curiam decision by an appellate court, without a written opinion, that refuses to review the decision of a lower court; amounts to reaffirmation of the lower court's opinion

permanent campaign description of presidential politics in which all presidential actions are taken with reelection in mind

plaintiff the individual or organization that brings a complaint in court

plea bargains negotiated agreements in criminal cases in which a defendant agrees to plead guilty in return for the state's agreement to reduce the severity of the criminal charge the defendent is facing

pluralism the theory that all interests are and should be free to compete for influence in the government. The outcome of this competition is compromise and moderation

plurality system a type of electoral system in which, to win a seat in the parliament or other representative body, a candidate need only receive the most votes in the election, not necessarily a majority of the votes cast

pocket veto a presidential veto that is automatically triggered if the president does not act on a given piece of legislation passed during the final ten days of a legislative session if Congress, by its adjournment, prevents the bill from returning

police power power reserved to the government to regulate the health, safety, and morals of its citizens

political action committee (PAC) a private group that raises and distributes funds for use in election campaigns

political equality the right to participate in politics equally, based on the principle of "one person, one vote"

political ideology a cohesive set of beliefs that form a general philosophy about the role of government

political parties organized groups that attempt to influence the government by electing their members to important government offices

politics conflict over the leadership, structure, and policies of governments

popular sovereignty a principle of democracy in which political authority rests ultimately in the hands of the people

pork barrel appropriations made by legislative bodies for local projects that are often not needed but that are created to help local representatives win reelection in their home districts

power influence over a government's leadership, organization, or policies

precedent prior case whose principles are used by judges as the basis for their decisions in present cases

preemption the principle that allows the national government to override state or local actions in certain policy areas

preferred freedoms certain protections in the Bill of Rights, such as free speech and free press, that are considered to be critically important and crucial to the process of incorporation

primary elections elections used to select a party's candidate for the general election

priming preparing the public to take a particular view of an event or political actor

private bill a proposal in Congress to provide a specific person with some kind of relief, such as a special exemption from immigration quotas

privileges and immunities clause provision from Article IV, Section 2 of the Constitution, that a state cannot discriminate against someone from another state or give its own residents special privileges

probability sampling a method used by pollsters to select a sample in which every individual in the population has an equal probability of being selected as a respondent so that the correct weight can be given to all segments of the population

procedural liberties restraints on how the government is supposed to act; for example, citizens are guaranteed the due process of law

proportional representation a multiple-member district system that allows each political party representation in proportion to its percentage of the total vote

public law cases in private law, civil law, or criminal law in which one party to the dispute argues that a license is unfair, a law is inequitable or unconstitutional, or an agency has acted unfairly, violated a procedure, or gone beyond its jurisdiction

public opinion citizens' attitudes about political issues, leaders, institutions, and events

public opinion polls scientific instruments for measuring public opinion

public policy a law, rule, statute, or edict that expresses the government's goals and provides for rewards and punishments to promote their attainment

purposive benefits selective benefits of group membership that emphasize the purpose and accomplishments of the group

push polling a polling technique in which the questions are designed to shape the respondent's opinion

rallying effect the generally favorable reaction of the public to presidential actions taken in foreign policy, or more precisely, to decisions made during international crises

random digit dialing polls in which respondents are selected at random from a list of ten-digit telephone numbers, with every effort made to avoid bias in the construction of the sample

random sampling a method of measuring popular opinion whereby a small group of people, randomly selected from the population as a whole, may be considered representative, as long as every person had an equal chance of being picked

recall removal of a public official by popular vote

redistricting the process of redrawing election districts and redistributing legislative representatives. This happens every ten years to reflect shifts in population or in response to legal challenges to existing districts

referendum the practice of referring a measure proposed or passed by a legislature to the vote of the electorate for approval or rejection

regulation a technique of control in which the government adopts rules imposing restrictions on the conduct of private citizens

regulatory tax a tax whose primary purpose is not to raise revenue but to influence conduct; for example, a heavy tax on gasoline to discourage recreational driving

representative democracy/republic a system of government in which the populace selects representatives, who play a significant role in governmental decision making

reserved powers powers, derived from the Tenth Amendment to the Constitution, that are not specifically delegated to the national government or denied to the states

revenue agencies agencies responsible for collecting taxes. Examples include the Internal Revenue Service for income taxes, the U.S. Customs Service for tariffs and other taxes on imported goods, and the Bureau of Alcohol, Tobacco, and Firearms for collection of taxes on the sales of those particular products

revenue sharing the process by which one unit of government yields a portion of its tax income to another unit of government, according to an established formula. Revenue sharing typically involves the national government providing money to state governments

right to privacy the right to be let alone, which has been interpreted by the Supreme Court to entail free access to birth control and abortions

roll-call vote a vote in which each legislator's yes or no vote is recorded as the clerk calls the names of the members alphabetically

rulemaking a quasilegislative administrative process that produces regulations by government agencies

sample a small group selected by researchers to represent the most important characteristics of an entire population

select committee a (usually) temporary legislative committee set up to highlight or investigate a particular issue or address an issue not within the jurisdiction of existing committees

selection bias polling error that arises when the sample is not representative of the population being studied, which create errors in overrepresenting or underrepresenting some opinions

senatorial courtesy the practice whereby the president, before formally nominating a person for a federal judgeship, seeks the indication that senators from the candidate's own state support the nomination

seniority priority or status ranking given to an individual on the basis of length of continuous service on a committee in Congress

separate but equal rule doctrine that public accommodations could be segregated by race but still be equal

separation of powers the division of governmental power among several institutions that must cooperate in decision making

shadow welfare state social benefits that private employers offer to their workers, such as medical insurance and pensions

single-member district an electorate that is allowed to select only one representative from each district; the normal method of representation in the United States

slander an oral statement, made in "reckless disregard of the truth," which is considered damaging to the victim because it is "malicious, scandalous, and defamatory"

Social Security a contributory welfare program into which working Americans contribute a percentage of their wages, and from which they receive cash benefits after retirement

sociological representation a type of representation in which representatives have the same racial, ethnic, religious, or educational backgrounds as their constituents. It is based on the principle that if two individuals are similar in background, character, interests, and perspectives, then one could correctly represent the other's views

soft money money contributed directly to political parties for voter registration

solicitor general the top government lawyer in all cases before the Supreme Court where the government is a party

solidary benefits selective benefits of a group membership that emphasize friendship, networking, and consciousness-raising

speaker of the House the chief presiding officer of the House of Representatives. The speaker is elected at the beginning of every Congress on a straight party vote. The speaker is the most important party and House leader, and can influence the legislative agenda, the fate of individual pieces of legislation, and members' positions within the House

speech plus speech accompanied by conduct such as sit-ins, picketing, and demonstrations; protection of this form of speech under the First Amendment is conditional, and restrictions imposed by state or local authorities are acceptable if properly balanced by considerations of public order

spoils system government jobs given out based on political connections rather than merit

standing committee a permanent committee with the power to propose and write legislation that covers a particular subject, such as finance or appropriations

stare decisis literally, "let the decision stand." The doctrine that a previous decision by a court applies as a precedent in similar cases until that decision is overruled

states' rights the principle that the states should oppose the increasing authority of the national government. This principle was most popular in the period before the Civil War

strict scrutiny test, used by the Supreme Court in racial discrimination cases and other cases involving civil liberties and civil rights, which places the burden of proof on the government rather than on the challengers to show that the law in question is constitutional

subsidies government grants of cash or other valuable commodities such as land to individuals or organizations; used to promote activities desired by the government, to reward political support, or to buy off political opposition

substantive liberties restraints on what the government shall and shall not have the power to do

suffrage the right to vote; also called franchise

Supplemental Security Income (SSI) a program providing a minimum monthly income to people who pass a "means test" and who are sixty-five or older, blind, or disabled. Financed from general revenues rather than from Social Security contributions

supremacy clause Article VI of the Constitution, which states that laws passed by the national government and all treaties are the supreme law of the land and superior to all laws adopted by any state or any subdivision

supreme court the highest court in a particular state or in the United States. This court primarily serves an appellate function

tax expenditures government subsidies provided to employers and employees through tax deductions for amounts spent on health insurance and other benefits; these represent one way the government helps to ensure the social welfare of the middle class

Temporary Assistance to Needy Families (TANF) a federal block grant that replaced the AFDC program in 1996

term limits legally prescribed limits on the number of terms an elected official can serve

third parties parties that organize to compete against the two major American political parties

Three-fifths Compromise the agreement reached at the Constitutional Convention of 1787 that stipulated that for purposes of the apportionment of congressional seats, every slave would be counted as three-fifths of a person

totalitarian government a system of rule in which the government recognizes no formal limits on its power and seeks to absorb or eliminate other social institutions that might challenge it

trial court the first court to hear a criminal or civil case

turnout the percentage of eligible individuals who actually vote

two-party system a political system in which only two parties have a realistic opportunity to compete effectively for control

tyranny oppressive and unjust government that employs cruel and unjust use of power and authority

unfunded mandates regulations or conditions for receiving grants that impose costs on state and local governments for which they are not reimbursed by the federal government

Uniform Commercial Code code used in many states in the area of contract law to reduce interstate differences in judicial decisions

unilateralism a foreign policy that seeks to avoid international alliances, entanglements, and permanent commitments in favor of independence, neutrality, and freedom of action

unitary system a centralized government system in which lower levels of government have little power independent of the national government

United Nations (UN) an organization of nations founded in 1945 to serve as a channel for negotiation and a means of settling international disputes peacefully. The UN has had frequent successes in providing a forum for negotiation and on some occasions a means of preventing international conflicts from spreading. On a number of occasions, the UN has been a convenient cover for U.S. foreign policy goals

veto the president's constitutional power to turn down acts of Congress. A presidential veto may be overridden by a two-thirds vote of each house of Congress

Virginia Plan a framework for the Constitution, introduced by Edmund Randolph, which called for representation in the national legislature based upon the population of each state

War Powers Resolution a resolution of Congress that the president can send troops into action abroad only by authorization of Congress, or if American troops are already under attack or serious threat

whip system a communications network in each house of Congress; whips take polls of the membership in order to learn their intentions on specific legislative issues and to assist the majority and minority leaders in various tasks

White House staff analysts and advisers to the president, often given the title "special assistant"

writ of *certiorari* a decision of at least four of the nine Supreme Court justices to review a decision of a lower court; from the Latin "to make more certain"

writ of *habeas corpus* a court order that the individual in custody be brought into court and shown the cause for detention. *Habeas corpus* is guaranteed by the Constitution and can be suspended only in cases of rebellion or invasion

ENDNOTES

CHAPTER 1

1. Jeffrey R. Young, "Students' Political Awareness Hits Highest Level in a Decade," *The Chronicle of Higher Education,* January 30, 2004, A30.

2. Michael Walzer, *Spheres of Justice* (New York: Basic Books. 1983), p. 304.

3. See Eugen Weber, *Peasants into Frenchmen: The Modernization of Rural France, 1870–1914* (Stanford, CA: Stanford University Press, 1976), chap. 5.

4. See V. O. Key, *Politics, Parties, and Pressure Groups* (New York: Crowell, 1964), p. 201.

5. Harold Lasswell, *Politics: Who Gets What, When, How* (New York: Meridian Books, 1958).

6. Herbert McClosky and John Zaller, *The American Ethos: Public Attitudes toward Capitalism and Democracy* (Cambridge, MA: Harvard University Press, 1984), p. 19.

7. J. R. Pole, *The Pursuit of Equality in American History* (Berkeley, CA: University of California Press, 1978), p. 19.

CHAPTER 2

1. Michael Kammen, *A Machine that Would Go of Itself* (New York: Vintage, 1986), p. 22.

2. The social makeup of colonial America and some of the social conflicts that divided colonial society are discussed in Jackson Turner Main, *The Social Structure of Revolutionary America* (Princeton, NJ: Princeton University Press, 1965).

3. George B. Tindall and David E. Shi, *America: A Narrative History*, 3rd ed. (New York: Norton, 1992), p. 194.

4. For a discussion of events leading up to the Revolution, see Charles M. Andrews, *The Colonial Background of the American Revolution* (New Haven, CT: Yale University Press, 1924).

5. See Carl Becker, *The Declaration of Independence* (New York: Knopf, 1942).

6. See Merrill Jensen, *The Articles of Confederation* (Madison, WI: University of Wisconsin Press, 1970).

7. Reported in Samuel E. Morrison, Henry Steele Commager, and William Leuchtenberg, *The Growth of the American Republic* (New York: Oxford University Press, 1969), vol. 1, p. 244.

8. Quoted in Morrison et al., *The Growth of the American Republic*, vol. 1, p. 242.

9. Charles A. Beard, *An Economic Interpretation of the Constitution of the United States* (New York: Macmillan, 1913).

10. Madison's notes, along with the somewhat less complete records kept by several other participants in the convention, are available in a four-volume set. See Max Farrand, ed., *The Records of the Federal Convention of 1787*, 4 vols., rev. ed. (New Haven, CT: Yale University Press, 1966).

11. Farrand, ed., *The Records of the Federal Convention of 1787*, vol. 2. p. 10.

12. E. M. Earle, ed., *The Federalist* (New York: Modern Library, 1937), No. 71.

13. Earle, ed., *The Federalist*, No. 62.

14. Max Farrand, *The Framing of the Constitution of the United States* (New Haven, CT: Yale University Press, 1962), p. 49.

15. Richard E. Neustadt, *Presidential Power* (New York: Wiley, 1960), p. 33.

16. Melancton Smith, quoted in Herbert J. Storing, *What the Anti-Federalists Were For* (Chicago: University of Chicago, 1981), p. 17.

17. Earle, ed., *The Federalist*, No. 57.

18. "Essays of Brutus," No. 15, in Storing, ed., *The Complete Anti-Federalist*.

19. Earle, ed., *The Federalist*, No. 10.

20. Earle, ed., *The Federalist*, No. 51.

21. Garry Wills, *A Necessary Evil* (New York: Simon and Schuster, 1999), p. 297.

22. Observation by Colonel George Mason, delegate from Virginia, early during the convention period. Quoted in Farrand, ed., *The Records of the Federal Convention of 1787*, vol. 1, pp. 202–3.

23. Clinton Rossiter, ed., *The Federalist Papers* (New York: New American Library, 1961), No. 43, p. 278.

24. The Fourteenth Amendment is included in this table as well as in Table 2.3 because it seeks not only to define citizenship but *seems* to intend also that this definition of citizenship includes, along with the right to vote, other rights of the Bill of Rights, regardless of the state in which the citizen resides. A great deal more will be said about this in Chapter 4.

CHAPTER 3

1. Andre Henderson, "Cruise Control," *Governing*, February 1995, p. 39.

2. Ken I. Kersch, "Full Faith and Credit for Same-Sex Marriages?" *Political Science Quarterly*, 112 (Spring 1997), pp. 117–36; Joan Biskupic, "Once Unthinkable, Now under Debate," *Washington Post*, September 3, 1996, p. Al.

3. Linda Greenhouse, "Supreme Court Paved Way for Marriage Ruling with Sodomy Law Decision," *New York Times*, November 19, 2003, p. A24.

4. Yvonne Abraham, "Gay-Marriage Rule Eased," *Boston Globe*, May 5, 2004, p. 1.

5. *Hicklin v. Orbeck*, 437 U.S. 518 (1978).

6. *Sweeny v. Woodall*, 344 U.S. 86 (1953).

7. Marlise Simons, "France Won't Extradite American Convicted of Murder," *New York Times*, December 5, 1997, p. A9.

8. A good discussion of the constitutional position of local governments is in York Willbern, *The Withering Away of the City* (Bloomington, IN: Indiana University Press, 1971). For more on the structure and theory of federalism, see Thomas R. Dye, *American Federalism: Competition among Governments* (Lexington, MA: Lexington Books, 1990), chap. 1; and Martha Derthick, "Up-to-Date in Kansas City: Reflections on American Federalism" (the 1992 John Gaus Lecture), *PS: Political Science & Politics* 25 (December 1992), pp. 671–75.

9. For a good treatment of the contrast between national political stability and social instability, see Samuel P. Huntington, *Political Order in Changing Societies* (New Haven, CT: Yale University Press, 1968), chap. 2.

10. *McCulloch v. Maryland*, 4 Wheaton 316 (1819).

11. *Gibbons v. Ogden*, 9 Wheaton 1 (1824).

12. The Sherman Antitrust Act, adopted in 1890, for example, was enacted not to restrict commerce, but rather to protect it from monopolies, or trusts, so as to prevent unfair trade practices, and to enable the market again to become self-regulating. Moreover, the Supreme Court sought to uphold liberty of contract to protect businesses. For example, in *Lochner v. New York*, 198 U.S. 45 (1905), the Court invalidated a New York law regulating the sanitary conditions and hours of labor of bakers on the grounds that the law interfered with liberty of contract.

13. Kenneth T. Palmer, "The Evolution of Grant Policies," in *The Changing Politics of Federal Grants*, by Lawrence D. Brown, James W. Fossett, and Kenneth T. Palmer (Washington, DC: Brookings, 1984), p. 15.

14. Palmer, "The Evolution of Grant Policies," p. 6.

15. The key case in this process of expanding the power of the national government is generally considered to be *NLRB v. Jones & Laughlin Steel Corporation*, 301 U.S. 1 (1937), in which the Supreme Court approved federal regulation of the workplace and thereby virtually eliminated interstate commerce as a limit on the national government's power.

16. *U.S. v. Darby Lumber Co.*, 312 U.S. 100 (1941).

17. W. John Moore, "Pleading the 10th," *National Journal*, July 29, 1995, p. 1940.

18. *Printz v. United States*, 521 U.S. 898 (1997).

19. *Seminole Indian Tribe v. Florida*, 517 U.S. 44 (1996).

20. *Federal Maritime Commission v. Carolina State Ports Authority*, 535 U.S. 743 (2002).

21. *Nevada Department of Human Resources v. Hibbs*, 538 U.S. 721 (2003).

22. Morton Grozdins, *The American System*, ed. Daniel J. Elazar (Chicago: Rand McNally, 1966).

23. See Terry Sanford, *Storm Over the States* (New York: McGraw-Hill, 1967).

24. James L. Sundquist with David W. Davis, *Making Federalism Work* (Washington, DC: Brookings, 1969), p. 271. Wallace was mistrusted by the architects of the War on Poverty because he was a strong proponent of racial segregation. He believed in "states' rights," which meant that states, not the federal government, should decide what liberty and equality meant.

25. See Don Kettl, *The Regulation of American Federalism* (Baton Rouge, LA: Louisiana State University Press, 1983).

26. Eliza Newlin Carney, "Power Grab," *National Journal*, April 11, 1998, p. 798.

27. See Advisory Commission on Intergovernmental Relations, *Federal Regulation of State and Local Governments: The Mixed Record of the 1980s* (Washington, DC: Advisory Commission on Intergovernmental Relations, July 1993).

28. Advisory Commission on Intergovernmental Relations, *Federal Regulation of State and Local Governments*, p. iii.

29. Advisory Commission on Intergovernmental Relations, *Federal Regulation of State and Local Governments*, p. 51.

30. Robert Frank, "Proposed Block Grants Seen Unlikely to Cure Management Problems," *Wall Street Journal*, May 1, 1995, p. 1.

31. Judith Havemann, "Scholars Question Whether Welfare Shift Is Reform," *Washington Post*, April 20, 1995, p. A8.

32. U.S. Committee on Federalism and National Purpose, *To Form a More Perfect Union* (Washington, DC: National Conference on Social Welfare, 1985). See also the discussion in Paul E. Peterson, *The Price of Federalism* (Washington, DC: Brookings, 1995), esp. chap. 8.

33. Malcolm Gladwell, "In States' Experiments, a Cutting Contest," *New York Times*, March 10, 1995, p. 6.

34. The phrase "laboratories of democracy" was coined by Supreme Court justice Louis Brandeis in his dissenting opinion in *New State Ice Co. v. Liebman*, 285 U.S. 262 (1932).

35. Jason DeParle, "Life after Welfare," *New York Times*, August 29, 1999, p. 1.

CHAPTER 4

1. Clinton Rossiter, ed., *The Federalist Papers* (New York: New American Library, 1961), No. 84. p. 513.

2. Rossiter, ed., *The Federalist Papers*, No. 84, p. 513.

3. Let there be no confusion about the words "liberty" and "freedom." They are synonymous and interchangeable. "Freedom" comes from the German, *Freiheit*. "Liberty" is from the French, *liberté*. Although people sometimes try to make them appear to be different, both of them have equal concern with the absence of restraints on individual choices of action.

4. *Barron v. Baltimore*, 7 Peters 243, 246 (1833).

5. The Fourteenth Amendment also seems designed to introduce civil rights. The final clause of the all-important Section 1 provides that no state can "deny to any person within its jurisdiction the equal protection of the laws." It is reasonable to conclude that the purpose of this provision was to obligate the state governments as well as the national government to take *positive* actions to protect citizens from arbitrary and discriminatory actions, at least those based on race.

6. For example, *The Slaughterhouse Cases*, 16 Wallace 36 (1883).

7. *Chicago, Burlington and Quincy Railroad Company v. Chicago*, 166 U.S. 226 (1897).

8. *Gitlow v. New York*, 268 U.S. 652 (1925).

9. *Near v. Minnesota*, 283 U.S. 697 (1931); *Hague v. C.I.O.*, 307 U.S. 496 (1939).

10. Quoted in Abraham, *Freedom and the Court*, p. 14.

11. Abington School District v. Schempp, 374 U.S. 203 (1963).

12. *Engel v. Vitale*, 370 U.S. 421 (1962).

13. *Doe v. Santa Fe Independent School District*, 530 U.S. 290 (2000).

14. *Wallace v. Jaffree*, 472 U.S. 38 (1985).

15. *Lynch v. Donnelly*, 465 U.S. 668 (1984).

16. *Zelman v. Simmons-Harris*, 536 U.S. 639 (2002).

17. *West Virginia State Board of Education v. Barnette*, 319 U.S. 624 (1943). The case it reversed was *Minersville School District v. Gobitis*, 310 U.S. 586 (1940).

18. *Employment Division, Department of Human Resources of Oregon v. Smith*, 494 U.S. 872 (1990).

19. *Wisconsin v. Yoder*, 406 U.S. 205 (1972).

20. *U.S. v. Carolene Products Company*, 304 U.S. 144 (1938), note 4. This footnote is one of the Court's most important doctrines. See Alfred H. Kelly, Winfred A. Harbison, and Herman Belz, *The American Constitution: Its Origins and Development*, 7th ed. (New York: Norton, 1991), vol. 2, pp. 519–23.

21. *Schenk v. U.S.*, 249 U.S. 47 (1919).

22. *Stromberg v. California*, 283 U.S. 359 (1931).

23. *Texas v. Johnson*, 488 U.S. 884 (1989).

24. *United States v. Eichman*, 496 U.S. 310 (1990).

25. *Virginia v. Black*, 528 U.S. 343 (2003).

26. For a good general discussion of "speech plus," see Louis Fisher, *American Constitutional Law* (New York: McGraw-Hill, 1990), pp. 544–46. The case upholding the buffer zone against the abortion protesters is *Madsen v. Women's Health Center*, 114 S.Ct. 2516 (1994).

27. *Near v. Minnesota*, 283 U.S. 697 (1931).

28. *New York Times v. U.S.*, 403 U.S. 731 (1971).

29. *New York Times v. Sullivan*, 376 U.S. 254 (1964).

30. *Roth v. U.S.*, 354 U.S. 476 (1957).

31. Concurring opinion in *Jacobellis v. Ohio*, 378 U.S. 184 (1964).

32. *Miller v. California*, 413 U.S. 15 (1973).

33. *Reno v. American Civil Liberties Union*, 521 U.S. 844 (1997).

34. *U.S. v. American Library Association*, 539 U.S. 194 (2003).

35. *Chaplinsky v. State of New Hampshire*, 315 U.S. 568 (1942). This case was reaffirmed in a much more famous and important case decided at the height of the cold war, when the Supreme Court held that "there is no substantial public interest in permitting certain kinds of utterances: the lewd and obscene, the profane, the libelous, and the insulting or 'fighting' words—those which by their very utterance inflict injury or tend to incite an immediate breach of the peace."

36. *Broadcasting Company v. Acting Attorney General*, 405 U.S. 1000 (1972).

37. *Board of Trustees of the State University of New York v. Fox*, 492 U.S. 469 (1989). This case arose from an attempt to sell Tupperware in a dormitory on the State University of New York (SUNY) Cortland campus.

38. *City Council v. Taxpayers for Vincent*, 466 U.S. 789 (1984).

39. *Posadas de Puerto Rico Associates v. Tourism Company of Puerto Rico*, 479 U.S. 328 (1986).

40. *U.S. v. Miller*, 307 U.S. 174 (1939). This view has been accepted in over forty lower federal court decisions from the 1940s to the present.

41. *Presser v. Illinois*, 116 U.S. 252 (1886).

42. The handgun ban that was unsuccessfully challenged as a violation of the Second Amendment was enacted by the village of Morton Grove. The Supreme Court refused to hear an appeal from the federal court of appeals, which upheld the handgun ban. *Quilici v. Village of Morton Grove*, 695 F. 2d 261 (7th Cir. 1982); cert. denied, 464 U.S. 863 (1983).

43. *Horton v. California,* 496 U.S. 128 (1990).

44. *Mapp v. Ohio,* 367 U.S. 643 (1961). Although Mapp went free in this case, she was later convicted in New York on narcotics trafficking charges and served nine years of a twenty-year sentence.

45. For a good discussion of the issue, see Fisher, *American Constitutional Law,* pp. 884–89.

46. *Gideon v. Wainwright,* 372 U.S. 335 (1963). For a full account of the story of the trial and release of Clarence Earl Gideon, see Anthony Lewis, *Gideon's Trumpet* (New York: Random House, 1964). See also David O'Brien, *Storm Center,* 2nd ed. (New York: Norton, 1990).

47. *Furman v. Georgia,* 408 U.S. 238 (1972).

48. *Gregg v. Georgia,* 428 U.S. 153 (1976).

49. *Griswold v. Connecticut,* 381 U.S. 479 (1965).

50. *Griswold v. Connecticut,* concurring opinion. In 1972, the Court extended the privacy right to unmarried women: *Eisenstadt v. Baird,* 405 U.S. 438 (1972).

51. *Roe v. Wade,* 410 U.S. 113 (1973).

52. *Lawrence v. Texas,* 539 U.S. 558 (2003).

53. *Missouri ex rel. Gaines v. Canada,* 305 U.S. 337 (1938).

54. *Sweatt v. Painter,* 339 U.S. 629 (1950).

55. *Smith v. Allwright,* 321 U.S. 649 (1944).

56. *Shelley v. Kraemer,* 334 U.S. 1 (1948).

57. *Brown v. Board of Education of Topeka, Kansas,* 347 U.S. 483 (1954).

58. For good treatments of this long stretch of the struggle of the federal courts to integrate the schools, see Paul Brest and Sanford Levinson, *Processes of Constitutional Decision-Making: Cases and Materials,* 2nd ed. (Boston: Little, Brown, 1983), pp. 471–80; and Alfred Kelly et al., *The American Constitution: Its Origins and Development,* 6th ed. (New York: Norton, 1983), pp. 610–16.

59. Pierre Thomas, "Denny's to Settle Bias Cases," *Washington Post,* May 24, 1994, p. A1.

60. See Hamil Harris, "For Blacks, Cabs Can Be Hard to Get," *Washington Post,* July 21, 1994, p. J1.

61. See especially *Katzenbach v. McClung,* 379 U.S. 294 (1964). Almost immediately after passage of the Civil Rights Act of 1964, a case was brought challenging the validity of Title II, which covered discrimination in public accommodations. Ollie's Barbecue was a neighborhood restaurant in Birmingham, Alabama. It was located eleven blocks away from an interstate highway and even farther from railroad and bus stations. Its table service was for whites only; there was only a take-out service for blacks. The Supreme Court agreed that Ollie's was strictly an intrastate restaurant, but since a substantial proportion of its food and other supplies were bought from companies outside the state of Alabama, there was a sufficient connection to interstate commerce; therefore, racial discrimination at such restaurants would "impose commercial burdens of national magnitude upon interstate commerce." Although this case involved Title II, it had direct bearing on the constitutionality of Title VII.

62. In 1970, this act was amended to outlaw for five years literacy tests as a condition for voting in all states.

63. See Douglas S. Massey and Nancy A. Denton, *American Apartheid: Segregation and the Making of the Underclass* (Cambridge, MA: Harvard University Press, 1993), chap. 7.

64. See Jane J. Mansbridge, *Why We Lost the ERA* (Chicago: University of Chicago Press, 1986); and Gilbert Steiner, *Constitutional Inequality* (Washington, DC: Brookings, 1985).

65. See *Frontiero v. Richardson,* 411 U.S. 677 (1973).

66. *Meritor Savings Bank v. Vinson,* 477 U.S. 57 (1986).

67. *Harris v. Forklift Systems, Inc.,* 510 U.S. 17 (1993).

68. *Burlington Industries v. Ellerth,* 524 U.S. 742 (1998); *Faragher v. City of Boca Raton,* 524 U.S. 775 (1998).

69. *Franklin v. Gwinnett County Public Schools,* 503 U.S. 60 (1992).

70. *U.S. v. Virginia,* 518 U.S. 515 (1996).

71. *Lau v. Nichols,* 414 U.S. 563 (1974).

72. Dick Kirschten, "Not Black and White," *National Journal,* March 2, 1991, p. 497.

73. See the discussion in Robert A Katzmann, *Institutional Disability: The Saga of Transportation Policy for the Disabled* (Washington, DC: Brookings, 1986).

74. For example, after pressure from the Justice Department, one of the nation's largest rental-car companies agreed to make special hand-controls available to any customer requesting them. See "Avis Agrees to Equip Cars for Disabled," *Los Angeles Times,* September 2, 1994, p. D1.

75. *Bowers v. Hardwick,* 478 U.S. 186 (1986).

76. Quoted in Joan Biskupic, "Gay Rights Activists Seek a Supreme Court Test Case," *Washington Post,* December 19, 1993, p. A1.

77. *Romer v. Evans,* 517 U.S. 620 (1996).

78. *Lawrence v. Texas,* 539 U.S. 558 (2003).

79. For excellent coverage of the political and constitutional issues surrounding the actions of states on same-sex marriage, see Kenneth Kersch, "Full Faith and Credit for Same-Sex Marriages?" *Political Science Quarterly,* 112, 117–36 (Spring 1997).

80. From Lyndon B. Johnson, *The Vantage Point* (New York: Holt, Rinehart, and Winston, 1971), p. 166.

81. The Department of Health, Education, and Welfare (HEW) was the cabinet department charged with administering most federal social programs. In 1980, when education programs were transferred to the newly created Department of Education, HEW was renamed the Department of Health and Human Services.

82. *Regents of the University of California v. Bakke,* 438 U.S. 265 (1978).

83. See, for example, *United Steelworkers v. Weber,* 443 U.S. 193 (1979); and *Fullilove v. Klutznick,* 448 U.S. 448 (1980).

84. *Ward's Cove v. Atonio,* 490 U.S. 642 (1989).

85. *Grutter v. Bollinger,* 539 U.S. 306 (2003).

86. *Gratz v. Bollinger,* 539 U.S. 244 (2003).

CHAPTER 5

1. The Gallup Organization, "Gallup Social and Economic Indicators," at www.gallup.com/poll/indicators/indguns.asp.

2. For a discussion of the political beliefs of Americans, see Harry Holloway and John George, *Public Opinion* (New York: St.

Martin's, 1986). See also Paul R. Abramson, *Political Attitudes in America* (San Francisco: Freeman, 1983).

3. See Angus Campbell et al., *The American Voter* (New York: Wiley, 1960), p. 147.

4. Elisabeth Noelle-Neumann, *The Spiral of Silence* (Chicago: University of Chicago Press, 1984).

5. Albert H. Cantril, *The Opinion Connection* (Washington, DC: CQ Press, 1991), p. 207.

6. David Morris, "Opinions Split over Amendment to Ban Same-Sex Marriages," ABCNEWS.com, February 24, 2004.

7. Michael Robinson, "Television and American Politics 1956–1976," *Public Interest* 48 (Summer 1977), p. 23.

8. Cantril, *The Opinion Connection*, pp. 45–47.

9. Gerald F. Seib and Michael K. Frisby, "Selling Sacrifice," *Wall Street Journal*, February 5, 1993, p. 1.

10. Michael K. Frisby, "Clinton Seeks Strategic Edge with Opinion Polls," *Wall Street Journal*, June 24, 1996, p. A16.

11. James Carney, "Playing by the Numbers," *Time*, April 11, 1994, p. 40.

12. Mark Hertsgaard, *On Bended Knee* (New York: Farrar Strous Giroux, 1988), pp. 48–49.

13. See Gillian Peele, *Revival and Reaction* (Oxford, U.K.: Clarendon, 1985). Also see Connie Paige, *The Right-to-Lifers* (New York: Summit, 1983).

14. Herbert Asher, *Polling and the Public* (Washington, DC: CQ Press, 2001), p. 64.

15. John Goyder, Keith Warriner, and Susan Miller, "Evaluating Socioeconomic Status Bias in Survey Nonresponse," *Journal of Officiating Statistics*, Vol. 18, No. 1, 2002.

16. Michael Kagay and Janet Elder, "Numbers Are No Problem for Pollsters, Words Are," *New York Times*, August 9, 1992, p. E6.

17. William Saletan, "Push Me, Poll You," *Slate*, February 15, 2000.

18. "Dial S for Smear," *Memphis Commercial Appeal*, September 22, 1996, p. 6B.

19. Benjamin I. Page and Robert Y. Shapiro, "Effects of Public Opinion on Policy," *American Political Science Review* 77, March 1983: 175–90.

20. Robert A. Erikson, Gerald Wright, and John McIver, *Statehouse Democracy: Public Opinion and Democracy in the American States* (New York: Cambridge University Press, 1994).

21. The results of separate studies by the political scientists Lawrence Jacobs, Robert Shapiro, and Alan Monroe were reported by Richard Morin in "Which Comes First, the Politician or the Poll?" *Washington Post National Weekly Edition*, February 10, 1997, p. 35.

22. Benjamin Ginsberg and Martin Shefter, *Politics by Other Means* (New York: Basic Books, 1990), p. 24.

23. See the discussions in Gary Paul Gates, *Air Time* (New York: Harper & Row, 1978); Edward Jay Epstein, *News from Nowhere* (New York: Random House, 1973); Michael Parenti, *Inventing Reality* (New York: St. Martin's, 1986); Herbert Gans, *Deciding What's News* (New York: Vintage, 1980); and W. Lance

Bennett, *News: The Politics of Illusion* (New York: Longman, 1986).

24. David Firestone, "Steven Brill Strikes a Nerve in News Media," *New York Times*, June 20, 1998, p. 4.

25. See Tom Burnes, "The Organization of Public Opinion," in Mass Communication and Society, ed. James Curran (Beverly Hills, CA: Sage, 1979), pp. 44–230. See also David Altheide, Creating Reality (Beverly Hills, CA: Sage, 1976).

26. David Garrow, *Protest at Selma* (New Haven, CT: Yale University Press, 1978).

27. Quoted in Stephen Ansolabehere, Roy Behr, and Shanto Iyengar, *The Media Game* (New York: MacMillan, 1993), p. 142.

28. Robert J. Spitzer, "Clinton's Impeachment Will Have Few Consequences for the Presidency," *PS: Political Science and Politics* 32 (September 1999), pp. 541–45.

29. For a discussion of framing, see Amy Jasperson, et al., "Framing and the Public Agenda," *Political Communication*, vol. 15, no. 2, pp. 205–224.

30. Kathleen Hall Jamieson and Paul Waldman, *The Press Effect* (New York: Oxford University Press, 2003), p. 61.

31. Jamieson and Waldman, *The Press Effect*, p. 56.

32. Pew Research Center, *Cable and Internet Loom Large in Fragmented Political News Universe*, January 11, 2004.

33. Samantha M. Shapiro, "The Dean Connection," *New York Times Magazine*, December 7, 2003, p. 58.

34. Jonah Goldberg, "Reporters Hate Guns," *Brill's Content*, February 2000, p. 53.

35. Jeff Cohen, "NRA Defines Debate," *Brill's Content*, February 2000, p. 52.

36. Doris Graber, *Mass Media and American Politics* (Washington, DC: CQ Press, 1993), p. 384.

37. Philip M. Taylor, *War and the Media* (Manchester, UK: Manchester University Press, 1992), pp. 67–75.

38. Herbert I. Schiller, *The Mind Manager* (Boston: Beacon Press, 1973); Edward S. Herman and Noam Chomsky, *Manufacturing Consent* (New York: Pantheon, 1988).

39. Graber, *Mass Media and American Politics*, p. 53.

40. Michael J. Robinson and Margaret A. Sheehan, *Over the Wire and on TV* (New York: Sage, 1983); Thomas E. Patterson, *Out of Order* (New York: Knopf, 1993).

CHAPTER 6

1. See Richard Hofstadter, *The Idea of a Party System* (Berkeley, CA: University of California Press, 1969).

2. Alan Greenblatt, "With Major Issues Fading, Capitol Life Lures Fewer," *Congressional Quarterly Weekly Report*, October 25, 1997, p. 2625.

3. See Walter Dean Burnham, *Critical Elections and the Mainsprings of American Electoral Politics* (New York: Norton, 1970). See also James L. Sundquist, *Dynamics of the Party System* (Washington, DC: Brookings, 1983).

4. Benjamin Ginsberg, *The Consequences of Consent* (New York: Random House, 1982), chap. 4.

5. For a discussion of third parties in the United States, see Daniel Mazmanian, *Third Parties in Presidential Election* (Washington, DC: Brookings, 1974).

6. See Maurice Duverger, *Political Parties* (New York: Wiley, 1954).

7. Robert Jackman, "Political Institutions and Voter Turnout in the Democracies," *American Political Science Review* 81 (June 1987), p. 420.

8. Helen Dewar, "'Motor Voter' Agreement Is Reached," *Washington Post,* April 28, 1993, p. A6.

9. Erik Austin and Jerome Chubb, *Political Facts of the United States since 1789* (New York: Columbia University Press, 1986), pp. 378–79.

10. *League of United Latin American Citizens v. Wilson,* CV-94-7569 (C.D. Calif.) (1995).

11. Jonathan Salant, "Million-Dollar Campaigns Proliferate in 105th," *Congressional Quarterly Weekly Report,* December 21, 1996, pp. 3448–51.

12. U.S. Federal Election Commission, "Financing the 1996 Presidential Campaign," Internet Release, April 28, 1998.

13. FEC reports.

14. FEC reports.

15. *Buckley v. Valeo,* 424 U.S. 1 (1976).

16. David Broder and Ruth Marcus, "Wielding Third Force in Politics," *Washington Post,* September 20, 1997, p. 1.

CHAPTER 7

1. Alexis de Tocqueville, *Democracy in America* (New York: Random House, 1955), vol. 1, chap. 12; vol. 2, chap. 5.

2. Clinton Rossiter, ed., *The Federalist Papers* (New York: New American Library, 1961), No. 10, p. 83.

3. Rossiter, ed., *Federalist Papers,* No. 10.

4. The best statement of the pluralist view is in David Truman, *The Governmental Process* (New York: Knopf, 1951), chap. 2.

5. E. E. Schattschneider, *The Semisovereign People* (New York: Holt, Rinehart, and Winston, 1960), p. 35.

6. Betsy Wagner and David Bowermaster, "B.S. Economics," *Washington Monthly,* November 1992, pp. 19–21.

7. Mancur Olson, *The Logic of Collective Action* (Cambridge, MA: Harvard University Press, 1965).

8. Kay Lehman Schlozman and John T. Tierney, *Organized Interests and American Democracy* (New York: Harper & Row, 1986), p. 60.

9. John Herbers, "Special Interests Gaining Power as Voter Disillusionment Grows," *New York Times,* November 14, 1978.

10. Rich Lowry, "How the Right Rose," *National Review* 66 (December 11, 1995), pp. 64–76.

11. David D. Kirkpatrick, "Bush Campaign Seeks Help From Congregations," *New York Times,* June 3, 2004, p. A1.

12. For discussions of lobbying, see Allan J. Cigler and Burdett A. Loomis, eds., *Interest Group Politics* (Washington, DC: Congressional Quarterly Press, 1983). See also Jeffrey M. Berry,

Lobbying for the People (Princeton, NJ: Princeton University Press, 1977).

13. "The Swarming Lobbyists," *Time,* August 7, 1978, p. 15.

14. Leslie Wayne and Michael Moss, "Bailout for Airlines Showed the Weight of a Mighty Lobby," *New York Times,* October 10, 2001, p. A1.

15. John P. Heinz, Edward O. Laumann, Robert L. Nelson, and Robert H. Salisbury, *The Hollow Core: Private Interests in National Policy Making* (Cambridge, MA: Harvard University Press, 1993), p. 96. See also Schlozman and Tierney, *Organized Interests and American Democracy,* chap. 13.

16. A number of important policy domains, such as the environmental and welfare arenas, are controlled, not by a highly structured and unified iron triangle, but by rival issue networks. These networks consist of like-minded politicians, consultants, public officials, political activists, and interest groups who have some concern with the issues in question. Activists and interest groups recognized as being involved in the area are sometimes called "stakeholders," and are customarily invited to testify before congressional committees or give their views to government agencies considering action in their domain.

17. *Roe v. Wade,* 410 U.S. 113 (1973).

18. *Webster v. Reproductive Health Services,* 492 U.S. 490 (1989).

19. *Brown v. Board of Education of Topeka, Kansas,* 347 U.S. 483 (1954).

20. See, for example, *Duke Power Co. v. Carolina Environmental Study Group,* 438 U.S. 59 (1978).

21. E. Pendleton Herring, *Group Representation before Congress* (New York: McGraw-Hill, 1936).

22. Ann Devroy, "Gay Rights Leaders Meet President in Oval Office: White House Tries to Play Down Session," *Washington Post,* April 17, 1993, p. 1.

23. Michael Weisskopf, "Energized by Pulpit or Passion, the Public is Calling," *Washington Post,* February 1, 1993, p. 1.

24. Richard L. Burke, "Religious-Right Candidates Gain as GOP Turnout Rises," *New York Times,* November 12, 1994, p. 10.

25. Elisabeth R. Gerber, *The Populist Paradox* (Princeton: Princeton University Press, 1999), p.6.

26. Olson, *The Logic of Collective Action.*

CHAPTER 8

1. "Public Confidence in Selected Institutions," *National Institute of Justice Journal,* September 1997, p. 11.

2. Alan L. Clem, *Congress: Powers, Processes, and Politics* (Pacific Grove, CA: Brooks/Cole, 1989), p. 243.

3. Roger Davidson, "Invitation to Struggle," *Annals of the American Academy of Political and Social Science* 499 (September 1988), 11.

4. Historian Garry Wills refers to the idea that the three branches were designed to be co-equal as an "extraordinary misperception." *A Necessary Evil* (New York: Simon and Schuster, 1999), p. 84.

5. For data on occupational backgrounds of the members of the 105th Congress, see *Congressional Quarterly Weekly Report,* January 4, 1997.

6. Marian D. Irish and James Prothro, *The Politics of American Democracy,* 5th ed. (Englewood Cliffs, NJ: Prentice Hall, 1971), p. 352.

7. For some interesting empirical evidence see Angus Campbell, Philip Converse, Warren Miller, and Donald Stokes, *Elections and the Political Order* (New York: Wiley, 1966), chap. 11.

8. Congressional Quarterly, *Guide to the Congress of the United States,* 3rd ed. (Washington, DC: Congressional Quarterly Press, 1982), p. 599.

9. John S. Saloma, *Congress and the New Politics* (Boston: Little, Brown, 1969), pp. 184–85. A 1977 official report using less detailed categories came up with almost the same impression of Congress's workload. Commission on Administrative Review, *Administrative Reorganization and Legislative Management,* House Doc. #95-232 (September 28, 1977), vol. 2, especially pp. 17–19.

10. See Barbara C. Burrell, *A Woman's Place Is in the House: Campaigning for Congress in the Feminist Era* (Ann Arbor, MI: University of Michigan Press, 1994); and David Broder, "Key to Women's Political Parity: Running," *Washington Post,* September 8, 1994, p. A17.

11. "Did Redistricting Sink the Democrats?" *National Journal,* December 17, 1994, p. 2984.

12. *Miller v. Johnson,* 515 U.S. 900 (1995).

13. Timothy Eagan, "Built with Steel, Perhaps, but Greased with Pork," *New York Times,* April 10, 2004, p. A1.

14. www.house.gov/stark/services.html

15. Congressional Quarterly, *Guide to the Congress of the United States,* 2nd ed. (Washington, DC: Congressional Quarterly Press, 1976), pp. 229–310.

16. Richard Fenno, Jr., *Home Style: House Members in Their Districts* (Boston: Little, Brown, 1978).

17. See John W. Kingdon, *Congressmen's Voting Decisions* (New York: Harper & Row, 1973), chap. 3; and R. Douglas Arnold, *The Logic of Congressional Action* (New Haven, CT: Yale University Press, 1990).

18. Daniel Franklin, "Tommy Boggs and the Death of Health Care Reform," *Washington Monthly,* April 1995, p. 36.

19. Peter H. Stone, "Follow the Leaders," *National Journal,* June 24, 1995, p. 1641.

20. Holly Idelson, "Signs Point to Greater Loyalty on Both Sides of the Aisle," *Congressional Quarterly Weekly Report,* December 19, 1992, p. 3849.

21. Carl Hulse, "Even Some in G.O.P. Call for More Oversight of Bush," *New York Times,* May 31, 2004, p. A13.

22. Robert J. Spitzer, "The Presidency: The Clinton Crisis and Its Consequences," in *The Clinton Scandal and the Future of American Government,* eds. Mark J. Rozell and Clyde Wilcox (Washington, DC: Georgetown University Press, 2000), pp. 7–10.

23. Carroll J. Doherty, "Impeachment: How It Would Work," *Congressional Quarterly Weekly Report,* January 31, 1998, p. 222.

CHAPTER 9

1. Richard Morin and Claudia Deane, "Public Blames Clinton, Gives Record Support," *Washington Post,* February 15, 1999, p. A1.

2. Eric Pianin, "Clinton, Hill GOP Turn to Agendas," *Washington Post,* February 14, 1999, p. A24; Robert J Spitzer, "Clinton's Impeachment Will Have Few Consequences for the Presidency," *PS: Political Science and Politics,* 32 (September 1999), 541–45.

3. Morin and Deane, "Public Blames Clinton."

4. *In re Neagle,* 135 U.S. 1 (1890).

5. James G. Randall, *Constitutional Problems under Lincoln* (New York: Appleton, 1926), ch. 1.

6. Edward S. Corwin, *The President: Office and Powers,* 4th rev. ed. (New York: New York University Press, 1957), p. 229.

7. These statutes are contained mainly in Title 10 of the United States Code, Sections 331, 332, and 333.

8. The best study covering all aspects of the domestic use of the military is that of Adam Yarmolinsky, *The Military Establishment* (New York: Harper & Row, 1971). Probably the most famous instance of a president's unilateral use of the power to protect a state "against domestic violence" was in dealing with the Pullman Strike of 1894. The famous Supreme Court case that ensued was *In re Debs,* 158 U.S. 564 (1895).

9. In *United States v. Pink,* 315 U.S. 203 (1942), the Supreme Court confirmed that an executive agreement is the legal equivalent of a treaty, despite the absence of Senate approval. This case approved the executive agreement that was used to establish diplomatic relations with the Soviet Union in 1933. An executive agreement, not a treaty, was used in 1940 to exchange "fifty over age destroyers" for ninety-nine-year leases on some important military bases.

10. There is a third source of presidential power implied from the provision for "faithful execution of the laws." This is the president's power to impound funds—that is, to refuse to spend money Congress has appropriated for certain purposes. One author referred to this as a "retroactive veto power" (Robert E. Goosetree, "The Power of the President to Impound Appropriated Funds," *American University Law Review,* January 1962). Many modern presidents used this impoundment power freely and to considerable effect, and Congress occasionally delegated such power to the president by statute. But in reaction to the Watergate scandal, Congress adopted the Budget and Impoundment Control Act of 1974, which was designed to circumscribe the president's ability to impound funds by requiring that the president spend all appropriated funds unless both houses of Congress consent to an impoundment within forty-five days of a presidential request. Therefore, since 1974, the use of impoundment has declined significantly. Presidents have either had to bite their tongues and accept unwanted appropriations or had to revert to the older and more dependable but politically limited method of vetoing the entire bill.

11. For a different perspective, see William F. Grover, *The President as Prisoner: A Structural Critique of the Carter and Reagan Years* (Albany, NY: State University of New York Press, 1988).

12. For more on the veto, see Robert J. Spitzer, *The Presidential Veto: Touchstone of the American Presidency* (Albany, NY: State University of New York Press, 1988).

13. A substantial portion of this section is taken from Theodore J. Lowi, *The Personal President* (Ithaca, NY: Cornell University Press, 1985), pp. 141–50.

14. All the figures since 1967, and probably 1957, are understated, because additional White House staff members were on "detail" service from the military and other departments (some secretly assigned) and are not counted here because they were not on the White House payroll.

15. Article I, Section 3, provides that "The Vice-President . . . shall be President of the Senate, but shall have no Vote, unless they be equally divided." This is the only vote the vice president is allowed.

16. Shirley Anne Warshaw, *The Keys to Power* (New York: Longman, 2000), pp. 100–108.

17. Richard Neustadt, *Presidential Power* (New York: Wiley, 1960), p. 26.

18. For a more detailed review of the New Deal coalition in comparison with later coalitions, see Thomas Ferguson and Joel Rogers, *Right Turn: The Decline of the Democrats and the Future of American Politics* (New York: Hill & Wang, 1986), chap. 2. For updates on the group basis of presidential politics, see Thomas Ferguson, "Money and Politics," in *Handbooks to the Modern Worlds: The United States,* vol. 2, ed. Godfrey Hodgson (New York: Facts on File, 1992), pp. 1060–84; and Lucius J. Barker, ed., "Black Electoral Politics," *National Political Science Review,* vol. 2 (New Brunswick, NJ: Transaction Publishers, 1990).

19. Study cited in Ann Devroy, "Despite Panetta Pep Talk, White House Aides See Daunting Task," *Washington Post,* January 8, 1995, p. A4.

CHAPTER 10

1. Philip Shenon, "Establishing New Agency Is Expected to Take Years," *New York Times,* November 20, 2002, p. A14.

2. U.S. Bureau of the Census, *Statistical Abstract of the United States, 1997* (Washington, DC: U.S. Government Printing Office, 1997), pp. 348, 355.

3. Quoted in Leonard D. White, *The Republican Era* (New York: Free Press, 1958), p. 6.

4. As of 1998, salaries for GS-15 federal employees in Washington, D.C., could range from $77,798 to $101,142; salaries for the Senior Executive Service could range between $110,700 and $151,800 annually. Office of Personnel Management, Salaries and Wages web page, www.opm.gov/oca/payrates/index.htm (accessed on May 11, 1998).

5. See Paul Peterson, *The Price of Federalism* (Washington, DC: Brookings, 1995), for a recent argument that "redistribution" is the distinctive function of the national government in the American federal system.

6. *Budget of the United States Government, FY 1998: Analytical Perspectives* (Washington, DC: U.S. Government Printing Office, 1997), Table 12-2, p. 219.

7. For an excellent political analysis of the Fed, see Donald Kettl, *Leadership at the Fed* (New Haven, CT: Yale University Press, 1986).

8. George E. Berkley, *The Craft of Public Administration* (Boston: Allyn & Bacon, 1975), p. 417. Emphasis added.

9. Correspondent Kelli Arena, "Overhauling the IRS," CNN Financial Network, March 7, 1997.

10. See William Keller, *The Liberals and J. Edgar Hoover* (Princeton, NJ: Princeton University Press, 1989). See also Victor Navasky, *Kennedy Justice* (New York: Atheneum, 1971), chap. 2 and p. 8.

11. For more detail, consult John E. Harr, *The Professional Diplomat* (Princeton, NJ: Princeton University Press, 1972), p. 11; and Nicholas Horrock, "The CIA Has Neighbors in the 'Intelligence Community,'" *New York Times,* June 29, 1975, sec. 4, p. 2. See also Roger Hilsman, *The Politics of Policy Making in Defense and Foreign Affairs,* 3rd ed. (Englewood Cliffs, NJ: Prentice Hall, 1993).

12. Carl Hulse, "House Approves $447 Billion in Spending for Military," *New York Times,* May 21, 2004, p. A16.

13. The title was inspired by a book by Charles Hyneman, *Bureaucracy in a Democracy* (New York: Harper, 1950). For a more recent effort to describe the federal bureaucracy and to provide some guidelines for improvement, see Patricia W. Ingraham and Donald F. Kettl, eds., *Agenda for Excellence: Public Service in America* (Chatham, NJ: Chatham House, 1992).

14. Clinton Rossiter, ed., *The Federalist Papers* (New York: New American Library, 1961), No. 51, p. 322.

15. The title of this section was inspired by Peri Arnold, *Making the Managerial Presidency* (Princeton, NJ: Princeton University Press, 1986).

16. See Richard Nathan, *The Plot That Failed: Nixon and the Administrative Presidency* (New York: Wiley, 1975), pp. 68–76.

17. For more details and evaluations, see David Rosenbloom, *Public Administration* (New York: Random House, 1986), pp. 186–221; Charles H. Levine and Rosslyn Kleeman, "The Quiet Crisis in the American Public Service," in *Agenda for Excellence: Public Service in America,* ed. Patricia Ingraham and Donald Kettl (Chatham, NJ: Chatham House, 1992); and Patricia Ingraham and David Rosenbloom, "The State of Merit in the Federal Government," in *Agenda for Excellence.*

18. Lester Salamon and Alan Abramson, "Governance: The Politics of Retrenchment," in *The Reagan Record,* ed. John Palmer and Isabel Sawhill (Cambridge, MA: Ballinger, 1984), p. 40.

19. Colin Campbell, "The White House and the Presidency under the 'Let's Deal' President," in *The Bush Presidency: First Appraisals,* ed. Colin Campbell and Bert A. Rockman (Chatham, NJ: Chatham House, 1991), pp. 185–222.

20. See National Performance Review Savings, www.npr.gov/library/review.html (accessed on October 15, 1997).

21. Joshua Chaffin, "Democrats Probe High Cost of Halliburton," Financial Times, February 17, 2004, p. 10; Laura Rich, "On the Job in Iraq," *New York Times,* May 23, 2004, pp. 3–6.

22. Richard E. Cohen, "Crackup of the Committees," *National Journal,* July 31, 1999, p. 2214.

23. The Office of Technology Assessment (OTA) was a fourth research agency serving Congress until 1995. It was one of the first agencies scheduled for elimination by the 104th Congress. Until 1983, Congress had still another tool of legislative oversight: the legislative veto. Each agency operating under such provisions was obliged to submit to Congress every proposed decision or rule, which would then lie before both chambers for thirty to sixty days. If Congress took no action by one-house or two-house resolution explicitly to veto the proposed measure during the prescribed period, it became law. In 1983, the Supreme Court declared the legislative veto unconstitutional on the grounds that it violated the separation of powers—the resolutions Congress passed to exercise its veto were not subject to presidential veto, as required by the Constitution. See *Immigration and Naturalization Service v. Chadha,* 462 U.S. 919 (1983).

CHAPTER 11

1. See Richard Neely, *How Courts Govern America* (New Haven, CT: Yale University Press, 1981).

2. U.S. Bureau of the Census, *Statistical Abstract of the United States* (Washington, DC: Government Printing Office, 1995).

3. Neil A. Lewis, "Deal Ends Impasse over Judicial Nominees," *New York Times,* May 19, 2004, p. A19.

4. Robert Scigliano, *The Supreme Court and the Presidency* (New York: Free Press, 1971), p. 161. For an interesting critique of the solicitor general's role during the Reagan administration, see Lincoln Caplan, "Annals of the Law," *New Yorker,* August 17, 1987, pp. 30–62.

5. Edward Lazarus, *Closed Chambers* (New York: Times Books, 1998), p. 6.

6. Max Farrand, *The Framing of the Constitution of the United States* (New Haven, CT: Yale University Press, 1913), p. 157.

7. C. Herman Pritchett, *The American Constitution* (New York: McGraw-Hill, 1959), p. 138.

8. The Supreme Court affirmed this review power in *Martin v. Hunter's Lessee,* 1 Wheat. 304 (1816).

9. *Brown v. Board of Education,* 347 U.S. 483 (1954); *Loving v. Virginia,* 388 U.S. 1 (1967).

10. *Griswold v. Connecticut,* 381 U.S. 479 (1965).

11. *Gideon v. Wainwright,* 372 U.S. 335 (1963).

12. *Engel v. Vitale,* 370 U.S. 421 (1962); *Gideon v. Wainwright,* 372 U.S. 335 (1963); *Escobedo v. Illinois,* 378 U.S. 478 (1964); and *Miranda v. Arizona,* 384 U.S. 436 (1966).

13. *Baker v. Carr,* 369 U.S. 186 (1962).

14. Walter F. Murphy, "The Supreme Court of the United States," in *Encyclopedia of the American Judicial System,* ed. Robert J. Janosik (New York: Scribner's, 1987).

15. *Smith v. Allwright,* 321 U.S. 649 (1994).

16. Clinton Rossiter, ed., *The Federalist Papers* (New York: New American Library, 1961), No. 10, p. 78.

CHAPTER 12

1. Robert Shapiro, *Cut and Invest: A Budget Strategy for the New Economy* (Washington, DC: Progressive Policy Institute, 1995), p. 15.

2. "The Arms Industry—Markets and Maginot Lines," *Economist,* October 28, 1995, pp. 23–25.

3. For an evaluation of the policy of withholding subsidies to carry out desegregation laws, see Gary Orfield, *Must We Bus?* (Washington, DC: Brookings Institution, 1978). For an evaluation of the use of subsidies to encourage work or to calm political unrest, see Frances Fox Piven and Richard Cloward, *Regulating the Poor: The Functions of Public Welfare* (New York: Random House, 1971).

4. For an evaluation of the politics of eminent domain, see Theodore J. Lowi and Benjamin Ginsberg, *Poliscide* (New York: Macmillan, 1976), p. 235 and *passim,* and especially chaps. 11 and 12, written by Julia and Thomas Vitullo-Martin.

5. The figures cited are for 1997.

6. House Ways and Means Committee Print, WMCP: 105-7, *1998 Green Book,* from U.S. GPO Online via GPO Access at www.access.gpo.gov/congress/wm001.html (accessed June 1998). The 1999 cash assistance figures are from the State Policy Documentation Project of the Center for Law and Social Policy, available at www.spdp.org/tanf/cat-fin.htm#fin (accessed January 21, 2000).

7. Ways and Means Committee Print, WMCP: 105-7, *1998 Green Book,* from U.S. GPO Online via GPO Access at www.access.gpo.gov/congress/wm001.html (accessed June 1998).

8. Robert Pear, "Welfare Spending Shows Huge Shift," *New York Times,* October 13, 2003, p. A1.

9. Ibid.

10. Rebecca M. Blank, "Evaluating Welfare Reform in the United States," *Journal of Economic Literature,* vol. XL (December 2002): 1105–66.

11. Robert Pear, "House Democrats Propose Making the '96 Welfare Law an Antipoverty Weapon," *New York Times,* January 24, 2002, p. A22.

12. Robin Toner, "Welfare Chief Is Hoping to Promote Marriage," *New York Times,* February 19, 2002, p. A1.

13. U.S. Bureau of the Census, *Statistical Abstract of the United States, 1997* (Washington, DC: U.S. Government Printing Office, 1997), p. 45.

14. See, for example. Theodore R. Marmor, Jerry L. Mashaw, and Philip L. Harvey, *America's Misunderstood Welfare State* (New York: Basic Books, 1990), p. 156.

15. Burdett A. Loomis and Allen J. Cigler, "Introduction: The Changing Nature of Interest Group Politics," in *Interest Group Politics,* 4th ed., ed. Burdett A. Loomis and Allan J. Cigler (Washington, DC: Congressional Quarterly Press, 1995), p. 12.

16. See Senator Bob Kerrey's remarks quoted in David S. Broder, "Deficit Doomsday," *Washington Post,* August 7, 1994, p. C9.

17. See Beth Stevens, "Blurring the Boundaries: How the Federal Government Has Influenced Welfare Benefits in the Private Sector," in *The Politics of Social Policy in the United States,* ed. Margaret Weir, Ann Orloff, and Theda Skocpol (Princeton, NJ: Princeton University Press, 1988), pp. 122–48.

18. Frances Fox Piven and Richard Cloward, *Poor People's Movements* (New York: Pantheon, 1977), chap. 5.

19. There were a couple of minor precedents. One was the Smith-Hughes Act of 1917, which made federal funds available to the states for vocational education at the elementary and secondary levels. Second, the Lanham Act of 1940 made federal funds available to schools in "federally impacted areas," that is, areas with an unusually large number of government employees and/or where the local tax base was reduced by large amounts of government-owned property.

20. For an analysis of employment and training initiatives since the 1930s, see Margaret Weir, *Politics and Jobs* (Princeton, NJ: Princeton University Press, 1992).

21. Morton Keller, *Affairs of State: Public Life in Nineteenth Century America* (Cambridge, MA: Belknap Press of Harvard University Press, 1977), p. 500.

22. John E. Schwarz, *America's Hidden Success,* 2nd ed. (New York: Norton, 1988), pp. 41–42.

CHAPTER 13

1. Alexis de Tocqueville, *Democracy in America,* trans. Phillips Bradley (New York: Vintage, 1945; original published 1835), vol. 1, p. 243.

2. Under President George H. W. Bush, for example, Dick Cheney left the House to become secretary of defense; under President Clinton, Senator Lloyd Bentsen and Representative Les Aspin left Congress to become the secretaries of the treasury and defense, respectively.

3. Raymond A. Bauer, Ithiel de Sola Pool, and Lewis Anthony Dexter, *American Business and Public Policy: The Politics of Foreign Trade,* 2nd ed. (Chicago: Aldine-Atherton, 1972).

4. Brenda Holzinger, "Power Politics: Public Policy, Federalism, and Hydroelectric Power," unpublished Ph.D. dissertation, Cornell University, 1997.

5. For further discussion of the vulnerability of modern presidents to the people through the media, see Theodore Lowi, *The Personal President: Power Invested, Promise Unfulfilled* (Ithaca, NY: Cornell University Press, 1985); Jeffrey K. Tulis, *The Rhetorical Presidency* (Princeton, NJ: Princeton University Press, 1987); Samuel Kernell, *Going Public: New Strategies of Presidential Leadership* (Washington, DC: Congressional Quarterly Press, 1986); Richard Rose, *The Postmodern President: The White House Meets the World* (Chatham, NJ: Chatham House, 1988); and George C. Edwards, *The Public Presidency: The Pursuit of Popular Support* (New York: St. Martin's, 1983).

6. A full version of the text of the farewell address, along with a discussion of the contribution to it made by Hamilton and Madison, will be found in Daniel J. Boorstin, ed., *An American Primer* (Chicago: University of Chicago Press, 1966), vol. 1, pp. 192–210.

7. John G. Stoessinger, *Crusaders and Pragmatists: Movers of Modern American Foreign Policy* (New York: Norton, 1985), pp. 21, 34.

8. Hans Morgenthau, *Politics among Nations,* 2nd ed. (New York: Knopf, 1956), p. 505.

9. See Lowi, *The Personal President,* pp. 167–69.

10. In 1997, the next five biggest contributors were Japan (16.0 percent), Germany (9 percent), France (6.7 percent), the United Kingdom (5.6 percent), and the Russian Federation (4.4 percent). These figures do not include many specific UN operations and organizations, nor the U.S. contributions to these programs. *1998 Information Please Almanac* (Boston: Information Please LLC, 1998), pp. 348–49.

11. There was, in fact, an angry dispute over a "surplus" of at least $2.2 billion, on the basis of which Japan and others demanded a rebate. *Report of the Secretary of Defense to the President and Congress* (Washington, DC: U.S. Government Printing Office, 1992), p. 26.

12. Not all American policy makers agree that the UN is a worthy instrument of American foreign policy. The UN is on the verge of bankruptcy, partly because the United States owes the UN nearly $1.5 billion in dues. For a review, see Barbara Crossette, "U.N., Facing Bankruptcy, Plans to Cut Payroll by Ten Percent," *New York Times,* February 6, 1996, p. A3.

13. "IMF: Sleeve-Rolling Time," *Economist,* May 2, 1992, pp. 98–99.

14. Quoted in John Lewis Gaddis, *The United States and the Origins of the Cold War* (New York: Columbia University Press, 1972), p. 21.

15. Robert A. Pastor, *Congress and the Politics of U.S. Foreign Economic Policy* (Berkeley, CA: University of California Press, 1980), pp. 256–80.

16. George Quester, *The Continuing Problem of International Politics* (Hinsdale, IL: Dryden Press, 1974), p. 229.

17. The Warsaw Pact was signed in 1955 by the Soviet Union, the German Democratic Republic (East Germany), Poland, Hungary, Czechoslovakia, Romania, Bulgaria, and Albania. Albania later dropped out. The Warsaw Pact was terminated in 1991.

18. "Arms for Sale," *Newsweek,* April 8, 1991, pp. 22–27.

19. The original theory of containment was articulated by former ambassador and scholar George Kennan in a famous article published under the pseudonym Mr. X, "The Sources of Soviet Conduct," *Foreign Affairs 25* (1947), p. 556.

20. Richard Barnet, "Reflections," *New Yorker,* March 9, 1987, p. 82.

21. Thomas L. Friedman, "14 Big Macs Later . . . ," *New York Times,* December 31, 1995, sec. 4, p. 9.

ANSWER KEY

CHAPTER 1
1. b
2. c
3. b
4. d
5. d

CHAPTER 2
1. b
2. b
3. b
4. b
5. c
6. c
7. d
8. d
9. d
10. a

CHAPTER 3
1. b
2. c
3. d
4. c
5. c
6. b
7. a
8. d
9. c
10. d

CHAPTER 4
1. c
2. a
3. d
4. a
5. c
6. a
7. b
8. c
9. d
10. a

CHAPTER 5
1. c
2. a
3. d
4. c
5. d
6. b
7. b
8. d
9. a
10. b

CHAPTER 6
1. a
2. d
3. c
4. c
5. a
6. c
7. d
8. c
9. b
10. a

CHAPTER 7
1. a
2. d
3. c
4. a
5. a
6. c
7. d
8. d
9. b
10. a

CHAPTER 8
1. a
2. c
3. a
4. c
5. b
6. a
7. a
8. c

CHAPTER 9
1. b
2. a
3. a
4. b
5. a
6. a
7. b
8. c

CHAPTER 10
1. b
2. a
3. a
4. b
5. a

CHAPTER 11
1. a
2. b
3. d
4. a
5. c
6. c
7. a
8. d
9. a

CHAPTER 12
1. b
2. c
3. c
4. c
5. a
6. c
7. d
8. c
9. d
10. a

CHAPTER 13
1. b
2. d
3. b
4. c
5. c
6. c
7. c
8. d
9. a

ILLUSTRATION CREDITS

The Role of Government in Your Daily Life: Sagel & Kranefeld/ zefa/Corbis; Royalty-Free/Corbis; Royalty-Free/Corbis; Marc Asnin/Corbis Saba; Meeke/Corbis.

Separation of Powers in Action: AP/Wide World Photos; AP/ Wide World Photos; AP/Wide World Photos; Supreme Court Historical Society; AP/Wide World Photos; AP/Wide World Photos.

The Federal Marriage Amendment: AP/Wide World Photos; Carlos Avila Gonzalez/San Francisco Chronicle/Corbis; Rick Friedman/Corbis; Jodi Hilton/Corbis.

Limiting Federal Power in Favor of States: PEMCO Webster and Stevens Collection, Museum of History and Industry, Seattle/ Corbis; Billy E. Barnes/Stock Boston; AP/Wide World Photos; Reuters/Corbis; AP/Wide World Photos.

Should States Set the Speed Limit? AP/Wide World Photos; AP/Wide World Photos; AP/Wide World Photos; AP/Wide World Photos.

How the First Amendment Guarantees Freedom of Religion: AP/Wide World Photos; AP/Wide World Photos; AP/Wide World Photos; Win McNamee/Reuters/Corbis.

How the Constitution Protects Those Accused of a Crime: AP/ Wide World Photos; AP/Wide World Photos; Bettmann/Corbis; Bettmann/Corbis; AP/Wide World Photos; AP/Wide World Photos.

Cause and Effect in the Civil Rights Movement: Bettmann/ Corbis; Bettmann/Corbis; Bettmann/Corbis; Bettmann/Corbis; Flip Schulke/Corbis; Bettmann/Corbis.

How Presidents Shape Public Opinion: Bettmann/Corbis; By permission of Bob Gorrell and Creators Syndicate; AP/Wide World Photos; Brooks Kraft/Corbis.

Is the Media Biased? AP/Wide World Photos; Marc Asnin/Corbis Saba; AP/Wide World Photos; AP/Wide World Photos.

The Role of Political Parties in Contemporary Politics: AP/ Wide World Photos; Brown Brothers; AP/Wide World Photos; AP/Wide World Photos; AP/Wide World Photos.

The 2004 Presidential Campaign: Jeff Topping/Reuters/Corbis; AP/Wide World Photos; AP/Wide World Photos; AP/Wide World Photos; AP/Wide World Photos.

How Lobbyists Help Interest Groups Gain Influence: Carol T. Powers/White House/TimePix/Getty Images; AP/Wide World Photos; AP/Wide World Photos; AP/Wide World Photos; AP/Wide World Photos; AP/Wide World Photos.

Pork Barrel Politics: Royalty-Free/Corbis; AP/Wide World Photos; AP/Wide World Photos; AP/Wide World Photos; AP/Wide World Photos.

How Congress Decides: AP/Wide World Photos; Corbis; AP/ Wide World Photos; AP/Wide World Photos; AP/Wide World Photos; AP/Wide World Photos.

The President's Permanent Campaign: Bettmann/Corbis; Bettmann/Corbis; AP/Wide World Photos; Larry Downing/Reuters/Corbis.

Creating the Department of Homeland Security: AP/Wide World Photos; MAI/TimePix/Getty Images; AP/Wide World Photos; AP/Wide World Photos; Greg Smith/Corbis Saba; AP/Wide World Photos.

How Judges Are Appointed: Bettmann/Corbis; Bettmann/Corbis; AP/Wide World Photos; AP/Wide World Photos.

The Supreme Court in Action: AP/Wide World Photos; AP/Wide World Photos; AP/Wide World Photos; AP/Wide World Photos; Jason Reed/Reuters/Corbis; Erich Schilegel/Dallas Morning News/Corbis.

Who Gets What from Social Security: AP/Wide World Photos; AP/Wide World Photos; AP/Wide World Photos; AP/Wide World Photos; Lester Lefkowitz/Corbis.

Making and Shaping Foreign Policy: AP/Wide World Photos; AP/Wide World Photos; AP/Wide World Photos; AP/Wide World Photos.

The War with Iraq: AP/Wide World Photos; Getty Images; AP/Wide World Photos; AP/Wide World Photos; AP/Wide World Photos; Oleg Popov/Reuters/Corbis.

INDEX